To the Memory of
My Parents

and

G.O. Smith and James Guthrie
who all inspired what follows

and also

**For Harry, Catherine,
And their future Corinthian generation**

Sport
and the Law

Second Edition

by

Edward Grayson MA (OXON)

of the Middle Temple and of the South Eastern Circuit, Barrister
President, British Associaiton for Sport and Law
Fellow of the Royal Society of Medicine

Foreword by

The Rt Hon The Lord Howell of Aston

The Former Minister of State for Sport and Recreation

United Kingdom	Butterworth & Co (Publishers) Ltd, Halsbury House, 35 Chancery Lane, LONDON WC2A 1EL and 4 Hill Street, EDINBURGH EH2 3JZ
Australia	Butterworths, SYDNEY, MELBOURNE, BRISBANE, ADELAIDE, PERTH, CANBERRA and HOBART
Canada	Butterworths Canada Ltd, TORONTO and VANCOUVER
Ireland	Butterworth (Ireland) Ltd, DUBLIN
Malaysia	Malayan Law Journal Sdn Bhd, KUALA LUMPUR
New Zealand	Butterworths of New Zealand Ltd, WELLINGTON and AUCKLAND
Puerto Rico	Butterworth of Puerto Rico, Inc, SAN JUAN
Singapore	Butterworths Asia, SINGAPORE
South Africa	Butterworths Publishers (Pty) Ltd, DURBAN
USA	Butterworth Legal Publishers, CARLSBAD, California and SALEM, New Hampshire

© Butterworth & Co (Publishers) Ltd 1994

A CIP Catalogue record for this book is available from the British Library.

First edition published 1988

ISBN 0 406 01145 1

Printed by Clays Ltd, St Ives plc

Foreword by the Rt Hon the Lord Howell of Aston

The second edition of Edward Grayson's *Sport and the Law* is most welcome and an indispensable guide for all who have need to consider the ramifications of this minefield.

For members of Governing Bodies of Sport *Grayson* should be compulsory reading. He focuses attention upon the relationship between Sport and the Law in a manner which should cause them all to consider their responsibilities anew. As he says 'the law does not stop at the touchline' which is a reality too long ignored by many administrators of the old school — 'leave us to look after our own affairs, we can sort things out'.

Well, they can't. The case histories quoted by Grayson make sombre reading. Serious injury can no more be ignored on the sports field than anywhere else. And when it occurs these players are obviously concerned about any damage they may have suffered, physically and financially.

Then too, schools and clubs, parents and players may all have good cause to consider their responsibilities. Not only in this country but in Europe and internationally. Part III of this edition provides a good insight into these comparatively new areas of sporting jurisprudence while part II has some fascinating comment about Personal Relationships.

Of course, sponsorship and commercial advantage are subjects which dominate professional sport these days. Edward Grayson offers some vital insights to those caught up on such matters and guidance of great fascination for those of us who wish to follow sport as it becomes more and more tangled up in these thickets.

For many years Edward Grayson has been a sole voice in sport, and in the law, spelling out the dangers and the truths about the consequences of the law for all those who participate in sport. He has performed yet another service to both his great passions by updating his classic book which underlines the first importance of ethical considerations in sport and spells out the legal consequences for those who depart from them.

Denis Howell

'To many Lawyers it will seem that it is all to the good that legal principles and procedure should be discussed in public in any guise.'

Lord Atkin: Introduction to Uncommon Law
by A. P. Herbert (1935)

Preface

This book's purpose is expressly,

> 'To create a level of awareness among all readers of the extent to which ...
> the law can and should come to the help of sport; and indeed, how sport
> with its high public profile and image can come to the help of the law. For
> sport without rules and their control creates chaos. Society without laws
> and their enforcement means anarchy'.

The wide range of those readers is explained extensively in the
Introduction which follows this Preface, at pages xxxiv–xxxv.

Among them could be the bright-eyed civil servant who quizzed the
Joint Department of the Environment and Department of Education and
Science Seminar in 1986, 'How do you define sport?'. It had been hosted
by the Central Council of Physical Recreation (CCPR) and the then Under-
Secretary of State at the Department of the Environment who held the
popularly-styled Sports Minister's government portfolio, Mr Richard
Tracey MP. Three years earlier in 1983 an answer had been provided in a
Loughborough College lecture by the then British Olympic Association
Chairman, the late Sir Denis Follows. 'It is indefinable'.

Furthermore, sport, with medicine and music, like Tauber's song, goes
round the world; and from across the Atlantic, one of America's greatest
gifts to Anglo-Saxon culture, as judge, jurist, legal historian and
practitioner, Oliver Wendell Holmes Jr., explained in the opening
paragraph of his tome on *The Common Law,* with a theme comparable to
Glenn Miller's *Moonlight Serenade,* 'The life of the law has not been logic;
it has been experience'. He echoed an earlier attribution to the English
sage of the previous century, Dr Samuel Johnson: 'the Law is the last Result
of Publick Wisdom, acting upon publick Experience' (from *Dr Johnson
and the Law* by Sir Arnold McNair, KC).

To-day, these two intricate interlocking disciplines in a secular-
orientated society create the most vivid and dynamic demonstrations of
the contrasts between civilised and uncivilised conduct. Yet neither of them
can be understood without an awareness or constant reminder of how they
each operate in two different dimensions, reflecting Disraeli's *Two
Nations.* Sport absorbs two divergent and differing layers; as a public

commercial entertainment divorced in spirit, attitudes and ethics from its grass roots at school, club and village green levels. The law portrays its traditional Parliamentary and case law precedents on the one hand, and, on the other hand, the self-created codes of rules for playing and administering sport within its governing bodies and club regulations.

They overlap when the transgressors of rules of play on the field and malpractices off it fall foul of wider laws. For contrary to mythology and many misconceptions, and also many wishes within sporting administrative and playing circles, the law of the land does not stop at the touchline or board or committee room.

Different sports create different criteria for self-regulation. From golf at all pro-am levels, with its honourable built-in written and unwritten self-disciplines, to the intolerable and too often tolerated outrages elsewhere of criminally and civilly actionable violence. Thus, this second Butterworths edition of *Sport and the Law* appears six years after its first edition of 1988, which in turn built upon the earlier foundation stone in 1978 of a 76-page *Sunday Telegraph* booklet under the same title which followed on from a three-part series in that same paper a year earlier in 1977.

On each of the two earlier occasions no precedents existed for attempting to structure what is now conveniently but incorrectly categorised in our current soundbite syndrome society as Sportslaw, as a moment's thought will recognise. For certainly sport, as distinct from one of its more easily recognisable elements, physical recreation, embraces nearly every legal category which is identifiable in *Halsbury's* 52 volumes of the *Laws of England*. Its development is reflected almost daily in general as well as in the business and sports pages; from the crowd disasters at Bradford, Heysel, and Hillsborough, via Manchester United Plc's record-breaking profits to the self-inflicted cruciate ligament injury suffered by Paul Gascoigne when lunging recklessly and unlawfully against a Nottingham Forest opponent in the FA Cup Final. The rapid growth within fifteen years from a three-part newspaper series to the 506 pages here of text and Appendices reflects within a smaller timescale the corpus of legislation and litigation for nearly a century which has followed the inevitable collision between motor vehicle manufacturers' products and the communities who are forced to absorb them. Its logical and almost inevitable consequences have been the revolutionary recommendations of the *Royal Commission on Environmental Pollution* which exploded on an unsuspecting road and car users culture while these pages were in their final proof stages (Cmd 2674).

The earliest of those laws regulating vehicular traffic in the United Kingdom are found a century ago in Victorian pioneering days of public entertainment sport. That was when the social, class and economic distinctions between Playing gentlemen and gentlemen Players helped to mark off the paid professional from the privately funded or subsidised amateur; before his or her status in our time has been preserved artificially by trust funds and contorted eligibility rules and regulations. The public *and* private sport in England of that period inspired Baron Pierre de Coubertin to revive the concept of the Olympic Games in 1896 with the ideal expressed in the words of the Bishop of Pennsylvania in St Paul's Cathedral, London, on 19 July 1908, preaching on the occasion of the fourth Olympic Games, after their revival, in the spirit of St Paul's own First Letter to the *Corinthians*, Chapter 9, Verse 24:25, with which this book's main text ends at page 429:

> 'The important thing in the Olympic Games is not so much to have been victorious as to have taken part'.

That ideal and the true ethic of playing sport according to the rules and fair play were embodied in the Association football club founded in 1882 under the title of Corinthians. Comprising amateur playing professional schoolmasters, doctors, lawyers amongst others, able to indulge their time away from gainful occupations, they competed against and with their professional contemporaries in the field and off it in international elevens. The letters to me as a Second World War hero-worshipping schoolboy from one of their greatest performers who was in effect the Gary Lineker of his day as England's centre-forward, and also an outstanding university cricketer, G O Smith, after he had retired from the headmastership of the future King William III's preparatory school, Ludgrove, inspired their publication as *Corinthians and Cricketers*.

That in turn led to the accidental discovery of how professional footballers and cricketers were subject to different taxation laws relating to their benefit awards, and in due course to a successful attempt to abolish the anomaly. It had enthusiastic encouragement of Sir Stanley Rous who had re-drafted the Laws of the Game as the Football Association secretary, before becoming President of FIFA, and James Guthrie, captain of Portsmouth's 1939 FA Cup-winning team. He was then chairman of the then Association of Professional Football Players' and Trainers' Union (now the Professional Footballers' Association (PFA)); and in the recently published *Football and the Commons People*, which chronicles former and current MP's devotion to 'The People's Game', it is recorded (at page 26) of the popularly known Jimmy Guthrie, over the pen of the one-time Minister in Harold Wilson's 1964 Government, J P W (later Sir William) Mallalieu, who was as much MP for his beloved Huddersfield Town Football Club as he was for his differing Huddersfield constituencies and constituents between 1945 and 1979:

> 'He did more than any individual to improve the working conditions of professional footballers'.

That accidental discovery was how *Sport and the Law* began for the author as a coherent subject. The detailed explanation is set out in the last Appendix here, Appendix 15.

The contrast between the climate that inspired that correspondence, away from the current complexities of drugs, violence, commerce and political exploitation which dominate sport to-day, has led to an awareness and realistic belief in one route back to the Corinthian ideals. That is through the Rule of Law within sport, as played and administered by the schoolmasters, doctors and lawyers who have done so much to create it. Hence the first Appendix, 'The Corinthian Ideal' by a modern Corinthian and Cricketer, Hubert Doggart, heir to the heritage created by more than one of an earlier vintage, and also the second Appendix, by yet another Corinthian and Cricketer who forever will be recalled by lawyers and law students as the representative defendant in cricket's landmark Packer litigation, *Greig v Insole* [1979] 3 All ER 449, [1978] 1 WLR 302, Douglas Insole.

These and all the other equally admirable and valuable and valued Appendices from their distinguished contributors, together with the texts which precede them have all been crystallised with a brilliant simplicity justifying application of that overused description, when Simon Barnes wrote in *The Times* of 31 August during the 1994 Commonwealth Games and its drug problems as cited in the *Introduction*, at page lx.

'Sporting bodies were originally established to organise a bit of serious fun; these days the same organisations are trying to run billion quid industries.
    It is hardly surprising that things get out of step sometimes. And, as the spiral tightens and quickens, the anomalies will come at us more and more often'.

These thoughts were echoed with equal brilliance a few weeks later by a New York sportscaster and journalist, Anne Liguori, on Cliff Morgan's magnetically attractive BBC Radio 4 *Sport on Four* Saturday morning programme, cited on more than one occasion in these page. She analysed the strike action leading to the abandonment of the American baseball, ice hockey and possibly basketball seasons (15 October 1994):

'The business of American sport has evolved into a billion dollar industry...the business of sports ego and greed have changed the face of American sport forever.'

Inevitably, therefore, the question arises: could all this happen here if it has not happened already, at the *public commercial entertainment* as distinct from grass roots levels?

That Simon Barnes spiral since the first Butterworth edition in 1988 has thereby demanded a re-structuring of the chapters which were created on that occasion with no guidelines or precedents to shape them. It is explained in detail at page xxxiii of the *Introduction* which follows. For the legislative and litigation *principles* which stake out the subject-matter do not change fundamentally. Their application to individual circumstances which *illustrate* them comprise the principal additional changes since 1988.

Perhaps the most dramatic and vivid illuminations hit the London High Court while these final pages were being prepared during June and October 1994. First, Mr Justice Drake dismissed the personal injuries claim of Paul Elliott, the Chelsea footballer, against Dean Saunders and Liverpool Football Club. Subsequently Mr Justice Collins recorded a settlement of the action brought by John O'Neill of Norwich City against John Fashanu and Wimbledon Football Club, in each of which I must declare a professional interest as one of each Plaintiff's legal team. In the most authoritative and balanced overall judicial assessment of the relationship between the two disciplines which can yet be found anywhere, in language which is applicable to all sport and sporting disputes, Drake J explained in an early part of his judgment,

'Because this case has understandably attracted a great deal of public interest, I will first make a few general observations about the relationship of the law and sport. I have no doubt that there is a lot of public support for the view that the law should be kept away from sport. Amateur sport is primarily for the enjoyment of those taking part, professional sport, primarily for the entertainment of spectators. But in both cases there is some natural feeling of repugnance when what happens during a sporting event is made the subject of legal proceedings. I understand and sympathise with that view and I would certainly not encourage law suits arising from any sporting activities unless there are very good grounds to justify them. But it does not take much reflection to show that it would be wholly wrong to deny an injured party the right to claim compensation in the courts if there is no other way in which he, or she, can obtain it.

In the case of a professional, a serious injury may bring his career to an end, as happened with the plaintiff in this case. But exactly the same position may arise with an amateur player. The student badly injured while playing for his school, university or college, or teaching hospital, may lose the prospect of becoming an eminent doctor, lawyer or other professional expert. In each case both the professional and the amateur, if the injury was caused by another player acting in a wholly unacceptable manner, for example, by intending to cause injury, or being reckless, not caring whether or not injury was caused, then surely it is right that the injured person should be able to claim compensation'.

Barely three months after Elliott's High Court experience another career-wrecked professional international footballer, John O'Neill, of

Norwich City, sued John Fashanu and Wimbledon Football Club, claiming £150,000 damages for cruciate ligament injuries caused by an alleged assault and/or reckless negligence. After O'Neill's case was closed on his behalf by Nigel Baker QC, and the assault (but not the negligence) allegation was withdrawn, the action was settled in full for £70,000 inclusive of costs before the defendants gave any evidence. It followed a pattern set at Lewes Assizes in 1969 and London's High Court in 1970. Rees J adjudicated £5,400 damages and costs in favour of the *amateur* playing plaintiff (see *Lewis v Brookshaw* (1970) 120 NLJ 143).

Subsequent comments about the need for a Compensation Scheme analogous to the Solicitors' Indemnity Fund had surfaced after the Elliott judgment. They emerged again following the successful settlement of John O'Neill's action, without any indication from any executive source, apart from the Professional Footballer's Association, of a will to create one from the monies, sponsored or otherwise, awash within the game, to avoid similar court proceedings. If any other organisation, such as the Institute of Sports Sponsorship and the Institute of Professional Sport, each of which might be expected to have expressed an equal concern with this serious issue which is now in the public domain for debate, has made any effective attempts to tackle such a less easily soluble than it is clearly identifiable problem, there has been an unfortunate reluctance to disclose them.

Furthermore, within the compensation framework 'the injured person' as a victim of negligence or other culpable criteria, to which Mr Justice Drake's last sentence was targeted, must also include those who have suffered not only from physical but also administrative abuse. Thus, a few weeks after Elliott's case, but before O'Neill's, three minor League Welsh football clubs, who had been barred from playing on their home territories were forced to share English grounds because of administrative and tribunal decisions by the Football Association of Wales, with serious consequential financial losses. These were held by Jacob J to be in restraint of trade, in line with the celebrated decisions established in the earlier football [*Eastham*] and cricket [*Packer*] cases which are to be found in the pages which follow; and compensation in its widest possible form of injunctive relief was capable of being obtained only from the Chancery Division of the High Court. The judgment was delivered on 26 July 1994 and reported in the *New Law Journal*: 7 October 1994, Vol 144, page 1351 [*Newport AFC Ltd & Others v Football Association of Wales Ltd*].

As if to convert that successful restraint of trade interlocutory try against the Football Association of Wales into a goal against the Welsh Rugby Union and International Rugby Football Board, a restraint of trade writ was issued against each governing body ultimately in the final stages of these page proof corrections shortly before publication. This was an attempt to bar the rugby union *amateur* authorities from preventing a return to its fold by Stuart Evans, a former Welsh prop forward, who had experienced a brief professional career with the professional St Helens Rugby League club. Coinciding with the Sports (Discrimination) Bill introduced into the House of Commons earlier during the 1994 Parliamentary session, to outlaw discrimination against participants in sport by governing bodies, the two processes illustrate the law merging at legislative Parliamentary and litigation levels for protecting participants in sport, and in sport itself.

These current developments demonstrate the dynamic growth of the subject which explodes new material nearly every day. Indeed, they are illustrative of the need to keep abreast of what are now almost daily developments in this rapidly exploding world-wide penalty area, with two recent contrasting court rulings from Kipling's East and West, which now disprove his century-old concept, 'Never the twain shall meet'.

A Moscow court in late September was reported on the BBC World Service (21 September) to have ruled that a decision by the Russian Amateur Athletics federation to disqualify world hurdles champion Lyudmilla Narozhilenko was unlawful. The Federation's General-Secretary, Vladimir Usachev said that it would appeal, having acted according to the rules of the *International* Federation.

A month later, as recorded in *The Times*, for 1 November the *International* Federation was reported as having successfully resisted in the USA Supreme Court Harry (Butch) Reynolds' appeal against the reversal of the Federation's successful appeal against an Ohio Court's initial verdict in his favour (explained throughout the following pages). This had invalidated a Federation three-year ban for alleged drug offences.

Furthermore, as if to avoid not getting in on the act after a seven year gestation period since the Home Office's stated intended proposals for steroid legislative prohibition on 12 September 1987, as explained below, the Home Secretary (but significantly *not* any Minister from the Department of National Heritage: see Appendix 7) on 2 November disclosed details for tackling this particular sporting and social abuse. Proposals were announced in terms of general principles to be particularised in detail after these pages appear.

Finally, and consistent with precedent from the first edition's Preface, the last week of preparing this text for publication before the final proof stages experienced the following events which illustrate the pattern which has been unfolding with every passing day, and is hardly likely to cease after it has appeared.

(1) It began with a BBC television *Panorama* programme containing disputed and contentious commercial material about an internationally-renowned professional football personality, respected for his coaching and managerial skills. An earlier programme from

the same service in similar strain had reportedly incurred the receipt of a writ for libel.

(2) At about the same time an equally internationally-respected footballing personality was summarily dismissed from his managerial role with a club of historic traditions, but in the early stages of a four-year contract period.

(3) Violence on a rugby union field in South Wales involving the local Neath club and a visiting South African touring side inspired *The Times* to invite the former Metropolitan Police Chief Superintendent and a leading rugby union referee who had walked off the pitch during a match at Bristol in protest at violence in the course of play, George Crawford, to contribute his thoughts for a solution. He exploded them appropriately on Guy Fawkes Day, 5 November, advocating direct police intervention if no other *effective* sanction from referees or administrators would stem an uninterrupted flow of high profiled brutality. He concluded with the similar question raised earlier in the year by the High Master of St Paul's School in a letter to *The Times* cited at page xxv of the Introduction,

> 'At a time when rugby is attempting to display to the youth of this world that this is the game they should play, what signals are being received by the parents of those the game is targeting?'

(4) Later, during the same day, an enquirer on the popular BBC *Radio 5 Live*, 6.06 Saturday evening programme, posed the question whether the UEFA (Union of European Football Associations) three-player minimum quota of only three 'foreign' or non-nationals for each UEFA cup competition team within national football association criteria, and two other less rigidly defined, could be *ultra vires*? The answer did not lend itself to an 'instant coffee' -styled reply. It raised complex and potentially arguable issues under the Treaty of Rome: article 7 prohibiting discrimination; article 48 guaranteeing free movement of workers (who include professional sporting employees); and articles 85 and 86, prohibiting distortion of competition and abuse of a dominant position.

When these and similar issues surface again after publication, as they are almost certainly likely to do, arrangements have been made to up-date this text every quarter within the pages of the *New Law Journal*, separate and apart from continuation of the *All England Law Reports Annual Review*. The law within this text, as distinct from later illustrations of it, is stated as at the end of World Cup month 31 July 1994. This Preface has been completed almost symbolically on Guy Fawkes Day 1994; and as

before expressed for the first edition in the words of Lord Hailsham of St
Marylebone as Mr Quintin Hogg, QC, MP, when head of chambers, citing
the advice of his father, the first Viscount Hailsham, 'You are paid for
your opinions. Never for your doubts'. What follows except where
corroborated by others, are my own opinions.

Edward Grayson
4 Paper Buildings
Temple
London
EC4Y 7EX

EXTRAS IN EXTRA TIME

If any evidence would ever be required of sport's reluctance to distance itself
from the law in continuation of the pattern which unfolded during the week
ending on this Preface's cut-off date on Guy Fawkes Day, 5 November 1994,
the disputed allegations which surfaced only hours later surrounding Bruce
Grobbelaar's goal-keeping practices (and will inevitably survive the
publication of these pages before they are finally assessed) identify it at four
separate legal levels. They also provide the perfect answer in case the need
exists for explaining Why and How the law serves sport, which appears
throughout these pages, but has yet to pierce the minds of all who challenge
and question the necessity for their connection.

1. The FA's quest for legal guidance to steer it through the minefield of
    highly-profiled published material which correspondingly demands
    the concept of innocence until guilty is proved.

2. The recognition of its obligation to observe the rules of natural justice
    and the right to be heard at domestic administrative tribunals.

3. The corollary of libel writs consistent with the denial of such
    allegations.

4. Contemplated criminal investigations following alleged police
    enquiries consistent with precedents from comparable cases
    concerning professional football in the past.

Such threads which continue to entwine sport and the law do not differ
in substance from the warning of impending crowd disasters with their
built-in legal liabilities, sounded in his *Daily Mail* column by the late and
great constructively-campaigning journalist, J L Manning, during 1969.
As detailed later in the text he foreshadowed the tragic crowd fatalities of
the subsequent twenty years, with their judicial reports and Parliamentary

legislation and civil litigation after the lawyers had sifted the evidence which led to the law being changed for the general public benefit and compensation awards to victims following Ibrox (Wheatley: 1971), Bradford (Popplewell: 1985), Hillsborough (Taylor: 1989/1990).

They also do not differ in substance from the landmark litigation judgments led by the lawyers which emancipated women racehorse trainers from the male chauvinism of the Jockey Club (*Nagle v Field* (1966)), and professional football from its feudal controls in *Eastham's* (1963) and *Banks'* (1955) cases, which the equally late and great constructively-campaigning administrator, James Guthrie, claimed to be the shackles for the last bonded men in Britain. Contrary to the title built-in to the refrain *The Song is Ended but the melody lingers on*, the magic and fun within sport will always need the harmony between sport and the law, on and off the fields of play, to prevent the music and romantic joy which sport brings to the health and education of society at all levels from descending into barbaric depths to which so many participants, agents, administrators, and thoughtless commentators would direct its destruction.

Acknowledgements

'Many are called but few are chosen' is as appropriate for authors' acknowledgements as it is to the traditional prospects for pupil, and indeed, practising, barristers. So many different snatches of conversations and soundbites have contributed to these pages that to name all sources is impossible, and selection would be even more invidious than choosing a gallery of all-time sporting or legal heroes.

For self-evident reasons, of which some will be seen by the reader and others are personal to the author, the task of preparing these pages has been lightened by all those whose citations and attributions appear in the text: The Rt Hon Lord Howell of Aston for once more generously writing a foreword from his standpoint as the longest and most experienced serving British government minister ever concerned with sport; each one of the contributors who has generously made time for the valuable Appendices which are attributed to them; The Hon. Mr Justice Drake for the classically balanced part of his judgment in the highly profiled professional footballer's personal injury action of *Elliott v Saunders and Liverpool*, illustrated later by *O'Neill v Fashanu and Wimbledon* (in each of which I must disclose a professional interest), where he crystallised as cited at page xxvi of the *Introduction*, Why and How sport and the law benefit each other; Peter Hildreth, for his Olympian knowledge and experience of the international and domestic athletic scenes; Denis Campbell in addition to Herbert Kerrigan QC's Appendix for chronicling continually Scotland's Procurator-fiscal's successful application of the Rule of Law in court for the protection of sport. The former Metropolitan Police Chief Superintendent and leading Rugby Union referee George Crawford for recognising the need in appropriate circumstances to uphold the Rule of Law on the field of play. Hayden Opie, from Melbourne University and President of ANZSLA (Australian and New Zealand Sports Law Association) and Malcolm Holmes QC of the New South Wales Bar for an antipodean perspective; Fiona Miller for her EU sport initiatives; Tony O'Brien for insurance realities in sport; Jeff Butterfield of the Rugby Club of London and Cliff Morgan from Rugby Union with Maurice Oldroyd of the British *Amateur* Rugby League Association, for adherence to the concept of the Corinthian ideal for all sport; John Gale and Tim Gale for theatrical confirmation of *amateur* talents' capacity for co-existence without losing their status and enjoyment at different levels from the world of professionalism, traditionally performing on public commercial entertainment stages; Cheryl West and Rachel Heyhoe Flint for VAT and liquor licensing initiatives. My learned friends and professional colleagues at 4 Paper Buildings, Temple; Peter Caton, for his personal recollections of the most immortal Corinthian among all Corinthians and Cricketers, C B Fry; and Anthony Ewans QC, William Hughes, Richard Jory, and Rosina Cottage, for their differing individual experiences from a form of football played paradoxically with hands as well as feet. Peter Carter-Ruck for his sustained encouragement from the earliest days in initiating *The Royal Baccarat Scandal* with its historic saga of cheating in sport, and for the citation from his *Memoirs of a Libel Lawyer*; Charles Woodhouse, Maurice Watkins, Robert Stinson, Mark Gay, Alan Grossett, Julia Bracewell and Raymond Farrell, for their insight into the background of sporting administration; and not least from a younger generation of practising solicitors my son, Harry Grayson, for his industrious library researches, in addition to his Appendix, and Catherine Bond, in addition to her own Appendix, for her profound insight into the whole interaction between sport and law and its base for the Corinthian ideal in sport and society, explained in Hubert Doggart's Appendix. Without her enthusiasm and enlightened interest and support, this second edition could not have been completed within the framework of practising professional commitments.

For my Publishers no author can ever have been better served by their unique understanding, alone with my friend and adviser Barry Kernon, of the logistical problems in preparing a text of this complexity with workshop accommodation disruptions outside my professional chambers at 4 Paper Buildings and domestic residence at No 1 Brick Court, where, together with British Rail Inter-City travelling facilities, the bulk of what follows has been prepared alongside the daily and nightly demands of practice at the Bar while keeping abreast of the daily and indeed nightly developments of sport and the law!

Contents

Introduction

WHY

HOW

WHY

The Rule of Law within Sport

Bobby Moore, CBE, England's winning World Cup soccer captain in 1966 died on 24 February 1993 at the tragically early age of 51. On the road to that unforgettable 4-2 Wembley Stadium victory over West Germany, Moore's great Brazilian opponent, Pele, was assaulted out of the competition in the manner described by Pele's own words eleven years later cited at page 258 of the following text in *My Life and the Beautiful Game* [1977]:

> '...I had been the target of merciless attacks from Zechev of Bulgaria throughout the entire game... Morais, of Portugal, had a field day fouling

me, eventually putting me out of the game. He tripped me, and when I was stumbling to the ground he leaped at me, feet first, and cut me down completely. It wasn't until I actually saw the films of the game that I realised what a terribly vicious double-foul it was'.

Objectively and more recently, Brian Glanville, football's leading international chronicler, has explained in *The Story of the World Cup* (1993):

'...there was no excuse, not even that of cynical necessity, for Morais to chop down Pele. Later, Pele would say that it was only when he saw the incident on film that he realised how bad it was. He would swear, then, never to play in the World Cup again. The indulgent, flaccid English referee, George McCabe allowed Morais to stay on the field, so that now Portugal were virtually playing against ten men.'

This contrast with the 1994 World Cup competition, played under the long overdue FIFA directions to referees to penalise tackles from behind by players with no prospect of gaining the ball, could not have been more vivid. Yet if any overseas footballer, rugby player or any other body-contact sport competitor from outside the United Kingdom arrives at these shores, during 1994 and after, with the belief that this FIFA 1994 directive has changed what should have happened, but did not happen to Morais in 1966, he or she (and the ladies are not immune: see page 219) will be in for a shock. For under the applicable law in and outside administrative sporting council chambers, Morais in 1966 was, and in 1994 would be, subject to disciplinary sanctions within the game, and civil and criminal liabilities in the courts. Any who doubt this may not be aware of how Scotland has given a lead based on long established precedents in Britain since 1878.

At the time of writing during the close season of 1994 the Procurator Fiscal has charged the former record £4m transfer fee holder Duncan Ferguson, when playing for Dundee United, with an assault prosecution after allegedly head-butting a Raith Rovers opponent during the course of a professional Scottish League match. Six-figure agreed damages awards from injuries suffered by professional footballers during the course of play were summarised by the Scottish solicitor associated with one or more of them, Alistair Duff, in the *New Law Journal* for 13 May 1994:

1   In 1982, J *Brown v V Pelosi and St Johnstone Football Club*:

2   In 1993, *I Durrant v N Simpson and Aberdeen Football Club*, and

3   In 1993, *S Murray v J Dolan and Motherwell Football Club*

Since then, as recorded in the *Daily Telegraph* for 14 October 1994, the sum of £70,000 was agreed to be paid 'without admission of liability' to the former Northern Ireland international defender, John O'Neill, by John Fashanu and Wimbledon Football Club, 'in full and final settlement of his claims, including costs and interest, after withdrawal of an assault (but not a negligence) allegation following evidence of an alleged negligent tackle causing injuries when O'Neill was playing for Norwich City against Wimbledon in December 1987.

In turn they were all based upon long-standing principles contained in a London Court of Appeal affirmation of a Warwick County Court judge's £4,000 damages award. That was for injuries suffered by a local Midlands Sunday League player for a broken leg caused by a foul tackle penalised by the referee, reported as *Condon v Basi* [1985] 2 All ER 453, in line with *Lewis v Brookshaw* 120 NLJ 413, threaded throughout these pages.

These examples are the mere tip of an iceberg evidenced by the Annual Reports in 1980 and 1987 of the Criminal Injuries Compensation Board, to be contrasted with the opinion expressed to Simon Barnes in *The Times* 21 September 1992 (after an international Rugby player was acquitted at Kingston Crown Court of an assault charge) by the former Chief Executive of the Football Association, Ted Croker,

'I have always opposed people who seek to bring too much law into sport. I believe very much that sport should govern itself on the field of play'.

How international and domestic sport has been proved at times to be unfit to govern itself, off as well as on the field of play, appears from the principles, precedents and reasoning behind the examples cited above and below which can be found threaded throughout these pages. They illuminate the key to the whole subject within its ethical, moral, political and legal contexts. For any abdication of the Rule of Law within Sport (ie the Laws and Rules of Play *backed up by penal playing and effective disciplinary sanctions*) creates chaos. Concurrently and consistently alongside it, abandonment of the Rule of Law in Society (ie Parliament, common law and equity) results in anarchy. Thus, the reason *why* the wider Rule of Law in society has to fill the gaps left by Sport is the frequent absence of any effective and thoughtful sanction, policy, or philosophy for penalising offences committed within it at both playing and administrative levels, and the need to destroy the myth that victims of sporting violence during play consent or are *volens* to it.

The most vivid and only really *effective* attempt to impose a sanction *within* sport to hit the public mind and eye in recent times, akin to penalising breaches of road traffic and safety laws, has been FIFA's elimination from the 1994 World Cup competition of the criminal and civilly actionable violence which destroyed Pele's participation during the 1966 competition, for which no offender was punished. It stemmed from a little publicised in legal form set of Specific Instructions for Referees following *directions* from the *International Football Association Board* (the game's parliament),as distinct from any alteration or amendment to the Laws of the Game, after its AGM at FIFA House, Zurich, Switzerland, on 5 March 1994. These concerned *inter alia* details of the *reckless challenges* about elbows and *kicking an opponent* based on *tackling from behind* with little or no attempt to play the ball which breached Law XII. They became binding through the world as *from 1 July 1994*; but the said *International Football Association Board* gave FIFA permission to implement them as from the first World Cup match on 17 June 1994.

Without amending the Laws of the Game they directed referees to apply *sanctions* available to them under the Laws, and particularly Law XII relating to violent play, to take effect internationally as from 1 July 1994. Their significance was illuminated by a perceptive summary from the *Guardian's* football correspondent, David Lacey in the following way during the 1994 World Cup competition:

> 'Those criticising the officials now would appear to have forgotten the way weak refereeing allowed Pele to be kicked out of the 1966 World Cup, how the start of the 1978 final was soured by the angry Dutch reaction to Argentina's sport of gamesmanship over the protective case on Van der Kerkhof's injured forearm, Schumacher's assault on Battiston in the 1982 semi-finals which went unpunished, and the anarchy to which the 1990 final descended.
>
> A fine line between firmness and fussiness clearly needs to be drawn. The present tournament is poised to become one of the best ever played.'

If that is the final verdict, any lasting benefits can be seen to be due to the belated recognition by the International Football Association *Board* of the need not only to identify the provisions of Law XII, but also for the *will to implement them with appropriate sanctions*. The 1994 FA Cup Final schoolmaster referee, David Elleray, had operated them within minutes of the game's commencement to penalise a Chelsea offender with a yellow card after 'up-ending' Manchester United's Ryan Giggs. Afterwards, when criticised for having imposed this sanction and also awarding two penalties which opened the scoring towards Manchester United's 4-0 victory, he explained how his duty was to protect the integrity of the game, as well as the safety of the players. These criteria showed a more profound appreciation for the *Board's* directive than the purpose expressed by FIFA's General Secretary, J S Blatter, in his *'Mandatory Instructions to Referees and Linesmen'* dated 25 July 1994 to all National Associations affiliated to FIFA, including the four United Kingdom Associations, to extend the World Cup precedent. It ended with anticipated thanks for 'continued co-operation in striving to make our sport increasingly more attractive'. Too many commentators, including Herr Blatter, failed to recognise, as David Lacey and David Elleray have explained, that elimination of violent foul play restores not only 'more attractive' play. It also results inevitably in protecting the integrity of the game, the health of the players at all levels from the grass roots upwards, and, of course, an attempt to return to the Corinthian ideal of sport which ensures it, nearly thirty years after the unpunished outrageous violence suffered by Pele in that 1966 World Cup tournament destroyed it.

Significantly, and almost symbolically, nearly a year to the day after Bobby Moore's death, the British Government's Law Commission on 23 February 1994 published a Consultation Paper No 134 entitled *Consent and Offences Against the Person,* inviting comments on whether or not outlawing consent inter alia to sporting violence required legislation. Its foundation so far as sport is concerned was based upon misinformed judicial and professional readings of long-established precedents since 1878 spanning nearly 120 years, rendering such statutory intervention unnecessary as explained on pages xxvii–xxviii below. It appeared quite coincidentally on a day when the national press at all levels lavishly illustrated the injuries suffered by a naval rating's broken nose caused in the course of an inter-services rugby match during Royal Navy service. This created the first ever traceable court martial for rugby-field violence, and resulted in a conviction and sentence of detention and reduction in rank [*RN v Russell* (1994) *The Times* 23 February].

The armed services, of course, with their need to sustain discipline, and the schools with their own need to distinguish right from wrong when preparing their pupils for civilised behaviour, are more likely than the generally untrained volunteer administrators of sporting governing bodies, dominated by the jungle law of commerce, to recognise the need to uphold the Rule of Law in Sport, on and off the field. Thus, not far removed in time from the Law Commission's Consultation Paper and that naval court-martial conviction, the High Master of St Paul's School, R S Baldock, felt constrained to write to *The Times* Sports' letters' editor after witnessing on television unacceptable misconduct by international rugby players in early 1994, enquiring what parents were going to allow their sons to continue to to play rugby football. Almost concurrently the former Principal of the FA School of Excellence at Lilleshall and former captain of the memorable Oxbridge FA *Amateur* Cup winning team of 1951 and 1953, Pegasus (on each occasion before 100,000 crowds at Wembley Stadium), and housemaster at Malvern College, Denis Saunders, wrote to the *Daily Telegraph* after a televised production of the England international team manager's language limitations, enquiring how could the teaching professions educate their pupils with such profane examples when that one hour of television exposure 'undid all the good work that the Football Association are doing to try to improve the image of the game'! Later in 1994, Denis Saunders' Headmaster, Roy Chapman, opened the annual Headmasters' Conference of Independent Schools at Bournemouth with a wider claim, equally applicable to the state school system, for filling a moral vacuum in society created by a lack of public leadership to create role models of behaviour for younger generations to admire and follow, citing specific examples from the sporting scene.

Yet how the law is applied to sport within a game's administrative control and ultimately by the courts to distinguish between right and wrong was illuminated clearly by a relatively recent Reading football ground case during 1991.

HOW

Sport and the law in action

On Tuesday 19 March 1991, Mr Justice Drake in the High Court in London ordered £250,000 damages to police officers injured by soccer hooligans. He began his judgment in the following way:

> 'On Saturday, April 7th 1984 there was an outbreak of horrible and terrifying violence at Reading Football Stadium at Elm Park Reading. The occasion was the fourth division match between Reading and Bristol City, likely to arouse particular excitement and tension because it was nearing the end of the season and both Clubs had promotion hopes.'

During the course of his judgment leading to that £250,000 damages award he explained *how*, before the trial before him occurred, a Commission of FA Council members (with my own emphasis)

> 'came to the conclusion that the Reading Football Club had taken all reasonable precautions in accordance with the requirements of Rule 33 and therefore no disciplinary action was to be taken. A similar conclusion was reached in respect of Bristol City Football Club. The hearing appears to have been conducted within the day on which it was held. It is, of course, clear that the *evidence* before the FA Commission was nowhere near as full as that which I have heard, nor was it tested by cross-examination by experienced counsel. Furthermore, the Football Association were considering *disciplinary* charges under the FA Rules, whilst I have to consider *civil claims for damages* under the Occupiers Liability Act and at common law. Accordingly, the decision of the Football Association Commission is of limited relevance to the action, but I have referred to it as part of the history of events.' [Cunningham and Others v Reading Football Club Limited [19 March, 1991, unreported transcript pages 9-10].

In comparable jurisprudential circumstances when John Fashanu of Wimbledon was charged by the Football Association during December 1993 with misconduct under its domestic administrative rule, resulting from an elbow to head injury suffered by the Tottenham Hotspur captain, Gary Mabutt, the Football Association Commission of Inquiry exonerated Fashanu. It was not satisfied that its own self-imposed criterion of intention existed. On that point, however, no clarification emerged about whether or not the criminal burden of proof to the level of certainty or the civil burden of proof requiring a balance of probabilities was applied. Furthermore, in a comprehensive interview given to Jonathan McLeod in the solicitors' professional weekly journal, the *Law Society's Gazette* for 29 March 1994 at page 11 by one of the Football Association's leading legal advisers, who allowed himself to be described as a 'commercial litigator who spends nearly a third of his time handling contentious work for the FA', he also explained:

'A rule change to prevent the types of soccer injury suffered by Spurs centre back Gary Mabbutt and Torquay defender John Uzzell would be "extraordinarily difficult to draft"'.

This apparent abject abdication of responsibility appeared to be completely unaware of the two immediately recent developments before such a well-publicised confession, which can help to solve the difficulty in perpetuity, as explained below.

(1) The *International Football Association Board's* directions on 5 March (cited on pages xxiii–xxiv above) expressly emphasised the difference between not implementing any 'rule change' and the simple expedient of using the existing referees' sanctions to enforce the game's long-established Law XII for penalising violent play. As Philip Don, England's World Cup referee, explained to Michael Parkinson in the *Daily Telegraph* during the opening days of the 1994-95 season,

'The laws weren't changed. All that FIFA did was to remind referees of what their responsibilities are'.

(2) The Law Commission's Consultation Paper No 134 entitled *Consent and Offences against the Person* published two weeks earlier on 28 February, cited at page xxv above, where the element of *reckless* as distinct from *intentional causes* of injury was clearly emphasised.

For that Law Commission's contemporaneous Consultation Paper No.134 entitled Consent *and Offences against the Person*, which surfaced during the preparation of this second edition of *Sport and the Law*, explained at page 37 in paragraph 10.14, with my own emphasis:

'While exercising all the caution proper in approaching a direction to a jury given in a case over a hundred years old, it is notable that Bramwell LJ in

Bradshaw characterised as unlawful not only conduct intended to cause serious hurt, but also conduct where the defendant "knew that, in charging as he did, he might produce serious injury and was indifferent and *reckless* as to whether he would produce serious injury or not". It is submitted that that general view must be correct, at least to the extent that the possibility of convicting a sports player for *reckless*, as opposed to intentional, injury is not excluded. The thuggery that the Court of Appeal has rightly seen as criminal when committed on the sports field is not necessarily limited, and is not stated in any of the cases to be limited, to intentional injury'.

Indeed, that needlessly cautious commentary and explanation was required only because a House of Lords judicial caveat on Bramwell LJ's direction to the jury in *R v Bradshaw* (1878) 14 Cox C C 83 surfaced in a mainly non-sporting case of *R v Brown* [1993] 2 WLR 556 which had inspired that Consultation Paper; and that caution could have been avoided if any one of the phalanx of practitioners instructed in the case had been sufficiently industrious in research to direct the House of Lords Judicial Committee to the relatively recent Court of Appeal Criminal Division specific affirmation of *Bradshaw* in *R v Venna* [1975] 3 All ER 788. It held that *recklessly-* as well as intentionally-caused criminal injury to be equally culpable. It does not appear to have been cited to their Lordships according to the list of authorities in *Brown* at pages 557-558.

Additionally, that Consultation Paper has been concerned only with the criminal as distinct from the civil law liability for negligence in relation to football injuries. The elements of *recklessness* also exist with a duty owed by one player, whether professional or amateur, to another, as explained by Sir John (as he then was) Donaldson, Master of the Rolls, in the Court of Appeal decision in Condon v Basi [1985] 2 All ER 453 and refined further by Mr Justice Drake in his well publicised judgment in *Elliott v Saunders and Liverpool Football Club* [New Law Journal 5 August 1994: p 1094 and p xxxi below]. In that case he did not follow the gratuitously obiter Court of Appeal comment that a higher duty was owed by a player in a [then] first division football match than that of a player in a local league; it was not necessary for the decision of the court.

More significantly, as already cited in the Preface, he explained not merely once for both amateur and professional players how in each case:

'if the injury was caused by another player acting in a wholly unacceptable manner, for example, by intending to cause injury, or being reckless, not caring whether or not injury was caused, then surely it is right that the injured person should be able to claim compensation'.

[Page 4 of transcript.]

He re-affirmed it by explaining:

'There is no doubt at all, and the parties to this action agree, that the law does provide an injured sportsman with the right to claim compensation. The right is a very old one'

[Page 5 of transcript],

and reference was made in general terms to the now near 120 years old practice of criminal prosecutions cited above, which are now being enthusiastically and justifiably applied by the Procurator-Fiscal in Scotland to both football codes, separate and apart from the substantial damages awards recorded also North of the Border by Alistair Duff, specified at page xxii above.

These facts of sporting and legal life were ignored by or unknown to the many ill-informed commentators on Mr Justice Drake's decision on Paul Elliott's claim, both inside and outside the legal profession, who wrote and spoke with great insensitivity to the victim's physical and career suffering until the £70,000 settlement award to John O'Neill three months later cited at page xxiii hereof above. He suffered similar injuries to those experienced by Paul Elliott when he had the misfortune to collide with John Fashanu of Wimbledon within 20 minutes of his debut after having been transferred from Leicester City to Norwich City during the course of a then First Division Football League match. Clive White in *The Independent* for 14 October 1994 graphically recorded the disinformation which earlier had surfaced by explaining:

'The door to litigation over injuries appeared to have been firmly shut after the Elliott-Saunders case in June when the judge found against the plaintiff, but O'Neill's £70,000 award, after agreeing to withdraw his allegation of assault [but not of negligence] against Fashanu would seem to have pushed it ajar. "It's a door on a very loose hinge at the moment", Graham Kelly, the Football Association's chief executive, said'.

Indeed, Mr Kelly may not know how for 120 years in this particular penalty area the door has been wide open, in the memorable aphorism of Maule J 'Like the Ritz Hotel...open to all.'

As White concluded,

'During two days in court, Mr Justice Collins heard witnesses describe Fashanu's tackle as dangerous and, according to the former Northern Ireland manager, Billy Bingham, a deliberate attempt to injure. The Defence case was based on the argument that O'Neill, in choosing to play football, accepted the inevitable risks involved'.

From a jurisprudential and evidential interest, at the outset of the trial Mr Justice Collins acceded to the application of Nigel Baker QC on behalf of the Plaintiff for leave to adduce evidence of the First Defendant's disciplinary record in evidence at the hearing. Reliance was placed on the

Court of Appeal's decision in the entertainment industry's copyright action of *Mood Music Publishing Co Ltd v De Wolfe Ltd* [1976] 1 Ch 119 referred to in the submissions. In due course, after the Plaintiff's case had been closed, before any evidence was tendered by either Defendant, the £70,000 offer was accepted in full and final settlement of his claim 'without any admission of liability' after Nigel Baker QC withdrew the assault but not the negligence allegation.

Developing sport and the law

Thus, this second edition is required in order to explain and focus the kaleidoscopically constantly changing world of sport and law. Many different forces affect sport and those forces, gathering momentum even before the first edition in 1988, have exploded to change the face of sport since then. Such forces can consist of individual's actions, sporting administrations changing the rules of sport, and also national disasters which have also produced massive repercussions in the sports where they have occurred. Understandably, when Ben Johnson was first caught for taking the banned anabolic steroid stanozolol, the athletics world inevitably became introspective looking at the problem and seeing how extensive banned practices were in athletics. The Canadian Government earned universal congratulations on its *Commission of Inquiry into the use of Drugs and banned practices intended to increase Athletic Performance*, which led to a report by Mr Justice Dubin in 1990. This was a thorough and revealing report which sought to explain the problems within athletics and is a deeply self-critical report which sought to provide answers to a great problem. (See later chapter 7 for a fuller explanation.) A less intense and more ambivalent reaction around the world followed the FIFA World Cup expulsion of Diego Maradonna from the 1994 World Cup Competition, and his suspension of fifteen months which in reality ended his career.

Furthermore, when Bobby Moore died on 24 February 1993 at the tragically early age of 51 Britain lost not only one of its great ambassadors of sport but a great sportsman as well. Much of the press and media coverage of his life from his friends and other admirers concentrated on his character and sporting example and integrity rather than on his prodigious sporting prowess. In the same vale of tears a few months later, Danny Blanchflower and his great Tottenham Hotspur mentor, Arthur Rowe, and the England captain Billy Wright followed an earlier departure to the great 'Referee in the Sky' at Tyneside of Newcastle United's folk hero, 'Wor Jackie' Milburn, who all evoked identical echoes. This coverage was consistent with the sporting public's aching nostalgia for a return to the Corinthian ideal and spirit within sport. Indeed, one of the countless tributes to Wright from his contemporaries synthesised the true spirit of sport when Ken Jones explained in the *Independent* on 5 September after the death of Wright during the preceding week-end,

'Although proud to be a professional, there was always something essentially Corinthian about the conscientious purpose that enabled Wright to complete his career as a ruggedly efficient defender without ever incurring a referee's wrath. The game was all to Wright and remained so until his death, at 70, on Saturday.'

What that Corinthian ideal and spirit means is seen in the first Appendix contributed by Hubert Doggart, a 'Corinthian and Cricketer', son of a distinguished former Corinthian, Graham Doggart, who died in harness as the Football Association chairman, after having played for England as an amateur amongst professionals, and also in the Central Council of Physical Recreation's universally adopted Charter for Fair Play in Sport, consistent in principle with it as reproduced in Appendix 13, but silent on *sanctions* for enforcement. The result of that sustained nostalgic coverage proved that society still holds these values dear and the way in which a person plays sport is more important than the results. These, and also FIFA's Fair Play initiative in 1994 which contrasts starkly with Pele's World Cup suffering in 1966 and as witnessed world-wide on television, are two of the many reasons why this second Butterworth's edition of *Sport and the Law* demands a different angle of approach from its predecessor. The first edition ended six years ago, at a cut-off date of Battle of Britain Conclusion Day 31 October 1987. History now repeats itself at the end of Word Cup month, 31 July 1994.

On that earlier occasion there were no guide lines, no precedents. The territory covered was uncharted. The chapter headings and their contents were structured from scratch. Furthermore, many within both Sport and the Law could not see any need for bringing the law into sport believing, with the author, that it ought always to be enjoyed for fun, and, at times, as a spectators' entertainment. Indeed, they were generally hostile to such a position. For whatever the true meaning and the position of sport in society may be, if ever all of its elements can be defined, too many thought that sport was cocooned in a world of its own, sealed off from reality and the Rule of Law. The vagaries and limitations upon human conduct and contact, however, preclude such idealism in an ever-growing intensely competitive and commercially orientated sporting climate.

Thus, the creation of a book which explored that theme required explanation and justification, notwithstanding the existence for over a century of intervention by the courts, and of Parliament, in relation to specific sporting issues. I was placed in a defensive position six years ago in 1988 in order to justify the subject of Sport and the Law. That defence was against a combination of abuse, insult, ignorance, ridicule and hostility linked to the traditional arrogance of feudalism based on an absence of awareness of the past which has permeated so much of sporting administration and still lingers today.

The intervening six years, however, have changed all that. Indeed, anyone who seeks to challenge the need for the Law to partner Sport for the benefit of each discipline in 1994 should examine his or her conscience and study the 'Sport and the Law' section in the *All England Law Reports Annual Review* annually since the first edition cut-off date in 1987.

Today no-one can argue that the subject of Sport and the Law does not exist. The courts have functioned at every level, including and since 1987, from the House of Lords downwards with judgments affecting the law in relation to sporting issues of charities, companies, crime, domestic and disciplinary tribunals, personal injuries, taxation and VAT, to take a random sample. Parliament has been forced to legislate for additional safety requirements after the Hillsborough, Sheffield, disaster. The *All England Law Reports Annual Review* continues regularly to survey developments from the previous year, and the British Association for Sport and the Law's formation at Old Trafford on 6 February 1993, the 35th anniversary of the Munich air crash which decimated Sir Matt Busby's Manchester United 'Babes' team, emerged almost inevitably. Its balanced base between acadaemia and practice at Manchester Metropolitan University falls into line with the British Association for Sport and Medicine. No longer can the law relating to sport be regarded as a novelty.

Indeed, Sport and the Law has moved from novelty to reality within the sixteen years since it first appeared in 1977. Under that title, in a three part newspaper feature, a series of *Sunday Telegraph* articles was converted into a 76 page booklet during the following year in 1978, with forewords by the then Sports Council Chairman, and former British Lion, Dick Jeeps, CBE, and the then Solicitor General, Sir Michael Havers, QC, MP. Ten years later Butterworths published its 15 Chapters and 10 Appendices with forewords by Lord Havers, as the former Attorney-General and Lord Chancellor, and the then Rt Hon Denis (now Lord) Howell, Britain's longest serving Minister for Sport. The contents and structure of the fifteen chapters' subject matter, which are retained here but re-grouped (with the addition of EC Law and UK Sport), were created with no guide-lines, no precedents and no natural principles or philosophies in the manner recognisable through traditional legal textbooks.

Yet the law of the land should not be seen to be something which interferes with sporting rules. The law can benefit sport in so many different ways, primarily because it underpins society by differentiating between right and wrong. Sport also has its individual rules, and all sport and its administration are shrouded by statutory rules and common law and equity. Accordingly the law should be embraced as an important element of sport which can protect people who have been harmed and also be used to form an effective framework to and for the successful administration of sport. This latter aspect was crystallised so succinctly by the late Mr Justice Shearman over a century ago cited at page 199 below from his classic Badminton Library, *Athletics and Football*. He wrote it as a young practising barrister after an outstanding Oxford University sporting career which he sustained until he died in 1930 as President of the then Amateur Athletic Association.

Structuring sport and the law

Against that background, the policy decision was taken to retain from the first edition the original chapter headings and their contents, but to re-arrange and frame them in the sections which are categorised in the following way:

Part I.	*Overview: explaining the thrust and direction of this second edition*	(chapters 1-3)
Part II.	*Personal Relationships*	(chapters 4-8)
Part III.	*International Sport*	(chapters 9-10)
Part IV.	*Administration*	(chapters 11-12)
Part V.	*Commerce*	(chapters 13-14)
Part VI.	*Conclusion*	(chapter 15)

In the process of that chapter re-arrangement six further features have now emerged for explanation here, by way of Introduction, separate and apart from that Overview section. They were not apparent for the first edition's original structuring but since then have developed more sharply while these pages have been in the course of preparation. They demonstrate the depths and dimensions of the ties which bind Sport and the Law together for the benefit of each other in particular, and society generally, as a leitmotiv for the pattern of the book. They are conveniently summarised under their individual descriptions here thus:

(1) Nature of the subject xxxvii
(2) Complexity of the subject xxxviii
(3) Sustained lack of Government philosophy xliii
(4) Definition or description xlvii
(5) Corinthian values li
(6) Moral, Social, Political and Legal Issues lviii

Notwithstanding these headings which have surfaced imperceptibly since the first edition was published in January 1988 after its cut-off date on 31 October 1987, the purpose and target area of the book and the applicable legal principles relating to it have remained unchanged from how they were explained initially in Chapter 1 Genesis to that first edition. They are now repeated substantially below as before, with extended explanations in square brackets, as a prelude to that *Overview* section and those six further features for this second edition:

'The purpose of this book is to create a level of awareness among all readers of the extent to which those ties [between sport and the law] exist; and the need to be aware that there are many times when the law can and should come to the help of sport; and, indeed, how sport, with its high public profile and image can come to the help of law. For sport without rules and their control creates chaos. Society without law and its enforcement means anarchy.

That level of awareness is the overriding intention [for practical as distinct from arid academic purposes]. Any quest for more detailed knowledge and advice must and should demand deeper enquiries for which these pages have not been designed to respond. They are intended to be used as a signpost directing attention to easily identifiable legal areas and principles which may not otherwise easily or readily be recognisable as relevant to sport and sporting problems and issues [which require effective action]. Halsbury's Laws of England and Halsbury's Statutes [which respectively specify the detailed case law litigation and legislation] are to be found in every public library.

Thus the target area for this book is not only the present and future Prime Ministers of the United Kingdom, but also everyone who is concerned with, affected by or interested in whatever is believed or understood to be sport (which Sir Denis Follows, the country's leading sports administrator, claimed in 1983, three years after the Moscow Olympics, 'defies definition'). That means lawyers, administrators, players referees, umpires, trainers, doctors, physiotherapists, chemists, clubs, coaches, school teachers, students, supporters, parents, police and other public services, local government and leisure and recreation centre managers, tea ladies and team agents, politicians, property developers and speculators, criminal classes of all categories, commercial and physical, and the world at large, of all ages, from the cradle to the grave; in fact, participants at every level from aspiring and fading stars and administrators with feet and heads of clay to all who know that in the beginning and at the end, sport exists for fun and the never changing ideal embodied in *mens sana in corpore sano*: a healthy mind in a healthy body.

Comprehensively they can be consolidated into six clearly identifiable categories. The first five specified above; lawyers, administrators, players, referees and umpires are interdependent upon each other; and upon them exclusively, all the remainder concerned must depend. For without lawyers there would be no creation of and guidance for the rules or laws within which all sport must be played. Without administrators, mostly unpaid and unappreciated, and also often sadly untrained, play could not be organised; and without players, referees and umpires to apply the rules and laws there would be no need for any codes of conduct or practice to exist at all.

Players and sporting participants throughout the world at all levels and in every age bracket are identifiable in two recognisable categories: professional and amateur. They in turn give rise to class, economic, social and technical and also to legal foundations for analysis, debate and discussion, as we shall see in Chapter 13 Sponsored Gentlemen and Players. Furthermore, playing within the spirit and letter of the laws of any game has become identifiable with a classical concept of sporting idealism recognised universally as Corinthian. Fair play is its beacon, and justice in the law beams it to a wider society.'

Further, the need to preserve that Corinthian ideal and tradition provides the key to why the law has been pulled into sport for its protection and those who suffer from abuses within it. For when modern organised sport unfolded in the Victorian era from what at school playing fields and village green levels are still its grass roots, the Rule of Law was recognised generally in society and accepted in sport by both the gentlemen Players and the playing Gentlemen. There was no need for disciplinary bodies which to-day are required to regulate cheating by violence or drugs for which inadequate control by governing bodies today demands the attention of the courts. For while these pages were being prepared during the end of 1993 and early 1994 a surge of resentment surfaced from within the national British games by players at the sharp end against the abdication of responsibility by sporting governing bodies manned frequently by untrained volunteers relying on paid executives to demand effective operation of their own laws of play.

At the mythically incorruptible cricket temple the Northampton player Alan Lamb had been fined £5,000 by the Test and County Cricket Board for allegations of cheating by Pakistan bowlers through tampering with the ball in breach of Law 42.4 and 5 relating to Unfair Play and abuse of the ball. During and after libel proceedings against him were settled and withdrawn, a general impression of cheating within the *public* game emerged, corroborated subsequently by Imran Khan's disclosures and Michael Atherton's admitted 'suspicious' TV circumstances (accompanied by a denial of cheating), notwithstanding inadequate attempts to eradicate or at least control it by the Test and County Cricket Board and the International Cricket Council. The grass roots levels at track and field athletic clubs *publicly* disclosed disturbed and sustained concern before, throughout, and after the British Athletic Federation's investigation and recorded verdict into what will always be known as the Norman-Temple suicide affair. Within domestic football the Professional Footballers' Association and other responsible voices condemned injuries caused by elbow to head collisions which the Chief Executive of the Football Association had testified in the *R v Blissett* (1992) *The Times*, 5 December prosecution was in effect an accepted practice (and now for 1994-1995 season and onwards is to be outlawed). Subsequently on the opening day of the 1994-95 season after the World Cup *The Times* Football Correspondent, Rob Hughes, wrote:

> 'From the field of play it was distressing to hear Neil Ruddock, the Liverpool defender, greet the new code of conduct with the words, "Defenders like me had better get used to suspensions". Precisely. Had the FA not been so indulgent, had it not gone to court two years ago [ie in *R v Blissett*] to condone reckless use of the elbow, Ruddick would not have started last season...Ruddick performed a reckless foul in a pre-season match breaking the cheek-bone of Beardsley'.

After the ill-fated and foul-studded New Zealand rugby tour during 1993 it was left to the England captain and Harlequins hero, Will Carling, to initiate the public condemnation of the visiting internationals as a dirty side when the Rugby Union authorities at Twickenham earlier had voiced unwisely their displeasure diplomatically in *private* to the New Zealand authorities, and thereby created a needlessly wrong impression with the general public. For as the distinguished *Times* newspaper rugby correspondent, David Hands, wrote in a feature article 'it may take litigation to change such a caste of mind and that will not be far away, even in New Zealand'. This was re-emphasised in the *Daily Telegraph* a few days later during the season of goodwill by Stuart Barnes, the England international stand-off half, when he wrote,

> 'Players know themselves what aggression is permissible or otherwise and if someone oversteps the mark the victim should consider legal action as a serious option. A crime deliberately committed on a sports field belongs more in a court room than on a rugby pitch. No fair-minded players would object to such action and it is certainly more likely to eradicate the odd psychopath who will always graze on the rugby pitch, than the hot air that currently fills our winter reading'.

Indeed, subsequent events throughout 1994 involving South African conflicts on rugby fields with England and New Zealand opponents more than confirmed this warning.

Accordingly, if sport and its rulers cannot or will not try to preserve that Corinthian tradition, which the citations throughout this Introduction and the inspiration for this book demonstrate is an ideal realistically recognised and capable of attainment to aim for, if not always achieved, then the courts can and will do it for them, through the law of the land at both criminal and civil levels, and certainly if adequate compensation is required. This last point was emphasised by Mr Justice Drake at the commencement of his judgment in Paul Elliott's unsuccessful personal injuries action for damages against Dean Saunders and Liverpool Football Club (supra, page xxxviii). For he explained twice at the outset of his judgment that the courts as a last resort are inevitable 'if there is no other way' for compensating injured victims of playing misconduct which transgresses actionable civil and criminal laws [*New Law Journal* 5 August 1994: p1101]. The 'other way' of a Compensation Scheme analogous to the Solicitors' Indemnity Fund, was aired after this judgment and again three months later in October 1994, when the advisers to John Fashanu and Wimbledon Football Club agreed to settle for £70,000 a claim for personal injuries brought by John O'Neill after he had been injured when playing for Norwich City in a First Division Football League game during 1989. The professional football game's sponsored and transfer fee funds have the capacity to pay for it. Whether the moral will and intellectual capacity exist to implement it by those empowered to do so at executive is another question, and remains to be seen after the publication of this book.

(1)   Nature of the subject

No subject exists which jurisprudentially can be called sports law. As a soundbite headline, shorthand description, it has no juridical foundation; for common law and equity create no concept of law exclusively relating to sport. Each area of law applicable to sport does not differ from how it is found in any other social or jurisprudential category; agency; administrative law; agriculture; building; companies; charities; crime; contract; entertainment; environment; intellectual property; personal injuries; physical education; real and personal property; restraint of trade; sponsorship; tort; tax and VAT, and every other known legal area. Parliament has legislated in recent years for crowd safety and protection against football hooligans and recreational environmental despoilation. When sport hits the legal and political buffers, conventional and ordinary principles affecting the nature of the appropriate sporting issue concerned including parliamentary legislation are triggered into action.

Furthermore, as I have explained in the Introduction to my Butterworths *All England Law Reports Annual Review 1992*:

'It seems that practitioners in all branches of the profession - the judiciary, barristers and solicitors - fail frequently to comprehend the complex interplay between sporting and legal structures and how judicial and procedural elements interact upon them. Academics often ignore or fail to recognise the historic evidence from the past and the practical essential evidential and procedural subtleties required for success in the courts. Thus, the idea that the legal issues surfacing within sport can be regarded as a relaxation, a doddle or a diversionary fun exercise removed from more recondite and complex professional experiences is a fallacy, and nothing could be further from reality. The collective and individual illustrations from

1992 explain why - covering as they did, charities, company, commercial, contract and property rights, criminal and civil liabilities, judicial review and procedure, tort and VAT.'

Indeed, a clear cut example appears from the list of almost lemming-like successive abortive applications for judicial review, analysed in Catherine Bond's Appendix when blocked by binding precedent at present from the Court of Appeal in *Law v National Greyhound Racing Club Ltd* [1983] 3 All ER 300. Conversely, a graphic illustration of the way in which these conventional and ordinary principles are identifiable for sporting situations appear in the unreported transcript of a judgment from Sir Michael Davies sitting as an additional High Court judge in early 1993 when he awarded £13,055.72 agreed damages to a plaintiff injured in a Karate related accident. He commented at the outset that the amount involved merited transference of the claim to the County Court with its jurisdiction up to £50,000, and that it seemed

'That an application on request was made on behalf of the defendant to the judge in charge of the non-jury list to retain the matter in the High Court.....I suspect that the judge in charge of the list was told that this case was of great importance in the important world of karate and involved great questions of principle. Having heard all the evidence, I am totally confident it is nothing of the sort. No great question of principle arises. There is a straightforward question of fact to be decided. The law, which is found enshrined in one decision of the Court of Appeal to which I will refer [*Condon v Basi*], is, in my view, crystal clear. The court has to find the facts, apply the law and that is the end of it'. [*Champion v Brown* (1993) 24 February QBD.]

(2)   Complexity of the subject

Nevertheless, within the special framework, a review of the law as it developed for the sporting scene during 1992 in both the *New Law Journal* for 15 January 1993 and in that *All England Law Reports Annual Review* for 1992 (published in 1993) stumbled upon a hitherto unidentified development: the frequency with which practitioners are or ought to be ruled offside or no-balled for their mis-application of the law or procedure in practice. The House of Lords in *Re Guild v Commissioners of Inland Revenue*, reversed the lower court and for the first time extended the Recreational Charities Act 1958 for interests of social welfare to include a sporting purpose (without defining sport!) ([1992] 2 All ER 10: 27 February 1992). It became the ninth occasion out of ten in the sixty-five years since the celebrated tax-free cricketers' case in Sey*mour v Reed* [1927], when the House of Lords Judicial Committee has reversed the Court of Appeal (and often a trial judge as well). This can be seen in tabulated form in Appendix 10. Eleven months later in the same year of 1992 in *The Times* (Tuesday 5 December 1992) three landmark court decisions of general as well as professional legal sporting interest hit the headlines, to expose the legal professions' own area for lending itself open to critical scrutiny in this context.

In a well-publicised abortive attempt to obtain judicial review against the Jockey Club (*R v Disciplinary Committee of the Jockey Club ex parte the Aga Khan* [1993] All ER 853), the Court of Appeal pointed to a more appropriate route by way of contract which should have been taken on behalf of the famous racehorse owner instead of the precedent-barred process, after a debatable disqualification for alleged drug abuse; evidence by the Football Association's chief administrator was given on behalf of an acquitted defendant in a criminal trial concerning a football field injury in *R v Blissett* which was heavily criticised from within and outside the game itself, or should have been objected to by the prosecution and disallowed by the trial judge as inadmissible, or at least the subject of a rebuttal testimony; and the International Amateur Athletic Federation allowed a default judgment for £18m against it in Ohio, USA, District Court, to be obtained by the disciplined athlete, Harry 'Butch' Reynolds, on the debateable basis that no assets within the USA existed for its satisfaction (which has since then been overturned on appeal by the Association and re-affirmed on a further appeal to the Supreme Court by Reynolds).

It therefore follows that the subject-matter for understanding and practising the law relating to sport requires not only a knowledge of the applicable substantive law. It also requires recognition of the appropriate legal litigation procedure and strategy and tactics; the rules of admissible and inadmissible applicable, appropriate and relevant evidence, and the concept of one of Scotland's most renowned practitioners Sir Walter Scott:

'A lawyer without history or literature is a mechanic, a mere working mason;
if he possesses some knowledge of these, he may venture to call himself an
architect.' (As explained by Counsellor Pleydell in *Guy Mannering*.)

The almost perverse persistent refusal by practitioners in both branches of the profession to recognise or understand the rejection by the courts since *Law v National Greyhound Racing Club Ltd* [1983] 3 All ER 300 of the judicial review machinery to sporting governing bodies' decisions can be prayed in aid here, too, in addition to its citation under (1) **Nature of the Subject**, at page xxxviii above. The details are self-evidently explained in Catherine Bond's critical analysis at Appendix 9 which nevertheless illustrates a consistent pattern of erroneous *procedural* decisions comprising 100% failures by each of the applicants' legal advisers to load their clients' legal guns correctly: analagous to the attribution in Sellar and Yeatman's celebrated *1066 And All That*: 'Failed BA (Oxon)'.

Significantly, too, the Law Commission's *Report on Administrative Law, Judicial Review and Statutory Appeals* (No 226) published on 26 October 1994 during the final stages of preparation of these pages, did not consider this dimension. No doubt because no-one thought fit to raise it for consideration under the wider issue for Law Reform (see para 1.1, page 1) within the framework of the Law Commission's formal Fifth Programme.

Furthermore, internationally, and socially, with a global village created by international competition, television and transport, Sport and the Law today involves inevitably an international flavour entwined at the higher profiled levels with show-business. The worlds of soccer and Olympic Games competitions are processed in the media with international opera performers: and a complex network of commercial contract arrangements underlines the multi-faceted relationships which regulate the inter-action between participants and governing bodies.

Thus, while on one hand, top level sport is becoming constantly more commercialised and corrupt by cheating through violence and drugs against the Laws and Rules of Play, on the other hand, sport at its grass roots, the traditional sport played in villages, clubs and with the lesser facilities in state as well as from the flourishing independent schools, is still thriving at varying levels of activity within the Laws and Rules of Play. Million pound sponsorship and television deals are not subjects which *directly* concern commercially most people personally. Yet legal issues are just as alive away from the falsely glamorised and monied side of sport. Legal issues emerge which are often ignored by, or unknown to, many grass roots administrators: namely, responsibilities for children, coaching, disabled, and medical developments, rate reliefs for recreational charitable activities and school playing fields to name but a few, all have a special significance to sport. All of these were treated in the first edition under their individual Chapter headings and are updated here under their new group headings, in order to create a more definitive structure to the whole subject.

In the intervening six years since the first edition, in 1988, civil and criminal court incursions into sport have surfaced at almost every level, and in all areas of recreational activity to protect and compensate victims injured by gratuitous violence for whom no remedy exists within sport itself. The extent to which this has occurred appears with the five Chapters 4-8 inclusive which are now regrouped within the section Personal Relationships: and the same six-year period has witnessed legislative and litigation developments in nearly every other chapter comprising each of the other sections.

Of no less concern must be recognition of the quantum of injustice whether at playing or administrative levels, which is unknown and uncharted, because victims, whether of violence or administrative malpractice, cannot afford the costs of legal services, whether for a domestic tribunal, arbitration panel or court of law, unless funded by civil legal aid or as a witness in a state prosecution process. This, of course reflects a wider drama which the Master of the Rolls, Sir Thomas Bingham, described graphically as a 'cancer eating at the heart' of the administration of justice in a lecture to the University of Birmingham [(1994) *The Times* 5 March, p.5]. It is also emphasised by the number of occasions identified in Appendix 10 when the House of Lords, with an almost inevitable regularity, overrules lower court decisions on sporting issues with a legal flavour. Yet new sporting legal issues develop nearly every day: from ball-tamperings and sledging in cricket to Grand National and boardroom football fiascos, with the welcome developing success of women in all disciplines, from Olympic athletic triumphs to World Cup successes in cricket, equestrian events and rugby union, to the Curtis Cup in golf. This in turn still requires attacks on male bastions which appears in Chapter 8, *Women in Sport and the Law* and the Appendices 4 and 12 summarising respectively the ultimate future recognition generally of women's contribution comprehensively to sport by Julia Bracewell, with the continuing erosion of sex discrimination in sport and the repayments of VAT erroneously claimed in breach of EEC directives.

A more widely-targeted Sports (Discrimination) Bill was published and received its first reading in the house of Commons during June 1994. Its aim is to outlaw discrimination by the governing body of any sport against anyone solely because of participation in any other completely separate sport. More immediately, it is aimed at the prohibitions on amateur rugby union players experimenting in the in the form of trials, or with attempts to return from, professional Rugby League connections to rugby union participation at any level. The understandable battle to preserve rugby union's amateur status alongside its emergence as a world-wide televised branch of the entertainment industry nevertheless appears to ignore or be unaware of the long-established precedents from the traditional theatre and film industry. The thousand or so regular fee earning, Equity card carrying, professionals in the United Kingdom are swamped numerically by the amateur Thespians who tread the boards for fun, in a comparable pattern experienced by amateur musicians and singers who never intend to join the professional ranks. In the same cultural seam of communal activity, the distinguished *Sunday Times* internationally renowned rugby union correspondent, Stephen Jones, identified in his 1993 award winning Sports Book of the Year, *Endless Winter: the Inside Story of the Rugby Revolution:*

> 'millions of the lovely little beaverers:...who vividly demonstrate their affection for the game and its ambience by spending every leisure minute in the exhausting process of providing the fitting backdrop for players at

·all levels to come out on the rugby field and play. They still do, these heroes.
Every week. For nothing.'

It is possible that the understandable defenders of the faith for the true
spirit of amateur rugby have failed to recognise these precedents for
preserving its integrity while allowing the talents and sacrifices of time
and family and employment commitments by the relative handful of
players involved at the high profiled and globally televised entertainment
level to be rewarded for the pleasure they bring to millions and also the
funding for salaried administrators, and stadia developments.

Finally, as yet another example, if ever one were needed, of the dynamic
manner in which the law comes to the aid of sport, or at least of the
participants in it, David Hands, *The Times* respected Rugby Union
correspondent, recorded a further application of established legal principles
to the sporting scene in the final stages of page proof corrections. On 25
October 1994 he reported the issue of a restraint of trade writ against the
IRFB from a former Wales prop Stuart Evans who played rugby for St Helens
seeking re-instatement against the discrimination inherent in the Bill. This
remedy, of course, is eligible even to participants in erroneously-styled
amateur activities, as Scott J held in a usually unannounced section by
sporting administrators of his judgment in the drugs case of *Gasser v IAAF*.
He found unequivocally the International *Amateur* Athletic Federation to
be subject to the restraint of trade principles [chapter 11, page 304].

Finally, during the course of preparing these pages, a more subtle and
generally unnoticed universally form of sports injury syndrome
unconnected with violence or drug abuse began to emerge, namely, sports
injury caused from overuse and stress and neglect or inconsistency from
governing bodies. It first came to my attention at the Football Association-
Royal College of Surgeons medical conference at Lilleshall on two
occasions during the early 1990s. It was later confirmed by the
internationally-renowned athletics coach Frank Dick. Finally, illumination
came from the cavalier and irresponsible attitude of governing bodies.

For younger generations, the FA's experience was significant. Some
candidates for the FA School of Excellence at Lilleshall were rejected as
physically unfit from overuse and over stress on their developing bodies,
bones and muscles. For adults, the greater competitive and sponsorship
demands created a comparable problem; and at governing body level the
cricket authorities at Lord's Test and County Cricket Board were content
to send representative teams overseas without any or adequate professional
medical services at doctor level, notwithstanding the less financially
benefited women's sources recognition of the need.

Rugby football particularly increased the competitive framework for
what used to be regarded as an amateur-played friendly club rivalry, with
weekly identified increasing levels of injury; and the Football Association

turned on its head its own Memorandum and Articles of Association 'to protect the game...from abuses' by charging Manchester United and Leeds United with misconduct for withdrawing their younger players from representative international competition at the end of a long and arduous professional season in 1993 in order to prevent the overuse and abuse syndrome affecting long-term health care. In the end a moderate reprimand reflected the FA's belated recognition of reality.

Such injurious consequences within modern sporting disciplines are consistent with Sir Walter Scott's concept of a 'mere working mason' aspect of modern public and not so public sport, geared to greed and commercial exploitation. They are distinguishable from the need to adapt his other concept of an architect's mantle which would recognise the differential between present day market led forces and the earlier pioneering conditions of an age of innocence when sporting concepts were free from current trends and thought, now concentrated on an excessive but erroneous belief in sport as no more than a branch of the entertainment industry.

No greater example of the need for concentrated thought emerged than in 1989, when the Hillsborough disaster at Sheffield Wednesday's football ground spawned a British Government judicial inquiry by the then Lord Justice Taylor. This in turn was followed by concurrent and consequential legislation and litigation. The legislation has led to far-reaching changes in the organisation of public entertainment, football matches and stadia in order to encourage public safety. The disaster raised the interplay between moral, political, social and legal issues. These were the issues which Lord Hailsham of St Marylebone (creator during 1962 of the role of a Government Minister with responsibility for sport) dealt with during the time when the first edition was being prepared during 1987, as cited on page lix hereafter.

(3)   Sustained lack of Government philosophy

During a House of Lords debate on Sports Facilities initiated by Lord Dean of Beswick on 9 June 1993 a claim was made by Lord Addington:

> 'We want a more cohesive approach from the Government, and leadership from the centre. At present, we do not know where we are going'.

This echoed the thoughts of Lord Hailsham of St Marylebone thirty years earlier when he created the role of a Minister with responsibility for sport in 1962 when he recognised the absence of any

> 'coherent body of doctrine, perhaps even a philosophy of Government encouragement'.

Parliamentary action since then has been primarily a knee-jerk reaction to crowd disasters as evidenced after Ibrox (1971) by the Safety of Sports Ground Act 1975, after Bradford (1985) the Fire Safety and Safety of Places of Sport Act 1987, and after Hillsborough (1989) the Football Supporters Act 1990.

More significantly during the June 1993 Parliamentary debate Viscount Astor [now in 1994 a Parliamentary Under-Secretary in the Department of National Heritage] on behalf of the Government explained:

'Our policy remains firm that, before playing-fields are disposed of by local authorities, the local authorities should take account of long-term community needs.'

By inference, long term community needs means that the playing-fields should be preserved for the benefit of the community. However the then Secretary of State for Education, John Patten, had proposed already that the School Premises Regulations should no longer apply as far as a minimum standard for teaching and recreation were concerned. This produced a response from the then Secretary of State for National Heritage, in whose department resided the Minister for Sport as an Under-Secretary, that it was:

'a cost-cutting device with potentially disastrous results for team games and the ability to deliver the PE requirements of the national curriculum.'

To compound the confusion in the previous month of April 1993 a joint circular from the Department of Education and the Welsh Office produced a Guidance for Local Authorities on the issue of Disposal of Land for less than the best consideration that can be reasonably obtained. The three government departments here identified thereby possess overlapping functions for the provision and disposal of the grass root levels of all British and international sport playing fields. Thus, the sustained absence of a 'coherent body of doctrine, perhaps even a philosophy of government encouragement' over now more than a thirty-year period is self-evidently illuminated at its most essential level, and is re-affirmed by the chart of fifteen overlapping Government departments, in addition to the monolithic complex of the Department of National Heritage, all of which cumulatively are concerned directly with sport and recreation in Appendix 7. This was re-affirmed when the 1994 appointee to the Secretary of State status in the Department of National Heritage, Stephen Dorrell, MP, was reported in his local constituency newspaper, the *Leicester Mercury* for 21 July 1994, in answer to a question about his participation in sport as saying 'No, not if I can help it'! Subsequently he compounded this with an extraordinary announcement while these pages were being processed on

Friday 19 August that 'extra public spending should go on health and education rather than the arts, historic monuments and sport'! (*The Times*: 20 August 1994, p 8), thus ignoring the natural interaction between health, education and sport.

A back to basics course here in the true nature of sport at least would appear to be desirable for an elementary enlightenment in thiscrucial cultural area of national concern, welfare and, indeed, heritage! His arrival followed closely upon the announcement by his Under-Secretary on 9 July 1994 in the House of Commons. Ian Sproat, MP, of a fundamental re-structuring of Sports Councils throughout the United Kingdom, of which precise details will be announced after publication of this edition. Nothing contained in it modifies in any way at all, or infers any possible expected modification to, the essentially active participation of the fifteen government departments, separate and apart from the multi-fragmented Department of National Heritage, involved in Sport and Recreation identified in Appendix 7.

School and club partners

Furthermore, while these pages have been passing through their final proof stages a final point linked to a sustained lack of Government philosophy would appear to have justified the early planning decision for this edition to project Chapter 4, *Parent School and Club Partners* to the top of the detailed chapters pile. The failure of the United Kingdom's four home international Football Associations to qualify for FIFA's 1994 USA World Cup Competition was being compounded by the events of the disastrous week which ended during the Easter holiday and All Fools Day, when England's Test Match cricketers were crushed by a near record minimum score of 46 in the West Indies, and Great Britain's Davis Cup tennis team was defeated by Portuguese opponents, a defeat further compounded by the ultimate ejection from the competition by Roumania in July 1994.

Many detailed and reasoned explanations of personal, coaching, and administrative attitudes in different sporting disciplines will be floated after these pages have appeared. It is arguable however that few thoughtful analysts will disagree with the wisdom words of Lord Deedes, the former *Daily Telegraph* editor, journalist and Government Minister under three Prime Ministers, Churchill, Eden and MacMillan, in the decade spanning 1954 to 1964, which embraced the Central Council for Physical Recreation's Report of its Wolfenden Committee *Sport and the Community* published in 1960. Writing in his Weekly Notebook column on Easter Monday, 4 April 1994, he observed under the heading 'Little wonder we keep losing':

'Is there not an extraordinary contrast between the concern we feel over dismal sporting losses, such as our cricketers have been suffering in the West Indies, and our apparent indifference to what is happening to sport in our schools? The decline of games at our national schools, coupled with the selling off of their playing fields, has been going on long enough to show up in the sporting arena.

Independent schools have kept sport going but against increasing handicaps. Summer terms have been shortened and have become devoted to examinations on which future careers may depend. So cricket takes second place. We lack the systems of Australia and South Africa which help give good sporting performers at school further opportunities.

Discussion has recently centred on whether the national schools' curriculum can afford one or two hours a week for sport. How in the world do we hope to turn out winners on such a formula?

We can still turn out world competitors at golf - for which no national schools, and only a few independent schools, have ever catered. The Lawn Tennis Association, on the other hand, has spent a fortune in search of talent - vainly. Our Davis Cup team has just lost to the Portuguese [and as noted above ultimately to Roumania: EG].

Unless we can kindle more enthusiasm for sport in school, I doubt we shall count among serious competitors. Those who condemn competitive school games on the grounds that some children are bound to be on the losing side, have condemned this country's sportsmen and women to be permanent losers.'

Ironically, chapter 3 of that *Wolfenden Committee Report* in 1960 identified under a heading 'Some Special Factors and Problems Examined' (a) The Gap in paragraph 53: at page 25, with my own emphasis:

'...The one of which we treat first has been brought to our notice by a great many of the organisations and individuals who have submitted evidence to us. For example, the National Council for School's Sports (which is concerned with athletics, boxing, cricket, Association and Rugby football and swimming) has emphasised to us its sense of the inadequacy of the provision made for post-school sport and the *weakness of the links between school and adult clubs.*

54. This problem to which we refer as "The Gap", is the first of the gaps listed by the Albemarle Committee (Albermarle Report, Paragraph 148) [*The Youth Service in England and Wales* (also 1960)]. In the context of the present inquiry, "the Gap" stands for the manifest *break* between, on the one hand, the participation in recreative physical activities which is normal for boys and girls at school, and. on the other hand, their participation in *similar* (though not necessarily identical) *activities some years later when they are more adult'.

By a coincidence of timing at the end of the week which had begun with Lord Deedes' assessment, the junior government Minister at the Department of National Heritage, Ian Sproat, MP, unveiled a well publicised 8,000 word report for reviving competitive sports in secondary schools. It did not appear to have been published in consultation with the Department of Education and Science dealing with teachers contracts and the unions, nor with the Department of the Environment concerned with planning elements for preserving or buying back school playing fields. It also did not appear to be aware of the Gap exposed nearly 35 years ago by both the Albermarle and Wolfenden Reports, of 1960. That gap, however, also did not appear to be within the knowledge of the genuinely sports loving Prime Minister John Major when he explained to the Conservative Party Conference on the anniversary of the Battle of Hastings, 14 October 1994, how the National Education Curriculum would include sport, and physical education, to be experienced in every school by children from five to sixteen, linked to a hope for the preservation of school playing fields by local authorities.

Hence the earliest possible location in the text which follows this Introduction of Chapter 4, Parent, School and Club Partners, to head Part II of the chapter structure, *Personal Relationships*. Further hence *plus ça change, plus c'est la même chose* (the more things change the more they are the same)!

(4) Definition or description

A House of Commons Environmental Committee Report to the House of Commons in February 1986 on the workings of the Sports Council included a written memorandum from its then Director-General, John Wheatley, dated 30 October 1985, entitled 'Financing of Sport in the United Kingdom'. It stated under the head of definition in paragraph 2:

'A study of the financing of sport produces a problem of definition. There is no single list of activities which would meet with universal agreement. Many years ago sport was felt by some to encompass hunting, shooting and fishing. A much wider view is now taken by many people.'

and the same paragraph concluded with financial references

'from a variety of sources which have adopted different definitions.'

Two years earlier in 1983, Sir Denis Follows, a wise and experienced administrator with three renowned sporting bodies; the British Olympic Association, the Central Council of Physical Recreation and the Football Association, delivered a memorable Philip Noel-Baker Memorial Lecture at Loughborough College entitled *Whither Sport*. Among its many valuable thoughts was the

> 'conclusion, after years of trying, that sport defies definition. The Sports Council tried it and gave it up as a bad job.'

In the intervening six years since I cited each of these two quotations in the first edition I have begun to consider that a more realistic approach was provided by a great jurist, Lord Bryce, in his *Studies in History and Jurisprudence* , Vol 11, p181 where he observed:

> 'there are some conceptions which it is safer to describe than to attempt to define.'

Sport is one of them. Thus when Lord Hailsham of St Marylebone in his memoirs, *A Sparrow's Flight*, explained

> 'Sport, I believe...is an essential part of education. Years later, in my judicial capacity as Lord Chancellor, I was part-author of a judgment which authenticated the legal status of a fund for Association Football as a charitable trust [*IRC v McMillan* [1980] 1 AC 1]. Organised sport is undoubtedly part of our national culture. In mountain-climbing, cricket and most kinds of football, in hunting, fishing and game shooting, the British were the pioneers in the field of sport as it burgeoned in the nineteenth century. In a sense there is no such thing as sport. There is only a heterogeneous list of pastimes, with different governing bodies, different ethics, and different and constantly varying needs. There are funds to pay for the training and fares of Olympic athletes, there are demands for sports centres, problems of law and order connected with sporting contests, questions relating to the safety of sports grounds, varying views about bloodsports, boxing, horse racing and many other topics. All this and more I canvassed in Cabinet and urged the need of a small secretariat under a minister who might be more a liaison officer than a government spokesman. Whether I was right or wrong in the views I then expressed I do not know. Things have developed on rather different lines. But I soon discovered that I had talked myself into a job, and was myself the first to attempt the task I had tried to outline.'

By contrast, Professor Sir Ludwig Guttman the pioneering creator of the Spinal Injuries Clinic and the Disabled Olympic Games at Stoke Mandeville Hospital in Buckinghamshire in his *Textbook of Sport for the Disabled*, included among others this attempt by Unesco:

> 'Any physical activity which has the character of play and involves a struggle with oneself or others, or a confrontation with natural elements, is sport. If this activity involves competition it must be performed with a spirit of sportsmanship. There can be no true sport without fair play. All rules must be observed with this in mind.'

Within that context it has become inevitable to conclude at least that sport includes the elements of health, education, competition and the Rule of Law. More elaborately, in typically bureaucratic Brussels-speak, the Council of Europe has offered to the world in its own *European Sports Charter* definition while ignoring the Rule of Law and Guttman's 'rules to be observed':

> '"Sport" means all forms of physical activity which, through casual or organised participation, aim at expressing or improving physical fitness and mutual well-being, forming social relationships or obtaining results in competition at all levels.'

Indeed, 'results in competition at all levels' without the Rule of Law or 'rules to be observed' comes close to winning at all costs, the antithesis of true sport, Corinthian or otherwise.

Of equal importance is what Sport is *not*, also as described by Sir Denis Follows in that Loughborough College Lecture now more than a decade ago in 1983:

> 'Sport at top level has become much more part of the entertainment world and particularly so during the past thirty years. We have reached the age where sport at top level has become almost completely show biz - the cult of the individual, high salaries, the desire to present the game as a spectacle - with more money, less sportsmanship, more emphasis on winning - and all this has largely come about through television.'

This quotation partially explains why the term sport is indefinable. The meaning, function and reason for sport is changing along with the evolution of society in general; and a convenient cameo framing and explaining in part how this has occurred emerged during the *Times* obituary of the Corinthian-styled professional Billy Wright after recalling his playing triumphs with his beloved Wolverhampton Wanderers and England during the later 1950s, on 5 September 1994:

> 'By then he had revealed that there was more to him than a Boy's Own hero by his marriage to Joy Beverley, the eldest of the singing Beverley Sisters. It is difficult now when sports personalities, film and pop stars inhabit the same cultural and social milieus and earn similar fees to realise quite how unlikely such a liaison seemed in the 1950s, when footballers were generally perceived as being on a par with the working men who made up the majority of their audiences, and were paid accordingly.'

The current obsession with the trial on and by television of the American football entertainer, O J Simpson, crystallises the merger of those two cultures to-day. Sadly, that

> 'something essentially Corinthian about the conscious purpose that enabled Wright to complete his career as a ruggedly efficient defender without incurring a referee's wrath,'

cited from Ken Jones' *Independent* obiuary tribute at page xxxi, above, conflicts with the obscenely offensive posturings, with which so many self-styled sporting entertainers to-day corrupt their hero-worshipping adulators without any disciplinary disapproval by administrative authorities or many quiescent media commentators. It also reflects the contrast between much of current obscene humour and entertainment generally with the natural fun and joy dispensed by Morecombe and Wise, Frankie Howerd and the Flanagan and Allen Crazy Gang experiences.

What is sport?

Indeed, almost a year to the day on 5 December 1992 after that hat-trick of debateable sporting legal decisions explained at pages 21 to 22 above was reported simultaneously, the celebrated *Daily Mail* columnist and award winning Sportswriter of the Year, Ian Wooldridge, identified, on Cliff Morgan's BBC *Sport on Four* radio programme, while these pages were being prepared during 1993 following elimination of all the United Kingdom national soccer teams from the 1994 World Soccer Cup competition,

> 'A subject so profound that Cliff Morgan could devote the next six of these Saturday morning programmes to it. Does Sport still exist?
> Well it does; but you have to go out into the suburbs and shires to find it. Village cricket, soccer on Hackney Marshes, Old Boys rugger teams getting legless afterwards, point-to-pointing, county golf, darts leagues in Dorset.
> What we have been watching in the frenetic World Cup soccer action this week was hardly about sport at all. It was all about [a] high performance branch of the entertainment industry.
> The significance of crucial goals had less to do with national honour than balance sheets. How much a national football association would reap. How much the players would rip-off in bonuses and commercial contracts. Agents and airline representatives were more agitated than anyone. Their percentages and balance sheets were on the line.
> I have to accept, though, that this is what 'sport' has become. I shed no tears for England's elimination for a number of reasons. In their group they were palpably not good enough to get through. Like many I am relieved that their recidivist camp followers, small in number, but paranoically xenophobic, will be relieved of the necessity to smash up American towns; and though it may be a small point to some, I was simply disgusted, when for a few additional pieces of silver our national Football Association hatched a travel deal with an American Airline, instead of contracting one of our own.'

Cliff Morgan himself topped this admirable synthesis with what he described as a passing thought from an old Welsh proverb which hits the target: (as translated) 'endeavour is of no use without inspiration, without genius.'

If genius is unto the eye of the beholder, the converse of inspiration, desperation, was seen almost concurrently with the three national games of soccer, rugby and cricket. The concern cited at pages xxxv–xxxvi hereof above by the Professional Footballers' Association and England's Rugby Union captain, with misconduct on their respective fields of play, had an unhappy echo when the Allan Lamb libel action settled out of court appeared to confirm that cheating at cricket in breach of the Laws of the Game was accepted universally, and ultimately confirmed by revelations published during early 1994 in a biography of the charismatic former Pakistan cricket captain and Sussex County Cricket Club all-rounder, Imran Khan. A far cry, indeed, from Corinthian values still upheld at Tolworth in the suburbs of Surrey, by Corinthian-Casuals Football Club.

(5) Corinthian values

The Corinthian Casuals are well known in general sporting circles to have been the amalgamation of two amateur football clubs founded originally in the last two decades of Victorian England. United on the eve of the Second World War in 1939 the senior of the two, Corinthians, has contributed a meaning in the English language of the ideal conception of fair play within which the Rule of Law for games are played, and the present club carries this belief into action each week at its semi-rural ground at Tolworth in Surrey.

Indeed, when a biography was published in 1986 of one of the most celebrated of modern French international rugby players, Jean-Pierre Rives, by Peter Bills, it was subtitled "A Modern Corinthian". It would have been difficult to convey the same meaning and provide a sub-title from the rugby game's much admired and respected crusading equivalent to Corinthians and Corinthian-Casuals, the Barbarians!

Their principal sources of recruitment as amateur players who competed against professional opponents and shared their places in the England international teams of the pioneering Victorian and early Edwardian era before 1914, were schoolmasters, doctors and lawyers. A schoolboy Second World War correspondence that I had enjoyed with one of their leading personalities, G O Smith, who played 21 times for England between 1894 and 1901 when only three international games against the other three home countries were played each season, was published as *Corinthians and Cricketers*. C B Fry contributed the Foreword. Among their ranks were distinguished medical and legal practitioners whose significance is explained in Appendix 1 by a modern Corinthian and Cricketer, Hubert Doggart, OBE, President of the English Schools Cricket Association. Fry and G O Smith were schoolmasters, Fry commanding the Merchant Training Ship Mercury on Hampshire's River Hamble, and G O Smith becoming headmaster of Ludgrove School, where the future King of England during the 1980s and 1990s became a pupil. Significantly, perhaps but not surprisingly, at no time during that correspondence between a hero-worshipping schoolboy and his *beau ideal* from the Golden Age of the Victorian creative era did it touch upon or ever contemplate the modern problems in sport of violence, drugs (its own VD), commercial and political corruption.

The schoolmaster Corinthians taught their pupils the difference between right and wrong. The doctors were never required to develop in the now important emerging specialisation of Sports Medicine, and the practising lawyers were never required to provide their services for protecting the Rule of Law for the benefit of sport and the victims of breaches of playing laws within it. The patronage and philanthropy which then funded such sport which did not fund itself were not subjected to the sponsorship and agency pressures explained above by Follows and criticised in the citations hereafter by the late Peter Coni QC and the late Ron Pickering. Their values of fair play linked to healthy recreational activity within the Rules of play and the Laws of any game were identifiable without a need to consider any moral issues based on the Corinthian concept and ethic in the manner Pickering explained during a memorable 1985 CCPR address, cited below.

Lawyers participating in sport

Administratively behind closed doors and actively on playing fields the legal profession has served and serviced sport to its undoubted benefit throughout the century in which the scenario has been revolutionised since the young Shearman's Badminton Library, *Athletics and Football* pioneering publication in 1887. Cricket's first knight, Sir Francis Lacey, was a non-practising barrister who was MCC secretary at a crucial period of cricket's post-First World War expansion. He was followed during the Second World War on a caretaker basis at Lord's by Sir Pelham Warner, proud of his Inner Temple membership. John Sparrow of Lincoln's Inn and later Warden of All Souls College, Oxford, was no less proud of his membership of Old Wykhamist Arthur Dunn Cup winning XIs of 1929 and 1931 and a chronicler during the 1950s of football reports for the Observer. An earlier Arthur Dunn Cup winning Wykhamist, was the immortal Douglas Jardine in goal during 1920, before his solicitor training helped to prepare his analysis of the leg theory tactics with which the Ashes were won in 1932-33, and then withstand later in 1933, with the same moral and physical courage which he displayed to captain all his teams, the fast bowling of another immortal legendary sporting lawyer, the great Trinidadian all-rounder Learie Constantine. He in turn became a practising barrister, a peer of the realm, an Honorary Bencher of Middle Temple, and Plaintiff in the celebrated Second World War exposé in London's High Court of the social hypocrisy inherent in the USA race relations discrimination practised at the time during 1944 as explained in Chapter 15 *Whither Sport and the Law* at page 417, below. Before then, one of Jardine's most popular successors as Surrey County Cricket Club captain in 1939 was Monty Garland-Wells, also a solicitor and goalkeeper, for Corinthians and England's amateur International XI in 1930.

A little-known or remembered solicitor, Ebenezer Cobb Morley, who practised from 3, King's Bench Walk, Temple, is attributed in Bryon Butler's *Official History of the Football Association* (1991) with having initiated the concept of an association for the FA's foundation in 1863, and creation of a coherent set of rules now the Laws of the Game, analogous to the MCC's control until even to-day for cricket. The present President of the Endsleigh Football League, Gordon Mckeag, followed his solicitor father, Alderman William Mckeag, into the family practice and also until recently, chairmanship of Newcastle United. The Football League, now the Endsleigh Football League, was developed through its earliest years by another father and son solicitor family, this time from Lancashire, Charles and Harold Sutcliffe. Alongside them the Sheffield solicitor Sir Charles Clegg progressed to the FA chairmanship in between the two world wars during the 1919-1939 period while coining the memorable concept for both Sport and the Law: 'No one ever got lost on a straight road'; and he in turn was followed by G O Smith and C B Fry's immortal Corinthian solicitor, Charles Wreford Brown, and more recently by Sir Bert Millichip. Today, the in-house solicitor to the British Olympic Association, Bruce Mellstrom, competes for the Old Carthusians in the Arthur Dunn Cup Competition. One of his opponents and Secretary of the Old Etonians in that competition, when not practising full-time at the Bar is James Scobie, who inherits a great lineage from the Hon Alfred Lyttelton, KC, the first ever Double International to play football and cricket for England (great uncle of Humphrey Lyttelton) and FA Cup finalist who died while a Cabinet Minister. Within the track and field scenario, Sydney Wooderson, a practising solicitor, and holder of more than one world record before and after the Second World War, became [Sir] Roger Bannister's inspiration for breaking the four minute mile barrier in 1954. One of Bannister's predecessors in the Inter-Varsity sports at the White City after the Second World War, David Dixon, has doubled up as a practising solicitor and honorary secretary to the Commonwealth Games Federation. They in turn were all preceded by Harold Abrahams, a between the two World Wars hero of *Chariots of Fire*, barrister, administrator and communicator. Two solicitors, Nicholas Halstead and Allan Jay, became respectively President and Team Manager of the Amateur Fencing Association; a third, Robert Stinson, has for many years been Honorary

Treasurer of the International Amateur Athletic Federation. and a fourth, Charles Woodhouse, became chairman after years of playing and administrative service with the Surrey Cricket championship.

Uniquely among practising lawyers, Harold Hardman, while he was a qualified solicitor, won an Olympic Games gold-medal for the United Kingdom's soccer side's victory against Holland in the 1908 Olympic Games tournament, after appearing for Everton in two FA Cup Finals and before steering Manchester United and Matt Busby into European Competition against Football League opposition as chairman of Manchester United in 1956. Today, Manchester United's present glory is administered by a Board of Directors, which includes E Maurice Watkins, a practising solicitor and one of the founder members of the British Association for Sport and the Law together with the author and two members of the Law School at Manchester Metropolitan University, Peter Reyburn the then Head of the Department of Law, and Raymond Farrell who created a unit dedicated to Sport and the Law there.

A decade after Manchester United's formation as Newton Heath in 1878 and around the time of what is now the Endsleigh Football League's foundation in 1888, England's soccer International XI was built around four Corinthian practising lawyers, whose services were not required in the cause of sport. W R Moon (solicitor) in goal, the brothers Walters, A M (solicitor) and P M (Chancery barrister and later Lincoln's Inn Bencher) —'morning' and 'afternoon' as they were called—at full back; and at centre-forward before G O Smith, Tinsley Lindley, a Midland Circuit barrister whose photograph in wig and gown alongside Montague Shearman looks out from a montage on the Derby Crown Court Counsel's robing-room wall to-day. More recently in the Pegasus decade of the 1950s England's *amateur* International XI defence was based upon a Cambridge University goalkeeper captain who later qualified and still practises as a solicitor, M. J. Pinner.

The British Boxing Board of Control has been squired by successive generations of practising King's and Queen's Counsel who have seen that Queensberry Rules are regularly maintained. The Lawn Tennis Association was presided over in recent years by Sir Carl Aarvold, a former rugby international and presiding judge at the Old Bailey, London's Central Criminal Court. A Chancery Queen's Counsel, Allan Hayman, became president of the International Lawn Tennis Federation. A Midland Circuit Queen's Counsel, Barry Appleby, who is now a Circuit Judge, steered the Nottingham Forest Football Club Committee into corporate status; and his brother circuiteer W A Sime QC captained their county cricket XI while practising at the Bar and before his promotion to the Circuit Bench. From Wales, the retired former Deputy Lord Chief Justice Tasker Watkins, VC is the present President of the Welsh Rugby Union and Vernon Pugh QC, as chairman of the

International Rugby Football Board [IRFB] has the unenviable headache to-day of reconciling Northern and Southern hemisphere attitudes to payments for participating with the Rugby Union game. Lord Griffiths of Govilon in the county of Gwent played for Glamorgan in the county cricket championship after gaining Cambridge blues for cricket and golf and before becoming the only holder in sporting history simultaneously of the MCC presidency and captaincy of the Royal and Ancient Golf Club of St Andrews.

The author of the Taylor Report on Hillsborough, now as Lord Chief Justice, may not be aware how two of his predecessors contributed to sports administration. Lord Alverstone at the turn of the century held office with the newly-formed Amateur Football Alliance and at Kennington Oval after running for Cambridge University; and Lord Goddard will be recalled by many officiating at London's now demolished White City, for the Inter-Varsity sports, after gaining his athletics Blue four decades earlier.

Finally, one of the most visionary of modern sports administrators who embodied the true values of Sport and the Law and the Corinthian ethic with his administration of the Henley Royal Regatta, until his untimely death at the age of 57, was the late Peter Coni, QC. Coni's *Times* obituary explained how he:

'... strongly disapproved of the commercialisation of sport arguing that, once big money came into play, the advertisers, the agents and the sponsors followed.'

'Once you sell your soul you are lost' - he told one interviewer.

'The tail begins to wag the dog. When you depend on a sponsor, there's nothing to stop them telling you the deal's off unless their can-can girls are allowed into your enclosure.'

Values in sport

Only a few weeks before Coni died, the former editor of *Wisden's Cricketers' Almanack*, Graeme Wright, published a book with the title, *Betrayal: the struggle for cricket's soul'*. In it he attacked, *at the public level*, the market-led destruction of traditional sporting values of playing by the rules and fair play in style. It recalled a warning given to the whole of British sport by one of its most revered and best remembered practitioners and commentators, the late Ron Pickering. During the course of an address to the CCPR annual conference at Bournemouth nearly a decade ago in November 1985 he rocked his audience with certain comments under the title 'The Image of British Sport':

'Is this the problem; that the gap cannot be bridged between C B Fry and Daley Thompson, or the Corinthian-Casuals and Manchester United, or have the ground rules changed? Have we slipped down the slippery path that far that there is no return? I don't honestly believe so or I wouldn't just be wasting my time or yours saying simply I told you so. But I believe Peter Corrigan was right when he said recently in the *Observer*:"Sport took its soul to the pawnbrokers so long ago that finding the redemption ticket is not going to be easy."

It is not going to be easy, it will need a massive re-think by all that are genuinely concerned with sport. That in turn will need a massive and exciting focal point in my view. The only thing I can think of is the Birmingham bid for the 1992 Olympic Games. Someone might think up other initiatives.'"

Pickering provided the key to those other initiatives by his references to C B Fry and the Corinthian Casuals. For together they epitomised the ideal of Health, Education, Competition and the Rule of Law for redeeming sport's soul from the commercially orientated sponsoring pawnbrokers; and one, indeed the only, effective and practical proposal for providing an effective sanction within the sponsorship world for redeeming sport's soul was provided by a former playing member of Corinthian-Casuals who was also a member of the Great Britain Olympic Games squad in 1960 and Cambridge University soccer 'Blue', David Miller. In *The Times* on the opening day of the new Barclays League football season he wrote on 15 August 1987,

'I wish that Barclays, with their vested interest, would have conditional clauses written into the prize money benefits which penalise bad behaviour on and off the field.'

Thus the promoting and sponsoring companies are in a powerful position to benefit sport when sport fails to benefit and protect itself. FIFA's Fair Play sponsorship during the 1994 World Cup was a welcome initiative in that direction. One day a commercially vested interest organisation will have the intellectual and moral courage to direct its legal advisers to insert those conditional clauses ideally identified by David Miller's Corinthian concept with the appropriate penal sanctions for any material breach of them; or alternatively a legal adviser ready to accept the mantle of the true sporting legal heritage at pages lii–lv, as distinct from those concerned only with marketing sport as a mess of pottage, may yet enlighten a client with the significance which Miller's magic formula could yet have on its future welfare and all within it.

Seven years later towards the end of 1993 he began a *Times* series under the heading of 'Leadership in Britain' which could equally have been titled 'The lost Leadership of British Sport':

'...the reality is that much of British sport, on and off the field, is in a mess. Competitively, administratively, morally, British organisations head towards the 21st century in confusion: fragmented, arguing, jealous and left behind in the field of international leadership.

Britain, which gave organised sport to the world, which formulated most of the rules, where the Corinthian spirit epitomised attitudes that were universally admired, is a languishing power'.

Significantly, too, in the summer of 1993, the doyen of cricket writers, E W Swanton, who included many active Corinthians and Cricketers in the XIs selected under his supervision, wrote on 6 August , in the *Daily Telegraph*,

'The TCCB letters to counties for calling for a concerted effort to halt deteriorating standards of behaviour on the field will be applauded by all closest to the game.

Not only is a warning note necessary in respect of the first-class counties but it would be equally timely, if not more so, regarding league cricketers countrywide.

As the TCCB Discipline committee chairman, Peter Bromage, points out the umpires have a clear law to administer, No 43, Para 13, that on Unfair Play, now the longest of all. David Graveney, the players' representative on this committee, is warmly supportive of the TCCB letter, as is Tim Curtis, chairman of the Cricketers' Association'.

Finally, as if to re-assure advocates of the Corinthian ideal that they are not chasing an idle dream, Ronald Atkin in the *Sunday Telegraph* for 24 April 1994, wrote of England's cricket captain on the recent England A tour of South Africa under the banner headline, 'Corinthian classic patiently awaits his Test opportunity',

'The first sighting of John Crawley offers heartening reassurance that cricket has not, after all, mislaid the Corinthian mould that produced Dexter and May'.

Three months later at the height of the summer sporting season when the film *Chariots of Fire* was shown on television, the distinguished film critic, Barry Norman, wrote in the *Radio Times* of its producer David Puttnam's belief:

' in an age when everyone from governments down behaved expediently, when the end was unquestionably assumed to justify the means whatever they might be, it was time to resurrect and re-examine older, cleaner values proved splendidly correct.

Because essentially that's what *Chariots* is about. On the surface, of course, it concerns the winning and losing of races and medals and men striving to achieve their utmost potential. And on that level alone it works extremely well.

But the much more thoughtful subtext involves us with people who behave honourably and decently, who instinctively know the difference between right and wrong and are not prepared, for the sake of personal convenience, to colour them both in the same shade of grey.

In effect, and long before John Major thought of it, Puttnam was taking us back to basics. It may not in the end have achieved anything — expediency is still the watchword — but it was a noble try.'

(6)   Moral, Social, Political and Legal Issues

Summarised in the following way, Pickering said:

> 'Even young children, when they pick sides to play, establish rules that make the game fair and equal for all... but without the principle of fair play it is not sport ... As the rewards grow it is easy to see the pressures to cheat, to be greedy and to accept a lowering of moral standards. This debases the role model which should be the 'shop window' for tomorrow's participants and champions. When 60 per cent of British players admit they would commit a "professional" foul to stop a likely goal, we as a nation can hardly be shocked at Italian soccer players accepting bribes or American cyclists being body doped. They are part of the same moral issue.'

Also part of that moral issue was the conclusion arrived at by the Canadian judicial inquiry into the drug cheating scandal after the 1988 Seoul Olympic Games. Mr Justice Dubin recorded:

> 'Cheating in sport, I fear, is partially a reflection of today's society. Drugs and the unprincipled pursuit of wealth and fame at any cost now threaten our very social fabric. It is little wonder that immorality has reached into sport as well. Of course, cheating as such is not a new phenomenon in Olympic competition, but the methods used to cheat have become more and more innovative and more pervasive.'

No less innovative and pervasive has been the less condemned concept of cheating by violence. During the 1970s this escalated and in a remarkable contribution to the *Daily Express* on Tuesday 25 August 1987 at pages 30-31 the former Leeds United and Eire international footballer John Giles, wrote of his club's progress throughout the 1970s:

> 'I can now see clearly enough that we stretched the rules to breaking point ... we went too far, too ruthless. I went too far ... we did and we prospered. We never thought there might be a day when we would wonder if the price was too high.'

A decade later but also during 1987, the retiring Lord Chancellor and creator of the role of a Government Minister with responsibility for Sport, Lord Hailsham of St Marylebone, in his Carlton Lecture entitled: 'Morality, Law and Politics' explained:

> 'It has been our fortune, good or bad, to live in an age of conflict, violence and confusion, one in which old certainties have faded into agnosticism, when new fanaticisms, new bigotries have arisen and new sources of political power or disruption have first challenged and sometimes overthrown established authority ... At the heart of the problem lies the uncertain frontier between morality, politics and the law, the framework of an ordered and civilised life.'

That contention applies equally to sport, with its baseline for all activity within the Rule of Law with which this book alone is concerned. National politics obtrude only when converted into law or confused by conflicting government departments or successive governmental lack of coherent policies. Any reader enquiring of what David Miller rightly has described as the 'fragmented, arguing and jealous' elements in what has become the world of sporting politics should look elsewhere beyond these pages. Nevertheless South African sport straddled both international and sporting politics while the world-wide sports boycott and progressive initiatives within South African sport contributed undoubtedly to crumble to destruction the legal basis of the morally indefensible national apartheid policy. For morality underpins the whole sporting ethic, and may not appear always within the diverse commercial elements which dominate the public sporting scene above school and general grass root levels.

The fragmented elements forming those diverse and divergent commercial elements clearly reflect also the frequently untrained volunteer base of service to sport in the United Kingdom, and perhaps throughout the world, which is both its strength and weakness. Strength, because without its depth sport could never be administered adequately in sufficient numbers. Weakness, because it lacks the cohesive identity of peer groups evidenced by the armed services and traditional professions. The Army, Navy, RAF, clergy, doctors, dentists and lawyers all impose uniform codes of conduct and practice which potential transgressors can recognise as deterrents against misconduct. No comparable cohesive sanction with an effective penal policy from a *peer* group appears *generally* to exist, except among the Professional Golfers Association.

Thus employers' federations with feudal overtones are epitomised by the Jockey Club's formal inquiry headed by one of its own members into the great Grand National fiasco of 1993. The TCCB fined Allan Lamb for telling the truth about ball tampering in breach of cricket's law 42 prohibiting it: and Ray Illingworth, the England Team Manager, fined the team captain Michael Atherton £1,000 for dirt in his pocket and £1,000 for lying to the Umpire, when neither action created a breach of any known

Rule or Law within or without the game. For unless and until a homogeneous awareness and consistency can be brought to bear upon the minds of the general level of untrained volunteer sporting administrators and their paid equivalents to a civil service, the need for professional legal services will always be required to fill this vacuum which very few within sport itself are ready to recognise, notwithstanding the fragmented movement towards establishing a British Court for Arbitration in Sport.

Simon Barnes in *The Times* at the height of the Commonwealth Games drugs development in 1994 identified the realities when he explained:

'Sport is caught up in a spiral of inflation: inflation of interest, inflation of media coverage, inflation of financial possibilities for all concerned. Each one of these feeds on the others's increase: the radius of the spiral decreases, the velocity increases, and round and round and round we whizz, dizzy, disorientated and sometimes more than a trifle sick.

Groggy sporting administrators find themselves at permanent loggerheads with life as they seek to reconcile the two great irreconcilables: the value of sport and its ever-increasing price.

As sport is seen more than ever before, is followed more closely and is contested more intensely, so more things go wrong, and more things are seen to go wrong.

Sporting bodies were originally established to organise a bit of serious fun: these days, the same organisations are trying to run billion-quid industries.

It is hardly surprising that things get out of step sometimes. And, as the spiral tightens and quickens, the anomalies will come at us more and more often.' (31 August 1994)

In this context, and particularly the often and, indeed, usually overlooked or ignored, differential between sport at the entertainment global village or as a vehicle or medium for fun at the grass roots and school levels, The *Independent* newspaper's Chief Sports Correspondent Ken Jones, wrote from a lifetime's and family experiences after England cricket captain, Michael Atherton, had been fined controversially for dissent by an Australian Text Match Referee, although no complaint had been made by the Test Match Umpire who had dismissed Atherton, lbw, against South Africa at the Oval,

'while no case can be made for blatant dissent, the pernicious commercial influences of modern sport place an inordinate strain on today's performers, making it increasingly difficult for them to honour a resurgence of puritanism.

It is not only absurd, it is unjust to expect people who earn a living at a game and frequently are called upon to fulfil national as well as local expectations in the glare of television, to comply with a nonchalant code of behaviour that was drawn up for privileged amateurs.

Is it not possible that if Michael Atherton had smilingly vacated the crease

against South Africa at the Oval last week instead of incurring a fine for
mildly resenting the decision that saw him out first ball, questions would
have been asked about his commitment?

If the difference between winning and losing turns on an umpire's
perception, a referee's interpretation, a linesman's call, it takes considerable
character not to blow up.'

Such realistic thoughts on dissent at the public as distinct from the
private level do not diminish in any way at all the need for adherence to
the Rule of Law within sport for the elimination of criminal and civilly
actionable violent foul play.

Coincidentally and almost symbolically many of those issues on which
this Introduction has concentrated have crystallised in a remarkable way
during the final stages of correcting the main text in the days which
annually precede and succeed the sporting calendar's festival around the
Easter holiday period. The Grand National, FA and Scottish FA Cup Semi-
Finals and climaxes to the Rugby Union and Rugby League seasons all
excite emotions and enthusiasms. Yet less agreeable reminders of the
circumstances which have led to the creation of this book and its subject-
matter continued to surface.

The *Scotsman* (8 April) reported Sheriff Peter Hamilton's interpretation
of an admitted rugby assault in Haddington Sheriff Court creating a smashed
jaw and cheekbone 'borders on the realm of thuggery'''. At that time a rugby
union playing field manslaughter prosecution was en route to London's
Central Criminal Court at the Old Bailey. It resulted in an aquittal, but sadly
confirmed a prophecy when The Times (12 April) recorded a nine months
custodial sentence at Croydon Crown Court for an admitted wounding to
an amateur soccer referee whose life was saved by an emergency operation
to remove a clot from his brain. The victim said:

> 'The way that violence is on the football pitch has been growing recently,
> I am sure that someone is going to be killed'.

The following day, Alan Coren, the former editor of Punch, began a
feature in The Times (13 April)

> 'Last Saturday I watched a really cracking football match ... Utterly
> professional. Totally committed. Prodigiously physical. Impressively
> cynical. Above all, unstintingly competitive, and not a player on the field
> over 12 years old... sport has changed, and competition has changed, and it
> is too late to change either of them back.'

Nevertheless, such understandable pessimism contrasts with the
remarkably enlightened letter in the *Guardian* two days earlier, 11 April,
under the head '*Miscellany*', from Sammy Prebble, Kingston-upon-
Thames:

'I am 12 years old, so could some sensible grown-up answer a question for me? Why is it that when an overpaid loud-mouthed yob breaks his leg in Italy he is treated like a hero and carried home in luxury for first-class medical treatment? Yet when a beautiful and gentle creature breaks its leg when being forced to jump over a huge fence, we shoot it.'

The answer, of course, lies in the Oscar Wilde recognition of the cynic who understands the price of everything and the value of nothing.

All of this, of course, is sadly nothing more than a re-affirmation and up-date of what the late, lamented and much loved Ron Pickering told the CCPR representative governing bodies of sport nearly a decade ago in November 1985 as cited at page lvi above,

'Is this the problem; that the gap cannot be bridged between C B Fry and Daley Thompson, or the Corinthian-Casuals and Manchester United?'

It also ties in with the citation at the end of the next opening Chapter to the book, 1. Genesis, from the *London Evening Standard* symposium published in 1991, *Sporting Spite: Rebels and Rebellion in World Sport*, compiled by its eminent team of sports writers. Michael Herd, assistant editor and head of sport, wrote in the Introduction:

'All things considered, this is the appropriate time for sport's ruling bodies to declare enough is enough ... is there a way back to a golden age, to the Corinthian era?'

The simple answer is, of course: through the Rule of Law, notwithstanding the hostility to and rejection of it by too many of 'sport's ruling bodies'.

Accordingly when the honorary legal adviser to the Central Council of Physical Recreation, and to so many sporting governing bodies, Charles Woodhouse, a partner in the solicitors firm of Messrs Farrer & Co, read a paper on the Sport and the Law theme to the CCPR Annual Conference at Birmingham in December 1987 on the eve of publication of the first edition of this book, the then Chief Executive of the Football Association, Ted Croker, complained (as he repeated to Simon Barnes nearly five years later in September 1992 cited at page xxiii above) that he did not approve of police intervention into football affairs, particularly on the field of play, (notwithstanding the unremitting violence which was continuing at all levels of his game at that period, and particularly in the course of play as confirmed by the Criminal Injuries Compensation Board a few days later, cited at pages 158–159 below); and that it was all the fault of Edward Grayson who invented Sport and the Law.

I had not been aware of such a perception until that time. The invention was not intentional. How it occurred unintentionally and almost accidentally, but with hindsight, almost inevitably, appears in the opening chapter of *Genesis* with which this book still begins.

Part I

Overview

Chapter 1

Genesis

1 INTRODUCTION

Sport and the Law's inevitable birth occurred during the early 1950s
with an authentic legal-sporting pedigree. It was bred by *Corinthians
and Cricketers* out of the then Association Football Players' and
Trainers' Union (now the Professional Footballers' Association:
PFA) and the joint Oxbridge soccer club, Pegasus.

The name Corinthians was taken over a century ago as a classical
foundation for the world's most famous amateur football club of all
time: the Corinthians Football Club. Its title has survived the amalgamation with their amateur brother-in-arms, the Casuals FC on the
eve of the Second World War in 1939. Brazil's leading football club,
Sporting Club Corinthians Paulista, has adopted the name; and
letters received by the author during a wartime schoolboy friendship
and correspondence with two of its most celebrated members, who
also distinguished themselves as cricketers, C B Fry and G O Smith,
led to the book entitled *Corinthians and Cricketers*. It was first
published during the middle 1950s. To commemorate the centenary
of both clubs during the 1982–83 soccer season an updated version
was published: *Corinthian-Casuals and Cricketers*.

With hindsight, that enlightened correspondence between an enthusiastic enquiring schoolboy and particularly England's greatest
centre-forward of 40–50 years earlier, G O Smith, who had retired
from the headmastership of Ludgrove School, in Berkshire, where
England's future King William III is at present being educated, had
one significant omission in to-day's context. Whilst it covered conventional topics such as tactics, techniques, training and personalities
from W G Grace, C B Fry and Ranji to Steve Bloomer, and even
contemplated future post-war problems such as a two-division
County Cricket Championship, it never had the slightest thought for
the modern issues of violence, drugs, commercial exploitation and
political violation. Even during the Second World War (Hitler's war),
progressive ideas on sport breathed an air of innocence.

3

2 CORINTHIANS

Corinthian-Casuals, Cricketers and Pegasus

By the time when these modern 'Letters *from* Corinthians' were being prepared during the late 1940s and early 1950s for general readership, the heirs to the traditional sources were found under two separate footballing flags: Corinthian-Casuals and the newly formed Oxbridge foundation, Pegasus. After the Second World War had ended in 1945 an Oxford don, Dr H W Thompson (later and more widely known before he died in 1983 as Sir Harold Thompson FRS, CBE, Professor of Spectroscopy and Chairman of the Football Association), amalgamated the two Oxbridge soccer clubs, Oxford University Centaurs and Cambridge University Falcons. Christened Pegasus by his wife, Penelope, an Oxford classics scholar, its meteoric decade of romantic sporting glory upheld *two* profound Corinthian traditions. One was the inclusion of Test Match cricketers within its playing membership who were selected on meritorious grounds: P B H May, D J Insole, F C M Alexander, D B Carr, G H G Doggart, and A C Smith (the first four of whom were Test Match captains). The other was the forging of close links with outstanding professional football guides, philosophers and friends: Arthur Rowe, Vic Buckingham, Billy Nicholson from Tottenham Hotspur, George Ainsley from a pre-1939 Leeds United, and Joe Mercer of many clubs and England, in addition to many others. When Pegasus flew to its two Wembley successes in the (now defunct) FA Amateur Cup Final ties of 1951 and 1953, 100,000 crowds attended (on each occasion) just before Sir Roger Bannister's four minute mile in 1954 around Pegasus' Oxford Iffley Road playing arena.

The story of the *amateur* Cup Final triumphs is told in the final chapter of both publications, and 40 years on modern readers who are conditioned by crowd controls following Bradford, Heysel and Hillsborough crowd disasters, may find the size of those Wembley Stadium crowds to be astonishing. Three years after the second triumph, in 1956, some of the club's founder members, including D J Insole from Cambridge University (later the nominee defendant in the *Greig v Insole* [1978] 1 WLR 302 Packer litigation, now its University representative on the FA Council) appeared before an 80,000 crowd at the same place on the same occasion in Corinthian-Casuals colours.

Pegasus' Oxbridge captain throughout his all too short career, Denis Saunders, one of Billy Nicholson's coaching pupils, has progressed via the Corinthian traditions as a housemaster of Malvern College in Worcestershire, to Principal of England's future professional footballers at the FA-General Motors-sponsored FA

National School of Excellence at the Lilleshall National Sports Centre in Shropshire. Those amateur and professional links have thus been perpetuated also at grass-roots levels.

These triumphs were chronicled by the author only after a badly broken leg during Oxford University's soccer trials which, followed by inadequate treatment, allowed time for diversions of energies from active sport and examination studies to frame an historical setting to share those Corinthian letters with a wider readership. Research prior to publication, but after call to the Bar by Middle Temple and commencement of legal practice in Lincoln's Inn, produced two sporting legal puzzles connected directly with the Corinthian-cricketing and Pegasus texts which appeared to demand solutions. Each concerned the attitudes of the Inland Revenue authorities at the time towards two separate sporting taxation 'penalty' areas.

With hindsight they were for the author the earliest professional threads which started to bind the law with sport, and drew him gradually and inevitably to varying levels of friendships and publications which have led ultimately to the writing of this book. Jurisprudentially they are the true beginnings of what has unfolded and emerged as this dynamic, developing area of sport and the law.

Its real origins, however, can be traced to that personal injury and the inadequacies of its treatment. Time lost from studies in hospital for recuperation and during convalescence produced an emerging awareness then which has now been crystalised in the three chapters: Chapter 6, p 145 'Participation problems'; Chapter 7, p 191, 'Sports medicine and the law'; and Chapter 12, p 311, 'Administrative advice'.

For players, it illuminated the often misapplied latin tag, *volenti non fit injuria*. The author's own ill-timed tackle, stemming from blunted reflexes after the pre-term vacation, missed the ball; the foot hit the bone-hard Iffley Road playing surface resulting in a broken fibula. It created no legal liability of the kind which now follows. This is all too rarely recognised and it is also condemned at the public level, notwithstanding the concurrent criminal and civil liability inherent in the descriptions, 'professional foul', 'cynical foul', 'over-competitiveness'.

The wrong hospital advice and inadequate treatment were given to the then undergraduate author who was told to walk on the leg while the plaster was being set. This pointed to disaster, until parental intervention and insistence obtained the release from such gross medical negligence. Removal from Oxford to London and specialist orthopaedic surgery saved the limb. The initial medical neglect created a clear legal liability. Parental wisdom on behalf of a then legal infant (below the age of 21 at that time, now 18) declined to enforce it.

That experience demonstrates for players, administrators and sporting medicare personnel the importance of adequate insurance. For the author it also proved at an early age, and with startling clarity, how the law is not available to all. This event had occurred before Parliament's limited legal aid legislation in 1950 (and its further controversial cutbacks in 1993) but it demonstrates how inadequate financial resources preclude access to professional services to mount a claim. The hollow ring to Magna Carta's proclamation, 'To no one will we deny, delay, or refuse, right or justice' became self-evident. Maule J's aphorism still applies: 'The Law Courts like the Ritz Hotel are open to all.'

3 SPORT AND THE LAW IS BORN

Also open to all, for anyone genuinely concerned with the beneficial progress of sport generally and association football in particular, were in the 1950s the pages of the then monthly *FA Bulletin* during the secretaryship of the former schoolmaster and international soccer referee Sir Stanley Rous, CBE. He encouraged investigation of the solution to a legal paradox upon which the author had stumbled coincidentally and fortuitously during research preparations for *Corinthians and Cricketers*. It concerned Denis Compton of Arsenal, Middlesex, England's Test Match XIs; and wartime and victory soccer international XIs.

He was every games player's sporting hero of that period as the beau ideal of footballing and cricketing professionalism with the Corinthian style of enthusiasm laced with skill and fair play. As a county cricketer, his benefit payments from an admiring public were tax-free because of the well-known House of Lords ruling in *Seymour v Reed* [1927] AC 554 which had overturned a Court of Appeal reversal of an experienced taxation judge, Rowlatt J (and thus restored the judgment). As a professional footballer, however, his benefit was subject to tax as part of his income. This too, was based on earlier litigation and also on the nature of his footballer's contract and the Football League and FA regulations which were incorporated into it.

Detailed explanations of how the position was resolved in practice outside the Football League are more suited to the penultimate Chapter 14, 'No fine on fun' and also Appendix 15.

Suffice it to say here that the paradox produced two articles which tackled the problem head-on, while the author was also wrestling with an appropriate formula to present the correspondence with G O Smith, a great Corinthian sportsman of Queen Victoria's England, the country's centre-forward and captain (also an outstanding University batsman). The first was encouraged by Sir

Stanley Rous, CBE, then FA Secretary and Chairman of the Central
Council of Physical Recreation, ultimately President of FIFA and
contributor on the subject to the then *FA Bulletin*. It appeared
in April 1953 under the title *Taxation of Player's Benefits*. Later
in the same year the more professional publication, *Rating and
Income Tax*, allowed extensions of the same arguments with more
formal and traditional citations and sources. They are included in
Appendix 15.

The basic theme throughout each article was that the House of
Lords' decision in *Seymour v Reed* [1927] AC 554 freed from income
tax liabilities the *public funding sources, extraneous to a contract of
employment*, of a benefit cricket match granted to the Kent County
Cricket Club's opening batsman, James Seymour, for the traditional
Canterbury Cricket Week match against Hampshire in 1920. At that
time the professional footballer's comparable contract of employment contained discretionary and/or *contractual claims* for benefit
payments. The then legal advisers to contemporary football players
had perversely attempted to apply the *Seymour v Reed non-contractual* circumstances to their own contrasting situation on two separate
occasions before the author became aware of the position while
preparing *Corinthians and Cricketers* (see *Davis v Harrison* [1927] 43
TLR 623: and *Corbett v Duff; Dale v Duff; Feeburg v Abbott*; [1941] 1
KB 730).

It was clear to the author that so long as the professional footballers' contract of employment contained references to a benefit
claim, there was no chance of the revenue authorities or the Courts
equating the two professional sporting categories in respect of relief
for the two kinds of benefits. Indeed, at about the same time, the
situation was re-emphasised and re-affirmed by the London Court of
Appeal in the contemporary circumstances concerning a claim for tax
relief by an Australian Test Match cricketer who received public
funded collections, also under his contract of employment, while
playing Lancashire League cricket (see *Moorhouse v Dooland* [1955] 1
All ER 93). The only possible solution for professional football was
to follow cricket's precedent and take the benefit out of the contract
of employment. It was achieved in the following way.

Denis Compton's goalkeeper colleague in the 1950 FA Cup final
against Liverpool, George Swindin, was a committee member of the
then Association Football Players' and Trainers' Union of which the
chairman was the former Portsmouth FC captain, James Guthrie.
When Swindin moved to Peterborough United as player-manager
during the early 1950s, prior to returning subsequently to Arsenal as
manager, the United at that time was a progressive club outside the
Football League to which it was later elected in 1960. The Midland
Counties Football League in which it played had no comparable

regulations to the Football League players' contracts for testimonial or benefit payments. A special Peterborough United Benefit Fund Committee extraneous to the Club was created. The club's ground was hired to the Benefit Fund Committee to exclude the club from all arrangements. Two benefit matches in 1956 were arranged for the benefit of players, including the club captain Norman Rigby; and three years later the *Seymour v Reed* principle was applied by the Special Commissioners of Inland Revenue, to discharge the local income tax inspector's assessment, *Rigby v IRC* (1959) (unreported except in the Peterborough *Citizen and Advertiser*: 16 June, 24 July).

After Peterborough United were elected to the Football League in 1960 the Football League regulations were amended to delete the contractual element in the professional footballers' benefits to equate them with the professional cricketers. Any future Denis Comptons would no longer experience the sporting legal anomaly which existed needlessly between 1927 and 1956, primarily because of the absence of any apparent awareness on the part of the professional footballers' then legal or tax advisers during the intervening years of the simple solution: deletion of the *contractual or discretionary* entitlement, based upon the small print of the Football League Regulations to which the standard contract of employment was subject.

These tax publications led to meetings, and ultimately friendship, with the then Chairman of the Association Football Players' and Trainers' Union, Jimmy Guthrie. In 1939 he had captained the last pre-war FA Cup winning team, Portsmouth, to an unexpected 4–1 victory over a youthful Wolverhampton Wanderers team, known to the football world as Buckley's (not Busby's) Babes, because of the youth policy of the then team manager, Major Frank Buckley. Guthrie's persistence in discovering and attempting to solve serious sporting issues included not only the paradox produced by different taxation attitudes towards professional football and cricket benefits with the aid of Peterborough United (then outside both the Football League and also Compton's area of competitive employment with Arsenal) and its player-manager, George Swindin, who had been Denis Compton's Arsenal goalkeeping colleague, and, by that crucial time had become a fellow Union committee member. Guthrie was also responsible for launching the first real attack on the restraint of trade vice in the retain and transfer system of the professional footballer's contract of employment in Aldershot County Court proceedings during 1955. For he now placed his Union behind defending a claim in Aldershot County Court for possession of club premises against one of its players, Ralph Banks, and it was a prelude to the better known *Eastham* case and Mr Justice Wilberforce's landmark judgment eight years later in 1963 (*Eastham v Newcastle United* [1964] Ch 413).

Banks had been transferred to Aldershot for £500 from Bolton Wanderers after he had played left-back against Stanley Matthews in the 1953 Coronation Cup Final which led to Matthews' coveted FA Cup winners' medal in the dramatic finish which witnessed his team's, Blackpool's, 4–3 victory. At Aldershot he disputed a wages offer and in lieu thereof hoped to accept a more favourable offer from Weymouth who were unable to afford Aldershot's wish to recoup their own earlier £500 transfer fee paid to Bolton Wanderers. Although his contract of employment for 12 months from 30 June 1954 to 30 June 1955 had terminated at the date of the court action in October 1955, his Football Association registration permitted Aldershot's retention of his services under the FA Rules. The county court Judge, H H Judge Percy Rawlins, who had just been transferred to the Aldershot County Court circuit from his west country circuit base, refused leave procedurally for Banks to join the FA as a defendant to a counterclaim and plead that the club's possession claim was based upon an unenforceable contract in restraint of trade and thereby tainted with illegality. He ordered the FA to attend through counsel and a representative to assist him on the contractual arrangements.

A possession order was made with effect from five months from the date of judgment on 28 October 1955; but evidence was provided by a future FA deputy secretary, Douglas Hawes, in answer to a question by the judge that Banks was under a 'penalty'; ie the retain and transfer system was equivalent to a perpetually renewable lease built into the football governing body rules to which the professional players' contracts were tied.

In his judgment H H Judge Percy Rawlins said,

> 'It may very well be, although I am not going to decide it, that as the defendant alleges the rules of the Football Association place an intolerable burden upon some professional footballers. But it may well be that as the Football Association says, the rules were necessary for the protection of footballers because the Football Association exists to some extent to protect footballers and to prevent their exploitation.'

(*Aldershot Football Club v Banks*, Aldershot News, 4 November 1955.)

An appeal to the Court of Appeal was under consideration when as Guthrie in his own version *Soccer Rebel* [1976] page 74 explained: 'Aldershot, perhaps under guidance or orders, gave Banks a free transfer'; to the club he wished to join, Weymouth. Eight years later Wilberforce J in 1963 converted that 'penalty' testified by the FA's representative and H H Judge Rawlins' impression of an 'intolerable burden', arising out of the FA's retention of a player's services after his employment contract had expired, into an unenforceable restraint of trade category (*Eastham v Newcastle United Football Club, Football Association and Football League* [1964] Ch 413).

These were the first occasions when the restraint of trade issue was ever raised in the English courts for professional sport. Over forty years earlier a challenge to the system was made on behalf of a professional footballer, Harry Kingaby, who was dissatisfied with his position at the Aston Villa Club, *Kingaby v Aston Villa* (1912) Times, 29 March. Restraint of trade, however, was neither pleaded nor argued.

At that period before 1914 the restrictive elements which today are understood to create a restraint of trade situation between master and servant were already recognised in the legal world (see *Leather Cloth Co v Larsont* (1869) LR 9 Eq 345 at 354; *Mitchel v Reynolds* (1711) 1 PWms 181; 18 Sm LC (13 Edn) 462). Unfortunately that was not how it appeared to those who advised the plaintiff, Kingaby. No claim was formulated which challenged the restrictive practice per se. A claim was pleaded for damages for

(1)   loss of employment; and

(2)   maliciously charging an excessive transfer fee.

The trial judge, Mr Justice A T Lawrence (who later became the first Lord Trevethin as Lord Chief Justice in 1921 in contentious political circumstances under Lloyd George's premiership), non-suited the plaintiff and withdrew the case from the jury. He ruled there was no cause of action and confirmed the transfer fee and system under attack to be permissible under the terms of contract of employment (*Kingaby v Aston Villa* (1912) Times, 28 March).

Eight years after *Aldershot v Banks* when the restraint of trade issue was fully pleaded and established, in Eastham's case ([1964] Ch 413 at 445) the trial judge, Wilberforce J explained (with the author's emphasis on the pleading issue)

> 'Kingaby brought an action arising out of the fact that the club had placed an excessive transfer fee upon him. This seems to be the only reported case affecting the rules of the Football League. The case is shortly reported in 'The Times,' 28 March, but *I have seen the pleadings*, from which it appears that the action was for damages for breach of contract, damages for conspiracy, damages for maliciously procuring breaches of contract and an injunction. A T Lawrence J refused to allow the case to go to the jury because, as reported, he said *no tort against the plaintiff* had been committed and *there was no evidence of malice*. I find the case of no assistance.'

It is certainly arguable today in 1994 that if the restraint of trade had been properly pleaded and argued in 1912 the claim based on the then traditional and established authorities would have succeeded. Yet the perversity which used to permeate more than it appears to do to-day, the unawareness in sporting legal areas of the true legal issues, was illuminated after the restraint of trade and other principles were re-affirmed in the celebrated Packer litigation thirteen years after the *Eastham* landmark verdict in *Greig v Insole* [1978] 1 WLR 302.

The former secretary to the MCC and the co-defendant with the Test and County Cricket Board (TCCB) in the Packer litigation, the International Cricket Council (ICC), Jack Bailey wrote in *Conflict in Cricket* (1989)

> 'As the world knows, ICC and TCCB lost a case which, by the time all the witnesses had been called and the closing speeches had been made by both sides, and Mr Justice Slade had given his comprehensive and enlightening judgment, had lasted thirty-two days. The cricket authorities had lost on every point of law involved, although they had emerged with some credit from a moral standpoint. Had it all been worth it? Or rather, had we anything to show for the damages and costs awarded against us, amounting to some £250,000 (later shared equally between ICC and TCCB) apart from a vast amount of publicity for cricket all over the world?
>
> Well, for one thing, it had been a lesson. It had taught the cricket authorities that good intentions, if not paving the road to hell, certainly are not enough when it comes to the law of the land.
>
> We also learnt the law regarding inducement to breach of legal contract and what was reasonable in the cricket world, both to protect established cricket and to prevent unlawful restraint of trade.'

It is understandable that the cricketing establishment via the ICC and TCCB could have been unaware of the trial run to establish restraint of trade in the Aldershot County Court by Ralph Banks with the backing of Guthrie and his Union. It is beyond belief that thirteen years after *Eastham's* landmark decision the then legal advisers to cricket's establishment had not apparently recognised, alerted its clients to, or even understood the restraint of trade application to professional sport.

4 DEVELOPING SPORT AND THE LAW

Concurrent with these economic, employment, industrial and important taxation legal sporting issues was the wider and much farther reaching factor which commanded the Inland Revenue's attention: the Pegasus windfalls from the FA Amateur Cup travels for which the two 100,000 crowds at Wembley Stadium in 1951 and 1953 produced sufficient income to create a prima facie liability to tax. This was consistent with established precedents of over sixty years' unchallenged authority that sport clubs profiting from public funding beyond its private subscriptions were assessable to income tax (*Carlisle & Silloth Golf Club v Smith* [1913] 3 KB 75). Pegasus however,

with its Oxbridge structure, was no ordinary club. It contained all the
elements of classical physical education concepts which are built into
the ideal of a healthy mind in a healthy body: *mens sana in corpore
sano*.

That was the basis of a judgment delivered by Mr Justice Eve in the
High Court during the First World War in the year when W G Grace
and Victor Trumper both died, 1915 (*Re Mariette* [1915] 2 Ch 284).
He upheld as being validly charitable separate bequests for establish-
ing a fives court and an athletics prize at Aldenham School, near
Elstree in Hertfordshire. For reasons which can be attributed only to
unawareness among British sporting administrators between the two
World Wars (1919–1939), it does not appear to have been applied as it
could have been in court until the New South Wales Equity Court in
Australia (more recently concerned during 1986 with well publicised
British Government security issues in the Peter Wright *Spycatcher*
trial) applied the principles enunciated by Eve J for Aldenham School
to a bequest in favour of Sydney University Rugby Football Club
(*Kearins v Kearins* (1957) SR 286 (NSW)). (In this year, too, the
Central Council of Physical Recreation appointed a Committee
under Sir John Wolfenden which produced in 1960 a far-reaching
Report on *Sport and the Community*, which in turn led ultimately to
the creation of the Sports Council in 1972.)

Dining beneath the portrait of Eve J in the hall of Exeter College,
Oxford, in the immediate post-Second World War period after 1945
for nearly three years, concentrated the author's attention on his
decision in *Re Mariette* ([1915] 2 Ch 284). Gradually the author
became aware during periodic researches of the absence of its citation
or reliance upon it throughout the forty year period until its resurrection in Australia by McLelland J to benefit Sydney University Rugby
Football Club, during 1957 (*Kearins v Kearins* (1957) SR 286 (NSW)).
Spurred on by this unexpected antipodean bonus from the other
football game, Pegasus through its creative and driving force the then
Dr (later Sir Harold) Thompson was advised jointly, by the author
and the late Hubert Monroe, QC, subsequently the Presiding Tax
Commissioner, to tackle the Inland Revenue charitable status offices
at Bootle in an attempt to protect the club's profits obtained after its
Amateur Cup Final triumphs as a joint Oxbridge club team in 1951
and 1953 before those 100,000 crowds on each occasion. Because of
the lack of funds recorded above, it had to act contrary to its cup-tie
character when games were won after early errors and on this occasion concede defeat after the joint advice was rejected by the Inland
Revenue authorities.

A decade later Sir Stanley Rous's successor as FA Secretary, Denis
Follows (later Sir Denis Follows, chairman of the British Olympic
Association and Treasurer of the Central Council of Physical

Recreation), who was aware of the then Council's charitable status, commissioned from the author a contribution on *Football and the Law* to an *FA Manual of Administration* in the early 1970s. The opportunity was taken to explain the concept of physical education as a legal charity, and how

> '*educational* foundations could claim to qualify. At one time thoughts existed for Pegasus FC'.

On 30 October 1972, the Charity Commissioners registered an FA Youth Trust Deed; and after the eight-year battle to obtain a reversal of its rejection by the Inland Revenue, the Chancery judge and a Court of Appeal Majority, the House of Lords endorsed the judgment of Eve J as 'stimulating and instructive' (*IRC v McMullan* [1980] 1 All ER 884 at 892; letters b–c).

Curiously, and for reasons which are not clear, *Kearins* was not cited at any level of the FA Youth Trust Deed court disputes. Yet its judgment, too, was vindicated. Nearly thirty years later, as we shall see in Chapter 6, 'Participation problems', Australian authorities were relied upon by London's Court of Appeal to apply the principles of common law negligence to an award of £4,000 damages for a badly broken leg from a deliberate foul tackle in an amateur soccer match, and uphold the decision of a county court judge (*Condon v Basi* [1985] 2 All ER 453).

That contrast over a nearly thirty-year span from Australian sources for British courts between rugby charity (1957) and soccer playing violence (1988) exemplifies the sinister shadows which were taking shape throughout the sporting world, on as well as off the fields of play. This was while the more subtle sporting legal knots with taxation elements were being untied after the author had become entangled with them through Pegasus and professional players under Guthrie's guidance during the 1950s.

In 1969, the late J L Manning, an outstanding campaigning journalist, and son of an equally distinguished sporting journalist, Lionel Manning, recognised the appalling gaps in British crowd safety requirements after a relatively minor accident when a crush barrier collapsed in 1969 during a soccer match at Watford's homely ground in Hertfordshire, before the club's admirable progress throughout the later 1970s and 1980s. An invitation by Manning to the author to examine the correct legal position for his *Daily Mail* column resulted in the discovery that two British Government Reports which had recommended licensing systems after a crowd overflow at the first-ever Wembley Stadium FA Cup Final in 1923 (Cmnd 2088 (1924)), and thirty-three fatalities in 1946 during a Bolton Wanderers FA Cup-Tie (Cmnd 6846 (1947)) had produced the traditional Whitehall inactivity.

South America in 1964 and 1968 had recorded, respectively, 301 people killed and 500 injured after one match at Lima, Peru, and 71 people killed and about 200 injured at Buenos Aires in Argentina. Accordingly, when the Ibrox, Glasgow, disaster in 1971 caused 66 deaths and over 140 injuries, Manning did not have to shout very loudly, in the London *Evening Standard* to which he had moved, to steer Parliament into a third Government Report (from Lord Wheatley: Cmnd 4952 (1972)). This followed those two earlier Government Reports upon which no action had been taken: the Wembley Stadium FA Cup Final Report in 1923 and the Bolton Wanderers versus Stoke City 6th round FA Cup-tie Report in 1946. At last the Safety of Sports Grounds Act 1975 followed the Wheatley Report.

Among players, during soccer's World Cup Competition in 1966, the foul play chickens came home to roost, bred by the self-styled permissive society which the then Chancellor of the Exchequer in 1969, the then Roy Jenkins MP, later claimed unwisely during a well-publicised speech to Abingdon Labour Party to be the 'civilised society' ((1969) *The Times*, 21 July p 3). The Brazilian international player, Pelé, was seen on television and video recordings throughout the world to have been criminally and brutally assaulted out of the competition by Bulgarian and Portuguese opponents who have been later identified and recorded below in Pelé's own words at Chapter 9, p 258, International Interaction, without any effective retribution. *The Times* Senior Sports Correspondent, David Miller, recalled in his survey of that series, The Boys of '66, how the author had pinpointed the illegality in the *FA Year-Book 1967–68*. In 1969 a conviction at Maidstone Assizes for manslaughter after a local Essex footballer had fatally punched another caused the author to contribute a different form of article: 'Crimes of Soccer Violence', and *R v Southby* published in the *Police Review* for February 1969, Vol 77, p 110.

5 SPORT AND THE LAW ARRIVES

A year later, the first recorded substantial damage award of £4,500 for foul play on the soccer field resulted in an analysis by the author for the *New Law Journal* (1970 Vol 120, p 413 *Lewis v Brookshaw*). Concurrent with these violent physical developments on the field, behind the scenes, protracted and contentious negotiations, unknown to the author, were taking place for the transfer of the CCPR's assets to the newly-to-be-formed government-funded Sport's Council while preserving the CCPR's identity under an on-going contractual relationship which exists to the present day.

Nevertheless, physical violence persisted, and after the Scottish international rugby referee, Norman Sanson, was obliged in 1977 to send off two players for fighting in the Wales–Ireland international at

Cardiff, a commission from the *Sunday Telegraph* to assess and recommend remedies for the violence engulfing all body-contact sports resulted in a series published there entitled 'Sport and the Law'. The legal emphasis thus had shifted a long way from the taxation imbalance between professional footballers' and cricketers' benefits, restraint of trade, and the concept of Pegasus, as a sporting educational charity a quarter-of-a-century earlier during the early 1950s. To present the law in sport against a more comprehensive perspective, the series was converted a year later in 1978 into a more general survey under the same title in booklet form. It is the genesis for the present text.

On that occasion two Forewords were contributed. The former Lord Chancellor, Lord Havers (writing in his capacity as a then former Solicitor-General, before becoming Attorney-General), recorded:

'If the rule book is torn up or vicious fouls go unpunished then the sporting element is destroyed and fun for both the player and the spectator is lost.'

The then Chairman of the Sports Council, and a former Rugby Union President and captain of England, Dick Jeeps CBE, wrote:

'Sport belongs to the real world and its rapid development in recent years has made ignorance of the law among decision makers unacceptable.'

If only to preserve that fun element, in addition to alerting decision makers at all levels to the legal consequences of their actions, a partnership between sport and the law is essential. The events during the past 16 years since 1978 have done nothing to diminish that need. A senior FA councillor told the author shortly after the *Sunday Telegraph* publication appeared, 'You lawyers keep out of sport: we can take care of it all.' He has hardly been confirmed by the urgent calls made upon the courts and Parliament to try to put out the social fires which his own game's abject administration failed to control. The extent of this intervention is rarely outside public exposure and continues almost daily during preparation of this text. Indeed Leicester Crown Court throughout mid-summer and near autumn of 1993 was occupied for two months with the Public Order Act 1986 application to the Leicester City versus Newcastle United crowd disturbance at the end of the 1991–92 soccer season. Within the author's personal and professional knowledge it did not command national attention, but it was of great concern to the local community, sporting and otherwise (*Leicester Mercury* 28 August 1993). The database of intelligence and video evidence monitors the extent to which these experiences to a lesser or greater degree continue to exist. Indeed, the national media know we have become too immune to such experiences to bother to record them generally.

The misconception behind that quoted FA councillor's line of thought, or lack of it, reflects a wider confusion explained by the former Lord Chancellor and creator in 1962 of the role of government Minister with responsibility for Sport, Lord Hailsham of St Marylebone, in his Carlton Lecture 'Morality, Law and Politics', delivered shortly after his departure from office in June 1987. Discussing 'Values', he explained:

> 'It has been our fortune, good or bad, to live in an age of conflict, violence and confusion, one in which old certainties have faded into agnosticism, when new fanaticisms, new bigotries have arisen and new sources of political power or disruption have first challenged and sometimes overthrown established authority. Partly this has been due to the speed of travel, and partly, possibly as a result of the conflicts which this produces, by a decline in religious belief in the West, overawed as it is by the triumphs of its own science and technology. But, although science and technology are capable of demolishing, up to a point, certain types of superstition, they are not by themselves capable of creating a new system of values, and, if the old systems of value are to be re-established, the need for them will have at the least to be restated in the light of prevailing confusion and doubt. At the heart of the problem lies the uncertain frontier between morality, politics and law, the framework of an ordered and civilised life.'

For sport, however, the problem should be non-existent. As *Britain: 1991*, an official handbook prepared by the Central Office of Information for the Foreign and Commonwealth Office, explains at the beginning of Section 26 entitled 'Sport and Recreation':

> 'The British invented and codified the rules of many of the sports and games which are now played all over the world.'

When these rules are breached, as Lord Hailsham's successor, Lord Havers, observed, 'the sporting element is destroyed'. In a sporting context they can be identified and categorised at four separate levels:
(1)   playing laws;
        for players and participants to play
(2)   playing penal laws;
        for referees, umpires to control and discipline play
(3)   administrative laws;
        for fair and sensible organisation and control
(4)   national laws;
        the overriding control for justice and fair play at all the above three levels.
Because a Welsh international rugby union player in the autumn of

1985 punched a defenceless opponent during the course of a club rugby match without being seen by the referee:

(1)   there was a clear breach of rugby playing laws

(2)   this was not disciplined by the referee in control, and

(3)   was ignored by club administrators (*R v Bishop* (1986) Times, 12 October).

Accordingly, as a last resort the national law was invoked. The ultimate plea of guilty to a common assault resulted in an immediate custodial sentence reduced to a conditional discharge on appeal. Since then the tariff of criminal violence on playing fields at rugby and soccer football has progressively increased to the present penalty of 18 months custody. Damage awards have oscillated between the £4,000 tariff for a broken leg in amateur football in 1970 (*Lewis v Brookshaw* 120 NLJ 413) to a reported £900,000, cut on enquiry to nearer £250,000, (*Murray v Dolan and Motherwell FC* (1993) Scotsman, 24 November) out of court settlement for a professional player, and the £18.3m awarded to the American athlete Butch Reynolds in the Columbus, Ohio courts which was reversed on appeal but subject to a further appeal reportedly contemplated to the Supreme Court, America's equivalent to the House of Lords (*Daily Mail*, 21 May 1994). (See Chapter 7, 'Sports medicine and the law,' pp 215–216, for an explanation of this damages award and Chapter 11, 'Fair play and reason in court'.)

Such developments reflect a pattern throughout the 1970s, 1980s and now into the 1990s in which sport mirrors the general social climate of its time. Thus Stephen Pile, writing in *The Sunday Telegraph Review* on 8 November 1992 on the occasion of the launch of UK Gold, which he described as 'the all-repeats satellite channel', recalled

'I have now watched the first episode of every major soap, drama and comedy series in the past 20 years. And they make a fascinating study of social history. Here, in half-hour chunks, we can see the brutalisation of British life over two decades.

The shift from *Terry and June* (all sweetness and light in the 1970s, laughing affectionately at British incompetence) to *Eastenders* and *The Bill*, where everyone is snarling with anger and frustation all the time, is disturbing to watch when laid end-to-end.'

In the previous year the balanced and comprehensively experienced team of the London *Evening Standard* sports writers prepared and published a remarkable and illuminating anthology which confirmed the shift in emphasis from the days of the author's school-boy's innocence reflected in his hero-worshipping correspondence published as *Corinthians and Cricketers* initially in 1955 with the self-evident sordidness of to-day's amoral *public* sporting climate under the title *Sporting Spite: Rebels and Rebellion in World Sport*. The admirable introduction by the paper's assistant editor and head of sport, Michael Herd, contained this passage at page 11:

> 'Isn't it time to reflect on what has happened to sport? I suggest we have allowed ourselves to confuse the pursuit of sporting excellence with the scramble for money or political prestige. And as a result too many of us today condone what seems to be an irresistible compulsion for participants to behave badly. Let there be no doubt, though, that whatever external pressures exist, at the end of the day each participant is able to act according to his own moral values.
>
> As fists and four-letter words fly, is sport a mirror of our society in which, with arrogance and disdain, rules are bent so that Authority is tested? Do we all see what we can get away with on the field of play and off it? Perhaps E M Forster was correct when he wrote that it is international sport that has helped to kick the world downhill?
>
> All things considered, this is the appropriate time [1991] for sport's ruling bodies to declare enough is enough. How much violence will be tolerated before rugby and other sports act to replace anarchy with authority? At the very moment that baseness seems to have become a daily feature of our sporting lives, is there a way back to a golden age, to the Corinthian era? Some will say that sport should not look over its shoulder while the rest of the world makes what is declared as progress. But surely we want to return to the good old days?'

The answer to what might appear to be a rhetorical, at most a wistful question is simple: of course we do, with the overriding criteria, namely a return to the Rule of Law within sport itself, as the only 'way back to a golden age, to the Corinthian era'; which in turn is Sport and the Law's own 'Back to Basics'. Until this happens, the unnecessary and sickening sequence caused by the abdication of authority by 'sport's ruling bodies', which is summarised in Chapter 6, 'Participation Problems' at pp 161–165, continues unabated with a mounting regularity.

Each year since publication of the first Butterworths edition in early 1988 Sport and the Law has progressed. The *All England Law Reports Annual Review* contains a Sport and the Law Section; and the 35th anniversary of the Munich airport disaster on 6 February 1993 witnessed the creation of the British Association for Sport and Law at Old Trafford, Manchester under the aegis of the Sports Law Unit at the Law Department of the Manchester Metropolitan University.

If Sport and the Law could not be regarded before that occasion as having arrived at a mature age since its birth in the *FA Bulletin* for April 1953, it can certainly do so now.

Chapter 2

Progressive perspective

INTRODUCTION

The British Association for Sport and Law's foundation on 6 February 1993 symbolises recognition of the subject Sport and the Law. Nevertheless, it is vital to be constantly mindful of the range of issues connected with Sport, Law, and Sport and the Law: and this chapter aims to discuss those wider issues that surround the genesis of Sport and the Law: a discussion that is required because it is difficult to understand all the elements which continue to affect sport in a modern day environment without recognising their depth and complexity. The author's Sport and the Law contributions to the *All England Law Reports Annual Review* from 1987 onwards point the way in which the subject will inevitably develop in the years ahead. Criminal, civil and fiscal litigation surfaces regularly alongside Parliamentary attention in its legislative and debating capacities. Yet at one particular point, the relationship of the law and sport in the constitutional legal context remains static, and indeed, perversely confusing, in the United Kingdom at least; namely at government levels in Whitehall and Westminster.

At the end of the first page and top of the second page in the Chapter 1, 'Genesis' for the first Butterworths edition of *Sport and the Law*, it was necessary to explain

> 'an expanding and exploding world of sport at the end of the twentieth century as part of a wider recreational and leisure scene. This is the absence of any "coherent body of doctrine, perhaps even a philosophy of government encouragement"; to cite the words first used to describe how ... in the early 1960s, "a need, not for a Ministry, but for a focal point under a Minister", exists to identify "government responsibility for sport": per Lord Hailsham of St Marylebone writing in *The Door Wherein I Went*. He "was left to organise the first government unit of this kind" in 1962 when Minister for Science and Technology in the Government of Mr Harold Macmillan (later Lord Stockton) ... that need has outgrown the constitutional legal status of a junior government Minister at the level of Parliamentary Under-Secretary in the Department of the Environment, with only 20 per cent of his time available for sport and recreation matters. The remaining 80 per cent is allocated to

"Gypsies and Gypsy site provision"
"mineral planning ... with onshore exploration work"
"planning matters, planning appeals"
"new towns, those which are still new town corporations"
"royal parks and palaces"
"ancient monuments and historic buildings, and the area called heritage"
"European Regional Development Fund money which comes into the Department of the Environment, and indeed for some matters on derelict land"
(evidence, 11 December 1985: Mr Richard Tracy MP, to House of Commons Environment Committee: HC 198-iii at page 105, col 1, para 321).'

Thirty years later the evidence from a House of Lords debate on Sports Facilities on 9 June 1993 was that no progress at all had been made. Furthermore in relation to the most fundamental aspect of how Westminster and Whitehall view what Britain's longest serving Sports Minister, Lord (Denis) Howell of Aston, recognised in that debate (Hansard House of Lords 9 June Col 1025)

'about sport and recreation ... that it is a social service'

was followed by the claim (col 1027):

'what we need is a strong statement from the Government on the philosophy and purpose that they envisage for physical education within the school curriculum. We do not have such a philosophy and we suffer as a result.'

Sixteen months later at the Conservative Party Conference in October 1994 as already explained in the Introduction (page xlvii) the genuinely sports-loving Prime Minister John Major recognised this lacuna by announcing a National Education Curriculum to include sport and physical education for every schoolchild between the ages of five and sixteen, although qualified by a hope for preservation by local authorities of their school playing fields. Thus the capacity to sustain it depends upon the available facilities and resources at all levels. Indeed, only a few days before the 9 June 1993 debate an extraordinary disclosure in the *Independent* recorded how:

(1)   John Patten, Secretary of State for Education, proposed that the School Premises Regulations should no longer apply so far as minimum standards for teaching and recreation were concerned;

(2)   Peter Brooke, the then Secretary of State for National Heritage warned him

'not to underestimate the "flak" from the sports and playing fields lobby,'

and that they would see it

'as a cost-saving device with potentially disastrous results for team games and the ability to deliver the PE requirements of the national curriculum.'

Furthermore,

(3) an earlier Joint Circular from the Department of the Environment and Welsh office dated 16 April 1993 purported to give Guidance for local Authorities as its title stated in relation to 'Disposal of land for less than the best consideration that can reasonably be obtained.'

When the author enquired from Lord Howell whether it is correct to view this as a serious situation he produced the response, irrespective of Home Office for Public Order and other specialist government departments such as the Ministry of Agriculture, Fisheries and Food (MAFF) for angling and water sports, that (in relation at least to playing fields)

'Sport and recreation now covers three government departments. I do not think they talk to each other!'

And as he explained in a recent *Observer* contribution

'we do not have a Minister for Sport these days we have Ministers for Sporting occasions.' [Appendix 7, surveying the overall Government concern with British sport, more than confirms this claim.]

Clearly, one of the causes for this confusion is the absence of a concise and convenient definition for sport.

In 1980 the author himself tried it and failed when reviewing for the Sports Council publication *Sport and Leisure*, then *Sport and Recreation*, a valuable enquiry by Professor McIntosh entitled *Fair Play: Ethics in Sport and Recreation*. What emerged, however, is that if definition is impossible, description is everything. For while sport to many who view it through traditional eyes and minds is a healthy vehicle for fair play, others have corrupted it through the triple diseases of drugs, violence and commerce, which destroy its healthy honest foundation. Thus, in the process of that review, the author structured the following pyramid as a guideline to the facets which constitute sport. The base elements of this pyramid are shaped and conditioned by the upper echelons.

Violence
Internationalism
Politics and Power
Commercialism
Entertainment
Healthy Competition
Free - For - All Fun

The impetus for such structuring came from the Foreword by Sir
Roger Bannister, the pioneer who broke the four-minute mile barrier
as an undergraduate amateur, and progressed to Master of Pem-
broke College, Oxford from where he has recently retired. He wrote
of not only

> 'Sport, which occupies the professional time of a few and the spare time
> of many, is a fit study for ethics.'

but also

> 'Internationally it is becoming increasingly complex to organise and
> regulate and has become fraught with commercial and political pres-
> sures or even, as in the Munich Olympics, terrorism.'

Subsequent Olympic and Commonwealth Games have confirmed
this judgment from the later 1970s with every passing year, and the
pyramid justifies sectional attention, with violence at its apex.

Parallel with the pyramid proposal is the categorisation created by
Sir Denis Follows' own umbrella sporting association, the Central
Council of Physical Recreation (CCPR). Its own sub-divisions are
structured in the following way:

Games and Sports	: the traditional concept
Major Spectator Sports	: the public interest
Movement and Dance	: art or sport, or both, eg Torvill and Dean
Outdoor Pursuits	: rural sports out of town
Water Recreation	: rivers, lakes and all round island coasts
Interested Organisations	: the multitudinous residue, with Sports Council government-funded grants

In turn these approach the 'fundamental distinctions between rural
and urban and between aristocratic and plebeian' identified by Strutt
in 1801 and developed in Chapter 3, 'Under starter's orders', at p 80.

The pyramid structure with the passage of more than ten years since it was first conceived is still based on realities consistent with current experiences. Indeed, the intervening years have confirmed it. For the reader unfamiliar with Sir Denis Follows' concept of the indefineability of sport it will be appropriate to approach it within the present context at three separate stages, namely:

(1) the different layers of levels of the *sport* pyramid beginning at the top;

(2) the different layers of levels of *law* which are appropriate to sport;

(3) the crucial role of law in the playing and *administrative structures* of all sports.

The different layers or levels of the sport pyramid are consistent with Sir Roger Bannister's awareness that sport 'is becoming increasingly complex to organise and regulate'. The different levels or layers of law which are appropriate and applicable to sport were also identified and expanded in Chapter 1 Genesis (pages 16–17) through David Bishop's experiences, namely:

(i)   basic playing laws, eg rules prohibiting unfair or foul play

(ii)   playing penal laws, eg immediate field sanctions, ie dismissals sinbins;

(iii) administrative laws, eg disciplinary tribunals, ie suspensions, life-bans

(iv)   national laws, eg civil or criminal.

The crucial quality or true meaning of law generally at all levels or layers was further assessed from across the Atlantic by one of America's leading examples of a practising jurist, Professor Roscoe Pound, one-time Dean of Harvard Law School among many other distinguished offices. Writing in a series of Cambridge University lectures in *Interpretations of Legal History* he explained (at page 153):

> '... the science of law ... must be more than an organising and systematizing of a body of legal precepts. There are three things to consider, which may not be looked at wholly apart from each other and yet must not be confused by ambiguous use of the term "law". Putting them in the chronological order of their development, these are, the administration of justice, the legal order and law.'

Applied to the sporting scene, Roscoe Pound's three elements can be recognised clearly when identified with easily recognised illustrations in line with the more restrictive assessment set out above.

(1)   *the administration of justice:*

    (i)   balanced refereeing and umpiring for play

    (ii)   balanced disciplining administration in committee rooms and council chambers

(2)   *legal order:* playing and administrative laws for all games and play

(3)   *law:* as defined further by Pound below with concepts generally and sportingly applicable

> 'Law is the body of knowledge and experience with the aid of which this part of social engineering (ie the administration of justice and the legal order) is carried on. It is more than a body of rules. It has rules and principles and conceptions and standards for conduct and for decision but it has also doctrines and modes of professional thought and professional rules of art by which the precepts for conduct and decision are applied and given effect.'

Against those sporting and legal categories the Sport pyramid can be assessed.

LEVEL OF THE SPORTS PYRAMID

1 Violence

To ignore or deny this category rejects the evidence proved by the Munich massacre in 1972, the Heysel Stadium stampede in 1985, and the track record of British football followers which created their unenviable reputations during the years preceding this last disaster, and indeed, since then, too. Violence is an unfortunate apex of the pyramid. It is debatable whether it should exist at this level at the top of the pile. Nevertheless it affects all aspects of sport throughout the world.

Indeed, with a prophetic vision, George Orwell had written in *The Sporting Spirit* after the Second World War in 1945,

> 'Serious sport has nothing to do with fair play. It is bound up with hatred, jealousy, boastfulness, and disregard of all rules and sadistic pleasure in witnessing violence; in other words it is war minus the shooting.'

The shooting between El Salvador and Honduras at the time of the qualifying rounds for the World Soccer Competition in Mexico during 1970 coincided with the games between the two countries at that stage of the tournament; but although the occasion is cited often as an example of sport resulting in war, there is also a contrasting argument that a third match play-off took place amicably during the fighting period and in fact contributed to a reconciliation. Orwell's awareness of sport's 'disregard of all rules' was written before the higher levels of the pyramid merged to dominate sport's public persona.

2 Internationalism

Modern international sport began formally on 3 October 1872 with the Football Association's resolution:

> 'In order to further the interests of the Association in Scotland, it was decided during the current season that a team should be sent to Glasgow to represent England.'

Thus began the earliest regular international sporting fixture in the world. Five years later in the winter of 1876–77 the first cricket tour from England, through MCC, took place in Australia, followed by the first return visit in 1880, and creation of the mythical 'Ashes' at Kennington Oval in 1882. In 1886 the Four Home British Rugby Unions combined to form the International Rugby Board. In 1896, Baron de Coubertin recreated the Olympic Games from his enthusiasm and inspiration fired by his admiration for the athleticism of the English public school and collegiate university system which he had explored extensively. The foundation of FIFA, the Fédération Internationale de Football Association, followed in Paris during 1904.

A year later in 1905, the non-Government funded British Olympic Association was formed in anticipation of joining the 1908 Olympic Games to be held in Rome. When Rome withdrew as the host city, an Anglo-French trade exhibition at London's White City (then not sacrificed as a sporting centre on the high altar of property development) led to the United Kingdom's replacement for the first time. In the following year, 1909, the three leading cricket countries, England (represented by MCC), Australia and South Africa, formed the *Imperial* Cricket Conference. South Africa's membership lapsed when it withdrew nationally from the Commonwealth in 1961. After the restructured and retitled *International* Cricket Conference replaced it in 1965, applications by the South African governing cricket authority for joining as a new member failed regularly until its re-admission after the formal abolition of apartheid in the early 1990s, because of political opposition to its country's national apartheid policies, notwithstanding justifiable claims to have satisfied the International Cricket Conference's own *sporting cricketing standards* of non-discrimination. With this entwining of sport with politics, a new dimension emphasised what has been recognised by realists as a direct consequence of the First World War.

3 Politics and power

The First World War not only tore up the European map; it enmeshed the USA in the fight for it. The old British empire, now the Commonwealth, joined the mother country automatically in the name of the King Emperor, George V, on its own entry into battle with the Kaiser's Germany. By the time it ended in 1918, with united Imperial heroism and sacrifices in all war zones, the new international horizons heralded profound constitutional, national and political changes. The Versailles Treaty in 1919 contained the seeds for European nationalism which spawned Mussolini's fascism in Italy, Hitler's Nazism in Germany and their blatant exploitations of sporting events for political purposes.

With hindsight it is now possible to identify how three separate strands of events during the 1920s were unwinding to bind sport with national politics inextricably during the run up to the Second World War in 1939, and its near irrevocable cementation after it in the Empire, Europe and international sporting contests.

Firstly, the old Empire's priceless contribution to defeating the Kaiser inspired a nascent nationalism which culminated in self-government following from three Imperial Conferences, the Statute of Westminster in 1931, the former Dominions' individual roles alongside the mother country at the time of Edward VIII's abdication in 1936 and entry into the Second World War against Hitler's Germany. Within this progression the 1932–33 MCC cricket tour of Australia, under the aggressively thoughtful leadership of the amateur playing professional solicitor captain, Douglas Jardine, exploded into a political crisis which locked the former Dominion Office (now the Foreign and Commonwealth Office) in Whitehall with leading Australian national and cricketing politicians at all levels. It transcended the immediately successful object of winning the Ashes by four Test Matches to one and curtailing the undoubted batting talents of the then 22-year-old Donald Bradman.

Secondly, during the two following years, Mussolini concerned himself personally with substantial bonuses, (including exemption from military service,) which were offered to Italy's international football team, for its 1–1 draw with England in Rome during 1933 and the return fixture at Arsenal's North London stadium in 1934. England won 4–2 in what has become known in football circles as the Battle of Highbury. England's captain Hapgood, has recorded it as 'the dirtiest game I ever played in,' and Sir Stanley Matthews looked back upon it as 'the roughest in which I have ever taken part'.

Thirdly in December 1935, the Trades Union Congress tried to ban the visit by Germany's national team to North London's other national football centre at Tottenham Hotspur's White Hart Lane ground. It was not the fixture which produced the objections but the possibility of processions and demonstrations in an area bordering upon deeply populated Jewish communities who had been alerted to Hitler's horrendous practices. The German Ambassador called at the Foreign Office to discuss a cancellation and the Home Secretary, then Sir John (later Viscount) Simon, and later a wartime Lord Chancellor, wrote in *The Times* with an innocence touching upon naivety;

'Wednesday's match has no political significance whatever ... It is a game of football, which nobody need attend unless he wishes, and I hope that all who take an interest in it from any side will do their utmost to discourage the idea that a sporting fixture in this country has any political implications.' [Nearly 60 years later in 1994, the fixture booked to be played on Hitler's birthday, 30 April, was cancelled realistically for recognised political reasons.]

Whatever was the attitude 'in this country' during 1935, Germany was preparing its own showcase for politico-sporting posturing with the Berlin Olympics barely six months later in 1936. Two years later in 1938 England's footballers, still captained by Hapgood, were advised by Britain's Ambassador, Sir Neville Henderson, to give the Nazi salute in Berlin's Olympic Stadium four months ahead of the Munich 'piece of paper' of appeasement. The England team saluted with shame, but there was nothing shameful about their salutary victory 6–3. The 103,000 German crowd was stunned.

This sustained politicisation of sport continued even after the Second World War had ended in 1945. The Moscow Dynamo football tour of the United Kingdom was welcomed by football followers with the warmth shared universally by sporting aficionados. It chilled as a prelude to the Cold War with the realisation explained by Mr Colm Brogan in *Our New Masters* (1947) that the team was 'here to demonstrate the superiority of Stalinite football over bourgeois football, and the superiority of Russia over Britain.' The visitors' sustained persistence in playing a makeshift postwar Arsenal XI in the fog at Tottenham Hotspur's White Hart Lane ground, with the referee on one touchline, and the two linesmen on the other, symbolised the enigmatic attitudes which shrouded East–West relationships thereafter. Thirty-three years later Sir Stanley Rous wrote in his memoirs *Football World* (1978):

'Russia is now the country that looks on sport as a means of furthering its political aims.'

In the nearly fifty years which followed that Moscow Dynamo tour, Olympic and Commonwealth Games and international sport generally have been bedevilled by political poisoning of the sporting atmosphere. With the honourable and memorable exception of the late Sir Denis Follows' resistence to the non-sporting Mrs Thatcher's opposition to the Moscow Olympics, sport has supinely accepted this in a manner which more enlightened and intelligent administrative leadership could have avoided through recourse to the law which has consistently protected victims of sport in oppression within and without it as these pages will demonstrate. Taiwan proved this when its national badminton and athletics governing bodies applied successfully to the English courts for acceptance within their respective international governing bodies which had rejected them until the law was invoked successfully. As we shall see in Chapter 9, 'International interaction', the means required a legal interpretation of the rule-book; the purpose and consequence were political (*Shen Fu Chang v Stellan Mohlin* (1977) (badminton) unreported except at [1981] 3 All ER 324 g-h; and *Reel v Holder* [1981] 3 All ER 321, CA (athletics)). For reasons explained more fully in Chapter 9, the House of Lords in *Wheeler v Leicester City Council* overruled two other appeal court judges and the first instance judge to uphold Browne-Wilkinson LJ's dissenting judgment and to adjudicate as offside the Leicester City Council's ban on the Leicester Rugby Club's use of council playing premises. This happened because its players, selected for the honour of wearing England's white shirt, exercised their freedom of choice to tour South Africa.

If a sufficiently determined administrative will, of the kind demonstrated by Sir Denis Follows against a Prime Minister alien to and never comprehending any aspect of sport existed, the political spoilsports who trespass upon sport's traditional administrative apathy and ineptitude could be defeated. For deliberately and intentionally interfering with contractual relations as well as providing compensation for breach of contract, the law of tort can be structured to protect international as well as domestic sport from the political interference which has progressively been permitted to erode the true spirit of sporting comradeship for too long. One reason, of course, has been the hostage given by *public* sport to commercial interests, and the inevitable financial risks inherent in litigation costs. The shading from political to commercial layers in the pyramid became a natural one when Parliamentary activity in the sporting sphere accelerated at an unprecedented rate, for amending legislation which resulted in the Fire Safety and Safety of Places of Sport Act 1987, alongside preparations for and the hearing in Leeds Crown Court of the compensation claims for the Bradford City fire disaster, and the subsequent crowd control legislation following Lord Justice Taylor's Report and the Hillsborough disaster.

4 Commercialism

Commerce and sport are so wedded in the public mind that it is often forgotten how vast areas of sport from school to club levels are dependent upon voluntary service and private funding, without the vast sums now pumped annually into sport and monitored by expensive reports and inquiries. The Government-funded Report from the Monopolies and Mergers Commission to the Secretary for Trade and Industry in July 1976 'on the supply in Great Britain of the services of managing greyhound tracks' contained at page 56 in paragraph 7.7 what the author and many others may consider to be a realistic ideal. It cited the evidence from Peter Lawson, the General Secretary of the Central Council of Physical Recreation (CCPR) (which includes amongst its members, as representing a major spectator sport, the National Greyhound Racing Club which was at the heart of the Report). He was recorded there to have said of the CCPR:

'It regarded a voluntary body, run by eminent people with no financial interest in it themselves, as the best way of controlling a sport, even when there is a major betting interest.'

a test which the NGR satisfied. The intervening near twenty years experience, however, demand the caveat of subject always to adequate administrative and professional advice.

Practical realities in the 1980s precluded such idealism being generally applied. In November 1983, the CCPR itself published *The Howell Report* from a committee of enquiry into sports sponsorship. Ironically it contained a specific recommendation for Government reference to the Office of Fair Trading to examine whether any monopoly situations exist between certain marketing and sporting associations. Curiously so far it has been ignored. In February 1986, a controversial House of Commons Report from an Environment Committee appointed under House of Commons SO 99 in December 1983 contained evidence from the Sports Council, sport's government funded agency equivalent to the Arts Council, that sponsorship funds amounting to an estimated £134 million were received by sport in 1985; and in August 1986 a market analyst's report from Mintel estimated an increase to £140 million. These figures were separate from the Sports Council's additional parliamentary evidence during 1985 of the following sources separate from sponsorship:

(a)   local authority capital expenditure (£186 million in 1982–83);

(b)   net revenue expenditure (£650 million in 1984–85), which included the costs of public parks, only some of which could be allocated to sport particularly as distinct from recreation generally;

(c)   central government grants to the four Sports Councils for the four home national countries which amounted in 1985–86 to £39 million;

(d)   government financial assistance to deprived areas for sport and recreation through the Urban Programme and Partnership grants comprising £31 million in 1985–86.

More significantly, the Parliamentary Report recorded that

> 'In 1983/84 the Government recovered an estimated £624 million in income tax and NI contributions from those employed in sport (excluding sports goods, manufacturing), £477 million in betting duty, and £280 million in VAT mainly from the commercial sector.'

More recently in its Annual Report 1992/93 the Sports Council explained:

> 'A study commissioned by the council last year revealed:–
> - the value-added (or output) attributable to sport-related activity exceeds £8 billion per year, or around 1.7% of Gross Domestic Product;
> - consumer expenditure on sport and related items is now touching the £10 billion per year mark, representing a growth rate of some 11% per year between 1985 and 1990;
> - sport provides nearly half a million jobs in the UK;
> - domestic tourists and overseas visitors spend over £14 billion a year in the UK, of which over £1.5 billion occurs directly as a result of sport.'

In 1985 a Sports Council Olympic Review advised £5.5m funding for Britain's Olympic prestige. Its Annual Report for 1992/93 recorded:

> 'In the past twelve months a concerted effort has been made to achieve a more favourable VAT and tax status for the Association. In addition, the BOA has actively campaigned for the establishment of a national lottery. It has helped to unite British sport, creating an effective lobby to guarantee a fair share of any potential new revenue for sport. Leaping to a personal best, then, has not proved too stiff a challenge for the Association over the past twelve months in established areas of finance. In addition the bar has been set higher in several new areas.'

Commercial sources therefore cannot be ignored. If they are to be harnessed most effectively and beneficially they require skilled professional structuring. Sponsorship is in the beginning and at the end a business deal which must be geared to clear contractual foundations as we shall see in Chapter 13, 'Sponsored gentlemen and players'; and the whole of sports funding in the later 1990s should be framed with an eye to the tax, VAT, and charitable situations at both national and local levels to be explained in Chapter 14, 'No fine on fun'. That particular title is taken from the polemical attack by the late Sir Alan Herbert on a greatly resented Entertainment Tax; and this leads logically to the next layer or level of the pyramid.

5 Entertainment

Sir Denis Follows in his Loughborough College lecture explained how

'Sport at top level has become much more part and parcel of the entertainment world and particularly so during the past thirty years. We have reached the stage where sport at top level has become almost completely show business with everything one associates with show biz – the cult of the individual, high salaries, the desire to present the game as a spectacle – with more money, less sportsmanship, more emphasis on winning – and all this has largely come about through television.'

His conclusion contained this express warning:

'I have no fear for the future of sport at grass root level. But I do profess a fear for sport at top level.
In my lifetime I have more or less seen an entertainment industry born and die. I refer to the cinema. Is there any God given gift that protects League Football and County Cricket from such a fate?'

In the eleven years which have passed since those thoughts, the fluctuating mobility of different sponsors entering and departing from these two national and other sporting institutions, such as longstanding provincial tennis tournaments, point to the authenticity within Sir Denis' apprehensions about *sport at top level*, and an issue yet to be resolved in 1994. His lack of fear for the grass roots stemmed from his knowledge that it is there that the true meaning of sport exists forever, with healthy competition and free-for-all fun.

Yet even here, too, the years since Follows spoke in 1983 had witnessed changing attitudes to education in sport, creating such dangers and apprehensions as the monopolistic control of public entertainment sport by television, commerce and sponsorship which previously did not exist. No greater proof is needed than the conference and seminar during November 1986 mounted in successive weeks by, respectively, the CCPR and the two government departments concerned, Education and Environment, concerning sport in schools and the apprehensions of Lord Deedes during Easter Week-end 1994 cited already at pages xlv–xlvi of the Introduction.

6 Healthy competition

Every sporting competitor should know the difference between healthy and sickening activities. Unfortunately, the corruption of language among media, professional sport commentators and observers has transferred the euphemism for unfair conduct and play from the professional foul, now recognised as a criminally and civilly actionable assault, to a 'good' or 'keen' competitor. Description once more, rather than definition, is appropriate for accurate understanding. One commentary which stands the ultimate test of time was coined by the doyen of modern all-round sporting chroniclers, Bernard Darwin, who trained as a barrister, practised as a golfer and had many other sporting attributes. Under the title *British Sport and Games*, published by the British Council in a *British Life and Thought* series at the outset of the Second World War during 1940 and revised when it ended in 1945, he wrote nearly fifty years ago with words requiring no modifications to-day:

> 'As long as there is competition in any walk of life, so there will be some sharp practice, but at least it is today generally and severely frowned upon where once it was almost admired.'

He continued interrogatively,

> 'What exactly are the ideals which make us call the man who lives up to them "a good sportsman"? One of them and that the chief, because almost everything else is comprised in it, is "to set the game above the prize", to enjoy the contest or the adventure first of all for its own sake. It is one that in its sternest and narrowest sense is scarcely possible to live up to. Everybody must want to win; that desire is part of the joy of the contest, whether it be with the beasts of the chase or with a human adversary, and those who have such desire are far better otherwise occupied. There is a certain maxim, or rather aspiration, too often quoted, which in its literal meaning is almost absurd – "May the best side win!". It is one which must, if we are honest, be accompanied by another unspoken wish, namely, that ours may prove the best side. Otherwise it is an anaemic thing. Of course we want our own side to win. We should be poor creatures if we did not and poor players. The point is, I take it, that we must not want it too much and in the wrong way. First of all we must not want to win by an excessive sharpness. Games must have rules and rules must be kept, but there will always come moments when it is well not to insist too much upon breaches of them, but rather to put the blind eye to the telescope. As to when those moments arise, there will always be differences of opinion. This much at least can be said, that the rules of games are not made for those who mean to break but for those who mean to observe them. You cannot legislate for cheating.'

Nearly fifty years on the last sentence requires qualification. The need to legislate for cheating marks the difference between recognising regrettably that unfair and unhealthy competitors do exist, and carrying on unconsciously as if they do not. The minority who step out of line have to be lassoed, coralled and above all else sanctioned until they learn the norm of good behaviour or forever be outlawed and banished, to allow the silent majority within a setting of Healthy Competition their free-for-all fun.

7 Free-for-all fun

In 1986 a publication prepared by the National Coaching Foundation and the Association for Children's Play and Recreation-Playboard was entitled *Play the Game*. An introductory section entitled 'A New Perspective on winning and losing' explained under these sections

'What is needed is a new view of competition which emphasises the personal challenges and rewards:

of trying to do better than last time

of persistence

of setting one's goals and finding the discipline to pursue them

of co-operation of playing for the team

of sheer athletic joy.'

Under the fun concept it explained

'Keeping the fun in sport can be extremely hard. Rather than measure the value of sport in terms of whether a child can win or not, score or not, defeat or be defeated, emphasis should be on the development of a sense of personal worth and achievement ...

When competition is kept in perspective, there is room for fun in the pursuit of victory – or more accurately, the pursuit of victory is fun.'

These concepts may be elusive. From different sides of the Atlantic and from different points in time they can be summarised in well known standards familiar to some, perhaps not so well known to others. From America, Grantland Rice wrote,

'For when the One Great Scorer comes
To write against your name,
He marks – not that you won or lost –
But how you played the game.'

In similar style, Sir Henry Newbolt explained

'There's a breathless hush in the Close to-night –
Ten to make and the match to win –
A bumping pitch and a blinding light,
An hour to play and the last man in.
And it's not for the sake of a ribboned coat,
Or the selfish hope of a season's fame,
But his Captain's hand on his shoulder smote –
"Play up, play up, and play the game?" '

Out-dated? Old hat? Or, in the end, nearer to the true meaning of sport than the higher echelons in that pyramid:

Entertainment
Commercialism
Politics and Power
Internationalism
Violence

or the modern cult-concept, sponsored sport? Each reader must judge for himself, or herself. For as we shall see in Chapter 8, the women are rapidly 'catching up the men'.

THE LEVELS OF LAW APPLICABLE TO SPORT

Against the background of the above perspective of the levels and layers of sporting operations, how does the law fit in or function? To some the answer may be clear-cut; but a moment's reflection should establish that it cannot be as simple as superficial minds would suggest. For sport in its widest, broadest meaning acknowledges the laws' existence at one or more of four separate levels, already explained:

(i)   basic *playing* laws, eg rules prohibiting unfair or foul play;

(ii)   playing *penal* laws, eg immediate field sanctions, ie dismissals sin-bins;

(iii) *administrative* laws, eg disciplinary tribunals, ie suspensions, life-bans;

(iv)   *national* laws, eg civil or criminal.

Thus a World Cup or Test Match offence against the laws of a particular game, such as the assaults by Portuguese and Bulgarian footballers on Pelé in England during the World Cup Competition of 1966, and the threats to bowl in an intimidatory fashion as explained in Chapter 9, 'International interaction', could or would (subject to any advantage discretion by a referee or prosecuting or litigating source),

(a)   breach a playing law;

(b)   activate a penal playing law;

(c)   initiate an administrative law;

(d)   operate a civil or criminal law.

Thus, *R v Bishop* (1986) illustrates (a), (c) and (d). Because the *referee* did not see the admitted criminal common assault on the rugby field, the offence was initially charged and prosecuted as an assault occasioning actual bodily harm. This was not pursued in the Crown Court where a plea of common assault was the basis of a one month's custodial sentence reduced on appeal to a suspended sentence and thus (b) *could not function*. Furthermore, at one stage the administrative law operated by the Welsh Rugby Union resulting in a season's ban was under consideration for a High Court application during late 1986 and early 1987 resulting in no further action being taken.

For lawyers, however, this alignment may justifiably be considered too restrictive. Yet even if sport is approached from a wider legal spectrum, the practical and ultimate result would be the same. Hence, the application of every restricted legal category, (a) to (d) inclusive above, to the sporting scene within Pound's wider concept at page 24 (supra) as 'part of social engineering'. Furthermore, beyond sport, this covers the whole legal spectrum from divorce in family life to drunken and drugged drivers as the apex of anti-social misconduct.

Pound's concluding comment is a natural prelude to the next stage, namely, the crucial role which law has played in the playing and administrative structure of sport. He wrote:

'Like the engineer's formulas, they [ie the law's "doctrines and modes of professional thought and professional rules of art"] represent experience, scientific formulations of experience, and logical development of the formulations; but also inventive skill in conceiving new devices and formulating their requirements by means of a developed technique.'

Another great American practitioner and jurist, Oliver Wendell Holmes, coined the concept in the opening pages of his work on *The Common Law*: 'The life of the law is not logic, it is experience.' Experience, expediency and experiment through law produced the structure and the framework for modern sport, as we shall now see. Sadly, however, the manner in which it is both played and administered in our time merits the condemnation of a celebrated source nearer home, with Kipling's immortal couplet [*The Islanders* (1902)]:

'Then ye returned to your trinkets; then ye contented your souls With the flannelled fools at the wicket or the muddied oafs at the goals.'

CRUCIAL ROLE OF LAW IN THE PLAYING AND ADMINISTRATIVE STRUCTURES OF ALL SPORT

Not without significance *The Oxford Companion to Sports and Games* – explains 'Archery can claim the oldest ancestry of any sport actively pursued today.'

Its practice and usage in the interests of national security meant that effective and authentic legislation protected its survival while outlawing other sports and pastimes. Latimer preaching before Henry VIII declared,

> 'The art of shooting hath been in times past much esteemed in this realme: it is a gift of God, that he was given us to excell all other nations withal – It hath been Goddes instruements whereby he hath gyven victories agaynste our enemyes.'

Edward III forbade the playing of idle games, including football, because they interfered with archery practice, and an Act of 1541 was similarly motivated. It not only made illegal a great variety of customary pastimes, but also ordained that every man under sixty years of age, 'not lame, decrepit or maimed', should possess and use a bow and train up his children and servants in the art.

Modern competitive archery runs true to form with so many other modern sports, and a fall-out from the social progress of emerging leisure pursuits during the mid and later nineteenth century. The first Grand National Archery Meeting was held at York in 1844, and in 1861 the Grand National Archery Society was founded to assume responsibility for this meeting and in due course became the official governing body for archery in the United Kingdom.

Comparable with archery in antiquity, and in one historic instance for national security, is bowls. Contemporaneous evidence confirms Sir Francis Drake's memorable reply to news of the Spanish Armada's sighting off Plymouth Hoe on 19 July 1588, 'There is plenty of time to win this game and thrash the Spaniards, too'; as he did.

Nearly three centuries passed, however, before a Glasgow solicitor during 1848–49, W W Mitchell, was charged to prepare a code which has become standard for what is now a universally popular game within the capacity of all generations and both sexes.

The most popular of all sports with a parallel for antiquity alongside any other, horse racing, was structured with the foundation of the Jockey Club in 1750 to regulate control of the potential corruption from gaming and commercial exploitation. As we shall see, with its disciplinary and drug controls it had almost a century's start on other governing bodies in keeping offenders against its Rules of Racing either in line or warning them off the Turf on Newmarket Heath. Cricket's first dedication of the Laws of the Game are attributable in 1774 to the club which played at the Artillery Ground now used by the Honourable Artillery Company. MCC's foundation in 1787 ultimately took over and has retained trusteeship and copyright of the Laws; although in 1968 it surrendered autonomy for government funding purposes of the domestic English game to the Cricket Council and under it, to the Test and County Cricket Board (TCCB).

These club and professional sources available to the leisured society of the times inevitably created a class basis for developing British sport. This mould began to crack only when the rapacious fiscal legislation after 1945 allowed commercial predators and business sponsorship to replace the earlier pioneering patronage. The first organised athletics meeting originated at Exeter College, Oxford in 1850, as if to anticipate the vintage period of the 1950s when its ancient walls contained Roger Bannister, to break the four-minute mile barrier; Denis Saunders, captain of the two Pegasus Oxbridge FA Amateur Cup-winning teams before two 100,000 Wembley crowds; and John McGregor or Kendall-Carpenter, England's future rugby captain and Rugby Union President.

From Cambridge University in 1862 came the final thread to link the differing school rules for playing football in anticipation of the FA's foundation in 1863; and the Gentlemen and Players division epitomised the public fabric of nearly all popular pastimes in their formative years. Dr Arnold's mid-nineteenth century concept of *mens sana in corpore sano* guided those who created the urban, industrial and overseas clubs formed for amateur joys. The public demand and spectator appeal converted them into professional industries by legislative changes of the emerging public bodies such as the FA, Rugby League and the County Cricket Championship. Even Baron de Coubertin's vision of an athletic dream which grew into the modern Olympic Games from 1896 was inspired from these privileged and elitist sources.

Underlying and running throughout this unfolding pattern and progression was the constitutional legal core described so aptly by the judge who was required to sentence the last women to be hanged before Ruth Ellis, Edith Thompson. Montague (later Mr Justice) Shearman was an outstanding Oxford University athlete who later became President of the Amateur Athletic Association until he died in 1900. Author of a classic sporting textbook in the Badminton Library, *Athletics and Football*, he wrote as a young practising barrister a century ago (during 1887) in a chapter entitled 'Athletic Government' which is equally applicable to all sports:

'One of the most remarkable features about modern English Athletic life is the capacity of the athlete for self-government. As soon as any game or sport becomes popular in any district, or throughout the

country, clubs are formed; the clubs conglomerate into district associations; and the latter finally become gathered into a national governing
body. All these bodies, from the smallest club to the largest association,
are the outcome of voluntary effort; they are worked, as a rule, in a
sensible and businesslike manner, and the officers, in almost every case,
are unpaid. Football, cricket, cycling, athletics, paper-chasing, have all
their governing bodies; and at a week's notice the best team in any sport
can be picked from the whole country, or the popular opinion as to any
change or innovation in the sport ascertained. All this discipline and
organisation is so well known nowadays as to excite little notice; but
when fairly considered, it is really marvellous and most creditable to the
capacity and sound sense of the English sportsman.'

Victorian modesty must have prevented him from also saying what
the author will say to fill the gap. It was also due in no small way to the
lawyers at all levels and the sense of justice and fair play among the
lay administrators, many from the teaching profession, who combined to create the administrative structures and playing laws which
have been adapted universally throughout the world.

Shearman himself played a major role in the development of
amateur athletics in the years long before modern accountancy
ingenuity has converted them at the public level into trust fund
athletics. Cricket's first knight, Sir Francis Lacey, was MCC's non-
practising barrister secretary who received his accolade in 1926. That
was the year in which Harry Altham from Winchester College produced the first edition of his classic *History of Cricket* before creating
the MCC coaching scheme, and later attaining Presidency of that
Club and also of his beloved Hampshire County Cricket Club. In that
year, too, a Watford Grammar school-master began his public refereeing career before gaining the highest honours within soccer as Sir
Stanley Rous and ultimately re-writing the Laws of the Game and
inventing the ingenious diagonal system of refereeing control to
worldwide acclaim. More recently, Upjohn J's judgment in *Football
League Ltd v Littlewood Pools Ltd* ([1959] 2 All ER 546) explains the
skill in creating the copyright contained in the League's fixture com-
pilation from the solicitor son, Harold Sutcliffe, of a former Football
League President and solicitor, Charles E Sutcliffe, in its formative
years of the last century. These examples can be multiplied in every
British sport at national and local levels.

The two World Wars inevitably operated as a catalyst upon the
development of British sport which reflected their impact on society
generally. They also mark the general unawareness of understanding
within sport of how the law was available to benefit it before and
during the inter-war years period. As we will see later in Chapter 6,
'Participation problems', the advisers to the Plaintiff (Kingaby) in
the crucial litigation before 1914 did not apparently recognise or

understand the difference in applying the law of restraint of trade in contract, from conspiracy in tort to the professional footballers' retain and transfer contracts which were perpetually renewable analogous to a lease at the employer's discretion – *Kingaby v Aston Villa FC* (supra).

The landmark sporting education charity decision in favour of athletics and a fives court at Aldenham School was propounded by Eve J in line with his former College's contribution to amateur sport, Exeter College, Oxford ([1915] 2 Ch 284). Outside Australia it was also not always followed, recognised or understood in court generally by the sporting world until the Charity Commissioners registered the FA Youth Trust Deed in 1972. Thereafter eight years of contested litigation passed before its endorsement and approval by the House of Lords in *IRC v McMullen* ([1981] AC 1). Finally, as we shall see in Chapter 11, 'Fair play and reason in court', even the great and courageous Sir Patrick Hastings, advocate supreme with Norman Birkett, in the inter-war years, and after too, could not find a way to overturn an oppressive FA disciplinary tribunal verdict on the Arsenal Football club chairman, Sir Henry Norris, in the manner which is utilised today by *declaratory judgments* on grounds of denying natural justice as distinct from the at present inapplicable judicial review machinery. Libel was the only relief pursued and more often lost than won, as he experienced on that occasion (*Norris v FA* (1929)) and later in the better known and reported judgments concerning the Pony Turf Club and the Jockey Club, also arising out of the libel claims; respectively *Cookson v Harwood* (1931) [1932] 2 KB 478 and *Chapman v Ellesmere* [1932] 2 KB 431.

Natural justice was not unknown to the courts at that time (see *Maclean v The Workers Union* [1929] 1 Ch 602 at 605); but its applicability to sporting and even more general situations was not recognised as it has become today. Indeed, it was in yet another sporting libel action after the Second World War, again attempting unsuccessfully to attack a sporting disciplinary tribunal (the Jockey Club again: *Russell v Duke of Norfolk* [1949] 1 All ER 109) that Lord Denning MR (at pp 119–20), in what Professor Lowell has called 'a forceful but scarcely cited obiter',

> 'was quietly laying the groundwork for the acceptance of a number of the basic principles behind'

the breaches of natural justice created by the Brighton Watch Committee, as established by the House of Lords' judgment fifteen years later in its police corruption case of *Ridge v Baldwin* [1964] AC 40. This we shall see in Chapter 11, 'Fair play and reason in court'.

Concurrently with sport's tentative and (except for professional cricketers' tax-free benefits triumph in the House of Lords during

1927) generally *un*successful court appearances after the First World War, two other parallel developments emerged, consistent with a national awareness of the advantages of physical education. As a precedent for RA Butler's Education Act of 1944, before the Second World War ended in 1945, the Education Act 1918 was passed during August, three months prior to the 11 November Armistice Day. Conceived throughout under the guidance of the Minister and eminent educationist, historian and statesman, H A L Fisher, and consolidated three years later by the Education Act 1921, the legislation extended earlier legislation for public education to include physical and social recreational education at varying levels.

In 1925 the privately-funded National Playing Fields Association was created under the patronage of the then H R H Duke of York, later H M King George VI, a year before he played at Wimbledon; and a letter to Yachting Monthly inspired the first Round Britain Fastnet Rock race.

By the mid-1930s, at a time of developing military nationalism in Europe and mass unemployment, an uneasy awareness was felt of a gap in the nation's physical culture, created by an imbalance when compared with Nazi Germany and Fascist Italy, and a lack of coordination for physical and mental health. Against this background the creative vision and genius of a thirty-year-old physical education teacher, Phyllis Colson, conceived the idea of a nationally coordinated 'umbrella' body of sporting organisations. Thus was born in 1935 the Central Council of Recreative Physical Training (later and now the Central Council of Physical Recreation – the CCPR). A starting gift from private sources covered its initial expenses of £300.

Backed by the then Board of Education (now the Department for Education and Science), under the patronage of the King (George V) and Queen (Mary), with the Prince of Wales (Edward VIII) as its Vice-Patron, and Lord Astor, its President, its launch was auspicious, and the initial council members included Stanley Rous. The new Jubilee Trust created after 25 years' reign of the present Queen's grandfather contributed £1,000 in February 1936, and a few months later the NPFA added an equal sum and free accommodation.

The Board of Education's parallel involvement became apparent with first a circular in January 1936 encouraging inter alia *Physical Education for Persons no longer attending school*; a Memorandum a year later in January 1937 on *Physical Training and Recreation*, explaining the Government's proposals for the development and extension of the facilities available, and a final enactment, in the first few weeks of Mr Neville Chamberlain's Conservative Party premiership, of the Physical Training and Recreation Act on 13 July 1937. This was the first statute dedicated exclusively and specifically to activities identified in its title (although Public Health legislation since 1875 under Disraeli's Conservative Government had entered into this area fragmentarily). This innovative enactment authorised the then Board of Education to grant aid to voluntary recreational organisations and two years later on the eve of the Second World War the Social and Physical Training Grant Regulations of 1939 extended it to

'(a) the provision and maintenance of facilities for social and physical training in England or Wales, including payment of leaders, instructors and wardens, and the hiring and equipment of premises;

(b) training of leaders, etc; and

(c) incidental expenses of organisation and administration.'

The war years catalyst carried into battle on the home and service fronts the mixture of voluntary and national service which is the leitmotiv for the mixed economy of today and the keystone for the future funding of leisure and recreation in the community. Sporting rivalries between branches of the armed services and combined services fixtures had been threaded into traditional sporting calendars for decades. In 1938 they were joined by ENSA, the Entertainments National Service Association. In 1939, CEMA, the Council for the Encouragement of Music and Arts, was formed with a mixture of Government and private sources, including the American Pilgrim Trust. When the Pilgrim Trust pulled out in 1942 CEMA's funding became exclusively grant-aided from the Ministry of Education, alongside the 1937 statutory public funds for Physical and Recreation Training.

Thus the scene was set for the logical pattern which unfolded after the Second World War. In June 1945, a month following the European War's end, CEMA's conversion was approved 'to encourage knowledge, understanding and practice of the arts ... With the name of the Arts Council of Great Britain.' Unfortunately, a decision was made to transfer it from the Education Ministry to the Treasury. From there it was transferred back to the Education portfolio until it became the Office of Arts and Libraries in the 1980s and to-day is linked with Sport and Lotteries within the Department of National Heritage.

The initial grant in 1946–47 was £350,000. The funding of £101m by 1985 was argued by Arts lobbyists to be insufficient; and arguments were fuelled by the uncertain constitutional status in the 1980s of the Minister responsible for its administration with the belief created by the dual roles of *appearing* to be a spending Minister for the Arts and a budgeting Minister linked to Treasury constraints/

control until in April 1992, alongside a hotch-pot of other cultural areas, including sport, it was shunted into the Department of National Heritage. With a Minister at the Cabinet table and Parliamentary Under-Secretaries in both the House of Commons and House of Lords they are now all committed collectively to wider heritage areas than those described before the House of Commons Environment Committee as cited at page 20, above (see also Appendix 7) by the then Sports Minister and his limited areas of activities.

Furthermore, this new Department of National Heritage and its Minister and civil servants have no *direct* control or jurisdiction over school sport (Department for Science and Education), planning supervision over playing fields (Department of Environment), sports medicine (Department of Health and Social Security) – the key areas for the future of sport. Thus, the sporting scenario became even more complex than the Arts background.

The original CCRPT became the CCPR in 1944. In 1957 it appointed a committee under the chairmanship of Sir John Wolfenden to report on the future of sporting administration 'in promoting the general welfare of the community'. In 1958 Parliament passed the Recreational Charities Act to widen the scope of charitable status in a context built-in to its title.

Before the Wolfenden Committee reported in 1960, the Conservative Party's 1959 General Election Manifesto contained a commitment to *The Use of Leisure* specifying.

'Measures will be taken to encourage Youth Leadership and the provision of attractive youth clubs, more playing fields, and better facilities for sport.'

The Labour Party's official election booklet, entitled *Leisure for Living*, declared the Party's policy to form a Sports Council within the then Ministry of Education, with an income of £5m to spend.

In 1960 the CCPR's Wolfenden Report ended with 57 paragraphs of Conclusions and Recommendations. They included £5m 'as the amount to be distributed in any one year' by a Sports Development council. Two years later in 1962, a full quarter-of-a-century after the first direct government entry on the playing field and physical recreation and training areas under the 1937 legislation, Lord Hailsham of St Marylebone (*before* his three periods as Lord Chancellor in the 1970s and 1980s) was Minister for Science and Technology in Mr Macmillan's Cabinet. He explained in *The Door Wherein I Went* (at page 207) how he recognised the time had arrived for another leap forward in this crucial area of national activity:

'It occurred during a Cabinet Meeting in which government responsibility for Sport was being discussed. It was being said that, properly speaking, responsibility for sport was being shared between quite a number of departments and authorities, education, local government, universities, the services, and all the voluntary bodies dealing with athletics, from the Olympic and Commonwealth Games and League and Cup football at the top, to badminton, fives and even chess at the most refined and esoteric end of the spectrum. I pointed out that recreation generally presented a complex of problems out of which modern government was not wholly free to opt, and which government funds were, in fact, and were likely to continue to be, committed in one way or another in coaching, in the provision of playing-fields, in matters of safety at racecourses and football grounds. I waxed eloquent on this subject, talking of the fares for Olympic competitors and many other topics. I suggested that there was need, not for a Ministry but for a focal point under a Minister, for a coherent body of doctrine, perhaps even a philosophy of government encouragement. Paradoxically, I thought there was in fact a kind of analogy in the way in which I had tried to administer government science, making use of independent expertise, but not seeking to impose regulation or central administration. My eloquence had its effect on the Prime Minister and, before I knew where I was, I was left to organise the first government unit of this kind under Sir John Lang, who had been Secretary of the Admiralty when I was First Lord. As in most of the other things I have done in public life, except the Party chairmanship, I always strive to work through other people with the minimum of fuss, as I find that this is the best way to get things done. This particular activity was a minor matter, and I thought comparatively little of it at the time since it occurred at a period when other things were occupying my mind [as a Cabinet Minister].'

Belief that 'This particular activity was a minor matter' was, in the context of traditional Whitehall and Westminster thinking, then, as well as now, understandable.

The first ever Wembley FA Cup Final stadium crowd overflow was in 1923 where an estimated crowd of 125,000 gathered at a stadium equipped for 93,000. A government inquiry was established as there were 1,000 casualties but thankfully no fatalities. Its report (Cmd 2088) in 1924 recommended a stadium licensing system and fire precautions. Nothing happened. After 33 were crushed to death in a crowd overflow in 1946 during the Bolton Wanderers versus Stoke City FA Cup-tie a further government report made similar recommendations (Cmd 6846). Again nothing happened.

During the later 1960s an experienced and perceptive journalist, the late J L Manning, son of an equally respected Fleet Street practitioner Lionel Manning, warned vigorously in the *Daily Mail* that no legal liability protected crowd safety positively. Nothing happened apart from ridicule. Then came Ibrox in 1971, with 66 deaths; another report in 1972 (Cmnd 4952), and at last something did happen: a Highway Code-styled Green Guide in 1973 without legal effect but with common-sense recommendations for stadia safety and the Safety of Sports Grounds Act 1975 with limited provisions confined to First and Second Division Football League Clubs, Wembley Stadium and Murrayfield, Edinburgh.

Contemporaneously with the above inactivity on the safety scene, Lord Hailsham's concept took shape administratively. After the 1964 General Election and a change of Government, the Sports Ministry portfolio was handed to a former Football League referee, now the Rt Hon Lord Howell of Aston. He was appointed initially as a junior under-secretary at the Department of Education and Science (with responsibility for sport). After his reappointment two years later in 1966 following his Party's further General Election success, and before the arrival in 1970 of Mr Heath's Government, he was promoted to the role of Minister of State at the Ministry of Housing and Local Government, taking that responsibility for sport with him to a different department.

A four-year period as Opposition Spokesman for Local Government and Sport preceded his return to office in February 1974 for a further five-year period until 1979. On that occasion as Minister of State at the Department of the Environment, he had responsibilities to sport and recreation as well as the countryside, environmental policy, water resources and the Property Services Agency.

Denis Howell has thereby held the sports ministry portfolio for a cumulative period of eleven years, a longer span than that experienced by any other occupant of this nationally important but constitutionally junior government role. Indeed, those eleven years are only four short of the collective tenure of all other fourteen holders of the office since the start of Mrs Thatcher's first Government in 1979. Significantly, his generous and friendly public advice given in the *Independent* newspaper (20 June 1987) after the General Election of 1987 to the seventh and youngest appointee, Colin Moynihan MP, a former Olympic Games rowing cox, included the following warning note:

> 'The problems ahead are formidable and deepening. He will need to find resources as yet untapped if he is to steer the nation through seas quite unlike the calm waters in which he is used to coxing his boat . . . On the international political stage, cricket and rugby will demand more of his time than the 20 per cent allocated by his predecessor to the whole of his portfolio.'

Domestically Denis Howell was responsible during his first ministerial period for implementing the Wolfenden Report's recommendations in 1960 to create a Sports Council by establishing an advisory Sports Council in 1965, of which he became chairman. This occurred prior to the grant of a Royal Charter in 1971 (when his immediate successor, then Eldon Griffiths MP, occupied the ministerial chair) to what became the executive Sports Council.

1972 witnessed not only the transition of Phyllis Colson's 1935 CCPR creation as a collective focal point for the governance of British sport to the Sport's Council for England. Sports Councils for Scotland, Wales and Northern Ireland were structured concurrently with Royal Charters and linked to their respective government offices for funding. Each of the other three home countries retains its equivalent to the CCPR separate from its national Sports Council.

The hard core legal basis for that transition was a contract signed in 1972 under the title of Heads of Agreement by the representatives of the Sports Councils and the CCPR. It was re-affirmed in January 1985 by a document headed Memorandum Agreement produced in evidence to and published in an appendix (No 5, pages 117–118) by a House of Commons Environment Committee Report on the Sports Council and its associated public bodies in early 1986 (HC 241). The contract guaranteed the funding by the Sports Council of the CCPR, which was restructured. The Sports Council inherited from the original CCPR its valuable assets, including its properties, journal, the priceless experience of its professional staffs, and the charitable trusts for administering the National Recreational Centres on land and water.

The Sports Council's prime objectives, as summarised in the House of Commons Committee's Report (para 15, page x):

'as set out in its Royal Charter, are to encourage mass participation in sport and to promote excellence in sporting achievement. Clearly these aims are interlocked. The greater the number of people participating in sport the more chance there is of excellence emerging. The higher the achievements of the top performers, the greater the number of those who will be inspired to emulate them.'

In 1972 the CCPR was restructured, with HRH The Duke of Edinburgh continuing in office as an active President. A new Central Committee elected Denis Howell as its Chairman in 1973, where he stayed until his reappointment as Minister in 1974. Its present role and objectives were summarised in a written Memorandum of evidence to the House of Commons Committee by its General Secretary, Peter Lawson, thus:

(1) to constitute a standing forum of national governing and representative bodies;

(2) to support the work of the specialist sports bodies and to bring them together with other interested organisations; and

(3) to act as a consultative body to the Sports Council.

This last function was illustrated vividly on two occasions in the years immediately before the House of Commons Committee's Report. Both linked the Sports Council directly, yet were ignored by the Committee's Report. One was contained in the Sports Council's written evidence, the other forms the CCPR's oral testimony.

The written Memorandum of evidence from the Sports Council (pages 81–82) generously acknowledged and adopted the CCPR's proposal in its Paragraph 33

'that a non-profit distributing body having the purpose of developing and controlling a sport or recreation activity for the public benefit should enjoy tax exemption.'

This issue is considered further at Chapter 14, 'No fine on fun'.

In 1981 the CCPR established its own Committee of Enquiry into sports sponsorship under the chairmanship of Denis Howell. Its members included the Sports Council's Director General, John Wheatley, and the subsequent Sports Minister, Colin Moynihan MP. Its report, published as The Howell Report in November 1983 contained 73 Conclusions and Recommendations. These compared consistently with the 77 conclusions and recommendations from a House of Commons Education, Science and Arts Committee Report published a year earlier in October 1982 on the Public and Private Funding of the Arts. (1982 HC 49–1, Ch XIII; pp cxxic–cxxix). They each contrast sharply with the mere nine conclusions and recommendations of the House of Commons Environment Committee on the Sports Council and its associated public bodies (1986 HC 241, Ch 3 pp xxix–xxx).

The Government's Response published in July 1986 to the House of Commons Committee's Sports Council Report (HC 504) recognised in the context of

'the efficient structure of sport ... some overlapping functions between the Sports Council and the Central Council for [sic] Physical Recreation (CCPR) and with the other main sporting agencies, such as the British Olympic Association and the Sports Aid Foundation. As the Committee found, the structure of sport is a crowded one, having developed over the last century and relying now, for the most part, on long-held traditions and customs.'

Reliance was also placed heavily on public as well as private funds in the manner experienced by the Arts. Before 1971, as the CCPR Memorandum to the House of Commons Committee explained (page 34, Question 1)

'the majority of public funds allocated for sports purposes were dispersed by the Department of Education and Science, largely through the CCPR.'

Its continued funding is sustained by the 1972 Heads of Agreement, alongside sponsorship and subscription sources from its constituent governing body members, approximately 300. The Heads of Agreement were negotiated at arm's length at the time of the 1972 reorganisation of the CCPR and have been the subject of almost continuous contention since then.

The Government's Response also welcomed the House of Commons Committee's endorsement

> 'of DOE funding for sport, of the role of the Sports Council and of the division of responsibilities between the Government and its sponsored body.'

ie the Sport's Council. The extent of that funding can be seen in the contrasts between the time of the Royal Charter in 1971 and the date of that Government Response, in July 1986.

In 1971 the initial allocation of Government funds to the Sports Council was £3m. By 1985 it had grown to £30m. Underpinning it at that date in 1985 was a sponsorship source attributed to well over £100m a year. Furthermore, during early 1986 the campaign by Birmingham City Council for the 1992 Olympic Games was underwritten by a Government guarantee for any financial shortfall and in due course the bid by Manchester received comparable support. This publicly funded intervention was separate and apart from a continuing complaint of payment of corporation tax and VAT by non-profit-making organisations such as the British Olympic Association. Only pressure from the Central Council of Physical Recreation and a Kent County Playing Fields senior member who had been associated with the European Commission, Ernest Virgo, and advice from Andrew Park QC, resulted in exposing HM Customs and Excise breaches of EC Directives leading to the Treasury's intention ultimately to exempt from VAT certain non-profit-making organisations and local authorities concerned with sport and physical recreation (see also Chapter 14, 'No fine on fun').

The emergence of central government in sporting recreation fields reached its climax with prime ministerial, Home Office and judicial intervention in 1985 after the football crowd tragedies of that year. In 1976, the emerging professional and differing bodies of Recreation Management resulted in a Department of the Environment Committee which took eight years to gestate all relevant facts. The Department published its Final Report in early 1984. A few months earlier in 1983, a discussion paper on behalf of all government agencies concerned with sporting recreation and leisure activities under the title of the Chairman's Policy Group published its *Leisure Policy for the Future*, under the chairmanship of the Sports Council's Chairman, Mr Dick Jeeps CBE.

Each of these publicly funded publications purported to identify the areas of government involvement with leisure services. The corroborative evidence which identifies the complexity of government involved is graphically illustrated in Appendix 7. During the early 1990s a new Government department with the title of Department of National Heritage was created after the General Election of 1992. Within the period of hardly more than two years which have passed before the date of publication of this edition no less than seven different Government Ministers have been allocated the portfolio for the Minister with Responsibility for Sport. Furthermore, as Appendix 7 demonstrates, even within the heterogeneous conglomerate of the Department of National Heritage, the Sport and Recreation Division is merely part of an Arts, National Lottery and Sport Group, alongside fifteen other Government Departments concerned with Sport.

Against this background it can be seen how sport and recreation and leisure have travelled in space and substance since the Minister for Science and Education in 1962, Viscount Hailsham, thought 'that recreation generally presented a complex of problems out of which government was not wholly free to opt'. The range of that complexity will emerge from the pages which follow, both in the private and public sector in addition to what must have become apparent on even a superficial reading of the text so far.

The Chapter 5, 'Public protection', demonstrates the urgency with which Parliament has reacted in 1985 and 1986 and the later 1980s and early 1990s to the consequences of successive parliamentary failures since 1924 to activate methods for crowd safety, apart from the relatively ineffectual interludes with the then Green Guide of 1973 and the halfhearted Safety of Sports Grounds Act 1975. By limiting its implementation to First and Second Division Football League grounds and national stadiums, it demonstrated a total unawareness of and disregard for the system of promotion and relegation that has operated throughout the Football League since the Second Division was added in 1890 to the First Division created in 1888.

The promotion of Bradford City in May 1985 from the Third Division to the Second Division meant that forty-eight hours after its disastrous fire, its ground would have come under starter's orders for the safety provisions of the 1975 enactment. Knowledge of fluctuating sporting fortunes commonly known to the general public for promotion and relegation issues may possibly have escaped the attention of Whitehall and Westminster. The legislation, however, was Home Office responsibility. The Minister with responsibility for Sport had no concern constitutionally or legislatively with its innovation or implementation. If the 1975 Act had provided for *all* Football League Clubs to be designated and licensed, the Bradford

City tragedy might have been more likely to be avoided (ie subject to correct procedures being followed), and a more heightened awareness of safety requirements might have prevented the Hillsborough disaster of 1989 or mitigated the quantity of fatalities and injuries.

Thus, thirty years after Lord Hailsham conceived the idea of a 'focal point under a Minister, for a coherent body of doctrine, perhaps even a philosophy of government encouragement,' the question must now be asked: 'Is a further leap forward now required by the mere pressure of events?' It must be asked, whatever may be the personal thoughts of the mandarins at Whitehall and Westminster who would never know the difference between a Gentleman and Player or distinguish a Corinthian from a Harlequin, or comprehend how sport has progressed within the changing perspective of the last three decades.

The manner in which the constitutional role and status of the erroneously named Sports Minister has fluctuated since it was created is seen from the list and departmental duties of the incumbents, to date, below.

Indeed, no greater indictment of the current chaos which pervades Whitehall and Westminster's lack of a comprehensive and intelligent approach to sport and recreation has appeared than the facts known throughout the sporting world which surfaced for the enlightenment of the general public in the report prepared under section 6 of the National Audit Act 1983 for presentation to the House of Commons in accordance with section 9, and dated 23 December 1993 (although not published until 14 January 1994: HMSO 131), from the Comptroller and Auditor General, Sir John Bourn, while these pages were in their last stage of preparation.

The report, entitled *The Sports Council: Initiatives to improve Financial Management and Control and Value for Money*, states in paragraph 1.7, under the heading 'Restructuring of the Sports Council',

'In November 1991 the Government issued a document, Sport and Active Recreation, which set out their policies and priorities for sport. These included the restructuring of the Council into a Sports Council for England and a United Kingdom Sports Commission. During the course of the National Audit Office's examination the Government announced that it no longer intended to proceed with the planned restructuring. Instead, fresh arrangements were to be considered to ensure a United Kingdom dimension for sport. Following on from this, the activities and general structure of the Council will also be reviewed.'

Seven months later on 8 July 1994 the Under-Secretary of State for the Department of National Heritage, Iain Sproat MP, announced the establishment in the next financial year of a new United Kingdom

Sports Council, separate from the Sports Councils for Scotland, Wales and Northern Ireland. The detailed mechanism will be unveiled after publication of these pages but whatever develops must be questioned in the light of the number of *seven* Government Ministers holding the portfolio of the Minister with the responsibility for Sport between 1992 and 1994, and also of the valuable cameo and insight into the dead hand of Government inaction which comes from one of the most unlikely of true sporting sources. Jemina Parry-Jones is a director of the National Birds of Prey Centre in Newent, Gloucestershire, and the daughter of Philip Glasier, one of the best-known falconers and author of a recognised classic in its field, *Falconry and Hawking*. Jemina Parry-Jones' own *Falconry: Care, Captive Breeding and Conservation* (1981) explains in relation to DoE inspections under the Wildlife and Countryside Act 1981, at page 179,

> 'Sadly the government system for running the Civil Service in general is now very outdated. It seems that as soon as someone in any governmental department gets to know and understand the system they promptly get moved to a different job and department [NB see list of junior Ministers, below]. Any business that was run in this way would be bankrupt very quickly. But this is the way the system works at the moment and so it has to be accepted.'

If Lord Hailsham's conception had existed in responsible form and structure from the time of the 1924 Wembley Stadium Committee Report's recommendation for a stadium licensing system and fire precautions, would 33 spectators have died at Bolton in 1946, 66 at Ibrox in 1971, 59 at Bradford and one schoolboy at Birmingham in 1985, and 95 at Hillsborough, Sheffield in 1989, apart from the thousands of others injured and bereaved during the same period? Parliamentarians and their acolytes who savour the flavour of hospitality tents and boxes at sporting events may ponder the question and answer during their next refreshment interval. Alternatively they may care to wait until they have read Chapter 5, 'Public protection'.

COMPLETE LIST OF MINISTERS WITH
RESPONSIBILITY FOR SPORT TO DATE

(as at 31 July 1994)

Minister	Period	Constitutional status
Rt Hon Viscount Hailsham	1962–1964	Minister with special responsibility for sport (1959–64; Minister for Science and Technology)
Rt Hon Lord Howell MP	1964–1969	Joint parliamentary under-secretary of State, Dept of Education and Science (with responsibility for sport)
	1969–1970	Minister of State, Ministry of Housing and Local Govt (with responsibility for sport)
Sir Eldon Griffiths MP	1970–1974	Parliamentary under-secretary of State, DoE Minister for Sport
Rt Hon Lord Howell of Aston Manor	1974–1979	Minister of State, DoE (responsibility for environment, water resources and sport)
Sir Hector Monro AE, JP, DL, MP	1979–1981	Parliamentary under-secretary of State, DoE (with special responsibility for sport)
Sir Neil MacFarlane MP	1981–1985	Parliamentary under-secretary of State, DoE (with special responsibility for sport for children's play, 1983–1985)
Richard Tracey JP, MP	1985–1987	Parliamentary under-secretary of State, DoE (with special responsibility for sport)
Hon Colin Moynihan MP	1987–1990	Parliamentary under-secretary, DoE (with qualified responsibility for sport)
Sir David Trippier RD, JP, MP	1987–1989	Parliamentary under-secretary, DoE (for Inner Cities and Urban Development with urban development grant-aid responsibility for sport)
Robert Atkins MP	1990–1992	Parliamentary under-secretary of State
Rt Hon David Mellor QC, MP	1992–1993	⎫ Secretary of State for National Heritage with responsibility inter alia for sport
Peter Brooke MP	1993–1994	⎬
Rt Hon Stephen Dorrell MP	1994–	⎭
Robert Key MP	1992–1993	⎫ Parliamentary under-secretary DNH
Ian Sproate MP	1993–	⎬
Viscount Astor	1994–	

Chapter 3

Under starter's orders

INTRODUCTION

The great Grand National Steeplechase starting tape fiasco in 1993 and the England versus Pakistan Lord's Test Match alleged tampered cricket ball imbroglio of 1992 illuminate the starting point for understanding how such complex subjects as Sport and the Law merge with and interact upon each other. Independently each occasion with its international repercussions created a potential minefield for legal issues. The Grand National for negligence and/or breach of contract for any financial damage suffered from the loss of an indefinable period of preparation and training to attain peak level fitness for horse and rider on the great day; the Lord's Test Match ball accusations for defamation proceedings in London's High Court and revelations of alleged cheating by unfair and illegal ball-tampering, during the libel action *Nawaz v Lamb* ((1993) Times, 16–19 November).

The two disciplines of Sport and the Law demand different levels of understanding by lawyer and layman alike, and they differ in proportion to the different levels of involvement required by each of them. Therefore this chapter serves as an overview for all those who may not comprehend how the law intertwines with sport. It gives a bird's eye view of the subject as a whole and introduces the non-legal reader to some of the many overlapping issues as examples of what is often not recognised as a labyrinthine network of interlocking elements.

In sport, players are expected to know and play according to the Laws, penalties and sanctions for their enforcement of each game within which their performances occur. All participants, from coaches and trainers to doctors and physiotherapists within and without a commercially orientated competitive climate, are progressively required to recognise the demands of drug control and testing, together with the regulatory limitations upon personal medication. Administrators need to know the different legal categories applicable to their particular spheres of action. Secretaries should possess an awareness of the whole spectrum affecting their duties with the necessity to seek specialist advice whether exemplified by a simple sponsorship or insurance contract or a planning application, to name but a few; treasurers should have at least some basic familiarity with taxation and VAT and easy accessibility to specialist accountancy services relating to particular requirements. Finally, all lawyers concerned with legal practice in this minefield area, solicitors, counsel and judges, should also be expected to have an understanding of the available substantive law, evidence and procedure applicable to the appropriate circumstances in issue in addition to the sporting subtleties and techniques, such as expert evidence relating to a particular situation. Profound experiences and precedent prove that this ideal is not always achieved, as these pages illustrate.

Transcending all such self-evident categories is the often overlooked or forgotten reality that the overwhelming majority of public and private domestic and international sporting controlling and governing bodies are part-time operators, some with a love for sport itself, others on an ego trip for self-aggrandisement, separate and apart from a full-time secretariat. Thus the Jockey Club and Aintree Racecourse authorities had ignored earlier warnings about the inherent defects in a flag-waving hand-start elastic tape control for initiating effectively the world's oldest and most celebrated steeplechase before a global television audience at a time when Wimbledon's All England Lawn Tennis and Croquet Club had progressed to electronic line outs and the electronic eye had arrived to assist the cricket adjudication by a third umpire. Correspondingly, the suspect tampered Test Match cricket ball remained under lock and key at Lord's cricket ground without any attempt by the International Cricket Conference to allay the apprehensions in the public mind about the extent or prevalence of the practice in issue.

At Law, the procedural precedent blockage from a ten year-old Court of Appeal decision in *Law v National Greyhound Racing Club Ltd* [1983] 3 All ER 300 unseated the attempt by the Aga Khan's legal advisers to challenge by the inapplicable judicial review route, instead of by breach of contract, the Jockey Club's disqualification on a disputed drug testing process of his filly Alysa's 1989 Epsom Oaks triumph, as explained in more detail in the pages of the Introduction and in the Judicial Review Appendix 9. Correspondingly the Football Association's Chief Executive was allowed unchallenged to give arguably inadmissible and rebuttable evidence on the basis of his lack of expert knowledge of the technical issues relating to coaching and refereeing expertise involved in a criminal prosecution for grievous bodily harm, allegedly caused by an acquitted professional footballer against another in a criminal trial at Salisbury Crown Court, as criticised by the author in various* legal sources† before the Introduction in this text (*R v Blissett* (1992); Times, 5 December).

* *New Law Journal* 15 January 1993; *Solicitor's Journal* 2 July 1993.
† *Legal Executive* July 1993; *All England Law Reports Annual Review 1992* (published 1993).

Each of these examples illustrates the wisdom words of one of Britain's most revered jurists, F W Maitland, when he began his celebrated Lectures under the head of Dissertations:

'Let us remember one of Maine's most striking phrases: 'So great is the ascendancy of the Law of Actions in the infancy of Courts of Justice, that substantive law has at first the look of being gradually secreted in the intersteces of procedure'.'

The constructive analysis of the Judicial Review procedural machinery in Appendix 9 by Catherine Bond demonstrates how this operates. Anyone wishing to explore 'substantive law' in greater detail than the limitations of space which these pages permits, for which a level of awareness alone has been attempted here, should refer to the 52 volumes of *Halsbury's Laws of England*. Each one contains material applicable to Sport and the Law.

Concurrently with Maitland's quotation from Maine is the equally applicable aphorism already cited in the Introduction here above from Scotland's most celebrated legal chronicler and renowned historical novelist who was also a Writer to the Signet, Sir Walter Scott. He created for one his best known characters Counsellor Playdell in Guy Mannering the oft-recalled words:

'A lawyer without history or literature is a mechanic, a mere working mason; if he possesses some knowledge of these, he may venture to call himself an architect.'

2 HISTORICAL BACKGROUND

Against that background the manner in which Sport and the Law combine today is the result of the off-field story of post-Second World War public and professional British sport. One of persistent and sustained erosion of feudal controls by sporting governing bodies over their members evidenced by the table set out at the end of Chapter 11 at pages 308–309. Indeed, when Parker LJ confirmed the plaintiff tennis player Ian Currie's right to pursue his appeal against Essex County Lawn Tennis Association, he explained, 'This is a developing area of the law' (*Currie v Barton and Rippon* (1987) Times, 29 July, p 42).

That erosion of feudalism for public and professional sport was spearheaded initially after the Second World War by James Guthrie's politico-legal campaign to emancipate professional footballers from their roles as the 'last bonded men in Britain', and later by Florence Nagle's successful challenge in the courts to the Jockey Club's refusal to grant racehorse trainers' licences to women in their own names.

Their ultimate triumphs created a better balance between the governance of public and professional British participants by their administrative controllers and their comparable social position in the world outside, beyond committee rooms and council chambers, as we shall see in Chapter 6, 'Participation problems'. If the imagination, resourcefulness and will demonstrated by pioneers such as Guthrie and Nagle had been used more frequently to challenge 'decisions by the regulating bodies' (a judicially critical phase) before and after the Second World War, British sport's general development after it would not have been retarded in the manner exposed by comparisons in the international scene, especially in the high profile and publicised areas evidenced by cricket, rugby, soccer and lawn tennis.

Indeed, as we shall see in Chapter 4, 'Parent, school and club partners', parents and other guardians of children, sporting and physical education interests can rely upon Parliamentary and charity law, as a last resort, to challenge the decisions of local authorities, school governors and teaching staff if appropriate circumstances permit. In this way they can overturn obstructive and socially divisive decisions by sources which dispute the traditional existence of competitive games and playing fields to accommodate them. If the correct law is invoked to protect sport and its wider realm of physical education at this level then British sporting talent domestically and internationally will be in a position for the first time to realise its full potential, at present denied through a mixture of parental or general unawareness and obstructive attitudes alien to the nation's true sporting spirit and heritage.

For just as medicine demands doctors trained and experienced in their own disciplines for patients to be treated skilfully when they need and seek advice, so, too, does sport need the law to fill the gaps which sport itself cannot reach. Furthermore, sport needs an awareness in all cases to recognise when such a need arises, both at Parliamentary and litigation levels.

Judicial decisions have demonstrated an unawareness among lawyers and people in sport of the extent to which the law can help sport to benefit itself and the community it serves. In the years which have witnessed sport's explosion at the public level since the Second World War, planning and property, personal injuries, professional players' benefits and testimonials, charities, contracts, crimes, torts and tribunals have all illuminated this position through diverse and debatable judicial verdicts. Each of these conventional legal topics can create its own jurisprudential problems for practitioners without bedevilment by the imp which lurks within so many sporting contests out of court to create for litigation lawyers what is so well known as 'the glorious uncertainty of the game'. When this spills over into the legal arena, the consequences can be expensive and far-reaching not only for individuals and sporting organisations, but for society in general.

Examples will leap out from every chapter which follows. The extent to which they have accumulated during the last thirty or so years suggests that while tradition has preserved the conventional custom that sport is a relaxation and recreation from more pressing and heavily committed affairs of the day, it has often ignored or been totally unaware of the gravity of the burdens which have developed progressively while sport is obliged to fit into a general legal framework.

Within the last twenty-five years the most popular of sporting activities in the United Kingdom have publicly or within the professional knowledge of the legal profession manifested the need to resolve differences of opinion among sporting administrators and their advisers and lawyers to a degree which demonstrates the need for that clear-cut awareness and understanding of the available substantive law, evidence and procedure applicable to the appropriate circumstances in issue.

Horseracing (twice), cricket (twice), rugby (thrice) and soccer (eight times), prove this pattern of unawareness, since 1962, summarised in tabulated form set out at the end of Chapter 11, pages 308–309. It explains within the standard or level of burden of proof required for criminal trials, to a degree of satisfaction so that the reader can be sure, or sure beyond reasonable doubt, how the needs of society in the amoral climate of the last two decades of the twentieth century demand sport and the law, and the law and sport, to co-operate more effectively and efficiently than might be indicated by errors from the past that occurred through lack of care, thought and understanding.

Lord Denning flashed an oblique light on a generally unidentified problem area in the more recent of the two leading cricket-ball-out-of-the-ground cases from Linz in County Durham (*Miller v Jackson* [1977] 1 QB 966); (the Cheetham Cricket Club ground at Manchester providing the other sixteen years earlier (*Bolton v Stone* [1951] AC 850)). The ultimate decision considered in detail in Chapter 5, 'Public protection' (infra at pages 117–122), was not relied upon in a later Court of Appeal verdict relating to noise nuisance from water-ski activities (*Kennaway v Thompson* [1980] 3 All ER 329). For present purposes, however, Lord Denning illuminated the existing lacunae in many minds and experiences more subtly than the clear-cut examples which follow here with an expression of surprise that opposition had not existed to a planning application (the arm of law which was flexed to block the asset stripping attempt on Fulham Football Club's Craven Cottage ground development scheme for residential accommodation in early 1987). For ease of reading in an ascending order of legal and sporting complexities they will be illustrated in the following sequence. These examples are wide-ranging and apparently unconnected. The thread that runs though them is the subject of Sport and Law.

(1) planning and property (Lord Denning's citation);

(2) amateur rugby regulations (Court of Appeal);

(3) crime (Newport Crown Court);

(4) contract (High Court);

(5) benefits (House of Lords);

(6) charities and rating (House of Lords);

(7) race relations and politics (House of Lords);

(8) tribunals (High Court);

(9) personal injuries (Court of Appeal)

(10) evidence (Court of Appeal);

(11) facts (Committee on Legal Education, House of Lords);

(12) Parliament

Furthermore, as will be seen, in three instances (ie professional footballers' contracts, professional footballers' benefits, and charitable educational sporting trusts) the development of sport in general was retarded for respectively fifty, thirty and forty years because of inadequate and ill-considered applications or non-applications of the law to sport to an extent which would have changed the face and fate of British sport today if it had been properly served, as it clearly was not, by its administrators or by the advice they received; and in each of the above categories differences of judicial impressions required variations of earlier judgments by appellate courts.

1 Planning and property

Miller v Jackson (supra) was a householder's civil claim against an adjoining local cricket club that cricket balls hit out of the ground created a physical and legal nuisance. A local High Court judge on circuit in his authorised discretion granted an injunction. The Court of Appeal discharged it and approved in substitution an agreed amount of £400 damages for nuisance. The reasoning and also the result were not followed three years later by another Court of Appeal in a water-ski noise-nuisance case (*Kennaway v Thompson*, supra and infra, and in Chapter 5, 'Public protection', at p 122). On that later occasion a £15,000 damages awarded by the circuit High Court judge was replaced by an injunction in qualified terms.

The significant subtlety commented upon by Lord Denning ([1977] 1 QB 966 at p 976) and referred to in a discerning note in the Modern Law Review, (Vol 41 1978 at pp 334–337) was,

> 'I must say that I am surprised that the developers of the housing estate [ie adjoining the ground] were allowed to build the houses so close to the cricket ground. No doubt they wanted to make the most of their site and put up as many houses as they could for their own profit. The planning authorities ought not to have allowed it.
>
> The houses ought to have been so sited as not to interfere with the cricket. But the houses have been built and we have to reckon with the consequences.'

Lord Denning's stricture pre-supposed that an objection was made by the cricket club to the appropriate planning authority on behalf of the estate developers. The absence of any evidence during any of the judgements in the Court of Appeal or at first instance that such an objection had been lodged, or that any appeal had been made to the Minister under the provisions of the existing Town and Country Planning legislation, justifies the inference that no effective attempt was ever made to protect the club's position in the manner manifested by Lord Denning's surprise. The outcome of any such contemplated objection can never be guaranteed. On appropriate evidence and the burden of proof in civil cases (ie the balance of probabilities as distinct from the higher criminal burden of proof (supra)), it is at least arguable that Lord Denning's practical approach to the club's problem if operated at the correct time could have had at least modified or qualified, if not completely altered, the ultimate results, ie siting or with physical safeguards from protective netting to avoid the nuisance. Slough County Court during 1994 witnessed a comparable circumstance when His Honour Judge Nigel Hague QC refused an injunction to restrain cricket balls hitting an adjoining property (*Lacey v Parker and Boyle* (for Jordans CC) (1994) 144 New Law Journal 785 10 June).

2 Amateur rugby regulations

More clear-cut and easily explicable than the contingencies of planning law objections are two relatively recent examples from the less simple form of football based on the Rules associated with Rugby School and the amateur game to which it gave its name as distinct from the professional Rugby League version from which the amateur Union administration is expressly dissociated. One concerned a

Court of Appeal's decision that a High Court judge had not directed a jury with sufficient clarity in a civil libel action upon the correct interpretation of the Regulations relating to amateur status of the International Rugby Football Board, of which the Welsh Rugby Football Union was a constituent member. The other concerned a debatable and disputable direction by a Welsh Crown Court judge to a jury in the first-ever criminal trial for assault on a rugby field which resulted in a conviction.

During 1979 and by a libel action tried in 1982 the famous Welsh rugby union footballer, Dr J P R Williams (now Mr J P R Williams FRCS) complained that he and his amateur status had been defamed by two articles written in the *Daily Telegraph* by its then rugby football correspondent, John Reason. At a four-day trial the jury found unanimously that the plaintiff had been libelled and Russell J gave judgment for £20,000 in respect of two separate alleged libels, £12,000 for one and £8,000 for the other. In the Court of Appeal an application by the defendants for leave to adduce fresh evidence which had not been called during the trial was dismissed. It did accede, however, to an alternative submission and ordered a re-trial on a separate and exclusively legal ground involving the game's administrative laws. For present purposes it suffices to explain that the regulations within the amateur rugby union game, both internationally and domestically, are complex. For the purpose of deciding whether or not to order a re-trial once the issue of fresh evidence had been dismissed, the leading judgment of the Court of Appeal of Stephenson LJ explained in three separate ways how reluctantly it was obliged to direct the trial to take place all over again in the spirit that Lord Atkin once said (in *Res Behari Lal v The King Emperor* (1933) 50 TLR at p 2) in a Privy Council appeal from the Commonwealth: 'Finality is a good thing, but justice is better' (*Williams v Reason and Daily Telegraph* [1988] 1 All ER 262).

When introducing the issue of the basis for ordering a retrial in the earlier part of his judgment, Stephenson LJ explained (at p 264)

'The only grounds of appeal are that the judge misdirected the jury as to the true interpretation of the relevant regulation, or that, if he did not, he failed to put to the jury adequately the defendant's defence that the plaintiff was nevertheless in breach of the regulation.'

He continued (at p 271) that the judge left

'to the jury both the interpretation of the [International Rugby Football Board] regulations (which he should not have done) and the decision of what evidence to believe and what inferences to draw from the oral and documentary evidence. But I have come to the reluctant conclusion with great regret that the trial went wrong, so seriously wrong as to require a new trial before another judge and jury, as I have already indicated.'

Finally, after explaining, also at p 271, that

'The first issue in the case, the construction of the board's rules and regulations, was indisputably a matter for the judge. The law is stated as follows in 12 Halsbury's Laws (4th edn), para 1461 ...'

Stephenson L J concluded with two separate passages at p 24, thus:

'[The judge] should have decided it conclusively. As it was, he left it to the jury to decide' (letter A).
... The judge himself should have insisted on determining the true meaning of the regulation himself. As he did not, this court has to consider and decide its true meaning. If the meaning which he invited the jury to give was wrong, we have no choice but to allow the appeal and order a new trial subject to O.
59 rll (2) [of the Rules of the Supreme Court]'

All three judges, Stephenson, O'Connor and Purchas L J, agreed that the trial went wrong when the judge failed to address the jury about the appropriate regulations.

For reasons of expenditure no retrial was heard. On that point the real issue of defamation and the plaintiff's amateur status was never decided. It also illuminated the prohibitive cost of litigation and consequences of judicial error. Legal aid has never existed for defamation; and the range of public funding at all levels will dominate public debates for a long time after these pages appear. Legal aid is available however for malicious falsehood in which different levels of proof from defamation are required.

3 Crime

Before *Williams v Reason and The Daily Telegraph Ltd*, an earlier illustration of judicial error connected with Welsh rugby emerged during the first ever prosecution for a criminal assault on a rugby field, during 1977. The principles upon which an offence of that kind could be proved had existed for nearly a century and are dealt with more particularly in detail in Chapter 6, 'Participation problems' (and see particularly *R v Bradshaw* (1978) 14 Cox; *R v Moore* (1898) 14 TLR 229 and re-affirmed more recently in *R v Venna* [1975] 3 All ER 788). Here it suffices to explain that deliberate and/or reckless tackling causing injury and particularly in breach of playing laws of any game prima facie creates an offence, both civil and criminal.

In *R v Billinghurst* ([1977] Crim LR 553), the defendant had been charged in the Newport, South Wales, Crown Court with inflicting grievous bodily harm upon an opponent during the course of a game. Serious injury was caused, and, as the trial judge said in summing-up to the jury,

> 'There is no dispute, on the evidence of the defendant himself, that that was not done in the course of playing the game at all. That is to say, not when struggling to get the ball, or to prevent [the victim] getting the ball, or anything of that kind.' (unreported transcript: p 3B)

In due course the jury convicted. Because the trial was the first of its kind in the United Kingdom, the judge understandably imposed a nine month sentence of imprisonment, suspended for two years, with an indication that 'Maybe the Criminal Injuries Compensation Board would be involved' (p 8F).

Equally understandable but technically wrong, however, because of the novelty at that time in 1977 of prosecuting for such an offence, is the commencement of that section of the summing-up when the judge left for consideration of the jury

> 'where the line has to be drawn between that to which a person taking part in a rugby game is to be deemed to be consenting, and that to which he is not deemed to consent.'

In other words, taking into account what was an admitted assault, in an off-the-ball-incident with serious injuries, was it something to which the victim consented? The jury in its Welsh wisdom rejected this divergence from the correct legal concept.

The summing up was technically wrong because it conflicted with the laws of playing rugby football, which do not condone deliberate foul play. Indeed, the Law Commission Consultation Paper, 'No Consent and Offences Against the Person' specifically refers in footnote 134 to paragraph 11 inter alia

> 'Law 26(3) of the Laws of the Game of Rugby Football 1993/94 [which] forbids a wide range of dangerous play, including by sub-laws (3)(b)–(c), wilful hacking, kicking and tripping, and early, late or dangerous tackling.'

Furthermore, the summing up was also technically wrong in its conflict with the criminal law of the land. As the Court of Appeal explained in *R v Donovan* ([1934] 2 KB 498 at 507),

> 'If an act is unlawful in the sense of being in itself a criminal act, it is plain that it cannot be rendered lawful because the person to whose detriment it is done consents to it. No person can license another to commit crime.'

(See also generally *A-G's Reference (No 6 of 1980)* [1981] QB 715 and *R v Brown* [1993] 2 WLR 556.) If the error was understandable in 1977 because of the novelty at that time of such a prosecution, no similar mitigation exists in 1994. *Volenti non fit injuria* is one of the few well-known legacies of legal Latin jargon understood beyond the boundaries of the law courts and offices. It has no place in deliberate and/or reckless breaches of playing laws of any game, just as it has no place in the criminal law of the United Kingdom as cited above. This fact appeared to be more immediately recognisable in late 1993 by the England rugby captain, than by the visiting New Zealand All Black-tourists whom he condemned as 'mostly a dirty side'.

4 Contract

The simpler form of football, soccer, created its own complexities of an 'own goal' nature when the professional players combined to tackle employment restrictions before the First World War. Harry Kingaby was the player nominated to challenge the contractual nexus between himself and Aston Villa, his employer club. This existed within a cartel-monopolistic system controlled by the confederation of employer clubs within the Football League competition and the overriding governing control of the Football Association which administered amateur as well as professional clubs and competitions. Aston Villa placed a transfer fee upon his services for his release to any other club, which prevented the free movement he desired.

As already explained at page 10 above in Chapter 1, 'Genesis', the trial judge, Mr Justice A T Lawrence non-suited the plaintiff and withdrew the case from the jury. He ruled there was no cause of action and confirmed the transfer fee to be permissible under the terms of contract of employment (*Kingaby v Aston Villa* (1913) Times 28 March).

So far as the two authorities, the Football League and the Football Association, were concerned, their restrictive employment system was apparently and complacently vindicated (see *The Story of the Football League* (1938) and *The History of the Football Association* (1953)). Dissatisfaction in society generally after the Second World War disturbed the pattern of conventional acceptability among all sections of the community and within the game. Under the aggressive chairmanship of James Guthrie, who had captained the last pre-war FA Cup winning team, Portsmouth in 1939, the Players Union (formally the Association Footballers' and Trainers' Union) encouraged the restraint of trade issue in a county court claim at Aldershot. One of their players who had played in the 1953 FA Cup Final for Bolton Wanderers against Blackpool and Stanley Matthews, desired a transfer. Aldershot imposed a requisite fee, and claimed possession of his club house. The defence challenged the possession claim to be vitiated by a tainted and unenforceable contract of employment in restraint of trade. It failed, but the judgment of Judge Percy Rawlins in granting a deferred possession order delayed for five months said:

> 'It may very well be, although I am not going to decide it, that as the defendant alleges, the rules of the Football Association place an intolerable burden upon some professional footballers.' *Aldershot Football Club v Banks (Aldershot News, 4 November 1955)*

Consideration was given to pursuing an appeal. Within a month, before a decision was concluded, the defendant had achieved his free transfer. The local chronicle commented:

> 'Until the whole complicated, outdated transfer system is overhauled, the Banks case will never be really closed.' (*Aldershot News*, 25 November 1955)

Eight years later, it came nearer to closure with the well-publicised judgment of Wilberforce J in *Eastham v Newcastle United FC and The Football Association, The Football League and certain footballing personalities* ([1963] 3 All ER 139). The restraint of trade defence which had been abortively raised legally but with realistic results in the Aldershot County Court, and ignored before the First World War in *Kingaby's case*, was itself now vindicated.

Three years later it was extended to a more general right to work when Florence Nagle was permitted by the Court of Appeal to pursue her claim against the Jockey Club for authority to obtain a trainer's licence in her own name, in lieu of her head lad (*Nagle v Fielden* [1966] 1 All ER 689). By the time, therefore, in 1977, when Mr Kerry Packer arrived on the professional cricket stage, the law had moved a long way forwards in sporting industrial relations from the unsatisfactory state in which it had been allowed to remain unchallenged between 1912 and 1955. When England's cricketing establishment decided in 1977 to interfere with existing contractual relationships and impose positive restraints affecting the Packer 'rebels' there were many who recognized the twin torts of inducting breach of contract and restraint of trade which appeared inevitable for the five hour judgment of Slade J after 31 days of witness and advocacy submissions. The £250,000 bill of costs in many cricketing lawyers' eyes was avoidable with foresight at the time of legal conflict and not with the hindsight of wisdom after an event (see *Greig v Insole*).

An inevitable thought must cross many minds if the action by Harry Kingaby in 1912 for varied permutations which missed the open goal of restraint of trade is looked at in the light of the inexorable and inevitable consequences of the claims by *Banks* (1955), *Eastham* (1963), *Nagle* (1966), *Greig* (1978): how would modern British sport have developed in the intervening crucial formative years if the present established rights of contractual freedom had been established when the opportunity in 1912 was seen, and missed, by mis-reading the legal small print among the existing cases in the Golden Age of playing sport, but not advising upon it, before 1914?

The answer may be impossible to consider; but a similar question arises from two further examples of another missed open goal for football and a hit wicket for cricket at respectively the players' benefit and sporting educational charity levels. Both are affected by rulings from the highest judicial tribunal in the House of Lords; *Seymour v Reed* (infra) benefits, *IRC v McMullen* (infra) charities. Professional football players' benefits contain a story of either unawareness or apathy for over thirty years from 1927 until 1959. Sporting education charities contain a story of another lost opportunity on the road to the Chancery Division of the High Court of Justice in London from the Sussex County Cricket Club's historic headquarters at Hove.

5 Benefits

One of cricket's happiest journeys in the law courts, although not without a struggle of Test Match proportions, was its ultimate achievement of tax-free benefits for professional cricketers; with a corresponding saga of more than thirty lost and wasted years while professional footballers sought an equality which eluded them through an apparent unawareness of their potential opportunities during the intervening years. The simple and clear-cut background legal story with a slightly more complex history is illustrated by the more recent and topical decision in London's High Court when Brightman J began his judgment in *Moore v Griffiths* ([1978] 3 All ER 399 at 403)

'In 1966 England won the association football World Cup for the first but not, one hopes, last time.'

The successful appeal by Bobby Moore, from the General Income Tax Commissioners, concerned a one-off payment by the Football Association to England's captain and his 21 playing colleagues for that triumph. It filled a legal gap which should have been plugged over forty years earlier if those who had been involved with professional footballers' affairs before and during the Second World War had understood properly the true legal nature of their own financial employment conditions by comparison with those which were known for professional cricketers.

Bobby Moore's bonus of £1,000 together with similar sums to his fellow squad members was held by Brightman J to have

'had the quality of a testimonial or accolade rather than the quality of remuneration for services rendered' (at p 409: b–c).

That was how the House of Lords in 1927 regarded the payments to the Kent County Cricket Club's opening batsman, James Seymour, on the occasion of the benefit match granted to him by the club committee for the traditional Canterbury Cricket Match against Hampshire in 1920 (*Seymour v Reed* [1927] AC 554).

Likewise, the principle enunciated by Brightman J was how the Special Commissioners of Income Tax in 1959 viewed the payments made to the Peterborough United Football Club captain, Norman Rigby, in their decision (unreported excepted for the Peterborough *Citizen and Advertiser* 16 June 1959 and 24 July 1959). They discharged assessments made upon payments received by him and fellow Peterborough United players from two testimonial matches arranged during 1956 in circumstances directly analogous to those experienced by James Seymour at Canterbury in 1920. The time lapse of 32 years between *Seymour v Reed* and *Rigby v Inland Revenue Commissioners* is a classic example of the levels of unawareness.

In 1927, shortly after the House of Lords had overruled the Court of Appeal in *Seymour*'s case to restore the judgment of an experienced and respected revenue authority, the same judge, Rowlatt J, was required to adjudicate upon the testimonial benefits paid to an Everton footballer, George Harrison. Because the payments were built in to the player's contract of employment via the Football League Regulations, Rowlatt J was obliged to differentiate the situation from Seymour's Canterbury Cricket Week match.

'He has earned this just as much as he earned anything else in the service of the club' (*Davis v Harrison* (1927) 11 TC 707 at 723).

Fourteen years later during the Second World War in 1941 the same fate was felt by three other professional footballers, Billy Dale and Billy Corbett of Manchester City and Alf Feebury of Notts County, when they applied abortively on the same contractual basis before Lawrence J (later Lawrence LJ, the Presiding Judge at the Nuremberg War Trials) and then the first Lord Oaksey, (*Dale v Duff, Corbett v Duff, Feebury v Abbot* [1941] 1 KB 730, [1941] 1 All ER 312, 23 TC 763). There was no alternative but for the distinction between the contractual footballing element and the non contractual public subscription cricketing funding to be emphasised for the second time after the House of Lords judgment. Why nothing was ever done in the intervening years to attempt amendments to the Football League contractual regulations after the two abortive High Court attempts failed has never been explained.

As already explained above, after Peterborough United were elected to the Football League in 1960 the Football League regulations were amended to delete the contractual element in the professional footballers' benefits to equate them with the professional cricketers.

Cricket's own battle had lasted seven years while the Inland Revenue challenged the source of James Seymour's benefit funding from public and other donations. In due course it was invested by the beneficiary in the purchase of a farm.

The Revenue assessed it as income. The General Commissioners discharged the assessment; Rowlatt J upheld their discharge. His judgment was reversed by the Court of Appeal, who in due course were overruled by the House of Lords. The original contention and Commissioners' conclusion as a personal gift were thereby confirmed finally in the highest tribunal.

6 Charities and rates

Fifty odd years later in 1980 a parallel procedural pattern emerged. As already explained briefly in Chapter 1, 'Genesis', a later unanimous House of Lords verdict overruled a Court of Appeal majority, a High Court judgment, and restored another ruling by Commissioners; on this occasion the Charity Commissioners' approval of the FA Youth Trust Deed, notwithstanding Inland Revenue objections. For in 1972 the Charity Commissioners registered it. Walton J upheld a Revenue objection to its charitable status. A Court of Appeal majority confirmed the judgment but in due course they were all overruled by the House of Lords, to restore the original registration and the Commissioners' conclusion for charitable status (*IRC v McMullen* [1981] AC 1). Yet it is at least arguable that here is a further example of lost and wasted years in the development of British sport because of an unawareness and lack of understanding of the true manner in which the law and sport merge for the mutual advantage of each other. The factual foundation for this contention begins only six months after the House of Lords ruling in *Seymour v Reed* on 24 May 1927. For on 22 November 1927 a will made on that date by a testator in Hove, Sussex, gave a legacy value of £300

'To the Sussex County Cricket Club ... of Funding Loan in trust to pay the interest yearly to the Nursery Fund.'

Eighteen months later on 17 April and 15 May 1929 it was respectively argued and rejected as a charitable request (*Re Patten:*

Westminster Bank Limited v Carlyon [1929] 2 Ch 276). Yet only four years earlier on 25 February 1925, the same judge Romer J had upheld as validly charitable a £300 bequest to form the nucleus of a regimental fund for the regiment, the 6th Dragoon Guards (the Caribiniers), of that particular testator,

> 'for the promotion of sport (including in that term only shooting, fishing, cricket and polo).' (*Re Gray Todd v Taylor* [1925] Ch 362)

The story of how the Sussex County Cricket Club and its advisers took the wrong route in their legal submissions before Romer J in 1929, and thereby missed the chance to steer sporting educational charities into general judicial approval fifty odd years before the House of Lords gave their blessings in the FA Youth Trust case during 1980 [*McMullen v IRC* supra] begins with a claim from two outstanding sporting legal academicians, in 1969 that,

> 'The chart of decisions on sport is erratic'

ie concerning charities (*Hanbury's Modern Equity*, 9th Edition by R H Maudsley. Cf author's structure of chart in Appendix 11).

Professor Harold Hanbury was not only Oxford University's Vinerian Professor of Law among other academic honours. He was also Honorary Treasurer of the Oxford University Association Football Club for twenty-five years. Professor Ronald Maudsley was not only Professor of Law in London and American Universities. He had also been awarded Double Blues at Oxford for cricket and golf, and later shared the Warwickshire County Cricket Club captaincy with H E 'Tom' Dollery during Varsity vacations. They were therefore ideally equipped for their joint assessment.

It emerged from a sporting reading of the Parliamentary and judicial mixture which has shaped charity law in the United Kingdom to its present position in the late twentieth century. By 1929 a pattern had developed based upon the refinement given to charitable categories enacted in a Statute of Queen Elizabeth I, known generally as the Charitable Uses Act 1601, by a celebrated classification (per Lord Macnaghten: *IRC v Pemsel* [1891] AC 531) in 1891 which formulated four heads applicable today,

(1)   Relief of poverty

(2)   Advancement of education

(3)   Advancement of religion

(4)   General public good.

Four years later in 1895 a Court of Appeal upheld a judicial finding

that a mere prize for yacht-racing was not validly charitable
(although today a Royal Yachting Association Trust is registered
with the Charity Commissioners under the second head of education,
see *Re Nottage* [1895] Ch 649). The First World War witnessed a
landmark decision which the House of Lords in 1980 warmly welcomed in its FA Youth Trust decision. This was the decision of Eve J
that bequests for building a fives or squash courts and an annual
athletics sports prize for Aldenham School in Hertfordshire was
validly charitable. It was based on the *mens sana in corpore sano*
principle (*Re Mariette* [1915] 2 Ch 284, 288). Ten years later in 1925
Romer J applied it completely to the Carabiniers bequest saying,

> 'One might equally say that no person can be trained to be an efficient
> and useful soldier unless as much attention is given to the development
> of his body as to the development of his mind,'

and he followed it with a specific citation from Eve J, of the self-
evident advantages and benefits of physical education (*Re Gray*
supra, at p 368–369).

Another four years later in 1929 Romer J was primed for receiving
similar arguments on behalf of the Sussex County Cricket Club
Funding Loan bequest 'in trust to pay the interest yearly to the
Nursery Fund.' What happened? As the judgment records at 389,

> 'As regards the trust for the benefit of the Nursery Fund of the Sussex
> County Cricket Club it was argued that the trust is one for the "support-
> ation aid and help of young tradesmen, handicraftsmen and persons
> decayed" within the meaning of the statute of Elizabeth. In my opinion
> a professional cricketer is neither a tradesman, a handicraftsman nor a
> person decayed, and though undoubtedly, as a result of the adminis-
> tration of the fund, boys all of the working or lower middle classes and
> not well off financially may be embarked upon life as professional
> cricketers, it is, I think, reasonably clear that the object of the fund is the
> encouragement of the game of cricket and nothing else, and it has been
> held by authorities that are binding upon me that such a bequest is not
> charitable.'

Yet the evidence and legal precedents from different disciplines from
sporting or educational charities or trusts all pointed in the opposite
direction following the same judge's earlier finding for the Army. As
his judgment explained earlier at p 286, it appeared on the evidence
tendered before him that the Sussex County Cricket Club in the year
1908 established a special fund

> 'which has ever since been maintained by voluntary contributions and
> subscriptions for the purpose of teaching and coaching young cricketers
> in the game of cricket so as to enable them to earn their livelihood by
> becoming cricket professionals and of furthering the interest of cricket

as a national game, such fund being known as the Nursery Fund. All the
moneys received for the fund are spent in the payment of a professional
cricketer in teaching and coaching young cricketers in the game of
cricket and in paying the incidental travelling and other expenses incurred in connection with his employment. It is stated that during the
past seven years thirty-one boys or thereabouts mainly between the ages
of seventeen and twenty-one have by means of the said fund received
instruction in the said game, and that about twenty-one of these boys
are now being employed as professional cricketers by the Club or by
other clubs and schools in the county of Sussex and other parts of the
south of England, and Mr Godfree, who is a member of the Committee
of the Club, says that the parents of the boys so taught are, he believes,
all of the working or the lower middle classes and not well off
financially.'

The combined threads of teaching, coaching, ages of 17–21, schools,
and 'not well off financially' point inexorably and inevitably to the
established categories from 1891 of advancement of education and
relief of poverty. A legacy for 'poor men of the trade of a tinplate
worker' was held with 'no reasonable doubt [to be] a charitable
legacy' (*Re White's Trusts* [1886] 33 Ch D 449 at 454). In *Roberts v
Gray* ([1913] 1 KB 520), a contract claim concerning an apprenticed
billiards player, the Court of Appeal unanimously followed established authorities in the words of the then Master of Rolls, Cozens-
Hardy MR at p 525,

'education must not be taken in its narrow technical sense as merely
meaning education to enable a man by the work of his hand to hereafter
maintain himself as an artisan, but has a much wider meaning than that;
it applies to education and instruction in the social state in which the
infant [apprentice] is, and in which he may expect to find himself when
he become an adult.'

With these citations, the available evidence and Romer J's own
application of the Aldenham School judgment to the Army bequest
in 1925 it is difficult to see how he would have failed to have been
attracted by the argument that the apprenticed cricketers 'of the
working or the lower middle classes and not well off financially'
qualified for charitable status. The opportunity was lost and thus the
dice were loaded against the serious attempts during the later 1950s to
establish the joint Oxbridge FA *Amateur* Cup winning club Pegasus,
with its object of advancing the game at university level, within the
charitable educational setting after its Cup triumphs in 1951 and
1953.

The first Lord Oaksey in the City of Glasgow Police Athletic
Association judgments of the House of Lords stood apart from his
brother Law Lords with a strong dissenting judgment in 1953 when
they distinguished the subject-matter from the Army Officers bequest

upheld by Romer J in 1925 to reject its charitable status claim (*IRC v City of Glasgow Police Athletic Association* [1953] AC 380 at 397). A glimmer of light shone from the New South Wales, Australia, Equity Court in *Kearins v Kearins* (1957) when a bequest to Sydney University Rugby Football Club was upheld as charitable because of the Aldenham School judgment of Eve J; and in 1958 Parliament passed the Recreational Charities Act which widened the scope for social purposes as a charitable basis. No funds existed for Pegasus, a strictly amateur Oxbridge club, to fight a law-suit advised against the Inland Revenue during the late 1950s in the hope of preserving the profits from its two 100,000 Wembley Stadium crowd attendances and from the cup-ties leading up to them in 1951 and 1953. The author reiterated their claim two decades later when responding to a commission for Sir Denis Follows to contribute a section on *Football and the Law* in the newly conceived *FA Manual of Administration*. Written in 1971, edited by Sir Denis with his schoolmaster's pen, it appeared thus (at pp 154–155) in 1972;

'(viii) **Charities**
One form of registration which hitherto has not troubled the football world and the world of sport is with the Charity Commissioners. This arises from basically a long established approach by the courts that sport as such is not a valid charitable object allowing it to qualify for charitable status and thereby charitable relief from taxation. House of Lords judgments have contributed to this thinking but Parliament by the Recreational Charities Act of 1958 has given fresh impetus to those who thought that the law had gone too far away from what should be the right approach to a highly technical and complex subject. Certainly sport associated with education and service discipline has been granted charitable status and any Old Boys' Club or others associated with educational foundations could claim to qualify. At one time thoughts existed in this direction for Pegasus FC after its FA Amateur Cup Final triumphs in 1951 and 1953; but as time went by the team's raison d'être and playing strength dwindled and the interesting reasoning behind this never fructified. The benefit, of course, is the very real one of freedom from the burden of income tax and the encouragement of bequests, grants and donations for this purpose. Any secretary or official sufficiently interested to pursue the matter further as a layman is advised to consult his local library or write to H M Stationery Office and study the House of Lords debate on the motion Charities and Charity Law as reported in Hansard (Parliamentary Debates): House of Lords: Wednesday 30 June 1971, columns 323–401. In one equally unknown and obscure realm of law freedom from income tax does exist in the football world: for certain players' benefits.'

In the same year (1972), Sir Denis registered the FA Youth Trust Deed. Eight years later the House of Lords followed and applied Eve J from 1915. The Lord Chancellor, Lord Hailsham of St Marylebone, did not specify Sussex County Cricket Club or its advisers when he explained ([1981] AC 1 at 17),

'I do not think that the courts have as yet explored the extent to which elements of organisation, instruction, or the disciplined inculcation of information, instruction or skill may limit the whole concept of education ... But it is clear to me that the decision in *Re Mariette* is not to be read in a sense which confines its application for ever to gifts to a particular institution.'

Sadly, *Re Mariette* was never mentioned in *Re Patten*, the Sussex case, and neither was *Re Gray*, Romer J's own decision. Yet even if Romer J had been persuaded to follow them for Sussex CCC, would sport have taken advantage of the possibilities it would have opened up? For when the Lord Chancellor, Lord Hailsham of St Marylebone, in the FA Youth Trust case thought the courts have not 'as yet explored ...', he was identifying the profession which services those courts, and initiates their intervention, rather than the judiciary who respond to chart the course of charities and other developing and emerging legal areas.

The comprehensive manner in which the House of Lords applied the concepts of physical recreation to the principles of standard charity law and practice, together with the absence of sufficient evidence on the issue of recreation, prevented the FA Youth Trust Deed judgments in any of the courts being able to consider the Recreational Charities Act 1960 (a state of affairs untouched by human legal hands until *Re Guild* [1992] and see p 97 and Appendix 11, page 485). This will be considered more appropriately in Chapter 14, 'No fine on fun'. Furthermore, Chapter 4, 'Parent, school and club partners', will explain the availability and applicability of charity law for rate relief to the advantage of sporting bodies, clubs, and the community generally.

7 Race relations

Five years after the Youth Trust Deed judicial opinions, the House of Lords was again brought on to the sporting stage with legislation enacted during the reign of Queen Elizabeth II, as distinct from the charity legislation of Queen Elizabeth I, ie the Race Relations Act 1970 (*Wheeler v Leicester City Council* [1985] AC 1054). The relevance of this sensitive and developing area of law here is merely to emphasise the need for careful and thoughtful co-ordination of sport and the law. More appropriately it is considered in detail under Chapter 9, 'International interaction'. Here, it is mentioned solely to record the course it took procedurally.

The Leicester City Council sought to withdraw its facilities to the local rugby club for usage of its practice ground at Welford Road because players had exercised their free choice to tour South Africa with the England national representative team. An application for judicial review to Forbes J failed. So, too, did an appeal to the Court of Appeal (Brown-Wilkinson LJ dissenting). The House of Lords, unanimously overruled the Court of Appeal majority and Forbes J, and the Leicester City Council's decision. The conflict of judicial opinion here explains the manner in which sport and the law must be regarded as a developing rather than a static or contracting area. It is considered in greater detail in Chapter 9, 'International Interaction' at pp 262–264 below. It can also be read in the light of the great West Indian cricketer Learie Constantine's High Court triumph 50 years ago during the Second World War, after American armed services personnel inspired discrimination against him at London's Imperial Hotel, Russell Square, as explained in Chapter 15, 'Whither Sport and the Law' at p 417 (below).

8 Tribunals

The House of Lords unanimity for soccer's charitable status in 1980 would have been some compensation for the FA's defeat a year earlier by Cantley J in 1979 in the High Court. He had expunged the suspension imposed by a disciplinary tribunal upon the former national team manager, Don Revie (*Revie v The Football Association* (1979) Times, 14 December) which is dealt with more appropriately and in more detail under Chapter 11, 'Fair play and reason in court'. The significance of that judgment here is that this was the third time within a quarter-of-a-century when decisions of soccer's ruling body's disciplinary tribunals had been reversed in the High Court. During 1962 from the north-east of England the High Court was called upon to reverse its suspensions upon first the players and then officials and the club itself at Sunderland (*Elliott & others v the FA & others* (1962) Times, 12 April; *Ditchburn & others v the FA & others* (1962) Times 22 June). Cantley J's reversal of the ban upon the former England team manager Don Revie (*Revie v FA* (1979)) because of fundamental procedural tribunal errors (see Chapter 11) confirmed the need for care and caution in yet a further developing legal area essential to the efficient and effective administration of the world of sport. More recently, the Football Association of Wales Ltd was held in London's Chancery Division of the High Court to be in restraint of trade after administrative and tribunal decisions banned three minor league football clubs from playing on their own local grounds: *Newport AFC Ltd & Others v Football Association of Wales Ltd* (1994) 144 *New Law Journal* 1351, 7 October.

9 Personal injuries

That significant FA Tribunal year of 1962 also witnessed one of the rarer and perhaps more mundane necessities for the co-ordinating roles of sport and the law; the input and assessment of evidence. *Wooldridge v Sumner* ([1963] 2 QB 43) was a decision of great importance arising out of the White City National Horse Show of the Year. The claim was for personal injuries suffered by a photographer discharging his professional duties within the arena when he was injured by a competing horse. Barry J awarded £6,000 damages against the competitor, but dismissed a claim against the organisers. The case is full of legal nuggets which will be more fully discussed and cited elsewhere (Chapter 5, 'Public protection' and Chapter 6, 'Participation problems'). Here it is important and relevant for a rarely recognised but none the less important area of judicial intervention. For the Court of Appeal reversed the trial judge's finding simply and solely on the ground that in assessing the evidence he had drawn the wrong inference of fact from it, and thereby had erroneously attributed negligence when the evidence pointed to error of judgment as distinct from negligence. As Sellers LJ said at p 52

'it provides a striking illustration and reminder of how uncertain can be the raw material of a court's inquiry, the evidence'.

Diplock LJ, at p 60 explained

'The relevant events took place in the course of a few seconds; all or some of them were seen by 12 different witnesses including the rider and the injured man, and, as is inevitable when honest witnesses give their recollections of what occurred in a very brief space of time, there were wide divergences in their respective accounts. In such a case an appellate court will not lightly disturb the findings of the trial judge as to what in fact occurred.'

On that occasion the appellate tribunal, after six days of forensic arguments and a reserved judgment running to over twenty pages, did feel obliged to disturb the trial judge's findings; but two decades later in *Condon v Basi* ([1985] 2 All ER 453) a later Court of Appeal applied an Australian precedent (*Rootes v Shelton* [1968] ALR 33) to extend the frontiers of sporting injury damages liability to common law negligence, and confirm the judgment of H H Judge Wooton in the Warwick County Court (see in Chapter 6, 'Participation problems').

More recently an unreported High Court judgment agreed a damages award of £30,557, of which £7,000 were general damages and the rest special damages for injuries received in a Karate practice session. Sir Michael Davies began his judgment, leading to a finding of negligence as pleaded in the claims:

'I suspect that the judge in charge of the list was told that this was was of great importance in the important world of Karate and involved great questions of principle. Having heard all the evidence I am totally confident it is nothing of the sort. No great question of principle arises. There is a straightforward question of fact to be decided. The law, which is found enshrined in one decision of the Court of Appeal to which I will refer, is, in my view crystal clear [ie *Condon v Basi*, supra]. The court has to find the facts, apply the law, and that is the end of it.'
[*Champion v Brown* (1993) Unreported, 24 February.]

Thus the two high-profiled football cases of *Elliott v Saunders and Liverpool Football Club Ltd* (1994) and *O'Neill v Fashanu and Wimbledon Football Club Ltd* (1994) Times, 14 October, were illustrative of the same *general* legal criteria.

10 Evidence

The hard real world of admissible facts brings into play the crucial role and law of admissible evidence. For practical purposes it is often the decisive element in contested litigation. When Sam Weller tried to explain that

'the soldier said Ven they ordered him three hundred and fifty lashes.'

he was rebuffed

' "you must not tell us what the soldier, or any other man, said, sir" interposed the judge: "it's not evidence".'

Textbooks from deservedly distinguished and eminent sources have continually analysed and assessed the juridical and admissible nature of evidence. Equally important for the litigant and the lawyer is the *collection* of it. Without intending to digress into the continuing contention about a fused or divided legal profession, the undisputed fact remains that collation and co-ordination of evidence is as essential and often difficult for operating a legal system as the ultimate presentation in court or advising on legal issues and preparing documents out of court. The *Williams v Reason and Daily Telegraph* (supra) Court of Appeal conclusions which refused leave to admit fresh evidence in the Court of Appeal is one example of the desirability to get all the eggs together in the same basket at the outset of any contested issues before trials begin. The *Wooldridge v Sumner* (supra) verdict by the Court of Appeal because the trial judge drew the wrong inference of fact from the extensive evidence tendered before him is another example, this time of the need to try and assist the tribunal as much as possible with as much available and admissible evidence as can be achieved. To-day this includes authentically proved video evidence.

A different version of extracting from evidence the wrong inference of fact occurred in an important action about a disputed will and codicil when the trial judge failed to sum up the essential facts correctly to the jury. The House of Lords at the end of 1958 reversed a majority Court of Appeal confirmation of the judge's summing up and found that this happened in a case which attracted much general attention at the time on 20 May 1957. It began in circumstances which created the original and more unorthodox sporting situation, tinged with a touch of undoubted criminality, known as the 'Colonel who debagged the Solicitor' (*Wintle v Nye* [1959] 1 All ER 552).

Purists who may object to its inclusion within a sporting legal context may be unaware of two sequels which do not appear in any law reports. Immediately after the House of Lords decision Lincoln's Inn barristers, dining in Hall in the presence of HRH Princess Margaret, drank a toast in honour of the Colonel and to his success. They also sent a jeroboam of champagne to him and to his ex-cavalry campaigner, ex-trooper Cedric (Spike) Mays who had helped his preparations, with a signed menu card inscribed 'for the successful amateurs to drink the health of the losing professionals.' Subsequently the serving colonel of their regiment, the Royal Dragoons, sent them both the regimental sports tie, dark blue, with golden eagles – the regimental badge. It was awarded only to those who represented 'the regiment in sporting events' (*Last Post*, Spike Mays (1974) p 81; *The Last Englishman*, A D Wintle (1986) p 283).

The key facts in the probate action for the estate of Colonel Wintle's cousin concerned a complicated will and codicil drawn up by the defendant solicitor. She had been nursed by the Colonel's sister for many years before she died. The sister was left far less interest in the cousin's estate under the will and codicil than what the solicitor received under them. Personal knowledge of his family convinced the Colonel that the testatrix had not appreciated or known the contents of either document when she signed them. He failed to obtain any satisfaction from the solicitor to redress the imbalance between himself and the Colonel's sister; but he could not sue because he was not linked legally to the estate and the signed documents. He therefore planned a campaign with military precision to place himself in the litigation riding seat.

A hoaxed invitation for tea effected a meeting between the two men. The Colonel ordered the solicitor to take off his trousers, ejected him on to the highway at Hove in Sussex, then 'exhibited the trousers in the trophy room of [his] club, telephoned the police, the Press and Nye's partner . . . and then went home and sat back with a large whisky awaiting results.' *Wintle*, (p 273)

They soon came. He was arrested later the same evening; charged with common assault, and appeared ultimately before Byrne J at Lewes Assizes, where he pleaded guilty. A six month's custodial sentence was imposed and served (in contrast to *R v David Bishop* (see p 35); one month reduced on appeal to a suspended sentence for punching on the head a defenceless rugby opponent lying on the ground). The worldwide publicity resulted in an assignment to Colonel Wintle of family interests under the will and codicil creating a right to challenge them in the Probate Division of the High Court of Justice. The only issue, per the Lord Chancellor, Lord Simonds ([1959] 1 All ER 557 C-D) was

'whether the testatrix knew and approved of the contents of (i) the will and (ii) the codicil.'

Neither fraud nor undue influence was alleged.

The jury answered 'Yes' to questions related to both elements after days of legal argument, evidence and a summing-up by Barnard J. A Court of Appeal majority rejected an appeal, after a further six days' argument with a reserved judgment on the seventh. The dissenting judgment of Sellers LJ was approved by the House of Lords reserved judgment after a further six days' argument on the basis (per Lord Simonds at p 557: G-H) that

'The summing-up of the evidence substantially negatived the law which the learned judge had in terms enunciated.'

In brief, the House of Lords (p 559: G-H) agreed unanimously that the jury was not

'directed to view the [evidential basis of the] transaction with the vigilance and jealousy which the law requires.'

Its verdict was formally set aside, with consequential advantages to the Colonel's sister. Fifteen years later in *Wooldridge v Summer*, Sellers LJ was a member of the Court which reversed the trial judge on comparable circumstances of judicial error. That judicial mishap was an illuminating corollary to another and perhaps generally lesser known reason for erroneous verdicts and ultimate injustice: insufficient facts. The courts discourage litigation replays with additional facts which could have been obtained and used in evidence on a first hearing. This is why the Court of Appeal refused a retrial on the ground of additional evidence which it heard on behalf of the *Daily Telegraph's* appeal against the £25,000 damages libel award by the jury in favour of the Welsh international J P R Williams. It adjudicated that the additional evidence which it heard on oath could have been obtained for use at the original trial and thereby rejected a re-trial on this ground, although it ordered one for the reason already explained in detail (p 60 supra) ie that the judge had failed to direct the jury correctly on the relevant rugby regulations about amateurism (pp 60–61, supra). No retrial ever took place, with the risks of costs as one of the matters leading to that position.

11 Facts

Against this background all readers ought to know how a crucial but oft-forgotten *Report of the Committee on Legal Education* (Cmnd 4595), commissioned by Lord Gardiner, Lord Chancellor in 1967, and completed for his successor, Lord Hailsham of St Marylebone in 1971, under the chairmanship of Mr Justice (later Lord Justice) Ormrod, explained the realities underlying this aspect of the administration of justice, in para 91 at page 38, thus (with the author's own emphasis):

> 'The raw material of every *practising lawyer* is facts, and a great deal of his time will be spent, whether he is a judge or a barrister or a solicitor, *in finding the facts.* The law cannot be properly applied until they are ascertained. If the facts are wrong, the advice of the most learned lawyer will be, at best, worthless – and may be dangerous. Facts, therefore are of crucial importance to the practising lawyer at all levels, and his ability to *handle* facts is among his most essential skills. The *handling* of facts has many aspects. The practitioner must first *obtain* the client's instructions and the surrounding facts, and then *investigate* and *scrutinise* them for accuracy. Analysis of all the available data, to separate the *relevant* from the irrelevant and to perceive the relation between one set of facts and another and so to check reliability or expose errors, is an essential process in every case. In every case, also, he must *synthesise* his facts in order to present them lucidly and cogently, whether as an advocate, or as a pleader, or as a draftsman, or as a negotiator, or even as a letter writer.* All stages of these processes will of course be controlled and informed by his knowledge of the relevant law, without which the exercise would be futile.

The emphasis on italicised words here is made deliberately. To *find, obtain, handle, investigate, scrutinise* and *synthesise* relevant facts is a process in which both branches of practising lawyers depend upon other people for providing the facts. The need to excavate for them, and also corroborative witnesses in support, becomes more burdensome with every passing decade as visual aid and television erosions

* The raw material etc formerly on p 28.

of independent and inquiring thought processes paralyse or inhibit
the general public's capacity to communicate coherently, and sometimes, too, the investigator's ability to pursue with sufficient depth.
The ideal of a Sherlock Holmes with Dr Watson to eliminate the
probable, or a Perry Mason's facility to whistle up a Paul Drake-style
assistant who can fly off to all corners of the globe for information at
a moment's notice, is hardly possible for practitioners whose clients
are tied to a legal aid budget, or even for those with no cash limit. The
client outside both of these categories, unable to afford legal services,
makes a mockery of Magna Carta: 'to no one shall we deny justice':
Colonel Wintle's triumph, recognised by Lincoln's Inn barristers and
his regimental Colonel, was to battle in the Court of Appeal and the
House of Lords, assisted only by ex-trooper Cedric (Spike) Mays
(although he had been represented by distinguished Counsel at the
trial).

Thus, all who enter the lottery of litigation should somehow be
primed with the golden advice given in the presence of counsel and
their client by the late Simon Burns. He was the wise and skilled
solicitor who steered the appeal to the House of Lords of Reginald
Woolmington to reverse the Court of Criminal Appeal and quash a
murder conviction when the Lord Chancellor, Viscount Sankey LC,
expressed the immortal words,

> 'Throughout the web of the English Criminal Law one gold thread is
> always to be seen, that it is the duty of the prosecution to prove the
> prisoner's guilt' (*Woolmington v DPP* [1935] AC 462 at 481 and 483).

He also had a knack of explaining to difficult and inarticulate clients
in his soft and slow Humberside burr,

> 'Mr Client. When you've fought the case and lost it, please don't come
> back to us and explain "If the barrister had only known about x, or y or
> z, we could have won the case." You must tell us, now, while there is still
> time to investigate, and evaluate, what you haven't told us so far.'

The chapters which now follow are relied upon for direct testimony as
evidence, as well as the inference of fact to be drawn from them; that
those who persist in believing that sport has nothing to do with law,
and that law can be divorced from sport, do so at peril to themselves and all whom they seek to serve. No area of society is un-
affected by legal issues. Sport is no exception. The pattern and
applicable legal areas selected for these pages have been chosen from
professional experiences and observation as being most likely to
affect and concern the widest possible readership to be interested.
Every specialist sport and every legal speciality will doubtless expect
far fuller treatment. That is not the purpose of this book. A level of

general awareness is the aim for a gap which the ever increasing interaction and interrelation between sport and the law is almost daily proving to exist on daily published evidence.

12 Parliament

The previous two chapters ('Genesis' and 'Progressive perspective'), identified the extent to which Parliament as the United Kingdom's supreme law-making body is a source of legislation affecting sport; and further examples will emerge during the remainder of the text. What merits attention in this general survey is an often overlooked aspect of the position generally, explained in a little cited reference during Lord Hailsham's Carlton Lecture:

> '... in a free country it is a seldom cited but almost universal principle that an action is lawful unless prohibited by some positive rule of law or public policy, prescribed by statute or customary law.'

For controlling the excesses of personal and sporting misconduct and neglect Parliament has acted prohibitively during the later 1980s and early 1990s to a greater extent *in a short period* than during any earlier era of Britain's sporting and national history. It has begun to act positively on fiscal issues to alleviate the revenue and VAT burdens which are annually the subject of pleas from sporting sources. Chapter 14, 'No fine on fun', explores some of them.

Thirty years ago, Professor Peter McIntosh in his most valuable but little-known *Sport in Society* (1963) summarised succinctly the first comprehensive chronicle of the British sporting scene, Joseph Strutt's *The Sports and Pastimes of the People of England*. McIntosh explained how Strutt's survey 'from the earliest period to the present time' [1801]

> 'classified sports under three broad headings:
> "rural exercises practised by persons of rank",
> "rural exercises generally practised" and
> "pastimes usually exercised in towns and cities, or places adjoining them," He [Strutt] was perhaps imposing upon the past those geographical and social distinctions which he drew from observation of the society at the end of the eighteenth century. Nevertheless he found it possible without distorting his evidence to notice in the sports of the Middle Ages these fundamental distinctions between rural and urban and between aristocratic and plebeian.'

These 'fundamental distinctions' explain the pattern of the extensive Parliamentary control of sport, leisure and physical education from medieval times to the beginnings of modern sport in industrial Britain and elsewhere a century ago. National security demanded the protection of archery by Parliamentary prohibitions on football and other pursuits which were diverting time from practising and preparing skills with bows and arrows. Concurrent with that pattern of legislation was the area described in 1962 a year before McIntosh's summary, as a

> 'complex hotch-pot of statutory enactments which have been built-up over the years',

namely, *The Game Laws of this country* (per Col James N Vallance OBE, TD, Chairman, Wildfowlers' Association of Great Britain and Northern Ireland). That complaint echoed the immortal *Commentaries on the Laws of England* two centuries earlier where Sir William Blackstone recorded in 1765 (Book iv: pp 174–175)

> 'The statutes for preserving the game are many and various, and not a little obscure and intricate'.

He explained the offence

> 'of destroying such beasts and fowls, as are ranked under the denomination of game,'

to be one

> 'which the sportsmen of England seem to think of the highest importance; and a matter, perhaps the only one, of general and national concern; associations have been formed all over the kingdom to prevent its destructive process ...'

That prevention to protect the species and the landed sporting property rights which accompanied it by criminal penal sanctions inspired the network of Game Law legislation which survives today. Blackstone explained, with a reflection of an enlightened eighteenth-century Oxford attitude from his chair as the first Vinerian Professor, which created the lectures on which his commentaries were based before his leading judicial appointments, in the then Court of Common Pleas,

> 'the only rational footing, upon which we can consider it was a crime is, that in low and indigent persons it promotes idleness, and takes them away from their proper employments and callings; which is an offence against the public police [sic!] and economy of the commonwealth.'

The protection from that legislation shaped the gaming laws which created the ground rules between poachers and landowners and their gamekeepers, with Parliamentary and contractual permissions for licence holders to catch and sell game. Alongside, or because of this parliamentary control of rural sporting activities, landowners carved out their own areas of sporting rights and enjoyment within the framework of the property land laws. These created the exploitation of fishing, gaming and shooting rights through boundaries; easements, licences, profits a prendre and restrictive covenants which belong to the realm of real property and real estate law, where the detailed crucial creative conveyancing documents are found. Their protection comes from enforcement by the remedies of damages and injunctions of the civil wrongs of trespass (particularly against hunting and anti-hunt saboteurs), nuisance and negligence, together with conventional criminal offences of assault, malicious damage, and more specialised statutory offences in this legislative field such as the long-standing Night Poaching Acts, the Protection of Animals Act 1911, the Salmon and Freshwater Fisheries Act 1923 and more recently the Wildlife and Countryside Act 1981.

This blend of common law landed property rights and Parliamentary enactments which have catered down the years for protection and commercial exploitation of rural sports belong to the same legal stable which more recently has sired and applied to the commercial world of urban and industrialised sponsored sports the intellectual property rights found in copyright, franchising, patents and trade mark laws, and considered in Chapter 13, 'Sponsored gentlemen and players'.

Violent criminal elements more recently (and particularly since the acquiescence by light-headed and light-minded pseudo-intellectuals in a permissive society masquerading as a progressive or so-called civilised society since the 1960s) have poisoned certain urban and even rural sporting areas; and these have demanded special criminal sanctions. Accordingly, they have absorbed more concentrated Parliamentary time than any other period of Britain's sporting or social history. Thus, the Parliament which ended with the General Election of 1987 produced in its final year

(1)   Two Reports, Interim (Cmnd 9585) and Final (Cmnd 9710), from Mr Justice Popplewell on Crowd Control during 1985 and 1986.

(2)   The Sporting Events (Control of Alcohol etc) Act 1985.

(3)   The Public Order Act 1986.

(4)   The Fire Safety and Safety of Places of Sport Act 1987.

(5)   An improved Green Guide Code for sports ground safety.

Since then, two further statutes have been implemented to tackle the never-ending criminal element poisoning the soccer scene.

(6)   The Football Spectators Act 1989

(7)   The Football Offences Act 1991

CONCLUSIONS

Looking back on this chapter, 'Under starter's orders', is there any message for practitioners, administrators, academics and others at whom the book is aimed? In the author's submission there is; because it has been, and throughout these pages it will again be necessary, to turn back the clock: to explain and examine procedural legal processes with their relevant evidence and try to demonstrate how verdicts are reached.

In that context they illustrate three basic elements which must provide a consistent legal and juridical thread or pattern throughout this book, and, it is suggested, for any understanding of how the law functions in practice and particularly within an emerging and not easily recognisable or identifiable area such as sport and the law – history, procedure and evidence, and appropriately admissible facts.

Sir Walter Scott focuses the historical setting. Maitland, quoting Maine, identified the procedural significance; and many within the law often forget the key role for ascertainment and excavation of the admissible evidence and facts. The extent to which this vital process is taught, if at all, in law schools is at present limited in scope, but beginning to be recognised by the professional governing bodies in harmony with University Law Schools. A similar question of equal importance concerns the extent to which, if at all, sport and physical education are taught in schools in Britain today.

That is why the relationships between a Parents, Schools and Club partnership must be considered together in the next chapter.

Part II

Personal relationships

Chapter 4

Parent, school and club partners

INTRODUCTION

Sir Denis Follows as long ago now as 1983 recognised in his valedictory lecture at Loughborough College the then developing trend which has distorted and overshadowed the picture and concept of true sport *at the public level.*

> 'Sport at top level has become much more part and parcel of the entertainment world and particularly so during the past thirty years. We have reached the stage where sport at top level has become almost completely show business with everything one associates with show biz – the cult of the individual, high salaries, the desire to present the game as a spectacle – with more money, less sportsmanship, more emphasis on winning and all this has largely come about through television.'

The corollary to this is one of the more fundamental attitudes which exists in many households today. Previous generations may have ignored what Lord Howell in his Foreword to the First Edition described as 'the social and ethical considerations which sport presents in our everyday life'. Ethical considerations are relevant to sport at all levels. Parents now recognise that a career in professional sport, for the limited few with a potential talent capable of being nurtured and developed, can be as rewarding, profitable and self-fulfilling as any conventional and traditional trade or profession. Yet sporting talents may never achieve their full potential without adequate coaching, teaching and premises at school level provided from within the bureaucratic framework of the government Department for Education, as distinct from the portfolio attributable to a junior Minister in the Department of National Heritage associated with sport and a rag-bag of the *non*-sporting activities.

Finally, for the great majority of sports participants, the natural enjoyment and fun to be shared require a need for facilities and coaching services. Thus, the integration of Parents, Schools and Clubs is as crucial for the personal happiness and self-fulfilment of all concerned with sport and recreation as it is for the ultimate performance of national representatives.

Accordingly, of equal importance to the safety element explained in the next chapter in the public protection of sport is the dimension of safeguarding the future of schools, school playing fields, playgrounds and competitive sport in schools. These demand even greater attention. No need exists for any who cares for British sport to explain or justify the contention. In this context, however, it is worth recalling how the founder of the modern Olympic Games based his own ideal upon the games ethic of the Victorian English public school system.

In *This Great Symbol: Pierre de Coubertin and the Origins of the Modern Olympic Games*, his biographer. Professor John J Macaloon, of the University of Chicago explains (p 79) how de Coubertin erroneously attributed to Dr Arnold of Rugby School the images of sporting emphasis created by Arnold's best known pupil there, Thomas Hughes, in *Tom Brown's Schooldays*, and how,

> 'In the memories of 1880s Englishmen, Arnold had indeed become associated with athletic games ... Coubertin's identification of Arnold with education sport was an illusion in Freud's sense of the term: a deep and multiply determined wish fulfilled. Coubertin needed a link between school reform, social and moral education, and athletic games; and he needed that link embodied in a single, distant, exotic, kind and fatherly figure of patriotic and progressive genius to serve him as an image and the new France as a model. Because he needed Arnold to be this man, so he made him to be.'

Arnold's personal priorities were first religion, second character and moral leadership, and third intellectual excellence. His impact socially and educationally has been enduring, beyond the inspiration for de Coubertin's resurrection of the Olympic Games in 1896. A few years and also half-a-century later four unpublicised examples from renowned celebrities illustrate the significance of sport in education at different times and at different levels in the social hierarchy. These lead into section 76 of the Education Act 1944, a little known enactment which could have fundamental effects on British sport and physical education if parents and people concerned with and about the future welfare of British sport were aware of it. The under or non-usage of it to date confirms another level of unawareness.

PARENTS AND SCHOOLS

The younger generation of the Sitwell family, Sir Sacheverell, Sir Osbert and Dame Edith, were among Britain's literary leaders during the earlier part of the twentieth century. When Sir Osbert Sitwell's parents discovered 'that the headmaster was the most famous dribbler in England' (The Scarlet Tree) they were converted to their choice of preparatory school for his early education at the century's turn. The school was Ludgrove, then at Cockfosters near Barnet. Hertfordshire. It has now long been settled in its Second World War home at Wokingham in Berkshire. The headmaster was G O Smith, legendary amateur centre-forward for England on twenty occasions alongside the equally memorable professional players such as Steve Bloomer (Derby County), Ernest 'Nudger' Needham (Sheffield United), and John Goodall (Preston North End). Nearly half a century later, Bobby Charlton's grandfather, a member of the famous Northumberland Milburn family, persuaded the headmaster, Mr Hunter, at Ashington Primary School that his grandson's entry to Morpeth Grammar School after passing the eleven plus examination would deny his grandson the continued development of soccer because rugby was the school's traditional game; and, as Charlton himself recorded in *This Game of Soccer* (1967) 'Much to my relief I was switched to Bedlington Grammar – and soccer.'

Consistent with that pattern, during the later 1980s and early 1990s, it emerged that parental choice destined England's professional soccer captain, Gary Lineker, to attend the City of Leicester Boys School. This school had a soccer tradition as distinct from a more popular rugby-orientated tradition in the same city; and his rugby playing counterpart, Will Carling, was switched from Shrewsbury's great soccer heritage to Sedbergh and its rugby playing inheritance.

None of these profound choices needed or at their respective times would have been able to make use of Parliament's provision for such entitlements today under the Education Act 1944, enacted during the latter period of the Second World War.

Section 76 provides:

'In the exercise and performance of all powers and duties conferred and imposed on them by this Act (the Secretary of State) and local education authorities *shall have regard to the principle that, so far as is compatible with the provision of efficient instruction and training and the avoidance of unreasonable public expenditure, pupils are to be educated in accordance with the wishes of their parents.*'
(Author's emphasis)

Section 99 contains a limited sanction for enforcing this section. It creates a complaints procedure to the Secretary of State, who 'may make an order' for such enforcement of section 76 as is appropriate and practicable.

Furthermore, without resiling in any form and indeed by way of affirmation the Education Act 1980 provides under the heading (again with the author's emphasis).

'6 Parental preferences
(1) Every local education authority shall make arrangements for enabling *the parent* of a child in the area of the authority *to express a*

*preference as to the school at which he wishes education to be provided
for his child* in the exercise of the authority's functions and *to give
reasons for his preference.*

(2) Subject to subsection (3) below, it shall be the duty of a local
education authority and of the governors of a county or voluntary
school to comply with any preference expressed in accordance with
the arrangements.

(3) The duty imposed by subsection (2) above does not apply–
   (a) if compliance with the preference would prejudice the provision
       of efficient education or the efficient use of resources:
   (b) if the preferred school is an aided or special agreement school
       and compliance with the preference would be incompatible with
       any arrangements between the governors and the local edu-
       cation authority [made under subsection (6) below] or
   (c) if the arrangements for admission to the preferred school are
       based wholly or partly on selection by reference to ability or
       aptitude and compliance with the preference would be incom-
       patible with selection under the arrangements.

Section 76

It has been used in non-recreational circumstances on varied occasions with varying success during the last four decades for situations ranging from religion to policy making decisions about
schools. Five may be cited as illustrating a general approach.

Watt v Kesteven County Council ([1955] 1 QB 408) established that
section 76 laid down the generalities to be regarded along with other
considerations, including a power to make exceptions. If that basis
for action fails to motivate the local authority, then the practical
availability of a complaint to the Minister to exercise his default
powers under section 99 also exists. The Courts can still be used if he
or the local authority exercise their Parliamentary powers capri-
ciously or unreasonably (*Associated Provincial Picture Houses Ltd v
Wednesbury Corporation* [1948] 1 KB 223); and *Cummings v Birkenhead Corporation* [1971] 2 All ER 881 confirmed that parental wishes
are only one factor to be taken into consideration.

Both of these precedents come from the sensitive area of religious
education. The more robust traditional sporting sphere, with its
crucial impact on national health and fitness should and could have
better results for sport and physical education if challenged on the
right sporting and education issues and in the right circumstances of
for example, unreasonable, illogical, and spurious egalitarian politi-
cally-motivated objections to sporting competition in schools. Thus,
a school or teaching staff or governing body which denies pupils the
undoubted advantages of competitive sport because of, for example,
an unnatural or half-thought out social theory about egalitarianism
or an equally debatable premise, could be justifiably and perhaps
successfully challenged by parents under section 76. Further, if either

local or national government officials were to ignore the forces of parental and public opinion, separate and apart from general national as well as sporting issues involved, there would be two further avenues available to parents:

(1)   a right of referral by complaint to the Minister under section 99, and

(2)   as a last resort, an overriding control of judicial review by the courts.

These provisions would have been available for the happy-go-lucky six-year-old schoolgirl certified as terrified of attending gymnastic classes but under threat of compulsion to attend by Suffolk County Council (*Daily Telegraph*, 16 October 1992). The capacity of parents to enforce the law depends, of course, upon the financial capacity to sustain litigation in addition to the will to pursue it. This was illustrated when parent-ratepayers objected to the London Borough of Enfield's proposals to change the system of education and character of schools within the borough. They brought an action to restrain the council from acting on its proposals. The parents succeeded in part with an injunction; but they were referred back to the Minister under section 99 of the Education Act 1944 enforcing their rights under section 76 (*Bradbury v London Borough of Enfield* [1967] 3 All ER 434). Costs, however, were awarded in favour of the plaintiff parent-ratepayers.

Three recent cases since the first edition also illustrate how this parliamentary machinery can be operated effectively, and significantly, because public bodies are involved, as distinct from private sporting governing institutions, by the process known as judicial review.

In *Harvey v Strathclyde Regional Council* ((1989) Independent, 6 July) the House of Lords upheld a decision of the First Division of the Court of Session (which had overruled the Lord Ordinary) to confirm that an education authority in the Paisley outskirts of Glasgow had in fact had regard to Scotland's equivalent under section 28(1) of the Education (Scotland) Act 1980 to section 76 of the Education Act 1944 applicable to England and Wales for educating children in accordance with their parents' wishes. For it has consulted extensively with the parents and taken account of the parent representations before reaching a decision to discontinue a school even though the decision conflicted with the desires of most of the parents. The proceedings were initiated by a schoolgirl's mother who objected to the closure of the school and the transfer of pupils to another school.

A few months later the report surfaced of the London Queen's Bench Division having allowed an application for judicial review by school governors who opposed the local authority's policy which 'went against' the statutory duty under section 6 of the Education Act 1980 to comply with parental preferences for a school for their child (*R v Greenwich London Borough Council, ex parte Governors of John Ball Primary School* (1989) Times, 16 November).

More recently, and again in a non-sporting context, section 76 of the Education Act 1944 and section 6 of the Education Act 1980, for considering parental prejudices, were recognised as available in appropriate circumstances during the course of a successful application geared to section 55(4) of the Education Act 1944 for judicial review relating to a legitimate expectation for consultation by a local education authority with parents in respect of travelling expenses outside the local education authority's district (*R v Rochdale Metropolitan Borough Council, ex parte Schemet* (1992) Times, 9 September, Roche J) and see also Butterworths *Law of Education*, 9th edn, edited by Peter Liell and John Saunders (Volume 3, paragraph F213).

Finally, in *R v Essex County Council, ex parte C* ((1993) Times, 9 December) the Court of Appeal dismissed an appeal from Jowett J who had refused a mother's application for judicial review seeking free transport under section 55 of the Education Act 1944 for a child 'with special needs' to facilitate his attendance at the school of his parents' choice. In particular the Court explained that parental choice under section 76 of the 1944 Act was subject, inter alia, to 'the avoidance of unreasonable public expenditure'.

These are undoubted legal rights for enforcement under section 76 of the Education Act 1944 and section 6 of the Education Act 1980 created by Parliament and capable of enforcement through the courts. They have been preserved intact by the monumental Education Reform Act 1988 (238 sections; 13 Schedules) which pays token lip service to physical education as a foundation subject within the National Curriculum under section 3(1)(a) and also by the Education Act 1993 (308 sections; 21 Schedules) which ignores physical education entirely. They are all available to Parent Teacher Associations (PTAs) who have been concerned about extreme politically or socially debatable decisions to diminish or demolish competitive sports within and against other schools, without any apparent hope or means for challenging them. Local authorities, school teachers and governors who have hitherto considered their controversial attitudes to be immune from any effective challenge and decisions should be in no doubt about the potential parental capacity to attack successfully and to rout an intransigent enemy on this particular front. Finally, although the no less convoluted Statutory Instrument SI 1992/603 The Education (National Curriculum) (Attainment Target and Programmes of Study in Physical Education) Order 1992 provides in generally vague terms for such programmes and an attainment target, availability or rather non-availability of facilities for these purposes is not provided for them.

Another important sphere in schools is the equally contentious issue about preservation or sale of surplus school fields. The issue involves a mixture of local economic and political policies with some legal safeguards which are linked to planning law. Objectors to such policies are entitled to be vigilant for and alerted to action upon applications under the Town and Country Planning Acts by developers for change of use, particularly following a Domesday Book Register of school playing fields as explained on page 102 below.

(1) Dual use of facilities

In 1983 the Environment Committee of the House of Commons was appointed to examine, inter alia, associated public bodies connected with the Department of the Environment, identifying expenditure, administration and policy. Its slender report and examination of evidence published in February 1986 on the Sports Council as an associated public body makes light reading compared with the erudite report from the Education, Science and Arts Committee of the House of Commons published in October 1982 on the Public and Private Funding of the Arts (HC 49). Nevertheless, at page xxii in Paragraph 56, the Sports Council Environment Committee report did conclude:

'56. Everyone is agreed that more dual use of school sports facilities would be desirable. There would be a net saving of public money and probably other benefits for all concerned. The way forward has been shown in many places. The difficulties involved can be solved by officials if they are given a lead and persuaded to shed Departmental protectionism. What is needed is a greater firmness by Ministers on what is in the public interest. We were glad to hear that Mr Richard Tracey [then Under-Secretary at the DoE with responsibility for sport] thought the same and intended to have discussions with Ministerial colleagues in the DES. We strongly urge all Ministers concerned to bring these discussions to a successful and speedy conclusion and to place the public good before sectional Departmental interests.'

(2) School playing fields and school games

The result of the Committee's 1986 recommendation for government ministerial co-ordination and co-operation was a joint seminar at the DoE organised by the two departments in December 1986. The conclusion was the establishment of a Forum of Commission. Yet throughout the proceedings no recognition was given at any stage by the conventional educational, environmental and recreational or

Government sources in attendance that the present law suffices to provide answers for many of the clearly identifiable problems. It exists positively and negatively. Negatively, those same planning laws which were used in March 1987 by Hammersmith and Fulham Council to warn Fulham Football & Athletic Company's proposed asset strippers to 'keep off the Craven Cottage grass,' are equally available to any group of local objectors in any part of the country to protest to local authorities who may be seduced by the financial offerings from similar property predators to local authorities for selling off school playing fields.

No doubt, following from the Environment Committee's recommendation, a year later, March 1987, witnessed a joint Sports Council – Arts Council production entitled 'Getting it together: guidance on housing sports and arts activities in the same building' with a joint Foreword from the then respective Chairmen, John Smith, CBE and Sir William Rees-Mogg. Whatever resulted from such a guidance required further attention which is still unresolved at the time of writing (early-1994).

A Foreword from the then Minister for Sport, Robert Atkins, housed in the Department for Education in a 1991 publication entitled, 'A Sporting Double: School and Community' explained how a study entitled 'The Dual Use of School Sports Facilities' was published in June 1987 and this in turn led to the 1991 production,

> 'designed to help local education authorities, school governors and headmasters introduce or extend dual use provision in their schools. Recreation authorities and sports organisations will also find it useful in considering this possibility with their local schools.'

It concluded, at 1991 with the aspiration how,

> 'The guidance builds on the initiatives which the Department of Education and Science and the Environment (before the transference of government sports issues to the Department of National Heritage after the 1992 General Election), the Sports Council and others have developed over the years and as a result we hope that an increasing number of school sports facilities will be opened up for the benefit of the whole community.'

Unfortunately the wishes from the then Ministers for Sport and Education and Science at that 1991 date and at the time of writing in early-1994, have been overtaken by the conflict in Government circles which surfaced in July 1993. The Secretary of State for Education John Patten proposed that existing School Premises Regulations should no longer apply so far as minimum standards for teaching and recreation space were concerned. The Minister for National Heritage housing the Government Sports Unit, Peter Brooke, was reported as seeing it 'as a cost-saving device with potentially disastrous results for team games and the ability to deliver the PE requirements of the national curriculum,'

as provided for in the Education Reform Act 1988.

This tension at Ministerial level in mid-1993 is wholly consistent with the administrative government indecisiveness which has followed from the House of Commons Environment Committee's conclusions in February 1986. It also contrasted with the claim made at the CCPR's Annual Conference in November 1993 by the House of Lords representative of the Department of National Heritage, Baroness Trumpington, that the 1993 Education Act with 308 sections allowed dual use partners such as the sports council and local authorities to enter into agreements with school governing bodies for the joint management of school facilities. Their implementation and application however, would be a matter for the Department for Education.

A classic example appears for preservation in Chapter 12, 'Administrative advice' at pages 314–316 which was tracked by the *Daily Mail*'s award-winning Ian Woolridge's 1987 campaign for preserving the War Memorial Recreation Ground at New Milton, near Brockenhurst and Southampton from the attempted transfer of 3.6 acres of oak fringed-grass with a car park for a supermarket.

The effect of such objection formalised under the Town and Country Planning Acts 1945–71, would be to cause an inspector to conduct an inquiry, usually in public. This in turn would permit evidence to be called in support by any objectors, as well as for the applicants. The developer's plans would be scrutinised within the context of local, school and general environmental and social needs. The inspector would report formally to the Minister, in whose hands the overriding decision would be made: at the Government department which houses the so-called Sports Minister in his constitutional role as Under-Secretary at the Department of Environment (not, and never since Lord Hailsham's conception of the role, at the Department for Education and Science).

All planning applications have to be advertised and notice given for the purpose of objections being lodged within a specified timescale. Accordingly, the rapes of school playing fields are subject to ministerial control under Parliamentary law and are controlled by the courts in the event of capricious or unreasonable ministerial misconduct. This is only if the victims are ready, willing and minded to operate the mechanisms advised by Lord Denning in *Miller v Jackson*, cited at p 59, infra.

Positively, section 53 of the Education Act 1944, (as amended by the Education Act 1980, s38 (6), Sch 7) contains provisions to facilitate recreation and social and physical training. Indeed, it contains a specific duty which is self-evident, namely,

'**53.** (1) It shall be the duty of every local education authority to secure that the facilities for primary secondary and further education provided for their area include adequate facilities for recreation and social and physical training, and for that purpose a local education authority ... may establish maintain and manage, or assist the establishment, maintenance and management of camps, holiday classes, playing fields, play centres, and other places (including playgrounds, gymnasiums, and swimming baths not appropriated to any school or college), at which facilities for recreation and for such training as aforesaid are available for persons for whom primary secondary or further education is provided by the authority, and may organise games, expeditions and other activities for such persons, and may defray or contribute towards the expenses thereof.

(2) A local education authority, in making arrangements for the provision of facilities or the organisation of activities under the powers conferred on them by the last foregoing subsection shall, in particular, have regard to the expediency of co-operating with any voluntary societies or bodies whose objects include the provision or the organisation of activities of a similar character.

(3) The Minister may make regulations empowering local education authorities to provide for pupils in attendance at any school or county college maintained by them such articles of clothing suitable for the physical training provided at the school or college as may be prescribed.

(4) Sections one and two of the Physical Training and Recreation Act, 1937 (which relate to National Advisory Councils and local committees and sub-committees for the promotion of physical training), and so much of section three of that Act as relates to the grants committee, to recommendations of that committee, and to consultation with such Councils as aforesaid, shall cease to have effect.'

That duty in substance creates a foundation and link for threading local education facilities with a community, whether through a club or not; and if any doubt or uncertainty could be raised it would be dispelled by the more recent provision under the Education (No 2) Act 1986, which received the Royal Assent on 7 November 1986. It was designed specifically to meet this particular problem of dual use facilities, and was announced for this purpose at the CCPR Annual Conference at that time, ie providing for the use of school premises outside school hours by members of the community served by the school.

Section 42 provides:

'That articles of government for every county and maintained special school shall provide–

   (a) for the use of school premises at all times other than during any
      school session, or break between sessions on the same day, to be
      under the control of the governing body:
   (b) for the governing body to exercise control subject to any direction
      given to them by the local authority and in so doing to have regard
      to the desirability of the premises being made available (when not
      required by or in connection with the school) for use by members of
      the community served by the school.'

It was implemented on 1 September 1987 (SI 1987/344 C8). How the
section has been operated varies inevitably between local authorities.
A comparable sanction to section 99 of the Education Act 1944, does
not exist: and the ultimate power for enforcement may be required at
ballot boxes during the period of local elections.

   At the time of writing, uncertainty overshadows the extent of
future usage because of financial restraints. A similar situation exists
for the equally important potential nexus between clubs and schools
sport. This is turn brings into focus again the significance of physical
education as a charitable concept. Linked to the local Government
Finance Act 1988, it contains the key for clubs which seek to fill the
gap caused by teachers' strikes or reluctance to provide out of school
facilities in their own time with club coaching facilities. Such legitimate substitutes to replace physical recreation arrangements ab-
dicated by the teaching profession justify clubs to claim under the
Local Government Finance Act 1988. There are advantages, mandatory or discretionary, which are dependant upon an application of
the law relating to charities, now established by the House of Lords
ruling in the FA Youth Trust Deed decision to extend to physical
education for young people (*IRC v McMullan* [1984] AC1), and
extended by the more recent House of Lords in *Guild v IRC* [1992] 2
All ER 10. These decisions absorb the 'interests of social welfare'
criteria under the Recreational Charities Act, 1958 to include 'some
similar purpose in connection with sport' related to a bequest 'to be
used in connection with the Sports Centre [then] in North Berwick'.

(3) Schools: club sport, schools and rates

Sections 47 (1) and (2) and 48 of the Local Government Finance Act
provide for rate relief by local authorities when premises are linked to
charitable purposes; now as guided by the House of Lords.

   This is consistent with the position for opposing planning applications on change of use for school premises, which is considered in
detail under Chapter 12, 'Administrative advice', and, because it
creates a form of local tax, also under Chapter 14, 'No fine on fun'. In
the context of school sport, however, the relevance of education and
sporting charity law can be seen for clubs which structure their affairs

and premises to provide the crucial coaching, teaching and training facilities in order to obtain the correct benefits.

A perfectly legitimate arrangement was recommended at a CCPR seminar in 1980 after the House of Lords judgment in the FA Youth Trust Deed case by a Charity Commissioner. He advocated hiving-off a section of a sports club's premises and affairs to qualify for charitable purposes generally. This is equally applicable and available for rating purposes. Indeed it was validly established for VAT purposes when two sections of a bowls club at Watchet in Somerset successfully separated their indoor from their outdoor sections under the appropriate governing bodies (see Chapter 14, 'No fine on fun').

As we shall see in Chapters 12, 'Administrative advice', and 14, 'No fine on fun', the discretion has been operated advantageously in certain local authority areas and rejected in others. What may not be readily realised, which emerged by an omission from a valuable *Times* newspaper series during early December 1986, was recognition of the problem by the Wolfenden Committee Report on Sport in 1960 commissioned by the then CCPR. At the end of a detailed Paragraph 160, it concluded on page 64:

'We therefore would urge most strongly that local authorities should examine the claims of sports bodies for rating relief with the utmost sympathy and should treat them more generously rather than less generously than in the past. For the provision of maintenance of a facility for physical recreation on the part of a voluntary body may in a very real sense relieve the local authority of its own responsibility to provide such facilities, as laid down by various Parliamentary enactments, including Section 53 of the Education Act 1944.'

That section 53 cited at page 96 above created a duty to provide 'facilities ... for social and physical training.' Thus, the wheel of history goes full circle. More than thirty years after the Report (which led ultimately to the Sports Council's creation), the need for its recommendations for rate reliefs ties in with the growing concern for the future of sport in schools and clubs. With the growing politicisation of sport generally, the ultimate sanction could yet be at local election times if the discretion allowed under legal remedies is not operated with 'the utmost sympathy' recommended as long ago as 1960. That sympathy was certainly recognised by the House of Lords judicial committee after the majority judges in the High Court and Court of Appeal had failed to demonstrate it for charitable legal sporting status (*IRC v McMullan* supra, pp 71–72), and again when overruling the Inner House of Scotland's Court of Session in *Guild v IRC* [1992] 2 All ER 10 (supra).

(4) Physical education and charitable status and the courts

In 1980 the House of Lords judicial committee in *IRC v McMullan* ([1981] AC 1) confirmed that the Charity Commissioners' registration (eight years earlier in 1972) of an FA Youth Trust Deed was a validly registrable charity. This emphasised that physical education is legally regarded as educational for eligibility to charitable status. The taxation advantages for it are considered in Chapter 14, 'No fine on fun', and the consequences for rating of sports clubs are considered there, too, as well as below.

The real significance is seen in a cameo of dialogue between counsel and one of the two Court of Appeal majority judges overruled by the House of Lords in the interim journey from that 1972 registration to the 1980 winning post at Westminster:

> '*Appeal Judge*: Are you really saying that physical education is education like Latin and Greek?
>
> *Counsel*: Yes, my Lord.'

The Court of Appeal 2–1 majority judges, the first instance judge, and the Inland Revenue Commissioners, had all rejected the Charity Commissioners' registration of the FA Youth Trust Deed. The necessity for the House of Lords to be called upon to rule, as it did unanimously with all five judicial opinions, demonstrated vividly the gap between differing legal attitudes to this vital area of national interest. Physical education has always been linked to national health in the manner that sport and recreation legislatively and historically have been geared to the interests of national security in the United Kingdom, with priority given to archery over banned football in medieval times, and recognition of the need for national fitness built into the Fisher Education Acts of 1918 and 1921 at the end of the First World War; the Physical Training and Recreation Act 1937 in the years leading up to the outbreak of the Second World War; and, as we have seen above in the specific provisions of the Butler Education Act 1944, conceived and enacted during the peak years of the Second World War.

The final judicial score was 6–3 in favour of the FA Youth Trust. At half-time stage in the Court of Appeal ([1979] 1 All ER 588) it was 1–3 against the religion, education and general public good. During the interim period, while awaiting the result of the Court of Appeal's reserved judgment, the author had commented 'Many consider that sport qualifies for them all, both realistically and cynically' (*Sport and the Law* (1978)). In a commercially oriented society lacking spiritual leadership that conclusion is re-affirmed here.

Indicative of the differing and limited attitudes are the thoughts contained in the leading House of Lords judgment delivered by the Lord Chancellor, Lord Hailsham of St Marylebone, ([1981] AC 1) at page 17:

'I do not think that the courts have as yet explored the extent to which elements of organisation, instruction or the disciplined inculcation of information, instruction or skill may limit the whole concepts of education. I believe that in some ways it will prove more extensive, in others more restrictive than has been thought hitherto. But it is clear to me at least that the decision in *Re Mariette* [1915] 2 Ch 284 is not to be read in a sense which confines its application forever to gifts to a particular institution.'

Edgar Mariette was an Aldenham School housemaster who had made his will in 1908 containing bequests to the school he had served as boy and teacher, for building a court and athletics prize. Eight years later in 1915 when the casualty lists from the First World War battlefronts were extended by newsvendor placards at different ends of the Commonwealth announcing the deaths of Victor Trumper at the early age of 36 and W G Grace at 67, London's High Court in the Chancery Division heard contending arguments for and against the Mariette legacies. Mr Justice Eve had no reputation equivalent to the recently retired Lord Chief Justice, Lord Alverstone, who had created a sporting track record as athletics Blue, administrator, and author; but he was a product of Exeter College, Oxford, where modern competitive athletics began in 1850. His judgment of less than two pages in the Law Reports ([1915] 2 Ch 284) was warmly endorsed by the House of Lords in the FA Youth Trust Deed case, ignored until then by many British sporting governing bodies, but relied upon in Australia after the Second World War to validate a bequest to the Sydney University Rugby Football Club (in *Kearins v Kearins* (1957) SR 286 (NSW)). It is reproduced in toto in Appendix 11. For present purposes the key passage of legal and educational sporting principles is contained in the following sequences, at pages 288–289:

'The object of this charity is the education, in the widest sense, of boys and young men between the ages of ten and nineteen. No one of sense could be found to suggest that between those ages any boy can be properly educated unless at least as much attention is given to the development of his body as is given to the development of his mind. It is necessary, therefore, in any satisfactory system of education to provide for both mental and bodily occupation, mental occupation by means of the classics and those other less inviting studies to which a portion of the day is devoted, and bodily occupation by means of regular organised games: To leave 200 boys at large and to their own devices during their leisure hours would probably result in their quickly relapsing into something approaching barbarism. For these reasons I think it is essential that in a school of learning of this description, a school receiving and retaining as boarders boys of these ages, there should be organised games as part of the daily routine, and I do not see how the other part of the education can be successfully carried on without them.'

Forty-two years later McLelland J in the New South Wales Equity Court applied this precedent in *Kearins* (supra) to a bequest of £2,000 'for fostering the sport of Rugby Union at Sydney University'. Curiously it was not cited in any of the three court hearings of the FA Youth Trust Deed case, (although as we shall see later in the chapter relating to actionable sporting negligence in personal injuries Australian authorities are eminently persuasive citations for United Kingdom courts). As he explained:

> 'I cannot see any difference in principle between the provision of the means of bodily and physical development for school children or young men at school and such provision who attend the university who are, for the most part, young men and women. Participation in the sporting activities of the University has, I think, always been regarded as an important element in the development of men and women at the university, not only in respect of bodily and physical development but also as part of a well-balanced student.'

That attitude is consistent with Eve J's judgment before it and Lord Hailsham's opinion afterwards. The extension of the Recreational Charities Act 1958 'interests of social welfare' to include after a bequest 'to be used in connection with the sports centre [then] in North Berwick' also a concept of 'some similar purpose in connection with sport', creates a legal googly yet to be bowled to the whole world of sport and the law [*Guild v IRC* [1992] 2 All ER 10].

Nevertheless the Central Council of Physical Recreation's annual conference in November 1986 publicised the verdict of the Secondary Heads' Association that for British sport in schools.

> 'It is time to say there is a crisis in many parts of Britain. Not everywhere but in enough areas for us to be concerned as a nation.'

In March 1987 that general warning was particularised with a detailed report. For this chapter, it suffices to explain summarily how

– 95 per cent of schools have suffered a 'rapid decline' in weekend and after-school sports fixtures in the past two years:

– 75 per cent of pupils have no opportunity to learn to swim at school;

– 40 per cent of schools have inadequate facilities for dance and gymnastics;

– so few schools employ groundsmen that nearly half of all playing fields are substandard by department of education and science criteria;

– only one teacher in 10 apart from specialist PE teachers helps out with school sports. In many schools help is non-existent;

- children aged 12–14 have on average only two hours of exercise a
 week and 65 per cent of sixth-formers can opt out of PE and
 games.

At the same time, the CCPR itself estimated that 547 school playing
fields in whole or in part have been, or are about to be, sold. Subsequently, when a Domesday Book Register of School Playing Fields
was published under the impetus of the Central Council of Physical
Recreation, the National Playing Fields Association and Sports
Council in October 1993, it showed that outside London 404 sites
(about 1.75% of the total) were then currently under threat from
development with planning permission either already granted or
being sought: but it did not identify past playing field losses.

The reasons for these unhappy developments are complex and are
reflective of wider political and industrial problems surrounding the
British educational picture, of which sport has always been a crucial
segment. At the time of the March 1987 report the CCPR secretary,
Peter Lawson, was reported as saying:

'Competitive sport in schools is going down the tube fast. The decline
was exacerbated by the teachers' dispute, when games went by the
board. Success in sport can transform pupil's lives and encourage them
to try harder in academic subjects.'

Many reasons can be advanced for the overall position, but for sport
it may be suggested with confidence that the problems are concentrated on the following separate and interconnecting areas:

(a) industrial differences of approach to teachers' working conditions and pay between the profession, employers and
 Government;
(b) the conflict between traditional outside school hours recreational activities with developing family, social and industrial
 demands upon teachers;
(c) the novel attitude from different sources which challenges the
 authenticity and value of competitive sport in a nation which
 has given sport to the world;
(d) availability and preservation of school premises;
(e) dual use facilities for premises between schools and club industrial and social activities.

Finally at the end of the DoE and DES joint seminar in December
1986 the author enquired of the senior DES representatives whether
there existed within the Department a separate section for Physical
Education: the cryptic answer was. 'No. We also don't have one for
maths and Latin. Why should we?' In 1991 a House of Commons
Education, Science and Arts Committee endorsed the value of 'Sport

in Schools' with special recommendations and in March 1994 the CCPR published a 'Charter for School Sport'.

One area which is never prayed in aid, however, is the only weapon which can be used effectively: the law. This illustrates another level of unawareness of the extent to which the law applies and is available when operated for the benefit of sport, and the society they both serve. Against a background of Parliamentary legislation and that overwhelming judicial approach to physical and sporting education in the United Kingdom, the wider more generally recognisable responsibilities within sporting education also need attention.

RESPONSIBILITIES

(1) Introductory

Arrangements for facilities and premises which blend parents and schools with outside agencies simplifies application of the appropriate law. Parliamentary enactments and the common law and equity applied by the judges do not differentiate between different levels or categories of activities or disciplines. Schoolteachers, club coaches and both amateur and professional players are all subject to the same duties of care to guard against foreseeable risks, breaches of which causing damage, injury or loss, create the tort of negligence. Education authorities, clubs, governing bodies and promoters and entrepreneurs are subject to identical responsibilities for safety of premises and equipment; and all are equal and subject to liability under the criminal law. Different disciplines, recreation facilities and sporting situations must create differing examples. The principles are common to all of them. The illustrations cannot be exhaustive and others will no doubt occur and also apply to whatever results from extending the National Curriculum already referred to at p xlvii of the Introduction.

(2) Supervisory

The supervisory roles of the teacher at school or the coach in sport or any form of physical recreation are identified in law, morality and spirituality. All generations in any civilised society are heirs to their own traditions and act in loco parentis to their successors. The teacher and coach positively assume an authority for which the law and society hold them responsible, legally and morally.

The author recalls enquiring of the wife of a Southern England Football League Club chairman, who had been a distinguished and prominent legal practitioner, whether any of her husband's director colleagues acted as a personnel adviser to young players who sought fame and fortune away from their northern homes. The incredulity with which the question was received suggested to the author this particular board of directors had never considered the point and the corollary may well be that the whole concept of acting in loco parentis as football directors and perhaps even to committee members is as alien to them as *mens sana in corpore sano*.

The law's approach is simple and clear-cut. Teachers, coaches, physical educationists and all who act in loco parentis take on board the essential elements establishing the law relating to liability for civil negligence, ie:

    (a)   a duty of care
    (b)   to guard against foreseeable risks which
    (c)   if resulting in foreseeable damage
    (d)   creates a breach of duty
    (e)   with consequential liability for negligence.

Finally in the well-publicised rugby schoolboy drama of *Van Oppen v Clerk* and the *Bedford Charity Trustees* [1989] 1 All ER 273: affirmed [1989] 3 All ER 389 CA, Boreham J rejected (1) on the evidence a claim for alleged negligent coaching and (2) affirmed by the Court of Appeal, a claim for non-insurance on the basis that there was no higher duty on a school than on a parent to insure. On the evidence, however, a claim based on actionable non-disclosure appears to have been available, as explained in *New Law Journal* 1988 Vol 138 pp 532–533.

The test of in loco parentis varies with different generations and age groups. The changing attitudes to corporal punishment and the claims to chastise and censure are illustrative of this; and it may well be argued that conflicting opinions could exist about the level of care which is both blameworthy and blameless. Within this negligence formula the only guide must be the existing cases until the law is tested with special circumstances and developing disciplines such as hang-gliding or the martial arts, whose activities have yet to be considered in reported cases. Against this background, the most recent relevant and appropriate citations can be summarised in the manner considered in Chapter 5, 'Public protection'. Closer analysis of these and other cases will disclose differing dicta from judges for defining different categories, ie coaches, supervisors, teachers. These must be tailored to any special identifiable situation, subject to any overriding House of Lords or Parliamentary guidelines which may yet emerge. For present purposes, the intention must be to sustain the theme throughout this book: a level of awareness.

1932
Unprecedented striking in a school playground of golf ball which hit eye of fellow pupil inside a school building causing injury.

Decision
No liability
Principle
School and staff exonerated from responsibility which could not have been prevented even by supervision.

Citation
Langham v Governors of Wellingborough School and Fryer (1932) 101 LKJB 513, 147 LT 91: 96 JP 236: 30 LGR 276.

1936
Schoolboy during vaulting horse gymnastic training at school landed in 'a stumble' suffering personal injury.

Decision
Local Authority liable
Principle
Lack of promptitude by games master to prevent stumble when or after vaulting created lack of care causing accident and negligence.

Citation
Gibbs v Barking Corporation (1936) All ER 115.

1938
Fee paying adult, participating in physical training class wearing rubber shoes, slipped on fairly highly polished floor (suitable for dancing but not for physical exercise) which caused personal injury.

Decision
Organising local authority council liable
Principle
(1) Council failed in duty to provide a floor which was reasonably safe in circumstances creating danger beyond usual degree of playing a game; (2) *volenti non fit injuria* defence rejected because of consent to risk of this added danger beyond ordinary hazard lawfully practised.

Citation
Gillmore v London County Council (1938) 4 All ER 331; 55 TLR 95, 159 LT 615.

1939
Unanticipated action by child at swimming bath. Let go suddenly of a springboard to which she had been clinging, thereby disrupting preparation to jump from it by another child who suffered injury.

Decision
No liability
Principle
Action not capable of anticipation, irrespective of adequacy of supervision, for which evidence was equivocal and not definitive.

Citation
Clark v Bethnal Green Corp (1939) 55 TLR 519.

1939
School pupil injured when fielding at cricket, under supervision of dual-role teacher also acting as umpire. Evidence conflict between: (1) Plaintiff (pupil's) – claim of placed at 'silly mid-on' (facing batsman) (2) Defendant's (per the master) of 'square leg' location (at right angles to wicket) and moving close to batsman of own accord.

Decision
Liability proved
Principle
Umpire duties precluded exercise of sufficient supervisory care as master in charge. They conflicted with need to prevent boy to be very considerably less than 10 yards from wicket (as adjudged by court). This was a dangerous situation in the circumstances; and also in judgment of failure 'to exercise the care which the law required from a master in charge of pupils in these circumstances.'

Citation
Barfoot v East Sussex County Cl (unreported: *The Head's Legal Guide*: Para 3–111) [Croner Publications]. *Caught in Court*: 1989 John Scott p 221. NB Scott's industrious researches revealed that the trial judge, Humphreys J (Shrewsbury School XI) awarded damages for the Plaintiff Schoolboy after deciding 'with fear and trembling and with as much courage as I can assume', to disagree with the expert evidence testimony of the famous Sussex and England all-round player, Maurice Tate.

1947
School game of 'touch' played in room with insufficient space and one participant placed hand unwittingly through glass partition causing injury.

Decision
Liability proved.
Principle
Reasonable and prudent father would have contemplated possibility of such an accident.

Citation
Ralph v LCC (1947) 63 TLR 546 CA, 111 JP 548

1968
Horseplay during schoolbreak caused forseeable injury of eye from discarded elastic

Decision
Liability proved
Principle
(1) Reasonable prudent parent principle (above)

Citation
Beaumont v Surrey County Council (1968) 66 LGR 580: 112 SJ 704

rope because of breakdown in usually adequate school supervision.

not applied to headmaster of school with 900 pupils. (2) Duty breached, to take all reasonable and proper steps to prevent injury between pupils, bearing in mind known propensities of boys or girls between ages 11 and 18.

1981
12-year-old pupil with dislocated hip and unfit for physical training of which teacher advised. Wrongful persuasion that permission authorised and disability caused awkward movement resulting in injury.

Decision
Liability proved
Decision
Double failure: (1) to observe awkward movements. (2) to supervise properly within special category as disabled or crippled child.

Citation
Moore v Hampshire County Council (1981) 80 LGR 481 C.

1981
18-year-old gymnast injured when using trampoline facilities in gymnasium during period of supervision at gymnasium club.

Decision
Out of court settlement
Principle
No admission of liability on negligence allegation. Claim formulated for £350,000. Insurance policy ceiling at £250,000. Settlement of claim for £250,000, with denial on negligence liability that supervision inadequate.

Citation
Tracey Moore v Redditch and Bromsgrove Gymnast Club (unreported: but recorded for purpose of emphasising the value of insurance for victim and insured).

1984
15-year-old rugby playing schoolboy injured during school game by high tackle from schoolmaster during instructional period, without any unfair play issue.

Decision
Liability proved
Principle
Teacher momentarily forgot playing with young schoolboys of lesser and smaller physique than himself.

Citation
Affuto Nartoy v Clarke & LLEA (1984) Times, 9 February

	Decision	Citation
1985 Soccer player injured by foul play in club match sued for wrongful assault and negligence in damages claim for broken leg.	Liability proved **Principle** Negligence proved and upheld in Court of Appeal because of duty owed by one competitor to another to play according to the rules was breached on this occasion by violent foul play.	*Condon v Basi* (1985) 2 All ER 453.
1988 Schoolboy injured by rugby tackle but not insured	Negligence not proved and alleged failure to insure rejected **Principle** Evidence of no negligence. No duty to insure equivalent to non-parental duty to insure	*Van Oppen v Clerk to the Bedford Charity Trustees* [1989] 1 AER 273 affirmed [1989] 3 All ER 389 CA.
1991 Schoolboy recovered damages against schoolteacher and governing body for broken neck in swimming bath injury	Liability proved **Principle** Inadequate supervision and guidance	*Gannon v Rotherham MBC and Others* Halsbury's Monthly Review July 1991 91/1717
1993	Negligence proved **Principles** Higher duty of care owed to athletes under disability than to able-bodied participants	*Morrell v Owen and others* Times, 14 December 1993.

In a valuable overview of the coaching and teaching field, under the heading 'Should coaches take care?', John Gardiner surveyed this supervisory scene from the widest possible perspective ((1993) *Sport and the Law Journal*, Nov, p 11; *New Law Journal*, 12 Nov, p 1598). The 1985 case citation is the natural link for the wider responsibilities, both criminal as well as civil, for the consequences of playing misconduct committed by one participant towards another. It was the first time that negligence in addition to civil or criminal assault was alleged in the United Kingdom courts, based upon an Australian precedent (*Rootes v Shelton* [1968] ALR 33). The principle applies to school as well as to adult activities. It is the appropriate stage to move on now to those wider responsibilities for playing participants beyond school and physical education per se, and also to wider public protection generally.

Chapter 5

Public protection

1 INTRODUCTION

When school and club partners in sport graduate as entertainers to attract spectators and spill over into environmental areas, the public interest and its protection become inevitable: this chapter therefore discusses the public protection of spectators and also participants in sport. Many disasters over the last few decades, often caused by both preventable misfortune and acts of God, have illuminated the issue.

Three national sports disasters within 20 years, Ibrox, Glasgow (1971), Bradford (1985) and Hillsborough (1989), were each followed by a judicial inquiry, litigation and legislation. These instances all point to three inevitable conclusions. One is the consistent knee-jerk reaction of horror at all levels of general social, sporting and political activity, too late for protection of the victims from the consequences of negligence by offending services. A second is the no less consistent application of Lord Hailsham's awareness now more than 30 years ago as cited throughout these pages of the absence of any 'coherent body of doctrine, perhaps even a philosophy or government encouragement'. Third is perhaps the most disturbing and unnerving yet hitherto unmentioned element in any of the nine official reports spawned by successive Governments and judicial inquiries since the now historic first-ever Wembley Stadium FA Cup Final of 1923 between Bolton Wanderers and West Ham United; a pattern of potential sports crowd mishaps traceable through the Law Reports can be seen for more than a century and a quarter. How much more has been lost and unreported in the mists of time may now never be known.

On 13 April 1866 the collapsed section of a grandstand at the celebrated Cheltenham National Hunt Festival resulted in what every law student recognises as the starting tape for personal injuries liability in negligence by occupiers of premises: *Francis v Cockerell* [1870] 5 QB 501. Thirty years later in 1896 another grandstand collapsed at Ewood Park, Blackburn, home of the famous Rovers. An incompetent contractor having been employed to repair it, the committee members of the then unincorporated association which constituted the club, were held personally liable in damages (*Brown v Lewis*

[1986] 12 TLR 455). A year later in 1897, Blackburn Rovers Football Club Limited was registered under the then Companies Act.

Five years onwards witnessed yet a third collapsed grandstand, with graver consequences. At Ibrox, Glasgow, disaster struck within ten minutes of the kick-off for the then traditional Scotland versus England soccer international on 5 April 1902. A new stand had been built for the occasion which consisted of wooden planking upon steep uprights. The swaying of the crowd trying to follow an attack by the Scottish forwards caused seven rows of planking, 30 yards wide, to collapse. The 40 feet drop to the ground below killed 26 people and injured 587. Every damages claim was met, *without* reported litigation, and the FA in London followed the Blackburn Rovers precedent to become registered as the Football Association Limited in 1903. Yet no Government Inquiry was created.

That was reserved for another potential disaster, after the First World War twenty years later at the 1923 FA Cup Final. An estimated 200,000 crowd officially recorded as 126,000 overflowed into a stadium equipped for less than 100,000. Miraculously no fatalities and a (relatively) mere 1,000 injured appear to have completed the casualties chronicled in a memorable contemporary essay from Robert Lynd entitled 'The Battle of Footerloo.'

'It would, perhaps, be an exaggeration to say that Wembley Park was turned into a battlefield: but as the stretcher-bearers bore the seeming corpses one after another through the crowd and out of the ground, it looked considerably more like a battlefield than like a football field.'

The outcome was a Government Report in 1924 under a former Home Secretary, Edward Shortt, KC, which contained recommendations ignored for half-a-century until the Safety of Sports Grounds Act 1975, following the second Ibrox Stadium disaster in 1971. The absence of any major sporting crowd tragedy at football grounds where the cluster of current crowd disasters have occurred is a reflection of the sporting social good behaviour between 1919 and 1939 while ground records were established in the inter-war years (as recorded in Appendix 1).

When the Second World War ended in 1945, followed by the Bolton Wanderers fatalities (33) in 1946 and the consequential Government Report in 1947 there began a sequence which ended with Lord Justice Taylor in 1990 beginning his Final Report on the Hillsborough, Sheffield disaster with

'It is a depressing and chastening fact that mine is the ninth official report covering crowd safety and control at football grounds ... why were [so many] recommendations and others not followed? I suggest two main reasons. First, insufficient concern and vigilance for the safety and well-being of spectators. This was compounded by a preoccupation with measures to control hooliganism. Secondly, complacency which led all parties to think that disaster as had not occurred on previous occasions it would not happen this time. But there is no point in holding inquiries or publishing guidance unless the recommendations are followed diligently'.

Legislation and a Green Guide Code for Safety have proliferated alongside the inevitable compensation claims following each national disaster identified already above and in the following pages. Furthermore, concurrent within the national calamities were the spiralling number of accidents at theme parks, leisure centres and general activity holiday centres, of equal concern for victims and their families as those from more publicised occasions.

During 1986, the Consumers Association *Which* magazine, the Sports Council's *Sport and Leisure* bi-monthly journal and the *Guardian* newspaper (3 August 1987, p 28) all advocated an inspectorate system of control: and the British Activity Holiday Association (BAHA), which was formed for cohesive control, was unable to discover which government department would or should be stirred to act. Once more, Lord Hailsham's absence of any 'coherent body of doctrine, perhaps even a philosophy or Government encouragement' became apparent.

2 TOWN AND COUNTRY TIES AND DIFFERENCES

In less dramatic contexts, however, Parliament at different times has been concerned with public protection in differing ways from time immemorial, alongside common law and equitable remedies, especially within a rural sporting perspective. Thus Peter McIntosh's assessment in 1962 of Joseph Strutt's antithesis from 1801 becomes appropriate once more when he contrasted

'rural exercises generally practised'

with

'Pastimes usually exercised in towns and cities or places adjoining them.'

Lord Hailsham's awareness in 1962 of the absence of any 'coherent body of doctrine, perhaps even a philosophy of government encouragement, led to his concept of a 'focal point under a Minister'. That absence means that modern legislation reacts to ad hoc situations without any underlying principles or pattern uniting the disparate sporting recreational and leisure interests. The following modern illustrations emphasise the point.

Date and Source	Purpose/Object	Origins	Sponsor
1991 Football (Offences) Act	Control of disorderly behaviour at football matches	Taylor Report	Home Office
1989 Football Spectators Act	Supervision of local authority functions under Safety of Sports Ground Act 1975	Taylor Report	Home Office
1986 Public Order Act	Public protection from violence	Social and football crowd hooliganism	Home office
1984–1987 Tall Ships Race	Inquiry headed by Richard Stone QC	19 lives lost: 67-year-old barque: *Marques*	Department of Transport
1984 Occupiers Liability Act	Protection of landowners to permit warning notices for recreational visitors but excluding liability	Pearson Commission (Cmnd 7054–1, paras 1546–50) Law Commission Report (Cmnd 6428)	Lord Chancellor Lord Hailsham of St Marylebone
1981 Wildlife and Countryside Act	Protection of environment and natural rural sources	Consolidating legislation	Ministry of Agriculture, Fisheries and Food
1979 Fastnet Yacht Race Report (Mr Justice Forbes)	Inquiry Report and Recommendations	15 lives lost: 24 boats abandoned	Royal Yachting Association and Royal Ocean Racing Club

3 RURAL AND WATER SPORTS

Such modern plurality is entirely consistent with the earliest legislation affecting rural sporting interests recorded by the English legal system's most traditional jurist and historian. Blackstone's eighteenth-century commentaries (Bk IV, Ch 13, p 174) identified gaming laws sanctions 'constituted by a variety of acts of parliament: which are so numerous and so confused, and the crime itself [killing game even upon their own estate] of so questionable a nature, that I shall not detain the reader with many observations thereof.'

Nearer our own time. Sir William Holdsworth's monumental *History of English Law* traced back to Richard II a fragmentation comparable to our own period when he wrote under the head of *Hunting and Game* (Vol 4, p 505):

'The legislation on this subject proceeded on many different principles. Sometimes it proceeded on the principle that assemblies for the purpose of hunting and sporting gave opportunities for riot and disorder; sometimes on the principle that hunting and sporting ought to be the privilege of the landowners, and that other classes ought to employ themselves in a manner more suited to their condition in life; and sometimes on the principle that it resulted in the wanton destruction of game. We can see all these principles underlying Richard II's statute on the subject [13 Rich II St 1 Ch 13] and they appear clearly enough in the various statutes of this period.'

Those different principles have a common denominator which echoes today's legislative examples above and is rooted in property law: the licence principle. It originated with the Royal prerogative recognised by Blackstone from its creation and the parcelling out of Forest Laws after the Norman Conquest, and survives today as an example in Hampshire's New Forest. It has been perpetuated for centuries by Parliament with an ebb and flow of restrictions and authorities for defining, preserving and killing different species of game; and it is structured to provide individual property ownership protection through the laws of civil trespass, criminal damage, poaching and the Public Order Act 1986.

For lawyers, surveyors, agents and other associated professional practitioners, the conveyancing machinery of freeholds, leaseholds, contractual licences, deeds of grant, easements, profits à prendre and incorporeal hereditaments are a staple diet. For lay readers, or the non-property-orientated lawyer, a former editor of one of the leading sporting journals *The Field*, Wilson Stephens, summarised the position succinctly in the *Guinness Guide to Field Sport* (pp 215–216) during 1974 thus:

'The difference between British law on the right to sport, and that which applies over much of the rest of the world, is the application of the principle of separate enjoyment. This means that to own land, to farm the land or exploit it in other ways, and to shoot or catch the game and fish upon it, are three different usages and may possess separate identities. He who owns the land, may, if he does not wish himself to farm it, let it to somebody who does. Similarly, if he does not wish to exercise his right to the sports it provides, he may let them, or sell these rights. Alternatively, he may sell the land and retain the sporting rights; or sell the land to one buyer and the sporting rights to another.

Elsewhere in Europe the right to sport has gone with the ownership of land, in most cases being inseparable from it. A consequence has been that the well-being of game, and inevitably of other wildlife, has varied with the interest of individual landowners in sport. There has been no monetary incentive, as there is in Britain, for a non-interested land-owner to maintain the environment in a condition favourable to game in order to let or sell at an enhanced price to those who are interested. Nor is there the incentive for buyers or lessees to do likewise in order to obtain the best results from what they are paying for ...

Fishing rights are held and traded in exactly the same manner as shooting rights. In English law a river is regarded as land which happens to be covered by water. There is no right of property in the water itself, but the owner of the land over which it flows is entitled to the natural benefits which it brings, and is protected against disturbance of this entitlement by pollution, diversion, or alteration of flow upstream. This lays upon him the responsibility of ensuring that no acts of his, or of his servants, disturb the enjoyment of these benefits by those downstream.'

Protection of those rights exists through a mixture of Parliamentary and common law and equity developments. Within the present limited context of establishing a level of awareness, public protection can most conveniently be seen through the better known sporting interests of hunting, shooting and fishing, and the contrasts and conflicts with watersports.

Hunting

No statute, with one qualification, prohibits or encourages the highly profiled foxhunting (other animals are served statutorily for closed and open seasons or periodic control, eg Badgers Act 1973; Deer Acts 1963, 1980 and 1987; and many varied statutes for salmon and other fishing). Hunts and their members until recently were generally be-lieved to be protected only by their readiness to enforce the civil law of trespass. Now they have the general advantages of the Public Order Act 1986. The one qualification is the rarely used section 1 (1)(a) of the Protection of Animals Act 1911. It creates a statutory exception to the offence to torture, infuriate or terrify a captive animal. This can include foxes, although proof of the offence may be difficult, and the protection here is for animals and animal lovers.

The Public Order Act 1986 was designed for wider social problems than anti-hunt saboteurs. Sections 4 and 5 and also section 39 purport to extend police powers where hitherto they had no power for acting against misconduct on private land. The criminal common law was also invoked during 1986 in original and unusual circumstances after activists had desecrated the grave of the 10th Duke of Beaufort on

Boxing Day 1984, ten months after he had died aged 83. Two offenders were charged and convicted at Bristol Crown Court on two counts of conspiracy at common law for attempting to dig up the Duke's remains. They were each imprisoned cumulatively for three years (*R v Curtin and Anor* (1986) Times, 12 June).

In the previous year the civil common law was operated against the Master of a West Country Hunt for a successful claim in damages and injunctions for hunting too close to land where its hounds were not welcome and it could be inferred that inadequate steps were taken to prevent them (*League Against Cruel Sports v Scott* [1985] 2 All ER 489). Over a century before that judgment it was established that hunt members entering land without permission, orally or by written licence or other authority, committed a trespass (*Paul v Summerhays* [1878] 4 QBD 9). Consistent with these remedies the Peterborough-based Fitzwilliam Hunt obtained an injunction against a hunt saboteur who had blown a trumpet and imitated hunt cries to mislead hounds, taking them out of the control of their owners and thereby causing a trespass to goods (*Fitzwilliam Land Company v Cracknell* (1993) *Peterborough Evening Telegraph* 9 September, 4 November). Subsequently a local authority's ban on hunting on ethical grounds was held to be unlawful in a judicial review as *ultra vires* its statutory powers (*R v Somerset County Council, ex p Ewings* (1994) QBD 9 Feb, [1994] 6442 NLJ 461.

Shooting

By contrast, any sport with built-in lethal products as its raison d'être is regulated by Parliamentary control, separate and apart from property licences to shoot on land not owned by the firearm possessor. The Firearms Acts 1968 and 1982 and statutory Rules specified in the first edition have since then been extended by the Firearms (Amendment) Act 1988 and the Firearms (Amendment) Regulations 1992, made under section 2(2) of the European Communities Act 1972 pursuant to Council Directive No 91/477/EEC. Cumulatively they regulate the control, acquisition and possession of firearms and shotguns generally. (See generally *Archbold* 1992 edition, paragraph 24–1 and 1993 second cumulative edition up to date to 1 April 1993.) Game licences for sporting rights owned or hired or purchased are required under the Game Licences Act 1860, which contains a built-in framework for forfeiture or suspension when the basis for the grant is breached, eg poaching, itself subject to a network of statutory provisions capable of ensnaring the unwary or careless country sportsperson. A responsible gundealer, gunsmith or a specialist publication such as *Gun Law* by Godfrey Sandys-Winsch, *The Law Relating to Firearms* by P T Clarke and J W Ellis or *Fair Game* by Parkes and Thornley should be consulted for any uncertainty.

Fishing

With splendid irony for the present text, Izaak Walton's sporting literary classic *The Compleat Angler* contains the opinion that there is,

> 'No life so happy and pleasant as the life of a well-governed angler, for when the lawyer is swallowed up with business, and the statesman is preventing or contriving plots, then we sit on cowslip banks, hear the birds sing, and possess ourselves in the quietness of silent silver streams.'

Of all sporting participants, none is as well served with legal literature and guidelines as those who throw a fishing line. Parliament has legislated extensively with substantial statutes from the Fisheries Act 1878 to the Salmon and Freshwater Fisheries Act 1975 and the Salmon Act 1986; and the courts have been ready to protect the sport and its participants and thereby the fish with injunctions against pollution, eg *Pride of Derby Angling Association v British Celanese* [1953] 1 All ER 179, which also included orders against Derby Corporation and the British Electricity Authority on the grounds of nuisance (see also *Nicholls v Ely Beet Sugar Factory* [1936] Ch 343).

More recently in a landmark test case decision at Swindon County Court in Wiltshire, £10,000 damages with £2,750 interest and costs were awarded by Judge Dyer for negligence and nuisance caused by a trout farm which was alleged to have let thousands of rainbow trout escape into a prime stretch of the River Kennet near Marlborough in Wiltshire. The complaint by the Savernake Fly Fishing Club against the former owners of the trout farm was that the voracious farm-reared rainbow trout had ruined 40% of the 1990 angling season because they pestered fishermen who were attempting to catch the more wily brown trout, and thereby damaging their sporting interests for which club membership cost £500 a year. The Anglers' Co-operative Association welcomed the decision as a precedent for similar cases in other parts of the country: *Broderick and Brown* (on behalf of the *Savernake Fly Fishing Club v Gale & Ainslie Ltd* (1993) Times, 30 March).

Furthermore, injunction proceedings have succeeded by anglers against unauthorised canoeists (*Rawson v Peters* (1973) EGD 259); and this raises the most significant and crucially important issue for the future of rural sport: How are the conflicting interests to be balanced to satisfy the needs of land and water users? The Sports Council and CCPR published a joint Water Sports Code sub-titled 'Some behaviour recommendations for water recreational users' towards the end of the 1970s; and more recently during the early 1980s the Sports Council with the cooperation of the National

Anglers' Council, the Water Space Amenity Commission and the British Canoe Union has published *Angling and Canoeing Statement of Intent*. Clearly the problem will not go away.

Indeed, without restraint on both sides it can only get worse in a violence-orientated society, notwithstanding Izaak Walton's idyllic tranquillity. Furthermore, it conveniently leads on to another aspect of the consequences of water sport activity: not merely to anglers on the banks, but householders too. This is the problem of noise, a common law private nuisance. It was highlighted by the successful claim in 1981 against the Cotswold Motor Racing Club which resulted in a Court of Appeal reversal of a £15,000 damages award by the trial judge, and replacing it with a modified and complex injunction (*Kennaway v Thompson* [1980] 3 All ER 329). It thereby returns the lawyer and the sporting participants to the general problem of public protection within the tiny space available for fun for 55 million British people. The issue falls into place conveniently under two separate headings, public protection outside sports premises, of which *Kennaway v Thompson* is one startling example, and public protection inside sports grounds and premises, clearly illuminated by the Bradford City tragedy.

4 PUBLIC PROTECTION OUTSIDE SPORTS PREMISES

Here the law is embedded exclusively in judicial precedents applied to the differing facts of differing games. In rural communities space problems create fewer difficulties than urban areas demonstrate. There the need to sustain a balance between public recreational and private proprietary interest has created regular judicial headaches in applying the common law of public and private nuisance. Understandably the cases fluctuate around the most popular ball games of cricket, football, golf and tennis.

Golf first entered the law reports in the early 1920s, cricket in the 1950s, football in the 1960s and cricket again in the 1970s. Watersports emerged too, as these pages show. Three leading cases explain the legal position. They deal with domestic rights in conflict with sporting occupancies for public protection. Miss Bessie Stone, Mrs Miller and Miss Kennaway are all enshrined in perpetuity throughout the law reports and text books as their problems required judicial clarification of a developing law to new situations.

Nuisance and negligence are the areas concerned. None of the ladies obtained what she had claimed: not because of any male chauvinism but because the vagaries of litigation must always depend upon special facts, differing human judicial attitudes, and, in the celebrated summary of the great American judge and jurist, Mr Justice Oliver Wendell Holmes: 'The life of the law is not logic: it is experience' (*The Common Law* (1881) p 1). In brief,

Miss Stone

failed to persuade a trial judge (that cricket balls hit out of a ground to adjoining land can be a remedy in civil law), succeeded in the Court of Appeal but lost her claim in the House of Lords

Mrs Miller

(with her husband) obtained from a trial judge an injunction but lost in the Court of Appeal with a substitution of damages

Miss Kennaway

failed to get a full injunction (for noise comprising a nuisance in law created by a boat and water ski races) but on appeal from a trial judge obtained a restricted injunction in addition to damages

How did this all arise? The answer requires an explanation briefly of the applicable legal principles, the differing facts, and the enigma of judicial variation. For the present context, the difference in law between nuisance and negligence must be recognised.

Legal nuisance involves an interference with the use of enjoyment of land. It can be public, which involves criminal law processes and sanctions; or private, which the sporting examples here illustrate on the initiative of an aggrieved complainant. Negligence, too, can involve criminal elements. Here the context concerns civil liability with three essential elements:

(i)   a duty of care recognised by law;
(ii)   breach of that duty by failure to apply foreseeable standards, and
(iii)   damage from that breach which is not too remote.

Against that legal background a sporting journey from Cheetham Cricket Ground near Manchester across the Pennines to another cricket ground at Linz, County Durham, and then down to Gloucestershire to a water-ski and motor boat course, illuminates the problems.

1947 was a vintage year for English cricket. Compton and Edrich broke all records and postwar crowds hit new peaks. On 9 August Miss Bessie Stone had stepped from her garden gateway on to the pavement of the highway when she was struck on the head by a cricket ball hit out of the adjoining Cheetham Cricket Ground by a visiting player, causing her injury. She sued for damages against representative club members (an accepted procedural practice against an unincorporated club membership which will become apparent in Chapter 14, 'Administrative advice'). Her claim therefore was based correctly on the two known allegations available to her in the law of civil wrongs known as torts:

(i)   negligence

(ii)   private nuisance

At the trial before Mr Justice Oliver, at the then Manchester Assizes, in December 1948, negligence was rejected and nuisance dismissed; in the learned judge's opinion a single isolated act causing direct damage could not properly be brought under the head of nuisance to a highway: but if he was wrong, the damages were provisionally assessed for £105. An appeal to the Court of Appeal confirmed the judge's reasoning and conclusion on negligence, but a reversal by a 2–1 majority on nuisance. The cricketing authorities were understandably concerned at the consequences beyond Cheetham and the Court of Appeal. A successful appeal was argued to the House of Lords by counsel specially instructed – Sir Walter Monckton, not only King Edward VIII's personal adviser at the time of the Abdication crisis, but also a distinguished school and club cricketer, future President of MCC and the Surrey County Cricket Club, and also Mr W A Sime, then captain of Nottinghamshire County Cricket Club and a future Crown Court Recorder. Juristically their Lordships ruled that the evidence of only six hits outside the ground in 28 years meant that the risk of repetition was not sufficiently foreseeable for negligence liability (*Bolton v Stone* [1951]AC850). Lord Oaksey, as Lord Justice Oaksey, the civilised world's Presiding Judge at the Nuremberg Trial of War Criminals, and father of the *Daily* and *Sunday Telegraph*'s John Oaksey, explained:

'the standard of care in the law of negligence is the standard of an ordinary careful man, ... He takes precautions against risks which are reasonably likely to happen.'

Distinguishing the facts from a golfing liability where subsequent interferences were proved (*Castle v St Augustine Links* (1922) 38 TLR 615), Lord Oaksey concluded (1951) AC 863),

'There are many footpaths and highways adjacent to cricket grounds and golf courses on to which cricket and golf balls are occasionally driven, but such risks are habitually treated both by the owners, committees of such cricket and golf courses and by the pedestrians who use the adjacent footpaths and highways as negligible and it is not, in my opinion, actionable negligence to take precaution to avoid such risks.'

More significant than the negligence result itself, however, was the manner in which the nuisance issue was considered by the House of Lords. Lords Porter (at p 860) and Reid (at p 868) considered that Miss Stone's counsel admitted that nuisance fell with the dismissal of negligence, although Lord Reid significantly said.

'I find it unnecessary to deal with the question of nuisance and reserve my opinion to what constitutes nuisance in cases of this character.'

With this specific reservation by the most revered and respected of modern Law Lords, any euphoria for cricket and the general sporting world should be tempered not only with the knowledge that the issue could be re-argued on different facts, but also by a note from one of the most distinguished of modern commentators, and by a usually unrecognised footnote to legal history.

Professor (Sir) Arthur Goodhart, who edited the *Law Quarterly Review* for 50 years, was described by Lord Denning in the centenary issue (1984) at page 514 as 'Beyond doubt the greatest jurist of our time.' In a contemporary analysis over his familiar initials, 'ALG' in Volume 5 (1951) at pages 460–464 under the title 'Is it cricket?', he began

'one cannot help feeling sympathy for Miss Stone,'

and ended,

'As the present case has given rise to some misunderstanding in the popular press it is to be hoped that it will be made clear to those responsible for cricket clubs, whether these are situated in a town or in the country, that they are under a duty to take reasonable care not to injure those persons who may be passing outside their ground and that the degree of care must depend on the facts of each particular case. It is, as we said at the beginning of this note unfortunate for Miss Stone that the facts in her case were on the borderline, and that it was necessary for three separate courts to consider them.'

Monckton's biography from the pen of F E Smith's son, the second Lord Birkenhead: *Walter Monckton, The Life of Viscount Monckton Brenchley* (1969), at page 267, commented on the position concerning nuisance issue with a reference from Miss Stone's plaintiff counsel, the late Mr H I Nelson KC.

'The outcome brought immense relief to all concerned with cricket clubs, but not to Mr Nelson who had represented the plaintiff with such conviction of the justice of her case. Although Lord Porter said that it had been conceded on behalf of the plaintiff that if the claim in negligence failed the claim in nuisance must also fail, Nelson had made no such concession, as Walter Monckton was afterwards to confirm.

It must seem strange (said Nelson) that to shoot with a gun, or a bow and arrow, or even, as has been held in one case, to permit a piece of beef fat to fly out of a butcher's doorway in the course of chopping meat, may render the perpetrator liable in nuisance to any user of the highway injured thereby, whilst a cricketer may deliberately hit cricket balls into the highway with impunity. Possibly at some future date a cricket ball so hit may cause a major disaster, and the whole question of liability be reopened. The cricket ball case certainly made the headlines. To associate the sacred game of cricket with nuisance was regarded by many as something akin to blasphemy'

(Mr H I Nelson to Lord Birkenhead).

Thirty years after Miss Bessie Stone's misfortune, cricket balls again hit the law reports as well as a complainant. The victims on this occasion were a local neighbourhood and Mr and Mrs Miller whose property adjoined the long established Linz Cricket Ground in County Durham. Balls hit out of the ground caused consternation and Mr Justice Reeve at Durham granted them an injunction against the club as well as modest damages. On appeal to the Court of Appeal the injunction was discharged to be replaced by an agreed damages award of £400. Yet again, it would be unwise for any cricket or sporting buffs to be overjoyed with the result. The appeal judges were not united in their approach, the academic lawyers criticised it, and a later Court of Appeal dealing with similar legal issues concerning different facts and a different sport emphatically refused to follow it (*Miller v Jackson* [1977] 3 All 338, not followed by *Kennaway v Thompson* [1980] 3 All ER 329).

The former Lord Chief Justice, Lord Lane, as Lord Justice Lane, was ready to uphold the injunction after delaying it to give the club time to accommodate the circumstances, and Lord Justice Cumming-Bruce, while not going that far in the remedy, agreed that negligence had been proved because there was a foreseeable risk (as distinct from the failure to establish this point against the Cheetham Club of injury to adjoining occupiers). Hence, the £400 agreed damages for negligence. Lord Denning, however, in a judgment which he has extracted without critical comment at the end of his publication *Landmarks in the Law* (1984) rejected both negligence and nuisance and would have dismissed the claim for damages. In particular did he rely upon the fact that plaintiffs were authors of their own misfortune in coming to the nuisance.

Three years later a different Court of Appeal was required to consider a damages award by Mr Justice Mais to a householder who complained about the noise from power boats and water-ski activities adjoining her property near Fairford in Gloucestershire. She, too, came to the nuisance, but the court held that the degree of noise overrode the public interest in the club's undoubtedly important sporting activities of an international nature. The injunction was limited in scope, and *Miller v Jackson* was specifically rejected as a binding precedent.

The most significant thread which binds both judgments is Lord Denning's built-in warning to all sporting organisations adjoining land potentially ripe for development. He said:

'I am surprised that the developers of the housing estate were allowed to build the houses so close to the cricket ground.... The planning authorities ought not to have allowed it. The houses ought to be so sited as not to interfere with the cricket. But the houses have been built and we have to reckon with the consequences.'

Similar considerations emerged in *Lacey v Parker and Boyle (for Jordans CC)* already discussed at page 59.

Lord Denning's realistic approach to the key practical sporting legal focus begs the question as to whether or not anyone ever objects to that particular form of planning application. Nevertheless, he identified what must become a more and more urgent problem in a tightly packed urban community encouraged by the Sports Council campaign, 'Sport for all'.

The cases which follow are merely illustrations and many others are to be found in the standard textbooks:

1922
Golf ball played from 13th tee parallel with Sandwich Road, Kent, much frequented by motor cars and taxi cabs, into which road golf ball was hit. Windscreen of passing taxi cab hit by ball and splintered glass, causing loss of driver's eye (*Castle v St Augustine's Links Ltd* (1922) 38 TLR 615)

Decision
Golf Club and player jointly liable for £450 damages and costs.
Principle
Tee and hole were public nuisance from the conditions and in the place where they were situated. No precedent for different facts: but slicing of ball into roadway not only a public danger but was the probable consequence from time to time of people driving from the tee.

1949
Stamford Bridge, Chelsea Supporters overflow into neighbouring garden properties after exclusion from Moscow Dynamo match in 1945 (*Munday v Metropolitan Police Receiver* [1949] 1 All ER 337)

Decision
Compensation against Receiver, Metropolitan Police.
Principle
Award under Riot Damages Act 1886 (still in force). Elements of riot proved under applicable law as at 1945–1949.

1950
Noise from Speedway track surrounding football ground disturbed occupiers of residential properties surrounding stadium (*Attorney General v Hastings Corporation* (1950) 94 Sol Jo 225)

Decision
Injunction against speedway noise obtained.
Principle
Nuisance to private interests overrode public interest in speedway competition.

1951
Cricket ball hit from Cheetham CC, Manchester to roadway on rare occasions. (*Bolton v Stone* [1951] AC 850)

Decision
No liability.
Principle
No negligence or nuisance. Remote risk of injury not reasonably to be anticipated.

1951
Widow of deceased motor car race marshall sued organisers of race in Jersey and executors of the crashed car driver who also died (*O'Dowd v Frazer-Nash* [1951] WLR 173)

Decision
No liability.
Principle
Organisers had taken all reasonable precautions. No negligence by driver for brake failure.

1961
Footballs kicked out of field by young children (from green used frequently for recreational purposes) on to adjoining roadway. Motorcyclist thereby caused to swerve fatally (*Hilder v Associated Portland Cement Manufacturers* [1961] 1 WLR 1434)

Decision
Field owners liable for negligence.
Principle
Failure to take reasonable care from reasonably anticipated danger to road users.

1968
Pedestrian walking along narrow public lane injured on head by golf ball (*Lamond v Glasgow Corporation* (1968) SLT 291)

Decision
Liability established for negligence.
Principle
Although no previous history of any accident, 6,000 shots a year played over fence should have created forecast of foreseeable happening.

1977
Cricket balls hit out of 70-year-old cricket club ground into adjoining gardens prevented occupants who had recently purchased house from using garden in summer (*Miller v Jackson* [1977] 1 QB 966)

Decision
Injunction discharged on appeal by Club, but £400 agreed damages for nuisance.
Principle
On appeal Club guilty of nuisance and negligence; but Appeal Court's discretion discharged injunction because public loss of cricket prevails over hardship from individual non-use of garden (see also pp 58–59 above for building development consent creating problem under Town and Country Planning laws).

1981
Power-boat racing noise upset neighbour who built a house adjoining watersports lake usage (*Kennaway v Thompson* [1980] 3 All ER 329)

Decision
Damages award by trial judge of £15,000 discharged on appeal by householder.
Principle
Courts do not approve the concept of wrongdoers purchasing potential to continue by merely paying for the injury. Injunction in modified but none the less effective terms to modify noise.

1994
Lacey v Parker & Boyle (for Jordans CC) (1994) 144 NLJ 785

Decision
Injunction refused.
Principle
Plaintiff came to the nuisance to which he objected when cricket balls damaged adjoining property.

5 PUBLIC PROTECTION INSIDE SPORTS GROUNDS AND PREMISES

A pattern of precedents can be seen which show how victims of accidents at sporting or recreational occasions have claimed for injuries, some successfully, others not so successfully. The codification under the Occupiers' Liability Acts 1957–1989 to create the common duty of care avoided thereafter the need to consider any implied term in a contract of entry to premises. This had been one of the legal arguments upon which the injured victim in the first seriously recorded report of a claim for damages due to defective sporting premises was able to recover damages, *Francis v Cockerell* (1870) 5 QB 501. On that occasion a grandstand collapsed at Cheltenham Races and the promoter was held liable for the default by the contractor of which the promoter was innocent. The other legal argument was the currently applicable basis for a claim of negligence.

This is in an area where the well-known legal concept of *volenti non fit injuria* comes into operation. It cannot apply to unlawful violent foul play on the field. It also does not apply to the ordinary hazards of attending sporting occasions. For unusual experiences which could have been foreseen a breach, then the 'common duty of care' can override the *volenti* position.

The reported cases which explain how the law operates in this area of public protection within the grounds and premises disclose two particular trends which run throughout this text. One is the crucial question of fact which is the first base to all live legal issues, both litigious and non-litigious. The other is the appellate structure which enables findings of fact to be disturbed on appeal. Three important cases illustrate features in each of the two categories under consideration. For the first, of protection within, they are as follows:

(1)   *Whitby v C J Brock* (1886) 4 TLR 241

(2)   *Hall v Brooklands Auto-Racing Club* [1933] 1 KB 205

(3)   *Wooldridge v Sumner* [1963] 2 QB 43

The first, *Whitby v Brock*, may be said to be on the fringe of sport with its location and subject-matter: the old Crystal Palace (before the fire in 1936), and bona fide fireworks (before being used in sporting metaphors). An injured visitor successfully obtained a damages award for injury by a firework on a jury's verdict. The judge, however, gave judgment for the defendants, and the plaintiff appealed successfully. During the course of the appeal hearing, the Master of the Rolls, Lord Esher (at page 242) observed.

> 'Surely there was negligence in letting off fireworks in such a way as to strike the Plaintiff.'

Counsel's response summarised the *volenti* principle:

> 'At a cricket match a spectator struck by a ball in the course of a game has no right of action, as he takes the risk on himself when he goes to a match.'

Over fifty years later in *Hall v Brooklands*, as we shall see below, the Court of Appeal extended this more elaborately.

In *Whitby v Brock*, however, the Court of Appeal unanimously decided that the jury's verdict was justifiable on the evidence and should be restored. Yet fifty years later in *Hall v Brooklands* the converse occurred which caused critical comments contemporaneously to be made of the ruling, and makes it a valuable source for citation of general principle but as a verdict, one which must be regarded as having been decided on its own special facts.

At the famous Brooklands race track near Weybridge in Surrey, a car hurtled over a crowd barrier and hit a spectator who claimed compensation. A jury, assisted by specialised engineering evidence, found for the plaintiff.

A strong Court of Appeal, Scrutton, Greer and Slessor, LJJ, read the evidence and its inferences differently and reversed the jury's finding (the converse to what happened in *Whitby*'s case). The points which are more significant for the professional and lay reader than the actual conclusion on the particular facts are the principles applicable to this important area of spectator sport which have stood the test of time and specify when the *volenti* principle does and does not apply to spectators at sporting events. When they were applied thirty years later in the case concerning the White City Horse Show, *Wooldridge v Sumner*, (supra) already considered in Chapter 3, 'Under starter's orders', above pp 73–74, the Court of Appeal decided that the experienced trial judge had drawn the wrong inferences of fact from the evidence. Once again it reversed a finding on this occasion to the disadvantage of the plaintiff, in whose favour the trial judge had awarded damages. It decided that an error of judgment rather than negligence caused the accident to a photographer inside the competition area when he was hit by a competitor's horse. The claim was against the rider and the show organisers, who were initially exonerated. Sellers LJ in the context of this claim against a competitor explained succinctly at page 56 the general proposition concerning liability to spectators by participants with words which are equally applicable to promoters operating the now statutory 'common duty of care':

> '... provided the competition or game is being performed within the rules and requirements of the sport by a person of adequate skill and competence the spectator does not expect his safety to be regarded by the participant.'

If these words are adapted to promoters as well, then the more detailed and elaborate explanation below from the earlier Court of Appeal judgment in *Hall v Brooklands* can be recognised more readily. Sellers LJ would have been equally accurate and consistent if he had been required to adjudicate, for example, after the Bradford City fire disaster and had said:

'... provided the competition or game is being performed within the rules and requirements of the sport [or particular organising activity] by a person [or organisation] of adequate skill and competence the spectator does not expect his safety to be regarded by the participant [or organiser, save in 1986 by the Bradford City legal requirements].'

Against those summaries of the cases the principles laid down in *Hall v Brooklands* and their applicability to a sequence of cases summarised in tabulated form can be read as a condensed understanding of this general area today, always to be qualified by the Bradford experience.

Scrutton LJ explained the position thus

'The question of the liability of the Brooklands Company raises questions which are of general application to any cases where landowners admit for payment to their land persons who desire to witness sports or competitions carried on thereon, if these sports may involve risk of danger to persons witnessing them. A spectator at Lord's or the Oval runs the risk of being hit by a cricket ball, or coming into collision with a fielder running hard to stop a ball from going over the boundary, and himself tumbling over the boundary in doing so. Spectators at football or hockey or polo matches run similar risks both from the ball and from collisions with players or polo ponies. Spectators who pay for admission to golf courses to witness important matches, though they keep beyond the boundaries required by the stewards, run the risk of the players slicing or pulling balls which may hit them with considerable velocity and damage. Those who pay for admission or seats in stands at a flying meeting run a risk of the performing aeroplanes falling on their heads. What is the liability of the person taking payment for permission to view these various sports?'

Here the liability of the person taking payment was the sole issue on appeal. In a later passage Lord Justice Scrutton in effect answers his own question after extracting the principle involved from earlier precedents, as

'... a promise to use reasonable care to ensure safety. What is reasonable care would depend on the perils which might be reasonably expected to occur, and the extent to which the ordinary spectator might be expected to appreciate and take the risk of such perils. Illustrations are the risk of being hit by a cricket ball at Lord's or the Oval, where any ordinary spectator in my view expects and takes the risk of a ball being hit with considerable force amongst the spectators and does not expect any structure which will prevent any ball from reaching the spectators. An even more common case is one which may be seen all over the country every Saturday afternoon, spectators admitted for payment to a field to witness a football or hockey match, and standing along a line near the touchline. No one expects the persons receiving payment to erect such structures or nets that no spectator can be hit by a ball kicked or hit violently [ie in those far off 1930s the learned judge had in mind "violently" within the playing laws of the game, eg of the cannon ball shooting epitomised by Ted Drake, or Eric Houghton or hitting of the Jim Smith/Arthur Wellard style; not today's ill tempered, dissenting, lawless, physical mobile body contact violence] from the field of play towards the spectators. The field is safe to stand on, and the spectators take the risk of the game.'

Lord Justice Greer, in words which also are still applicable, gave another approach to the same test with examples which are equally of value, referring to spectators and the promoter and/or occupier of premises.

'... both parties must have intended that the person paying for his licence to see a cricket match, or a race, takes upon himself the risk of unlikely and improbable accidents, provided that there has not been on the part of the occupier a failure to take usual precautions. I do not think it can be said that the contents of the contract made with every person who takes a ticket is different. I think it must be the same, and it must be judged by what any reasonable member of the public must have intended should be the term of the contract. The person concerned is sometimes described as "the man in the street", or "the man in the Clapham omnibus", or, as I recently read in an American author, "the man who takes the magazines home, and in the evening pushes the lawn mower in his short sleeves". Such a man taking a ticket to see a cricket match at Lord's would know quite well that he was not going to be encased in a steel frame which would protect him from the one in a million chance of a cricket ball dropping on his head. In the same way, the same man taking a ticket to see the Derby would know quite well that there would be no provision to prevent a horse which got out of hand from getting amongst the spectators, and would quite understand that he was himself bearing the risk of any such possible but improbable accident happening to himself.'

A representative pattern of cases for over a century, including those decided before the codification by the Occupiers' Liability Acts to create the 'common duty of care' illustrates the difficulties in establishing liability for injuries where no exceptional dangers or hazards were established.

1870
Collapsed Grandstand at
Cheltenham Races (*Francis v
Cockerell* [1820] 5 QB 501)

Decision
Judgment for spectator.
Principle
Negligently constructed stand for
which promoter vicariously liable.

1886
Firework injury at (old) Crystal
Palace (*Whitby v CJ Brock* (1886)
4 TLR 241)

Decision
Judgment for visitor.
Principle
Negligence proved.

1896
Collapsed grandstand at
Blackburn Rovers (*Brown v Lewis*
(1896) 12 TLR 455)

Decision
Judgment for spectator.
Principle
Negligent construction. Club
committee members made personally
liable.

1932
Polo player on pony ran through
a hedge at Ranelagh injuring a
spectator (*Piddington v Hastings*
(1932) Times, 12 March p 4)

Decision
Judgment for owners of premises.
Principle
No failure by premises owners to use
reasonable care.

1932
Motor race track. Contact of
wheels at 100 mph between two
Talbot racing cars caused one
apparently to leave the track and
go over rails at side of track (*Hall
v Brooklands Auto-Racing Club*
[1933] 1 KB 205)

Decision
Judgment for owners of premises
and competitors.
Principle
No evidence per Court of Appeal
that owners or competitors had
failed to take reasonable care.

1949
Ice hockey players stepped out of
or broke off from hockey game to
fight, injuring spectator with stick
(*Payne and Payne v Maple Leaf*
(1949) 1 DLR 369 (Canada))

Decision
Players liable.
Principle
No consent to breach of rules.

1951
Ice hockey puck hit six-year-old
rink-side spectator (*Murray v
Harringay Arena* [1951] 2 KB 529

Decision
Judgment for owners.
Principle
No lack of safety.

1962
Photographer at horse show
injured by winning horse
(*Wooldridge v Sumner* [1963] 2 QB
43)

Decision
Judgment for organisers and
competitor.
Principle
No lack of safety.

1971
Spectators injured at motor-cycle scramble meeting *Wilkes v Cheltenham Home Guard Motor Cycle and Light Car Club* [1971] 3 All ER 369, CA

Decision
No liability.
Principle
Almost inexplicable accident. Competitors and organisers exonerated from negligence. Competitor entitled to strain to win if not foolhardy.

1974
Spectators at 1971 Ibrox disaster (*Dougan v Rangers Football Club* (1974) Daily Telegraph, 24 October p 19)

Decision
Judgment for representatives of deceased victims. Glasgow Rangers liable.
Principle
Failed to exercise sufficient care to spectators in egress and handrails prior to 1975 Act.

1976
Discus hurled from practice net on athletics ground ricocheted from guy-rope and hit spectator standing well behind the net (*Wilkins v Smith* (1976) 73 LS Gaz 938)

Decision
Judgment for owners.
Principle
Duty fulfilled by keeping spectators out of the area of foreseeable deflection.

1987
Bradford City Fire disaster (see below)

Decision
Judgment for victims.
Principle
Negligence by Club and local Fire Authority.

1987
Sheffield United Special Police Services (*Harris v Sheffield United Football Club Limited* [1987] 2 All ER 838)

Decision
£51,699.54 liability to club to South Yorkshire Police Authority.
Principle
Special police services for soccer crowd problems chargeable for beyond normal public duty to maintain law and order.

1991
Cunningham v Reading FC Ltd (1991) Times, 20 March

Decision
Judgment for injured Police Officers from hooligans on Football Club premises.
Principle
Crowd law negligence and Occupiers Act 1957, s 2 (1), (2) established because of prior knowledge of club about a violent element among particular visiting supporters

1991
Alcock v Chief Constable of South Yorkshire Police [1991] 4 All ER 907.

Decision
Judgment for Defendant against Hillsborough claimants.
Principle
Only those present in stadium and not those watching on television qualified to claim disaster damages.

1993
Cook, Cochrane, Hampson v Doncaster Borough Council (1993) *Sporting Life* 16 July

Decision
Judgment for jockeys and racehorse owner for injuries resulting from open hole or underlying void in racetrack on occasion of 1989 St Leger autumn meeting.
Principle
Defendant corporation controlling owners of the racetrack surface liable for unsatisfactory conditions creating negligence liability.

These judicial pronouncements emphasise the vital and crucial difference between consenting to the normal risks of sporting events, and where no such consent occurs or can be inferred.

Furthermore, in *Cunningham v Reading FC Ltd*, Drake J (1991) Times, 20 March adjudicated that the exoneration by a one-day FA Commission of Inquiry of any culpability by the Defendant Club was irrelevant and of no value to his own judicial investigation into liability under common law negligence and the Occupiers Liability Act, for which the issues and evidence were entirely different. Substantial damages of £250,000 were awarded to five police officers who had been injured during an Association football match at Reading Football Clubs' ground when supporters of the visiting team rioted using concrete broken off from the terraces as weapons.

The position concerning public protection within grounds and premises can be summed up as follows. The spectator has no protection against a promoter who regulates his affairs safely or the player who performs within the rules of a particular game. On the other hand, the promoter or organiser who arranges negligently or the player who performs recklessly is at risk for a claim in negligence. Where the protection of the spectator outside sporting premises is concerned, the position here is covered by nuisance as well as negligence. Nuisance involves acts which affect adversely the public at large and negligence a duty of care to one's neighbours which is breached with consequential and foreseeable damage.

Negligence was the basis on which Sir Joseph Cantley brought his wealth of experience as Chairman of the Summerlands Isle of Man fire disaster Inquiry and the High Court trial judge in the dispute between England's former football manager Don Revie and the Football Association when he adjudicated in favour of the victims during test cases following the Bradford City fire disaster. He concluded that the club was two-thirds to blame for failing in its duty of care to spectators; and the local West Yorkshire Metropolitan Borough Council as the local fire authority had failed in its duty under the Fire Act 1971, and was one-third to blame (*Fletcher & Fletcher: Britton v (1) Bradford City Association Football Club (2) Health and Safety Executive, (3) West Yorkshire Metropolitan Council*) (Leeds Crown Court: 23 February 1987: Times, Daily Telegraph, 24 February 1987).

The unprecedented Parliamentary action upon urban and national sporting issues which followed so swiftly after the Bradford disaster ran concurrently with the urgent progress of the litigation. This emphasises the sharp contrast with the pattern of legislation for rural sports from their Norman Conquest origins in the Forest Laws attribution to a royal prerogative. Indeed, Stephen J's authoritative *History of the Criminal Law of England* claimed in 1883

'Between 1389 and 1832, or 443 years, about twenty acts were passed relating to game; and these collectively constituted the game laws when the present statute, 1 & 2 Will 4, c 32, which replaced all but one of them, was passed into law.'

Until 1975, Parliament had never entered *directly* on to the *public* sporting scene. It was that scene which caused Lord Hailsham to explain during 1962

'recreation generally presented a complexity of problems out of which modern Government was not free to opt.'

It had opted out after its own crowd safety reports in 1924 and 1946 following the Wembley Stadium and Bolton Wanderers eruptions respectively. Spurred by the late J L Manning's justifiable accusation of an unfilled gap in the public interest two years before the 66 fatalities at Ibrox, Glasgow, there was thereafter no alternative to further action. Lord Wheatley has described in his memoirs *One Man's Judgment* (p 177) how he was invited to report on the events and conclusions from them (not dissimilar from the post-Wembley and Bolton reports) which led directly to the Safety of Sports Grounds Act 1975 and the Green Guide equivalent to the Highway Code for crowd safety. These in turn proved inadequate as Bradford demonstrated, on the same day, when a 14-year-old schoolboy died during an imbroglio amounting to a riot between the notorious visiting Leeds United crowds and home team supporters at Birmingham City's ground. The Prime Minister, Mrs Thatcher, responded to the national sense of urgency. Mr Justice Popplewell, a former

Cambridge University cricket blue and noted games player and former practitioner in Queen's Bench personal injury cases, was commissioned to report. Within a year he had produced an Interim (Cmnd 9585) and a Final Report (Cmnd 9710), and Parliament subsequently enacted three new laws:

Sporting Events (Control of Alcohol etc) Act 1986

Public Order Act 1986

Fire Safety and Safety of Places of Sport Act 1987

and responded to Mr Justice Popplewell's recommendation for a new Green Guide.

BRADFORD, HILLSBOROUGH AND BEYOND

The Interim and Final Reports of Mr Justice Popplewell's Committee of Inquiry into Crowd Safety and Control at Sports Grounds (Cmnds 9585 and 9710) were based on evidence from over 200 oral, written and inspection sources. They contain all the factual and legal elements which are essential for understanding what is required for the belief expressed in the Introduction to the Final Report (para 13, page 2)

> 'that the paramount need is to protect the public by improving safety standards, and thereby restoring confidence among those who attend sporting events. This means that effective steps should be taken quickly. In this belief I commend my findings and recommendations for your consideration.'

The date of that Introduction is November 1985. Nearly a year later in November 1986 the litigation (*Fletcher & Britton v Bradford City Association Football Club & Others* (supra)) which followed from the facts presented in the two Reports, as two test cases to establish liability, emphasised and confirmed the key recommendation in paragraph 3.52 at page 23 that

> 'one authority must be given the responsibility for securing structural safety at undesignated sports grounds and stadia.'

During the course of counsel's opening speech for the plaintiff at Leeds Crown Court a similar 'Departmental interest clash or overlap' to that described in the House of Commons Environment Committee's complaint concerning governmental confusion over dual use of school playing fields emerged.

The four statutes concerning 'structural safety at undesignated sports grounds and stadia' cited below and in force at Bradford were enacted at different times over a span of fourteen years in isolation from each other. The Home Office was the Whitehall department concerned with the Fire Precautions Act 1971, the Safety of Sports Grounds Act 1975 and the Building Act 1984, delegating operation of all statutes to local authorities. The Department of Employment was concerned with the Health and Safety at Work Etc Act 1974, with its implementation delegated to HM Factories Inspectorate. Current Regulations in 1994 made under the Act in 1992, implementing an EC Directive (EEC 69/391) in the UK relate inter alia to risk assessment and protective measures.

The relevant detailed provisions *at the time of the Bradford City disaster*, summarised here for convenience in comprehensible form, functioned in the following way:

Fire Precautions Act 1971 s 10	Discretion to complain to a magistrates' court if premises subject to the Act cause the appropriate 'Fire Authority (to be) satisfied that the risk to persons in the case of fire' is so serious that prohibition or restriction ought to be imposed until remedied.
Safety of Sports Grounds Act 1975 s 10	Identical discretion to complain to magistrates' court where 'the risk to spectators at a sports ground is so great' that, similarly, prohibition or restriction ought to be imposed until remedied.
Health and Safety at Work Etc Act 1974 ss 3, 18, 21.	Obligation on employers and self-employed persons to ensure that 'persons not in their employment are not ... exposed to risks to their health and safety' with enforcement powers available to HM Factories Inspectorate.
Building Act 1984 s 77	Discretion to complain to magistrates' court in respect of overloaded building (eg the collapsed Ibrox grandstand at the time of the 1971 disaster).

As Mr Justice Popplewell's Final Report explained in Paragraph 3.47 at page 23,

'It appears that there are three authorities who have the power to deal with breaches of structural safety at undesignated sports grounds [*ie overwhelming majority of those outside the publicised professional and leading amateur stadia which are subject to special designated Government orders*]: the Health and Safety Executive (under section 3 of the Health and Safety at Work Etc Act 1974); a county council (under section 10 of the Safety of Sports Grounds Act 1975); and a district council under section 77 of the Building Act 1984.'

The Building Act 1984 did not arise during the Bradford City litigation, but the overlap of jurisdictions from the other three enactments caused Counsel in opening the trial for the representative plaintiffs to observe

'The general state of decay ought to have placed any regulatory authority on its guard.'

The claim against the club briefly was that it ignored notices of risk from those regulatory authorities: and against them was alleged lack of vigilance. The functional and operation difficulties in action or by concern in pursuing their knowledge of risk on an enforced avoidance of those 'regulatory authorities' were graphically expressed in the subsequent paragraphs of that Final Report, Paras 3.48–3.50 (inclusive at page 23) leading to the Recommendation for an integrated control.

'**3.48** It is also clear that while these authorities have the power to enforce provisions of their respective Acts, they have no duty to inspect the premises to ascertain whether there have been any breaches. This difficulty was highlighted by the events at Bradford referred to in my Interim Report [NB it also emerged during the judgment of Sir Joseph Cantley sitting as Deputy High Court judge on the Bradford City litigation].

3.49 It is in my view essential that one authority, and only one authority, should have the responsibility for the structural safety of undesignated sports grounds and stadia [ie those outside the limited Orders by statutory instrument made for the leading Football League and other nationally known stadia].

If not, there will not only be a duplication of efforts and waste of resources, but also a risk that no one will in fact inspect these grounds and stadia.

3.50 The necessary inspection must depend on the perception of risk, particularly having regard to other buildings within the jurisdiction of the particular authority. But a duty to inspect and ensure compliance with reasonable standards of safety is necessary.'

The absence of such a specific statutory duty did not preclude the claim for negligence against the three defendants in the special circumstances leading to the Bradford City fire disaster. The initial claim against the club for lack of reasonable care was founded on general common law negligence principles incorporated in the fifth of the seven statutes identified at the outset of this chapter, ie the Occupiers' Liability Acts 1959–1984, with additional claims based on failure to observe the Green Guide. Of that document the Interim Popplewell Report recorded in Paragraph 2.28 at page 10,

'Had the Green Guide been complied with this tragedy would not have occurred.'

In accordance with accepted litigation procedures, the Club brought within the action as additional parties:

(1)   the West Yorkshire Metropolitan Council and

(2)   the Health and Safety Executive

for breaches of their respective operations under their respective applicable enactments. They in turn alleged failure by the Club to respond to notices which it had received from regulatory authorities so that within this circuity the claim on behalf of and by innocent victims of the disaster revolved around what will be the logical corollary to both Popplewell Reports. They found the facts and made recommendations. The judge, Sir Joseph Cantley, was concerned with liability and blame.

Further developments in addition to the Bradford City litigation have occurred since the Final Popplewell Report published in early 1986 and the Final Taylor Report in 1990.

(1)   Two new revised Guides to Safety at Sports Grounds have been published by the Home Office and Scottish Office resulting from recommendations in the Interim as well as the Final Popplewell and Taylor Reports. The current edition in 1990 claims to provide

> 'guidance to ground management, local authorities and technical specialists such as engineers in order to assist them to assess how many spectators can be safely accommodated within a sports ground used for a sporting event.'

Like its precedent its contents comprise in effect a good house-keeping guide to sports ground safety, based upon sound building, construction and engineering principles. Ironically, and sadly, its principles are consistent with the evidence given to and the recommendations made by the Wembley Stadium Committee Report in 1924 (Cmnd 2088). Thus Paragraph 40 of more than sixty years antiquity stated

> 'We have been somewhat surprised to find that in many cases little or no precaution is taken against the risk of fire in stands. We do not suppose that either the risk or the consequences of fire would be so serious in an open stand as in a closed building, but we consider it most important that adequate arrangements should be made to deal with any outbreak which might occur.'

Chapter 13 of the new Guide between paragraphs 206–248 spells out the details for prevention. Alleged breaches of the old

Guide formed a substantial section of the claim for negligence against the Bradford City Club.

(2) The Sporting Events (Control of Alcohol etc) Act 1985 received the Royal Assent on the day after publication of the Interim Popplewell Report in July 1985. Its implementation has given extended power of closure and search, in addition creating offences in connection with alcohol on coaches and trains – and it will be further considered in Chapter 12, 'Administrative advice' (at p 325). It was passed to meet the social problems of soccer hooliganism, in the same climate which created the Public Order Act 1936 in response to Mosley's marches in London's East End before the Second World War. That enactment, and in particular section 5, has been substantially repealed and extended by the Public Order Act 1986. The Public Order Act 1986 gives discretionary (not mandatory) powers to the Courts to ban offenders from attending sporting matches.

(3) The current legislation is now an additional weapon in the legal armoury in the war against football hooliganism. It also has built in to it powers of extension by the Home Office, if, as already has been evidenced to the world at large on television, as well as to sporting observers, the danger signals from potential crowd explosions at boxing, cricket, and racehorse meetings are not defused sufficiently by longer-standing statutory powers or adverse consequences. Existing examples illustrate the point from the association football world. One from the Heysel Stadium experience in May 1985; the other from the riots at the Luton Town versus Millwall FA Cup tie a few weeks earlier, and a third from Europe generally.

(a) Heysel Stadium Extradition proceedings in Belgium were instituted against football followers from England on the initiative of Belgian authorities, after a three-tiered extradition ladder in London, from Chief Stipendiary Magistrate, Divisional Court to the House of Lords. A Belgian Parliamentary Commission of Equity cited in the Final Popplewell Report emphasised criticism of UEFA and Belgian footballing and other footballing authorities, against whom proceedings were initiated;

(b) Britain's former Minister with responsibilities for Sport, Mr (now Sir) Neil MacFarlane, criticised the FA in London for a lenient sentencing policy on the clubs associated with the violence at the Luton Town versus Millwall Cup Tie in early 1985 before the Bradford, Birmingham and Brussels disasters a few weeks later;

(c) *European Convention on spectator violence and misbehaviour at sports events and in particular at football matches* was cited in the Final Popplewell Report with ten key points geared to a coordinated teamwork structure with the comment in paragraph 1.47 (page 9):

> 'This is a blue-print for European football, which has lessons for our domestic game.'

All the circumstances emphasise that sporting authorities are in a position to regulate their affairs. Three examples from within the domestic English game, at Bristol, Brighton and Derby, prove this (see pages 141–145 below).

(4)   The Fire Safety and Safety of Places of Sport Act 1987 was among many statutes enacted before the General Election in June 1987. By a Commencement Order (SI 1987 No 1762) its principal provisions did not come into force until 1 January 1988. It contained 40 sections and five schedules, and therefore is too long to reproduce here. On its second reading in the House of Commons, Mr Douglas Hogg MP, as the Minister concerned, explained: 'Despite the complexity of the Bill ... its purpose is simple: to provide more effective protection from the dangers caused by fire and to ensure a higher standard of public safety at those sporting fixtures where a serious risk to public safety may exist' (HC Hansard: 30 March col 813). The impact of this enactment upon sporting and local authority recreational administration will clearly be formidable. The key substantive point for sport is the requirement of a safety certificate for a permanent stand which provides covered accommodation for 500 or more spectators at any category of sports ground. Procedurally, local authorities will be able to serve enforcement notices without an initial court application, as under the 1975 Act.

(5)   The Football Spectators Act 1989 received Royal Assent two years later on 16 November 1989, seven months and one day after the Sheffield Wednesday Hillsborough Stadium disaster on 15 April 1989. It was enacted just two months before Lord Justice Taylor's Final Report (Cm 962) was presented to Parliament on 10 January 1990 (with its basic proposals for all-seater stadia and rejection of non-sports comprehending Prime Minister Mrs Thatcher's unrealistic and unworkable so-called membership scheme; in essence a dog or motorist licensing scheme). This Act created a Football Licensing Authority and replaced the provisions of the Public Order Act 1986 for restriction and exclusion orders which the author had been

advocating analogously to road traffic offences since the Appendix 2 to the first edition (reproduced here as Appendix 12 and initially published in the 1978 *Sunday Telegraph Sport and the Law*).

(6) In 1991 the Football (Offences) Act was enacted to implement three of the many specific recommendations of the Final Taylor Report, namely throwing of missiles, racialist chanting and going on to football pitches without lawful authority or excuse. In due course by Statutory Instrument it was extended to UEFA and FA Premier League fixtures.

For the great majority of the 43,000 registered clubs at the Football Association's 16 Lancaster Gate headquarters, or those who meet Ian Wooldridge's brilliant criteria, cited in the Introduction here from Cliff Morgan's BBC *Sport on Four* radio programme, that sport exists at

> 'Village cricket, soccer on Hackney Marshes, Old Boys rugger teams getting legless afterwards, point-to-pointing, county golf, darts leagues in Dorset',

Lord Justice Taylor's 76 recommendations in that Final Report have no direct *administrative* application or significance. It contained 427 paragraphs, 8 appendices and nearly 120 pages and photographs. Nevertheless, the First Aid, Medical and Ambulance recommendations in paragraphs 64–68 inclusive, will be ignored by many at their peril in the context of current inevitable injuries off, as well as on, the field of play.

Two crucial sections applicable to subsequent events at the time of writing in early 1994 create a common thread throughout the whole sporting world which embrace athletics (and the Norman–Temple suicide inquest and published prelude scenario); cricket (and ball-tampering surfacing in Alan Lamb's libel action); horse racing (and the Grand National starting fiasco); rugby union football (and its rejection of the realities of semi-professionalism alongside apparent ignorance of violence) and soccer (with its Chief Executive's testimony in court acquiescing in violence). All of these as assessed by David Miller in the *Times* before and after Christmas/New Year 1993–1994 and Alan Hubbard in the *Observer* during early 1994 qualify for Lord Justice Taylor's strictures in his chapter 1 under the heading of 'Poor Leadership' in paragraph 55 and in chapter 2 at paragraph 132 under the heading 'Leadership and Example'.

The first of these at paragraph 55 demonstrates an understandable unawareness, as a pupil from a distinguished Northumberland rugby-playing school, of the Corinthian Casuals' retention of traditions at their own ground, Tolworth, Surrey.

'55. Then there is what happens on the pitch itself. Long departed are Corinthian Casual standards; accepting decisions of the referee without demur; affecting a modest diffidence on scoring a sensational goal. For many years now referees' decisions have been regularly challenged by spread arms and entreaties; even an unsensational goal has caused the scorer to be hugged and embraced all the way back to the centre spot. The cool self-control of Corinthian Casuals will never return. Perhaps we should not lament its departure since there is no harm in a reasonable show of joy in success. But, more recently, things have gone further. On scoring a goal a player nowadays often rushes straight towards the perimeter fencing and either affects to climb it or, with fists raised and shaking, goes on his knees to excite response from supporters. Little has been done to stop such demonstrations which are calculated to hype up the fans into hysteria.'

Subsequently he brought a refreshing touch of judicial realism to explain the consequences to all sporting participating offenders when he reported in paragraph 132 with words and thoughts of general application four years later in 1994:

'132. It is in the first instance up to the players themselves, then the referees, the managers and the club directors to stop both incitement and violence by players whether on or off the ball. The referees, managers and directors have power to do this. If and when they fail to use it, the FA must take a firm disciplinary line using their very full powers to fine those involved including the clubs and to penalise the clubs in points. If all else fails, there is no reason why violence on the pitch should have any immunity from the law of the land or from police action.'

Indeed, all of this was corroborated by his brother Law Lord, Lord Griffiths of Govilon in the County of Gwent, a former Cambridge University and Glamorganshire county cricket bowler, President of MCC and the Royal and Ancient (St Andrews), in a London *Evening Standard* interview (14 December 1993) after the New Zealand rugby tourist experiences:

'The law may be usefully employed to stop some of the excessive brutality in contact games ... I absolutely deplore stamping. I don't mind a bit if the law is employed so that people have it brought home to them that this is not part of the game'.

Such sentiments are echoed by the Law Commissions Consultation Paper No 134 on *Consent and Offences against the Person*.

Furthermore, even before Parliament felt forced to intervene on a national level, certain admirable local efforts were made, notwithstanding the pathetically inadequate attitude expressed to Lord

Justice Taylor as reported in paragraph 52 of his Final Report, which related to the administrative periods of the late Mr Croker at the Football Association and his successor Mr Kelly at the Football League:

'52. The FA and the FL have not seen it as their duty [in the past] to offer guidance to clubs on safety matters. In their written submission they said:
"Of course, both The FA and The Football League are concerned to ensure that crowd safety standards are the highest reasonably practicable. It is felt, however, that neither of these authorities should be charged with the responsibility of setting detailed safety standards or enforcing them."'

Accordingly, the gaps left by that abject abdication of public responsibility were filled by some at least of the professionally administered company-clubs in the fullest way.

The Bristol City Case (*Bristol City v Milins* (1978) Daily Telegraph, 31 January)

The Bristol City Football Club company demonstrated the private control of public places by seeking and obtaining an injunction in its local Bristol County Court restraining a 17-year-old supporter from entering or attempting to enter its Ashton Gate ground.

He had created a 'substantial' disturbance involving fighting during at least two City home games in 1977. After the first he was convicted in the magistrates' court of a Public Order Act offence. The Club sent his father a letter stating that he was banned from the ground for the rest of the current season. He later defied the ban by attending and being ejected from another match. Hence the injunction order.

The Brighton and Hove Albion Case (*R v Clark and Ors* (1985) Daily Telegraph, 10 April)

Easter Monday, 8 April 1985 witnessed a coastal fixture at Fratton Park, Portsmouth between the home club and Brighton and Hove Albion. Five Brighton followers from the East Sussex area near the famous Goldstone, Hove, ground were convicted with varying sentences of 14 days' imprisonment, 28 days' detention and £100 fines, for various Public Order Act offences of a conventional kind. Immediately after the sentences, from which no appeal was lodged, all five were banned for life from the Brighton ground. The Secretary of the Brighton & Hove Albion Club, Mr Ron Pavey, was reported as having said,

'We don't want these people at our ground. We declared that anyone convicted would be banned for life from the Goldstone ground and we will stick with that policy.'

Derby County (1986)

The Board now bans any supporter who misbehaves in the ground for five years. A letter is sent threatening an injunction against them if they come into the ground in breach of the ban. Anybody who is convicted of a criminal offence within the ground is now banned automatically for life.

Any doubts that the Public Order Act applies to premises which ordinarily could be regarded as private were dispelled in *Cawley v Frost* (supra) by Queen's Bench Divisional Court of the High Court of Justice (per Lord Widgery LCJ, Melford Stevenson J and Caulfield J). The facts and extracts from the judgments may assist professional as well as lay readers to explain what may appear to be a paradox or conflict between private and public elements.

After an evening match between Halifax Town and Preston North End in 1976 about 200 supporters of each club were prevented by police intervention from clashing on the speedway track between the stands and pitch. Among the arrests was one for using threatening words or behaviour in a *public* place whereby a breach of the peace was likely to be occasioned, contrary to section 5 of the Public Order Act 1956 (as amended).

The point was taken and upheld at a lower court that part of the playing area or speedway track was sufficiently distinguishable to lose the character of a *public* place. The High Court rejected this and three judges led by the Lord Chief Justice of England in the Divisional Court of the Queen's Bench Division, Lord Widgery LCJ, laid the law down thus:

> 'Where you have an establishment which is set up to provide for the public, such as the Halifax Town Football Club or Wembley Stadium, one ought to approach it on the basis that it is a public place in its entirety.' (*Cawley v Frost* (1971) 64 CHR 20)

Surprising as this decision and these pronouncements may be to the non-lawyer, they were recognised within the legal profession at least three years earlier. Anti-apartheid disrupters of a men's doubles match on No 2 Court at Wimbledon between Davidson and Bowrey and Pilic and Drysdale were required to obtain a House of Lords ruling that the local Wimbledon justices had rightly dismissed the charge against them for lack of sufficient evidence that they had been guilty of insulting behaviour (a High Court ruling having disagreed with the lay bench), and for the purposes of the House of Lords appeal it was conceded that No 2 Court at Wimbledon was a public place.

The legal process was initiated by a Metropolitan Police officer in the period long before the present Crown Prosecution Service began, involving the legal profession at all levels. (This was distinct from the time when police officers acted in a quasi-legal capacity by formulating charges and also the charges at the magistrates' court proceedings.) The defendant had entered the playing area to interrupt play. The House of Lords confirmed the local Wimbledon law justices' conclusion that the behaviour of interruption was not *insulting*. No argument was pleaded at any effective stage that the conduct was *abusive*. Yet on the basis that entrance to the ground was legal, either by invitation or by paid ticket, the status of entry created licence and licensee. It was abused by misconduct. Thus the charge of *abusive*, as distinct from *insulting* behaviour consistent with the provisions of section 5 of the Public Order Act 1936 whereby a breach of the peace was likely to have been occasioned would have been justified on the facts and at least arguably likely to have resulted in a conviction which would have been upheld by the higher courts. The ruling is therefore no more than an authority for (a) the facts of the particular case, (b) a confirmation of the construction approach to the meaning of insulting, and (c) for the agreement that private sporting premises are a public place (*Brutus v Cozens* [1973] AC 854).

One final set of enactments which require attention from the Popplewell complex of seven [now eight] identifiable and applicable statutes to sporting premises are the Occupiers' Liability Acts 1957–84. Passed initially in 1957 to codify the previous common law cases into a 'common duty of care' they were extended by the Act of 1984. This was enacted following two Royal Commission Reports in order to protect ramblers and recreational users of land from being treated as trespassers in rural districts.

Finally, during November 1993 in a different legal dimension an enterprising Bury, Lancashire, solicitor, Bernard Clayton, obtained an award of £101.75 damages and costs against Oldham Athletic Football Club from the Deputy District Judge in Bury County court, after he had been kept out of the ground with a valid ticket, when Manchester United were playing, because the defendant club had inadvertently admitted so many with forged tickets. The claim comprised not only a refund for the cost of the ticket, but also damages for wasted travelling expenses, unnecessary child-minding expenses, and loss of enjoyment, for which £25 was awarded, consistent with the Court of Appeal decisions in *Jarvis v Swans Tours Ltd* [1973] QB 233, [1973] 1 All ER 71 and *Jackson v Horizon Holidays Ltd* (1974) Times, 6 February. (Daily Mail, 16 November 1993.)

PERSONAL AND CROWD SAFETY CONCLUSION

Facts and evidence always are the only practical yardstick by which a situation can be assessed and judged legally. There are so many different situations which have given rise to injunctions and damages: a regatta, fairs, fire-works, circus, and noise from Earl's Court sideshows.

There are weapons in the legal armoury which have yet to be involved extensively in the struggle which has developed between a public suffering from uncontrolled crowd violence or other abuses and promoters, clubs and other organisers of sporting events who in the past have given an impression of failing to recognise their responsibilities beyond the narrow confines of their own backyards. One which has recently passed through Parliament as these pages are being processed in 1994 is the Criminal Justice and Public Order Act, which provides for an offence for a sale of tickets for designated Football matches by unauthorised persons. Another has been the creation of a Football Safety Officers Association. Its object under its Rules

> 'would be to improve safety at football grounds, promulgate best practice, enhance the role of safety stewards and continually develop safety officers' expertise.'

Only planned coordination between Parliament and all those ready to recognise responsibilities for public protection can prevent repetition of past disasters.

Crowd violence and hooliganism are the fall-out or pay-off from a permissive society of which football is a mere victim of exploitation. This practical solution is offered to try at least to contain and even perhaps eradicate what is a social as well as a sporting evil. Its direct relevance to playing as well as spectating emerges from Chapter 6, 'Participation problems'.

Chapter 6

Participation problems

1 INTRODUCTION

Participants in sport have no less claim to public protection than anyone else concerned with it: and within the context of these pages participation in sport means how a person approaches and plays the game. The concept of 'participation' involves a complexity of social issues which include the sportperson's amateur or professional status and the consequences arising out of this distinction. The requirement to obey the Rule of Law, however, demands the same standard of conduct, whether competing or indulging in any way at all within an amateur or professional environment.

Furthermore, this chapter demonstrates that all participants in sport are always at risk if they break the law of the land in the course of play. It also illuminates the developing reluctantly recognisable reality within sport that the law of the land does not stop at the touchline or boundary.

Behaviour in sport reflects behaviour in society generally. Thus, a violence-orientated society will inevitably create violent elements in sport and this chapter accordingly deals with the criminal and civil liability of offenders in sport.

Participation touches the law at every point of the sporting compass and for all ages. For in the same spirit which caused the late Mr John Hislop, in a memorable *Times* feature article during early 1987, to claim how it is often forgotten that without horses there would be no racing of the equine kind, correspondingly without participants there would be no sport of any kind.

According to the Sports Council's 'Sport in the Nineties: New Horizons' survey published in 1993:

'If children are taken into account, it is estimated that almost 36 million people (two-thirds of the entire British population) take part in sport and recreation;'

It is also explained:

'... 29 million adults took part in sport and recreation at least once a month in 1990. This represents almost two-thirds of the adult population of Great Britain, showing an increase of 2 million since 1987.'

Indeed, at the cut-off date for the manuscript for the first edition at October 1987 participation in United Kingdom sport and recreation involved about 22 million in all 'on at least one occasion a month,' explained John Wheatley, the then Director-General of the Sports Council at the CCPR Annual Conference in Bournemouth during November 1986. It embraced all generations, from the cradle to the grave. So, too, for all participants, do Parliament and the courts.

Furthermore, when John Wheatley produced his figures of 22 million participants, he also explained

> 'Many of these however clearly do not see the need to join the governing bodies of sport, though their interests are affected by those governing bodies,'

and

> 'There are now about 6.5m members of approximately 150,000 sports clubs of which about 110,000 clubs are affiliated to governing bodies of sport.'

He then demonstrated,

> 'In the United Kingdom, there are approximately 390 governing bodies of sport which exercise some measure of control or guidance in the four countries of the United Kingdom.

National Governing Bodies of Sport

Sports	UK	GB	E	E&W	W	S	NI	All Ireland	Total
75	54	39	41	7	66	77	79	32	395

> The number and character of the governing bodies reflect various backgrounds and produce a pattern of management of sport which demonstrates the vast range of interest and has some important consequences.'

At the time of writing in mid-1994, the Sports Council's latest figures, allowing for contraction and amalgamations of sporting governing bodies within a particular discipline, and the creation of more recently established foundations since the date of the first edition, have been varied to

Sports	UK	GB	E	W	Sc	NI	Total
108	42	53	59	66	77	84	489

One of the most important of those consequences explained by John Wheatley was recorded a quarter-of-a-century earlier in the Wolfenden Committee Report on Sport, 'Sport and the Community'

(1960), established by the CCPR. This led to the Sports Council's creation under Royal Charter in 1972, as we can see in Chapter 2, 'Progressive perspective'. The preceding years had led to a revolution in the nature and structure of the participatory role in sport *qua* amateur and professional. The Wolfenden Report in 1960 was faced with the dying days of the social and artificial antithesis between the professional and amateur status. Two years later (in 1962) the MCC abolished the formal distinctions between Gentlemen and Players. In turn a year before Wimbledon went 'Open' in 1963, the Wolfenden Committee endorsed (page 69, para 172):

> 'genuine amateurism which is worth preserving, namely, the wish to play a game for straightforward enjoyment, without any thought of money or of indirect financial gain. This is the element which is uppermost in the attitude of millions of humble games players; it is not snobbery or class distinction, nor does it imply any rebuke to those who perfectly legitimately play games for a living.'

This last contemporaneous comment identified the lingering social stigma which had clung to paid performers until money sport monopolised the public sporting scene from the mid-1960s onwards, notwithstanding the first professional sporting knighthoods to Sir Jack Hobbs and Sir Gordon Richards in the Coronation Honours list of 1953, followed by Sir Leonard Hutton in 1956 and subsequently Sir Stanley Matthews CBE in 1965, and the millionairess winners of the Wimbledon Ladies Tennis Championships. The Wolfenden majority concluded.

> 'There seems to be no reason why difficulties about the status of a very small number of players should lead to a solution which would prevent the millions who just want to play something from being amateurs, in the full sense of the word.'

More than three decades later, the difficulties have persisted, notwithstanding the refreshing readiness to recognise the charade of trust funds in public athletics. They still preserve the title 'amateur' in national and international governing bodies (eg the International AMATEUR Federation) and 'boot money' exists in amateur rugby. In October 1985, a Scottish schoolboy athlete initially lost his amateur status upon receiving a 10p bag of sweets as a prize for winning competitively, until public ridicule caused his reinstatement. At the present time of writing in mid-1994 the International Rugby Board members and the four home United Kingdom Rugby Unions – England, Scotland, Wales and All Ireland – have compromised the amateur and professional status. The Unions have argued that 'amateurism' has been preserved while players are allowed to earn money from associated activities 'connected' with rugby union as distinct from professional Rugby League football.

Throughout the later 1980s and early 1990s the gap between playing standards of rugby at the televised entertainment levels and school, club and other grass-roots categories has widened with each passing year. Yet what is often ignored is the comparable position where the *professional* stage and theatre function on a different plane qualitatively and quantitatively from the countless *amateur* thespians and choral, musical and operatic societies which flourish throughout the land. The amateur status and ethos merit and doubtless voice the wish of a great majority of rugby union players and club members for preservation as much as those whose skill and sacrifices in time and family and employment situations deserve compensation for the entertaining pleasure and value they provide for millions.

During the Second World War, Professor D W Brogan, writing for the American public in *The English People: Impressions and Observations* (1943), claimed correctly at the time (page 69):

'Professional football is by far the most important game from the spectator's point of view but it is only the cream of a very deep milk jug.'

With successive generations *all* sport perpetually gushes forth fresh sporting talents from a very deep well of milk; but money sport sours the cream at the top and frequently curdles it into unlawful social and commercial conduct, as we shall see throughout this chapter.

Every sporting participant initially carries an amateur sporting status. The majority millions retain it. Relatively few become paid professionals: and even fewer can afford to remain amateurs at the public participatory level as sporting heroes, or heroines, with professionally developed skills and techniques. Classic examples at different ends of the century are the immortal C B Fry, and the American banker, Charlie Fenwick, who rode the 40–1 outsider, Ben Nevis, to win the 1978 Aintree Grand National, or HRH The Princess Royal, competing for Great Britain in the Olympic Games, and winning the first race of the prestigious Diamond Day afternoon at Ascot on 'Ten No Trumps' at 9–1, in the Dresden Diamond Stakes ladies race in July 1987.

Against this background and perspective of the two participatory amateur and professional sporting categories, it must be emphasised that none can escape the applicable law, with its inevitable overlapping elements. Obvious areas for duplication include sporting responsibilities, civil and criminal misconduct, *off* as well as *on* the fields of play, and certain paradoxical situations, especially in relation to income tax (*Jarrold v Boustead* [1964] 3 All ER 76) and reputation involving defamation (*Tolley v Fry* [1931] AC 333), both of which with splendid irony, protect the amateur status commercially.

A valuable report from a CCPR Enquiry under the Chairmanship of Charles Palmer OBE into Amateur Status and Participation in Sport, published in 1988, highlighted the differentiations in attitudes with different governing bodies towards a status preserved in many circumstances by trust funds which many would consider incompatible with tradition and understanding. Towards the end of 1994, a Sports (Discrimination) Bill introduced in the House of Commons by Wakefield's Labour MP, Dennis Hinchcliffe, aims to undermine the artificial differentiations. It illustrates how Sport and the Law functions in Parliament.

2 PARTICIPATORY SPORT AND THE LAW

'It is as much in the interests of the Plaintiff himself as of any other contestant that there should be rules for clean fighting and that he should be protected against his adversary's misconduct in hitting below the belt or doing anything of the sort.'

With these words one of Lord Denning's predecessors as Master of the Rolls, Lord Hanworth, in 1933, and the Court of Appeal reversed Mackinnon J's judgment and thus rejected a claim by the then 18-year-old Irish heavyweight boxer, Jack Doyle, against the proprietors of the now demolished White City Stadium and the British Boxing Board of Control (1929) (*Doyle v White City Stadium Ltd* [1935] 1 KB 110). His professional boxing licence was suspended for six months, and his £3000 purse was forfeited under the small print of the fight contract after the referee had disqualified Doyle for foul fighting in a contest for the heavyweight championship of Great Britain. This was against the late Jack Petersen, who subsequently became the President of the British Boxing Board of Control. Doyle's lawyers had argued, because of their client's legal status as an infant, that forfeiture was a penalty which was contractually disadvantageous and thereby not beneficial to their client. The test then as now, since the Infants Relief Act 1874 and more recently under the Minors' Contracts Act 1987, has been that infants' contracts must be for beneficial necessaries.

Twenty years before Doyle's case an earlier Court of Appeal had upheld a trial judge's ruling about a different form of an infant's sporting contract. They had allowed a claim by a leading international billiards player, John Roberts, for breach of contract against the infant defendant who obtained advantages from the agreement arising out of a form of touring apprenticeship experiences. This was adjudged to be beneficial for necessary instruction and education towards future playing proficiency (*Roberts v Gray* [1913] 1 KB 520). It had been available but never used for the advantage of cricket apprentices as legatees in the mishandled charity claim by Sussex County Cricket Club's advisers already discussed above in Chapter 3, 'Under starters' orders' (*Re Patten* [1929] 2 Ch 276).

Doyle's Court of Appeal appearance is cited extensively in all leading practitioners' and student text books for the many-sided legal principles with which it bristles, concerning not only infants' contracts, but also the non-necessity to imply a contractual term for giving notice of alterations in administrative rules comprising the small print of the particular contract. All are silent, however, about Lord Hanworth's citation extracted above. So, too, are the memoirs of Doyle's celebrated leading counsel Serjeant Sullivan, *The Last Serjeant*. This was also the title to his status in legal rank, now extinct, but commemorated in the area known as Serjeant's Inn, just off Fleet Street. They do dwell extensively on one of Sullivan's even better known and non-sporting clients, Sir Roger Casement. He was hanged for treason. Lord Hanworth's words threading the true spirit of sport with law, and the law with sport, should also be 'hanged', as a warning against sporting treason, in every schoolroom dressing room, changing room, committee room, board room and club room throughout the land.

Such an ideal will not happen because of the conflicting commercial, criminal and personality interests which fluctuate through the varying layers of fun, healthy competition, professionalism, entertainment, internationalism and terrorism which comprise the pyramid structure which forms sport in the latter part of the twentieth century. As a reflection of the Law in Sport it transcends the rules and laws of all games. It is also illuminated most vividly by the extent to which the criminal and civil law of the land have had to be wheeled on to the playing battlefields throughout the 1970s and 1980s for protection of players and the sport itself. The principles of control by the courts were first established in 1878 (*R v Bradshaw* (1878) 14 Cox 83 and *R v Moore* (1898) 14 TLR 229) and subsequently gathered dust in musty leather bindings on library shelves for nearly a century after. They were reaffirmed more recently in a wider and non-sporting context by a more modern Court of Appeal Criminal Division in 1975 (*R v Venna* [1975] 3 All ER 788). The significance of *Venna*, which is particularised at page 156, below, is that it fills the gap left by Lord Mustill in the sado-masochistic case of *R v Brown* [1993] 2 All ER 75 at 109h–i, [1993] 2 WLR 556 at 592H–593D, and cited in extenso in the Law Commission Consultation Paper No 134 (on Consent and Offences Against the Person) when he is reported as saying after a survey of 'contact' sports, ex cathedra of *Bradshaw* (after no practitioner before him referred to Venna):

> 'This accords with my own instinct, but I must recognise that a direction at nisi prius, even by a great judge, cannot be given the same weight as a judgment on appeal, consequent upon full argument and reflection. The same comment may be made about *R v Moore* (1898) 14 TLR 229.'

These principles, broken down into language comprehensible to a jury and thus to any man, woman or child on the terraces, were first used in the 1978 *Sunday Telegraph* edition of this book. Repeated in the first ever British Sport and the Law conference at the University of Birmingham in July 1978, they have stood the test of time with extended usage and application since then. They are repeated here as a warning to all potential violent sporting offenders and those who would encourage them.

> 'From 1878 to 1978 the British, and, in particular, English and Welsh [NB since then, Scottish, too] Courts have sustained the same principles of reckless and deliberate violent action for players as they have applied to protecting spectators in deciding what are the consequences of rough and illegal play. Tackle fairly and there is no problem. Tackle foully but accidentally, eg slipping in the mud or on canvas, and there would be no legal liability; but tackle foully or hit below the belt with deliberation and/or recklessness and there is no doubt what the consequences would and should be: a criminal prosecution and claim for damages. If these thoughts are regarded as fanciful, consider the following examples.'

Those examples which followed in 1978 and which are now set out on pages 163–165 below consolidated both the criminal and civil liability illustrations at the time. Since then the violent acts in the course of play in so many different disciplines, but primarily at both traditional football codes, have caused an annual pilgrimage to all courts. This has occurred at every level: High Court, Crown Court, County Court, Magistrates' Court, Coroner's Court and Compensation Board. The easily available remedy of civil assault has been extended by a concurrent claim for negligence which was upheld by the Court of Appeal in *Condon v Basi* [1985] 2 All ER 453. Furthermore, Mr Simon Inglis' valuable researches for *Soccer in the Dock* have thrown up forgotten examples of off-field criminality, too.

Sadly, the optimism for self-regulation within sport itself which was expressed when the author first raised the possibilities of involving the courts' powers has not been fulfilled. In a *Police Review* article in 1969, the author first explained the reality of criminal conduct built-in to deliberate and reckless tackles following the prosecution for manslaughter of a player who killed an opponent with a blow struck during the course of a soccer game (*R v Southby* [1969] *Police Review*, 7 February, vol 77, p 110). In friendly terms the need to involve the courts was rebutted by a member of the FA staff, the late John Carvosso, in a contribution to the *FA News* (March 1969, p 288).

He claimed the absolute power on the field of the referee to be 'sufficient ... to deal with every contingency'. Ironically in the same issue, now more than twenty-five years ago, a need for action to control criminal foul play was crystallised by a more modern Corinthian and Cricketer than the author's schoolboy heroes, C B Fry and G O Smith. At page 297 an article entitled 'A Bad Example' was written under the authorship of A H Fabian in his capacity as a former Cambridge University (captain), Corinthians, Derby County and England amateur player, and a frequent co-author with Tom Whittaker, Arsenal's trainer and later manager. He also played cricket for Cambridge University and Middlesex and was a master at Highgate School. He suggested

> 'that it should be brought home to the star professional footballers that a responsibility they carry is the example they set to the young boys who will be the players of the future.'

In October 1986 when the Court of Appeal heard the Welsh Rugby International, David Bishop's appeal, it echoed those words: 'Local heroes have a responsibility to the game, their fellow players and to the public.' They were spoken by a former pupil at Highgate School during Fabian's mastership there, Lord Justice Brian Neil.

A decade after that *Police Review* initiative, in 1980, when another Welsh rugby international player, Paul Ringer, was sent off the field at Twickenham for striking an opponent outside the laws of play, letters to *The Times* from disparate sources concerned with the law and order confirmed the referee's verdict. Manchester's Chief Constable, James Anderton, explained the criminality; the master in charge of games at St Edward's School, Oxford, reiterated the bad example for boys, and an 80-year-old supporter voiced his concern for the future by comparison with the standards of the past. By the time of the Bishop affair in 1986, such outstanding Welsh International Rugby players as Clem Thomas in *The Observer* and Wilfred Wooller in the *Sunday Telegraph* were condemning selection committees and coaches for any field offences; and as we shall see, the legal consequences of their inactivity could be considerable. By the end of the decade the sentencing tariff for vicious criminality has escalated to 18 months immediate custodial imprisonment (*R v Lloyd*: Times 24 January 1989). A rugby hooker aged 28 who kicked the head with great force of an entirely innocent opposing winger who was lying on the ground (in a minor club game) after having released the ball on being tackled while the referee was watching the ball, appealed against his sentence at Bristol Crown Court. While dismissing the plea against sentence, in the Court of Appeal Criminal Division, Pill J explained:

> 'the game was not a licence for thuggery ... what the appellant did had nothing to do with rugby football or the play in progress. The Recorder's description of the appellant's action that it was a vicious barbaric act was justified. The sentence [of 18 months] was appropriate.'

This and many other cases cited below appear in the Law Commission's Consultation Paper No 134 (supra) at paragraph 10.13; and footnote 93 to paragraph 10.11 contains the following extract from both codes of football:

> '93 A wide range of dangerous acts is specifically forbidden by Law XII of the Rules of Association Football; the particular conduct in *Bradshaw* would seem to be outlawed by sub-laws (*c*) and (*d*), the "Advice to Referees" appended to which (1993 edition, p. 35) says "Jumping at an opponent and not jumping for the ball is a foul; there is no such thing as accidental jumping at an opponent". Law 26(3) of the Laws of the Game of Rugby Football 1993/94, similarly forbids a wide range of dangerous play, including, by sub-laws (3)(b)–(c), wilful hacking, kicking and tripping, and early, late or dangerous tackling.'

Accordingly, for ease and convenience of reference, the case summaries and illustrations of the basic principles outlined briefly below will be broken down into their own subdivisions of:

(1)   Criminal liability and

(2)   Civil and compensatory liabilities

Other chapters deal with the more commercially orientated aspects of participation problems, namely:

(i)   Status, reputation and compensation

(ii)   Contracts

(iii)   Finance

Criminality and civil liability are the key to keeping participants within the rules of play when adequate penal playing laws, eg the sin-bin principle (long-established for the potentially violent ice-hockey and water-polo, and introduced since 1982 to professional Rugby League Football) or the will to enforce and punish the existing laws against offenders, do not exist and fail to deter.

Criminal liability

The judicial principles applying the common law which have been sustained repeatedly for over a century from *Bradshaw* (1878) via *Moore* (1898) down to their reaffirmation in *Venna* (1975) did not appear to require application to the sporting scene until the violent explosion which publicly at least can be traced to the Bulgarian and Portuguese players' assault upon the Brazilian, Pelé, in England during the World Cup in 1966. The same principles were applied to the £4,000 damages award in 1970 by Rees J for a broken leg injured in a foul tackle in a local Sussex amateur game (*Lewis v Brookshaw* (1970) 120 NLJ, p 413). They could have been applied also to two notorious field dismissals by referees while the 1970s unfolded.

In 1974, during the FA Charity Shield match at Wembley Stadium the referee sent off two international soccer players for fighting on the field, ie assaulting each other: Kevin Keegan (Liverpool) and Billy Bremner (Leeds United) witnessed by millions of TV viewers. In 1977, at Cardiff's National Stadium, in the Wales versus Ireland rugby international game, for similar mutual assaults, the referee, Norman Sansom, dismissed Geoff Wheel (Wales) and Willie Duggan (Ireland). No really effective action was taken condemning such conduct within the course of that game, which was also witnessed extensively on television. A less charitable view, culminating in the comments of the England Rugby Captain, Will Carling, was taken of the New Zealand players' actions towards the end of 1993 during their tour of Britain.

Any mistaken belief that mobile body contact sport contained a built-in licence to commit crime, however, was soon to be dispelled. An amateur South Wales rugby player during early 1977 had the double misfortune during the course of a game (1) to break the leg of an opponent (2) who was a Borstal prison officer. The victim's principals were not content to lose his valuable professional services without an attempt to let similar offenders realise the consequences. That was how *R v Billingshurst* (supra) became the first ever rugby footballer to be prosecuted and ultimately convicted of the offence of assault occasioning actual bodily harm. The case was extensively reported in the popular and professional legal sources. By the time David Bishop, the Welsh international player, punched an opponent on the ground away from the ball during a club rugby match in South Wales neither he nor his club could claim that they were unaware of the legal consequences. No move was made by Bishop's club committee to discipline his conduct privately within the club membership's own internal capacity to regulate its own affairs. Accordingly, the prosecuting authorities had no alternative but to act upon the evidence and the complaint which led to the player's plea of guilty to the charge of common assault and ultimate prison sentence. This was varied on appeal from an immediate to a suspended sentence of one month, in abeyance for a year. His concurrent suspension by the Welsh Rugby Union, the game's governing body, was no different from experiences of any other practitioner such as a dentist, doctor or lawyer disciplined by his peers for a serious offence in a graver category than, for example, an isolated and single road traffic offence of speeding.

The legal principles applied when the South Wales prosecuting authorities prosecuted in 1977, *R v Billinghurst*, and 1985, *R v Bishop* were laid down with unequivocal clarity by two eminently respected and experienced Victorian criminal trial judges: Bramwell LJ who later became Lord Bramwell, and Hawkins J who is now recalled as Lord Brampton.

In *Bradshaw*'s case ([1878] 14 Cox CC 83), a jury acquitted a footballer in a friendly game on a manslaughter charge after evidence had been given from one of the two umpires then in charge of the game that no unfair play occurred. During prosecuting counsel's opening speech to the jury, Bramwell L J interrupted a reference to the game's rules to say (at p48)

'whether within the rules or not, the prisoner would be guilty of manslaughter if while committing an unlawful act he caused the death of the deceased.'

His summing-up (at p85) to the jury included these words:

'If a man is playing according to the rules and practice of the game and not going beyond it, it may be reasonable to infer that he is not actuated by any malicious motive or intention, and that he is not acting in a manner which he knows will be likely to be productive of death or injury. But, independent of the rules, if the prisoner intended to cause serious hurt to the deceased, or if he knew that, in charging as he did, he might produce serious injury and was indifferent and reckless as to whether he would produce serious injury or not, then the act would be unlawful. In either case he would be guilty of a criminal act and you must find him guilty; if you are of a contrary opinion you will acquit him.'

On the evidence the jury returned a verdict of Not Guilty.

Twenty years later in *Moore*'s case ([1898] 14 TLR 229) the evidence was that the accused jumped with his knees against the victim's back. This threw him violently against a knee of the goalkeeper, causing an internal rupture and ultimate death, a few days afterwards. He, too, was charged with manslaughter; and on this occasion the verdict was Guilty. Hawkins J's summing-up to the jury explained (at pp229–230) 'the rules of the game were quite immaterial' and 'it did not matter whether the prisoner broke the rules or not. Football was a lawful game, but it was a rough one and persons who played it must be careful to restrain themselves so as not to do bodily harm to any other person. No one had a right to use force which was likely to injure another, and if he did use such force and death resulted, the crime of manslaughter had been committed.'

'. . . If a blow were struck recklessly which caused a man to fall, and if in falling he struck against something and was injured and died, the person who struck the blow was guilty of manslaughter, even though the blow itself would not have caused injury.'

Nearly a century after *Bradshaw*'s case in *R v Venna* ([1975] 3 All ER 788), a more recent Court of Appeal dismissed appeals against convictions for assault occasioning actual bodily harm and Public Order offences in a non-sporting context. The reserved judgment after two days of legal argument included the following significant sentence (at p 793 f–g)

'*R v Bradshaw* (1878) 14 Cox CC 85 can be read as supporting the view that unlawful physical force applied recklessly constitutes a criminal assault.'

What constitutes 'recklessly' has been the subject of such subsequent gymnastics by the higher judiciary in the House of Lords that they moved the learned Editors of the leading practitioners' 'bible' in the criminal courts, *Archbold*, in their Preface to the 41st Edition [1982] at page v, to describe them as 'a challenge even to the most gifted of Her Majesty's trial judges'. (Since then, the current 1992 [44th] Edition spans 22 pages in paras 17–68 and 17–88 for discussing 'Reckless' – 'Recklessly', while preserving the *Bradshaw* test in Para 17–82.) 'Wildly impulsive' is the definition in *The Oxford Mini-dictionary*. Disregarding the consequences is the yardstick used by practitioners. For present purposes it would be advisable for each citation from Bramwell LJ, Hawkins J and the Court of Appeal in *Venna* to be hung alongside Lord Hanworth's words in *Doyle*'s case in the places mentioned above at p 150.

Before illustrating the application of these principles to prove criminal violence committed in the name of a game, it is appropriate to identify two developments which have occurred since this treasure trove of judicial wisdom has surfaced down the years. One is the corruption inherent in the bastard expression 'professional foul'. The other is the little known or cited revelation from the Government-funded Criminal Injuries Compensation Board.

The vice contained in the corrupting use of the term of professional foul is three-dimensional, or to adapt the standard sporting metaphor, it creates a corrupting hat-trick. *Archbold* (42nd Edn 1985, at p 2256 in para 27–156) explains:

> 'This word corrupting means dishonestly but purposely doing an act which the law forbids.'

Accordingly, the professional foul corrupts in three concurrent ways:

(1) the law of football, rugby or soccer;

(2) the law of the land, criminal and civil;

(3) the profession of playing games according to both sets of laws above.

It may also be said to be a corruption linguistically for all three reasons; but that debate need not be considered here. Suffice it to say that it should be expunged from the vocabulary of every self-respecting sportslover and condemned except to explain that what has been called a professional foul in the past is in reality an actionable criminal and civil assault.

The Criminal Injuries Compensation Board was created in 1964 to administer a compensation scheme for victims of violent crimes after public opinion brought pressure through a vigilant press campaign amidst a growing tide of violence demanding it. The scope is complex, but its jurisdiction certainly can cover both field and crowd violence from sporting activities in appropriate circumstances. Even the traditional legal age limitations for young offenders and victims can be modified, too. Regional centres exist and enquiries are best made first to the Criminal Injuries Compensation Board (England: Whittington House, 19 Alfred Place, London WC1E 7LG; Scotland: Blythswood House, 200 West Regent Street, Glasgow G2 4SW). By 1980 the tide of sporting violence had reached a sufficient level for inclusions of two paragraphs headed 'Football violence' in its Annual Report (paras 29 and 30).

Paragraph 30 concluded with a reminder of the devastating effect all too easily forgotten that criminal violence, which corrupts and poisons the sporting scene, *has upon the victims.*

> 'While there is now considerable public awareness of the existence and extent of football violence, we doubt whether the public is aware of the catastrophic effects which result from such criminal acts. The Board frequently deals with cases of people scarred for life, sometimes with cases of people seriously and permanently maimed and occasionally with people who are killed. We welcome the efforts which the courts, the police and many sporting organisations are taking to attempt to lessen the number of such crimes.'

The extent to which 'sporting organisations' are taking or encouraging attempts 'to lessen the number of such crimes,' both off and on playing fields, is debatable. The ambivalence of many rugby playing sources, for example, regrettably, in South Wales towards the prosecution of David Bishop, is paralleled only by the Football League's expulsion of Luton Town from its Littlewoods Cup Competition for attempting to exclude violent visiting supporters from its terraces, and stands.

Paragraph 29 explained the Board's developing involvement and the principles upon which it operates. It began with a general statement, and then provided an example which failed to meet its criteria. That required standard requires a civil standard of proof on the balance of probabilities. Since the example cited in the report, the civil law of liability for injuries as explained by the Court of Appeal in *Condon v Basi* has now extended the tort of negligence specifically to the playing in a field in a manner which leaves the Board's example from 1980 open to a fundamental reassessment and review. The Board is concerned with criminal injuries. The level of proof in criminal courts is certainly to a degree of sureness or satisfaction beyond reasonable doubt. The proof required by the Compensation Board is on the balance of probabilities: ie the civil burden of proof, the level or degree of proof required in civil cases. Because of the developments contained in extending the law of civil negligence explained below at page 174, to sporting violence, this example provided in Paragraph 29 has been overtaken by events and is deliberately omitted here to avoid any risk of confusing the reader. Paragraphs 29 and 30 with the concluding sentences cited above included with the author's own emphasis in the concluding paragraph reads as follows:

'**Football violence**
29. Public attention has been focussed recently upon the increasing pattern of mindless violence amongst both players and spectators. It results in injury to police and other people who are trying to keep the peace, to players and also to innocent bystanders. The phenomenon is not confined to professional soccer; amateur football, both association and rugby, is by no means immune and there are disturbing signs that the cricket field has growing problems in this respect. In our view, there is no doubt that a major contributory factor is the excessive consumption of alcohol amongst young spectators.

We are making an increasingly large number of awards to police officers who have been injured when attempting to restrain or arrest troublemakers, and to those we have referred to as innocent bystanders who are injured by bottles, beer cans and bricks indiscriminately thrown inside and outside the stadium.

We are also getting more and more applications arising out of alleged crimes of violence on the field of play itself. There is little problem when there is a proved "off the ball" incident: what raises far more difficulty is the alleged vicious or wild tackle. Here the alleged victim must prove either that there was an intention to injure him as opposed to a mere over-zealous desire to get the ball, or, and this is a very difficult matter in what is necessarily a heat of the moment situation, that the alleged assailant was guilty of "recklessness" within the meaning of *R v Venna* [1975] 3 All ER 788, [1976] QB 421, 61 Crim Ap R310; and other authorities.

30. Police, players, or spectators are not the only victims of injury arising out of sporting activities. In one recent case a full award was made to a referee who sent off a player for misbehaviour in a Sunday football match. The player returned onto the field of play and butted the referee with his head on the nose as a result of which the referee was knocked unconscious and sustained injury in the area of the nose.

Of course, the Board receives many applications from spectators assaulted on their way to and from football matches, often only because they are wearing a scarf or other emblem which indicates that they are supporters of the club playing against that "supported" by the assailant.

The wider problem of violence is one for the law-makers, the law-enforcers, and the clubs and associations concerned. There are signs that the clubs and associations are taking measures to cope with a problem which unfortunately shows no sign of going away.

While there is now considerable public awareness of the existence and extent of football violence, *we doubt whether the public are aware of the catastrophic effects which result from such criminal acts. The Board frequently deals with cases of people scarred for life, sometimes with cases of people seriously and permanently maimed and occasionally with cases of people who are killed. We welcome the efforts which the courts, the police and many sporting organisations are taking to attempt to lessen the number of such crimes.'*

Whatever efforts were made they clearly did not suffice to prevent a return to this area seven years later in the Annual Report for the year-end 31 March in 1987. It was presented to Parliament by the Home and Scottish Secretaries in December 1987. The then CICB Chairman Michael Ogden QC, began a section with the above citation against a marginal note at page 13 headed *Violence connected with sport.*

'37. For many years the Board has received a large number of applications from spectators assaulted at or in the vicinity of sporting events, notably as a result of violence at or near football grounds. In the last few years, the Board has received an increasing number of applications arising from violence among players, particularly during rugby or football matches.'

Also at page 14 it concluded

'We consider that it is in the interests of everyone that people who commit criminal offences on the playing fields should be prosecuted.

Anyone who considers that an injury upon him was caused by a criminal offence should draw the attention of the police to it. If he does not do so, he is unlikely to receive compensation from the Board.'

This last qualification identifies para 6(a) of the Scheme, which provides for withholding or reducing compensation for delay, non-disclosure to the police and other inhibitory factors.

Since that date in 1987 the Board has continued to make awards regularly without returning to the general commentary of its 1980 and 1987 Annual Reports. Yet notwithstanding such an authoritative source a continuing claim persists that the courts are not the forum for discussing criminal or civil liability (see *Solicitors' Journal* 1993 Vol 137 No 25 page 628: Simon Gardiner, and No 27 page 693: Edward Grayson and Catherine Bond). Furthermore, on 26 November 1991, the full Criminal Injuries Compensation Board at Nottingham granted a £15,000 interim award to a fully qualified physical education teacher who lost an eye in a third fifteen so-called friendly rugby game from a proven deliberate assault, upon it (CICB: *Mark Johnson* (1991) NLJ p 1725: *Halsbury's Laws* MR 92/594: *All ER Annual Review* 1992: p 313). Finally, while these pages were being prepared, criminal proceedings for unlawful killing on a North London rugby field were initiated and on a self-defence plea resulted in an acquittal; and the Law Commission Consultation Paper No 134 (supra) contains in paragraph 46.4 a graphic summary of the level of tolerance to be considered in the following way:

'**46.4** The process of participating in sport might be said to involve a certain amount of give and take; but, at the same time, there is a limit to the extent to which criminal sanctions can or should be withheld because of the attitude of the victim. We may give an example. Fast bowling in modern professional cricket is potentially extremely dangerous. To avoid or greatly minimise that danger batsmen are permitted, though not obliged, to wear a variety of protective clothing, particularly helmets. A batsman who declined to protect himself in that way would undoubtedly be creating a situation where a bowler bowling normally would be creating a significant risk of causing serious injury. That is, in the first place, a question for the cricket authorities; but the implication of the scheme that we provisionally propose is that a bowler who continued in his usual way and injured the batsman would be risking criminal liability, because above a certain level of hazard the consent or connivance of the victim is no defence. Similar considerations will apply, with increased force, if very fast, dangerous bowling is permitted in cricket at a lower level than the modern first-class game, particularly if the batsman's ability to cope with very fast bowling is obviously limited.'

This in turn recalls a valuable cameo captured by David Frith, the editor of *Wisden's Cricket Monthly* in his valuable book *The Fast*

Men (1975). At pages 139–140 he refers to the injured Sri Lankan batsman Sunil Wettimuny and the account

'related by Peter Marson of *The Times*, who wrote the following dialogue surrounding Wettimuny's arrival in hospital: "What happened to you?" "I was hit playing cricket." "Where?" "At The Oval." "Who did it?" "Thomson." At this point, and with the timing peculiar to officers of the law, a police sergeant who had chanced to be within earshot of the conversation interjected: "Do you wish to prefer charges?"'

David Frith commented (as at 1975)

'It raises an interesting point. A fast bowler who has written that he aims to hit batsmen could find himself in the position of an American ice hockey player who has recently faced a criminal charge of assault with a dangerous weapon (a hockey stick) during a match. The penalty, if convicted, is three years' jail.'

Just over a decade later in a Canadian citation referred to in *R v Brown* (supra) and also in the Law Commission Consultation Paper No 134:

'In *Regina v Ciccarelli* (Ontario Prov Ct 1988), Minnesota North Star Dino Ciccarelli was convicted of assault for his part in an incident which took place on 6 January 1988, in a National Hockey League game in Toronto, Ontario ... Ontario Provincial Court Judge Sidney Harris said, "It is time now that a message go out from the courts that violence in a hockey game or in any other circumstances is not acceptable in our society." Ciccarelli was sentenced to one day in jail and ordered to pay a $1,000 fine.'

SAMPLE SUMMARY OF CRIMINAL PROSECUTIONS FOR SPORTING VIOLENCE ON THE FIELD OF PLAY: 1878–1994

[NB Almost daily and frequently weekly referrals come the author's way from all parts of the United Kingdom to illustrate the increasing and sickening sequence of field violence which sadly inspired the London *Evening Standard*'s publication under its title *Sporting Spite: Rebels and Rebellion in World Sport* (1991), cited at p 18 (supra). The examples which follow could be multiplied countless times over to reflect a basic thread and principle.]

1878	Decision
Leicester Assizes	Acquittal.
Prosecution for unlawful soccer tackle: manslaughter charge (*R v Bradshaw* (1878) 14 Cox CC 83)	**Principle** Deliberate and/or reckless tackle not proved to jury. Rider by jury to tighten up tackling rules.

1882
Berkshire Quarter Sessions
Bare-knuckle prize fight.
Prosecution of spectators for
aiding and abetting in such fight
(*R v Coney* (1882) 8 QBD 534)

Decision
Conviction quashed for defective
summing up.
Principle
Blow struck in prize fight clearly an
assault, but playing with single sticks
or wrestling does not involve an
assault, nor does boxing with gloves
in the ordinary way. Consent of
illegal prize-fighters to interchange of
blows no defence.

1898
Leicester Assizes
Prosecution for unlawful soccer
tackle: murder (*R v Moore* (1898)
14 TLR 229)

Decision
Guilty. Manslaughter.
Principle
Deliberate and/or reckless tackle
outside laws of game proved.

1901
*Central Criminal Court: Old
Bailey*
Test case prosecution against
National Sporting Club for
illegality or legality of
Queensberry rules boxing
competition (*R v Roberts and Ors*
(1901) Daily Telegraph, 29 June)

Decision
Acquittal.
Principle
Boxing within the rules as distinct
from boxing until exhausted not
unlawful. See pp 172–173 below.

1969
*Maidstone Assizes (transferred
from Chelmsford)*
Prosecution for murder after
death from niggling blow in Essex
amateur soccer match (*R v
Southby* (1969) Police Review, 7
February, vol 77, p 110; NLJ
vol 120, p 413)

Decision
Guilty. Manslaughter.
Principle
Deliberate and/or reckless blow
outside laws of game proved.

1977
Lyons, France
Prosecution of rugby
international for field assault
(unreported)

Decision
Conviction (reversed on appeal).
Principle
Deliberate and/or reckless foul play
on field equals criminal conduct.

1978
Newport Crown Court
Prosecution for broken jaw in
rugby tackle

Decision
Conviction (not to be appealed).
Principle
As above – deliberate and/or reckless
foul play on field equals criminal
conduct.

The French connection deliberately inserted here has no binding authority on the English courts. Because the prosecution was supported by the French Rugby Union against one of its international players later selected to play against England in the International Rugby Tournament, the citation is inserted deliberately and non-recklessly to remind all aggressively minded players and their belligerently minded friends in the Press Box, as well as all other home sporting national bodies, of the potential and ultimate consequence of violent and unlawful conduct on sporting fields.

1980
Croydon Crown Court
Court of Appeal
Prosecution for three fractures to face in rugby tackle: Guilty plea (*R v Gingell* [1980] Com L Rev 661)

Decision
Immediate custodial sentence (six months).
Confirmed in principle, reduced to two on appeal because first precedent (quaere: why only six: why not more?).

1980
Wolverhampton Crown Court
Prosecution for gouging out eye in rugby tackle (*R v Doble* (unreported) Stafford Cr Ct, 8–10 Sept 1980)

Decision
Jury acquitted in spite of evidence.
Principle
Judge recommended victim to approach Criminal Injuries Compensation Board.

1982
Scottish Sherriff's Court
Prosecution of two opposing rugby captains: prosecuted on advice of Procurator-Fiscal (unreported)

Decision
No evidence offered against one. Other pleaded guilty: suspended sentence.
Principle
Action at last: against punch-up on field (hitherto not pursued by abdication of prosecution responsibilities and also by victims for younger generations).

1985
FA Tribunal
Complaint by one professional footballer of assault by another within framework of bringing game into disrepute under FA Rule 35(a) (unreported)

Decision
Not proven, but deposit returned to complainant on establishing prima facie case.
Principle
Action at last: recognition of existence of potential offence at professional level.

1985
*Dursley, Gloucestershire,
Magistrates' Court*
Private prosecution for broken leg
in soccer tackle (unreported)

Decision
Guilty: £180 fined with costs.
Principle
Action at last: by victim on own
initiative.

1985
Clacton, Essex Magistrates' Court
Prosecution against woman
footballer for breaking
opponent's jaw in women's
friendly soccer match

Decision
Guilty: £250 compensation and
costs.
Principle
Female of species can be as deadly as
the male!

1986
South Wales
Process initiated against Welsh
International rugby player for
alleged assault in club match

Decision
Guilty plea to common assault.
Principle
Action at last, long overdue, against
alleged offenders at public level. First
prosecution against international in
United Kingdom.

1985–86
*Newport Crown Court and Court
of Appeal*
Concussion from punch in off-
the-ball rugby union incident
(*R v Bishop* (1986) Times,
12 October)

Decision
Guilty plea to common assault.
Sentence: One month's custodial
imprisonment reduced without
reasons to one month's suspended
imprisonment.

1986
Cardiff Crown Court
Ear bitten after tackle in police
rugby union match. (*R v Johnson*
[1986] 8 CAR (5) 343) Inflicting
grievous bodily harm with intent
contrary to s 18 Offences against
the Person Act 1861

Decision
Convicted. Six months' custodial
imprisonment. Confirmed on appeal.

1988
Swindon Magistrates' Court
Broken jaw by professional
soccer player in tunnel after
match (*R v Kamara* (1988) The
Times, 15 April)

Decision
Guilty plea. Inflicting grievous bodily
harm contrary to s 20 Offences
against the Person Act 1961. £1200
fine £250 compensation and costs.

1988
Bristol Crown Court
Broken cheekbone caused by
amateur rugby player in club
match kicking opponent on
ground during course of play (*R v
Lloyd* (1988) Times,
13 September)

Decision
Conviction: grievous bodily harm 18
months' imprisonment.

1988
Wood Green Crown Court
Broken jaw by amateur soccer
player in 'friendly' match (*R v
Birkin* (1988) *Enfield Gazette*,
7 April)

Decision
Actual bodily harm.

1989
*St Albans Crown Court and Court
of Appeal*
Concussion from kick on head to
player on ground by soccer
opponent (*R v Chapman* (Court
of Appeal Criminal Division
transcripts))

Decision
Grievous bodily harm. Eighteen
months' custodial sentence.
Confirmed on appeal.

1991
Ct In Cum Bd
Eye gouged out from Rugby
Union foul play in line-out (1991)
NLJ 1725, Hals Laws MR 92/54)

Decision
Criminal liability admitted though
offender not identified. £15,000
interim compensation award.

1994
RN Plymouth Court Martial
Broken nose from Rugby Union
foul play (*RN v Russell* (1994)
Times, 23 February)

Decision
4 months detention. Reduced ranks.

1994
Court of Appeal Criminal Division
Facial fractures admitted
Probation and Compensation
Order [See also Ch 15, whither
Sport and the Law?, pp 425–426]
(*R v Piff* (1994) Guardian, 2
February)

Decision
Attorney-General's reference to
Court of Appeal Custodial Sentence
substituted. Compensation Order
cancelled.

Criminal liability: vicarious liability and responsibility

One final area of criminal liability for sporting violence which to date
has not yet arrived in court is the question of ultimate or final

responsibility. Responsibility vicariously for civil liability would certainly exist against coaches, committees and selectors with proof of
appropriate evidence of known violence. It has also been confirmed
by the American case of *Tomjanovich v California Sports Inc*
No H-78-243 (SD Tex 1979) see p 184, below. A similar response
equating criminal with civil liability and responsibility, subject
to the variations in the degree or level of evidence and proof required,
has yet to be tested in the courts for this particular sporting penalty
area. Nevertheless there is now appropriate precedent available from
the associated world of entertainment which the author suggests
can support the positive response to the referee's question. This
guidance is provided from *Wilcox v Jeffery* [1951] 1 All ER 464, that
if the appropriate evidence can exist of knowledge of proven violent
sporting offences and encouragement to persist is given by further
selection with no contrary warning of discouragement; then vicious
criminal liability can arise, in the circumstances discussed immediately below.

In 1949 a greatly admired United States musician and citizen,
Coleman Hawkins, a jazz saxophonist, was granted permission to
enter the United Kingdom under art 1 (4) of the Aliens Order 1920,
subject to a limitation against taking any employment, paid or unpaid. The owner of a monthly magazine, *Jazz Illustrated* was convicted at Bow Street Magistrates Court under art 18 (2) of the Order,
of aiding and abetting a breach of the condition of entry by encouraging a concert performance given by Coleman Hawkins.

The appeal against conviction was heard by a strong Divisional
Court in the King's Bench Division comprising the Lord Chief
Justice, Lord Goddard, Humphreys J and Devlin J (as he then was).
The facts included circumstances of active and more significantly
negative encouragement which Lord Goddard explained in his
characteristically robust and colourful style when rejecting the appeal
against conviction (at p 466):

> 'The appellant [Wilcox] clearly knew that it was an unlawful act for him
> [Coleman Hawkins] to play. He had gone there to hear him, and his
> presence and payment to go there was an encouragement. He went there
> to make use of the performance, because he went there, as the magis-
> trate finds and was justified in finding, to get "copy" for his newspaper.
> It might have been entirely different, as I say, if he had gone there and
> protested, saying:
> "The musicians' union do not like you foreigners coming here and
> playing and you ought to get off the stage".'

At that period, international mutual exclusivities among musicians
unions operated as keenly on both sides of the Atlantic as the recent
differences between the national acting unions manifested in the
dispute about the wife of Sir Andrew Lloyd-Webber, Sarah Brightman, performing in America. Lord Goddard continued:

'If he [Wilcox] had booed, it might have been some evidence that he was not aiding and abetting.'

More than 40 years on in the 1990s, the concept of a Lord Chief Justice recommending booing as a form of discouragement at a public performance is both indicative of the shift in social attitudes and also the change in climate surrounding light entertainment. Furthermore, Lord Goddard was not unfamiliar with the sporting scene. During the vintage Corinthian era he had obtained his running Blue for Oxford versus Cambridge in the Annual Athletics Inter-University Sports at Queen's Club in 1898 and for many occasions when the fixture was resumed in 1946 in the year of his appointment as Lord Chief Justice he was seen to be officiating near the winning post at the White City. The point was made clearly in *Wilcox v Jeffery* that negative as well as positive encouragement can comprise aiding and abetting; and although that ruling may one day be challenged the undoubted fact is that it is still cited in the leading practitioners' and academic books as an authentic authority, ie Glanville Williams, *Textbook of Criminal Law* (1983, 2nd edn, p 250), Smith & Hogan, *Criminal Law*: Part I. General Principles (1983, 5th edn, pp 122, 125); *Archbold* (42nd edn p 2308 at para 29.5). Accordingly, until it is over-ruled or distinguished by any court of comparable status sports, coaches, committees, and direct participating supporters of the selection of known violent playing offenders cannot say that they have not been warned of the full criminal consequences if their choice persists in offending by committing criminal offences, albeit misguidedly, in the name of a game. To what extent the same principles could apply to the selection of offenders with known violent proven criminal convictions outside sport is a further question which may yet have to be considered in the future if current violent sporting tendencies continue unabated. An admirable step in the right direction was the peremptory and public action by the Rugby Union executive in March 1987 to exclude from selection for the next rugby international players who had been associated with violent play during the Wales versus England international at Cardiff forty-eight hours earlier.

Finally separate and apart from these physical offences against the criminal law are others which happily are rarer in apparent extent, but none the less have to be recorded. As indicated above, the author is indebted to the industry of Mr Simon Inglis, recalling what had already been recorded by the author in official FA publications. Mr Inglis followed his own valuable and learned architectural and historical survey of *The Football Grounds of England and Wales* with no less a salutary reminder of the extent to which sport reflects society, in the later publication *Soccer in the Dock*. The chapter 'Power to the

People' recalls the assistance of campaigning newspapers to uncover financial (as distinct from physical) corruption with the professional game during the 1960s. Resulting from these and other energetic concurrent pursuits from additional sources, prosecutions of a different kind from those analysed above were mounted. They may be summarised thus:

1963	**Decision**
Doncaster Magistrates' Court	Fined maximum £50 each.
Prevention of Corruption Act	**Principle**
1906. 3 players charged with	FA ban permanently from football
attempting to fix a 3rd Division	and football management.
Football League match.	
1963	**Decision**
Rochdale Magistrates' Court	Fined £60.
Agent charged with offering	**Principle**
bribes to footballers.	Tip of iceberg during investigations.
1964	**Decision**
Mansfield Magistrates' Court	Guilty and custodial imprisonment
committal proceedings	for international footballers.
Nottingham Assizes	**Principle**
Conspiracy to corrupt.	International footballers not above the law.

3 CIVIL LIABILITY

Introduction

The corollary to the criminal process for broken limbs on sporting fields at any code is clearly a damages claim, with the corresponding burden of proof in civil claims geared to a balance of probabilities. That is distinct from the degree or level of satisfaction beyond reasonable doubt or satisfaction of sureness required for the necessary burden or proof in criminal trials.

Unlike the criminal liability lineage beginning in 1878, injury inflicted in the course of play by participants, as distinct from those caused by land occupiers or promoters, do not appear to have entered court reports until the beginning of the century, and particularly during the interwar years, 1919–39. In the Court of Appeal decision of *Wooldridge v Sumner* arising out of the White City National Horse Show of the Year, Diplock LJ (later Lord Diplock) said:

'It is a remarkable thing that in a nation where during the present century so many have spent so much of their leisure in watching other people take part in sport and pastimes there is an almost complete dearth of judicial authority as to the duty of care owed by the actual participants.'

Albeit, as he concluded,

'to the spectators.'

In that particular case, a professional photographer was the injured plaintiff.

Twenty-odd years later in *Condon v Basi*, the Master of the Rolls, Sir John Donaldson, commented in the early part of this judgment:

> 'It is said that there is no authority as to what is the standard of care which governs the conduct of players in competitive sport generally and above all, in a competitive sport whose rules and general background contemplate that there will be physical contact between the players, but that appears to be the position. This is somewhat surprising, but appears to be correct.'

What was 'said' on the occasion to the Master of the Rolls, was incomplete. On four earlier occasions one of the most self-disciplined of all sporting activities, golf, threaded a pattern of liability from which 'a standard of care which governs the conduct of players in competitive sport can be gauged' was clearly identifiable; and Diplock LJ's comment is explicable from six interlocking sources:

(1)   the absence of any legal aid until 1950 to assist litigants of slender-means for civil claims;

(2)   notwithstanding the existence since 1950 of that limited legal aid capacity, private litigants as distinct from institutions, multi-national organisations or sporting governing bodies can hardly run the risk of costs involved; indeed, even the FA was justified in asking the Sports Council and the CCPR to join their quest for charitable status on behalf of the rest of sport for the potential expense of its appeal to the House of Lords in 1979–80;

(3)   the absence at present in 1994 of any wish to contemplate an American-style contingency fund system for legal costs, which has at last been floated in outline form by the solicitors' governing body, the Law Society;

(4)   the general reluctance in more leisurely days to bring the law courts onto the playing fields before professional sport and commercial sponsorship created a conventional climate for litigation;

(5)   a continued reluctance generally to recognise that sport cannot be above the law, and that however magical and dramatic it may be, the ordinary rules of life and the law of the land are never suspended at any time of its existence;

(6)   the lesser quantum of persistent and sustained sporting field violence before 1962 compared with its progression permanently since then.

Boxing

One particular activity fuses the civil and criminal liabilities into a combined focus: boxing. This self-proclaimed Noble Art of Self-Defence contains in that descriptive title a legal issue common to both civil and criminal litigation (*R v Palmer*; *R v Turner*; *Lane v Holloway*). To-day the legality or illegality of boxing depends exclusively upon whether or not the evidence produced before a court creates a condition of sparring or prize fighting, from which modern boxing has evolved. So far as the Law Commission Consultation Paper No 134 (supra) is concerned, paragraphs 10.21 and 10.22 state:

> '**10.21**   The only explanation of injury and death continuing to be caused in boxing with complete impunity, at least as far as the criminal law is concerned, is that the immunity of boxing from the reach of the criminal law is now so firmly embedded in the law that only special legislation can change the position. We do not consider further in this Paper whether such legislation should be introduced, for two reasons. First, as we have already pointed out, the legality of boxing is a clear anomaly in the context of the general rules applying to sports and games that are described above, or in the context of any general rules for sports and games that might emerge from the study conducted through this Paper. Second, we fully recognise that whether or not boxing should continue to be legal is a hotly contested issue, already much-debated, that is not going to be resolved by any sort of appeal to the general law.
> **10.22**   Therefore, it is in our view for Parliament to take an entirely separate decision, in the light of the material sedulously put before it by the British Medical Association and others, as to whether boxing should continue to be lawful. We merely note that, in the event of boxing continuing to be lawful, and there being comprehensive legislation on offences against the person, it will be necessary specifically to provide in any such legislation that it is not criminal to kill or intentionally severely to injure another person in the course of a boxing bout.'

More realistic and meaningful in the welter of commentary after the death of the young super bantamweight boxer Bradley Stone on 2 April 1994 have been the recommendations of some of the British Boxing Board of Control's doctors and Neil Allen, the London *Evening Standard*'s boxing and athletics correspondent from his knowledge of all the competitions' drug-testing regulations. These are spot-check weight-tests during pre-title fight training to avoid dehydration and other health-damaging practices. In brief, a prize fight exists, and is illegal, if parties meet intending to fight until one gives in from exhaustion or injury is received whether gloves are used or not. A mere exhibition of skill in sparring, demonstrating the Noble Art, is not illegal (*R v Orton* (1978) 39 LT 293, 43 JP 72J).

A quintet of legal rulings over half a century from 1866 to 1911 demonstrates the differing degrees of evidence for the legal status of boxing, which in Britain has never been formally legalised. Nevertheless, one of the many valuable judgments from Australian courts has come as close as anything can be traced judicially for legitimising its existence. For in the Supreme Court of Victoria Mr Justice McInerney in *Pallante v Stadiums Property Limited* (No 1) [1976] VR 331 rejected a procedural application to strike out the statement of claim by a boxer who had received eyesight injuries when boxing under Australian Boxing Alliance Rules. He sued all persons other than his opponent, namely the promoter, his trainer, the matchmaker and referee. (See also Lord Mustill in *R v Brown* [1993] 2 WLR 556 at 592 F–G.)

The summary of the judgment at [1976] VR 332 vindicated boxing as 'not an unlawful and criminal activity so long as, whether for reward or not, it was conducted by a contestant as a boxing sport or contest, not from the motive of personal animosity, or at all events not predominantly from that motive, but predominantly as an exercise of boxing skill and physical condition in accordance with rules and in conditions the object of which was to ensure that the infliction of boxing harm was kept within reasonable bounds, so as to preclude or reduce, so far as is practicable, the risk of either contestant incurring serious head injury, and to ensure that victory should be achieved in accordance with rules by the person demonstrating the greater skill as a boxer.'

The ultimate result of the claim was never disclosed, and in the absence of contrary information, should be treated as having been settled. Two commercial cases in the English courts for events outside the boxing ring concerned management contracts and procedural remedies. In *Warren v Mendy* [1989] 3 All ER 103 injunctions were refused; *Watson v Prager* [1991] 3 All ER 487 concerned a stay of a restraint of trade action which resisted effectively an arbitration agreement tarnished by invalidity.

The English cases are summarised below.

1 1866 *R v Young* [1866] 10 Cox 370 held by Bramwell B at 373	After a trial following a boxing fatality, fighting with gloves in a private room, supported by medical evidence that the sparring with gloves is not dangerous, thereby did not create a breach of the peace or result in a manslaughter verdict. However, it had occurred to him that 'supposing there was no danger in the original encounter, the men fought on until they were in such a state of exhaustion that

it was probable they would fall and fall dangerously, and if death ensued from that it might amount to manslaughter.'

2 1878
R v Orton (1878) 39 LT 293

Court of Crown Cases Reserved (forerunner of Court of Criminal Appeal, now Court of Appeal Criminal Division) confirmed a jury's verdict which had considered evidence of the contest, including examination of the gloves used:

Kelly CB: 'No doubt the contestants wore gloves; but that did not prevent them from severely punishing each other.'

Danman J: 'The jury having examined the gloves and having the fact proved that the contestants severely mauled each other, they found rightly that this was a prize fight. The question was entirely one for the jury.'

3 1882
R v Coney [1882] 8 QBD 534

Court of Crown Cases Reserved confirmed
(1) a prize fight is illegal;
(2) all persons aiding and abetting are guilty of assault (although the evidence before the court did not qualify for a conviction);
(3) consent of the persons actually engaged in fighting the interchange of blows does not afford any answer to the criminal charge of assault (which is the *volenti non fit injuria* principle applied to criminal law: (see also *R v Donovan* [1934] 2 KB 498; no one can consent to crime).

4 1901
R v Roberts & Ors
Daily Telegraph &
other sources: 29 June 1901

Central Criminal Court (Old Bailey). Prosecution for manslaughter following fatal accident after head injury during gloved contest at fashionable National Sporting Club in London.
Grantham J's summing up to jury explained that
'he thought the weight of evidence went to show the fatal blow was caused not by a knock-out blow inflicted by Roberts, but by a fall on to the rope in the effort of the deceased victim, by throwing himself back, to avoid a blow.'
The jury's verdict in answer to specific questions formulated by the trial judge was

(1) accident; (2) boxing match; (3) not guilty
of manslaughter.

The decision was limited to the facts and
did not extend the principle which contrasts
illegal prize fighting with lawful sparring and
boxing. It is wrongly cited in sporting and
social texts as legitimising boxing, a technical
status which has never positively arisen. Hence
the ruling on the limited special facts: not
illegal.

5 1911
R v Driscoll and
Moran [British Boxing
Year-book 1985: p 12]

Birmingham Magistrates' Court: Jim Driscoll
and Owen Moran were summoned to show
cause why they should not be bound over to
keep the peace on the eve of a featherweight
title fight. Both were bound over and the
contest was delayed for two years, before it
was promoted and ended as a draw at the
National Sporting Club premises at King
Street, Covent Garden in London.

The last weapon in the legal armoury originates from a mixture of
common law and statute, the Justices of the Peace Act 1361. Its
availability to protect the peace of the realm applies not only to
participating contestants but also to the public at large. Thus it can be
used against boxing promoters' arrangements for stewarding the
developing problems of crowd conduct comparable to football hooliganism. Against that background of British boxing's law court appearances, the affinity with civil liability and damages can be
assessed. The issue of consent as defence to a civil claim for damages
was considered fully by the Court of Appeal Civil Division during a
civil claim of assault in *Lane v Holloway* ([1968] QB 379). It applies
equally effectively to the more frequently utilised remedy for claiming
civil damages against an offending participant of negligence; and also
to a lesser extent when the remedy provided by the law of nuisance
can be applied (ie by coming to the nuisance).

There are thus three separate heads under which damages can be
recovered for playing field injuries caused by participants:

(1)   assault and battery, technically trespass to the person;

(2)   negligence;

(3)   nuisance.

1 Assault and Battery (or trespass to the person)

This basis for a compensation award of civil damages is illustrated by
a colourful case arising out of a domestic dispute (*Lane v Holloway*

[1968] QB 379). The two most effective claims were for broken legs resulting from foul football play before *Condon v Basi* (supra), namely *Lewis v Brookshaw* (1970) 120 NLJ 143 and *Grundy v Gilbert* ((1978) Sunday Telegraph, 31 July, p 31). The contrast and legal difference between civil assault and negligence is explained clearly in separate passages from the section on tort in Volume 45 of Halsbury's Laws of England (4th Edn) and an extract from one of Lord Denning's judgments.

Civil assault distinguishable from negligence. The Tort section in Halsbury's Laws, under the joint editorship of the late Professor Harry Street and Professor N E Palmer explains (para 1310 at p 602):

'Assault is an intentional offer of force or violence to the person of another;'

and a footnote to this citation comments,

'There appears to be no decision in which mere negligence has been held sufficient to constitute an assault.'

Lord Denning in *Letang v Cooper* ([1965] 1 QB 232 at pp 239–240) explained that if an offender

'does not inflict injury intentionally, but only unintentionally, the Plaintiff has no cause of action in trespass. His only cause of action is negligence and then only on proof of want of reasonable care ... if intentional it is the tort of assault and battery. If negligent and causing damage, it is the tort of negligence.'

Battery is the actual as distinct from the intentional striking, and usually implies a prior assault. The form of pleading in court documents for the damages claim ideally includes 'assaulting and beating' (*Lane v Holloway* at p 38). *Condon v Basi* extended the frontiers of negligence to define a duty of care against causing foreseeable dangers owed by one participating competitor to another. The judgments were based on this plea. It also included in addition to negligence, a claim for assault and battery in the county court particulars of claim, which had begun the action *Lane v Holloway* ([1968] 1 QB 379).

The Court of Appeal was concerned with three separate legal issues arising out of a domestic punch-up at Dorchester in Dorset, where Judge Jefferies had dispensed his own brand of rough justice two centuries earlier. The facts concerned the consequences of retaliation by a young man's over-reaction with a violent blow causing serious injury and damage to a more elderly man after his insulting remarks. Each of the three legal issues has an importance generally and for sport particularly.

(1) Damages quantum, increased six-fold from £75 to £500.

(2) Consent to an injury (*volenti non fit injuria*).

(3) Claims based upon an unlawful act, ie fighting, cannot sustain a remedy (*ex turpi causa non oritur actio*).

Lord Denning dealt with that last legal point by explaining at page 386:

> 'Even if the fight started by being unlawful, I think that one of them can sue the other for damages for a subsequent injury if it was inflicted by a weapon or savage blow out of all proportion to the occasion;'

and with the second by agreeing

> 'that in an ordinary fight with fists there is no cause of action to either of them for any injury suffered. The reason is that each of the participants in a fight voluntarily takes upon himself the risk of incidental injuries to himself. *Volenti non fit injuria*. But he does not take on himself the risk of a savage blow out of all proportion to the occasion. The man who strikes a blow of such severity is liable in damages unless he can prove accident or self-defence.'

Salmon LJ at page 388 said of them

> 'There are recondite topics about which there is much learning;'

and at page 399:

> 'To say in circumstances such as those that *ex turpi causa non oritur actio* is a defence seems to me to be quite absurd. Academically of course one can see the argument, but one must look at it, I think, from a practical point of view. To say that this old gentleman was engaged jointly with the defendant in a criminal venture is a step which, like the judge, I feel wholly unable to take.'

Winn LJ at pages 395–396 cited two of 'the great criminal judges' in *R v Coney* (supra), Sir James Fitzjames Stephen and Hawkins J, concluding that Hawkins J in *R v Coney* said

> 'It is always a question for the jury in case of an indictment, as it was for this county court judge.
> ... So within the limits of his findings of fact it is for this court. I do not, having regard to those findings, regard what happened as a fight to which the plaintiff [victim] consented, to which he was *volens*. I regard it as a case where this young man [defendant] went down to thrash the other, older man.'

The actual citation by Winn LJ from Hawkins J and the prelude to it, are of sufficient significance to justify reproduction here as a classic statement of the common law which has stood the test of time for more than a century with approbation, and in principle, is applicable to both civil as well as criminal liability.

Hawkins J in *R v Coney* ([1882] 8 QBD at pages 554–555) explained:

'Nothing can be clearer to my mind than that every fight in which the object and intent of each of the combatants is to subdue the other by violent blows, is, or has a direct tendency to, a breach of the peace, and it matters not, in my opinion, whether such fight be a hostile fight begun and continued in anger, or a prize-fight for money or other advantage. In each case the object is the same, and in each case some amount of personal injury to one or both of the combatants is a probable consequence, and, although a prize-fight may not commence in anger, it is unquestionably calculated to rouse the angry feelings of both before its conclusion. I have no doubt then, that every such fight is illegal, and the parties to it may be prosecuted for assaults upon each other. Many authorities support this view. In *Rex v Ward*, the prisoner was tried for the slaughter of a man whom he had killed in a fight to which he had been challenged by the deceased for a public trial of skill in boxing. No unfairness was suggested, and yet it was held that the prisoner was properly convicted. To the same effect is the case of *R v Lewis*, in which Coleridge J, said "When two persons go out to strike each other, each is guilty of an assault." See also *R v Hunt*, per Alderson B, *R v Brown*, by the same learned Baron, and by Bramwell B, in *R v Young*.

The cases in which it has been held that persons may lawfully engage in friendly encounters not calculated to produce real injury to or to rouse angry passions in either, do not in the least militate against the view I have expressed; for such encounters are neither breaches of the peace nor are they calculated to be productive thereof, but if, under colour of a friendly encounter, the parties enter upon it with, or in the course of it form, the intention to conquer each other by violence calculated to produce mischief, regardless of whether hurt may be occasioned or not, as, for instance, if two men, pretending to engage in an amicable spar with glove, really have for their object the intention to beat each other until one of them be exhausted and subdued by force, and so engage in a conflict likely to end in a breach of the peace, each is liable to be prosecuted for an assault: *R v Orton*. Whether an encounter be of the character I have just referred to, or a mere friendly game, having no tendency, if fairly played, to produce any breach of the peace, is always a question for the jury in case of an indictment, or the magistrates in case of summary proceedings.'

Nearly a century later these principles were applied in substance to claims for damages for broken legs arising from foul tackles on soccer fields in *Lewis v Brookshaw* in 1970 and *Grunday v Gilbert* in 1977 as cited below. The author is also indebted to Hayden Opie, President of the Australian and New Zealand's Sports Law Association and a senior lecturer in Law at Melbourne University for drawing attention to their application as long ago as 1971 in *MacNamara v Duncan* (1971) 26 ALR 584.

1970 *Lewes Assizes* Civil action for damages for assault for broken leg in Sussex soccer match (*Lewis v Brookshaw* (1970) 120 NLJ 413)	**Decision** £5,400 damages and costs. **Principle** Deliberate and/or reckless foul play outside laws of game.
1971 *Supreme Court of Australia Capital Territory* Civil action for assault (trespass to the person) for head injury from intentional blow outside rules of play (*MacNamara v Duncan* (supra))	**Decision** A\$ 6,000 damages and costs. **Principle** Intentional blow to which no consent, even though probability of such acts known to occur.
1977 *Bodmin Crown Court* Civil action for damages for assault for broken leg in Cornwall soccer match (*Grundy v Gilbert* (1977) Sunday Telegraph, 31 July, p 31)	**Decision** Almost £4,000 damages and costs. **Principle** Deliberate and/or reckless foul play outside laws of game.

James Condon suffered a broken right leg from a foul tackle by Burdaver Basi in Leamington, Warwickshire, in a local league soccer match on Sunday 30 March 1984. The referee sent off the offender for serious foul play and the victim's lawyers were ready to sue not only, as pleaded in the form Particulars of Claim, for assault and battery, but also in the tort of negligence. To this we now turn.

2 Negligence

The essential elements from a developing lineage include not only the factors identified by Lord Denning in *Letang v Cooper* (supra) of

(1) unintentional injury;

(2) proof of want of reasonable care comprising breach of duty; but also the third element of:

(3) reasonable foreseeable risk of injury or damage.

Reliance was placed on Australian authorities where the remedy had been applied for recovery of damages suffered by one participant arising from a water-ski accident against another. This has been stated at page 169 above, notwithstanding that there was 'no authority as to what is the standard of care which governs the conduct of players in competitive sports generally.' Golf had provided a pattern on four occasions and ice hockey and motor rally driving among others. In two of the golfing cases the duty was owned to fellow participants: in two others to the wider public by a participant, and in a fifth under the law of public nuisance. Save and except for the nuisance example, the negligence cases in which liability was established by one competitor against another or beyond may be summarised as follows, with an asterisk against the fellow competitor/participatory victim precedent.

1927
Cleghorn v Oldham (1927) 43 TLR 465
Golfer not in course of play swings club during demonstration and injures person standing by.

Decision
Player liable.
Principle
Not in course of play. Defence rejected of consent to negligent act not unfair or vicious in recreation. Negligent misconduct actionable in recreation as in any other activity.

1949
Payne & Payne v Maple Leaf Gardens Ltd (1949) DLR 369 (Canada)
Ice Hockey players stepped out of or broke off from hockey game to fight, injuring spectator with stick.

Decision
Players liable.
Principle
No consent to breach of rules.

Pre-1962
Unreported decision of Seller LJ on South Eastern Circuit (see [1963] 1 QB 43 at 55) Golfer in four-ball hit into rough, losing the ball. Said: 'Out of it' and encouraged better players to proceed. Resumed after finding ball, causing injury as victim turned round at defendant's cry of 'Fore'.

Decision
Player liable.
Principle
Conduct outside the game; unnecessary for it; showed complete disregard for safety of those he knew were in line of danger from being hit from an unskilled instead of lofted shot over their heads.

1968
Pedestrian walking along narrow public lane injured on head by Golf ball (*Lamond v Glasgow Corporation* (1968) SLT 291)

Decision
Occupier liable for negligence.
Principle
Although no previous history of any accident, 6,000 shots a year played over fence should have created forecast of foreseeable happening.

1981/2
Harrison v Vincent [1982] RTR 8
Passenger in sidecar during motor
cycle and sidecar combination
race injured.

Decision
Motorcycle rider competitor and also
race organisers liable.
Principle
Rider and employers failed in duty to
take care of condition of competing
vehicle.

1982*
Bidwell v Parks
Lewes Crown Court (unreported,
except newspapers) French J.
Golfer in tournament injured by
ball hit from fellow competitor
without warning.

Decision
Fellow competitor golfer liable.
Principle
Dangerous for 24 handicap golfer to
take shot which could have gone
anywhere without warning.

1983
Hewish v Smailes
Epsom County Court (provided
by Court archives by H H Judge
John A Baker DL)

Decision
Head butt causing broken nose and
black eyes to 38-year-old local player
in local league match.
Principle
Civil assault (trespass to the person)
damages claim: £400 general
damages and £5.80 proved special
damages and costs.

1989
Vermont v Green (provided by Mr
Oliver Sie, Barrister) Basingstoke
County Court

Decision
Kick during course of play to
opponent causing two nights in
hospital adjudicated to have been
deliberate on spur of moment.
Principle
Civil assault (trespass to the person)
damages claim: £400 general
damages; but claim for aggravated
damages refused.

1989
*Thomas v Maguire and Queen's
Park Rangers* [1989] Daily
Mirror, 17 February, High Court,
London
Damaged ligaments to
professional footballer
(Tottenham Hotspur)

Decision
Negligence claim based on illegal
tackle.
Agreed damages £130,000 settled out
of court.

1990 *May v Strong* Teesside Crown Court (Halsbury's Laws MRE 92/62 All Eng AR (1991) p 313)	**Decision** £10,000 damages to 19-year-old semi-professional footballer (£6,000 pain, suffering and loss of earnings: for compound fracture of tibia and fibula £4000, special damages for net loss earnings for 9 months. **Principle** Serious foul play and violent conduct sent off field by referee = recklessness held by judge as assault.
1994 *O'Neill v Fashanu and Wimbledon Football Club Independent* 14 October, High Court, London. Settlement of claim without admission of liability	**Decision** Negligence claims bases on alleged illegal tackle. **Principle** £70,000 agreed out-of-court settlement of claim without admission of liability after plaintiff's case and first defendant's disciplinary record admitted in evidence by Collins J.

The non-citation of any of those sources before 1985 to the Court of Appeal in *Condon v Basi* [1985] could not prevent it from reconciling the test *defining* a competitor's duty of care owed to another competitor which was formulated by the Australian court in *Rootes v Skelton* (supra), with the differing formulae which can be extracted from comparable citations concerned with a competitor's duty to a bystander or spectator. Thus, in *Wooldridge v Summer* ([1963] 2 KB 43) which contained Sellers LJ's citation (1962) of his own finding of negligence by the golfer in the four-ball competition, the same learned appeal judge in that case also formulated a test for negligence by a competitor against a spectator which was considered without dissent in the finding of negligence by a motor cycle competitor towards his sidecar passenger in *Harrison v Vincent* (supra). Furthermore, during the last stages of preparation of these pages, two professional footballers' cases hit the headlines, which have been considered in depth already in the Preface and Introduction. In *Elliott v Saunders and Liverpool FC* [New Law Journal, 5 August 1994] Drake J rejected an obiter in *Condon v Basi* elevating a higher duty owed between professional footballers to each other, when he held generally that

'an intentional foul or mistake, or an error of judgment, may be enough to give rise to liability on the part of the defendant, but whether or not it does so, depends on the facts and circumstances of each individual case.'

After John O'Neill's agreed £70,000 out-of-court settlement of claim a few weeks later the *Independent*, 14 October 1994, explained in greater detail how the courts are generally continuing to award damages against players as they have since at least 1927 in the United Kingdom and also the Commonwealth by application of the traditional trilogy of

(1) duty of care which has been breached;

(2) by reason of failing to heed a foreseeable risk;

(3) resulting in injury or damage.

Indeed the New South Wales Supreme Court Common Law Division of Lee CJ, after an award of A$ 68,154.60 with costs against not only an offending player who broke an opponent's jaw in a professional rugby league match, but also the employer club (*Rogers v Bugden and Canterbury Bankston Club* (unreported) 14 December 1990 and see All ER Rev (1991) p 246), was subsequently affirmed on appeal with an increase for aggravated damages [1993] Australian Torts Rep 181–248 CA (NSW).

Furthermore, in *Johnston v Frazer* (1990) 21 NSWLR 89 the New South Wales appeal court upheld the trial judge's A$ 121,490 damages award for a broken thigh and back injuries caused by one horse crossing in front of two other runners under the guidance of a jockey held to have failed to have taken reasonable care for the safety of a fellow jockey in the relevant circumstances.

There remains, however, one final head of claim against a player participant which overlaps here, as it has overlapped already in an earlier chapter: nuisance.

3 Nuisance

The third golfing claim cited above from 1968 in which liability for negligence was established contains the flavour of a nuisance claim: for the injury was received when walking along a narrow public lane. Because it was argued and accepted judicially that the risk was foreseeable, the claim succeeded in 1968 in negligence against Glasgow Corporation, the occupiers of the links from where the ball was played. Nearly fifty years earlier, a taxi driver, George Thomas Castle, familiar to every law student, lost an eye when a golf ball from the St Augustine's golf links in Kent splintered his windscreen on 18 August 1919, when he was travelling along the highway adjoining the golf course. He claimed and recovered £452 damages against the golf club on the ground of nuisance (*Castle v St Augustine's Links Ltd* [1922] 38 TLR 615).

The claim was formulated and argued on the basis that the source of injury interfered with his enjoyment of the public thoroughfare bisecting the links. Sankey J (later Lord Chancellor) was satisfied that the location of

> 'the tee and the hole were a public nuisance under the conditions and in the place where they were situated.'

Because of the public element this remedy of nuisance was available to the injured plaintiff. It was a weapon in the legal armoury used successfully for the complainants in the cricket ball case of *Miller v Jackson* at Linz County Durham (supra) and the noise from the powerboat racing in *Kennaway v Thompson*. It will be recalled in the former case that after Reeve J had granted an injunction the Court of Appeal discharged it and an agreed sum of £400 was settled for the nuisance damages. In the latter case the damages award by Mais J of £15,000 for nuisance was replaced by a limited injunction, on a structured basis to restrain limited future nuisances. (More recently see *Lacey v Parker and Boyle (for Jordans CC)* (1994) 144 NLJ 188, page 59, above.)

Damages

The permutations of principles and formulae which are available for assessment of damages awards are generally outside the scope of this work. They will be found extensively in the specialist sources: *Mac-Gregor, Ogus* and Halsbury's Laws (4th Edn) Volume 12. In one respect, however, the courts have recognised that a sporting participant may require special consideration, separate and apart from the general recognition already available as explained by the Criminal Injuries Compensation Board (supra) for innocent victims of criminal violence.

In 1968 Thompson J in *Mulvain & Another v Joseph & Another* (infra) explained that the injury arising out of a road traffic accident to an American club professional golfer who was playing on a European tour raised novel and interesting questions of law. The injury to his hand impeded his opportunity to enhance his anticipated experience, publicity, prestige and money prizes from the tour. It required his return to America without completing his programmed tournaments. Damages were awarded under numerous special heads relating to the particular sporting profession:

(1)   loss of opportunity of competing in tournaments;

(2)   ensuing loss of experience and prestige which might have resulted in his becoming a tournament professional in America;

(3)   loss of a chance of winning prize money.

The limited report in the *Solicitors' Journal* of 22 November 1968

(*Mulvain & Another v Joseph & Another*) of Thompson J's judgment concludes

> 'The figure was bound to be speculative, but he would award under that head [broken down as numbered above] £1,000 damages against the taxi driver and owner [the defendants], including damages for disappointment felt by the plaintiff through the frustration of his plans.'

Additional damages for the usual head of pain and suffering were the significantly lesser amount of £140.

Accordingly, the fouling footballer who causes injury to an opponent in breach of the game's laws, and using the formulae available of *Condon v Basi*, an injured plaintiff could involve himself and/or an employing club in damages which could be substantial. Authority for *general* damages in sporting injuries is scarce, but see *Girvain v Inverness Farmers Dairy* (NLR, 19 Feb 1994, and Kenyon's Appendix). Furthermore, while these pages were being processed, a Criminal Injuries Court Board awarded a 31-year-old disabled athlete *fit to carry on his sport* but proscribed in the job market £70,000 general damages for pain, suffering, loss of amenity and loss of future earnings, applying the *Smith v Manchester City Council* ((1974) 118 Sol 50 397, 17 KIR ICH) formula for assessing general damages. Consistent with vicarious liability and responsibility at criminal law, this leads on naturally to a similar assessment for civil liability.

Civil liability: vicarious liability and responsibility

The civil law's concept of vicarious liability contains different elements and angles of approach from those in the criminal law. The distinction may not be self-evident to a layman, but it is easily recognised by lawyers through two separate strands resulting in an ultimate individual responsibility for clubs, directors, committee members or coaches, and potential individual financial liabilities.

(1) *Respondeat superior*, 'let the superior person answer', is the common law liability for acts done during the course of employment and direct contractual relationships.

(2) Agency opens up fields of liability which can be linked through three separate sources in the light of the undoubted existence of a negligence liability for personal violent foul play.

(i) *1896: Brown v Lewis* (1896) 12 TLR 455, Blackburn Rovers Football Club committee were held liable for their own personal negligence in having employed an incompetent person to repair a stand: and a year later in 1897 the club converted its legal status into that of a limited liability company.

(ii)   *1919: Williams v Curzon Syndicate Ltd* (1919) 35 TLR 475. Defendant proprietors of a residential club employed an old and dangerous criminal as a night porter, one Lister, who stole the plaintiff's jewellery from a safe in the club manager's office. The plaintiff alleged that the defendants were negligent in employing such a man without taking proper care to ascertain his record. Because they were found not to have used due care in engaging an old lag, they were liable to make good the plaintiff's loss.

(iii)   *1943: Bradley Egg Farm Ltd v Clifford* [1943] 2 All ER 378 at 386. The Executive Council of an unincorporated poultry society were held to be personally liable for the damage caused by a servant of the society who performed a contract negligently. Because the society were unincorporated and there was no legal or factual principal on whose behalf the council members could act (a position which will be explained more comprehensively in Chapter 14, 'Administrative advice') only those council members (as in the case of the Blackburn Rovers committee members) would be liable. Other members of the society were not liable.

(iv)   *1979*: In *Tomjanovich v California Sports Inc* No H-78-243 (SD Text 1979), the injured player, Tomjanovich, did not sue the other player, Kermit Washington. However, a lawsuit was brought against Washington's employer for injuries received when Washington punched Tomjanovich in the face during the professional basketball game. Substantial damages were awarded by a jury, and settled on appeal: but liability was proved on the principle of the employer's failing to curb the offender's 'dangerous tendencies' of what is known as 'enforcer' in the National Basketball Association (in accordance with the question posed by Air Vice-Marshall Lamb at page 165 (supra)).

(v)   *1990*: *Roger v Bugden and Canterbury Bankstown Club* (unreported) 14 December 1990 and see All ER Review (1991), p 246. In Australia, however, as explained at page 181 above, the New South Wales Supreme Court Common Law Division of Lee CJ is en route to appeal after an award of $A 68,154.60 with costs against not only an offending player who broke an opponent's jaw in a professional rugby league game, but also the employer club.

Accordingly, whereas the ultimate liability for vicarious criminal liability and responsibility is penal, the parallel result civilly is financial. The scope of potential compensation is explicable factually in human equations by the Criminal Injuries Compensation Board survey and when considering commercial compensation. Thompson J's judgment in *Mulvain v Joseph* (supra) gauges the measure of loss suffered by the American golfing professional prevented by injury to his hand from completing his European experiences and tour. To adapt the Lord Chancellor Lord Hailsham of St Marylebone's words in *IRC v McMullan* (supra), the courts and thereby the profession have not as yet begun to explore with any depth the scope for compensation flowing from playing field violence. Thus clubs, committees and coaches have been put on notice of the full financial consequences concurrent with the warning at page 166 above about the full criminal consequences through the selection of known offenders against the laws of the game, whether or not there has been a conviction against the laws of the land.

Ancillary awards
In addition to compensation claims for unlawful foul play are the remedies which exist at common law for protection of reputation and compensation through defamation damages, and Parliamentary provisions for industrial and insurance awards. The first two, defamation and industrial awards are more appropriately located in the comprehensive Chapter 14, 'Administrative advice'. National Insurance payments are a logical corollary to the heads of damages known to the common law.

The Courts' approval here can be seen in *R v National Insurance Commission, ex parte Michael* [1977] 1 WLR 109 (referred to in *Faulkner v Chief Adjudication Officer* (CA on appeal from Social Security Commissioner) unreported 18 March 1994), where a policeman's claim for a football injury was rejected – 'it was not part of his employment to play in this game of football': a preamble to the cases listed below.

National Insurance
Compensation
National Insurance (Industrial Injuries) legislation has existed since the 1946 Act implemented the 1942 war time Beveridge Report, replacing ultimately the late nineteenth century Worker's Compensation enactments. Social Security (formerly National Insurance) Commissioners adjudicate under a complex network of appellate procedures, but, in the industrial injury areas, they cover a pattern of precedents illustrating the fine legal distinctions essential for awarding state benefits to victims of industrial accidents.

Initial claims are dealt with by insurance officers working out of local offices of The Department of Health and Social Security. Their decisions against a claimant are appealable to local National

Insurance Tribunals covering the country and, thereafter, to the Social Security Commissioners sitting in London, Edinburgh, Cardiff and Belfast.

Their decisions (which, for England, Scotland and Wales, are reported at the discretion of the Chief Commissioner) include cases where claims have been allowed and disallowed, and the Clerk to each local tribunal has a set of these reports, which may be consulted by claimants and their representatives. (The style of citation appears below.)

The legal test for entitlement to benefit is that an employed earner should have suffered 'personal injury ... by accident arising out of and in the course of this ... employed earner's employment.' Sport arises thus:

National Insurance

(Industrial injury)

Claims	Circumstances
	Allowed
Football R (1) 13/51	Male nurse at mental hospital performing duty as employee in charge of patients able to play football. Injured during course of duty and, therefore, employment.
Cricket R (1) 3/57	Male nurse at mental hospital injured while duty working as member of cricket team for pleasure of patients and assisting recoveries. Employed as such.
Volleyball R (1) 68/51	London Fire Brigade fireman injured at volleyball during compulsory fitness training period: refusing to play creating liability for disciplinary action. *Held*: employed to play.
R (1) 13/66	Fireman employed at Royal Radar Establishment injured when playing volleyball during recreational period including long period of waiting, and for which required to be and remain physically fit. *Held*: part of employment.
R (1) 3/81	Police cadet injured when the police personnel carrier in which she was returning to training school after representing her cadet force in the Cadets National Swimming Championships was involved in an accident. *Held*: Entitled Participation in the championships was a training exercise which commenced and concluded at the training school.

R (1) 7/85 — Police officer normally worked as a finger-print officer. On day of accident was to have undertaken duties as a sailing instructor at a location 40 miles from normal place of work. Before setting out he telephoned the police station (from his home), as he was required to do, to confirm that no fingerprinting duties had arisen.

His employer reckoned his employment to have started from that time. On the journey to the sailing centre, riding his own motor cycle, he was involved in an accident.

Held: (by the Court of Appeal, reversing the Commissioner). At the time of the accident the claimant was in the course of his employment.

(Note: The Court of Appeal judgment appears in an appendix to the report of the Commissioner's decision which presently features in the loose leaf folder of 1985 printed decisions.)

Disallowed

Football
R (1) 57/51 — Policeman injured in representative match played during duty hours. No compulsion to play. Not part of employment.

R (1) 2/69 — Laboratory technician injured during game in employed hospital grounds in lunch hours. Temporary cessation of employment; thereby precluded claim.

R (1) 5/75 — Police officer held by Court of Appeal not employed when injured in representative match.

R (1) 2/80 — Fireman attending (under orders) a residential course at the Fire Service Technical College in Gloucestershire. Injured playing football in a match organised by the students which took place in the college grounds after the instructional sessions had ended.

Held: Not entitled. He had finished his work for the day – and was playing for his own pleasure and recreation.

R (1) 4/81 — Airline stewardess suffered accident (at Dacca) whilst playing tennis in a 'stop-over' period at a time when she was on call. It was contended, inter alia, that airline crews were required to participate in sporting activities in order to keep themselves fit.

Held: Not entitled. Not required by her contract of employment to play tennis. No 'in course of' employment (R (1) 13 fireman at volleyball) distinguished.

The legal refinements and distinctions which create these different decisions belong to a legal textbook and journal rather than the intended guidelines here. They indicate an area where the public are more likely than not to become involved with a legal claim. Within this context the Italian doctors' death certificate issued for the Italian professional boxing champion Angelo Jacopucci after his knockout by Britain's Alan Minter becomes recognisable with its tragic description: 'an accident at work.'

A schoolteacher out of class hours injured during school activities playing games would be eligible for an award; whereas a member of a works' team for fun probably not.

4 CONCLUSION

The principles of common law and statutory provisions set out above are of universal application. Sadly they are needed now to an extent which was non-existent in the days of a more stable and less violent society. The criminal law was generally quiescent for football field offences at soccer until 1969 (*R v Southby* (supra)) and in rugby until 1977 (*R v Billinghurst*). In 1930 the distinguished Cambridge don, Sir Percy Winfield, delivered his classic Tagore Law Lectures in the University of Calcutta (1931, Cambridge University Press). He was obliged to say at that central period between the two World Wars about the application of the doctrine of *volenti non fit injuria*

'to unlawful sports, operations, or processes, or to unlawful incidents in sports, etc, which are lawful.'

that

'The reported cases and *dicta* are scanty.'

Apart from the above citations within this chapter there are many more which have been excluded and which illustrate the principles involved without developing them, which is the editorial basis upon which the law reports are compiled. Nevertheless, neither reported cases nor dicta on the subject today can be considered scanty. Indeed, practitioners' and students' textbooks now consciously and self-consciously include specific sections for sporting issues and particularly consequences of violent play when hitherto they were ignored or absorbed into the general text.

Furthermore, each particular sport has its own self-determining internal regulations and rules exclusive to its own discipline which do not require attention of the courts unless they conflict with the law. This has occurred frequently in the past at the level of disciplinary tribunals. These will be dealt with in depth at Chapter 11, 'Fair play and reason in court'. In particular, at the time of Winfield's Tagore lectures and especially before the First World War the balance of

sporting literature quantitatively and in anthologies tilted towards
the traditional moneyed classes' areas of indulgence in field events,
'huntin', shootin' and fishin''. Each required an awareness of either
property laws, firearms law or game laws, linked by a common thread
of Parliamentary or contractual licensing, in the manner explained at
the beginning of Chapter 5, 'Public protection', above.

With the leisure explosion and the need to balance conflicting
sporting interest in a mixed urban-rural community within the framework of international competition, the amount of law outside the
general principles identified here must vary within each particular
sport. For illustration purposes only, a representative selection can be
summarised below, indicating topical issues but also matters of
permanent concern to the actual discipline involved and its
participants.

Horse Racing	Rule 180 (ii) of the Jockey Club's Rules of Racing empowering discretionary disqualification for banned substances, even from innocently used substances contained in chocolate Mars bars!
Motorcar Racing	FIA (Fédération Internationale de L'Automobile) regulations controlling designs of vehicles to prohibit excessive skirting of car bodies for additional road surface grip [and in 1994 more controversial and debatable mechanical requirements under surveillances while these pages are being processed finally at the time of the deaths of Ayrton Senna and Roland Ratzenberger].
Hunting	Animal Act 1971 consolidating and codifying common law obligations and remedies, of general application to keepers of all non-dangerous animals.
Shooting	Firearms legislation generally for national security and game law licences.
Fishing	Parliamentary and Common Market legislation for protection of offshore and Inland Waterways fishing.

The last category exemplifies the need for the level of awareness
among not only participants in the most numerically popular of all
participatory sports: angling. It also demands a concurrent awareness
among simultaneous participants: water-sport activities whose boats
can conflict with fishing lines, and offshore commercial operators in
breach of national and common market quotas.

If notwithstanding the contents of this chapter anyone should still
doubt the nature and extent of the problems for participants and their
administrators, coaches and managers and all others associated with
sport, they should reflect upon the following citation from the *Daily*

Telegraph sports column 'Sport Around the World' for Monday 15 July 1991. It contained the crucial following paragraphs:

> 'The worst violence in sport occurs on suburban club playing fields, according to a university survey in Australia – and the biggest problems are not restricted to the macho world of rugby league, rugby union, and Aussie rules.
>
> One of the most violent sports is men's lacrosse, and there are also many injuries in men's and women's soccer. Kicking is most commonplace in water polo, and elbowing is a problem in netball.
>
> Almost a third of all players felt the level of violence in their sport, including verbal abuse, was excessive, Prof Ray Vamplew, of Flinders University tells the *Sydney Morning Herald*. And more than half the spectators thought violence was excessive in the sport they were watching.
>
> "One of the worst problems", says Prof Vamplew, "is when you get down to the C and D grades, where players said umpires were biased and incompetent. Lots of umpires agreed with that. Professional sport was the best controlled by match officials and this was a key buffer against violence." '

Professor Vamplew has since transferred his Professional Chair to be the first in the United Kingdom for Sports History at the Simon de Montfort University, Leicester. More specifically, however, his 1991 opinion and evidence were corroborated in the London *Times* of 13 April 1991 by the celebrated writer and former editor of *Punch*, Alan Coren, with eye-witness testimony.

For how long such faith in the control of match officials will be justified, only time and the integrity and intelligence of professional administrators will tell.

Against all of that background the next chapter follows logically: 'Sports medicine and the law'.

Chapter 7

Sports medicine and the law

1 INTRODUCTION

The medical fall-out from violence, drugs and over-use and stress at all levels for participants in sport has highlighted Sports Medicine as a speciality within medicine which currently does not yet have the same status as other medical specialisations. Nevertheless, doctors concerned with sport are progressively pursuing the recognition that Sports Medicine has equal value to other identifiable medico-legal categories. Inevitably, the evolution of Sports Medicine must invoke the law as a close ally for the health of sport and the community. The National Sports Medicine Institute of the United Kingdom at St Bartholomew's Hospital, the British Association of Sport and Medicine and the Association of Chartered Physiotherapists in Sport are each recognised as an acceptable unit of medicine within society generally and the medical services particularly.

Two of the most important subjects in Sports Medicine and the Law are the unlawful use of violence and drugs. Cheating by drugs can have lethal consequences. Correspondingly, too, can cheating by violent foul play. When sports performers break their respective participatory laws or regulations to cheat by violence or drug absorption proved by medical or pharmacological evidence to a level of criminal or civilly actionable liability, the action from sporting governing bodies is minimal, with such violations sometimes even being ignored. When armed services personnel or practitioners in the standard professional callings of the clergy, law or medicine breach their codes of conduct or practice, they know the score and the ultimate sanction of expulsion.

The great Brazilian footballer Pele was brutally and criminally assaulted out of the 1966 World Cup on English playing fields without any sanction or effective action taken against the named Bulgarian and Portuguese offenders identified in his book *My Life and the Beautiful Game* cited at page 258. After the Canadian sprinter Ben Johnson was stripped of his Olympic Games title for drug abuse offences he was reinstated as if his misconduct had been condoned. It was only when he re-offended some five years later that a life ban could have been imposed. Ultimately, Johnson retired before this sanction was implemented.

The medical evidence for proving such serious and socially disastrous sporting situations is crucial provided that the medical role is recognised and identified. Dr Malcolm Bottomley, the Medical Officer to the British Athletics team and Medical Officer to the Bath University Medical Centre and also the Distance Learning course there for Sports Medicine, explained in 1990, writing in *Medicine, Sport and the Law* (Blackwell Scientific Publications) at page 165:

'There is no question that high levels of physical activity lead to physiological changes and patterns of illness and injury that are unfamiliar in the general practice of medicine. Sports Medicine is a speciality. It is to be hoped that its present struggles lead it to a mature status where it is recognised as a speciality in its own right and can fit into the conventional framework of medicine. Until then the present unsatisfactory state, where athletes' medical care is fragmented, uncoordinated and, unfortunately, sometimes contradictory, will continue.'

An example of how that 'present unsatisfactory state' exists within the framework is these two crucial issues which were identified at the end of Chapter 15 to the first edition, 'Whither Sport and the Law' and still remain as two of 'Sport's Four Vices'. To the more general pattern of Sports Medicine I now turn.

2 SPORTS MEDICINE GENERALLY

Bobby Moore CBE's status as England's World Cup-winning captain in 1966 means that he cannot be ignored when he wrote in the Foreword to a different kind of sports book, Dr Muir Gray's *Football Injuries* (1980)

'It has always been a bone of contention of mine that not enough has been, or is being done, to alleviate or treat injuries at the lower levels of football.'

No less renowned in football circles is Andy Gray, who became the only recipient ever of both the Player of the Year and Young Player of the Year awards in the same season from the Professional Footballers Association in 1977. His travels took him around the world with Dundee United, Aston Villa, Wolverhampton Wanderers, Everton and Scotland. His words, too, cannot be ignored when he wrote during 1986 in *Shades of Gray* at page 96:

'It's often said in dressing rooms that horses have better treatment than humans, and it's true as far as some football clubs go ... Happily, most clubs, especially first and second division sides, have tightened up on their medical care in recent seasons. But I could still name you a team of class players whose careers have been finished early because they were abused so badly.'

Happily, too, medicine in sport has progressed since those passages were written. Nevertheless, it is at least arguable that such progression has not been far or fast enough. Since Gray's elegy the Football Association National Rehabilitation and Sports Injuries Centre had been opened at the National Sports Centre in Lilleshall, Shropshire; HRH The Princess Royal, as President of the British Olympic Medical Centre, officiated at the opening of Northwick Park Hospital and Clinical Research Centre in Harrow on the outskirts of North London; a London Sports Medicine Institute which had been opened on the campus of St Bartholomew's Medical College in 1987 was converted into the National Institute of Sports Medicine in April 1992 and the Royal Society of Medicine in 1994 initiated a specialist sports section under the presidency of Sir Roger Bannister. Yet Dr Dan Tunstall Pedoe, the former medical director of the London Institute and medical adviser to the London Marathon explained to the *Daily Telegraph* (23 December 1986):

'Sports medicine has had virtually no official recognition or support from the health service. The average struggling athlete, let alone the serious amateur, is less well served here than in other countries, where there is government money for injuries and where there may be well-established sports clinics.'

This message was anticipated when Mr Donald A D Mcleod FRCS, Honorary Surgeon to the Scottish Rugby Football Union, wrote in his contribution to Dr Tony Dunnill and Dr Muir Gray's *Rugby Injuries* (1982) (the companion volume to Muir Gray's *Football Injuries*):

'There is a strong argument in favour of all responsible sporting bodies ensuring that the common injuries associated with their particular sport are identified and minimised, wherever practical, by legislation and education in conjunction with informed coaching. However, we must not lose sight of the fact that sport must retain a sense of advantage and achievement, essential components in the challenge of participation in sport.'

Not surprisingly, against this background, the National Sports Medicine Institute has three main objectives: the establishment of clinical services throughout the UK; the establishment of a tiered education system in sports medicine for doctors, medical undergraduates, paramedical staff, coaches, trainers, and members of the public who are involved in sport; and the establishment of a national research programme. It is the logical corollary to the conception 25 years ago in 1969 after a Royal Society of Medicine assessment of the general sporting injury scene, of Mr W E Tucker MVO, FRCS, a former rugby international and the leading sporting orthopaedic practitioner of his era who was also one of the founder members of the British Association of Sport and Medicine. He said that there should be an orthopaedic surgeon in each town which had the privilege of looking after the local football team. The Royal Society had estimated the social impact of sporting injuries within the UK at that time and had calculated 1,500,000 sporting injuries annually, with two outstanding consequences. Sufferers were unable to continue with their respective sports, and 10 per cent of the injuries caused absence from work (*Daily Telegraph*, 24 September 1969). This occurred before the Sports Council's creation and grant of a Royal Charter in 1971, with its later policies of 'Sport for All' and 'Ever Thought of Sport?'

Complete statistics are never available for this type of survey, partly because sport straddles every aspect of social behaviour for all generations, and so many different Government departments are involved, spanning health, education, environment, foreign affairs, public order, trade and industry (see Chapter 2, 'Progressive perspective' and Appendix 6). A more recent comment in the London *Times* (2 March 1984) under the heading of 'Medical Briefing' explained,

'With alarming frequency sportsmen are dropping dead as they play. Those who enjoy especially stressful games – squash for example – seem to be particularly vulnerable to unexpected heart attacks.'

It confirmed what the author was told around the same time by the Professor of Cardiovascular-Surgery at Oxford University:

'Those who play squash to keep fit often forget that it is more likely necessary to get fit to play squash!'

More recently, in 1990 the British Athletic Board's Director of Coaching, Frank Dick, assessed in a discussion paper leading to the National Institute's foundation, that 25% of Britain's medal-winning potential is lost through illness or injury and that 5%–10% of attendance at casualty departments of hospitals are caused by sports injuries. Yet in medical training the treatment of soft tissue injuries is inadequately taught. Furthermore, even before then he cited during 1989 the European Coaches Association's view that 'stress-related injuries were going to cripple European nations.' In that dimension the legal consequences have hitherto never been contemplated.

Closer to medical and clinical circumstances, the therapeutic value of the Sports Council's 'Sport for All' campaign can never be over-emphasised. A belief in sport for the disabled was a logical outcome of Sir Ludwig Guttman's conviction after the Second World War that work and recreation of all kinds greatly improved the mental, psychological and physical rehabilitation of spinally-injured patients. This was a logical sporting corollary to the late Sir Archibald McIndoe's earlier therapy in a non-sporting context at his world famous plastic surgery unit at East Grinstead's Queen Victoria Memorial Hospital in Sussex for the Second World War airmen whose burnt and shattered faces were re-structured to accelerate a return to normal life. His brilliant ancillary service to his surgical team for the mental, psychological and physical rehabilitation of his patients was to surround the wounded with the most beautiful and graceful nurses available, many of whom married their patients.

Parliament has attempted to keep pace with Guttman's initiatives through two little known and perhaps under-used enactments. Section 4 of the Chronically Sick and Disabled Persons Act 1970 requires public undertakings to provide access, parking and toilet facilities (including those relating to sport and recreation) which are practicable and reasonable for disabled persons needs. Section 5 of the Disabled Persons Act 1981 imposed duties on those who grant planning permission under section 29 of the Town and Country Planning Act 1971 (now section 76 of the Town and Country Planning Act 1990) to draw attention to the section 4 and other provisions of that 1970 Act for the benefits required for the disabled. Perhaps there are many centres, including the USA, which have in the past overlooked the needs and sporting requirements of the disabled.

These essential initiatives also demonstrate a healthy move towards understanding the practical and realistic requirements for the less fortunate minorities in the community. All the plaudits for the apparent financial triumph and profitability from the Los Angeles Olympic Games of 1984 ignored the disgrace which should shame its admirers for deciding that the 1984 Wheelchair Olympics, the Paralympics, failed to obtain any share of the bounty which was earned from the able-bodied Californian Olympics.

The Spirit of Stoke Mandeville: the story of Sir Ludwig Guttman by Susan Goodman (1986) recorded (at p 140) how

'The United States was the Olympic country in 1984 and it was anticipated that the Paralympic Games would be held there also. An appropriate site was located, and approved, at the University of Illinois in Campaigne. Then in April, to the dismay of everyone involved and particularly the competitors, it was announced that funds necessary to hold the Games could not, after all be raised in the United States. Joan Scruton, as Secretary General of the International Stoke Mandeville Games Federation, remembers a hastily convened meeting at the sports centre which was attended by representatives of foreign member nations. That day the decision was taken to mount the seventh Paralympics at Stoke Mandeville. The Games would not be cancelled; the hundreds of athletes who had trained hard towards this goal would not be disappointed; the Olympic flame would be lit for them as for the able-bodied.'

As Susan Goodman went on to record (at pp 140–141)

'Appropriately, those seventh World Wheelchair Games – but the first in the "World" category to be held in Britain in the Games' twenty-four years of existence – were dedicated to [Ludwig Guttman's] memory and to his vow: "We will build a sports stadium and an Olympic village so that the disabled athletes of the world will always have their own Olympic facilities here at Stoke Mandeville when other doors are closed to them".'

Guttman had allowed disabled competitors to fulfil their potential as athletes. Contrarily, some able-bodied athletes are knowingly destroying themselves by using dangerous substances to improve their performances. There are genuine problems which will be identified later in the chapter, 'International interaction', and will be further considered here, for reconciling lawful medically-prescribed drugs which breach sporting regulations and outlawing a blatant form of cheating. That is the essence of sport's drug issue, irrespective of the health hazard. Thus, in the definitive study of this dilemma, *Foul Play: Drug Abuse in Sports*, Tom Donohue and Neil Johnson (1986) explain that beta-blockers (at p 85)

'are widely used to treat high blood pressure and certain cardiac disorders such as "angina pectoris", a pain over the heart brought on by excessive exercise ... Theoretically, beta-blockers could be used by marksmen to reduce pre-competition tension; but owing to their potentially harmful effects and possible use as doping agents, the International Shooting Union placed beta-blockers on its list of banned substances.'

The wiser and vital legal problem for sports and, indeed, society in general which these developing areas create was crystallised comprehensively and advantageously for this chapter by the Sports Council's Medical Adviser, Dr Martyn Lucking, at a Sports Council Symposium on 'Drug Abuse in Sport' for sporting governing bodies held at King's College, London, on 27 March 1985. He explained:

'There is ignorance amongst a lot of medical practitioners in prescribing to athletes. A lot of them, even those in charge of major sports teams, do not know what is going on. It is very important that doctors are made terribly aware of the type of drugs which are banned and to be careful when prescribing to participating athletes not just at the event but during the training period. The Sports Council has been discussing at meetings white lists and black lists which are being drawn up. They will be circulated. The athletes themselves should be aware of this situation and know what drugs they can take and what they cannot take without contravening the laws of their sport.'

Eight years later in 1993, while this edition was being prepared, the internationally publicised drug offences before and after the Barcelona Olympic Games demonstrated how little has changed generally.

That charge of ignorance among medical practitioners by the Sports Council's own medical advisers brings the law in medicine directly into line with the law in sport. Yet medicine in sport mirrors the law in applying conventional professional standards and concepts to sporting situations.

Parliament has not yet concerned itself specifically with this particular developing area. The common law applied by judges has sufficed; and so far as is foreseeable, this must continue to fill the gap until Parliament is persuaded that legislation is required, especially for making illegal the use of steroids.

To date, sports medicine within the law and a need to open up levels of awareness can be identified under three overriding general categories. Specialist sub-divisions can doubtless be found. Current developments fit neatly into the following three divisions:

(1)   violence;

(2)   negligence;

(3)   drugs.

The first and last are not only clear-cut and self-evident: their prevention is essential for the general health of sport. The first has been considered in depth in Chapter 5, 'Public participation' and Chapter 6, 'Participation problems' for its legal consequences. The last, which goes to the root of so many social evils within modern societies, is an appropriate note on which to end this chapter. The second has the more easily and readily recognisable links with the law. It is also the most complex of all. Yet they all three interact within and upon each other. How they relate to each other has been shown already by the general observations cited here above on the sporting medical scene from England's World Cup-winning soccer captain and two leading orthopaedic surgeons involved with inherently violent play regulated by the Laws of the Game for rugby football. It is an appropriate note on which to begin examining in depth the inter-relationship between Sports Medicine and the Law.

3 VIOLENCE

This subject is discussed in detail in the previous Chapter 6, 'Participation problems'. In the Sports Medicine and the Law context it takes
on an important significance as the results of violence are inextricably
linked to medicine.

The *Sunday Telegraph* edition of *Sport and the Law* appeared in
1978, with its confirmation of the 1977 series of articles explaining
how deliberate and/or reckless violent foul play created criminal and
civilly-actionable liabilities. Shortly afterwards the social impact of
those malpractices was illuminated by two learned papers from different points of the playing and geographical compass in the British
Medical Association Journal for 23 December 1978. The distinguished rugby international player, as Dr J P R Williams (now Mr
J P R Williams FRCS), wrote from clinical examinations at his
surgery then at Bridgend in South Wales. These established from his
medical evidence based upon his rugby playing experiences that the
playing tactic of collapsing the scrum at rugby football caused cervi-
cal spinal injuries. In the same issue, two practitioners closely associated with the Guy's Hospital Athletics injuries clinic, Dr John Davies
and Dr Terence Gibson, explained how 30 per cent of their referrals
of rugby injuries were directly attributable to deliberate and/or reckless foul play.

In early 1992, the Arsenal and England team doctor, John Crane,
disclosed after an address given to the London (now the National)
Institute of Sports Medicine at St Bartholomew's Hospital in
London that he and his Arsenal and England physiotherapist colleague, Fred Street, established that 18 per cent of the injuries they
identified in the Arsenal dressing room were attributable to foul play.

Neither medical source specified, or perhaps neither knew, that the
medical evidence it had adduced created prima facie breaches of the
law justifying, on admissible evidence in court, criminal or civil
process in the United Kingdom courts. The century-old principles
had been established in *R v Bradshaw* ((1878) 14 Cox CC 83) and later
confirmed in *R v Venna* ([1975] 3 All ER 788) (and as explained in
Chapter 6, 'Participation problems').

Yet one beneficial result of the South Wales analysis was its impact
on the law-makers within the rugby union game. The injurious effects
of such a collapsed scrum sufficed to cause a change in the playing
laws of the game to identify and outlaw this particular offence. No
parallel change in the playing laws could legislate for the more general
deliberate and/or reckless violent play. Yet more effective administrative penal laws have fluctuated with varying degrees of discipline
to suspend or ban players from national to village green status to
meet the Honorary Scottish Rugby Union's consultant surgeon's

advocacy to 'minimise [injuries] wherever practical, by legislation.' Such action within a game such as rugby union football, can be as effective as any attempted Parliamentary sanction. Indeed, no better description of the limits to sporting legislation was given than the following judicial words of the then Montague Shearman, later Shearman J (who had the sombre task of sentencing Edith Thompson in 1922 as the last British woman to be hanged before Ruth Ellis, following the well-known Thompson-Bywaters murder trial):

> 'All that a governing body of sport can be expected to do is to keep order and punish open offences against its laws, and it can no more render its subjects good sportsmen and amateurs than an Act of Parliament can render citizens virtuous.'
>
> (*Athletics and Football: The Badminton Library* (1887) Athletics Government p 227):

Doctors practising or interested in the sporting scene can provide medical evidence which identifies areas where the sporting laws may require a reassessment as contemplated in Mr Donald A D Macleod's citation at page 193 here.

Finally, the legal practitioner familiar with personal injuries claims and cases will be aware of what the average sportsperson suffering from, or concerned administratively with, sporting issues may not know: that the medical evidence could be crucial in establishing or rejecting claims for compensation on violent foul play. Medical evidence assisted the awards in the three leading reported civil damages awards for broken legs in Chapter 6, 'Player participation'.

(1)   *Lewis v Brookshaw* (1970) Sussex, £5,400.

(2)   *Grundy v Gilbert* (1978) Bodmin, £4,000.

(3)   *Condon v Basi* (1985) Warwick, £4,900.

The level of quantum in these awards may appear capricious, or inadequate when compared with the Canadian citations referred to below. That problem raises separate and difficult legal questions extraneous to this chapter. What they prove is that on appropriate medical evidence, linked to equally appropriate and admissible general evidence, broken limbs can at least be compensated, and medical testimony in the form of agreed medical reports between the litigating parties, or oral medical evidence in court, is a crucial factor merging sports medicine with the law. It is even more significant in the realm of sporting medical negligence, to which this chapter now turns.

4 NEGLIGENCE

The English courts to date have been free from sporting medical negligence claims. This does not mean that no allegations of malpractice have ever been made. None so far has progressed to judgment; and even if such an event were to occur, the facts would have to result in a sufficiently novel point of law, or an illumination of an existing one with sufficient originality to merit an arrival for posterity and future citation in the appropriate Law Report. There is also a three-fold suggested explanation for the comment by Lord Diplock (as Diplock LJ) in *Wooldridge v Sumner* ([1963] 22 QB 43) about 'the duty of care owed by the actual participants to the spectators';

'It is a remarkable thing that in a nation where during the present century so many have spent so much of their leisure in watching other people take part in sports and pastimes there is an almost complete dearth of judicial authority.'

This is arguably explicable because of:

(1)   general reluctance to recognise sport cannot be above the law;

(2)   absence until 1950 of legal aid to assist litigants of slender means;

(3)   general reluctance in more leisurely days before professional sport entered the big money leagues to bring the law courts into the playing fields.

As the sporting scene explodes socially and athletic injuries demand specialist forms of medical attention, the present 'complete dearth of judicial authority' which Lord Diplock believed to exist could well diminish as the duties of care owed by the medical professional to sporting practitioners and administrators develop within the traditional foreseeability test, plus the causal connection with consequential damage, to create an alleged negligent medical act.

The categories of negligence are never closed, however, as the Court of Appeal under Sir John Donaldson MR illustrated in *Condon v Basi* ([1985] 2 All ER 453). It applied Australian judicial rulings to uphold a county court award of £4,900 damages for a leg broken in a foul soccer tackle, on the basis of breach of the duty of care in negligence owed by one player to another. This development occurred notwithstanding that the established facts were equally consistent with, and indeed also pleaded as, a civil assault. The categories of medical negligence have been most valuably and conveniently identified under the following eight separate headings by Professor J K Mason and Dr Alexander McCall Smith in the first edition (1981) of *Law and Medical Ethics* at Chapter 10 pages 126–142. Their equally valuable fourth edition published in 1994 does not require any adjustment from their Chapter 9 where the following structure re-adjusts to fit Chapter 7 here:

(a) *vicarious liability*

(b) *the reasonably skilful doctor: the usual practice: the custom test*

(c) *mis-diagnosis*

(d) *negligence in treatment*

(e) *the problem of the novice*

(f) *protecting the patient from himself*

(g) *res ipsa loquitur*

(h) *injuries caused by drugs* (the third main overriding category here linking sports medicine and the law).

Can they be applied to sport? Of course they can. The legal principle underlying every aspect of negligence with its duty of care-breach-foreseeability-causing-damage structure is constant for every different set of circumstances. All that sport does, as in every situation where the legal requirements appear for the first time, is to create a new level of awareness.

(a) Vicarious liability

The purely legal issues involved in vicarious liability and sport, the antithesis between general culpability and exclusion of liability for negligence both general and medical, emerged dramatically in 1958 during the Munich air crash disaster which destroyed the famous Busby Babes and the official travellers with the Manchester United football team's party. The conflict of legal liability causation between ice on the wings, or slush on the runway, dragged on for years. The vicarious liability there was contested between whether the air*port* and/or the air*craft* authorities were responsible ultimately in law for their officials' contribution to one of international sport's most poignant fatal disasters before the 1985 crowd tragedies in Europe and England. This dispute contrasted with the devoted attention and facilities and staff at the Munich hospital where Sir Matt Busby and his fellow victims were admitted. They demonstrated to the world how general medical care and skill responded in traditional style to an acute emergency, and earned universal acclaim and admiration.

Those experiences illuminated the overlapping legal areas as a result of the expansion of international sport and the higher frequency of travel. In the United Kingdom, vicarious liability for medical negligence at hospital level has suffered from near immunity because of the frequent charitable elements involved in funding hospitals to complete application (see *Roe v Minister of Health, Woolley v Minister of Health* [1954] 2 QB 66, [1954] 2 All ER 131; *Razzall v Snowball* [1954] 3 All ER 429 and *Higgins v North West Metropolitan Regional Hospital Board* [1955] 1 All ER 414). After that flurry of judicial activity, administrative arrangements were made between the various medical defence societies and the appropriate Government departments for apportionment of damages awarded and costs but since January 1990 the entire costs of negligence litigation are borne by the National Health Service (see generally Mason and McCall Smith: *Law and Medical Ethics*, 4th edn, page 197).

An example of the vicarious liability principle to non-hospital medical malpractice emerges vividly from the facts and awards by the British Columbia Court of Appeal. It upheld the trial judge on a claim by a 28-year-old Canadian professional ice-hockey player, Mike Robitaille, against his former employer hockey club, Vancouver, known as the 'Canucks' (see *Robitaille v Vancouver Hockey Club Ltd* [1981] DLR (3rd) 288).

Sustained complaints to various club officials and doctors of developing injuries suffered in play were rejected in what were found judicially to be arrogant and high-handed forms of conduct. The neglect proved resulted in considerable personal and professional losses and suffering. The doctors' nexus with the club to establish a relationship involving vicarious liability as there was a level of control and involvement comprised a relatively modest bonus of $2,500, season tickets, free parking and access to the club lounge. The appeal court upheld the trial judge's evidential findings that:

'the measure of control asserted by the defendant over the doctors in carrying out their work was substantial. The degree of control need not be complete in order to establish vicarious liability. In the case of a professional person, the absence of control and direction over the manner of doing the work is of little significance: *Morren v Swinton and Pendelbury Borough Council* [1965] 2 All ER 349, 351.'

Also confirmed were the trial judge's damages awards:

(1) $175,000 for loss of professional hockey income;

(2) $85,000 for loss of future income other than from professional hockey;

(3) $40,000 for the traditional pain, suffering and loss of enjoyment of life.

Of equal significance for all sportspersons was a concurrent approval by the appeal court of the trial judge's conclusion about the plaintiff's contributory negligence. He was held to be:

'20% at fault because his failure to take any action [ie, to complain] to protect his own interest was less than reasonable. There was evidence upon which Esson J could find that Robitaille was negligent ... the trial judge correctly distinguished cases ... which dealt with factory workers ... dealing here with a highly paid experienced modern day professional athlete and not a factory worker responding to the mores of olden times.'

The plaintiff's contributory negligence assessment by the Court of not pursuing his medical complaints to agencies outside the negligent club's control earlier than he did was possibly harsh. Nevertheless, the trial judge heard extensive oral evidence, and his final awards, which included aggravated and exemplary damages, demonstrated his ultimate awareness of the plaintiff's overriding and justifiable grievance for medical neglect which created a clear-cut vicarious liability.

This case should be contrasted with *Wilson v Vancouver Hockey Club* (1983 5 DLR (4n) 282 (BC SC) affirmed 22 DLR (4n 516), CA). The Ontario Court of Appeal affirmed the trial judge's decision that the doctor in the case was an independent contractor on the facts of the case and the club was exonerated from liability. This was because the evidence indicated that the doctor made his decision on treatment without advice from the management of the club, and because the doctor felt he served the interest of the players exclusively and that his primary obligation was to them as servants of the hockey club.

(b) The reasonably skilful doctor: the usual practice: the custom test

No other professional discipline can be more readily aware of the universal search for progressive treatment to alleviate suffering than medicine. The general public's and layman's awareness, too, cannot ignore the onward march of new frontiers: from Simpson with chloroform; Madame Curie with radiology; Pasteur and immunology, down to our own century and Banting, Best and Macleod with insulin, and the triumph of Chain, Florey and Fleming with penicillin.

In sports medicine, too, anyone who followed the public interest during the 1950s will recall the tension surrounding the fate of Mr Denis Compton's kneecap. Mr W E Tucker FRCS extracted it with his mixture of orthopaedic skill and international rugby playing experience (both functions inherited from an equally distinguished paternal practitioner in both activities). This allowed his patient to continue playing Test and County cricket with success and public acclaim. Mr Compton had already retired from an active professional football career with an FA Cup winners' medal and wartime international honours; and the novelty of the nature of this surgery was not concerned with his winter game (in which Paul Gascoigne's self-induced injury has commanded comparable current attentions). Nevertheless, the intervening years have witnessed contractions in periods of time from when a conventional cartilage operation for a footballer incapacitated the patient for weeks, to modern remedies which can return a player to training within days.

Against this background of inevitable mobility in thinking and equipment, what is the norm to apply? Each specialist area of medicine, more so than the law, has its own levels of knowledge with interdisciplinary connections. A trainer or physiotherapist would not be expected to have the same level of skill as an experienced physician or surgeon. The courts have moved on even since the first edition of Mason and McCall Smith: *Law and Medical Ethics* appeared in 1981, with two landmark House of Lords decisions on medical duties. It ruled on warning of risks (*Sidaway v Board of Governors of the Bethlem Royal Hospital and Maudsley Hospital* [1985] AC 871, [1985] 1 All ER 643) and conflicting medical opinions (*Maynard v West Midlands Regional Health Authority* [1985] All ER 635, [1985] 1 WLR 634). Yet on this basic issue of what is the usual or customary level of skill to apply, Lord Scarman and their Lordships reiterated long-established principles from the 1950s in two passages appropriate for citation here. For a detailed discussion of the debate about the quality and level of evidence for assessing medical liability generally see Kennedy & Grubb: *Medical Law*, 2nd edition 1994 at pages 465–468.

In *Sidaway* at page 649 he referred to a jury direction by McNair J in the leading case of *Bolam v Friern Hospital Management Committee* ([1957] 2 All ER 118, [1957] 1 WLR 582):

> 'as a rule that a doctor is not negligent if he acts in accordance with a practice accepted at the time as proper by a responsible body of medical opinion even though other doctors adopt a different practice. In short, the law imposes a duty of care; but the standard of care is a matter of medical judgment.'

In *Maynard* at page 638 he said:

> 'I do not think that words of the Lord President (Clyde) in *Hunter v Hanley* [1955] SLT 213 at 217 can be bettered: "In the realm of diagnosis there is ample scope for genuine difference of opinion and one man clearly is not negligent merely because his conclusion differs from that of other professional men ... The true test for establishing negligence in diagnosis or treatment on the part of a doctor is whether he has been proved to be guilty of failure as no doctor of ordinary skill would be guilty of acting with ordinary care".'

One unreported example of undoubted medical neglect for which the author's legal infancy and paternal restraint against litigation blocked the ultimate writ for neglect was cited here in Chapter 1, Genesis in the same spirit as Lord Haldane of Cloan's account in his posthumous memoirs of the Irish appeal case to the House of Lords. A novel point of real property law was argued extensively. Judgment was reserved; but as the first Lord Chancellor in a Labour Government explained (*Richard Burdon Haldane: an Autobiography* (1929) page 66):

'Unluckily, the next day was Derby Day, and the lay clients met on the racecourse, and were said to have settled the case there, so judgment was never delivered.'

The author's leg broken by accident in the Oxford University soccer trials resulted in treatment from a local hospital which included advice to walk upon the broken leg while the plaster was setting. In due course the broken limb lost its alignment, and an ulcer was created inside the plaster. Maternal wisdom caused a transfer to a London hospital, more specialised treatment and prevention of more serious consequences. Clearly the Oxford medical staff were legally negligent by today's judicial standards, and, indeed, by the standards of that particular period before Lord Scarman's citations appeared during the mid-1950s. The combination of personal legal infancy; the absence of legal aid; and parental advice, all merged to inhibit the justifiable proceedings for medical negligence against the appropriate Oxford hospital sources.

Furthermore, the Oxford University sporting authorities who had control of the Iffley Road ground where the injury occurred had no first aid or treatment facilities of any description. They too were, in the author's opinion today, also guilty of vicarious negligence. In the spirit of Lord Haldane's experience, however, judgment was never delivered, although perpetuation of this medical lacuna anywhere could well fill this particular legal gap at some time in the future.

(c) Mis-diagnosis

The potential danger for this category of negligence must be realised by all concerned with athletic injuries in every sport where judgments have to be made under pressures of time and circumstances, eg TV cameras and a crowded arena. *Mason and McCall Smith* explains

'A mistake in diagnosis will not be considered negligent if [the usual degrees of dealings with patients] standard of care is observed but will be treated as one of the non-culpable and inevitable hazards of practice.'

206 Sport and the Law

They cited in a footnote a judicial observation,

> 'unfortunate as it was that there was a wrong diagnosis, it was one of those misadventures, one of those chances, that life holds for people (*Crinon v Barnet Group Hospital Management Committee* (1959) The Times, 19 November).'

Canada, however, again provides a direct example of liability which was established, this time in the Ontario Court of Appeal. A 41-year-old tool and dye worker broke his right *ankle* when playing soccer with his young son. A negligently erroneous X-ray prescription for attention to the right *foot* was compounded by a cascade of consequential errors involving more than one medical practitioner, who successively consolidated earlier mis-diagnosis. This resulted in the appellate court's confirmation of the trial judge's ruling that 'one negligent doctor could be liable for the additional loss caused by the other'. The appeal court also upheld the damages award of $50,000 for the general damages, which included $34,465 for loss of income up to the date of trial. The successive mis-diagnoses proved very expensive for the doctors, who included a radiologist, as well as painful for the patient (*Price v Milawski, Murray and Castroyan* (1978) 82 DLR (3d) 130).

(d) Negligence in treatment

The examples above of the professional ice-hockey player, the author's personal Oxford University experiences and the 41-year-old soccer-playing father, all illustrate negligence in treatment. A grey area or border line exists between negligence and error of judgment. It was illuminated by the extensively reported judgments on the baby whose delivery was forced by being pulled out too hard with forceps and wedged, with resulted asphyxia and brain damage. The House of Lords refined Lord Denning's distinction between negligence and error of judgment when the trial judge's damages award of £100,000 was overturned on the basis that he drew the wrong inferences of fact from the oral and documentary evidence (*Whitehouse v Jordan* [1981] 1 All ER 267, [1981] 1 WLR 246, HL). Lord Fraser in the House of Lords explained at page 281:

> 'The true position ... depends on the nature of the error. If it is one that would not have been made by a reasonably competent professional man professing to have the standard and type of skill that the defendant holds himself out as having, and acting with ordinary care, then it is negligence. If, on the other hand, it is an error that such a man, acting with ordinary care, might have made, then it is non negligent.'

In *Whitehouse v Jordan* a conflict of medical testimony caused the Court of Appeal and the House of Lords to adjudicate that the very experienced trial judge had drawn the inferences of fact from the conflicting medical evidence. In sports medicine as a developing science and discipline, with varying levels of experiences for different sports and different parts of the anatomy, the possibilities of conflicting and genuine specialist opinions could exist. Speculation without real example cannot prophesy here. The legal formula has been laid down by the House of Lords in *Whitehouse v Jordan* and affirmed in the later opinions of *Maynard* and *Sidaway*. Sports medicine must lie with it until tested in the fire of evidenciary battles.

(e) The problem of the novice

Every professional is at first an amateur. The beginner must be guided by instructions. The standard laid down by the House of Lords (see *Sidaway*, above) 'accepted at the time as proper by a reasonable body of medical opinion' is comparable to the fledgling athlete and games player projected into action with veterans. Public allowances of limited sympathy for youth alongside maturity will not include forgiveness for sub-standard performances. The law does not differentiate either. If liability arises it could be vicarious for any employer or controller of a practitioner associated primarily or secondarily with medical services, whether as doctor, physiotherapist, trainer or traditional sponge man. The amateur club which permits an unqualified member to act as an ad hoc first aid assistant without any practical experience resulting in any serious or actionable injury is as much at risk as the hospital committee allowing an inexperienced practitioner to carry out complex operations usually reserved for the maturer staff (see *Brown v Lewis* (1898) 12 TLR 455 for committee member's liability when negligent sub-contracting causes liability).

(f) Protecting the patient from himself

This particular category in the reported cases is concerned with suicide attempts and tendencies. An analogy can apply to excessively enthusiastic athletes seeking performance enhancement from drugs or striving to return to action when not fully fit. Without firm medical guidance, emphasising the harmful consequences of the zest for play overriding the consequences of such medical advice, then a liability for negligence could well arise. The demands and stresses of competitive professional sport are particularly vulnerable in this category.

(g) Res ipsa loquitur

This penultimate stage in *Mason and McCall Smith*'s classification of medical negligence has veered between extreme critical and literal commentaries upon it in the House of Lords (*Ballard v North British Railway Co* (1923) SC (HL) 43 at 46). Lord Shaw of Dunfermline said in 1923:

> 'If that phrase had not been in Latin, nobody would have called it a principle ... The day for canonising Latin phrases has gone past.'

Lord Denning brought it all into focus as Denning LJ in a hospital negligence case (*Cassidy v Ministry of Health* [1951] 2 KB 343 at 365, [1951] 1 All ER 574 at 588, CA) with the judgment that the plaintiff in the case before him on appeal was entitled to say:

> 'I went into hospital to be cured of two stiff fingers. I have come out with four stiff fingers and my hand is useless. That should not have happened if due care had been used. Explain it if you can.'

Lord Normand in 1950 (*Barkway v South Wales Transport Co Ltd* [1950] 1 All ER 398 at 399) explained that it is:

> 'no more than a rule of evidence affecting onus. It is based on common-sense, and its purpose is to enable justice to be done when the facts bearing on causation and on the care exercised by the defendant are at the outset unknown to the plaintiff and are or ought to be within the knowledge of the defendant.'

Earlier, in an English Court of Appeal decision, Kennedy LJ explained:

> 'The teaching, as I understand, of that phrase ... is this, that there is, in the circumstances of the particular case, some evidence viewed not as a matter of conjecture, but of reasonable argument, which makes it more probable that there was some negligence, upon the facts as shown and undisputed, than that the occurrence took place without negligence.
> The res speaks because the facts stand unexplained, and therefore the natural and reasonable, not conjectural, inference from the facts shows that what has happened is reasonably to be attributed to some act of negligence on the part of somebody; that is, some want of reasonable care under the circumstances ... it means that the circumstances are, so to speak, eloquent of the negligence of somebody who brought about the state of things ... more consistent, reasonably interpreted, without further explanation, with your negligence than with any other cause of the accident happening.'

Finally, Canada provides one more graphic example which would have horrendous consequences for any athlete. The plaintiff entered hospital for treatment of a fractured ankle and left with amputated leg. No explanation existed. That evidence on applying the principles cited above pointed in one inevitable direction: negligence (*MacDonald v York County Hospital Corporation* [1972] 28 DLR (3d 521)).

(h) Injuries caused by drugs

'Compensation for injury by drugs is now regulated in the United Kingdom by the Consumer Protection Act 1987. This derives from the European Directive on product liability (Council Directive 85/374/EEC), the aim of which was to create strict liability for most injuries which were caused by defective products; this policy had long been advocated by commentators on compensation for personal injury. Under the terms of the Act, strict liability is borne primarily by the manufacturer of a defective product although the suppliers will also be held liable if they cannot identify the manufacturer.'

Thus did Mason and McCall Smith highlight an area illuminated with the widest general publicity through the Thalidomide tragedy. For sportspersons, and sports medical practitioners, however, the social evil inherent in the drug trade raises legal, medical and sporting administrative issues which were crystallised by two leading sports personalities in a manner discussed in Chapter 9, 'International interaction'. This crucial social as well as sporting problem cannot be emphasised too strongly for sport as one which extends beyond the level of medical injuries caused by incorrectly or negligently pre-scribed drugs into the wider and equally significant career injuries suffered by the sports patient's lawfully prescribed drug treatment under national legislation which conflicts with the sporting legislation of a sporting governing body.

Two examples which are cited in that chapter (Ron Angus (from judo) and Willie Johnston (football)) identified not only a developing area which has yet to be thought through between the three interlock-ing worlds of sport, medicine and the law: they crystallise and illumi-nate the revolution which has projected sport from a healthy, fun loving competitive and educative element to a ruthlessly commercial-ised sector of a high profile entertainment industry containing within it seeds of destruction for health, sport and society. They raise questions for the future which have yet to be acknowledged and faced by sport and society for which an answer can be provided only in part by the law. They are the reason why this chapter concludes with the questions they pose and why the heading comes at the end of this division of Sports Medicine and the Law into Violence, Negligence and Drugs.

The foundation for the claim that 'an answer can be provided only in part by law' was confirmed on St Leger Day, Doncaster, Saturday 12 September 1987. The Home Office announced that it had asked the Advisory Council on the Misuse of Drugs to consider whether steroids should be included in the Misuse of Drugs Act 1971. A bulletin entitled 'Drugs in Sport, a Reappraisal' from the Institute of Medical Ethics under its Director, Dr Richard Nicholson, claimed to raise two main questions:

(1)   Is it unethical for a sportsman to take drugs?

(2)   Is drug-taking so serious a problem that the governing bodies of sports need to draw up rules to prevent it, with punishments for contravention of the rules?

The premise on which the questions were posed challenged and canvassed within a sporting context wider issues than the health hazards beyond sport identified in *Foul Play, Drug Abuse in Sports* by Tom Donohue and Neil Johnson cited at page 221 below, or in Dr Ellen Grant's *The Bitter Pill: How safe is the 'perfect contraceptive'?*, referred to in Chapter 8, 'Women in Sport and the Law'. Finally, the August 1987 edition of the authoritative *Pacemaker International* journal, in a feature article entitled 'The Ugly Mask of Drugs' (page 50), explained the dangers for the breeding side of racing, that Bute and Lasix which are permitted under rules in most American racing states, 'may mask congenital deficiencies in horses that will later be passed on to their offspring, thus having a detrimental effect on the breed'. Indeed, in the context of this trespass upon nature and God's own territory, it is pertinent to enquire: are two-legged animals different from four-legged ones?

This important trio of publications prove the complexity of the subject and the need, perhaps in Britain at least, for an in-depth assessment based upon authentic evidence to the level and degree of quality which produced both celebrated Reports to which Sir John Wolfenden gave his name.

5 DRUGS

The symposium mounted in 1985 by the Sports Council at London University's King's College occurred when the Sport's Council's campaign for drug testing among sporting governing bodies was backed by a formidable body of oral, documentary and visual evidence. This explained graphically the adverse health consequences of rule breaking by cheats indulging in drug-taking throughout the sporting world at all levels, internationally and domestically. It was concerned primarily with the inter-relationship between the health and ethical sporting problems. It was not concerned directly with the wider legal aspects which are illuminated immediately below to expand sport's own conflict of laws situation, considered generally in Chapter 9, 'International interaction'.

January 1984 witnessed a *Sunday Telegraph* announcement from the British Judo Association that a dope test on Ron Angus, winner of the under 78 kilo category in the All-England Championship in December 1983, had proved positive. A sample contained traces of a stimulant, pseudo-Ephedrine.

Angus, who had dual Canadian-British nationality, claimed that the substance must have been contained in a sinus decongestant which he had taken under a lawful medical prescription by his Canadian doctor. Because he had breached the Association's requirements he was banned for life from competing in British championships.

Five months later, after he had taken legal advice, the *Daily Telegraph* reported that the High Court in London had lifted the ban with the Association's consent. It admitted that the absence of a hearing for Angus to explain his position breached the rules of natural justice, and the life ban was duly rescinded. The Association's rules have now been tightened to place the onus on competitors, and by implication, therefore, on their *personal doctors* to ensure that lawful medication does not contain banned substances (*Daily Telegraph*, 15 June 1984).

Even wider publicity was suffered by Scotland's international outside-left Willie Johnston, sent home in alleged disgrace from the 1978 FIFA World Cup. From the facts explained in his book *On the Wing* and in the medico-legal opinion expressed at the Sports Council Symposium, he appears to have suffered a gross injustice which should never have occurred.

His own *English* Football League club doctor had lawfully prescribed Reactivan pills for his nasal condition. The *Scottish* FA doctor had warned Johnston about drugs; but the footballer patient had not realised that his pills contained a stimulant called Fencamsamin, of which traces were found after a positive dope test, in breach of FIFA rules. His international football career was blighted without any apparent personal culpability on his part.

No complaint appears to have been made to FIFA by anyone on Johnston's behalf, and the fact that FIFA's registered office is in Switzerland takes it outside the United Kingdom Courts' jurisdiction. Thus Johnston could not directly have made a similar claim in Scotland against the disciplining governing body, FIFA, to that made successfully by Ron Angus against the British Judo Association, unless he had emulated John Cooke's claim and sued his own Scottish FA (see Chapter 9, 'International interaction', p 260).

Nevertheless, on the facts summarised above from Johnston's own account, he was undoubtedly innocent of any offence under the principles of British criminal law. Indeed, section 28(3)(b)(i) of the Misuse of Drugs Act 1971, says that any accused person shall be acquitted of a drug offence 'if he proves that he neither believed nor suspected nor had reason to suspect that the substance or product in question was a controlled drug' ie one of which the use is controlled by the Act, and thereby unlawful generally.

That sub-section, and others comparable to it in principle as laid down by Parliament, illustrates the problems which face sports participants who require drugs lawfully for medicinal purposes.

(1)   *How* are athletes and their personal doctors to know when a breach or potential breach of a sporting governing body's rules against drug abuse occurs?

(2)   *How* are sporting governing bodies to know that a failure to meet their own stringent rules for the protection of a particular sport does or does not arise from a lawful medicinal prescription?

(3)   *How* are lawyers to balance the interest of the sport in which they advise administrators with the need to respect the rights of individual competitors?

(4)   *What* is the patient to do when faced with what may become a conflict of personal health interests against the undoubted right in a free society to participate in healthy competition?

These questions cannot be shirked and have to be thought through within the framework of what lawyers recognise, usually in the international legal field, as a conflict of laws situation. Furthermore, with the explosion of international sport, and the concern of the World Health Organisation as well as international governing bodies about the problem, there is the added issue of international harmony for approaching solutions.

As sport becomes more commercially competitive within a TV-regulated global coverage, the necessity to keep sport within a healthy framework for itself and its participants demands a co-ordinated effort from everyone concerned along the lines suggested below. Without such a concord, recourse to the courts or some form of legal investigation would be bound to follow.

Doctors who treat patients competing athletically must familiarise themselves with the requirements of the particular sport in question, both at domestic and international level – and pass on this information to their patients.

Lawyers who advise administrators must see that any regulations to prevent cheating do not either transgress natural justice rules and the opportunity to be heard, or contravene the spirit of the British parliamentary defence that ignorance of the facts can be a defence in a drugs case.

Administrators should try, with doctors, pharmacists, lawyers and drug manufacturers, to attain a balance between the sport's rules and the individual's medicinal requirements, in the interests of fair play, health and the avoidance of cheating.

Competitors must familiarise themselves with their own medical requirements within the rules laid down by their particular sport.

The breakdown of this union has heralded a spate of sensational situations which are only the tip of a wider and deeper iceberg. Thus, after Ben Johnson was caught using steroids in the 1988 Seoul Olympics, the problem of the widespread use of steroids within sport was highlighted and the floodgates for legal consequences and liabilities were opened. Shortly after Johnson's positive test of the steroid stanozolol, the government of Canada appointed the Honourable Charles L Dubin to lead the *Commission of enquiry into the use of drugs and banned practices intended to enhance athletic performance.* This has been the most detailed and innovative legal report which has been published on this subject and the Canadian Government merits praise for instigating this. Chief Justice Dubin said of the problem in the report, 'the evidence shows that banned performance-enhancing substances and in particular anabolic steroids are being used by athletes in almost every sport, most extensively in weightlifting and track and field.'

Robert Armstrong QC, a member of the Canadian Bar Association and Commission Counsel to the Dubin Inquiry, stated at an International Symposium on sport and the law held in Monaco in 1991 that Canada had lost its innocence as a sporting nation in Seoul. The Dubin Inquiry showed that the use of drugs within sport had no national boundaries and after the report was published it was seen that most athletic countries of the world had lost their innocence. Dr Robert Kerr, a doctor practising in San Gabriel, testified before the Dubin Inquiry that he had prescribed anabolic steroids to approximately twenty medallists in the 1984 Olympics. Pat Connolly, a coach of the women's track team at the US Senate Judiciary on steroid abuse in the US, estimated that five out of ten gold medallists in the US men's Olympic track team used anabolic steroids at Seoul.

The most common forbidden performance-enhancing techniques

include taking steroids, human growth hormone and blood doping. Blood doping is where the athlete takes blood out of his own body and then re-injects it a few weeks later, days before the event in order to increase his oxygen carrying capacity, thereby improving performance. It must be constantly borne in mind that whilst these athletes are cheating themselves and the public, they are also preventing other athletes from achieving success. These banned practices are obviously adopted frequently by a significant number of athletes and only one deterrent exists which is in- and out-of-competition testing.

The Sports Council in London governs the dope testing in Britain with an accredited IOC Laboratory and has implemented one of the most stringent programmes in the world. In 1992 over 4,000 samples were taken from athletes in 53 different sports, with a higher number than ever before coming from out-of-competition testing. It is difficult to assess how effective dope testing is as a deterrent. Taking as a touchstone Ben Johnson, who was tested positive for the second time in March 1993 after suffering so much humiliation following the Seoul Olympics, it is apparent that for some athletes it is not an effective deterrent.

The prohibited use of steroids within sport has resulted in much litigation in recent years. Many athletes challenge bans imposed on them after a positive test. For example, a 25 year-old Swiss athlete, Sandra Gasser, who had attained international standard in the 800 metres and the 1500 metres, appealed to the Chancery Division of the High Court after she was suspended for two years from eligibility to enter athletics competitions held under IAAF rules, following a positive test of the metabolite of methyl testosterone at the 1987 World Championships in Rome. An Arbitration Panel of the IAAF affirmed the decision. Scott J refused declaratory relief by writ (not by the usually misconceived judicial review procedure) that the suspension was unreasonably in restraint of trade (although he accepted that the restraint of trade principles applied to the facts of the case).

More significantly, however, in his unreported judgment he made two observations to suggest that a different approach by the plaintiff's lawyers (as so often happens) might have had different consequences. First, he found in relation to one of the two tested samples of urine: 'The Panel might have found that the other explanation was too conjectural to be accepted. But no evidence to incline them to the view had been put before them by the plaintiff or the SLV.'

Second, he explained that the Panel:

'accepted the other explanation. They may have been wrong in doing so. They may have been wrong in regarding the identified procedural failure as not material. But unless they exceeded their jurisdiction, exceeded, that is to say, their terms of reference, the Plaintiff is stuck with their conclusions. Any remedy of appeal to the High Court under the Arbitration Acts is long since time-barred.'

Furthermore, Robert Armstrong QC, at an international symposium said that 'basically Dubin recommended that in order to have a fair right of appeal, athletes should be in a position to be able to test the scientific validity of the test results'. The question therefore remains, could *different evidence* in the *Gasser* case of the kind contemplated specifically by Scott J have produced a different result? For that reason the decision and reliance upon it as a binding precedent must always be challenged as based upon a debatable foundation because of apparent inadequate or insufficient preparation *in the eyes and mind* of the trial judge for reliance upon it by those who wish to challenge tribunal practices in this area.

Katrin Krabbe, from Germany, has successfully overturned one IAAF ban for drug abuse but in November 1993 appealed on legal technicalities unsuccessfully to an IAAF arbitration panel against a ban imposed on her for the alleged use of the drug Clenbuterol. Andrew Saxton and Andrew Davies are the two British weightlifters who were sent home from the Barcelona Olympics in 1992 for being tested positive for Clenbuterol. Davies and Saxton have argued that their use of the substance did not justify disqualification as the drug was not on the IOC's list of banned substances at the time of competition.

The British sprinter, Jason Livingstone, was also sent home from the Barcelona Olympics as he was tested positive for the drug methandianone in a random out-of-competition test before the Olympics. He appealed to the British Athletic Federation Appeals Panel which dismissed his appeal by a 2–1 majority in April/May 1993. In the appeal, there was some doubt cast over the positive test as, in fact, a metabolite of methandianone had been found, not the actual substance. Livingstone argued that just because a metabolite of the substance had been found, this was not conclusive proof that he had actually used methandianone. This view was supported by the evidence of Professor Arnold Beckett, previously a member of the IOC's medical commission. However, the majority of the panel felt that the evidence which was before them put beyond reasonable doubt that Livingstone had taken the drug and had indeed cheated.

In December 1992, Harry ('Butch') Reynolds obtained judgment in a Court in Ohio against the IAAF for damages for $27.3m for wrongfully banning him from athletics. Following a competition in Monaco in August 1990, Reynolds was randomly tested and it was found that he had traces of the anabolic steroid nandrolone in his urine. The IAAF did not seek to defend the proceedings and subsequently argued that the Ohio Court had no jurisdiction over the

IAAF and chose to ignore the judgment. It should be noted that the Ohio court accepted everything that Reynolds said in his complaint as correct since the proceedings were not defended. The award of damages therefore is not a result of conclusions based on evidence heard from both sides on the merits of the case and as such this massive award should not be taken as a measure of how such damages will be assessed in the future, or, indeed that the disqualification in the particular circumstances was invalid. Furthermore, in May 1994, the Ohio court judgment was successfully appealed, with yet further appeal to the American Supreme Court (equivalent to the House of Lords) reportedly being contemplated by Reynold's advisors (*Daily Mail*, 21 May 1994).

Another contentious example to illustrate the problem emerged after a rugby international between France and Wales in Paris during 1992. Anthony Clement and Jean-Baptiste Lafond were allegedly tested positive for the use of prohibited drugs. In due course, it emerged that Malcolm Downes, the Welsh Rugby Union honorary surgeon, had prescribed Clement drugs for sickness and dysentry. Lafond had been administered with Pholeodine for a cough by a French doctor.

In due course each player was exonerated, but what emerged is that the Welsh Rugby Union uses the same list of banned substances as the International Olympic Committee, which differs from the list adopted by the French Rugby Union. Correspondingly, after an international conference of rugby doctors (which the author attended to give legal guidance) had recommended criteria for drug testing, the International Rugby Board, which is not renowned for its consistency over discrepancies in financial compensation for loss of time from normal employment, required reminding of the necessity for creating sanctions for findings of positive tests.

Thus the battle against cheats who perform with forbidden performance-enhancing techniques will probably rage on into the next millenium. The detrimental side-effects of the use of steroids must be constantly stressed in order that sportspeople who are tempted to use them will understand that a better performance is not the only effect of this practice.

When yet another sportsperson is tested positive, the public become resigned to the view that certain sports are not 'clean' and subsequently suspect that innocent participants may themselves be cheating. Undoubtedly, the real victims of this crime are the competitors who choose to compete using their own natural resources and refuse to compromise their own integrity in order to be better, stronger or go faster.

On that issue an argument has been formulated by Catherine Bond that any proven loss by a competitor downgraded with consequential financial sponsorship disadvantages would have a cause of action for negligence giving rise to damages (see the *Independent on Sunday* and Bath University Distance Learning Course for Doctors). It can also be extended, at least within the United Kingdom, to the criminal liability of obtaining a pecuniary advantage by deception under section 15(1) of the Theft Act 1968.

Mr Justice Dubin's Report concluded:

'Cheating in sport, I fear, is partially a reflection of today's society. Drugs and the unprincipled pursuit of wealth and fame at any cost now threaten our very social fabric. It is little wonder the immorality has reached into sport as well. Of course, cheating as such is not a new phenomenon in Olympic competition, but the methods used to cheat have become more and more innovative and more pervasive. Moreover the use of drugs as the method of cheating has reached epidemic proportions.'

If there is a solution, then what better remedy can be found than the end of Hubert Doggart's Appendix on The Corinthian Ideal:

'Three groups whose efforts could be harnessed to stop the rot and ensure the survival, relatively intact, of the Corinthian ideal.
First, the doctors, whose Hippocratic oath can be construed as an upholding of the Corinthian ideal in medicine. Secondly, the lawyers, who once played without a thought that their services qua lawyers would be needed, but cannot now be sure. And, thirdly, school teachers, whose raison d'être could be called "the upholding of the Corinthian ideal in body, mind and soul".'

Finally, because drug abuse is a national and international health hazard, the British Government surely cannot opt out of taking an interest here, just as it is no longer ignoring its need to become involved with the problems of sporting crowd violence.

As a start, consideration could be given to whether the lethal and recognised use of any known sporting drug substances, in addition to those which are already prohibited, should be outlawed alongside LSD, heroin, cocaine and other evil substances. The proposals announced by the Home Office (on 12 September 1987) that anabolic steroids were under consideration for being added to the lists of prohibited drugs is clearly a step in the right direction. If this could be said to place British sport at a disadvantage internationally, the message from the Sports Council's symposium was loud and clear. If Britain gives the lead the rest of the world would certainly follow; and that would be in the interests of health and fair play, which in the end is what sport, in and out of court, is all about.

Chapter 8

Women in Sport and the Law

1 INTRODUCTION

Fair play and the traditionally identified fair sex have long been accepted and recognised as synonymous in sport, notwithstanding how Kipling anticipated by a century the battles of the sexes with his concept that

> 'the female of the species is deadlier than the male'

and he showed the same perception of human nature with his awareness of

> 'the flannelled fools at the wickets, or the muddied oafs at the goals,'

Yet although he lived until the year of Hitler's notorious Nazi Berlin Olympic Games of 1936 he could not have visualised when he wrote those memorable lines how the position of women within sport would become increasingly more important throughout the twentieth century. Nevertheless, he could have been aware of what Baroness Hollis of Heigham told the House of Lords on 24 April 1991 during a House of Lords debate on Sport and Active Recreation.

> 'Baron Pierre de Coubertin – the founder of modern Olympics – fought all his life to exclude women from sport. I understand that Mrs Pankhurst threatened to disrupt the 1908 London Olympics in the same inimitable and intimidating fashion in which she was interrupting the political meetings of Lloyd George and Churchill in order to get women admitted to the sports of tennis, archery and skating in those Olympics.'

She was able to tell the House, however, that

> 'By 1988 in Seoul, one-third of the competitors were women but they are still excluded from the triple jump, judo, the pentathlon and the pole vault; yet women have climbed Mount Everest and regularly beat men in marathon races.'

By 1990 the percentage of women over the age of 16 participating in sport (excluding walking) had increased from 52% in 1987 to 57%.

This compared with an increase in men's participation from 70% to 73% in the same period. Furthermore, women's participation in indoor sports has increased faster than men's and that gap between them was marginally closed.

Inevitably, therefore, there are certain outstanding legal issues which affect women in sport. These include sex discrimination which manifests itself in many different forms, including whether men who had undergone a sex change can ever be classed as a woman in a sporting context, and the use or effect of the contraceptive pill within sport.

Triple Olympic Games hurdler and Cambridge University Blue, Peter Hildreth, the experienced and respected former *Sunday Telegraph* athletics correspondent, commented on one of the many changing facets of women's position in sport and society (4 February 1986) which is still the subject of debate,

'One aspect of the drugs-in-sport controversy still to be fully examined is the contraceptive pill.'

Dr Ellen Grant in her controversial study, *The Bitter Pill: How safe is the 'Perfect Contraceptive'?* published first in 1985, has explained how

'Derivatives of this male hormone [artificial testosterone] are present in nearly all of today's pills' (page 18:1986 edition); 'although a few are derived from *artificial progesterone*',

and Hildreth continued,

'there is evidence that women athletes who use it, while not in breach of the rules, are nonetheless reaping the benefits of illegal doping.

The pill, a stress hormone, part of whose action is to reinforce the body's reserves at times of high physical demand, not only prevents loss of performance during menstruation but also triggers a variety of advantageous side-effects.

According to Dr John Guillebaud, author of the definitive text-book on the subject of the contraceptive pill, it stimulates an increase in the level of steroid hormone secretion from the adrenal and thyroid glands ...

In sport the pill has served its users not merely in its intended role of protection against conception but also by suppressing menstruation, in tiding them over those difficult times when training or competition would otherwise be curtailed.

There was a time when the unlucky coincidence of the cycle with championship dates was known to have a decisive bearing on medals. The arrival of the pill meant that one of the variables accounting for loss of form was effectively mitigated if not banished.'

However acceptable or debatable are the premises upon which Dr

Grant and Dr Guillebaud encourage Peter Hildreth's attitude as an athlete, the whole issue of the side-effects of man-or-woman-made drugs embraces the wider angle approached by a bulletin entitled *Drugs in Sport: A Reappraisal* from the Institute of Medical Ethics. This questioned during the mid-1980s

(1) Is it unethical for a sportsman to take drugs?

(2) Is drug-taking so serious a problem that the governing bodies of sports need to draw up rules to prevent it, with punishments for contravening the rules?

The events at the Seoul Olympics and thereafter, with the Canadian Government's Dubin Report as a watershed, create a self-evident response to the questions asked. For they do present a problem from which medical and pharmaceutical evidence cannot prevent an escape, in the manner identified at the end of the 'Sports medicine in the law' chapter. The Institute's bulletin canvassed within a sporting context wider sporting issues than the valuable study by Tom Dono-hue and Neil Johnson, *Foul Play: Drug Abuse in Sports*, cited in that chapter at p210 above. Equally it transcended the biological and physiological differences between men and women athletes and participants generally. Thus, Hildreth concluded,

> 'It may be no coincidence that these advances parallel the march of hormones as an aid to modern training for many sports. We are what we eat and the pill is made from male hormones. What more appropriate tool could there be in the hands of those intent on re-defining the boundaries of gender?'

The manner in which those boundaries have been re-defined is land-marked for sport and society in well-known precedents, to be detailed further below, which have reached the courts on both sides of the Atlantic. In 1977 Dr Renee Richards, the guide, philosopher, friend and intermittent coach over many years to the Wimbledon champion Martina Navratilova, was obliged to obtain injunction relief in New York against the United States tennis authorities. She succeeded in preventing their reliance on a sex-chromatin test for determining that she was a female after surgical sex-change treatment before which she had been Dr Richard Rasskind, a New York opthalmic surgeon. In 1960, London's High Court was required to adjudicate on a similar medico-legal phenomenon in a non-sporting context in *Corbett v Corbett* (ors Ashley) ([1970] 2 All ER 33) and it is now public knowledge how, unknown to many outside family circles, a dis-tinguished writer (around that latter period), James Morris, under-went similar surgery to become Jan Morris.

Concurrent with these medical revolutions there has emerged in recent years the climax to a social revolution which can be traced generally to John Stuart Mill's celebrated essay on the *Subjection of Women*, written in 1861 and published in 1869; It involves many issues embracing women's rights within sport and the law. Emily Wilding Davison's fatal collision with His Majesty King George V's horse. Amner, at Tattenham Corner during the Derby Stakes at Epsom in 1913; Florence Nagle's High Court triumph over Jockey Club intransigence and chauvinism in the Court of Appeal during 1966; and the Parliamentary sex equality legislation of 1970 and 1975 which flowed directly from Britain's entry into the Common Market pursuant to the European Communities Act 1972, and the consequential commitments under the Treaty of Rome.

All this is a far cry from the days when Mrs Martha Grace at Downend, near Bristol, bowled her three sons, E M, G F, and W G Grace, to cricketing immortality in the mid-1850s. Sex-chromatin tests and Parliamentary legislation for eligibility to play games would hardly have been contemplated as necessary. Nearly a century later in the days before the Second World War they would have been equally regarded as fanciful when Mrs Selina Blanchflower captained Belfast Ladies soccer team, while her two sons, Robert Daniel, and Jackie, at their mother's knee, learned the skills which projected both into soccer's history books with Northern Ireland's World Cup soccer teams and club triumphs respectively with Tottenham Hotspur and Manchester United in the later 1950s and early 1960s.

Furthermore, Barbara Cartland, in her foreword to the biography of the mother of Jackie Blanchflower's Manchester United colleague, Bobby Charlton, 'Cissie', explained how they owed as much to their mother's influence and encouragement as to their own undoubted talents.

Significantly one of the unexpected and unanticipated yet most welcome surprises from the development of women in sport has been the contrast in examples between women and men at the public entertainment level. It is universally recognised that the standards of behaviour by women in the sporting field surpasses that of men. How many women can the reader name who have smashed their tennis rackets down on the grass at Wimbledon in temper, sworn at the umpire and/or crowd in sheer frustration or provided such a poor example of behaviour that a parent would not wish his or her child to attend the world's greatest tennis tournament to see them play?

Yet a mere twenty-five years after the Blanchflower brothers' Celtic glories from over the water, sex legislation from Britain's Parliament had become essential. It was used most emphatically to expose and compensate for proven sexual discrimination within the crucial sporting area of Physical Education at the other source of Britain's Celtic pride, over the borders in Scotland.

An Industrial Tribunal, sitting in Glasgow during three January days in 1986 adjudicated on its reserved judgment dated 28 February 1986 in an unreported decision under the Sex Discrimination Act 1975 in *Miller v Strathclyde Regional Council* (Case No S/2582/85). It held,

(1) unanimously that the respondent Council had unlawfully discriminated against a superbly professional and experienced qualified applicant by not placing her on the short list of candidates to be interviewed for the position of Principal Teacher of Physical Education at Grange Academy, Kilmarnock; for which the Tribunal found it just and equitable to award the applicant the sum of £1,000 as compensation for injury to her feelings, and

(2) by a 2–1 majority, that the respondent Council had further discriminated against the applicant on the ground of her sex by not appointing her to that post; and, as compensation for her loss of earnings as a result of not being appointed to the promoted post, an additional £1,600 was ordered to be paid by the Council.

The total compensatory award was £2,600.

The full reasons for the Tribunal's verdict and awards comprise fifteen single line spaced typescript sheets. They included the following significant conclusions for the future of sporting administration excellence and physical education in the United Kingdom (Transcript pages 14 and 15),

'Having considered all of the evidence the Tribunal had no hesitation in holding that the reason why the applicant was not put on the short list to be interviewed for the post of Principal Teacher of Physical Education at Grange Academy was because of her sex. There was no doubt in the mind of the Tribunal that the applicant's qualifications and breadth of experience and range of interests were greater than any other candidate on the list of candidates and that she should have been on the short list;'

and

'The majority of the Tribunal in this case ... take the unusual view after careful thought, that the applicant would have been appointed to the post had it not been for the sex discrimination.'

Within the sporting sphere, separate and apart from the wider social implications generally, the full impact and value of these verdicts cannot be overstressed. Indeed, the important Final Report of the Recreation Management Training Committee published in 1984 by the Department of the Environment included in its Recommendation for 'the establishment of a single professional institution for leisure managers' (paragraph 7.41 at page 98), amongst its specific proposals that 'The institute should appoint an education committee', and additionally,

> 'The education committee should include in its membership representatives from the education field who are familiar with academic requirements' (Paragraph 7.43 at page 98).

Furthermore, the Government's Response to the House of Commons Environment Committee noted 'an imbalance between men and women on the Sports Council will be borne in mind when future appointments are made' (1986: No 504).

The consequences of unlawful sexual discrimination to circumscribe the scope for implementing such an important recommendation are self-evident. At a time when sporting prowess, physical fitness and communal health are matters of acute national concern and interest, these disclosures from a country with such great sporting pride and traditions as Scotland inherits, should alert all who profess an association with the national future in these areas of the hidden traps and dangers which may lurk undetected. This concealment would have continued but for the legal power granted by Parliament under the impetus of the Common Market and its Treaty of Rome. How this came about is a further mixture of social, economic and legal history which intertwine in clearly definable strands.

2 UNITED KINGDOM SEX DISCRIMINATION LAW GENERALLY

How the present law emerged and what it means today are summarised with Lord Denning's customary conciseness in *The Due Process of Law* (1979) at page 245, thus:

> '... there is growing apace the move for equality. We have the Equal Pay Act 1970 and the Sex Discrimination Act 1975. These were the direct result of our joining the Common Market. They were passed so as to fulfil our obligations under the Treaty of Rome. Whenever a woman does work of equal value to a man, she is entitled to pay equal to his. Whenever there is a job which she can do – she is entitled to apply for it and to get it on equal terms with a man. There must be no discrimination against her because she is a woman. Likewise there must be no discrimination against a man because he is a man. This was invoked when a bachelor Mr Jeremiah claimed that he was put on to dirty work when the women were not. I said in *Jeremiah v Ministry of Defence*: [19 October 1979: ultimately reported in [1979] 3 All ER 833 at 836]
> "Equality is the order of the day. In both directions. For both sexes. What is sauce for the goose is sauce for the gander".'

Clearly the complex ingredients which comprise the sporting sauces inevitably create a pot-pourri of issues and elements which are still taking shape within the pressure cookers of a rapidly changing society. The legal starting point today, however, must be the Common Market, and the Treaty of Rome to which the United Kingdom became inextricably tied by the European Communities Act 1972.

It was established as the European Economic Community (EEC) on 25 March 1957. In turn it had evolved from the European Coal and Steel Community (ECSC) first announced publicly in Paris on 9 May 1950, by Robert Schuman, the French Foreign Minister. Three years earlier in 1947 *The Character of England* had been published under the editorship of Sir Ernest Barker, Oxford University's Professor of Political Philosophy. In a chapter entitled 'Homes and Habits', the fashion historian James Laver explained: 'Women are now emancipated to a degree which would have frightened the pioneers of Feminism' (page 479). Yet nearly forty years later, *Miller v Strathclyde Regional Council* demonstrated the limits to that emancipation during the last decade and a half of the twentieth century. How they exist within the *sporting* legal framework is as always a mixture of statutory and judicial interpretation; and on this occasion they form a legacy of pioneering sacrifices and spirited independence and creativity which should never be forgotten; illustrated representatively by Emily Wilding Davison before the First World War, Florence Nagle after the Second World War, and Mrs Margaret Stack and her daughter Prunella Stack, and Phyllis Colson, between the two World Wars.

3 PIONEERING WOMEN IN SPORT AND THE LAW

Emily Wilding Davison may mean little to many of the modern generation. Eighty odd years ago she merited a near state funeral when her coffin travelled to its last resting place in Morpeth, Northumberland, after her death in Epsom General Hospital on Sunday 8 June 1913. At the Derby Stakes four days earlier on the traditional Wednesday afternoon she broke away from the crowd and ducked under the double rails at Tattenham Corner, running onto the racecourse as the horses raced down upon her. She dodged under the head of Agadir, ridden by a skilled jockey (and future trainer), Walter Earl, and threw up her hands to grab deliberately the horse owned by H M King George V, Amner. It turned a complete somersault, falling upon and injuring seriously its jockey, Herbert Jones. (Four years earlier for its owner's father, King Edward VII, Jones had won the race on

Minoru.) Emily Wilding Davison died four days later on 8 June 1913 from the injuries she received without recovering consciousness. Until she died the local police, who had arranged for her urgent arrival at the hospital, were considering her legal responsibilities.

At the Epsom coroner's inquest on Tuesday 10 June 1913, the jury returned a verdict that her death was caused by a fracture of the base of the skull, being accidentally knocked down by a horse through wilfully running on to the course during the progress of the race. The coroner recorded a verdict of death by misadventure.

Dame Christabelle Pankhurst, one of the leading militant suffragettes has recorded in her memoirs *Unshackled: The Story of How we Won the Vote* (edited by the Rt Hon Lord Pethick-Lawrence in 1959),

> 'Emily Davison paid with her life by making the whole world understand that women were in earnest for the vote. Probably in no other way and no other time could she so effectually have brought the concentrated attention of millions to bear upon the cause.'

Five years later with a post-war General Election in focus, Lloyd George's Government ended a 50-year campaign with the right to vote, for women over 30, enshrined in the Representation of the People Act 1918, and the right to become an MP under the Parliament (Qualification of Women) Act 1918. A year later the Sex Disqualification Removal Act 1919 unlocked universally all university and legal professional doors until then barred to women, to complete a legislative hat-trick which Emily Davison's supreme sacrifice undoubtedly precipitated. (Many women, and perhaps men, too, would not understand the true significance of sport in not only men's and boy's lives, but also the national psyche. They may not realise how much the women's liberation movements' inheritance today from the suffragette campaigners for social and economic emancipation owes to Emily Wilding Davison's awareness of the vital impact which sport can have in changing the law.) Those three statutes are a permanent memorial to the use she made of sport so dramatically, and tragically, and, indeed, unlawfully, for law reform and accelerating the march of history.

During the 1930s at a time of national unease and an awareness of the gap in the nation's physical culture structure, acknowledged by Parliament through the Physical Recreation and Training Act 1937, already explained in Chapter 2, 'Progressive perspective', three women left indelible footsteps in the sands of time with their visionary administrative creation. In 1935 Prunella Stack developed to a national stage, as a preamble to the Government legislation two years later, the foundation laid five years earlier by her mother, Mrs Mary

Bagot Stack, of the Women's League of Health and Beauty; and in that same Silver Jubilee Year of the reign of King George V and Queen Mary, a physical education teacher, Phyllis Colson, single-mindedly conceived the idea of a nationally co-ordinated 'umbrella' of sporting governing body organisations. Thus in 1935 was born the Central Council of Physical Recreation, whose crucial role as a forum for Britain's sporting governing bodies and for initiating vital projects and campaigns in the national interest has already been outlined in Chapter 2, 'Progressive perspective'.

The Second World War's absorption of women into every level of service and social life shattered any obstacles to recognising their capacity to cope with almost any role to challenge their talents. Women's rights campaigns which followed it concerned themselves with wider targets than sporting fields. Yet the racing world once more set the scene for a happier, but no less significant, breakthrough than that provided by Derby Day 1913, half-a-century later in 1966.

Florence Nagle had trained racehorses for many years before the mid-1960s in southern England. The limitations and fiction imposed by the Jockey Club's monopoly over controlling British horse racing caused licences to be granted to women trainers through their 'head lad' (often a man of middle age). Chapter 11, below, 'Fair, play and reason in court', explains how she was able, with her advisers, to avoid the *procedural* hurdles found before the Master in Chambers and single Judge on appeal, when the Court of Appeal comprising Lord Denning MR, Danckwerts and Salmon LJJ, gave her an un-interrupted ride (by reversing the orders of the earlier decisions, from which she had appealed). The Master and Judge had struck out her Statement of Claim which contained a declaration and injunction reliefs for the grant to her personally of a trainer's licence. The appeal court judgments which gave her leave to proceed with her claim extended the procedural issues of permission to carry on with her action into a landmark decision concerning the right to work, for all genders and for all generations. One often forgotten consequence from it appeared in 1983 when Mrs Jenny Pitman, in her own name, was able to train Corbière to win the Grand National as the first-ever woman trainer's triumph in that great event. Another consequence was the election of women members to the Jockey Club and the male bastions were further breached when the Jockey Club amended its Rules of Racing to accept women jockeys officially, or as they are now known, jockettes.

Four years later Parliament enacted the first stage of its anti-sex discriminatory legislation to bring Britain into line with Article 119 of the Treaty of Rome via the Equal Pay Act 1970. Thus the scene was set for the ultimate legislative confirmation with the Sex Discrimination Act 1975.

4 PARLIAMENTARY INTERVENTION

In a Court of Appeal decision, *Shields v E Coomes (Holdings) Ltd*
[1979] 1 All ER 456, which must be explained more particularly in its
correct chronological context below, at p 235, Lord Denning illuminated the interlocking complexities of this new dimensional legislation thus at page 463:

'The English statutes are plainly designed so as to implement the EEC
Treaty and the directives issued by the Council. They are the Sex
Discrimination Act 1975, to which is scheduled the Equal Pay Act 1970,
as amended. All came into force on 29th December 1975. They must all
be taken together. But the task of construing them is like fitting together
a jig-saw puzzle. The pieces are all jumbled up together, in two boxes.
One is labelled the Sex Discrimination Act 1975; the other, the Equal
Pay Act 1970. You pick up a piece from one box and try to fit it in. It
does not. So you try a piece from the other box. That does not fit either.
In despair you take a look at the picture by the makers. It is the guide
issued by the Home Office. Counsel on behalf of the Equal Opportunities Commission recommended especially para 3.18, which he says
will show the distinction between the two Acts. Even that will not make
you jump with joy. You will not find the missing pieces unless you are
very discriminating.'

In considering selective discrimination within the present perspective
of Women in Sport and the Law, it is sufficient to direct attention here
to Article 119 of the Treaty of Rome; the preludes to British Parliamentary legislation, and how the statutes generally and specifically
control the present legal structure.

Article 119 has been described as dealing with two issues:

'First it places an obligation on member states to do certain things with
regard to equal pay. Second it tries to define what equal pay actually
means. On both counts the wording of Article 119 and its implication
have aroused controversy.'

This controversy has not been directly concerned with sport. Indeed,
only one particular section from this network of enactments, namely
section 44 of the Sex Discrimination Act 1975, specifically identifies
sport; but the philosophy and interaction behind the various legislative pieces must be recognised for any attempted understanding of
them.

The full text of Article 119 reads as follows:

'Each member state shall during the first stage ensure and subsequently
maintain the application of the principle that men and women should
receive equal pay for equal work.
For the purpose of this article, "pay" means that ordinary basic or

minimum wage or salary and any other consideration whether in cash or in kind which the worker receives, directly or indirectly, in respect of his employment from his employer.

Equal pay without discrimination based on sex means:

(a) that pay for the same work at piece rates shall be calculated on the basis of the same unit of measurement.

(b) that pay for the same work at time rates shall be the same for the same job.'

When the then Home Secretary, Mr Roy Jenkins, introduced the legislation at the Second Reading in the House of Commons, he explained,

'Nothing in Part 1 itself makes discrimination unlawful ... It is only where a person discriminates in a situation dealt with subsequently in the Bill that discrimation is unlawful.'

Thus sex discrimination per se is not unlawful. What creates actionable consequences is discrimination in a welter of identifiable situations which may be conveniently categorised for the present limited purpose under the following headings set out in the statutory arrangement of sections at the commencement of the Sex Discrimination Act 1975:

(1) Employment

(2) Specified bodies such as trade unions, and various agencies

(3) Education

(4) Goods, facilities, services and premises

(5) Special conditions or arrangements and advertisements.

Employment including pay disputes under the Equal Pay Act are heard by industrial tribunals, with a right of appeal to an Employment Appeal Tribunal. All others are tried in county courts with appeals to the Court of Appeal.

Section 44 of the Sex Discrimination Act as mentioned above contains the sole section identifying sport in a very limited manner. It comes within Part V of the Act under a general heading alongside other categories including charities, insurance and other circumstances nominated as 'General Exceptions from Parts II to IV' (ie those covering employment, education and other unlawful discriminatory areas). It stated thus:

'Nothing in Parts II to IV shall, in relation to any sport, game or other activity of a competitive nature where the physical strength, stamina or physique of the average women puts her at a disadvantage to the average man, render unlawful any act related to the participation of a person as a competitor in events involving that activity which are confined to competitors of one sex.'

The key concepts here, of course, are the antithesis between 'the average woman' and 'the average man', and also 'competitors'. Both have been considered in the reported decisions of the tribunals and the courts. Both will doubtless have to be considered again. In a survey of the first decade's operation of the legislation from its inception on 31 December 1975 in *The Financial Times*, 3 January 1986, Lady Howe, the Equal Opportunity Commission's first deputy Chairman wrote,

'The legislation was neither perfect nor comprehensive.'

No reference was made to section 44. If it had been, the comment would have been justified that the first decade reflects an exploratory experience with a stop-go pattern. The reported cases illustrate a gradual move towards its beneficial application to sportswomen with the inevitable hiccups en route. Furthermore, a valuable survey by Dr Alice M Leonard for the Equal Opportunities Commission of the *First Eight Years* (1976–1983) (summarised in the *New Law Journal* 31 January 1986) of the tribunal referrals identifies in its fuller text sport alongside 'Literary, artistic' in the applicants' occupations for claims under both the 1970 and the 1975 Acts; and for men as well as women only 1 % of those who utilised the legislation are logged under these three comprehensive categories.

With such scant material no definable pattern can yet be traced; but the recorded cases in the various reported sources manifest a tentative approach bedevilled by the unrealistic delineation between 'the average woman' and 'the average man'. Women no less than men in sport demonstrate talents and qualities well above average which the slightest reflection can easily recognise. Indeed, this Parliamentary injection into sex legislation of the commercial shipping language of averaging suggests that the draftsman of the section and Parliament not only did not understand women in sport but could not have understood the above average skills which are the hallmark of true athleticism. A grandstand survey of some of these skills among women will explain and emphasise the point.

5 ABOVE AVERAGE GRANDSTAND VIEW

No legislation or litigation was ever needed for an adoring tennis public to share and enjoy the qualities demonstrated before, between and then after two World Wars. First through the Mesdames Lottie Dodd, Suzanne Lenglen, Helen Wills Moody, Betty Nuthall, Dorothy Round and Kay Stammers until the outbreak of the Second World War. Then after it, with the more publicly exposed televised performers such as Maureen Connolly, Louise Brough, Christine Evert, Ann Jones, Virginia Wade, Martina Navratilova, Steffi Graff, and Monica Seles.

Likewise, the athletics world and a wider public rejoiced at the Olympic triumph of the Dutch housewife and mother, Fanny Blankers-Koehn, who won four Gold medals at London's Wembley Stadium in 1948, Northern Ireland's Mary Peters' victory in 1972, and Fatima Whitbread's 1987 success. Many will also recall how, before the Second World War, Marjorie Pollard followed masculine footsteps to represent England's women cricket and hockey elevens before writing regularly for the *News Chronicle*, a tradition carried on more recently by Rachel Heyhoe Flint with cricket and The *Sunday Telegraph*. When England's lady cricketers won the Ladies World Cup Final at Lord's in 1993, the trophy was presented on the grass outfield as ladies are still excluded from certain areas of the Lord's pavilion: an echo of 30 years earlier when the Indian golf champion Papina Semgolum won the Durban Open golf championship and received his prizes outside in the pouring rain while his white competitors watched inside.

Laura Davies to-day follows a tradition when ladies' golf produced its inter-war years champions who played mixed foursomes on equal terms with their men golfing partners: Diana Fishwick and Joyce Wethered come readily to mind. After the Second World War Jeanne Bisgood became England's Ladies' Golf Champion while practising as a barrister from the Lincoln's Inn Chambers at 5 New Square, where she was succeeded as a tenant in the sport of practising tax law by Margaret Hilda Thatcher.

Amy Johnson flew into airspace and international public imagination before disappearing over the Thames Estuary on war service. Many differing generations will know how Sonia Henje and Esther Williams respectively skated and swam from their particular sporting disciplines into wider audiences at the cinema.

On horseback the women (and their horses, too) have produced their own fan clubs. From Pat Smythe and her Olympic and European successes on Flanagan to Virginia Leng, Lucinda Green and The Princess Royal as eventers, with The Princess Royal actively effective as a winning jockey and President of the British Olympic Association. Furthermore, Alison Dean's devotion in looking after the record-breaking classic colt, Reference Point, throughout his career, leading to the racecourse in triumphs in 1987, was a crucial factor in the superb teamwork organised at Henry Cecil's training stables at Warren Place, Newmarket. Also within the Olympic setting, women's fencing was the springboard from which Mary Glen Haig was elected to succeed the late Lord Burghley, Marquess of Exeter, to the much coveted position of one of Britain's two members on the International Olympic Committee.

Such examples as these can be multiplied by any sporting afficionado. (Apologies are extended herewith to all other ladies omitted solely for reasons of space. Each one mentioned, and so many others who merited inclusion, illustrate the antithesis between their own achievements and 'the average woman'.)

6 JUDICIAL INTERVENTION

What is the 'average woman' and what is the 'average man' in *this* context has yet to be fully investigated by the courts. A tentative approach to it was made in the unreported decision of the Court of Appeal which was concerned with whether or not a 12-year-old schoolgirl was discriminated against playing football with boys of her own age (see *Bennett v The Football Association Ltd and The Nottinghamshire FA* Court of Appeal transcript: No 591 of 1978). Tentative, because the issue and evidence called before the county court and accepted in the Court of Appeal was directed towards comparing and differentiating medically between boys and girls of 12 years of age, below and above the age of puberty. The conclusion was that the circumstances of the case proved existence of a disadvantage (the Act being silent on age levels).

The playing merits do not appear to have been argued of the 12-year-old plaintiff-contender for a place in the boys' team for which she had been selected. Yet Lord Denning (at page 2 of the transcript: No 591 of 1978) said 'She ran rings around the boys'; and a witness as recorded in the *Daily Telegraph* report of the county court hearing said she was 'a vicious tackler and once tackled a 15-year-old so hard he had to be supported and taken from the field'. This pointed, of course, to this particular plaintiff not being put 'at a disadvantage to the average' boy! Concentrating on what appeared to be a diversion in evidence from doctors about puberty, and without apparent arguments on above average skills, the Court of Appeal overruled the Deputy County Court Judge who had adjudicated and awarded £250 in favour of the 12-year-old 'vicious tackler' of 'a 15-year-old'. The trial judge had held that prior to puberty there is little difference in stamina between males and females and therefore the exception under section 44 did not apply. The Court of Appeal reversed this particular decision saying that 'woman' for the purposes of the Act was defined as a female of any age.

Two years later in *Greater London Council v Farrer* ([1980] ICR

266), the Employment Appeal tribunal at page 272 C-D per Slynn J said, of *Bennett*'s case,

> 'we read the decision of the Court of Appeal as applying to the particular facts before it'.

Certainly the imbalance between the medical evidence concerned with puberty and the apparent absence of argument on the evidence tending to prove the existence of above average athletic talents which did not disadvantage the female plaintiff leave this decision without any general guidance for further disputes in the manner stated above. Any schoolgirl footballers not caught through average talents by the exclusion clause in section 44 can at least consider their chances on different evidence and arguments of a replay. Furthermore, the Football Association have modified their restrictions and emulated the Jockey Club by admitting to its Council a representative of the Women's Football Association.

More generally, the Employment Appeal Tribunal in *GLC v Farrer* said of section 44 at page 272 C-D:

> 'it seems to us that this section is dealing with a situation in which men and women might both be playing in the same game or taking part in the same event. It is in that situation that the disadvantage of the woman because of physical strength, stamina or physique would become a relevant matter. It does not seem to us that this section is dealing with the situation where it is desired that a girl should play a game against a girl, or where teams of girls are to play teams of girls'.

Indeed, the circumstances of that particular case threw up the relevance of a specifically exempting section within the Sex Discrimination Act 1975. Section 51(1) exonerates any acts done under a statutory authority passed before the 1975 legislation. This applied to the London Government Act 1963. Schedule 12 of the Act created a right to impose restrictions on wrestling licences. It was invoked to prohibit women's wrestling. An industrial tribunal allowed an appeal by a woman wrestler, who was equipped physically and professionally to be licensed, against a promoter's rejection of her services because of the 1963 prohibition. The Employment Appeal Tribunal reversed the industrial tribunal.

Practical realities were the reason for the Amateur Swimming Association's rejection of the Oxford University woman waterpolo coach to play in the annual inter-Varsity men's match with Cambridge University. The precedent created by Sue Brown who coxed the Oxford University crew in the annual Boat Race was the basis of the claim for that plea. Rowing, of course, is a non-body contact sport. Waterpolo is not. Those who have experienced its rigours will respect and understand the reasons for discrimination against the Oxford University female coach:

'Waterpolo is a physical contact sport and Fiona [the coach] is involved in hard tackling. It's like Rugby in a pool.'
(See *The Daily Telegraph*: 4 March 1983.)

This may be contrasted with the selection by Oxford University in 1986 of another Fiona, Macdonald. She became the first woman to gain a golfing Blue. The only surprise in this example is that it has taken so long for this award to arrive (although the traditional competition for academic honours with the men has perhaps traditionally concentrated attention on the University's Schools comparisons rather than those at Iffley Road and Oxford's other games playing areas).

A more clear-cut pattern of decisions unfolded under the Sex Discrimination Act 1975 which did not involve the concept of the average woman in arriving at decisions.

In 1977 the first fully reported decision in this subject area concerned, appropriately, a professional solicitor sufficiently skilled to apply for a post as woman golf professional. The applicant armed with this double qualification failed to prove before an industrial tribunal, and on appeal to an Employment Appeal Tribunal, that a local authority had disregarded her professional golfing qualifications in competition with male applications for a local council coaching post.

Both Tribunals considered as an issue of fact and thereby concluded that no discrimination had existed when rejecting contentions that

(1)   certain interview questions

      and

(2)   confusion about interview arrangements for an appointment she was unable to attend

were discriminatory on the grounds of her sex (*V Saunders v Richmond-upon-Thames BC* [1977] IRLR, Vol 6, 362).

Also in 1977, however, a 22-year-old snooker player did satisfy a Sheffield County Court judge that a publican discriminated unlawfully against her sex when he refused to allow women in his premises to play snooker because

(1)   too many wanted to do so

      and

(2)   women ripped the snooker table cloths (*Rice v Chatteron* (1977) Times, 29 June). She obtained a nominal damages award of £10 and costs.

Two years later a similar result was achieved in Belfast under comparable Northern Ireland legislation on appeal from a county court judgment to the High Court. The Belfast YWCA banned young women from its snooker tables because of

(1) alleged inexperience with snooker cues and consideration that they would be more likely than young men to make a tear in the cloths of the snooker tables, which were very costly to repair, and

(2) talking and laughing to disturb the necessary silence for concentrating by other players.

One of the arguments justifying the discrimination by the Belfast YWCA was that private membership excluded the discriminatory legislation. The established facts proved that the snooker room and its facilities were open to temporary membership with no more selection requirements than an acceptable standard of behaviour and witness to enter the premises, as distinct from the more usual exclusivity created by club memberships. Notwithstanding prima facie sound reasons for the discrimination, it was held unlawfully in breach of Article 30 of the Sex Discrimination (No 1) Order 1976 which reflected the 1975 Act. Nominal damages of £25 and costs resulted (*Bateson v Belfast YWCA* (1980) NI 135).

Sandwiched between these two legal snooker table victories, for complainants about discrimination against playing that particular game, were Theresa Bennett's FA tackle and also the peripheral but sportingly connected decision of the Employment Appeal Tribunal and Court of Appeal concerning equal pay for a woman among many men counterhands in betting shops, already cited for general principles above (*Shields v E Coomes (Holdings) Ltd* [1979] 1 All ER 456). A claim for equal pay was rejected by a 2–1 majority of an industrial tribunal on the basis that differences of quality of work-loadings justified the inequality of which complaint was made. Particularly significant was that in troublesome areas the man counterhand worked longer hours in a protective role. The Employment Appeal Tribunal allowed an appeal by the woman complainant. When the respondent company appealed to the Court of Appeal it failed to obtain a reversal to the original tribunal's finding. The variation in pay was held to be discriminatory and not due to a material difference other than difference of sex, which would have justified the distinction within section 1 (3) of the Equal Pay Act 1970. As Bridge LJ concluded at page 473:

'if the company had employed persons specially trained as security guards who were recruited from either sex [to operate the protective function], entirely different considerations would arise, but that is certainly not the case'.

The following year, 1979, witnessed one step forward and another step backwards for the battle by the woman wrestler Sue Brittain, in her married name of Marjorie Farrar, for a licence. It failed as explained above because of the pre-1975 escape clause section 51 (1) which was properly operated by earlier legislation in 1963 (*Greater London Council v Farrar* [1980] ICR 266).

In 1980 and 1981 the breakthrough arrived with Mrs Belinda Petty, an experienced judo referee. She took on the British Judo Association at another industrial tribunal after she was banned from refereeing the All-England's *men's* contest, although still allowed to referee all-male club and area events and the *women's national* event.

The Association claimed, inter alia, that women did not have the strength to separate two hefty male fighters, and even arranged a demonstration as part of its evidence at the tribunal hearing to try to prove this. Indeed, one of the demonstrators said in testifying: 'I wouldn't feel happy on the mat with a woman refereeing. I think I would find the physical aspects of a woman controlling two hefty men on the mat a little degrading'. The tribunal rejected this and other arguments as an unlawful discrimination, and in October 1980 ruled that Mrs Petty's qualifications should be considered on her merits. The Employment Appeal Tribunal confirmed this decision in June 1981, stressing that it failed to see how provisions for refereeing related to the participation of competitors.

The Employment Appeal Tribunal found in its judgment [1981] ICR 660 at pages 665–6 per Browne-Wilkinson J:

'It is common ground that judo is a sport in which men and women ought not to compete one with the other. Section 44 saves from being unlawful "any act related to the participation of a person as a competitor in that activity," ie judo. Mr Beloff submitted that the "act" referred to (ie preventing women from refereeing men's events) was "related to" the participation of men as competitors. He said that the words "related to" were wide words – unnecessarily wide if all that was meant to be covered was a provision preventing competitors of both sexes from competing. In our view this is not correct. We cannot see how provisions as to referees relate to the "participation" of the competitors in the contest. They might, at a stretch, be said to relate to the sex of the competitors but not to those competitors' participation in the contest. We think that the words should be given their obvious meaning and not extended so as to cover any discrimination other than provisions designed to regulate who is to take part in the contest as a competitor. Any other construction would lead to great uncertainty: for example, would the section be extended to discrimination against the lady in the box office at a football ground? For these reasons we consider the decision of the industrial tribunal to be correct and we dismiss the appeal.'

Mrs Petty's successes in 1980 and 1981 were in effect the top score for sportswomen at half-time in the first decade which followed implementation of the 1975 Act. As the second decade got under way, at the time of writing the first edition during 1987, further developments were anticipated to occur to confirm the social revolution reflected in the exploding sporting scene.

In 1988 Sandra Priestley challenged the Social and Recreational Club (in *Priestley v Stork Margarine Social and Recreational Club*) at her place of work for operating an unwritten 'men only' rule in the snooker room. She maintained that the club was not private and therefore could not be exempted under section 29 of the Sex Discrimination Act 1975 which relates to discrimination in the provision of goods, facilities or services. Her case was upheld in the Birkenhead County Court by HHGP Crowe, QC on 24 June 1988 (unreported) because the club did not have a selection procedure, and any employee of the company to which the club was linked was automatically qualified to join. Furthermore, in 1992 the Leeds Industrial Tribunal judged that Susan Thompson, a top amateur pool player, had been discriminated against on the grounds of her sex; and furthermore, that she had been victimised in her rejection for membership by the Professional Pool Players Organisation (PPO). The tribunal observed that her rejection had been under 'the old pal's act' and that it seemed to be the case of the best woman player being regarded as as good as the worst man (23 March 1992: unreported). In due course at the 1992 AGM of the PPO her application for membership was accepted.

The full fall-out from Mrs Miller's triumph over Strathclyde Regional Council (see paragraph above) has yet to be assessed, if the result itself has yet percolated through the various layers of interdisciplinary sporting knowledge to those who would be expected to wish to know of it. For so far as the author is aware, above average sportswomen who compete professionally in the sporting marketplace alongside men for lucrative commercial prizes, such as darts or in the eventing fields, have yet to chance their arms or risk their costs or those of the Equal Opportunities Commission before tribunals. Lady Howe's comment that 'The legislation was neither perfect nor comprehensive' can be extended with even greater force to Women in Sport for its application. It may well be that the best is yet to come from these statutory innovations, stimulated by the *Brighton Declaration on Women and Sport* of May 1994 explained comprehensively by Julia Bracewell in Appendix 4.

Finally, attention to the social engineering of the EEC-inspired legislation should not divert attention from other equally important areas which can be overlooked for Women in Sport and the Law. One is a recent development at local club level, another is the conventional or standard legal scene: finally there is the impact of medicine and science.

7 WOMEN AND 'MALE' PRIVATE CLUBS

The Sex Discrimination Act 1975 effectively allows discrimination against women in private sporting clubs. Section 29 allows single sex clubs, or unequal membership rights in private clubs. Between 1976 and 1988 the Equal Opportunities Commission received some 2,000 complaints about the lower status and treatment of women members of private sports clubs. Private sports clubs such as some major golf clubs of national significance and the Marylebone Cricket Club still insist on excluding women from their membership. In *Priestley v Stork Margarine Social and Recreational Club* (supra), Mrs Priestley succeeded in becoming a member of the snooker club at her place of work because the club was not private. Significantly some major golf clubs and the MCC are private clubs per se, but have a public role in society: indeed it has been said of them, 'a private role with a public face'. Time alone may decide when generally accepted social attitudes will permeate such old-established institutions and force them to admit women as members.

While these pages were being prepared in 1993 a tangential decision affecting women's club membership rights took place when the West Kent Golf Club made a routine application for renewal of its liquor licence to the Club's bar under section 3(1) of the Licensing Act 1964. Local magistrates rejected the claim, which was affirmed on appeal in the Croydon Crown Court, because women were excluded from the bar. There is no binding precedent among lower court decisions, but as a persuasive weapon in the campaign for sporting and social equality among local clubs it could accelerate the pace comparable to the women's progress in track and field athletics (see *Daily Telegraph*, 25 May 1993, page 3).

8 STANDARD LEGAL SCENE

The novelty of acclimatising to the new dimensions for women's rights within the sporting as well as wider social setting should not divert attention from the continued application of traditional legal remedies and liabilities with a sporting flavour. Nothing in the legislation considered above affects them in any way whatever. As if to emphasise this position during the latter half of the first decade of this new era, the following five court appearances have concerned women in sport within a mixture of commercial, criminal and family contexts.

Commercial

1   During 1982/3 a dispute between the Women's Professional Golf Association and its then executive director landed both in the High Court on injunction proceedings until settled out of court in a customary way (*Edwards v WPGA; APP Publicity Promotions Ltd v CM Walker and others* (1982) Times/Daily Telegraph, November).

Criminal

2   In 1985 a woman footballer who broke an opponent's jaw in a woman's friendly (sic!) match on May Day was convicted of assault and ordered to pay £250 compensation by Clacton Magistrates (*Baker v Bridger*, (1985) *Daily Express*, May).
3   1986 recorded from America, in circumstances which would have been treated similarly in the United Kingdom, namely a fight between two women jockeys. One bit the arm of another who then required a tetanus injection. The Stewards imposed a £30 fine for 'causing a disturbance in the jockey's quarters', a TV room (*Calder Race Course, Miami*, (1986) *Daily Express*, 1 July).

Family

4   1981 witnessed divorce proceedings which doubtless are repeatable. A wife petitioned effectively on the ground of her husband's unreasonable behaviour based upon an excessive obsession with cricket, both participatively and statistically (Wolverhampton Divorce Court: *Rowley v Rowley*, (1981) Times/Daily Telegraph, 26 August).
5   1987 saw 'Golf was his mistress' when a wife petitioned successfully in the High Court Family Division (*Lane v Lane*, (1987) Daily Telegraph, 4 June).

Therefore nothing in the recent legislation suspends or qualifies in any way whatsoever the operation of the general law applicable to women whether in sport or outside it. What the legislation has tried to do with varying degrees of success is to outlaw sexual discrimination in certain proscribed situations, with sport singled out together with other limited areas under section 44 of the Sex Discrimination Act. This is yet to have further judicial treatment. Treatment of a more recognisable kind is perhaps the most appropriate note on which to end this never-ending development of sport and the law.

9 MEDICAL INTERVENTION FOR WOMEN IN SPORT AND THE LAW

London's High Court in 1960 witnessed a then unique claim to annul a marriage because of a sex change operation, when medical evidence proved that the female party to the marriage had been born a man. In *Corbett v Corbett (ors Ashley)* [1970] 2 All ER 33 Mr (later Lord Justice) Ormrod, himself trained as a doctor before being called to the Bar, was asked to adjudicate on this then unprecedented condition. In acceding to it he held that the party who had undergone a sex change operation

'is not a woman for the purpose of marriage but is a biological male and has been since birth.'

As we have already seen at the outset of this chapter unknown to many outside family circles as a distinguished writer, too, around that period, James Morris, underwent similar surgery to become Jan Morris; and almost a decade later sport caught up with this new medical phenomenon in the year Parliament passed the Sex Discrimination Act during 1975. Dr Richard Rasskind, a New York opthalmic surgeon, and a skilled tennis player, received similar surgical treatment to become after the operation Dr Renee Richards. Inevitably, the question emerged: what were the tennis authorities going to do about it?

For the next two years Dr Renee Richards shunted between various US tennis tournaments which were sufficiently enlightened to accept her entries with the knowledge of her transsexuality. Those which were not either rejected her outright, or conditional upon chromosome tests being factually or conveniently satisfied. The world-wide International Tennis Federation invoked Olympic Games tests which the doctor was unable to satisfy. When the locally based tennis authorities also required such stringent limitations upon entry the New York jurisdiction was invoked. In an action against the United States Tennis Association, the US Open Tennis Championship Committee and the Women's Tennis Association Inc, during 1977, Dr Richards claimed relief as a professional tennis player who had undergone sex reassignment surgery which had allegedly changed her sex from male to female. She sued for a preliminary injunction against the organisations

(1)   to prevent reliance on a sex-chromatin test for determination of whether she was female and thus

(2)   to permit her participation in the Women's Division of the US Open tournament.

The legal foundation of the action was that the condition breached the anti-discriminatory code built into the New York State equal opportunities legislation. After hearing a battery of conflicting medical and tennis evidence, Judge Alfred M Ascione held

'when an individual such as plaintiff [sic], a successful physician, a husband and father, finds it necessary for his own mental sanity to undergo a sex reassignment, the unfounded fears and misconceptions of defendants [sic] must surely give way to the overwhelming medical evidence that the person before him is now female'.

Accordingly, a requirement that the Plaintiff pass the sex-chromatin test in order to be eligible to participate in the tournament was grossly unfair, discriminatory and inequitable, and violated the Plaintiff's rights under the New York Human Rights Law, and granted the injunctions (*Richards v US Tennis ASSN & Ors* 1977: 400 NYS (2nd) 267).

Similar reliefs would have been available to Dr Richards at that time under British law if she had been subjected to similar conditions for a United Kingdom tournament. Not only could the Sex Discrimination Act 1975 have been invoked; as a result of the Court of Appeal's decision which acknowledged matrimonial sterilisation in *Bravery v Bravery* [1954] 3 All ER 59 (where a wife failed to obtain a cruelty degree because the majority of the court held that she had consented to her husband's vasectomy), Dr Richards could have argued that the condition to undergo a sex-chromatin test would comprise an incitement to commit or to attempt to commit a battery.

By the time Dr Richards arrived in Britain, however, she came with an entirely different professional tennis status; as coach and adviser to the future Wimbledon champion Martina Navratilova in 1972. This lasted for five years until Dr Richards retired from professional tennis and returned to her other profession, ophthalmic surgery. By then, in 1982, English courts had begun to consider 'the average woman'.

Ten years later in April 1993, also from the USA *The Times* reported, 10 March 1993:

'A 16 year-old-girl who hopes to become an Olympic boxer is at the centre of a sex-discrimination lawsuit filed on Monday by the American Civil Liberties Union (ACLU). The lawsuit, filed in Seattle on behalf of Jennifer McCleery, claims she is being prevented from boxing in violation of state anti-discrimination laws. She trains under the name Dallas Malloy. "Since I started boxing, I realized how much I love it," she said. "It's like any other sport to me and I feel it's my right to be able to compete with others." Kathleen Taylor, executive director of the ACLU of Washington, said the girl was only seeking the right to box against other women.'

Finally, in a crucially important feature in the *Guardian* of 31 December 1993 under the headline *Women runners pay price of overwork*, Duncan Mackay reflected the most important issue for the future of *all* sport at the public entertainment level in relation to women in particular when he wrote with a sub-title 'on the growing casualty list of a crowded cross-country programme':

'Britain's selectors will be anxiously scanning the results of tomorrow's women's race in the County Durham international cross-country at Beamish for signs of fresh talent.

With the approach of the world cross-country championships in Budapest on March 26 they have seen the country's best runners falling faster than needles off a Christmas tree.

Liz McColgan, Andrea Wallace, Lisa York, Gillian Stacey, Suzanne Rigg and Hayley Haining are long-term victims of injury or illness and Andrea Whitcombe has been unable to handle the huge expectations of her after she twice won the English national senior title as a teenager. All would have been strong candidates for places in Budapest.

The most alarming aspect is the age of some of them: York is 23, Whitcombe 22 and Stacey and Haining 21. In addition Sharon Murphy, who was 21st in the 1992 world junior cross-country championships as a 16-year-old, has not raced this winter because of illness. Paula Radcliffe and Jenny Clague, Britain's best young prospects, have also suffered from viruses and injuries and they are barely out of their teens.

Bud Baldaro, the national cross-country coach, is resigned. "I thought we would have a great team this year but now it is looking pretty thin," he admitted. His one consolation is that Jill Hunter, injured for the past year, should return.

Like Frank Dick, the national director of coaching, Baldaro believes that far too much stress is being imposed on runners expected to perform over country, track and road the year round. "Athletes are being pulled all over the place. If it is like this now, what is it going to be like in 1994 when the programme is even worse?"

The cross-country season has expanded rapidly in recent years with the introduction of an international Grand Prix circuit and next December, the first European championships.

The British Athletic Federation has not helped by adding events to the calendar. This season there are British and national championships and a separate UK world cross-country trial.

Baldaro is also concerned that there is still not enough medical back-up for elite athletes who break down. Fiona Truman, for example, was once Britain's best teenage runner and a member of the senior team that won silver medals in the 1988 world cross-country championships. But when she was injured she had to pay £1,000 for physiotherapy that was to no avail: her Achilles injury forced her to retire.

Britain's women distance runners are often trapped in a vicious circle. If they want to reach world class they need to run more than 100 training miles a week. But with sponsorship opportunities limited, especially for women – even McColgan found trouble finding a shoe contract before she won the 1991 world 10,000 metres title – they also have to race regularly to support themselves. This over-activity stretches their bodies to breaking point and increases the chances of injury or illness. The recent gain in form of runners from China has heaped further pressure on the home runners. Many coaches in Britain find it hard to believe that the Chinese could handle the huge training loads they are reported to undertake – around 170 miles a week – without resorting to performance-enhancing drugs.

Leading athletes tread a thin line between training hard and over-training. Unfortunately for Britain, too many women are on the wrong side of it.'

10 CONCLUSIONS

In retrospect a number of illustrations of the artificiality of 'the average woman' and 'average man' concepts in this chapter cannot be ignored. All are fundamental and inconclusive, but must be recognised.

The law which has been considered here and throughout the book is essentially Anglo-Saxon for traditional common law and equity-orientated legal systems. Overseas and particularly totalitarian and all those countries with government-funded and supported sporting systems which approach sport with a different traditional and practical standpoint from that recognised throughout the United Kingdom and by the inheritors of its attitudes cannot be ignored. There is also a differential in their approach to women. Lightheartedly but nevertheless significantly it was treated with depth and subtlety by Peter Ustinov in his satire, *The Love of Four Colonels*. Produced in 1951 and reflecting the Four-Power occupation of Germany by Great Britain, France, Russia and the USA it portrayed with that author's customary perception the different national characteristics built in to the title. How far and to what extent comparable different national attitudes to Women in Sport and the Law will become relevant is an issue which must surface at some time in the future. Its form could well emerge in the final illustrations with which this chapter began.

Baron de Coubertin in his dogmatic male chauvinism cited by Baroness Hollis of Heigham, defined the modern Olympic Games as being

'The solemn and periodic exultation of male athleticism with internationalism as a base, loyalty as a means, not for its setting, and female applause as regard'.

The Olympic Charter still retains the words:

'No discrimination is allowed against any country or person on grounds of race, religion or politics'.

Notably, the word 'gender' has been omitted and it is indeed true that there is still discrimination against women within the Olympic movement. They are still excluded from many events, for example, ice-hockey, modern pentathlon, baseball, wrestling, waterpolo and some track and field events.

Football on the other hand is moving towards potential inclusion, with FIFA taking initiatives within the IOC to include women's football in the Atlanta Games during 1996. The inaugural Women's Football World Cup took place in England in 1991; FIFA are keen to encourage the women's game in order to achieve Olympic Games status and while these pages were being completed England's women won the Women's Rugby Union World Championship (Times, 3 May 1994).

Peter Hildreth ended his assessment that 'One aspect of the drugs-in-sport controversy still to be fully examined is the contraceptive pill' with a concluding paragraph, however, which is not inappropriate to this chapter on Women in Sport and the Law:

'The general picture presented by women in sport, as in life itself, has been revolutionised. As we celebrate the silver jubilee of the pill it will be as well to reflect that while we have grown accustomed to her face, it is not quite the face we knew . . .'

Indeed, so far as *public* sport is concerned one may well ask; shall we ever see My Fair Lady again?

Part III

International sport

Chapter 9

International interaction

1 INTRODUCTION

International sport, like Tauber's song, goes round the world. Three different levels of comprehension and understanding know no boundaries in any land and any language. Sporting competition, medicine and music create a universal form of communication. International law for sport is gaining an ever-increasing importance and significance due to the impact of modern travel and television. Television viewers in the UK seem to be interested not only in watching the sides they support play abroad, but also television has opened up interest in many foreign sports which are either not played in the UK or played to a very limited extent. These sports include American football, Australian rules football, sumo wrestling and baseball.

Britain's practising lawyers in *general domestic practice* burdened with clients' problems need not be troubled generally in their daily grind with issues of an international flavour. The lawyer and any man or woman involved with sport today cannot dare to ignore them.

Air transport, satellite and cable television have shrunk the globe in a style comparable to the impact with which a century ago the road and rail networks facilitated the sports explosion in the United Kingdom to which every other country experiencing similar developments can point. While trains spread their network and the populace for creation of new towns and sporting centres, William Clarke took his All England Cricket XI to spread that game's gospel throughout the land. Professional football proliferated within the framework of the Football League, formed in 1888, the year in which Gladstone's Local Government Act created the earliest structured county boroughs, and horse race tracks were opened up to punters beyond local heaths and town moors. Now television brings the Sports Council's 'Sport for All' campaign to an international spectator and participatory level from stadia and arenas throughout the world.

2 INTERNATIONAL SPORT AND LAW GENERALLY

Sport knows no universal sporting Parliament comparable to the CCPR in London and the other home countries' equivalent bodies in

247

Scotland, Wales and Northern Ireland as a debating forum and/or meeting ground. Certainly no democratically elected body exists universally to legislate for sport. Each particular discipline has its own world governing body, some democratically elected, others existing as self-perpetuating oligarchies. The law affecting international sport therefore comes from the traditional domestic and international layers already identified in Chapter 1 'Genesis' and Chapter 2, 'Progressive perspective'

(1) playing

(2) playing penal

(3) administrative   } laws

(4) national

extended by this international dimension to two more widely embracing areas of

(5) international governing body

(6) overseas national   } laws

The first four above-listed categories in the United Kingdom do not differ when considered in an international context. David Bishop's prosecution by the South Wales police authority for assaulting an opponent, followed by his suspension by the Welsh Rugby Union, was the appropriate action for the harm done. Equally, equivalent action should have been implemented against the Bulgarian and Portuguese footballers on English football fields as they were in breach of soccer's playing and British national criminal laws during the World Cup competition in 1966. The Brazilian visitor to these shores, Pele, was the victim. He identified the offenders, who were witnessed by millions of TV and video watchers, in *My Life and the Beautiful Game* (Pele, 1977 with Robert L Fish), cited extensively below at page 258.

   They each breached

(1) playing

(2) playing penal

(4) national   } laws

(5) international governing body

(6) overseas national law

but no effective administrative action was taken under category (3) administrative laws above by the English or FIFA authorities in the manner which would inevitably exist to-day.

The referees and/or linesmen who saw all fouls and thus assaults did not dismiss the offenders from either game. The FIFA off-field administrators took no comparable action to that of the Welsh Rugby Union against David Bishop, as they clearly could have done, by suspending each player for the remainder of the tournament. On the other hand, other countries have enforced their own laws against British citizens. The extradition proceedings by the Belgian government to return the British citizens who committed criminal offences in the Heysel Stadium disaster is an example of how international law can apply to the international sporting scene (*Government of Belgium v Postlethwaite* [1987] 2 WLR 365).

A different international sporting legal problem, which is more appropriate to Chapter 7, 'Sports medicine and the law', is emerging through the sophisticated process developing with drug deceptions which reflect a wider medical problem for society generally. It arises when a conflict exists between prescribed lawful medical treatment for the use of drugs prohibited by domestic and international sporting governing bodies, and their medical justification. In one well publicised situation, an English Football League club professional footballer playing for Scotland, Willie Johnston in the World Cup competition during 1978 in South America was found guilty of breaching the world governing soccer body's (FIFA's) drug regulations. The available factual evidence points to a conflict or confusion of communication between the patient and his club or national team's medical advisers about any awareness that this lawfully prescribed drug was a prohibited substance under the FIFA drug regulations. Six years later in 1984, an All England British Judo Association champion with dual British/Canadian nationality was prescribed a lawful drug by a Canadian doctor which breached the Association's rules.

More recently in 1992 two rugby union international footballers were allegedly tested positive for the use of prohibited drugs after France played Wales in Paris. It emerged that the Welsh Rugby Union honorary surgeon had prescribed drugs for sickness and dysentry suffered by Anthony Clement and the French doctor had administered Pholeodine to Jean-Baptiste Lafond for a cough.

All of these four cases are dealt with in medical detail in Chapter 7. Here they illustrate the principle more widely recognised in international legal circles as a conflict of laws situation. Humiliation resulted in all cases. For the professional footballer a publicised return to Scotland for an administrative sports offence to which section 28 (3) (b) (i) of the Misuse of Drugs Act 1971 would have provided a defence in a British criminal court

'If he proves that he neither believed nor suspected nor had reason to suspect that the substance or product in use was a controlled drug.'

It was not a defence available to Willie Johnston before the court of world football's ruling body, and it does not appear to have been known to him or any advisers for use in mitigation of his sentence (punishments which should have been inflicted upon the players who criminally assaulted Pele but were supinely not implemented by that same world governing football body in 1966). For the British Judo Association, the humiliation resulted in a High Court retraction of a life ban from competing in the British championships. This was for the breach of a natural justice principle also experienced by the Football Association in its unjudicial administrative treatment of its former national team manager, Don Revie. These two cases are referred to in more detail respectively in Chapter 7, 'Sports medicine and the law' and Chapter 11, 'Fair play and reason in court'. Humiliation also resulted for the French Rugby Union which then operated a list of banned substances different from the Welsh Rugby Union's use of the International Olympic Committee's list.

These conflicts between lawfully prescribed drugs for authentic medicinal purposes and desirably prohibitive sports drug laws will not disappear, if at all, until a harmonisation formula can be devised between participants, doctors, administrators and lawyers. Until such an ideal occurs, these examples will illustrate sport's own special conflict of laws situation. The Canadian Government's 'Commission of Inquiry into the use of drugs and banned Practices intended to increase Athletic Performance', which produced the Report of Mr Justice Dubin after Ben Johnson was disqualified in the 1988 Olympic Games, analysed the problem. It could not and did not devise any effective remedial and/or ameliorative action.

Correspondingly, the undefended civil litigation, on its merits, by the IAAF against Harry 'Butch' Reynolds, explained towards the end of Chapter 7, 'Sports medicine and the law' has its decidedly international flavour, indicative of the global village, dominating International Sport today. Reynolds commenced proceedings in his home town court of Columbus, Ohio, USA (see page 216, above).

Rightly or wrongly the IAAF considered that it did not see what this had to do with Ohio and, in any case, did not think that justice could have been obtained in Reynolds' home town courts. It also considered the remoteness of Ohio from the realities of the situation when recognising how the drug sample in dispute was taken in Monte Carolo; the IAAF headquarters at the time were based in England (see *Reel v Holder* [1981] 3 All ER 321 for the jurisdiction point); the factual witnesses in the case were from France, and expert witnesses were German and English.

In the future, however, one simpler resolution to such problems (as explained by the author in the *New Law Journal* for May 3 1991) may lie with a little known jurisdiction which has existed since 1983, but surfaced to a wider audience during early 1991 at two separate international gatherings geared to sport and the law. The first, organised by a group of progressive Australian counsel from Selborne Chambers, Sydney, NSW, was held on the Olympic Committee's doorstep in Switzerland, and the other by the charitable arm of the IAAF, the International Amateur Athletic Foundation in Monaco. Each was enlightened by the developments disclosed by Dr Gilbert Schwaar, Secretary-General of the Court of Arbitration for Sport (CAS).

CAS was conceived by the President of the International Olympic committee, HE Snr Juan Antonio Samaranch, the former Spanish Ambassador in Moscow, in 1983 just before the 1984 Los Angeles Olympiad, when a wave of litigation – nearly all of it unsuccessful – brought the Olympic movement under severe pressure. The idea was to set up an arbitration institution which would deal with disputes directly or indirectly linked with sport. Although created by the IOC, which covers its running costs, the members are completely independent of the IOC in the exercise of their duties. They comprise a panel of 60 international jurists with a working knowledge of sport, selected equally from the IOC; international federations such as FIFA; the Association of National Olympic Committees; and by the President of the IOC from outside the other three areas.

The jurisdiction is open to sports bodies, individuals practising or teaching sport, businessmen, corporate bodies, public or private, who may all refer to the CAS with a view to attempting to settle any conflict by arbitration, provided the dispute has a bearing on private interests. Any problems of a technical nature arising during the practice of a particular sport, such as the competence of a referee's or umpire's decision, would remain within the jurisdiction of the appropriate international federation or domestic organisation concerned. Thus, the capacity to play appropriate times which brought amateur basketball players (*R v The British Basketball Association ex p Mickan and Cheesman* [1981] March 17 CAT 0111) or an amateur tennis player (*Curry v Barton & Rippon* (1987) Times, 27, 28 March and 29 July) before the English courts, would lie within the jurisdiction of CAS.

The 72 paragraphs of statutes contain a recognisable procedural code designated in Art 27:

> 'The arbitration proceedings shall consist of written submissions and an oral presentation.
> It may start with a summary procedure for the purpose of trying to reach a consideration'.

Although the usual pre-condition for costs is contained in the statutes (Arts 72, 73), they are silent on the crucial question of legal aid or assistance for submission to the CAS authority. When Dr Schwaar was questioned by the author at each of the conferences about this, his responses on both occasions were unequivocal. In the appropriate circumstances, the equivalent of legal aid or assistance would be forthcoming.

As travel and television contract the globe to bring international sport into every living room, the concept of an International Court of Arbitration for Sport on circuit need not be a fanciful one. National and international sport have travelled a long way since Florence Nagle caused the Jockey Club to re-assess its attitude to women trainers. At one time, India's judiciary has been invoked to consider the existence of that country's equivalent of the Britannic Assurance County Championship, the Ranji Trophy, and the Argentine international footballer Diego Maradona was contemplating an appeal against a world-wide ban against him for alleged drug abuse. The Court of Arbitration for Sport with its 60 sporting jurists would have been an appropriate tribunal for both cases.

A further development affecting the Court of Arbitration for Sport was reported from its Headquarters in Lausanne while these pages were in preparation during the summer of 1993.

A proposal was formulated to create a Supreme Council of International Sports Arbitration which, when established, will control the Court of Arbitration for Sport (CAS). Its enforcement required the agreement of the International Federations and implementing procedures to ensure that all concerned would agree the jurisdiction: and on the basis that such agreement in total or an amended form will ultimately be forthcoming, the full document is reproduced here.

Significantly, while the British government and Treasury has influenced the Lord Chancellor and his officials to restrict the availability of legal services throughout the community under the legal aid legislation referred to in Chapter 1, 'Genesis', at page 6 above, the last paragraph of the proposal explains how. Dr Gilbert Schwarn's offer expressed at the two international conferences in 1991 explained above has been extended.

'CREATION OF AN INSTITUTION WHICH ESSENTIALLY GUARANTEES THE ATHLETES RIGHTS ON THE JURISDICTIONAL LEVEL

In order to better safeguard the parties' rights in front of the Court of Arbitration for Sport (CAS), a "Supreme Council of International Sport Arbitration" is hereby created.

This decision makes the Court of Arbitration for Sport totally independent from the IOC by transferring to a new very high-level body the responsibility to ensure the total autonomy of the Court of Arbitration for Sport.

The Supreme Council will be composed of high-level jurists designated by the IOC, the International Federations, the National Olympic Committees (four per body) and four by the Athletes.

It will also include four eminent personalities co-opted by the Supreme Council itself.

The Supreme Council elects the President.

The Supreme Council performs the administrative and financial functions and duties necessary to the functioning of the Court of Arbitration for Sport (designation or confirmation of arbitrators, determination of the parties' contributions to the functioning of arbitration panels, contribution to the financing of the jurisdictional operations, etc.).

The Court of Arbitration for Sport shall be composed of two Chambers:
– one Chamber for Ordinary Arbitration;
– one Chamber for Appeal Arbitration.

The Chamber for Appeal Arbitration is responsible for the requests of arbitration for appeal made against the sports bodies, including in doping matters, on the basis of compulsory undertakings by all the athletes on the national and international level and of a clause of appeal provided for by the statutes of the organisation concerned.

In order to facilitate access to sports arbitral jurisdiction to persons even without resources, the creation of a "Legal Assistance Fund for Sports-related Arbitration" is also envisaged.
Lausanne, 21st June 1993'

Six months later this was converted to a

CODE OF SPORTS-RELATED ARBITRATION

without sustaining the existence of a 'Legal Assistance Fund for Sports-Related Arbitration' comparable to British Legal Aid.
Its preamble stated:

'The International Sports Federations, the National Olympic Committees, the International Olympic Committee and groups representing the athletes have set up a new structure and new rules of procedure in connection with sports arbitration, with the aim of facilitating the resolution of sports-related disputes, including doping-related disputes, provided that the IF's [International Federation's] regulations so permit or with their prior agreement.
    The Court of Arbitration for Sport (CAS) is now placed under the aegis of the International Council of Arbitration for Sport (ICAS).
    The ICAS is a foundation under Swiss law which has its seat in Lausanne. Its object is to ensure the total independence of the CAS and to safeguard all the rights of the parties before it. The ICAS is composed of 20 members, high-level jurists, performing their functions in a personal capacity, in total objectivity and independence. Their task is, in

particular, to appoint the personalities who appear on the list of CAS arbitrators and to keep a constant watch over the activities of the CAS court office. They themselves cannot act either as arbitrators or as counsel to the parties.

For its part, the task of the CAS is to secure the arbitral resolution of the disputes submitted to it. It does this through the intervention of Panels of arbitrators whose task is either to resolve disputes submitted in sole instance to the so-called ordinary procedure (Ordinary Arbitration Division), or to rule on appeals related to the decisions given by federations, associations or other sports bodies (Appeals Arbitration Division). It should be noted that the ICAS has the task of adopting and modifying not only its own statutes, but also those of the CAS.

Consequently, there now exists on a world-wide level a sports-related arbitration structure and procedure, together with an institution designed to settle disputes submitted to it, in total independence and fully respecting the rights of the parties, precisely because of the attachment of the CAS, charged with the resolution of disputes, to the ICAS, responsible for the smooth operation and financing of the former. This structure has been developed by specialists in arbitration after extensive consultation with all the interested parties.'

The extent to which this jurisdiction will be effective must depend upon the extent to which IF's [International Federation's] 'regulations so permit or with their prior agreement'.

One other harmonisation area in international sport which affects the United Kingdom is a corollary to the VAT conflict of laws area considered in Chapter 14, 'No fine on fun'. It will be recalled how the Celtic Football & Athletic Football Club Ltd and the Football Association Ltd were able effectively to rely upon UEFA competition regulations obliging them to reciprocate hospitality to opposing sporting competing bodies in order to refute HM Commissioners of Customs & Excise rejection of their claims for allowable entertainment input expenses under the appropriate VAT regulations. Now the Inland Revenue has entered the same area of international fiscal consistency.

The Financial Secretary to the Treasury, the Rt Hon Norman Lamont MP, responded with the following information in a written Parliamentary answer on 25 March 1987 to a question about information he had available as to what level of payment countries other than the UK formally levied the commencement of taxation (HC Written Answer, 25 March 1987, Hansard: Vol 113 col 212):

'Countries which have withholding arrangements include the USA, Canada, France, Germany, Australia, New Zealand, Belgium, Switzerland, Portugal, Spain, Finland, Norway and Sweden.
Generally, tax is withheld on all payments subject to the effect of the relevant double taxation agreement. For example, the UK–United

States of America convention exempts the visiting entertainer or sportsman from liability where the gross receipts do not exceed $15,000 (or
their sterling equivalent) in the tax year concerned.'

Consistent with this universality, Regulations were laid in the House
of Commons the following day, 26 March 1987, containing details of
the new rules for the withholding of tax at source on payments to
nonresident entertainers and sportsmen. They were introduced under
SI 1987/1530 as a witholding tax to take effect from 1 May 1987 and
consolidated in sections 555–558 of the Income and Corporation
Taxes Act 1988 and SI 1987/530. For this purpose a Foreign Entertainers Unit was set up to administer the new scheme on 5th Floor,
City House, 140, Edmund Street, Birmingham, B3 2JH (telephone
021–200–2616).

Notwithstanding the universality of this position, the overriding
tax burdens on British Sport generally (see Chapter 14, 'No fine on
fun') resulting in early 1991 in Peter Lawson, the CCPR's General
Secretary, at an International symposium on Sport and Law at
Monaco under the auspices of the International Athletic Federation,
the IAAF's charitable arm, claiming

'though in Britain we have mixed fortunes in our sports events and
competitions, there is one league that we have consistently headed for
many years, it is called the European Sports Taxation League'.

He was followed by John Lister, Honorary Treasurer of the British
Athletic Federation, who explained in the international sporting
context,

'The athlete witholding tax, the proper title is foreign entertainers tax, is
particularly disliked because as you would imagine we get no sympathy
at all from the likes of Mr Said Aouita or a variety of Kenyans when we
tell them well we are very, very sorry, but we have to deduct 25 per cent
British income tax from their appearance money. We get a very short
answer and the result is inevitably that we pay the tax which then
becomes an added cost to us. So we in sport in Britain are very much on
our own.' [See generally Chapter 14, 'No fine on fun'.]

Such aims for uniformity and consistency lead to three other areas
where a pattern of principle can be discerned in which sport can be
said to have been identified and recognised internationally in law; and
how it is always necessary to keep a level of awareness well in mind.
One concerns intervention by the English courts; another the arrival
of Common Market law at its legislative and litigation levels, and the
third concerns the never ending struggle by sport to prevent invasion
into its territory by alien trespassers seeking to exploit its existence for
naked political purposes.

For the first, Chapter 6 unfolded in its earlier pages the table of English court decisions against international sporting governing bodies which had failed to realise how the judges will assist victims of injustice and unlawful actions committed by sporting governing bodies. Soccer (FIFA), cricket (ICC), badminton (IBA) and athletics (IAAF) all received their come-uppances in the courts when acting contrary to the restraint of trade laws so far as soccer and cricket were concerned, and contrary to their own regulations in the badminton and athletics cases. They were all relied upon and identified by the *Daily Telegraph* racing editor, Tony Stafford, in a warning to the Jockey Club at Portman Square about the consequences of its reported intention to enforce the Royal Western India Turf Club's ban on an English jockey, Kevin Darley. He had been disciplined for his riding of the horse Sweet Success in Bombay. The incident turned sour when he complained that the Indian administrative procedures did not comply with the rules of natural justice. Past precedents within the international racing fraternity pointed to an international agreement which had allowed the automatic application of riding bans which had been imposed overseas to apply to the UK.

Tony Stafford pointed out the capacity of English courts to rule against unlawful actions by international sporting governing bodies; citing in particular Foster, J in the case of (*Cooke v The Football Association* (1972) Times, 24 March). Here the judge ruled FIFA's regulations to be in restraint of trade and also told the FA to withdraw from FIFA if the world body would not alter its rules 'to accord with the principles of English law' relating to restraint of trade. Stafford also reminded the Jockey Club of its own downfall in the Court of Appeal during 1966 at the persistence of Florence Nagle and her experienced legal advisers to establish women's rights for a trainer's licence in their own name (*Nagle v Fielden*, supra). Instead of automatically implementing Darley's three months' riding ban from India at Darley's behest the Jockey Club suspended it pending Darley's appeal in England to allow him to continue riding. When the Jockey Club ultimately confirmed the ban in a London hearing of the appeal to its own jurisdiction, three weeks alone were left of the original ban. If there had been an implementation of the full three months under an automatic suspension pursuant to the relevant international agreement there could well have been a re-run of the FA's further downfall experienced in 1979 when it was adjudged to have breached a natural justice principle in its treatment of its former national team manager (*Revie v The Football Association* (supra)). The Jockey Club's refusal to apply the Indian suspension automatically was another step on the road to fair play in sport and justice in the law at international level.

The second pattern of principle to be observed is the creeping encroachment of European Community law upon the European sporting scene. A free market for the participants in professional sports under Articles 48–51 of the Treaty of Rome overshadows the traditional planning for team structures in British professional football. In two cases the European Court of Justice has accepted jurisdiction for disputes concerning professional as distinct from amateur sport as an economic activity under Article 2 of the Treaty.

Finally, and by no means least, the point considered demonstrates the impact of English rugby players arguing that they should have unqualified freedom of movement. The Leicester Rugby Football Club lived up to its nickname of 'the Tigers' when it pursued the Leicester City Council through the High Court, the Court of Appeal and ultimately to the House of Lords to gain a unanimous verdict that the Council had improperly operated the Race Relations Act 1976. It had purported to suspend and ban the club from use of the council's own Welford Road Recreation Ground because three of its players had exercised their freedom of choice to accept an invitation from the Rugby Union at Twickenham to represent England on a rugby tour of South Africa (*Wheeler and others v Leicester City Council* [1985] 1 AC 1054).

In a general internationally mobile sporting world it can be seen from this summary and overview that the tentacles of international sport and law are gradually and almost inevitably creeping into the British domestic sporting scene. Notwithstanding their diversity they can still be fitted into the traditional legal framework of international law, namely,

(1) Public
(2) Private   law
(3) Conflicting

3 PUBLIC INTERNATIONAL LAW

Convention and tradition confines this area to relationships between states. Lord Radcliffe, a Lord of Appeal for fifteen years and Director General of the Ministry of Information during the Second World War, took a broader view when he spoke upon The Rights of Man after that war to the Grotius Society (1950, Vol 36, p5), founded in 1915 to promote the ideas of international law:

'I do not claim to know what international law is: but at least I am confident that, if it is to have any power over the hearts and minds of men, it cannot be just the body of rules that sovereign States are prepared from time to time to recognise in their dealings with each other. If it is to bind the conscience of mankind, it must be felt to have behind it the sanction of some less mundane authority. The protection that we can expect to get is indeed a matter for experts: but it is the protection that we ought to get that we dwell upon in our distress.'

Protection was the last thing that the outstanding international footballer, Pele, received from referees, or football received from its sovereign body, FIFA. There was no effective punishment of the offenders for Pele's 1966 World Cup distress expressed thus in *My Life and the Beautiful Game* (1977, Pele with Robert L Fish on pages 144–145)

'... against Bulgaria ... I had been the target of merciless attacks from Zechev of Bulgaria throughout the entire game. Zechev did everything he could physically to cripple me, and the referee, Jim Finney* gave neither me nor any of the others on our team the protection we had a right to expect from an official in a game.'

...

'Morais, of Portugal, had a field day fouling me, eventually putting me out of the game. He tripped me, and when I was stumbling to the ground he leaped at me, feet first, and cut me down completely. It wasn't until I actually saw the films of the game that I realised what a terribly vicious double-foul it was. The stands came to their feet screaming at the foul, but the English referee, George McCabe allowed Morais to remain on the field, although again, even in the most inexperienced league in the world, he would have been thrown out for either of the two fouls, let alone both. Dr Gosling and Mario Americo came to help me from the field, and Brazil went on to play with ten men and ended up eliminated from the tournament.'

Those impressions of what the films showed for Pele have been confirmed by the author's own viewing of the official film of the 1966 World Cup Competition, *Goal*, by its scriptwriter and the then *Sunday Times* football correspondent, Brian Glanville, and also by *The Times'* senior sportswriter, David Miller. The six legal consequences as set out previously could be considered in turn insurance. They were all repeated fourteen years later during the semi-final of the 1982 World Cup competition in Spain. The West German goalkeeper Schumacher assaulted the French defender, Battiston, in a manner condemned internationally by the sporting press. Yet as David Miller recorded in his book on the 1966 World Cup, *The Boys of '66: England's Lost Glory* at p 21,

---

* NB Jack Rollin, football's leading statistician and author of the *Guinness Book of Soccer Records*, in his *World Cup Triumph 1966* records the referee as Herr Tschenscher of West Germany. Pele's text is as cited above.

'Any dignified sport would have suspended for life the West German goalkeeper for his atrocious foul in the 1982 semi-final, which shamefully handicapped the French. From FIFA there was no more than a murmur.'

Battiston's 1982 West German experience and Pele's Portuguese and Bulgarian experiences in the 1966 World Cup created a classic combination of circumstances which could and should have demonstrated – but did not – how all six legal layers can be acted upon. These fouls merited the following sanctions:

(1) Playing – sending off from field;

(2) Playing penal laws – in breach of Law 12 of Association football – violent conduct or serious foul play;

(3) Administrative – suspension or dismissal from competition in the manner suffered by Scotland's star winger who was sent home from the 1978 World Cup in Argentina following a positive drugs test in breach of FIFA rules but lawfully prescribed under Parliament's Misuse of Drugs Act 1971 (see Chapter 7, 'Sports medicine and the law', infra);

(4) National – prosecution under Section 47 of the Offences Against the Person Act, 861, for assault occasioning actual bodily harm;

(5) International governing body – as in (2) above with censure upon referees and FIFA noted by David Miller for abdicating responsibilities;

(6) Overseas national laws as in (3) above, with the precedents from other violent visitors or criminal offenders to United Kingdom shores.

Nothing at all in fact ever happened. Furthermore, many participants of *all* sporting codes would argue that a comparable position existed towards the end of 1993 in what the England rugby union captain, Will Carling, described as 'dirty play' by the New Zealand tourists.

The offenders escaped back to their native lands without any effective punishment for their undoubted criminality. The reluctance of the prosecuting authorities in the Liverpool area (covering Goodison Park, where the Pele assaults occurred) to take action could conceivably have resulted from diplomatic sensitivities. Since then, in the next World Cup, at Mexico City in 1970, England's captain, Bobby Moore, was intimidated by a false charge of alleged theft in the Colombian capital of Bogota; and as the world knows, twenty years later, the South Wales prosecuting authority charged a Welsh international amateur rugby footballer with the offence identified and suffered by Pele. To those who supinely and irresponsibly say 'It's all part of the game', Pele's beautiful game and that of others – the game of ballet without music – there is one question to be answered. What should happen to any member of a dance routine chorus whipping the feet from under the legs of Fred Astaire and Ginger Rogers? Punishment or condonement? For 1994, FIFA's red card sanctions at last redresses the balance which had been out of kilter in 1966.

Sustaining Lord Radcliffe's yardstick for international law sanctions as 'the protection we ought to get that we dwell upon in our distress', it was granted by Foster J in the Chancery Division of London's High Court in 1972. A Sheffield-born former Manchester United player, John Cooke, found that his proposed transfer back to the County Palatine for service with Wigan Athletic, then outside the Football League, from Sligo Rovers in Eire, was blocked. This was due to FIFA's insistence on upholding the restrictive practices built in to the Republic of Ireland's FA and Football League provisions of a kind which Wilberforce J had declared to be in restraint of trade and unenforceable and thereby unlawful in the celebrated Eastham Case in 1963 (supra). FIFA's control covers the FA in London, the custodians of English soccer, with whom Wigan Athletic was registered. The FA were bound by contract and loyalty to FIFA to obey the world body's refusal to register the transfer from Sligo Rovers to Wigan Athletic: Cooke's employment contract was subject to Irish restrictions of the kind outlawed by Wilberforce J. With FIFA's registered offices in Switzerland outside the jurisdiction of the English courts, there was only one course open to Cooke's English lawyers at the time of commencing proceedings in advance of the judgement during 1972. They sued the FA for declarations attacking the FIFA overriding restrictive articles and confirming the Irish prohibitions. Foster J unshackled Cooke from his Eire and FIFA bonds in the spirit of Guthrie's campaign to free soccer slaves from being the last bonded men in Britain (*Cooke v The Football Association*: (1972) Times, 24 March). Four days later (28 March 1972) a letter to *The Times* from Mr David Green commented on FIFA's Article 14 which was held to be unlawful with its references to contracts subject to national Rules 'no matter how harsh the terms of the contract may be,' under English common law,

> 'And is it not, to adapt the words of Mr Justice Wilberforce in Eastham's case, incongruous to the spirit of an international sport, that any rule of an international governing body should be drafted in the revolting terms of Article 14.'

Pace David Miller, 'From FIFA there was no more than a murmur.' International cricket also acted unlawfully when the ICC unwisely combined with the TCC in restraint of trade. They attempted to block the Packer assault on professional cricket's limited economic employment terms by interfering with Packer's contractual relationships with his contracted players (*Greig v Insole* (supra)); and so, too, was the FA of Wales prohibition on the three junior league clubs, Newport AFC, Caernarfon Town and Colwyn Bay, against playing on their home grounds in the Principality (*Newport AFC Ltd and Others v FA Wales Ltd* (supra)).

4 PRIVATE INTERNATIONAL LAW

The other cases, listed at the beginning of Chapter 3, 'Under starter's orders', dealing with international governing bodies were concerned with the construction of governing body regulations. The purpose of the regulations was to meet Lord Radcliffe's criteria of 'the protection that we ought to get that we dwell upon in our distress'. On both occasions, the courts confirmed membership for Taiwan's governing sporting body of respectively the International Badminton Association and the then International Amateur Athletic Association (today more realistically an International Trust Fund or Trustee Athletic Association) (*Shen Fu Chang v Stellan Mohlin* (unreported) (1977) QBD, Goff J, except at [1981] 3 All ER 324g-h; *Reel v Holder* [1981] 3 All ER 321).

In the athletes' case Lord Denning MR said at page 323c

'I put on one side any thought of international politics. In international law Taiwan's claim is not recognised.'

Referring to the badminton case and Goff J's judgement Lord Denning confirmed at page 324g-h

'The judge, Robert Goff J, took the view, with which I agree, that we are not concerned with international law or with sovereignty. We are simply concerned with the interpretation of the rules of the IAAF;'

and he concluded with words with which Eveleigh LJ and Brandon LJ agreed,

'These courts can and should make a declaration in favour of Taiwan [of wrongful exclusion from IAAF membership in 1978] to that extent. We do not think this should give rise to any international complications. We are making a declaration on the meaning of the rules according to English law, which is the governing law.'

Five years later the Commonwealth Games Federation arrived in London's High Court to end with the ex cathedra obiter dictum of the Vice-Chancellor in the Chancery Division, Sir Nicholas Browne-

Wilkinson. He was concerned, without citation to him of the Court's emancipation of participants from feudal sporting bonds explained in Chapter 11, Fair Play and Reason in Court, only for a claim by a South African born participant to swim for England whose alleged English residence and domicile had been disputed. He ruled after a rushed interlocutory hearing that the Federation were right

(1) to give the word 'domicile' in article 34(3) of its constitution the ordinary popular meaning of the word and

(2) not to apply the legal meaning which would ordinarily be given to it under the English law of domicile.

He also ruled that even if the law of domicile's traditional legal meaning in tax and family law precedents, concerned with the effect of the legal location or base for a litigant, was the correct test, the full evidential requirements for proving the criteria making England the domicile of choice had been satisfied (*Cowley v Heatley and others* (1986) Times, 24 July). Once more, as in *Reel v Holder* (supra) the case turned on the true meaning of the rules, according to English law. His general strictures as cited below and based upon traditional judicial unawareness of how law today is essential for the health of sport, ie

 'sport would be better served if there was not running litigation at repeated intervals by people seeking to challenge the decisions of the regulating bodies'

become more inappropriate as every passing year demonstrates. This second edition emphasises how the law provides solutions which governing bodies and the judiciary cannot, or will not see.

5 ADMINISTRATIVE SPORTING ACTION

The decision of Leicester City Council to ban the Leicester Rugby Club from using its practice ground at Welford Road, Leicester, for twelve months must be evaluated in this administrative context. The decision was taken under the Race Relations Act 1976. Why? Three Leicester Rugby Club amateur players had exercised their right to tour South Africa with the England national rugby team; these three players held the view that their sporting activities were not relevant to the political situation in South Africa at that time. Mr Justice Forbes upheld this administrative local authority decision. So, too, did a Court of Appeal majority, Lord Justice Browne-Wilkinson (who later succeeded Sir Robert Megarry as Vice-Chancellor of the Chancery Division) dissenting. On appeal the House of Lords unanimously reversed the earlier rulings (*Wheeler v Leicester City Council* (supra)).

The Race Relations Act 1976 contained in section 71 a duty upon local authorities to carry out their functions with the need to promote good relations between persons of different racial groups, which existed in the Leicester City Council's territory. The existence, scope, interpretation and implementation of this section was the key legal issue. Lord Justice Browne-Wilkinson posed the contending antithesis in this section from his dissenting judgement:

'on a point of fundamental principle. The case raises a conflict between the two basic principles of a democratic society: viz, on the one hand, the right of a democratically elected body to conduct its affairs in accordance with its own view [i.e. Leicester City Council] and, on the other, the right to freedom of speech and conscience enjoyed by each individual in a democratic society;'

and he ultimately reached

'the conclusion that the decision of the council is unlawful since legally irrelevant matters were taken into account.'

In the House of Lords, to use a popular rugby metaphor, its judicial grand slam of five Law Lords' unanimous ruling was based on two fundamental premises:

(1) the Council's ban on the club's use of its practice ground at the Council's recreation premises was unreasonable and unfair and amounted to procedural impropriety within the now familiar principles set out in *Associated Picture Houses v Wednesbury Corporation* [1948] 1 KB 223.

(2) The Council's use of its statutory power was a misuse of power because the Council intended to and did in fact punish the club when they had not broken any law.

Just as the rugby players established they had not broken any laws, some cricketers could have argued this in 1982 when the Test and County Cricket Board banned England's Test cricketers who had earned their living professionally in South Africa. *Wisden's* Notes by the Editor (1983 Edition at page 80) recorded of those events how

'The Prime Minister ... Speaking in Parliament, Mrs Thatcher said "We do not have the power to prevent any sportsmen or women from visiting South Africa or anywhere else. If we did we would no longer be a free country".'

Correspondingly Lord Roskill said when delivering one of the two leading House of Lords opinions with words equally applicable to the arguably unlawful ban on the cricketers as they were to the undoubtedly unlawful ban on the Leicester Rugby Club's use of its Welford Road ground, (at p 1076)

> 'It is important to emphasise that there was nothing illegal in the action of the three members in joining the tour. The government policy recorded in the well known Gleneagles agreement has never been given the force of law at the instance of any government, whatever its political complexion, and a person who acts otherwise than in accordance with the principles of that agreement, commits no offence even though he may by his action earn the moral disapprobation of large numbers of his fellow citizens.'

A year later, the New Zealand Rugby Football Union was less effective in protecting its tour to South Africa in 1985. Here a complex network of interlocutory procedures ultimately resulted in a High Court injunction being granted with sufficient timing prior to the departure date to prevent the tour from taking place (*Finnigan and Another v New Zealand RFU* [1985] NZLR 185). An appeal to the Privy Council was academic and rejected. If time had been on the Union's side, it is arguable that the decision could have been reversed.

Since these dramatic and explosive legal issues were considered in controversial contexts the South African sporting scene has shifted with the legal dismantling of apartheid. Readmission to the community of international sport has now followed and the earlier texts from the first edition of this book dealing with the debatable interpretations of the so-called Gleneagles Agreement, the Commonwealth Declaration on Apartheid in Sport, may now be considered both otiose and obsolete. Certainly there are many who would consider that the sporting boycott imposed internationally on South Africa, whether legal or not, contributed to a wider and deeper national political change of scene and climate within South Africa. Furthermore, if the ultimate result has been to integrate blacks into South African sport and therefore society generally, then retrospectively the end may be said to have justified the means.

Thus, it is appropriate to end this chapter with its never ending march into the future with the words of one of the world's greatest and best loved international athletes of all time, Emile Zatopek from Czechoslovakia, in a BBC Radio 4 Sport on Four interview (Saturday 27 June 1987), reproduced here with the permission and assistance of the producer Peter Griffiths and its presenter Cliff Morgan. Zatopek began by saying in an interview with Ian Dark

'As a schoolboy I have had the good teachers who told us: England is the cradle of modern sport and I came to London, like, in to the cradle of modern sport.'

He ended with what should be a beacon for sports lovers throughout the world to ensure all those who are prepared to identify and fight the evil spirits outside sport waiting to destroy it as fun and joy.

'I esteem sport activity as really activity for good conditions, good health and happy life ...
  Sport activity: it is giving really a pleasure; by travelling; by meeting; by this friendship. It is greater than the victory. All the world, sportsmen are like brothers;'

and as a contemporary of Fanny Blankers-Koehn, he doubtless intended to include the sisters, too.

Tauber's own song may have ended; but the melody of international sport will linger on into eternity – this will be so long as international sport continues to be the catalyst which enables so many people to make new international friends without, it may be hoped, the need to resort to the law in court.

Chapter 10

Single European Market and UK sport

1 INTRODUCTION

The British Parliament's European Communities Act 1972 legislated (on 17 October 1972, to take effect on 1 January 1973), for Britain's entry into the Common Market, created by the Treaty of Rome. The Lord Chancellor in Britain's government at the time was Lord Hailsham of St Marylebone. He had already created the role of a Minister with responsibility for sport. Forty years earlier during the winter of 1932–3, his father Viscount Hailsham had been MCC President at the time of the so-called Bodyline crisis, when Test Matches between England and Australia dominated the international cricket scene. Sixty odd years before that, at Kennington Oval in South London in 1870, his grandfather, the first Quintin Hogg, and founder of the Regent Street Polytechnic, participated in the earliest traceable international soccer match between Scotland and England players. Today's sporting world sees that historic fixture lost in the mists of time and the traditional Ashes series are part of a world-wide International Cricket Council framework, within an exploding and expanding European political, sporting and legal scene.

2 COMMON MARKET CATEGORIES

The single European Act was signed in Luxembourg on 17 February 1986 and at The Hague on 28 February 1986. It came into force on 1 July 1987: and Article 4 of The Treaty created for The Community four separate institutions;

(1)   a European Parliament, with elected representatives from the Common Market countries;

(2)   a Council, of Government Ministers, one from each member state, the principal decision making body;

(3)   a Commission, of 17 members nominated by Government agreement, acting in the EC's interests, and not their nominating country, proposing policy and administration;

(4)   a Court of Justice of 13 judges, including one from each state, with the power to interpret EC Law.

Lord Denning has explained, almost symbolically in the present Sport and the Law context, in his volume entitled *What Next in the Law* (pp 295–296):

'...the principle of the supremacy of Community law. The Treaty, its Regulations and Directives, take priority over any of our English law. If there is any conflict or any inconsistency between Community law and English law, then Community law is to prevail.'

He expanded this in a judgment in *Bulmer v Bellinger SA* where he explained with his renowned colourful simplicity [1974] Ch 401 at 411

'... the Treaty (of Rome) concerns only those matters which have a European element, that is to say, matters which affect people or property in the nine countries of the common market besides ourselves. The Treaty does not touch any of the matters which concern solely England and the people in it. These are still governed by English law. They are not affected by the Treaty. But when we come to matters with a European element, the Treaty is like an incoming tide. It flows into the estuaries and up the rivers. It cannot be held back. Parliament has decreed that the Treaty is henceforward to be part of our law. It is equal in force to any statute...'

Clearly Lord Denning was referring to the Community law laid down by the Common Market Parliament in Brussels and the European Court of Justice at Luxembourg. It is a hybrid straddling both conventional national law and the two conventional forms of international law, public and private. Furthermore, since only seven years have passed since July 1987, the full impact of Europe on Sport and the Law in the United Kingdom cannot *at present* be appreciated or anticipated, particularly because the nature of the Common Market's purpose and philosophy is structured economically within its legal framework. For as the bulk of the 22 million British participants, associated with 'approximately 150,000 sports clubs of which about 110,000 clubs are affiliated to governing bodies of sport', as cited by the then Sports Council Director-General in 1986 at page 146 Ch 6 'Participation problems', are drawn from the non-profit making voluntary sector, the manner in which British sport outside the high profile commercially orientated branch of the entertainment industry will be affected by this new dimension to the English legal system cannot be assessed with any element of or accuracy or, indeed, confidence. This is exemplified by the Customs and Excise correction of its omission to operate the EEC Directive since 1990, as explained hereafter in Chapter 14, 'No fine on fun', and in Appendix 12.

This uncertainty is easily identifiable within Sport and the Law's own development within the United Kingdom. A full century elapsed between the judicial common law establishment of criminal liability for football field violence in *R v Bradshaw* (1878; supra) and its extension to Rugby Union in *R v Billinghurst* (1978; supra). Restraint of trade had to wait from its emergence in *Mitchell v Reynolds* (1711) 11 p Wms 181 and *Leather Cloth Co v Larsent* (1869) L R 9 Eq 345 before being pleaded and argued in *Aldershot Football Club v Banks* (1945 supra) and later in the *Eastham* (1963) and *Grieg v Insole* (1978) cases, having been ignored in the *Kingaby* saga (1912; supra and Mr Justice Eve's landmark *mens sana in corpore sano* sporting educational charity decision in *Marriette* (1915 supra), which was ignored in the arguments vainly seeking similar status for the Sussex County Cricket Clubs Nursery Fund in *Re Patten* (1929; supra), had to wait for its resurrection in 1957 for the Sydney University Rugby Club in *Kearins v Kearins* (supra) before achieving the highest accolade from the House of Lords in the FA Youth Trust affirmation of it in *IRC v McMullan* (supra).

Furthermore, as the hat trick of disasters during the end of 1992, explained in the Introduction, have demonstrated, even traditional attempts to apply the law in practice can be ruled offside. Add all of that to the manner in which the House of Lords has overruled lower courts in 75% of its referrals on sporting legal issues, and any confidence in applying EC law to UK sport when appropriate in the future must be muted. For another reversal of a lower court decision albeit on a *non*-sporting context, see *Marshall v Southampton and South-West Hampshire Health Authority (Teaching) (No 2)* (explained at page 271, below).

For present purposes, the level of awareness which is the leitmotiv throughout these pages is the most that can be aimed for here. More detailed assessment must await events which have to happen, apart from certain guidelines in the existing cases to date identified below.

3 COMMON MARKET SPORT AND LAW

Furthermore, Community law's supremacy over English, or in the special context which is being considered here, British law, is not confined to Brussels and Luxembourg. Chapter 14, 'No fine on fun', will show how the competition rules of the European Football Association, UEFA, enabled Scotland's Celtic Football Club and the Football Association in London to win their battles with H M Customs and Excise over whether or not business entertainment expenses of hotel accommodation should be allowed as recoverable input tax (*Celtic Football & Athletic Co Ltd v Customs and Excise Commissioners* [1983] STC 420, and LON/VAT Tribunal 83/484).

The basis for the Scottish Court of Session's and London VAT Tribunal's respective rulings was built into the UEFA competitions' respective rules. Those for the UEFA European Cup in Celtic's case, and those of the UEFA Youth Cup for the FA, both obliged the host country to provide accommodation which would be reciprocated on a return fixture. Thus, what would otherwise have been regarded as a non-claimable VAT input was justified by UEFA's administrative football law. The respective court and tribunal rulings resulted in favour of the two national football associations, resolving a conflict between UEFA law and Britain's VAT law as enacted by the British Parliament (under the then Finance Act which had created it in 1973, after Britain's Common Market entry, by the European Communities Act 1972).

Although this example of sport's administrative laws was not within Lord Denning's purview cited above, it illuminates the principle to be operated when their mandatory nature collides with a Parliamentary enactment, (or, perhaps it could be argued, a Customs and Excise interpretation of it.) In the present context of Common Market considerations, this collision between sporting European law and sport's administrative law is coincidental. An equally vivid illustration could come from FIFA or any other supra-national governing sporting body. It assists as a prelude to Lord Denning's more formal judicial explanation, in a fully reported case on the fringes of sport concerning a woman betting shop employee, *Shields v E Coombes Holdings Ltd* ([1978] 1 WLR 1408 at 1415). The woman succeeded in a claim for equal pay with male counterhands under Britain's Equal Pay Act 1970. The then Master of the Rolls developed the supremacy of Community Law when he applied Article 119 of the Treaty of Rome which creates an equal pay principle for men and women:

> 'It arises whenever there is a conflict of inconsistency between the law contained in an Article of the Treaty and the law contained in the internal law of one of the member states, whether passed before or after joining the Community. It says that in any such event the law of the Community shall prevail over that of the internal law of the member state.'

A similar experience occurred in *McCarthys Ltd v Smith* [1979] 3 All ER 325 [1980] ICR 672 at 692 affecting pay differential between men and women as a warehouse manager. Having failed before an industrial tribunal the complainant found support from Lord Denning, but a Court of Appeal majority, being less certain, caused a reference to the Court of Justice of the European Communities for a direct ruling under the provisions of Article 177 of the Treaty of Rome concerning that particular procedure.

As Lord Denning has explained in *What Next In the Law* (Butterworths: 1982 at p 299) of the European Court at Luxembourg:

'They adopted my view. The case came back to us – when we held that the woman manager was entitled to equal pay with her predecessor. I said (1980) ICR 672 at 692:

"The majority of the court felt that Article 119 was uncertain. So this court referred the problem to the European Court at Luxembourg. We have now been provided with the decision of that court. It is important now to declare and it must be made plain that the provisions of Article 119 of the EEC Treaty take priority over anything in our English statute on equal pay which is inconsistent with Article 119. That priority is given by our own law. It is given by the European Communities Act 1972 itself. Community law is now part of our law: and, whenever there is any inconsistency, Community law has priority. It is now supplanting English law. It is part of our law which overrides any other part which is inconsistent with it. I turn therefore to the decision given by the European Court. The answer they gave was that the man and the woman need not be employed at the same time (which had been argued against the woman in the case). The woman is entitled to equal pay for equal work, even when the women is employed after the man has left. That interpretation must now be given by all courts in England. It will apply in this case and in such cases hereafter."'

A decade and more after that landmark decision, in the wake of Sally Gunnell's claim that she is entitled to the same amount of payment as Linford Christie for her athletic appearances as a Barcelona Olympic Gold medallist, differentials and distinctions may well be argued successfully to exist because of different sponsorship agreements and crowd drawing power capacities. Nevertheless, the existence of these decisions from the English Court of Appeal and the European Court point the way ahead for sport to recognise the potentialities which the European umbrella can unfold.

More recently, in 1993, the European Court ruled that the English Parliament's compensation ceiling under the Sex Discrimination Act 1975, as amended, section 65(2) for wrongful dismissal was in breach of Community Law and decided in effect that consequences will require amending legislation in the UK Parliament (*Marshall v Southampton and South-West Hampshire Health Authority (Teaching) (No 2)* [1993] 4 All ER 536, [1993] 3 WLR 1054 ECJ and article 6 of Council Directive (76(20) EEC)).

Finally, in the wider, more commercially orientated area of articles 85 and 86 dealing with restrictive commercial agreements, one case at least with a sporting flavour concerned the service of coin operated amusement machines for public houses in what used to be known as the East Riding of Yorkshire, now known as Humberside. An interim injunction was extended until the trial of action for what the evidence established was a serious issue to be tried, based on Article 85 of the Treaty, for which damages would not have been an adequate remedy in accordance with the well established principles in *American*

Cyanamid Co v Ethican Ltd [1975] 1 All ER 504, per Sir Neil Lawson sitting as a judge of the High Court in *Cutsforth v Mansfield Inns Ltd* [1986] 1 All ER 577.

If ever the inevitable question is therefore asked – whatever has this got to do with sport – the answer is simple: everything. For just as rugby football and other mobile-body-contact sport players erroneously believed that they were above the law and immune from prosecution in the British Courts for violent foul play until the South Wales police put the prosecutor's boot into them dramatically in a conviction in 1977 (*R v Billingshurst* (supra)) so, too, could there be a corresponding belief of immunity from Community law. British sport, however, is affected by crucial decisions of the European Court of Justice.

The Common Market test for this purpose under Article 2 relates to 'the economic policies of member states' and therefore applies only to professional and not to amateur participants. This coincides with the English courts' attitude which limit the restraint of trade doctrine to professional sportspersons and not amateurs, who have no trade (formally and official, at least) to protect in sport, irrespective of whatever may be their activities outside it (*R v The British Basketball Association, ex p Mickan and Cheesman*, (1981) 17 March, CAT No 01116), although no universally comprehensive definition of amateur has yet been created. In *Gasser v IAAF* (supra) relating to a woman athlete's two year suspension for alleged drug offences, Scott J held that restraint of trade could apply to athletes in receipt of trust funds under the IAAF regulations (a body often realistically referred to as the International Trust Funds Association), but held on the facts that the restraint was reasonable in all the circumstances.

4 EC SPORT AND LAW DECISIONS/JUDGMENTS

The Common Market decisions of the European Court of Justice about sport appear in a number of judgements. One concerns 'pacers', the racing cyclists' equivalent to pacemakers in the horse racing or athletic worlds, in a Dutch cycling contest (*Walgrave and Koch v Union Cycliste Internationale* case 36/74, ECR [1974] 1405, [1975] 1 CLMR 320). The other originated from an Italian Court's reference to the European Court from a commercial dispute about payment for services to discover players outside Italy to play for a local Italian club, Rovigo (*Dona v Mantero*) case 13/76, ECR [1976] 1333, [1976] 2 CLMR 578). They both established without any qualification the important principle that the practice of professional sport is subject to Community Law and the jurisdiction of the European Court in so far as it constitutes an economic activity within the meaning of Article 2 of the EEC, ie

'It shall be the aim of the Community, by establishing a Common Market and progressively approximating the economic policies of Member States, to promote throughout the Community a harmonious development of economic activities, a continuous and balanced expansion, an increased stability, an accelerated raising of the standard of living and closer relations between its Member States.'

The Dutch cyclists' case arose because the international governing body controlling the sport made a new rule that in the world championships to be held in Spain (which was then not a member state), the pacer and the stayer had to be of the same nationality. The Court confirmed its jurisdictions over professional sporting issues but ruled that in spite of EEC Articles prohibiting discrimination (Articles 48–66) national teams could be selected on the basis of harmony of nationality. The Dutch national team accordingly was not competing in breach of Community law. Correspondingly, England's national representative sporting sides are justifiably able to discriminate on playing merit against potential candidates who play in England but are not English nationals (although the curious anomalies of registering South African-born cricketers to play international cricket for England are too well known to be repeated here).

The Italian professional football commercial dispute arose because the employing club chairman claimed that the plaintiff agent acted prematurely in signing players whose registrations were prohibited under a rule of the Italian Football Federation. This limited registrations of non-Italian national players within the Italian domestic competitions. This restriction was held to be prohibited by the anti-discriminatory EEC Articles and referred back to the Rovigo tribunal for further adjudication on the facts. Of equal significance was confirmation by citation of the Walgrave precedents that jurisdictions existed to adjudicate on matters concerning professional sport as an economic issue under Article 2 (supra).

Finally, a third precedent has emerged between a Belgian National Football coach wishing to coach a French football team. The French football authorities insisted on a French qualification. The European court to whom the issue was referred decided that any refusal to permit continuation of such work required stated reasons of authenticity, of which absence would be a breach of the Treaty, *Heylens v Union Nationale des Entraineurs* (1987) ECR 4097.

The majority of the domestic British sporting administrators may be unaware of these crucially important judicial decisions. However the application of EEC law to British sport is something which is in the knowledge of at least the professional association football world.

The progressive developments illuminate an unfolding growth area. The former Common Market Commissioner for Competition and Fair Trading, Mr Ivor Richard QC, was extensively reported towards the end of 1984 in the general as well as the sporting press to the effect that a free movement of professional footballers would be directed if not effected voluntarily by the commencement of season 1987–1988; and his successor, Mr Peter Sutherland, was reported in November 1985 as having instructed all clubs within the Community to be allowed to sign three non-national players immediately. Furthermore, it was also reported that UEFA had been told that the EEC wanted that number to be increased to five from the start of season 1986–1987, with total freedom to sign as many players as necessary from Common Market countries within three years (*Mail on Sunday*, 3 November 1985).

The consequences of such an edict were self-evident. There have been no legal restraints on wealthy overseas clubs obtaining the services of all the talented United Kingdom players; and as the then English Football League secretary, Mr Graham Kelly, was reported as saying:

'We will certainly be in grave danger of losing all our best players.'

The reaction from the office of the Commissioner, Mr Peter Sutherland, was:

'Players have their rights under community law ... if a player has the chance to secure his own future during a relatively short career then who are the Commission to stop him? We are trying to ensure that there is no restriction on freedom.'

These developments demonstrate the grey area which still exists at the date of writing following a purported agreement on 17 April 1991 between the Commission Vice-President Martin Gangenareux, responsible for internal market matters, and the Union of European Football Associations (UEFA). A limitation on the number of foreign players was challenged by a Belgian professional football player, Jean-Marc Bosman, in the European Court of Justice. The purported agreement was held not to be a legally binding act and thereby not justifiable and therefore the action was dismissed.

Undeterred by this red card, and in the tradition of United Kingdom restraint of trade litigation, from the Eastham and Packer precedents, Bosman has brought another action against UEFA and the Royal Football Club de Liege before a Belgian court. That court has referred the matter to the European Court of Justice, requesting its advice on whether the UEFA rules are compatible with EC law, and in particular with the provisions relating to free movement and competition.

As an illustration of the strict three foreign player regulations operated by UEFA the Leeds United versus VfB Stuttgart European Champions Cup fixture had to be replayed during the Autumn of 1992 because VfB Stuttgart, having fielded initially two players foreign to Germany, Dubajic and Sverisson, then added foreign substitutes, Knup and Fimabic, which thereby breached the three foreign player limit. The breach was no doubt inadvertent but emphasised the necessity for club administrators to have this particular competition requirement within sport itself, and potential problems created by the Common Market free movement of workers, in the forefront of everyone's mind connected with this particular tournament.

At the time of writing in early Summer 1994 an opinion from the European Court is still awaited on this issue: furthermore with these revelations, the thoughts of many sports-persons concerned with alleviating 'restriction on freedom' will turn to whether or not the England test cricketers, who had broken no law either nationally or administratively by playing cricket professionally in South Africa, were unlawfully discriminated against in breach of the EEC Treaty and thereby the European Communities Act 1972. Did the Test and County Cricket Board, the unsuccessful defendants in the Packer litigation in 1977, err again when it banned the players for a three-year period? There was at least an intellectually arguable case that the ban was in restraint of trade, although the decision contained a built-in defence of reasonability (in the alleged interest of international cricket). Furthermore, the anti-discriminatory legislation of the EEC Treaty contains in Article 48 (3) a proviso limiting freedom of movement 'on grounds of public policy, public security or public health'. Many arguments on both sides of this issue could be formulated in this area.

Article 86 of the Treaty was invoked by the Commission to which the Independent Television Association (ITVA) on 5 April 1989 had referred a purported granting by the Football Association at Lancaster Gate in London of exclusive permission to the BBC and a complex of companies, BSB, for televising football matches for which it owned the rights, and expressly excluding any other UK broadcaster at the Commissioner's request. The exclusivity clause is not only in breach of the competition Article 85 (i) but also an abuse of the FA's dominant position under Article 86 – see official Journal of the EC 3 AW 1993 (93) c 94/06).

A year earlier on 10 June 1992 in another television dispute the Scottish Football Association succeeded before the European Court of Justice in having annulled an earlier EC Commission decision requiring the broadcasting of peremptory information relating to alleged interference with Argentine Football Association matches (SFAV EC Commission [Official Journal EC: 10:7:98 ref 92/C 174(2)]). Also in 1992, a licensed French private television company also succeeded with the European Court of Justice in challenging an EC decision to refuse an injunction against the European Broadcasting Union *La Cinq SA VEC Commission (European Broadcasting Union intervening)* Case T–44/90 [1992] 4 CMLR 44.

CONCLUSION

Such economically orientated EC decisions are as relevant as they would be in more recognisable domestic jurisdictions. They illuminate how wide the range of sporting legal issues can be when different national legal issues converge.

Indeed, Lord Denning's incoming tide conceals icebergs which are beyond the scope of these pages, but include particularly in a commercial context such depths as diplomas for coaching, lotteries, animals, ocean-going sailing yachts (even used for sporting purposes concurrently with commercial enterprises: see chapter 14, 'No fun on fun', p 390) and VAT which will remain in the United Kingdom for only commercial and no longer for non-profit making sporting sources. This accords with Customs and Excise and H M Treasury developments to meet European requirements as explained in Appendix 12. Like the celebrated *Ole Man River*, Lord Denning's tide will keep rolling along, but for Sport and the Law, into territories undreamed of in the past.

Part IV

Administration

Part IV

Administration

Chapter 11

Fair play and reason in court

1 INTRODUCTION

Consistent with the gradual fusion of Parliamentary, common law and equity and EEC developments within sport, sport has attempted with varying degrees of success and failure to create its own mechanisms, jurisdictions, rules and regulations for controlling its administration.

The courts of law become the last resort for victims of maladministration and oppression to obtain justice when their application does not conform to common law or the equity rules of natural justice. This chapter therefore discusses how sporting governing bodies and those whom they purport to control forced the courts and judges to recognize the roles they have to play when fair play and reason in sporting committee rooms and council chambers fly out of their windows.

Notwithstanding that final goal, however,

'Justice can often be done in domestic tribunals better by a good layman than by a bad lawyer.'

That was how Lord Denning explained the courts' general reluctance to intervene in such proceedings. This also reflected the fact that nearly 100% of contested criminal matters in the United Kingdom are concluded either by lay justices guided on legal matters by professionally trained court clerks, or by juries directed on matters of law by the trial judge (the only exceptions being the legally qualified stipendiary magistrates adjudicating in densely populated communities). Lord Denning continued:

'This is essentially so in activities like football and other sports, where no points of law are likely to arise, and it is all part of the proper regulation of the game.' (*Enderby Town Football Club v The Football Association* [1971] 1 All ER 215.)

During 1989 Lord Denning's words were illuminated by a coincidence of administrative and legal experiences involving Swindon Town Football Club, the International Cricket Conference, the Test

279

and County Cricket Board and HH The Aga Khan. Each particular situation was well publicised at the relevant time. The connecting thread between them demonstrates the necessity for a level of awareness, the achievement of which is the object of this book.

Swindon Town Football Club was demoted from the First Division of the Football League to the Third Division in 1990 because of Boardroom financial irregularities. After a tentative High Court action was abandoned due to a realistic risk of high costs, the directors of the Club exercised their right *within the Football League Regulations* to attend before an Appeals Committee of Football Association Councillors. An impeccable hearing conducted by Lord Denning's concept of 'good laymen' resulted in a preservation of Swindon Town's Second Division status based on sound legal principles. Ironically, a spokesman for the Football League (whose own Regulations provided for this appellate structure) complained publicly afterwards that the Football Association had been expected to support the Football League. In fact the Football Association Appeals Committee did not support the Football League because they considered the penalty it had imposed to be too oppressive. As one of the Counsel representing Swindon Town, I pointed out in the sports correspondence columns of *The Times* (18 July 1990) the Football League's bizarre and unsporting attitude. I also questioned without any response or rebuttal, the fitness of the Football League to administer its competition when such an attitude exists. More recently Jacob J in London's Chancery Division of the High Court held the Football Association of Wales to have acted in restraint of trade when prohibiting three minor league football clubs from playing in their home grounds (*Newport AFC Ltd and Others v FA of Wales Ltd* (1994) 144 NLJ 1351).

Earlier in 1989 the former Secretary to the International Cricket Conference and MCC, Jack Bailey, published what he entitled *Conflicts in Cricket*. In revelatory pages 101–2, he wrote of the Packer litigation which had been fought out in 1977 and 1978 in the same Chancery Division of London's High Court as thirteen years earlier Mr Justice Wilberforce had applied the long-standing common law principles and equitable reliefs associated with restraints of trade to the professional football world. (*Eastham v Newcastle United Football Club Ltd and the Football Association* [1963] 3 All ER 139.)

> 'The cricket authorities had lost on every point of law involved, although they had emerged with some credit from a moral standpoint. Had it all been worth it? Or rather had we anything to show for the damages and costs awarded against us, amounting to some £250,000*

* and later passed on to the unfortunate MCC and County Cricket Club members in increased subscriptions, any one of whom could have told the then legal advisers of the ICC and TCCB that they were batting, bowling and fielding on a likely losing legal wicket from the start: and at least one solicitor county executive did!

(later shared equally between ICC and TCCB) apart from a vast amount of publicity for cricket all over the world?
   Well, for one thing, it had been a lesson. It had taught the cricket authorities that good intentions, if not paving the road to hell, are not enough when it comes to the law of the land ... A contract was a contract and if certain players were required they would have to be issued with legally binding contracts for a twelve-month period or longer.
   We also learnt the law regarding inducement of breach of legal contract and what was reasonable in the cricket world, both to protect established cricket and to prevent unlawful restraint of trade.
   ...
   During the case, and at a comparatively early stage, our counsel had entered a defence that ICC and TCCB were employers' associations and as such immune, as were trade unions under current law, from the charges against them. The rules and prime activities of both bodies were not held to constitute them as employers' associations, but almost as soon as the case was over TCCB set about amending their rules and constitution to enable them to qualify'.

It was not the fault of the 'good layman' who was the nominal defendant, Douglas Insole, that his experiences as a distinguished Corinthian-Casual amateur footballer, former Cambridge University soccer Blue, and ultimate representative of his University on the FA Council, had not prepared him for expensive professional advice resulting in that disastrous legal result thirteen years after the football landmark decision in the *Eastham* case during 1963.
   Correspondingly, it was not surprising that HH The Aga Khan battled in vain against the Jockey Club's disqualification of his filly Alysa, after winning the Epsom Oaks in 1989, by use of the judicial review machinery, when he was trapped by a precedent of the Court of Appeal in *Law v National Greyhound Racing Club Ltd* [1983] 3 All ER 300 that the judicial review procedure is not applicable to private sporting governing bodies. His legal advisers had chosen to argue his claim on this basis instead of the route recommended by the Court of Appeal by way of a writ for breach of contract earlier. As I have written in the *All England Law Reports Annual Review* for 1992, after he had lost on this inevitable ground in the Court of Appeal,

'It left him and his advisers with a recognition of his breach of contract remedies – and, in the absence of any application for leave to appeal to the House of Lords, or of any apparent intention ever to have tested this particular climate in the House of Lords – with the question, why on earth the traditional contract route had been ignored in favour of a procedure trapped by binding precedent (*R v Disciplinary Committee of the Jockey Club exp The Aga Khan* (1992) Times, 9 December).'

A careful analysis of how and why this has occurred appears in Catherine Bond's Appendix 9. It emphasises the warning of Woolf LJ (as he then was) at the Divisional Court level All ER Rev 1991, pp 313–314 that there was 'no relief which the court can provide on application for judicial review until the law is either changed by a higher court or by statutory intervention'.

2 LIBEL

Twenty-two years before *Enderby Town* in 1971, Lord Denning had prepared the ground for those conclusions as stated above with a prophetic foretaste of what lay ahead, given through a judgment concurring with the better known words of Tucker LJ, in the sporting libel action of *Russell v Duke of Norfolk* ([1949] 1 All ER 109, [1949] 65 TLR 225). It was the last of many unsuccessful attempts to use this particular remedy of defamation before a judge and jury to challenge sporting disciplinary tribunal decisions in the years 1919–39 between two World Wars. Domestic tribunal decisions can easily have adverse effects upon those who are subject to their verdicts. Thus, as this chapter explains, they emerged in the last fling of the Gentlemen v Players era through sensational libel actions at the time from the two sporting spheres where unashamed and unconcealed financial interests and investments predominated in two of the most high-profile professional sports, horse racing and association football.

Today libel has been replaced by declaratory judgments through an exclusively judge-made route identifiable in its own category of administrative law. Within the world of sport there is now an overlap between the general common law of economic torts which protect interference with employment and contractual relationships and the correct procedural remedies. Because mistakes by administrators and practitioners still continue as illustrated through the last thirty years from the worlds of football (*Eastham* and *Revie v The Football Association*, cricket (*Packer*) and racing (*Nagle* and the *Aga Khan*), an explanation of how the modern route was carved, which also highlights the errors made before it began and along the way, is the most suitable and helpful form of narrative, as guidance in avoiding similar disasters in the future.

Lord Denning's path to natural justice in the world of sport began with one of those many libel actions which appeared to pre-Second World War practitioners to be the most effective and, indeed, only, remedy for protecting reputations and clearing the name of victims defamed or otherwise harmed by debatable domestic tribunal disciplinary or administrative decisions. In the *Russell v Duke of Norfolk* trial the Court of Appeal considered a racing trainer's licence which was found to have been withdrawn after a properly conducted inquiry by the sport's ruling body, the Jockey Club. It decided that a drug had been administered to a horse named Boston Boro, and trained by James Russell, which ran in the John O'Gaunt Plate at the Lincoln Spring meeting of 1947 in the race before the traditional Lincolnshire Handicap (which is now run at Doncaster).

The finding of fact was to the effect that the trainer was guilty of negligence in not preventing the drug's administration. When the decision was published in the Racing Calendar that negative conclusion was omitted. It thereby allegedly created a contrary implication, namely, that the plaintiff himself was a party or privy to the more serious inference of active administration of the drug (per Asquith LJ [1949] 1 All ER at 118, [1949] 55 TLR at 231). The libel action failed on two conventional grounds:

(1) publication was privileged, and

(2) the plaintiff had consented to it contractually via the Rules of Racing, by which he was undoubtedly bound.

3 NATURAL JUSTICE AND RESTRAINT OF TRADE

In the Court of Appeal, however, Lord Denning took the first step on the road which has led to the modern law of natural justice in sport. It not only encourages, but also on the appropriate facts, enforces challenges to unjust and thereby unfair decisions by domestic sporting tribunals and their governing bodies. He explained the following pre-conditions ([1949] 1 All ER at 119–120, [1949] 55 TLR at 231–232):

(1) 'Common justice requires that before any man is found guilty of an offence carrying such consequences [as taking away his livelihood] there should be an enquiry at which he has opportunity of being heard.'
(2) 'The Jockey Club has a monopoly in an important field of human activity ...' [a point to which he was to return on more than one occasion, and particularly in the landmark decision of *Nagle v Fielden* [1966] 2 QB 633].
(3) '... whether the inquiry was held in accordance with the essentials of justice. That, in my opinion, is a conclusion of law ... It would be no easy matter for a jury to distinguish between the question whether there was a proper inquiry and the question whether the decision of the stewards [of the Jockey Club] was right or wrong; whereas a Judge is able to put aside the correctness of the decision as irrelevant. On this question I am entirely in agreement that there is only one conclusion possible on the evidence – namely, that the inquiry was in accordance with the principles of natural justice.'

That conclusion of law is summarised neatly in Halsbury's Laws of England [4th Edn] Volume 1, paragraph 64 at page 76, where justice in the law is married with fair play in sport by the following two sentences.

'Implicit in the concept of fair adjudication lie two critical principles, namely, that no man shall be a judge in his own cause (*nemo judex in causa sua*) and that no man shall be condemned unheard (*audi alteram partem*). These two principles, the rules of natural justice, must be observed by courts save where application is excluded expressly by necessary implication.'

Nevertheless, Lord Denning explained in *The Discipline of the Law* (page 150) in 1979, precisely thirty years after he first laid the trail in *Russell v Duke of Norfolk*, with the following paragraph under the head of 'Powers against own members' at the outset of the section 'Abuse of "group" powers'

'During the last 30 years, the Courts have done much to protect the individual member against injustice by the association itself. They have condemned Rules that are in unreasonable restraint of trade and held them to be invalid. They have overthrown the decisions of domestic tribunals which were unjust. They have interfered with the discretion of committees when exercised unfairly. They have, in accordance with their long tradition, upheld the weak and put down the "oppressor's wrong".'

The observant reader will note in that citation the additional road alongside the path of natural justice by which judges have protected the victims of administrative group oppression. In addition to surveillance of domestic tribunals by the courts he identifies injustice by the association itself and condemnation of 'Rules that are in unreasonable restraint of trade and held ... to be invalid'.

When he wrote in 1979 that extra dimension of unreasonable restraint of trade was fresh in every sporting lawyer's mind as well as in Lord Denning's, resulting from his twin offices of Master of the Rolls and President of Whitchurch Cricket Club. In the preceding year of 1978 Slade J had adjudicated in London's Chancery Division of the High Court against cricket's establishment in the celebrated *Packer* litigation. He upheld complaints through representative proceedings by three well-known players via procedural remedies of declaratory judgments that:

(1)   the International Cricket Conference (ICC) intended changes retrospectively of qualifying rules, and

(2)   the Test and County Cricket Board's proposed ban was both ultra vires and unlawfully in restraint of trade.

Concurrent with these judgments were further rulings brought by Packer's World Series Cricket Limited against the same governing bodies that their conduct was also an unlawful inducement to the contracted players concerned to break their contracts with the Australian-based management (*Greig v Insole* [1978] 1 WLR 302).

Coincidentally, in 1979 Cantley J in London's Queen Bench Division of the High Court adjudicated against the rejection by the Football Association of the plea made to it by the legal representatives of its former national team manager, Don Revie. A disciplinary tribunal of the FA had earlier spoken critically of Revie and thereby demonstrated a likelihood of bias thus breaching the elementary rules of natural justice. The tribunal banned Revie from football management activities for ten years. As Revie's leading counsel, Mr Gilbert Gray QC, has explained to the author, the disciplinary tribunal was formed by FA officers who were purporting to adjudicate on his client's conduct after he had withdrawn from his England team management contract. The High Court judgment expunged the ten-year ban which had been imposed on Revie because he had established the likelihood of bias ((1979) Times, 14 December).

The link between the two judgments of *Greig v Insole* and *Revie v The FA*, coming so close together in time and connecting the two national games, was the economic consequence of taking away a man's livelihood which had been recognised by Lord Denning initially in *Russell v Duke of Norfolk* in 1949, and crystallised by him in *The Discipline of the Law* in 1979. They had the following effect upon a sporting practitioner's livelihood of:

(1)   a governing body, by creating restrictive practices for working conditions and acting unreasonably in restraint of trade which can curtail or limit or even exclude the right to work, which Lord Denning, Danckwerts LJ and Salmon LJ identified in *Nagle v Fielden* [1966] 2 QB 633, and

(2)   a disciplinary tribunal purporting to impose periods of suspension and acting unfairly in breach of natural justice which can be equally damaging to that right to work.

Ironically for the FA, its official history published a quarter-of-a-century earlier to celebrate the ninetieth anniversary of its foundation in 1953, contained the following citation from the charge to the trial jury in *Russell v Duke of Norfolk* by the trial judge, the Lord Chief Justice, Lord Goddard. It was approved by the Court of Appeal, with a significant commentary on it by the author, Geoffrey Green. At p 349, he cited Lord Goddard to have directed the jury:

'Did Mr Russell receive a fair and honest hearing before the Stewards? Was the inquiry before the Stewards conducted fairly? Domestic tribunals, such as the Jockey Club, were not bound by procedure such as governed the courts of law, but in holding an inquiry into the conduct of a person they must act fairly and give the person to be brought before them a fair notice of the charge of, or complaint against him and an opportunity to defend himself'.

Green commented with much prescience for a non-lawyer in the light of subsequent judicial affirmation,

> 'The parallel between the Football Association and the Jockey Club in this matter is important since all Football Courts of Inquiry, all Commissions and Disciplinary Boards are domestic tribunals qualified to act under the Rules of The Football Association. The importance of strict adherence to the procedure laid down by the FA is, therefore, paramount.'

That passage was available to the FA's legal advisers when two sets of procedural errors were committed only a few years after Green wrote in 1953. Two Commissions of Inquiry purported to adjudicate upon the alleged irregularities about the affairs of the Sunderland Football Club and its officials and players during the later 1950s and early 1960s. Public acknowledgement of administrative errors with appropriate costs was duly made twice during 1962 in two separate statements made in separate actions brought by the players in one, and the club and officials in another, before two different judges in the Chancery Division of London's High Court, as we shall see below. It was still available to the different generation of FA Tribunal members twenty-five years later in the *Revie* case when the High Court was required to intervene in circumstances epitomised by the opening citation at the commencement of this chapter from Lord Denning in his judgment in one of the FA's happier court appearances when defending against *Enderby Town*.

How the law has developed in this crucial area for the victims of oppression from authoritarian sporting regimes is a classic example of the protection created by the courts without Parliamentary intervention when they are activated effectively by the correct procedural remedies operated by practitioners selecting the right and not the wrong legal remedies. It also illustrates once more how sport reflects a wider and more general development of the law not only for the benefit of sport itself but also for society generally, with the application to the narrow world of sport of the developing legal process from the larger world outside it.

4 THE JUDICIAL ROAD TO SPORTING JUSTICE

(1) Between two World Wars: 1919–39

In the years before, between and immediately after the two World Wars the feudalism inherent in the Gentlemen and Players amateur–

professional dichotomy, based upon its economic and social class distinctions, dominated the administration and much of the playing of British sport, particularly the two most professionally and commercially orientated and popularly practised pursuits, horse-racing and professional football. Indeed, at the time of writing in the early 1990s some would say that so far as a practical and practising gap between amateur administrators and professional practitioners is concerned, the divisions still exist in both areas in nearly all participatory sports. The need for a full-time paid director-general or secretary need not necessarily bridge these divisions if the administration is still subject to committee control.

Before 1939, with money and reputations at stake, and the control and remedies of the kind considered here available in the courts but unrecognised and unused by the practitioners instructed by victims of sporting administrative oppression, each sport inspired the inevitable litigation with ineffective results in the examples cited below. Professional footballers' advisers before 1919 had failed to choose the correct legal remedies to tackle the restraint of trade transfer system in *Kingaby v Aston Villa* during 1912 (supra); after 1919, in *Davis v Harrison* [1927] 43 TLR 623, they failed to equate professional cricketers' tax-free benefits with footballers, because the professional footballers' terms of employment incorporated a discretionary benefit claim by contractual ties instead of the non-contracted public appreciations, which contrasted with professional cricketers in the saga lasting from 1920 until the House of Lords final judgment in *Seymour v Reed* [1927] AC 554. Racing, too, had its revenue problems in the same year when a professional jockey's appreciation from a grateful winning owner was held to be liable to tax (*Wing v O'Connell* [1927] IR 84); and both sporting sources witnessed unsuccessful libel actions against the two ruling bodies, the FA and the Jockey Club, with a foretaste of what might have been if the correct procedural and substantive remedies had been considered.

Professional football was concerned with irregularities allegedly committed during the 1920s against the FA's own internal Rules and the Football League's parallel Regulations by the then Board of Directors of the Arsenal Football and Athletic Company Limited. The story is told in similar general terms without legal analysis by the former Arsenal *amateur* international player Bernard Joy in *Forward Arsenal* (1952) at pages 49–50, and by Geoffrey Green in *The History of the Football Association* (1953) before the passage cited above equating the FA's domestic tribunal procedures with the Jockey Club (page 285).

The FA's investigation into Arsenal's affairs resulted in suspensions of certain directors, including Mr G W Peachey, Mr J M

Humble, the Chairman, Sir Henry Norris, and the club itself was censured. As Bernard Joy wrote of the Chairman,

'It was unfortunate that his soccer interests ended on such an unhappy note, because he did as much as anyone to put Arsenal on the map by instigating the move from Woolwich to Highbury' (in 1913).

Two separate sets of proceedings were launched – one by Mr Peachey for company law relief in the Chancery Division of the High Court; the other by Sir Henry Norris in the Queen's Bench Division for libel and impugning the investigation. All were unsuccessful in circumstances which prima facie might have been handled differently to produce more advantageous results, ie they should have proceeded by the breach of natural justice route which was available even at that time instead of the by then conventional and almost obsessive faith, with adverse results, in defamation. The following examples illustrate how the governing bodies should and could have been taken to the courts, but were not.

Peachey's action was brought against the company-club to prevent the surviving directors implementing the FA's directives to the Board that the condemned men should 'not be permitted to continue in their positions as directors or to take part in the management of the club'. Injunctive relief was sought against the mechanism of the club's company meetings and share transactions. In the end he withdrew his claim against the club upon payment of his costs. For present day practitioners, however, the significance lies in the concession made by Peachey's Counsel as reported at the time:

'he did not think the findings of an outside body like the Football Association would be appealable against in that Court, or could scarcely be appealed against in any way. He should imagine that the Football Association could only be proceeded against by way of a libel action ... The decision of the Football Association in a matter of this sort was not a judicial position that could be against in that Court ... The Football Association purported to dismiss Mr Peachey from the board of directors ... The only ground alleged against Mr Peachey was that he had been remiss in his duty. This Mr Peachey denied, and although he attended the meeting of the Commission he was not asked a single question on the point ... Mr Peachey had acted in the way he had [ie of suing the club] because he was dissatisfied with the original finding by the Football Association ... He felt he was being hounded out.'

(*Daily Telegraph*, 17 November 1927, page 14.)

That revelation of 'not being asked a single question on the point' on the attendance by Mr Peachey at the Commission contained a prima facie complaint of a breach of natural justice. It was never pursued.

Ironically in the same Chancery Division of the High Court the then MP for the Govan division of Glasgow, Neil Maclean, was commencing proceedings by a writ alleging that he had been wrongly expelled by a trade union committee. He argued that the Trade Union had acted *ultra vires* its own rules and thereby unlawfully, and also that they were in breach of natural justice. Although the claim failed, Maughan J, later Lord Chancellor as Lord Maughan, reiterated in early 1929 in language appropriate to this text:

'the principles of fair play so deeply rooted in the minds of modern Englishman that a provision for an inquiry necessarily imports that the accused person should be given his chance of defence and explanation. On that point there is no difficulty.'

(*Maclean v The Workers Union* [1929] in Ch 602 at 625).

The idea expressed by Peachey's counsel that 'the Football Association could only be proceeded against by way of a libel action' was clearly shared by Sir Henry Norris's advisers. At the same time that Maughan J was hearing evidence and argument which led to his judgment (supra) during early 1929 in the Chancery Division of the High Court, Sir Henry Norris pursued the first of his two Queen's Bench Division actions against the FA. It was for libel based upon an imputation of alleged dishonesty for having received relatively small amounts of money from Arsenal FC in breach of the appropriate domestic rules and regulations.

The opening address by the eminent and experienced practitioner Sir Patrick Hastings KC to the then Lord Chief Justice, Lord Hewart and the jury, contained these ominous words:

'A Commission was set up which was remarkably appointed and amazingly conducted, but whether it was properly constituted and conducted did not affect the question of the alleged libel.'

Equally amazingly, however, after the libel action was lost, he told the court about a further action between the same parties which was in the court list which sought to impugn the appointment and proceedings of the commission appointed by the FA:

'in view of what had happened in the first case he felt that no useful purpose could be served by proceeding with the [second] action.'

Again, a prima breach of natural justice would appear to have existed at least for the purposes of argument and evidence, in the manner which later succeeded against the FA after the Second World War (twice during 1962 in the circumstances concerning the inquiries into Sunderland Football Club, a third time on behalf of Don Revie in 1979). On each occasion in 1927 and 1929 affecting Arsenal the available procedural route for obtaining an effective judgment against the FA appears to have been unrecognised or needlessly rejected.

Shortly afterwards during 1931 and 1932 Hastings was again concerned in a sporting libel action which was a forerunner of the *Russell v Norfolk* claim in 1949. *Chapman v Lord Ellesmere* ([1932] 2 KB 431) is cited extensively in all the leading practitioners' and students' textbooks on issue of privilege and damages. Here it is noteworthy principally for three reasons:

(1)   consistent with the Jockey Club's practice in *Russell*'s case, no criticism was, or appears likely to have been, made of the conduct of the domestic proceedings to create a complaint about natural justice;

(2)   the Jockey Club's conclusion that the trainer had been negligent in not safeguarding the admittedly doped horse was published in the Racing Calendar and elsewhere in a manner which could have justified readers in a belief of personal involvement: yet there was in fact no personal involvement in this case and the trainer was not given the opportunity to establish his innocence;

(3)   Hastings himself wrote in *Cases in Court* that the libel claim:

'... was the only method by which Mr Chapman could free his character from the implication placed upon it, and establish once and for all that he was completely innocent ... The public attention drawn to his unfortunate position by the overwhelming verdict of a jury must have gone a long way to wipe away the stigma of his warning-off notice.' [page 83].

It is a nice academic point in 1994 whether the same result might have been achieved for both Chapman in 1931 and Russell in 1949 today. If they had sought declaratory judgments identifying the discrepancies between the published Racing Calendars' version of the tribunal findings and the truth they could possibly have been successful in clearing their names. Had similar circumstances arisen today a claim against the publisher of the Jockey Club's rules for negligent misstatement would be justified under the Civil Law of negligence (as distinct from the Jockey Club rules), based on the landmark decision of the House of Lords in *Hedley Byrne & Co Ltd v Heller & Partners Ltd* [1964] AC 465.

One difference between the *Chapman* (1932) and *Russell* (1949) decisions which justified Hastings' comment 'to wipe away the stigma' was that at the trial Chapman succeeded initially against three sets of defendants: the Jockey Club, its agents Weatherby & Sons, who published the *Racing Calendar*, and *The Times* and other newspapers. The Court of Appeal reversed the jury's findings against the first two defendants (the Jockey Club and Weatherby) on the ground that the proceedings and publication respectively were privileged (consistent with the *Russell v Duke of Norfolk* findings). A retrial was ordered on the excessive damages awards against *The Times* and other news agencies (who were then not privileged but today would also be privileged under the Defamation Act 1952, Schedule 11, paragraph 8 (c)). Hastings' biographer, H Montgomery Hyde, wrote: 'No new trial took place as the parties came to terms.' Romer LJ [1932] 2 KB at page 477 noted that Hastings' forensic skills at the height of his advocacy powers had excited 'the jury [who] became "furious" and "hysterical"'' before awarding the damages which were ruled on appeal to have been excessive.

The remaining seven years after *Chapman*'s case, leading up to the outbreak of war in 1939, were free from challenges to the jurisdiction of sporting governing bodies, with one exception: this was *Doyle v White City Stadium Ltd* [1935] 1 KB 110 (see pages 149–50) (supra). There, the Court of Appeal overturned the trial judge and a plea for leniency on behalf of a disqualified boxer, pointing out that 'rules for clean fighting' were in his own as well as 'any other contestant's interests!': a lesson and moral overlooked by many modern ball game administrators at all levels. Indeed, the public attention drawn to *Chapman*'s case as recorded by Hastings could also have contributed to this absence of sporting disciplinary disputes. As Hastings also wrote in *Cases in Court*:

'At the same time the action may have done some good in the racing world by establishing, even more firmly than before, the absolute authority of the Jockey Club.'

Thus, other sporting bodies and the general public could understandably have misled themselves into the belief of the infallibility of all sporting governing bodies. If this belief existed, the post-war years should have dispelled it.

(2) After two World Wars: 1945 onwards

A year before the Second World War ended, in 1944, Mr A T Denning KC, a survivor of the First World War, was appointed to the High Court bench. In 1948 he was promoted to the Court of Appeal. In 1952, three years after *Russell*'s case, he took the first step along the widest possible road (beyond the narrow sporting scene) for the courts' control over power based bodies on which sport has been obliged to travel. It is traceable through

(1)   the well-known and much canvassed Court of Appeal judgments in *Abbott v Sullivan* ([1952] 1 All ER 226); *Lee v The Showman's Guild of Great Britain* ([1952] 2 QB 239) and many others through to the Vice-Chancellor, Sir Robert Megarry's comprehensive survey in *McInnes v Onslow Fane* ([1978] 1 WLR 1520) in the tribunal lane; and

(2)   also through the parallel economic pathway of restraint of trade and interference with the right to work stimulated by the little known county court action *Aldershot Football Club v Banks* (Aldershot News, 4 November 1955): Wilberforce J in *Eastham v Newcastle United* [1964] Ch 413; the Court of Appeal in *Nagle v Fielden* [1966] 2 QB 633; *Cook v FA and FIFA* [1972] 24 March, p 8 down to the *Packer* litigation in 1977 (interlocutory) and final judgment of Slade J (supra) in 1978, and many others, too, including, more recently, *Newport AFC Ltd and Others v FA of Wales Ltd* (1994) 144 NLJ 1351, 7 October.

Today, there *should* be few sporting bodies and sportspersons of all ages, sexes, denominations or disciplines unaware of the courts' overriding surveillance in these fields. Nevertheless, the extent to which the message has not yet been received was demonstrated towards the end of 1986 and 1987 by yet another dimension to the David Bishop rugby common assault saga. His Crown Court conviction and custodial sentence of one month, varied by the Court of Appeal Criminal Division to a suspended sentence of one month's imprisonment for two years, was followed by an 11 months' suspension imposed on him by the Welsh Rugby Union. Complaints that this was a needless intrusion by the sport's governing body overlooked the double jeopardy to which any practitioner in the learned professions or services is also subjected by his or her peers if convicted of serious criminal as distinct from minor offences.

The length of the Welsh Rugby Union's suspension of 11 months was also challenged. Bishop complained that it had been imposed without his having had an opportunity to be heard personally at the time when the suspension was imposed. His amateur status did not deprive his entitlement to natural justice. After reported proposals to challenge the initial decision in the High Court, the Welsh Rugby Union provided for a personal hearing attended by legal representatives. This sequence of events suggested that initially a denial of natural justice could have occurred on the occasion of the original decision to suspend the player, ie he was not present or represented or heard in his defence or aware of the nature of the disciplinary (as distinct from the court) charge against him.

In due course, the first finding was confirmed after a full and represented personal hearing. As soon as the result was known,

Bishop's advisers once more complained of injustice and again announced an intention once more to seek High Court intervention. On this occasion, the only apparent complaint could have been directed to the composition of the investigating tribunal itself on the lines laid down by Cantley J in *Revie*'s case, or against the actual conduct of the proceedings within the four walls of the hearing. The earliest published reports recorded that the proceedings begun in the Cardiff High Court Registry had been discontinued because of an irregularity. This would be consistent with the published statement of Bishop's advisers wishing to seek judicial review of the second and confirmatory verdict. In *Law v National Greyhound Racing Club Limited* [1983] 3 All ER 300, the Court of Appeal emphasised earlier decisions that the emerging procedural jurisdiction which the courts have evolved (known as judicial review) is confined to the review of activities of a public nature as distinct from a purely private or domestic nature. (See Appendix 8 for full discussion of this case.)

Thus the Leicester Rugby Club's successful challenge all the way up to the House of Lords concerned a public activity. The challenge was brought under the judicial review procedure against the purported ban by its local public authority, Leicester City Council, upon the club using council playing fields property, because the Club allowed its players to exercise their freedom of choice to wear England's white rugby shirt in South Africa. The Welsh Rugby Union's disciplinary committee decision on David Bishop, although concerned with a public issue, does not apply. Traditional High Court remedies suffice. That was how the post-war pattern began to unfold two years after *Russell*'s case in 1949.

Abbott v Sullivan (supra), which occupied the Court of Appeal for five days in 1951, was the starting gate for the courts to enter an arena in attempting to dispense justice among domestic tribunals purporting to act in disciplinary circumstances. This was the first time that domestic tribunals had been investigated in depth and there was a subsequent impact on sporting tribunals. Ultra vires conduct was established successfully against a disciplinary committee which caused a cornporter employed to remove grain from ships in London Docks to be removed from a register of corn porters. He could not obtain damages for it from a trial judge or from a Court of Appeal majority. Claims for defamation and procuring a breach of contract were dismissed. Lord Denning who dissented, however, considered it to be:

> 'not an ordinary contract case. It is a claim in an uncharted area on the border land of contract and tort';

and he thought the court 'should entertain the claim for damages' on the footing of contract.

Four months after *Abbott v Sullivan*, a different court in *Lee v The Showman's Guild of Great Britain* [1952 [swr] 2 QB 329 unanimously upheld the trial judge's verdict that a ruling by a disciplinary committee purporting to fine and ultimately expel a member on the basis of alleged unfair competition was ultra vires and void. Arguments that the committee had exclusive power under its rules to interpret them to the exclusion of the courts were dealt with by Lord Justice Romer saying:

'The proper tribunals for the determination of legal disputes in this country are the courts, and they are the only tribunals which by training and experience, and assisted by properly qualified advocates, are fitted for the task. The courts jealously uphold and safeguard the prima facie privilege of every man to report to them for the determination and enforcement of his legal rights.'

Two year later, in 1954, a sporting governing body's rules for the first time received the same treatment, albeit in a commercially based dispute as distinct from its disciplinary jurisdiction. Commercial claims in tort against certain officers of the British Amateur Weightlifters' Association by members were defended procedurally (as distinct from on the merits). This was consistent with the Court of Appeals principles set out in the *Showman's Guild*, Mr Justice Lynskey followed through by saying:

'The Parties can, of course, make a tribunal or council the final arbiter on questions of fact. They can leave questions of law to the decisions of a tribunal, but they cannot make it the final arbiter on questions of law. They cannot prevent its decisions being examined by the courts.'

(*Baker v Jones* [1954] 2 All ER 553 at 558–9.)

In the following year, 1955, the emphasis in court shifted for the first time from disciplinary proceedings to administrative oppression by a governing body's restrictive rules. James Guthrie was the constructively aggressive Chairman of the then Professional Football Players' and Trainers' Union (now the Professional Footballers' Association (PFA)). He had captained Portsmouth at Wembley, the last pre-war FA Cup-winning team, against Wolverhampton Wanderers, and he revived the players' fight for contractual freedom forty years after it had been thoughtlessly forfeited in the misconceived action during 1912. On that occasion it will be recalled how Harry Kingaby's claims against Aston Villa for damages for (1) loss of employment because of the transfer fee charged and also (2) maliciously charging an excessive transfer fee, were nonsuited by AT Lawrence J on the basis that (1) there was no cause of action and (2) no evidence of malice was proved. Guthrie now placed his union behind defending a claim in Aldershot County Court for possession of club premises against one of its players, Ralph Banks.

Banks had been transferred to Aldershot for £500 from Bolton Wanderers after he had played left-back against Stanley Matthews in the 1953 Coronation Cup Final in a dramatic finish which witnessed Matthews' team, Blackpool's 4–3 victory. At Aldershot he disputed a wages offer from Weymouth who were unable to afford Aldershot's wish to recoup their £500 transfer fee. Although his contract of employment for 12 months from 30 June 1954 to 30 June 1955 had terminated at the date of the court action in October 1955, his Football Association registration permitted Aldershot's retention of his services under the FA Rules. The county court Judge, HH Judge Percy Rawlins, who had just been transferred to the Aldershot County Court circuit from his west country circuit base, refused leave for Banks to join the FA as a defendant to a counterclaim and plead that the club's possession claim was based upon an unenforceable contract in restraint of trade and thereby tainted with illegality; but he ordered the FA to attend through counsel and a representative to assist him on the contractual arrangements.

A possession order was made with effect five months from the date of judgement on 28 October 1955; evidence was provided by a future FA deputy secretary, Douglas Hawes, in answer to a question by the judge that Banks was under a 'penalty'. (A 'penalty' in this context of the retain and transfer system was equivalent to a perpetually renewable lease built into the football governing body rules to which the professional players' contracts were tied.)

In his judgement HH Judge Percy Rawlins said,

> 'It may very well be, although I am not going to decide it, that as the defendant alleges the rules of the Football Association place an intolerable burden upon some professional footballers.. But it may well be that as the Football Association says, the rules were necessary for the protection of footballers because the Football Association exists to some extent to protect footballers and to prevent their exploitation.
>
> (*Aldershot Football Club v Banks*, (1955) Aldershot News, 4 November.

An appeal to the Court of Appeal was under consideration when as Guthrie in his own version (*Soccer Rebel* [1976] page 74) explained: 'Aldershot, perhaps under guidance or orders, gave Banks a free transfer'; to the club he wished to join, Weymouth. Seven years later Wilberforce J in 1962 converted that 'penalty' testified by the FA's representative and HH Judge Rawlin's impression of an 'intolerable burden' (arising out of the FA's feudal retention of a player's services after his employment contract had expired) into the category of an unenforceable restraint of trade (*Eastham v Newcastle United Football Club, Football Association and Football League* [1964] Ch 413).

Three months into the year following *Aldershot v Banks* [1955] the scene shifted back to disciplinary proceedings in the Queen's Bench Division of the High Court. Pilcher J adjudicated that the Stewards of the National Hunt Committee had acted ultra vires their own rules on three grounds.

(1)   They had disqualified and warned off a livery stable keeper for 'training and running' a horse under their jurisdiction which the Plaintiff had undoubtedly trained but did not run;
(2)   their indefinite disqualification breached their own rule requiring a specified time scale, and
(3)   the actual offences alleged were not subject to Regulations relied upon.

(*Davis v Carew-Pole* [1956] 2 All ER 524.)

By now the first decade of post-war sport had ended after a sports-starved nation had sustained its morale on the home front throughout the war years with substituted competitions for the traditional fixtures, which had resumed with a more intense and commercially organised combative spirit among administrators and players. The long-standing soccer rivalries in the north-east of England between Newcastle United, Middlesborough and Sunderland with maximum-wage ceiling restrictions inspired the Sunderland club into alleged irregularities and ultimate conflict with football's authorities reminiscent of the Arsenal Club's difficulties half-a-century earlier. In the year after Pilcher J's decision in *Davis v Carew-Pole*, a joint FA-Football League Commission of Inquiry was established in 1957 to investigate allegations that the club and many of its players and officials had allegedly side-stepped the archaic maximum-wage ceiling structures with 'under-the-counter-payments' which were outside the game's administrative laws. Draconian sentences of varying levels of severity were imposed by the Commission on the Directors, Manager and Players for alleged offences against the game's financial prohibitions. By the time when the joint FA-Football League Commission of Inquiry adjudicated ultimately, the players concerned had benefited from the legacy of union and legal organization left behind by Guthrie. He had been dismissed by his union in circumstances which caused the distinguished sporting MP for Huddersfield East, J P W Mallalieu, himself a former Oxford Rugby Blue, champion in Parliament for professional footballers, and son-in-law of Portsmouth's single FA Cup-winning manager, Jack Tinn, to write in 1976 at the beginning of *Soccer Rebel* under the heading of *A Single Minded Man*:

'I consider that Jimmy Guthrie did more than any other individual to improve the working conditions of professional footballers. I also consider that professional footballers have treated Jimmy Guthrie with gross ingratitude.'

When the FA-Football League Commission of Inquiry adjudicated, the Sunderland Club's own legal advisers were equipped to recognise the developments which created a different sporting legal climate from when the Arsenal advisers failed to use the weapons available to their clients in the legal armoury even in 1927 and 1929. Thus, in 1962 on two separate occasions the FA had to admit grave errors of procedure through counsel on two separate hearings in actions brought first by the players and then by Sunderland FC and its officials. These procedural errors required that all disciplinary punishments were expunged from the record. The fallacious belief of counsel in 1927 that 'the findings of an outside body like the Football Association would [not] be appealable against in court', and of Sir Patrick Hastings in 1929 that 'no useful purpose could be served by proceeding with the action' impugning disputed FA proceedings at that date, were now dead and buried along with the *Gentlemen v Players* fixture which MCC terminated during this same year of 1962. The courts were now more than ready to act if called upon to rectify the miscarriages of sporting maladministration of any kind, and the pattern of development unfolded rapidly.

A classic example occurred midway through the five years spanning Sunderland's saga of soccer injustice when professional Rugby League Football was similarly ruled offside, in early 1960. During a cup-tie on 13 February one of Keighley RFC's players, Jack Holmes, was sent off the field. On the following day, 14 February, the referee submitted his report to the appropriate disciplinary committee in accordance with the rules. On 15 February the committee met to hear the case, and suspended the player. Summary justice could not have acted more swiftly and summarily. On this occasion it was summary injustice.

No notification had been given to the club or to the player that the case was going to be considered. The referee's report was not received by the club until some time on 15 February; and it was not brought to the attention of Mr Holmes at all. Accordingly the club and player had no alternative but to go to court for 'a decision clearing him of the odium the suspension had naturally caused' (per Mr Ingress Bell QC). Mr Justice Danckwerts in the Chancery Division granted against members of

(1) the disciplinary committee, and
(2) the appeals committee of the Rugby Football League that
     (i)   the suspension was not valid, and
     (ii) they had no jurisdiction to hear the case further.

As *The Times* newspaper law report recorded, with the Judge's words which are as applicable today as they were more than three decades ago, in 1960:

> 'In his Lordship's view the hearing, or absence of hearing, by the disciplinary committee on 15 February was so unfair that it could not be treated as a valid decision. On the ground of natural justice it was the duty of a body like this to hear the player, and it should be the onus of the committee to notify him that the case would be heard on a certain day.'
>
> (*Keighley RFC Ltd & Anor v Cunningham & Ors* (1960) The Times, 25 May, page 5.)

The year after the FA's capitulations in 1962 to Sunderland FC's claims witnessed Wilberforce J's landmark decision in the *Eastham* case (supra) during 1963. (This outlawed the retain and transfer system attacked on the wrong battle lines in 1912. It confirmed the first shots fired effectively against it, appropriately in sight of the Aldershot military barracks, on behalf of Ralph Banks under Guthrie's generalship in 1955.) Three years later came the next landmark decision with the Court of Appeal's creation of the right to work in *Nagle v Fielden* (supra). The Court's decision was obtained on a procedural stage of the action after first the Queen's Bench master and then the Queen's Bench judge in Chambers had each ruled that the plaintiff, Florence Nagle's, statement of claim disclosed no cause of action (on different grounds which ultimately succeeded in the Court of Appeal). The far-reaching consequences were in substance as effective as if the action had been fought at trial with witnesses. The ultimate advantages for women's rights are considered in Chapter 8, 'Women in Sport and the Law'. The Jockey Club conceded defeat after resisting the claim until the Court of Appeal's unanimous reserved judgment. In a fascinating cameo published twenty years after in an interview given by Mrs Nagle to Sue Montgomery in *The Sporting Life* during 1986, she explained how, after the judgement, a number of Jockey Club members explained how they had been on her side all the time, although they had omitted to express support to her before the verdict. It is as easy to back litigation winners as it is to choose winning horses after the contest has concluded!

Sandwiched between those two landmark decisions of 1964 and 1966, Scotland came on stream with another example of unnatural justice in 1965. The Scottish Football Association failed, as the Jockey Club were to fail a year later, to obtain a procedural abandonment at half-time before a final judgement whistle on a claim against it in court by the St Johnstone Football Club. The Association had purported to censure and fine the Club £25 for arranging a benefit game for one of its players without formal authorisation. No notice was given of the intention to publish or even to attend on its disciplinary pronouncement. Lord Kilbrandon had no difficulty in applying the appropriate principles of natural justice to grant a declaration against the Association in Edinburgh's High Court, known as the Outer House (*St Johnstone Football Club v The Scottish Football Association Ltd* [1965] SLT 174).

By contrast with the decisions from the ball games and race track council chambers, the more cerebral world of contract bridge produced a text book example of how to conduct an investigation after the Executive Committee of the World Bridge Federation in 1965 announced alleged irregularities by British bridge players during the World Bridge Championship in Buenos Aires, South America. An Inquiry was established by the British Bridge League under the joint chairmanship of Sir John Foster, QC, MP, and General Lord Bourne. After a lengthy in-depth investigation attended by counsel instructed by solicitors, with the right to cross-examine witnesses, the charge of cheating by allegedly having used 'finger signals' was rejected, and the full account of the blueprint for such an ideal procedure appears in *Story of an Accusation* (1966) by one of the acquitted accused, the celebrated bridge practitioner and chronicler, Terence Reese.

By the end of the 1960s the fallacy of sporting administrative immunity from the due process of law had been fully illustrated. The FA, Scottish FA, Rugby Football League, Jockey Club and National Hunt Committee had all been scrutinised by the courts and found wanting in either their quasi-judicial or administrative capacities, and, in the case of the Football Association at both levels. The scene was therefore set for a review judicially by Lord Denning of the process he had identified in *Russell v Duke of Norfolk*. The opportunity arrived in another industrial case concerned with a trade union's expulsive conduct cited in the next paragraph. On the facts and evidence he dissented from his fellow appeal judges and the trial judge who was upheld by the Court of Appeal majority. The Court, apart from Lord Denning, was strongly criticised for its decision in the *Journal of Public Law*. Nevertheless the principles which Lord Denning summarized should be regarded (with one further refinement by the Vice-Chancellor, Sir Robert Megarry, eight years later in *McInnes v Onslow Fane* [1978] 1 WLR 1520), as the general and overriding guideline for all sporting governing bodies and tribunals with power to act fairly or unfairly, judicially or unjudicially.

In *Breen v AEU* ([1971] 2 KB 175 at pages 189–190), Lord Denning explained the position in clear terms which equates the court's control over private bodies with that over statutory authorities (subject always to the distinction identified in *Law v National Greyhound Racing Club Limited* (supra) that the process of judicial review is available against public but not private activities, in which latter category the courts place domestic sporting activities. The latter are regulated and controlled by the declarations and injunctions which are referred to by Lord Denning as 'the modern machinery for endorsing administrative law' (at the end of the following citation). Neither of Lord Denning's dissentient appeal judges dissociated themselves from his general survey. It began with a backward glance to the 'last 22 years', and thereby *Russell v Duke of Norfolk* (supra):

'there have been important developments in the last 22 years which have transformed the situation. It may truly now be said that we have a developed system of administrative law. These developments have been most marked in the review of decisions of statutory bodies: but they apply also to domestic bodies.

Take first statutory bodies. It is now well settled that a statutory body, which is entrusted by statute with a discretion, must act fairly. It does not matter whether its functions are described as judicial or quasi-judicial on the one hand, or as administrative on the other hand, or what you will. Still it must act fairly. It must, in a proper case, give a party a chance to be heard: see In re *HK (An Infant)* [1967] 2 QB 617, 630 by Lord Parker CJ in relation to immigration officers; and *R v Gaming Board for Great Britain, Ex parte Benaim and Khaida* [1970] 2 QB 417, 430 by us in relation to the gaming board. The discretion of a statutory body is never unfettered. It is a discretion which is to be exercised according to law. That means at least this: the statutory body must be guided by relevant considerations and not by irrelevant. If its decision is influenced by extraneous considerations which it ought not to have taken into account, then the decision cannot stand. No matter that the statutory body may have acted in good faith; nevertheless the decision will be set aside. That is established by *Padfield v Minister of Agriculture, Fisheries and Food* [1968] AC 997 which is a landmark in modern administrative law.

Does all this apply also to a domestic body? I think it does, at any rate when it is a body set up by one of the powerful associations which we see nowadays. Instances are readily to be found in the books, notably the Stock Exchange, the Jockey Club, the Football Association, and innumerable trade unions. All these delegate power to committees. These committees are domestic bodies which control the destinies of thousands. They have quite as much power as the statutory bodies of which I have been speaking. They can make or mar a man by their decisions. Not only by expelling him from membership, but also by refusing to admit him as a member: or, it may be, by refusal to grant a licence or to give their approval. Often their rules are framed so as to give them a discretion. They then claim that it is an unfettered discretion with which the courts have no right to interfere. They go too far. They claim too much. The Minister made the same claim in the *Padfield* Case, and was roundly rebuked by the House of Lords for his impudence. So should we treat this claim by trade unions. They are not above the law, but subject to it. Their rules are said to be a contract between the members and the union. So be it. If they are a contract, then it is an implied term that the discretion should be exercised fairly. But the rules are in reality more than a contract. They are a legislative code laid down by the council of the union to be obeyed by the members. This code should be subject to control by the courts just as much as a code laid down by Parliament itself. If the rules set up a domestic body and give it a discretion, it is to be implied that the body must exercise its discretion fairly. Even though its functions are not judicial or quasi-judicial, but only administrative, still it must act fairly. Should it not do so, the courts can review its decision, just as it can review the decision of a statutory body. The courts cannot grant the prerogative writs such as *certiorari* and *mandamus* against domestic bodies, but they can grant declarations and injunctions which are the modern machinery for enforcing administrative law.'

(*Breen v AEU* [1971] 2 KB 175 at 189–190.)

As the 1970s and 1980s unfolded, Lord Denning's assessment in *Breen*'s case of the progress since 1949 in the readiness of the courts to operate, and their example to be followed, become recognisable. In 1985 the jockey John Francome, who had been disciplined in 1979 for indiscreet disclosure to a bookmaker friend, explained in his recollections, *Born Lucky*:

'As with most private clubs the Jockey Club makes its own rules and then judges and penalises anyone who breaks them accordingly. Except for the fact that no press reporters are allowed, their enquiries are run on much the same lines as a normal court of law, with the Jockey Club Disciplinary Committee acting as judges, with solicitors who put their case and the defendants with solicitors put theirs.'

This account of natural justice at the Portman Square Headquarters of horse racing's ruling body is still subject to the criticism that no appeal procedure exists within its jurisdiction. Nevertheless, the above summary satisfies the courts' own standards and anyone aggrieved by Jockey Club justice has a direct route to the High Court.

Variations exist of the pattern which is now recognised by those who understand the relevant court requirements of judicial control over domestic tribunals. Examples of this emerged during the decades following *Breen v AEU*. In *Machin v The FA* [1983] Bristow J's ruling against a referee's report allegedly incorrectly recording a foul tackle was overruled by a Court of Appeal majority, on this occasion in favour of the FA. Lord Denning and Lawton LJ preferred to uphold the finality of a referee's factual finding, with Buckley LJ dissenting on the basis that the court was justified in drawing inferences of fact where an apparent perversity existed. More significantly, and for more permanent usage, all judges now accept unequivocally the use of television and video recording evidence. In 1987 the Charlton Athletic management did not appear to be aware of this. It protested publicly against such evidence when one of its players was disciplined and later exonerated for an alleged offence against a referee, recorded on camera but not witnessed by any FA official.

In 1978 Sir Robert Megarry, Vice-Chancellor, in *McInnes v Onslow Fane* ([1978] 3 All ER 211) rejected the grievances of an unsuccessful applicant to the British Boxing Board of Control for a promoter's licence. The lengthy reserved judgment absorbed the pattern of precedent which by then had developed in the nearly 40 years since *Russell v Duke of Norfolk* and structured the potential circumstances into three separate categories for which natural justice could or could not apply. He identified: (1) forfeiture situations such as deprivation of livelihood, for which judicial fair play rules must always apply; (2) application cases of the kind comparable to joining a club for which the rules of natural justice were not applicable (notwithstanding the right to work established in *Nagle v Fielden*), and (3) expectation cases such as renewal of a licence, where natural justice rules could apply ([1978] 3 All ER at 218). Certain observations in which he gratuitously echoed the sanctimonious words of the then Vice-Chancellor, Sir Nicholas Browne-Wilkinson in *Cowley v Commonwealth Games Federation* during 1986 (at page 26 supra), railing against the intervention by the courts against sporting governing bodies, were clearly made without any awareness of the National Hunt, Rugby League, *Sunderland* and *Eastham* for football and interlocutory *Packer* cricket precedents cited above, protecting sporting victims of oppressive maladministration.

By the 1980s, South African sporting associations brought the law on a stage highlighted by the House of Lords judgments in *Wheeler v Leicester City Council*. These are considered more appropriately in Chapter 9, 'International interaction'. As already explained, because a public activity was involved, the judicial review procedure was implemented. In 1986, when the Commonwealth Games Federation in Edinburgh rectified an earlier omission to ban the South African-born swimmer, Annette Cowley, by giving her an opportunity to be heard, they reconvened a meeting to remedy this earlier omission. The ultimate High Court hearing before Sir Nicholas Browne-Wilkinson, V-C, was concerned with issues of rules construction and the meaning of domicile within their provisions as distinct from any natural justice elements which had been implemented at the reconvened administrative meeting dealing with that issue (see *Cowley v Healey* (supra)). Four years earlier in 1982 the Test and County Cricket Board was surprisingly unchallenged when it banned celebrated

England cricketers for three years. They had toured and played as a team in South Africa. Notably they had admittedly broken no national or cricket law, or even the notoriously wrongly called Gleneagles Agreement. This, too, is considered more appropriately in Chapter 9, 'International interaction'; but it raised profound issues of conduct allegedly justifying procedural questions in restraint of trade; and if pursued to court the judgments in the *Eastham* and *Packer* cases of respectively Wilberforce J and Slade J would have been assessed within a new and different international context.

The international position was considered by Foster J in the Chancery Division of London's High Court, as we have already seen in Chapter 9, 'International interaction', (*Cook v The Football Association* (1972), Times, 24 March, page 8). On that occasion the FIFA rules were held to be in restraint of trade because the rules purported to repeat the Banks-Eastham registration restrictions preventing the Plaintiff transferring from Sligo Rovers in the Republic of Ireland to Wigan, then outside the Football League. The learned judge also directed that if the international body would not be bound by English law, then the FA as the representative defendant should leave the world body. Furthermore as Chapter 10, 'Single European Market and UK Sport', also explains, Common Market law transcends, regrettably many may consider, traditional common law rules/principles; and Article 48 creates a mandatory right for 'The free movement of workers' which has already been brought to the notice of all European football authorities.

Since January 1988 when the first edition of this work was published, Scott J (as he then was) has rejected two applications commenced by writ, and the Divisional Court and Court of Appeal have explained on more than one occasion that judicial review is not available against sporting governing bodies so long as *Law v The National Greyhound Racing Club* remains a binding precedent, namely, unless and until it is overruled by the House of Lords or legislation. As I have explained in Butterworths All England Law Reports Annual Review 1992:

> 'It would appear that there is a death wish or hypnotic eye which seduces sporting litigants into this no man's land of legal procedure with for them, fatal and doubtless costly, results'

unless prepared to challenge the procedure in the House of Lords.

In *Currie v Barton and anor* (1988) Times, 12 February, the Court of Appeal upheld Scott J's refusal to find that the denial of a personal hearing by an Essex County Lawn Tennis player banned for three years after a dispute with his non-playing captain was in breach of natural justice, because he had written a letter explaining his side of the story; and the House of Lords was never given an opportunity to consider whether this decision could have been added to its catalogue of reversal of lower court decisions summarised in Appendix 10. Indeed in *Memoires of a Libel Lawyer* my instructing solicitor on the appeal, Peter Carter-Ruck said 'We lost the case and I felt, and still feel, my client had suffered an injustice.' [Chapter 41, p 263.]

Four months later in an unreported but well-known decision in sporting administrative circles, Scott J refused to disturb an IAAF Arbitration Appeal Board's confirmation of a two-years ban on a 25-year-old Swiss athlete, Sandra Gasser, after she had been tested positively for anabolic steroids. The value of the judgment must be qualified because he explained that the Arbitration Panel:

'held that "the B sample was not tested in a proper and efficient manner according to normal laboratory practice" ... The Panel might have found that the other explanation was too conjectural to be accepted. But no evidence to incline them to that view had since been put before them by the Plaintiff or the SLV [The Swiss Federation] ... The Plaintiff is stuck with their conclusions. Any remedy of Appeal to the High Court under the Arbitration Acts is long since time-barred.' (*Gasser v IAAF* (1988) 15 June (unreported))

It should also be noted that Scott J accepted the Plaintiff's claim that restraint of trade was an appropriate cause of action, but he refused relief on the basis that the suspension had been reasonable in the circumstances. Four years later in 1992 the IAAF found itself on the receiving end of a Columbus, Ohio, USA court judgment in a case brought by an American track athlete Harry L 'Butch' Reynolds for injunctive relief and substantial damages, on the basis that he had been wrongly suspended after a positive drug test. The judgment was successfully appealed in the American Courts. For reasons of costs and absence of assets against which a judgment could be enforced the action was undefended and judgment was obtained in default of defence, and not on its merits and a further appeal to the Supreme Court is reportedly contemplated. At an international symposium organised by the International Athletic Foundation, Counsel for the Canadian Government Dubin Inquiry, Robert Armstrong pointed out it

'Basically recommended that in order to have a fair right of appeal, athletes should be in a position to be able to test the scientific validity of the test results.'

In the *Gasser* case Scott J inferred that this had not been exhausted by the complainant-plaintiff's evidence and may yet be taken to the Supreme Court. In the *Reynolds* case the IAAF had not contested the merits. Hence the limited value of both decisions.

Of greater significance in 1991 and 1992 were the abortive attempts to use the judicial review route to judicial relief. Rose J in *R v Football Association Ltd, ex parte Football League Ltd* [1993] 2 All ER 833, found that the FA was a domestic body whose powers arose from and duties existed in private law only. In *R v Disciplinary Committee of the Jockey Club* [1993] 2 All ER 853 the Court of Appeal unanimously held that any correct remedy was in contract by writ.

In a valuable Foreword to a series of essays in honour of Lord Denning: *The Judge and The Law* edited by Professor J L Jowell and J P W McAuslen [1984], his distinguished contemporary, Lord Devlin, has written:

> 'When Tom and I were young during the 1920s the law was stagnant: The old-fashioned judge looked to the letter of the statute and for the case on all fours. He knew that he had to do justice acccording to law. Either he assumed that the law when strictly applied would always do justice or else he decided that, if it did not, it was not his business to interfere. Today this is not the idea. No statement of the law, be it a precedent or a statute, is ever final; it is to be read in its context and its context can change.'

During the course of a procedural application in the Court of Appeal to proceed out of time in *Currie v Barton and Rippon* (supra), Parker LJ said, confirming the leave given by the Court of Appeal's Mr Registrar Adams, words which confirm Lord Devlin and are relevant to the themes of this chapter,

> 'The particular field of law which is here involved is a developing field. It is a field in which decisions have been made which would have been unthinkable a few years before they were made.'
>
> (*Currie v Barton and Rippon*, (1987) The Times, 29 July page 42.)

No context is changing more rapidly within society at the public level with a mixture of public interest and private activity than the whole world of sport. How sporting bodies have been brought to court during the 1970s, 1980s and 1990s is summarised below. As a summary, it is not offered as a comprehensive survey. Nevertheless it charts a pattern of which, within the purpose for which this book has been written, many may not be aware.

The *Revie* (1978) and *Cowley* (1986) Commonwealth Games examples demonstrate this. In *Enderby Town v FA* from which the opening citation of Lord Denning at the head of this chapter was extracted, legal representation was refused at the tribunal hearing and upheld by the Courts. For Revie, Cowley, and indeed, ultimately David Bishop, the tribunals allowed the lawyers to attend. In today's changing sporting scene even 'the good laymen' would be wise to be assisted by the services of a good lawyer if natural and, indeed, any justice is to be guaranteed for sport and its proper administration according to law. The common laws of tort relating to restraint of trade and breach of contract with which the Packer team bowled out cricket's establishment required more than just a good layman. That standard or level of excellence can suffice without any further assistance to operate the rules of natural justice and fair play if the following sound elementary rules of common sense extracted from the cases are implemented:

(1) avoid any risk of pre-judgment or prejudice or bias or likelihood of it;

(2) formulate and notify clearly, preferably in writing, any assertions needing reply;

(3) notify clearly, and preferably in writing, any date for investigation or hearing;

(4) act intra vires, within any rules, and not ultra vires, outside them;

(5) remember the right to be heard in defence of any allegation;

(6) in cases of difficulty or complexity, consider carefully any request for legal representation.

If these principles require illuminating or consolidation for the lay reader, and some lawyers, perhaps, too, no better source exists outside of sport than Sir Terence Rattigan's renowned dramatisation of *Archer-Shee v The King* (1910) in *The Winslow Boy*. The true story has become well-known from the play and film versions. It is told fully in the biographies of the great Irish advocate, Carson, by Edward Majoribanks (1932) and H Montgomery Hyde (1953), and in Rodney M Bennett's definitive study, *The Archer-Shees Against the Admiralty* (1973).

Carson led a personal as well as a professional crusade against the Admiralty to expunge a false accusation that a 13 year-old cadet had stolen a five shillings (25p) postal order from a fellow pupil at the Royal Naval College, Osborne, on the Isle of Wight. He had been expelled after investigations at which he had no opportunity to defend himself properly. When a bureaucratic blockade, lasting nearly two years, against a proper investigation of the facts was breached in the High Court, Carson's cross-examination of the Judge Advocate of the Fleet who was also Recorder of the Old Oxford Quarter Sessions (prior to the controversial Beeching Reforms under the Courts Act 1971), concentrated on a single point:

Q. You said you were Recorder of Oxford.
A. Yes.

Q. I suppose if you were to try a boy for theft as Recorder of Oxford you would give an opportunity for both sides of being heard.
A. I would not do otherwise.

On the following day the Admiralty surrendered. They had been exposed for failing to operate fair play and reason behind closed doors.

SUMMARY OF SOURCES CONFIRMING CITATIONS IN CHAPTER 11

Date	Sport	Issue/ Principle	Decision	Source
1971	Soccer	Claim for legal representation.	Court of Appeal Refused on facta and construction rules.	*Enderby Town v FA*
1973	Soccer	Claim that offence of foul tackle different in referee's report from evidence on admitted television evidence: alleged breach of natural justice.	Court of Appeal by 2–1 majority reversed experienced trial judge and held sufficient opportunity to know offence and deal with it at tribunal.	*Ernest Machin v FA*
1977	Cricket	Industrial issues overlapping. Attempt to ban players because of Packer innovations.	Court held in restraint of trade and unlawful inducing breach of contract. TULRA 1974 not applicable after late pleading amendment allowed.	*Greig v Insole: World Series Cricket v Insole*
1979	Horseracing	Bookmaker banned for 3 years	High Court confirmed no breach of natural justice.	*Banks v Jockey Club*
1979	Soccer	England team manager's protest about constitution of tribunal imposing 10 years' ban because of adverse attitudes to him personally expressed by tribunal members: objections overruled.	Court held tribunal hearing contrary to natural justice because of likelihood of bias among tribunal members.	*Revie v FA*
1983	Soccer	Brighton & Hove Albion FC captain challenged ineligibility for FA Cup Final because of points total totting up for disciplinary offences.	Court refused intervention on basis no breach of natural justice or other unlawful act.	*Foster v FA*

Date	Sport	Issue/Principle	Decision	Source
1984	Judo	Life ban because of positive drug test challenged on basis that lawful prescription conflicted with sporting governing body rules [NB: see also Ch 7: 'Sports medicine and the law'.]	High Court Consent Order rescinding ban and restoration of licence membership: Consent Order precluded detailed reasons, but natural justice breach arguable.	*Angus v British Judo Association and others*
1985	Rugby Union	Schoolmaster spanning amateur rugby union and professional rugby league threatened with forfeiture of status as amateur and administrative school sport committee membership.	Retraction upon Counter-threat by schoolmaster to Rugby Union of legal action; anticipated restraint of trade, interference with contract and potential libel.	*Ray French v Rugby Union & Lancashire Schools Rugby Union Committee*
1985	Soccer	Attempt to lift ban by UEFA (European football authority) on British clubs competing after Brussels disaster.	High Court refuse application as ultra vires power of defendant English FA to enforce application outside jurisdiction.	*Liverpool FC and others v FA* (unreported)
1987	Tennis	Court of Appeal leave to appeal when time had expired.	Leave granted. 'The particular field which is here involved is a developing field.'	*Currie v Barron and Rippon*, (1987) Times, 29 July.
1990	Soccer	Internal Appeals machinery operated effectively and successfully under Football League Regulations.	Appeal against oppressive demotion allowed by FA Appeals Committee.	*Swindon Town FC v Football League Ltd*
1994	Soccer	Restraint of trade prohibiting right to play on own territory	Declaratory judgment and injunction granted	*Newport AFC Ltd and others v FA Wales Ltd* (1994) 144 NLJ 1551, 7 October

Chapter 12

Administrative advice

1 INTRODUCTION

(1) Background

The Central Council of Physical Recreation for England and Wales deservedly enjoys a membership of 268 national organisations, 202 British-based and 66 constituted with a responsibility for England. Each governing body in turn has its own constituent members, which form a mass of sporting groups beyond accurate numerical assessment. The CCPR's former Treasurer, Sir Denis Follows, claimed towards the end of his 1983 Philip Noel-Baker Memorial Lecture, 'Whither Sport, the true nature of sport':

> 'sport ... remains with the masses. And this goes for all forms of physical recreation. There isn't enough money available to turn us all into professionals. So let us be generous: Say 1% of participants receive any financial reward for practising sport. It is with the remaining 99% that we should concern ourselves'.

Then he posed the crucial question and supplied the answer:

> 'Where is sport going? I say that at the top level it has ceased to be sport – it has become a branch of the entertainment industry. Whether it should go that way or not is for those in control of its destinies to determine, but for 99% of the participants, we, the devotees of sport and recreation, have a responsibility to ensure that the young of this country are brought up to observe the basic principles of fair play and sportsmanship – a respect for others and for authority: A recognition that in any sporting contest there must be losers as well as winners and that while we honour the winners, we applaud the efforts of the losers. This is essentially an educational process in which we all have a part to play.'

Sir Denis Follows, not everyone may know, was an educationist by heart, and by training. He began his professional life as a schoolteacher. So, too, did his no less distinguished predecessor, Sir Stanley Rous. So, too, did the immortal C B Fry, G O Smith, Harry Altham,

311

and so many other admired examples of the scholar-athlete remained schoolmasters all their lives. Therein lies the key to the crucial problem which faces British, and, indeed, international sport today, a problem which is so rarely recognised, or understood, in a world of public sport dominated by market forces and commercial predators: how to shift the balance of administering and controlling sport back to leaders and teachers of their calibre, and away from the political activists and money men, and women, too, who use and abuse sport and prostitute its real values, spelt out by Follows, as a medium for quick profits or spurious political purposes at domestic and international levels.

They seek to eradicate an alleged elitism from the British sporting scene and ignore the facts and traditions which focus the nation's attention and enthusiasms annually upon such events as the winners of the Derby, Grand National, Boat Race, Cup Final, Test Matches and all the other romantic and dramatic sporting struggles.

There is a well-established group of people who do not believe in competition and believe it is wrong to separate the winners from the losers because of differentials in talent and, above all, character.

The trespassers from political fields enter into sports' territories either knowing, or in their ignorance of sport, not knowing the resentment felt by such intrusions upon fundamental freedoms fought for successfully for centuries. It is arguable that all these invaders, and their commercial co-activists, take on sport as a soft touch. Sport itself has no effective political lobby. For reasons not the fault of successive Government Ministers responsible for sport, they have been relegated constitutionally, except during Denis Howell's periods as Minister of State, to the role of Under-Secretary with 80% of Ministers' time bespoken for other duties. If the masses, who are the real heirs to sport's rich traditions, are to protect their inheritance from the ravages of political and commercial marauders, then they must become aware of their right to do so within the law, and act upon it within the manner explained in this text. Thus while these pages were being prepared as explained at pp 20–21 in Chapter 2, 'Progressive perspective', the Secretary of State for Education, John Patten, announced that the School Premises Regulations should no longer apply so far as minimum standards for teaching and recreation were concerned. Yet the Secretary of State for National Heritage, Peter Brooke, and the National Playing Fields Association each explained the consequential inference of an invitation to sell recreational land to potential developers. For if the price of liberty is eternal vigilance, then the need for sport is an enlightened vision and awareness.

(2) Purpose

This chapter will embrace the difference between clubs and companies, charities and trusts, although to some extent these differences have emerged already within the earlier chapters. It will concentrate on summarising and emphasising what has already been identified, the need to control sport by the proper administrative reins which are held by the masses and their representatives. It will also explain briefly those areas of organisation where some accountancy, legal and medical and other professional disciplines' advice should be expected. For if any group of persons administering sport at any level, whether it be domestic or national, expects to do so without legal advice at least, then will they please consult the governing bodies at Lord's, Lancaster Gate, Portman Square and Twickenham.

There are also gaps which exist between public and private levels within sport which require special attention. Sport needs space to be played; and needs participants; parents share their children's development with the schools; schools in turn can benefit from liaising with clubs and local authorities should show deeper recognition of clubs' crucial role in filling the gaps left by teachers' wider problems as already explained in Chapter 4, 'Parent, school and club partners'.

This chapter will deal first with the rights of individuals who comprise the masses; then with the collective rights of clubs and companies and finally, with some of the extras which often make the difference to a cricket score. These final points could add a level of awareness which might otherwise be overlooked.

2 INDIVIDUAL SPORTING RIGHTS

(1) Playing Fields Planning
(2) Parents
(3) Schools
(4) Rate Reliefs

(1) Playing Fields Planning

Without space, organised outdoor sport could not exist. For at least a decade, the Central Council of Physical Recreation and the National Playing Fields Association have combined their attempts to prevent school and industrial playing fields rendered surplus by local authority and commercial policies from being sold off and destroyed as recreational outlets. Their need for support from every member of the community, 'the masses', was evidenced publicly by two dramatic experiences during 1987.

The Craven Cottage football ground in West London where Fulham have played since 1896 has many romantic sporting associations apart from its approach through Bishop's Park, its riverside site and the location for Edward Bulwer-Lytton's writing of *The Last Days of Pompeii.* To the property marketeers it was a prime site for redevelopment and the Last Days of Football at the Cottage. A network of transactions too complex for and irrelevant to this text had prepared the route for an orthodox deal. Its operators had overlooked the surprise expressed by Lord Denning in *Miller v Jackson* (supra) that the planning application for development outside the Linz, Co Durham cricket ground, had not been opposed. On this occasion the local authority's Planning Committee was alerted sufficiently by meetings at the local Hammersmith Town Hall and public opinion generally. The public pressure resulted ultimately in deferment of the planning application and renegotiation of the ground's ownership through a business consortium to preserve the ground for its more than ninety years usage for football purposes. The issues ended in London's Court of Appeal during 1992 when the trial judge was reversed. He had declared that the Club's directors and principal shareholders were entitled to give evidence to a public inquiry supporting a compulsory purchase order, although their testimony would be contrary to certain undertakings that they had given in an agreement under seal. The inquiry came within the witnesses (Public Inquiries) Protection Act 1892 and prohibiting testimony was argued and held to be contrary to public policy. A reserved judgment in the Appeal Court found there was no rule of public policy whereby a football club could ignore the undertakings given by the club's directors not to give evidence at the local council inquiry to support the council's compulsory purchase order at the inquiry and there was no rule of public policy rendering such an agreement illegal or unenforceable (*Fulham Football Club and others v Cabra Estates Plc* (1992) Times, 11 September; All ER Annual Review p 364).

Further south, on even more romantic territory bordering on Hampshire's ancient New Forest, another property operator cast its covetous eyes on the War Memorial Recreation Ground at New Milton, near Brockenhurst and Southampton. The intention of the London-based property company was to transform the 3.6 acres of oak-fringed grass into a car park for a supermarket. Its misfortune (or that of its market researchers) was an unawareness that, as Ian Wooldridge explained in the *Daily Mail* on St Leger Day, Doncaster, Saturday 12 September 1987,

'I learned such sport as I have ever been able to play there because New Milton is my home town.'

After he announced in August 1987 the proposed development through the pages of his celebrated inside sports column, which has more than once brought the Sportswriter of the Year Award, the story had moved over to the front page within a month. The director in charge of the project was quoted as saying, 'We are disappointed that emotion clouded the issue.' Wooldridge wrote,

'It certainly did. The emotion of a local population finally roused to the spectre of losing a town-centre recreation area bought by public subscription to honour its war-dead was such that a dithering town council met in special session on Wednesday evening [9 September] to reassess the issue.

Seventeen of the 18 town councillors turned up. They talked for only 15 minutes. They then voted 13–4 to send the developers packing. And by yesterday the developers acknowledged they had been beaten.'

Wooldridge continued with a most significant and heartwarming paragraph:

'Let Britain take note. It can be done. No issue in *Sportsmail's* pages over the past 25 years – be it soccer hooliganism, the antics of Mr McEnroe or even Zola Budd – provoked such angry and prolific responses as the test-case of New Milton's little public recreation ground. Letters arrived from all over Britain saying:
'The same is happening here'.
Hundreds wrote offering to add their signatures to New Milton's public protest petition organised by two local freedom fighters, 52-year-old Doreen Fernie and 79-year-old Bob Gates.
We had letters from former New Milton residents in Australia where the story was re-printed and from the Falkland Islands.
They came from people who had spent holidays in the friendly little town and had fond memories of enjoying a rare facility – a green lung with shady trees and bench seats right in the village centre.
Above all, we had letters from ex-Servicemen, some of whose relatives are commemorated on the Recreation Ground's war memorial'.

With citation of further sources from Second World War survivors and a tribute to Mrs Fernie and Mr Bob Gates, both awaiting hospital treatment, Wooldridge ended thus:

'They fought certainly on emotional grounds, to preserve a small patch of British Heritage and protect the huge right of the British people to resist cynical land development by those who will never need the facilities they destroy. If the *Daily Mail* assisted in that campaign then we are very proud.
All over the country, sports ground and public parks are in similar peril.

Many just disappear, the victims of public apathy as much as sharp-suited avarice.'
New Milton, Hampshire, has shown the national way.

The way is clear for all who are ready and willing to attack the twin enemies of sporting land; apathy of their neighbours and local authorities on the one hand and the 'sharpsuited avarice' on the other. Section 29 (2) of the Town and Country Planning Act 1971 marks the route. This enables any member of the public to make representations to the local planning authority within 21 days of the publication in the local press of any applications. If sufficiently orchestrated it could have the results explained by Wooldridge.

Even one objector can suffice to create a public inquiry by a Department of Environment Inspector. This was the experience of the Littlehampton Town Football Club who play in the Unijet Sussex County League. Their application for their playing area adjoining the then home of a local solicitor was to the appropriate planning authority, the West Sussex County Council, in 1964. Permission was sought to build a new dressing room and gymnasium accommodation in a corner of a sports field which the football club shared with the local archery, cricket, croquet, hockey and tennis clubs under a Queen Victoria Diamond Jubilee gift in 1897 from the then Duke of Norfolk. The trustees who administer the ground faced the opposition to the point of a formal Inquiry by the then Minister's government Inspector. At that time the application could have been abandoned, in the manner experienced at New Milton. The trustees pursued it, evidence was called, and ultimately the planning consent was rejected. The Inspector's report dismissing the appeal made it clear, however, that a fresh application signed for a different part of the ground would be favourably received.

In due course a fresh application was made successfully. Today a magnificent two storeyed structure built by private enterprise on a part of the ground authorised by the trustee-owners and also by the local authority justified the original application which, in effect, succeeded on a replay. The final result is a valuable example of the two dimensional use of the national planning laws in a local context. The beneficiaries of the planning permission granted for the Littlehampton Sports Field are the whole community and their visitors to that salubrious part of Sussex in an area administered now by Arun District Council for Sir Denis Follows' sporting 'masses'.

(2) Parents

The precedents from Bobby Charlton's grandfather and primary school headmaster, Sir Osbert Sitwell's parents, section 76 of the

Education Act 1944 and the Enfield School litigation were set out in Chapter 4, 'Parent, school and club partners'. They are referred to again here solely as a reminder and in the spirit of New Milton's victory over its property predators. Local authority bureaucrats and teaching ideologists are no less enemies of the nation's sporting heritage when the battle has to be fought for parental rights as laid down by Parliament in R A Butler's 1944 Education Act.

An individual parent, with sufficient private means to the extent which enabled Florence Nagle to take on the Jockey Club to the Court of Appeal in *Nagle v Fielden*, may not be stirred sufficiently to raise the battle flag alone against anti-competitive sporting school staffs and their local authorities. Parliamentary rights and recourse to the courts are available to Parent Teacher Associations and Parent Associations per se. They should reread Ian Wooldridge's message and consider how far it applies to their own children's and grand-children's futures for jousting with those who challenge at school level the national sporting heritage in Sir Denis Follows' message:

'This is essentially an education process in which all have a part to play.'

(3) Schools

Here, too, the precedents were set out in Chapter 4 at page 96. Section 53 of the Education Act 1944 implements a duty on 'every local education authority' to provide for facilities for recreation and social and physical training, thereby of sport; and since the first edition was published section 42 of the Education (No 2) Act 1986 has been implemented by SI 1987 No 344 with effect from 1 September 1987. This at least opens the doors to statutory authorisation for dual use of facilities

'(when not required by or in connection with the school) for use by members of the community served by the school'.

New Milton's spirit should be used to claim it as Paradise regained.

(4) Rate Reliefs

This area shades into the next section dealing with clubs. The formal legal status of clubs in relation to unincorporated associations is, except for taxation purposes, unknown to the law; but they function administratively only through their duly elected officers and trustees. Thus, each individual member can stir his or her club committee and officers into lawful and regrettably unlawful action.

Rate reliefs under the local Government Finance Act 1988 and the operation of section 47 in the light of the House of Lords guidelines for sporting educational charities (in the FA Youth Trust Deed and Recreational Charities Act decisions) were mentioned at page 97 in Chapter 4. Not every local authority would necessarily adopt the enlightened attitude shown by the Arun District Council in the past (as so shown in Chapter 14, 'No fine on fun') towards the Worthing Rugby Football Club and the Bognor Regis Town Football Club. Each of these sources provides coaching and thereby physical education for school children outside school hours. This is of course of benefit to the local community. Indeed, Worthing RFC claims to organise the biggest annual mini-rugby festival in the world with 1,000 young players participating on the day. Each club's coaching satisfies the education criteria for charitable status established in the Alderham school case of *Re Mariette*. (See Appendix 11). This was affirmed by the House of Lords in the FA Youth Trust Deed case of *IRV v McMullen* [1981] AC 1. Furthermore, when the concept of rate reliefs for sports clubs was floated at the Sports Council Recreation Management Seminar Conference in Harrogate during early 1986 and later at the joint DOE-DES Sport in Schools Seminar later that year, the reaction from other local authority sources was less than favourable.

In the last resort, however, for any local authority as well as for national government, power is with the people: the masses, at the ballot box. Those who care sufficiently should recognise their right which they hold in trust for all present and future younger generations. Above all, they should remember New Milton, Doreen Fernie, Bob Gates, Ian Wooldridge, and the Daily Mail, as they all took up the cudgels on behalf of the local community against commercial predators.

Before then, an earlier landmark decision took Arsenal Football Club to the House of Lords. A local litigant in person ratepayer challenged its rating valuation because of environmental interference: and won (*Arsenal Football Club Ltd v Ende* [1977] 2 WLR 944). This neighbouring attitude contrasts with the more recently published opinions expressed in *Fever Pitch* by a dedicated Arsenal follower, Nick Hornby.

3 COLLECTIVE RIGHTS: CLUBS AND COMPANIES

(1) General

Any reader and his or her associates who consider the time has come for the natural and normal progression towards treating clubs as companies will be following a precedent identified in the citation at pages 37–38 of Chapter 2, 'Progressive perspective' from Montague (later Mr Justice) Shearman's chapter 'Athletic Government' in his classic century-old sporting textbook in the Badminton Library: *Athletics and Football*. The initial discussion would be the form or structure which that collective action should take: club and company limited by shares, limited by guarantee, incorporation by royal charter, or friendly societies under recent legislation.

(2) Clubs

As a legal entity clubs are unknown to the law, except for the artificial formalities equating them with companies as corporations under revenue laws (see for example, *Worthing Rugby Football Club Trustees v IRC* [1987] STC 273).

The legal basis for a club is the contract which each member makes with another on joining the unincorporated association which remains (see Day J and Court of Appeal in *Steele v Gourlay* (1886) 3 TLR 772).

Because of this personal relationship, liabilities follow which usually are shared among the members either collectively or upon an indemnity basis. For example, the committee members of the Blackburn Rovers Football Club employed a negligent contractor. Personal injury was suffered due to a collapsed grandstand (see *Brown v Lewis* supra). The committee members were held personally liable and subsequently the club was converted a year later into an incorporated company which removed this liability. The company has a separate legal personality or identity from those who own it, a principle established by the House of Lords in 1897, the year in which Blackburn Rovers converted (see *Salomon v Salomon* [1897] AC 22). Consistent with that overriding negligence principle, the courts have recently progressed to recognition of a duty of care owed to a fellow member by an officer or member of a club performing a task on behalf of other members if he becomes aware of circumstances giving rise to the risk of injury. Thus a local sports club chairman (who had been warned when reserving an indoor five-a-side football pitch on local authority premises that it was in a dangerous condition creating a risk of injury to fellow members, but failed to warn them of it) was liable to a fellow member for loss suffered by him: *Jones v Northampton Borough Council* (1990) Times, 21 May; (1990) Independent, 25 May.

(3) Company limited by shares

Incorporation as distinct from an unincorporated status shifts the legal responsibility from individual members and committee members to the legal personality of the company, avoiding the personal liabilities of the kind experienced by the Blackburn Rovers committee in *Brown v Lewis* (except in extreme circumstances when company directors also can create a personal liability). Correspondingly Judge Brian Appleby QC has explained to the author that after his period as Chairman of the Nottingham Forest Football Club Committee, he was able to persuade its members that the risk of personal liabilities more than merited the surrender of its unique unincorporated association status within the Premier Football League. Thus it fell into line with all the other company/club structures.

The change of status also shifts control to the shareholders. Articles of Association can restrict transfers of shares and therefore control of the company. This emerged during litigation over a take-over bid that failed for control of Tottenham Hotspur during its doldrum years in the mid-1930s (*Berry and Stewart v Tottenham Hotspur Football and Athletic Co Ltd* [1935] Ch 718): and subsequently in the 1993 action replay of *Venables v Sugar* (May 1993). (*Edennote Plc, v Tottenham Hotspur Plc, Alan Sugar and Amshold Ltd*, 14 June 1993).

Conversely, after the Second World War, when a minority shareholding in the Bristol Rovers Football Club Limited became dissatisfied with the affairs of the organisation, it instituted one of the first recorded inquisitions into any company's affairs under the then new provisions of section 164 of the Companies Act 1948. The company and commercial issues were complex but one of the passages locked in time after nearly forty years has this insight into football club administration with this comment in the Board of Trade Report into the Inspection of Bristol Rovers Football Club Limited in 1951:

> 'in the Inspector's view too many members of the Board gave absorbed attention to the Team Manager's sphere of interest, to the exclusion of the legal, financial and administrative affairs.'
>
> (Report of A Frank Ward, FCA, Inspector appointed by Board of Trade: page 34)

Plus ça change, plus c'est la même chose?

As more and more shareholder supporters of football clubs have become dissatisfied with directors' administration of club affairs, the legal tussles between the shareholders have become more common-place. Indeed, the other Bristol club, City, was the cause of a 16-day High Court action in July 1978. Its former chairman failed to upset a resolution to increase the club-company's increased share capital but one of his supporters was awarded damages for improper voting use of 500 shares at a rate of £2.50 per share (*Hobbs & Leadbeatter v Castle, Bristol City Football Club Ltd and others*, (1978) Times, July 1978, page 2).

More recently in *Western Counties Construction Ltd v Witney*

Town Football and Social Club (1993) Times, 19 November, Morrit J on appeal from Oxford County Court confirmed rejection of a winding-up petition by creditors who failed to bring the club on the construction of its rules within section 220 of the Insolvency Act 1986 as an unregistered company; and the creditors' remedy lay against the individuals with whom their contracts had been made, and the appeal would accordingly be dismissed.

For clubs with limited financial resources one of the problems flowing from conversion to corporate liability status is the annual expenditure of filing the statutory documentary returns with the companies Registry and the formalities which require a working knowledge or awareness of company law, and the need for frequent legal and accountancy services. Furthermore, as the sample case histories here demonstrate, company formation gives power to the majority shareholders and so far as they co-exist, with the directors. An unincorporated association club structure leaves power with the members who appoint and dismiss the committee and trustees according to the rules, which ideally should be sufficiently clear to avoid differences of interpretation.

Conversely, it can be convenient for a local club with a friendly membership to form a company for a limited purpose, eg for the purpose of holding a lease of club premises to avoid the necessity of executing a succession of documents in the event of changes through social mobility, deaths or other departures of trustees in whom all club land must be vested for clubs under the Law of Property Act 1925, sections 34–36.

(4) Company limited by guarantee

This form of company is traditionally funded from group sources, subscriptions or fees and is progressively used by many professional, trade research, and other similar bodies. It is also increasingly used by governing sports bodies. In addition, it qualifies for exemption under section 35 of the Companies Act from use of the word 'limited' if its objects are

> 'the promotion of commerce, art, science, education, religion, charity or any profession and anything incidental or conducive to any of those objects'.

Sport per se is significantly absent from that list although it is arguable that sport is conducive to art, science, education or charity.

Accountancy and corporate information disclosure are less stringent than the requirements for a share company; and important differentials exist between the two types of company on member's liabilities in the circumstances of a winding-up. Potential candidates for this category could hardly be expected to contemplate it without specialist legal and accountancy advice.

(5) Company incorporated by royal charter

The source is a royal prerogative founded in common law. The word royal is not necessary for the title; and it does not appear in many corporations structured in this way, exemplified by the Sports Council and the Jockey Club. The qualifying standards for consideration must be self-evident from the standpoint of public interest.

(6) Friendly societies

This established structure with a benevolent philosophy has been revamped under the Friendly Societies Act 1992 to harmonise with UK insurance and company legislation and where applicable EC directives, with the concurrent creation of a Friendly Societies Commission. The starting point for enquiries should be 15 Great Marlborough Street, London, W1V 2AX.

4 EXTRAS

All areas of law affect administrators. The following topics have been chosen arbitrarily for discussion as they are the subjects which are most applicable to the administration of sport. This list can never be exhaustive because the needs of every individual, participant, club or company must differ dependent upon individual demands and requirements. Specialist textbooks will be found on every topic in every reasonably stocked public library; and such a source in any event should have on its shelves the comprehensive volumes of Halsbury's *Laws of England*, 4th Edn; Halsbury's Statutes, 4th Edn; The Digest, including Continuation Volumes and Reissue Volumes. The following are the most pertinent subjects:

(1)   Land, lease and licences
(2)   Liquor licences
(3)   Lotteries, betting and gaming
(4)   Libel, slander and copyright
(5)   Insurance
(6)   VAT refund

(1) Land, lease and licences

Consistent with the theme which must have become apparent throughout this text, sports clubs have no privileges when buying, selling or owning property. For real estate, and present purposes, the most significant subjects must be (i) ownership or title; (ii) easements or restrictive covenants; (iii) landlord and tenant and licence relationships.

(i) Ownership or title

All evidence of a company's or club's right to play on its ground whether a freehold, leasehold, peppercorn rental title or merely a licence, must be recorded in documents. In the beginning the services of a solicitor are essential and they would be no less necessary if points of dispute were to arise. Even freehold title today does not provide absolute right for owners to treat it indiscriminately.

(ii) Easements and restrictive covenants

Easement such as rights of way or rights to light or other equivalent legal privileges and restrictive covenants (which are in effect a form of negative easement) can be troublesome and frequently expensive irritants if not understood with clarity and handled expertly.

Restrictive covenants involving limitations and restrictions on land and building development are found more frequently in urban as distinct from rural areas. Parliament has laid down a procedural and substantive code for applying to various jurisdictions, and for this purpose the services of an architect and surveyor familiar with the local requirements would be essential.

(iii) Landlord and tenant licences

Parliament has imposed on ancient common law and equitable provisions complex legislation and formulae for which expert professional advice would be needed at some stage. The Football Association in the early 1950s after a number of court decisions clarified the position for its clubs, whereby agreements for occupiers and the hirers of property satisfied the requirements of a lease to invoke the protection of the Rents Act, whilst others failed to do so and thereby qualified for the lesser category of a licence with loss of Rent Act protection.

Those cases from the early 1950s which inspired the FA's initiative (*Errington v Errington* [1952] 1 All ER 149 and *Facchini v Bryson* [1952] 1 TLR 1386) excited much professional interest at the time. They sustained their drama with the House of Lords approval of some of the dicta in them when it delivered judgment in *Street v Mountford* [1985] 2 All ER 289.

Company and club premises can produce special headaches, and for business, by way of contrast with domestic accommodation, recent legislation has produced considerable commercial and professional legal problems. For example, when Newcastle United applied for consideration as a potential World Cup venue in 1966, it found itself involved with the local corporation over the terms of renewal of the lease on which St James Park has always been held. A lawn tennis club registered as a society under the Industrial and Provident Societies Act 1983 has been able to claim status as a business for protection under the Landlord and Tenant Act 1954 (*Addiscombe Garden Estates Ltd v Crabbe* [1958] 1 QB 513). Furthermore, in appropriate circumstances, the Landlord and Tenant Act 1954 provisions can be excluded by specific agreement (*Tottenham Hotspur Football & Athletic Co Ltd v Princegrove Publishers Ltd* [1974] 1 All ER 17.)

(2) Liquor Licences

Any practitioner familiar with the current edition of *Paterson's Licensing Acts*, containing over 1700 pages of text and appendices, will recognise the impossibility of attempting to embrace here any part of it. Different types of certificate exist for registration as well as different types of licences; supper, occasional, special or extended hours, together with the transfers of licences. One particular segment for which the then Lord Chief Justice, Lord Parker, said

> 'there have been a mass of authorities dealing with what can and cannot be a special occasion for the purpose of the Licensing Acts' (s 74(4), 1964) (*Lemon v Sargent* [1971] 3 All ER 936 at p 937).

Unfortunately, much seems to depend on the attitude of the local police and local justices. In Wales the local Chief Inspector failed in a High Court appeal against the grant of the justices to a hotelier who had obtained a special order of exemption under s 74(4) Licensing Act 1964 extending by one hour the permitted licensing hours for the match on Saturday 9 October 1971 so that refreshments might be supplied to the players and officials from the local football club following a home match. The justices held that the occasion in respect of which the application had been made was 'a special occasion'. The Divisional Court confirmed the justices' finding that this particular football match was quite independent of the activity of the hotelier. However, it was noted to be a borderline case (*R v Llanidloes (Lower) Justices, ex parte Thorogood* [1971] 3 All ER 932).

In Kent, a local golf club succeeded in the High Court against a refusal by the local justices to grant a special occasion licence. The key, as so often happens and in this jurisdiction particularly, is the relationship of the facts to the particular organisation and the local police approach. Thus in the Leicester courts, the local sporting clubs were trapped by a policy decision to oppose progressively increased applications by organisations not only including sport; and when Leicester City Football Club appealed to the High Court against a refusal to grant a special licence at their Filbert Street ground, before the match, during half-time and after the final whistle, in accordance with the practice over the previous seventeen years, Kennedy J held that on the evidence he was unable to intervene and overrule the justices; findings that the First Division matches were not 'special', although it appears the judgment included the recognition by the justices that an important fixture such as an FA Cup semi-final, might be treated differently (*Leicester Mercury*, 9 February 1985).

Since then, of course, Parliament has intervened with two interconnected enactments which in turn cross-refer in effect to two others. The Sporting Events (Control of Alcohol Etc) Act 1985, as amended by the Public Order Act 1986 under section 40 (1) and Schedule 1, creates a network of prohibitions for England and Wales against transporting and consuming alcohol at sporting events.

Section 30 of the Public Order Act 1986 gives courts the discretionary power to impose an exclusion order upon convictions for offences connected with football. This extends generally a principle which had been created six years earlier in 1980 for licensed premises generally, and also for Scotland, under two statutes of that year: the Licensed Premises (Exclusion of Certain Persons) Act 1980 and the Criminal Justice (Scotland) Act 1980, Part V, sections 68–77. It surely cannot be unfair to enquire how this lack of co-ordination at Whitehall and Westminster occurred. Was it because of the 20% limitation of time imposed upon a junior Parliamentary Under-Secretary or an unawareness at the Department of the Environment of the problems involved?

(3) Lotteries, betting and gaming

Consistent with the identification of the current edition of *Paterson's Licensing Acts* it is appropriate here to refer to the first edition of the *Law of Betting, Gaming and Lotteries* by Colin Milner Smith QC and Stephen Philip Monckom. Their volume contains 777 pages of text and appendices, and demonstrates the futility of any attempt to condense it here. The House of Lords, at the end of a procedural exercise straddling the Commercial Court with criminal procedure during 1980, laid down guidelines for identifying the requirements for a lawful lottery under legislation passed by Parliament four years earlier in the Lotteries and Amusement Act 1976 (*Imperial Tobacco Ltd v A-G* [1980] 1 All ER 866).

That enactment provided for three separate types of lottery with which event organisers and treasures should be familiar.

Section 3: Small lotteries incidental to exempt entertainments

Under this section sporting or athletics events are included in the exemptions which exist, but among other conditions the most crucial are that

(i)   no money prizes are permitted, and

(ii) tickets can be sold or issued and the result declared at the place and on the occasion concerned.

Section 4: Private lotteries

Private lotteries can only exist within the framework of a private organisation. The only people who are able to purchase tickets are the members of the club or organisation and only they themselves can appoint the promoter. The club or other private organisation alone can benefit and only the winning ticket purchaser will receive a prize.

Section 5: Public lotteries

This section specifies 'participation in or support of athletic sports or games or cultural activities'. Among other conditions it includes the total value of tickets (as amended by Statutory Instrument) to be £10,000 or less; registration with the Gaming Board; and the lottery is promoted on behalf of a club or society registered with the local authority.

The House of Lords in *Imperial Tobacco Ltd v AG* (supra) emphasised the essentiality of a distribution of prize by lot or chance and that the chance of winning was secured by a payment, contribution or consideration by those taking part.

Two years after the 1976 Act the *Royal Commission on Gambling* under Lord Rothschild's chairmanship reported in its *Conclusions* published in July 1978 (Cmnd 7200).

> 'Despite the good work being achieved through many lotteries, the situation we have discovered is scandalous. There is wholesale disregard of the law which is inadequate and confused, commercial exploitation to a totally unacceptable degree, gross lack of security and, we suspect, a good deal of plain dishonesty.'
>
> (Paragraph 12.134: page 194)

How far this Conclusion can be sustained or rejected nearly sixteen years later would depend upon evidence similar in quantity to that which appeared before the Commission. What it contains, however, is a built-in warning to avoid pitfalls, be careful and take professional guidance or advice.

Section 6 National Lottery

Chapters 12 and 13 in Volume 1 of the *Royal Commission on Gambling* (above) explained respectively at pages 163–164 and subsequently at page 227 the background to what was passed by Parliament as the National Lottery Act 1993 on 21 October 1993:

> '12.5 All lotteries must be considered from two aspects – as a form of fund-raising and as a form of gambling. It is commonly supposed that lotteries are an infallible means of raising funds with very little trouble. The truth is otherwise and there have been some costly failures through poor administration. The Isle of Man lottery in the 1960s was one example and there have been more recent cases, on a smaller scale, in Britain.
> 12.6 Attitudes to lotteries as a form of gambling have varied over the years. There was a time when it was commonly thought immoral that anyone should be able to gain a large sum of money at the expense of his fellows and without the exercise of any skill or effort on his part. This view is less common today [ie as at 1978] ... One reason for this change of attitude is the generally more tolerant attitude towards gambling under proper control that exists throughout the world today. Most Governments take the view that lotteries are a harmless form of gambling and also provide harmless entertainment....
> 12.9 State lotteries in Britain have had a long history extending from 1569 to 1826....
> 13.64 We conclude that there should be a single national lottery for good causes run by a National Lottery Board....
> 13.65 The good causes to benefit from the national lottery should not be defined in terms of organisations but of objectives which should be:
>   (i) Sport.
>   (ii) The Arts.
>   (iii) Other Deserving Causes.
> Nothing more elaborate is required.'

The Act extended the 'Other Deserving Causes' to comprise charities, national heritage and the Millennium Fund projecting local and national restoration schemes within the widest environmental range towards the year 2000. A Director-General, Peter Davis, was appointed by the Secretary of State for the Department of National Heritage, and as he explained in an interview with *Leisure Management* in December 1993, his first task was to produce a Draft Invitation to Apply (ITA) and Draft Licence to Run the National Lottery under the two-tier system for its administration under sections 5 and 6 of the Act. (See also pages 391–395.)

(4) Libel, slander and copyright

Once more the standard text books on the subjects indicate the scope of the areas which these topics cover: *Carter-Ruck on Libel and Slander* (4th edn Butterworth 1991); *Copinger and Skone James on Copyright*; *Gatley on Libel and Slander*;

There has been a cascade of writs issued for defamation in recent years, most of which are settled before they reach court. No general distinction in law affects the sporting scene. Only the relevance of the particular facts triggers any legal issue here, as in all other areas. Thus at the time of writing, the mystery of the alleged tampered cricket ball during the 1992 Lord's Test between England and Pakistan (now locked away in Lord's Pavilion) continued. Defamation proceedings due to Allan Lamb's comments concerning the state of the ball were begun and withdrawn after disputed evidence alleging breaches of cricket's laws 42.4 and 42.5 and consequential damage to the image of the game and integrity and romantic idealism at the *public* level.

Within the context of Sport and the Law there are two levels where organisers should be careful. One is ordinary administration. The other is conventional publication. In general it is essential to realise that programme criticisms, record announcements and every form of communication can create risk situations; libel for the written and slander for the word. A wrongful expulsion by a secretary resulted in judgment against officers and committee members responsible for the secretary's errors (*Birne v National Sporting Club Ltd & Ors* (1957) Times, 12 April, page 13).

In the 1930s one of the great anomalies arising out of the curious role of the amateur sportsman resulted in an award of damages to a famous amateur golf champion for a libel which had been published gratuitously, which expressed knowledge of the risk that payment and thereby professionalism could be inferred. Cyril Tolley claimed that a commercial advertisement in a national newspaper had impugned his amateur status by a cartoon depicting him with a chocolate bar sticking out of his trousers coupled with the caption:

'The caddie to Tolley said, Oh, Sir,
Good shot, Sir That ball, see it go, Sir,
My word how it flies,
Like a cartet of Frys,
They're handy, they're good, and priced low, Sir'.

(*Tolley v Fry* [1931] AC 333).

Procedurally the House of Lords ordered a retrial on the issue of damages; and the action was settled. The libel principle, however, was established on that occasion more than 60 years ago, to preserve a reputation and its amateur status; by to-day's commercial cultural standards, a near unbelievable exercise.

Nevertheless, the more recently publicised golfing libel action in Nottingham Crown Court, while these pages were being compiled, had a century-old echo with it for preserving a reputation for fair play and honour and rejecting cheating assertions (*Buckingham v Rusk and Dene* (Independent, 28 April 1994).

Thus in 1890 a distinguished nobleman and friend of the Prince of Wales and future King Edward VII, Sir William Gordon-Cumming, was accused of cheating at cards during a house party on the eve of the Doncaster St Leger Race meeting, the oldest classic horse race in the world. He sued for slander; called the Prince of Wales as a witness on his behalf, with harmful effect; and heard a biased summing-up by the Lord Chief Justice, Lord Coleridge, after a trial which lasted six days. He lost the action which he ought to have won. The procedural problems are reported in *Gordon-Cumming v Green and others* [1890–1] 7 TLR 409–410; and the full story was told in the *Royal Baccarat Scandal* by Lord Havers, Edward Grayson and Peter Shankland when it was first published in 1977.

Finally, to protect the organiser completely against any copyright infringement from musical entertainment at sporting occasions, whether from gramophone records or other forms of reproduction, then consultation should take place with the Performing Right Society Limited of 29 Berners Street, London, W1 (Tel: 081–580 5544) and the Phonographic Performance Limited Company at 14 Ganton Street, London W1 (Tel: 081–437 0311). An injunction was obtained against Rangers FC Supporters Club Greenock, for breaches of copyright under this head (1974, Scots Law Times 151); but if the amount charged is excessive a right of reference exists to the Performing Right Tribunal (*Performing Right Society Ltd v Aristidou*, (1978) Times, 6 July, page 12).

(5) Insurance

Normally there should be no difference from the normal everyday type of policy required for normal domestic or household needs. For the essence of good administration demands good housekeeping.

The usual type of household policy, tailored to the specialist sporting requirements, will cover property, theft and liability for personal injury; and the governing body of the appropriate sport will be the best source for such enquiry.

No limit for compensation need exist, subject to the amount of premium, for which cover can be obtained. Thus, pluvius policies for cricket benefit matches will be required whereas they will not need to be considered for indoor boxing tournaments where the risks of cancellation from training or other circumstances create liability to spectators and contestants involving different insurance elements. No limits exist to the potential permutations of cover, but the nature and wording of the insurance policies must be precisely thought out and formulated. The following points merely illustrate the needs of sporting policy holders; and a graphic example of the need for precision can be seen below after an unsuccessful claim in London's High Court for an alleged failure to insure against theft in respect of the disappearance of the Aga Khan's record-breaking 10 lengths Derby winner, Shergar, on 9 February 1983.

(a) Property insurance

To rebuild a grandstand or building after destruction by fire almost inevitably demands the expenditure for architects', surveyors' and similar consultants' fees and a suitable clause to cover these expenses can be added. Also a further example or experience occurred at Littlehampton. Although the ground and buildings were comprehensively covered by policies, a fire which burned down an old pavilion, housing all the club's kit and equipment, disclosed that the kit and equipment remained uninsured.

(b) Theft

Apart from conventional cover against chattels, a fidelity policy to protect club or company property against defaulting employees would also provide an additional safeguard via the insurers' inquiries about the bona fides of staff likely to handle valuables and cash; and while Mr Justice Rattee's High Court decision on Shergar in April 1994 was bloodstock related, the principle behind it had a wider lesson. The available reports from racing sources [*The Sporting Life: Racing Post* 27 April 1994] point to the Plaintiff co-owners of shares in the stallion, Coolmore Stud, Co. Tipperary, and others, believing that

(1)   as 'theft was exceedingly unlikely to happen' and

(2)   they had given no thought to insuring the Derby winner against theft and

(3)   the risk was considered so slim in the insurance world that theft cover was available as an 'extra goody' in many policies at no additional premium and

(4)   there was no implied terms that 'theft cover was included in the invitation to the bloodstock agents to obtain' 'mortality cover'.

Accordingly, the cover asked for in the Lloyd's open market had been obtained, and in the absence of the theft cover asked for there was no breach of duty to create negligence.

(c) Legal liability

This provides the widest scope for cover and costs. While the courts decide the law and quantum of damages for assessment of injury, whether to life, limb or reputation, the insurance companies track the decisions for evaluating the ultimate costs for assessing risks.

Hence, the majority if not all the cases listed under chapters 4, 5 and 6 would have been contested under the umbrella of an insurance policy; and further areas of legal liability into which sport and recreation may stray for attracting insurance move outside the self-imposed restraints in these pages of participation and spectatorship, where individuals or groups participate in activities away from spectator involvement: namely, such outdoor or supervisory worlds as playgrounds, potholing, rock-climbing and skateboarding.

Here, the disparate facts which are the key-note to litigation plot a zig-zag course of liability and non-liability; and skateboarding, which created such ambivalent reactions about whether it is a sport, a form of transport or a social and public menace during the later 1970s, formed its own Skateboard Association under the aegis of the Sports Council but was forced to go to Holland for adequate insurance facilities.

Finally, five other separate points need stressing:

(1)   All clubs should have a 'Public Liability' insurance in force, and it ought to include liability when the ground is loaned or hired for any purpose other than normal use, such as a religious crusade or a boxing tournament. Club activities outside the ground and overseas tours should also be covered.

(2)   To insure a club's liability to its employees, a separate policy is usually required. The premium is calculated at a rate per cent on the total wages and salaries, and this cover is additional to any benefits that can be obtained under the National Insurance Scheme (see Employers' Liability Compulsory Insurance Act 1969).

(3)   As so many clubs take part in overseas tours, secretaries should ensure, that, before they travel abroad, some sort of cover for medical expenses has been arranged. The cost of having a

comparatively minor operation in some foreign countries is enormous, and there is no equivalent of our National Health Service in many areas.

(4) Two complementary situations which can appeal to clubs and members collectively or individually are (a) group insurance schemes and (b) personal insurance which many participants obtain in particularly violent or physical pursuits supplementary to any other cover.

(5) Finally, a club committee and officers may find it prudent either by insurance or provision in their club rules to provide for general or specific indemnities. One example, and there could be countless others, where claims for damages arise, is in the field of defamation.

CONCLUSION

What emerges from this chapter is the complexity inherent in administering sport at any level: school, club or national institution. Furthermore, consistent with different areas of legal practice, sport, too, demands a knowledge by practitioners of the myriad minefields which can trap the unwary. Thus the litigation lawyer who lavishly believes that judicial review is a procedural avenue open to his or her client in sport should study the fate of the Aga Khan's abortive claim against the Jockey Club, and Catherine Bond's analysis in Appendix 9.

Part V

Commerce

Chapter 13

Sponsored Gentlemen and Players

1 INTRODUCTION

Almost every level of sporting administration today in the mid-1990s, domestically and internationally, looks to sponsorship for full or shared funding for its sustained existence. Sponsorship has an ever increasing importance within sport at both public and domestic levels. Sponsors seek out sport as it purports to promote a healthy and clean lifestyle for their products. Sport itself requires the money from sponsorship in order to invest money back into itself and also to reward the successful competitors. Sponsorship of major sporting events is keenly sought to the extent that modern day sport at the public entertainment level would be unimaginable without certain companies attaching themselves to the Olympics, cricket, soccer and horse-racing, to name but a few. Correspondingly many sporting school trips abroad would be unthinkable without parental and other sponsorship sources.

Sponsorship has no traditional legal status. Like sport itself, it leans more to description than delineation. There is no sponsorship statute and no private civil sponsorship case law per se exists at present independent of conventional commercial law (as distinct from VAT tribunal and High Court decisions).

As a factual phenomenon which has arrived on the sporting scene in particular, and the arts-leisure-recreation stage generally, sponsorship has now been recognised in the form of an important HM Treasury Memorandum of evidence. This was submitted to the Education, Science and Arts Committee of the House of Commons (supra, appointed under SO No 86A (Eighth Report 1982) HC 49-11) under the title of *Taxation in the Context of Private Sponsorship and of Gifts of Art Objects to Public and Private Institutions*, and thereby formally acknowledged authoritatively its existence. HM Customs and Excise have also recognised the existence of sponsorship in its VAT Leaflet No 701/41/90, 1 February 1990. Entitled 'Sponsorship' it provides specific guidance on 'how you must account for VAT on sponsorship income you receive.'

Each of these two authoritative sources has a crucial role to play in the functional operation of sponsorship. It qualifies in the appropriate circumstances acceptable to the Commissioners of Inland Revenue under the conventional tax laws and practices for tax reliefs. It is subject to VAT burdens and practices. These fiscal sources therefore point to sponsorship for what it is: a business-commercial concept used by the sponsor as a key promotional marketing tool.

Sponsorship's existence is vital for sport at regional and local as well as at national and international levels. It is also necessary to distinguish sponsorship from its associated ancillary advantages to sport and the arts-leisure-recreation scenario through the more familiar philanthropic and patronage methods of funding. Sponsorship is a legitimate taxation expenditure within a corporate or personal budget and as such it is distinguishable from the personal indulgence or whim of an enthusiastic benefactor. Indeed, according to the Central Council of Physical Recreation's associated body, The Institute of Sports Sponsorship, by 1989

'Currently over one thousand commercial companies in the United Kingdom between them subscribe over £200 million in various sponsorship schemes – a clear sign both of how important sport has become as a means of promoting commercial interests and how greatly organised sport now relies on commercial backing.'

When Barclays Bank Plc replaced the *Today* newspaper as sponsor for the Football League's centenary season of 1987–88 to create the Barclays League, the then chairman of Barclays Bank, Sir John Quinton, explained that he was a season-ticket holder at Tottenham Hotspur, but that the sponsorship deal was

'a decision made for hard-headed commercial reasons with clear business objectives in mind.'

Those objectives were stated with the claims

'We believe that the Barclays League Championship is an ideal promotional vehicle for us for a number of reasons. It appeals to youth – and young people are a key recruitment area for the bank. It involves clubs from throughout the country – and Barclays has at least one branch in every town where a league club is located. It is an event which is of interest to all ages and all sociological groups – and Barclays is keen to increase its market share in a number of target sectors. It offers more matches during a longer season than any other sports event in the UK, has 14 live televised matches during this season and offers enormous scope for our local branches and branch staff to become involved.
    Having said all that, football is also rather special in this country. Whatever its problems in recent years, it remains our national game and the local League club remains a vital part of the community. We are pleased our sponsorship can help to ensure the continued health of the game and indeed encourage its rebirth as a great family entertainment.'

These thoughts and attitudes from one of British soccer's highest profile sponsors were consistent with the approach from the Gillette toiletry company seen by some as the modern pioneers of nationally recognised sports sponsorship in the United Kingdom. The late Gordon Ross, who was involved closely at its inception in 1963 with the famous cricket competition The Gillette Cup, explained the mutual benefits from this ideal liaison between sport and commerce in his book *The Gillette Cup: 1963 to 1980.*

The trophy was inaugurated the year after the artificial distinctions between Gentlemen and Players were abolished in 1962 by MCC, prior to its own surrender of authority (apart from continued control of cricket's Laws) to the Test and County Cricket Board and the National Cricket Association for all aspects of the amateur game, during the later 1960s as we have seen in Chapter 2, 'Progressive perspective'. Initiated, as Ross wrote, 'rather too much of a mouthful for the sports pages of the newspapers', as 'The First-Class Counties Knock-Out Competition for the Gillette Cup', it was simplified in the press as 'the KO Cup'. Ultimately it was titled formally 'The Gillette Cup', which, after eighteen finals, because of its outstanding success, led ultimately to its demise.

Ross wrote of the relationship between Gillette and cricket:

'The manner in which Gillette acted, in the lowest possible commercial key and with meticulous care and responsibility, produced a confidence which established a happy marriage between cricket and the sponsor. Sponsorship in cricket grew gradually as a result of this sensitive approach, but few could have anticipated its final ramifications in the form of Packer's brash and gimmicky mass-media promotion.'

In his closing pages under the chapter heading of 'Reflections', Ross wrote interrogatively with words which have a message for all sponsors who wish to follow the impeccable trail blazed by Gillette's sponsorship. This trail has since been littered with less mutually beneficial results to sport and commerce,

'People may ask, "What did Gillette derive from the Gillette Cup and why [sic!] they get out of it?"
    This is a question that can only be answered if it is broadened to ask, "Why do companies sponsor sport – or the arts for that matter?"
    Obviously the prime reason for doing so is the publicity which is given to the company name. There are two ways of looking at that. First, the company wishes to project a good image of itself by association with a well regarded national event; in Gillette's case the advantage of association with a clean, masculine game is beneficial for its products. But the second consideration carries limitation with it and is the more important: the use of the company's name is only really valuable when the name is the same as the trade mark under which its products are sold, or .

in the case of a company not selling goods, is the same as the business name under which it trades.

Thus the multifarious activities of the Unilever organisation would probably render a Unilever Cup worthless, but the Cornhill Tests must be of considerable value. In Gillette's case two things happened as the eighteen years went by: the number of its products sold under trade marks other than Gillette increased with the company's diversification: and research showed that the public was beginning to associate the Gillette Cup less and less with products using the trademark Gillette, or even with the company itself. The competition was becoming a national institution set apart from the company's business. Exact measurement of such things is impossible but that seemed to be the trend.'

Ross continued with an example from the horse-racing scene in illustrating what he called 'The other reason for sponsoring is the altruistic one' which, as we shall see, is more accurately a form of patronage. He explained,

'In days gone by, wealthy individuals were able to sponsor sporting events (Lord Derby is a good example in the horseracing world). In today's economic climate, and with the growth of national events and the media, sponsorship by individuals is virtually impossible and their place as generous citizens is now taken by large companies. It is a proper activity for them and one from which they can derive credit. This was originally why Gillette came in.

In the famous offer letter of 4 September 1962 [which clinched earlier negotiations] they wrote of the company's "general desire to identify itself with the promotion of British sport and to make some tangible contribution to the future of first-class cricket."

That is the way it went, and Richard Burton [initially the company's legal adviser and subsequently Chairman] echoed this at a BBC television interview the night before the last final when he said:

"It cannot be measured in advertising terms. The memory I would like to leave is one where both sides, cricket and Gillette, had a very happy partnership.".'

Ross concluded his chapter and the book with a prophetic last paragraph:

'In leaving cricket, Gillette knew that they would not be inflicting any damage on the game itself. What they had created, with the help of cricket's administrators, was an extremely valuable commercial proposition, and its attraction was very quickly appreciated by a number of companies who competed for it when it became known that the competition was on the maket. The altruistic motive had been fulfilled – and the Gillette Cup will remain always an historical landmark in the folklore of cricket.'

Historically sponsorship began almost a century after cricket's earlier pioneering precedent for what in effect was an international sponsorship, in 1861. Before tracing backwards to that starting point and subsequent developments throughout the intervening years, it is essential to recognise the legal basis for modern sponsorship, and its distinction, with well-known examples, from closely associated categories with which it can easily be confused, namely philanthropy and patronage.

2 LEGAL AND FACTUAL FOUNDATIONS AND DISTINCTIONS

The essence of an effective sponsorship arrangement must be the sponsorship contract. A simple example from the professional football world is published at pages 352–353 below, with permission of the Aston Villa club, together with a check list of the nuts and bolts of a sponsorship contract which was contained in evidence published in the most valuable Howell Report from the CCPR towards the end of 1983. See pages 350–351 below.

Additional associated legal categories which constantly arise involve copyright licensing, passing-off, patents, trusts, and others in addition to taxes and VAT. For example in 1990, the BBC failed in a claim for exclusivity and breach of copyright under section 16 of the Copyright, Designs and Patents Act 1988 when British Satellite Broadcasting Ltd used short excerpts from the BBC's live broadcasts of soccer World Cup matches to show highlights of matches in its sports news programmes. After six days of evidence and legal argument, Scott J in a reserved judgment held that this amounted to 'fair dealing ... for the purpose of reporting current events' and was therefore protected by section 30 (2) of the 1988 Act because the World Cup matches were current events and inter alia the material was used in genuine news reports, (*BBC v BSB Ltd* [1991] 3 All ER 833).

Sponsorship is a growth area to such an extent that since the year of England's World Cup Soccer triumph in 1966, taken as a well-known and identifiable starting point, nearly a dozen in-depth authoritative studies have surfaced to which reference will be made at various stages in this chapter. The aim of this chapter is to provide a general level of awareness and as such only an outline and overview with easily recognisable illustrations can be attempted here.

For an in-depth analysis of the comprehensive legal issues involved, the reader is referred to *Sponsorship of Sport, Arts and Leisure: Law, Tax and Business Relationships* (1984 Stephen Townley and Edward Grayson), the only *legal* survey of the sports sponsorship scene published to date in the United Kingdom. In 1987, Iain C

Baillie, a member of the New York Bar and a Chartered Patent Agent published *Licensing: A Practical Guide for the Businessman* and in 1989 and 1990, Deborah Fosbrook and Adrian C Laing published two volumes of *The Media Contracts Handbook: A Master Contract Reference Book* for use within the Media Industry. Cumulatively they provided 75 specimen precedents, with a warning in their Introduction to Volume 2 under the heading of 'Sponsorship Generally'.

> 'There is no standard type of sponsorship deal. We have chosen particular circumstances which commonly involve the advancement of money by a commercial company to an individual, agent or association in return for media exposure of the sponsor's product, name, trademark or logo'.

Within the present survey for this particular chapter, three fundamental differentials which are frequently ignored, overlooked or unknown, must be recognised.

(1) Sponsorship can be as important for local and regional institutions and their activities as the often overvalued national and international sources.

(2) Sponsorship can be applied and accepted for legitimate tax deductible purposes in six different circumstances or levels, ie
  (i)   Personal individuals or team groups (eg Torvill and Dean by Nottingham Corporation or Watford Football Club by Iveco)
  (ii) Governing bodies (eg Football League by Barclays Bank Plc)
  (iii) Events (eg NatWest Bank Trophy in succession to the Gillette Cup)
  (iv) Product (eg Brylcreem by Denis Compton or tennis equipment by individual performers at Wimbledon or elsewhere)
  (v)   Long-term or one-off within time limits.
  (vi) Local, Regional or National in scope and range

(3) Sponsorship is not
  (a) Philanthropy
  (b) Patronage.

Terminology and definitions

The significance of each of these three different elements above will emerge during this chapter, but the last two concepts will be dealt with first because of the confusion which can be caused by not understanding the distinction between philanthropy and patronage. The borderline between philanthropy and patronage can be blurred, but they are both to be distinguished sharply from sponsorship. That distinction was explained conveniently in a second *Economist Intelligence Unit* (EIU) *Special Report on Sponsorship* (1980/81) by Jean Simkins at p 5. Distinguishing the sponsorship concept from that of patronage, the point is made there that

'the terms are sometimes interchanged and it is not unusual to refer to patronage by individuals (as opposed to organisations) as sponsorship, as in the case of sponsored walks for charity. In general, however, the term patronage in connection with commercial enterprises is applied to financial or material assistance given without the expectation of any return even in the form of publicity.'

Then the contrast is rightly made with

'Sponsorship [as being] essentially a business deal, which is intended to be for the advantage of sponsor and sponsored. If successfully designed and carried out, with properly defined objectives, sponsorship arrangements can be of real benefit to both parties and, at the same time, be of benefit to the community in providing events and facilities which would otherwise not be available. It is desirable to keep a clear distinction between sponsorship and patronage ventures, and to regard them as quite separate activities to which different criteria apply.'

The framework for such successful design, carrying out and properly defined objectives is always contractual. Barclays Bank Plc stepped into the breach left by a dispute over the contractual arrangements between the Football League and *Today*. The review of the 1986 Commonwealth Games at Edinburgh under the title *Unfriendly Games: Boycotted and Broke* (1986) by Derek Bateman and Derek Douglas, two experienced Scottish journalists, identified an assessment of the management of organisation by the distinguished consultants Cooper and Lybrand, commissioned by Mr Robert Maxwell. They recorded at page 43

'He must have been astonished [on reading the consultants' report] at the incompetence which led to "uncertainty as to whether contracts and in particular contracts that are part of a wider sponsorship arrangement have actually been signed, and the contents of those contracts.".'

Contractually styled documents are not essential for philanthropy or patronage: indeed in law they are inconsistent with such bounty (*Balfour v Balfour* [1919] 2 KB 571). Nevertheless in the current economic and social climate about disputed rights, clarification and certainty in documentary form are always desirable. Alternatively, symbolic or inferred inscriptions would suffice. Two classic sporting examples suffice, and demonstrate differences from sponsorship.

(a) Philanthropy

Philanthropy describes the act of donation without the expectation of receiving any form of gain in return. It is illustrated by a direct link between one of Fleet Street's landmarks in London which continues to survive time's ravages and the departures to Docklands and elsewhere of its newspaper associations. The sign of the Three Squirrels, outside the branch of Barclays Bank Plc, at No 19, represents how it is known and labelled and listed in the telephone directory as Goslings Branch.

For over three hundred years it has served the legal, literary and journalist professions, with its proud saga of two families, Gosling and Sharpe, who dominated the branch until the amalgamation with the Gurney, Backhouse and Barclay families to form the present structure in 1896. The best-known member of the Gosling family beyond the banking fringe was Robert Cunliffe Gosling who died prematurely after surgery in 1923 aged 53.

In the last decade of Queen Victoria's England he had been a double cricket and soccer Blue at Cambridge, and when only three soccer home international matches were played each season. He was capped five times on merit as an amateur forward alongside such renowned professionals as Bassett (West Bromwich Albion), Bloomer (Derby County), Goodall (Preston North End), Spikesley (Sheffield Wednesday), to name a few. C B Fry wrote in *Life Worth Living* of R C Gosling, that he was a

> 'magnificent forward ... very fast, skilful and unselfish. Otherwise he was an MFH with a princely income, and played in perfectly valeted brown boots which must have cost him a fiver. He aided the Corinthians in their reputation up North as a team of toffs. We were suspected of being Guards officers and young squires.'

Gosling was part of the Essex county squierarchy, later President of the County Cricket Club, a JP and High Sheriff, and mourned deeply by his tenant farmers and retainers when he died in 1923. In 1902, after the early death aged 41 of his fellow Old Etonian Arthur Dunn, founder of Ludgrove School (mentioned at page 89 in Chapter 4, 'Parent, School and Club Partners'), Gosling donated a trophy. It is inscribed

'In Memoriam'
The Arthur Dunn Challenge Cup

It has been played for annually, except for interruption from two World Wars, enthusiastically, and as we shall see in Chapter 15, 'Whither Sport and the Law'?, ferociously, by Old Boys XI's from the leading public schools. The donation by Gosling in memory of his friend had no sponsorship or patronage strings attached. It was a gift. It was philanthropy. The Arthur Dunn Challenge Cup, unknown to many, is the second oldest knock-out soccer cup competition in the world after the FA Cup, the FA having faced reality in 1974 to abolish its Amateur Cup Competition created in 1894.

(b) Patronage

Patronage is a step beyond philanthropy where donors do not expect to achieve gain, but allow their name to be associated with the subject matter of a donation.

In the year before Gosling's gift of the Arthur Dunn Cup during 1902, professional boxing had survived its trauma recorded in Chapter 6, 'Participation problems', at p 172, of the jury's acquittal at the Central Criminal Court of defendants charged with manslaughter following a death in the ring at the National Sporting Club, which claimed to be the headquarters of professional boxing at its premises in King Street, Covent Garden (*R v Roberts and ors* [1901] supra). The Club's limited finances also placed it at a disadvantage for competing with commercial promoters and boxers' managers for services of the leading fighters to entertain Club members and their guests. Something more tangible than a naked commercial reward was required to redress this financial imbalance. For at that stage at the beginning of this century, no equivalent honour or trophy existed for professional boxing at any weight equivalent to the FA Challenge Cup Competition, which was conceived in 1871, from the precedent of Harrow School's Cock-House knock-out competition. Indeed after a mere thirty years it had attracted a crowd of 110,000 to the Final tie at Crystal Palace in 1901, albeit with a London club, Tottenham Hotspur (then in the Southern League) from outside the Football League playing Sheffield United.

The National Sporting Club's active President was a celebrated all round sportsman and sports lover, the 5th Earl of Lonsdale. He provided generous donations and presided over the administrative structuring for the different weight divisions, into which boxing had been organised. The proposal to award a belt of honour to the winner of each National Sporting Championship fight at the appropriate weight, with the winner on three occasions at the same weight becoming the property owner of the prize, was adopted. After the demise of the Club in the later 1920s and establishment of the British Board of Boxing Control (1929) the Board took over the award of what are now known throughout the world as the Lonsdale Belts. The Board's first award was to the British flyweight champion from Scotland, Benny Lynch in 1936. The Club's first award was made in 1909 to the

British lightweight champion Freddie Welsh. A conflict of evidence exists in boxing sources about the formal title of the original belts before the Board's present designation with the name of their donor who undoubtedly paid for the original foundation during his active Presidency of the Club. He patronised it with his presence as well as his bounty and sought no reward beyond his sporting satisfaction.

Lord Lonsdale's indulgence was the converse of the circumstances which stirred Dr Johnson's rebuff in 1754 to Lord Chesterfield ten years after rejection of support for the doctor's Dictionary preparation

> 'Is not a patron my lord, one who looks with unconcern on a man struggling for life in the water, and when he has reached ground encumbers him with help? The notice which you have been pleased to take of my labours, had it been early, had been kind – but it has been delayed until I am indifferent, and cannot enjoy it; till I am solitary and cannot impart it; till I am known, and do not want it.'

3 SPONSORSHIP ORIGINS

Barely a century after Dr Johnson's patronage commentary the first example of modern sponsorship appeared in 1861, in turn almost a century before the Gillette initiative in 1962. *Sponsorship of Sport, Arts and Leisure*, by Stephen Townley and Edward Grayson, explains in its opening pages under the heading 'Historical Perspective' how cricket provides the precedents from its early growth as a public sport in the nineteenth century, via the personality cult clinging to Dr Grace and his exploitation of cricket while retaining his amateur status, down to the subsidised amateurism, during the years between two World Wars, from entrepreneurs enthusiastically devoted to cricket such as Sir Julien Cahn, ready to employ the Gentlemen to facilitate their continuing as subsidised amateur Players on the county championship circuit.

In 1861 expatriate Englishmen, Felix Spiers and Christopher Pond, had established substantial catering contracts for their supply of refreshments to the Melbourne and Ballarate Railway. To publicise their enterprises they sent an agent to England. Charles Dickens was invited to provide a series of public readings as a method of advertisement. When these failed to materialise the then finest and first ever English cricket team to tour Australia was arranged. It was assembled through the organisation of Surrey County Cricket Club's Secretary, William Burrup, and captained by H H Stephenson, also of Surrey. It succeeded on and off the field to such an extent that during the Australian winter Messers Spiers and Pond returned to Britain to create a famous catering company until its ultimate absorption by the Express Dairy Group.

About the same time other enterprising cricket sponsors, John Wisden and James Lillywhite, conceived the idea of advertising their sports goods, shops and equipment through annual publications. The name of one survives in print, the other in London's lights as a store; and the dusty sporting bookshelves confirm this pattern from Gamages and Spalding to other examples from our own times. In 1895 the professional doctor, W G Grace, playing cricket as an amateur, surprisingly retained that status with Gloucestershire and England while also retaining £9,073 8s 3d from three separate sources. During that forty-eighth year of his life Grace scored his hundredth 100 runs and for the first time by any batsman, he also scored 1,000 runs in May. As Grahame Parker's *Gloucestershire road: A history of Gloucester County Club* (published in 1983 in association with National Westminster Bank Plc) records:

'The *Daily Telegraph* launched a National Shilling Testimonial which brought him £4,281 9s 1d. There were others. GCCC added £100, £1 for each century perhaps, but a scant reward for his formidable contribution to their affairs. The Club was in the throes of a financial crisis. However, they did give him a Century of Centuries Dinner at the Victoria Rooms, Bristol on 24 June. The total of all the donations came to £9,073 8s 3d. Some amateur!'

In 1981, two years before Parker's county history, Eric Midwinter's biography *W G Grace: His Life and Times* noted

'A shrewd cartoon showed WG thanking Sir Edward Lawson [the *Telegraph* proprietor and later Lord Burnham] who is saying, "Don't mention it, doctor, look what you've done for my circulation".'

In the following year of 1896 he captained the Gentlemen against the Players for each match played, at Lord's and the Oval. He also captained England, as an amateur of course, in the three Test Matches against the visiting Australians captained by G H S Trott.

Another modern sporting historian, Gerald Howat, has been equally forthcoming over the mystery which once shrouded the overnight conversion of Grace's memorable Gloucestershire all-rounder successor during the winter of 1937 from Hammond, WR, professional cricketer and former professional footballer with Bristol Rovers, to Mr W R Hammond, amateur in 1938. This created his eligibility to captain England against Australia led by Don Bradman, the Gentlemen of England against the Players, and Gloucestershire in the County Cricket Championship (unsponsored) during the summer of 1938, and England in South Africa during the winter of 1938–39.

Howat explains with candour how Hammond was invited to join the Board of Directors of an expanding firm of motor tyre suppliers which had begun after the First World War, namely Marsham Tyres.

'Hammond's value to Marsham Tyres lay in the contacts he was able to make. Bill Pope, a fellow-director and subsequently managing director after the second world war, remembered the contribution he made to the firm:
"Whether on cricket tours or playing in England, on the golf course or at some dinner, he brought us business. He had an easy manner, a memory for names and, of course, great prestige. In the continuing growth years of 1938 and 1939, despite the European political uncertainty, he was involved as our firm's main outside 'contact' man".'

Howat explains that

'Pope admitted that the glamour of bringing in business appealed to Hammond more than the routine of following it up, but his job remained clear – to get the orders. He was popular with the firm's representatives and surviving photographs show him smiling at golfing functions and office gatherings. In attracting to their ranks one of the best-known figures in England, Marsham Tyres had done themselves a service. By 1939, an expansion programme which some had felt to be too ambitious had proved over-modest. New production facilities could scarcely meet increasing demand.'

During that summer of 1938 television cameras were at Lord's when Hammond scored his unforgettable 240 against Australia on Friday 24 and Saturday 25 June. The Pavilion rose to grant the standing acclamation given intuitively at the end of only the most specially styled innings. Very few at the time were aware that on the evidence now adduced by Gerald Howat's biography it is at least arguable that it had been sponsored by Marsham Tyres.

When the war ended, a more public but subtle form of sports sponsorship developed whereby the manufacturers of Brylcreem used the unnamed and unidentified photograph of Denis Compton, taking advantage of his cricketing image in 1948, with bat and head and shoulders, fully aware also of his reputation as a war time international footballer. Sales increased enormously and as Peter Hunt, Director of Public Affairs for Coca-Cola's Northern Europe Export Corporation explained,

'from Compton it was an obvious thing for Brylcreem to do something for cricket itself. And so appropriately, the County Cups were inaugurated. They were named after the manufacturing company, which was then County Laboratories.'

Ultimately it became part of the Beecham group, but after a similar experience to Gillette's success and perhaps ambivalence in the public mind and eye between sport and the initial nature of the sponsored product, Brylcreem and the parent group, Beechams, withdrew from cricket. Significantly, Hunt commented when he spoke and published in 1966, in the fourth year of the Gillette initiative,

'It also became known that Gillette were intending to spend a fair amount in introducing their own awards in cricket and it was felt there was no room for two such sponsorships unless Brylcreem were prepared to invest a considerably increased amount of money.'

That potential conflict between two competing sponsors in the same field leads directly back to the succession of Barclays Bank Plc to the *Today* newspaper at the beginning of the Football League Championship Centenary season, and the nature of the contractual row which exploded because of the publicised disagreement over the terms of the Football League contract with the *Today* newspaper. A contract is the key to all sponsorship arrangements, as it must be to all intelligent and validly intended and binding commercial arrangements.

4 SPONSORSHIP CONTRACTS: THE KEY TO SUCCESS OR FAILURE

Barclays Bank's arrival on the football sponsorship scene during August 1987 deflected attention from the dispute which erupted publicly during the withdrawal by the *Today* newspaper of its sponsorship of the Football League Championship competition. In October 1986, through its then parent company News UK, it had hurriedly replaced Canon (UK) Ltd after the start of the 1986–87 soccer season as the competition's sponsor. On Monday 3 August 1987 the *Today* columns announced that it had

' "told the Football League that it is proposing to end its sponsorship contract with them."
   This follows the League's failure to live up to its side of the agreement despite five months of complaints from *Today*.
   The League immediately announced it would seek legal advice. The deal was signed last season by News UK, the owners of *Today*. Since then the paper has become part of News International.'

The charges and counter-charges between the respective parties of repudiation can be assessed only by reference to the contract terms. Only if the dispute arrives in court will a final judgment be possible. Within the present context of avoiding conflicting sponsorship investment, however, and with the Brylcreem-Beecham policy in mind it is significant that the *Daily Telegraph* recorded the conflicting sides of this key issue on Monday 3 August 1987 at page 21 through its football correspondent Colin Gibson, thus:

'The major grievance ... voiced at meetings with League officials regularly since the signing has been the introduction of a sponsor for the centenary celebrations, though the League refute the charge. *Today* claim that they were never told that Mercantile Credit were to be allowed to sponsor the centenary events for £250,000.

Graham Kelly the League Secretary (and later and now Chief Executive of the Football Association) said yesterday

"The centenary events are a separate matter entirely. *Today* are the sponsors of the League Championship. The centenary celebrations are seven or eight special events and we hoped that the two sponsorships (ie for the championship sponsored by *Today* and the centenary game applicable here] would complement each other".'

That hope would certainly appear to have more chance of fulfilment with the replacement by Barclays very swiftly after the *Today* withdrawal in the week after the centenary celebration game at Wembley Stadium. Its then chairman, Mr (now Sir) John Quinton, announced at the time when the objectives stated at the commencement of this chapter were explained:

'As you know, our subsidiary company Mercantile Credit led the way with its sponsorship of the League's centenary celebrations. I know that they are well pleased with the sponsorship and I am sure that Barclays' sponsorship of the League Championship combined with Mercantile Credit's involvement with the centenary will give the Barclays Group a unique double and a unique opportunity for cooperation.'

The closer nexus between the two banking companies than that between a newspaper and an unconnected merchant bank is self-evident. Significantly, the point about shared sponsorship recognised by the Brylcreem-Beecham awareness of Gillette's arrival on the cricket scene is one of the many specified in the contract check list published in the CCPR's *Howell Report* provided for it by the sports sponsorship consultant David Way and reproduced in full here on pp 350–351 (*Howell Report*, 31, Chapter 5, 'Governing Bodies').

For under the subheading of 'Contracts' at that page in the Report the comment is made with an almost prophetic anticipation of the current football conflict:

'In this modern sporting world, governing bodies will find themselves involved in sophisticated contractual negotiations which are crucial to their financial stability. The need for watertight contracts and the employment, if necessary, of sound professional advice cannot be over-emphasised.'

Indeed, the same guidance is applicable to everyone entering into a sponsorship deal which goes beyond the simple clear-cut provisions of the Aston Villa styled situation which is also reproduced at pages 352–353.

Point 14 of the contract check list emphasises with prescience for the Football League-*Today* dispute,

'Shared sponsorships should be avoided, but if an event has more than one then arrangements concerning all sponsor benefits must be agreed beforehand. This applies especially to identification in the title, print and television bannering.'

It is also arguable that sponsors of individual sponsored beneficiaries, such as for the multiple sandwich board atmosphere which permeates professional lawn tennis players at Wimbledon, will also have such guidance in mind at their negotiation and contract signing stages.

Associated with and ancillary to this overriding need for thoughtful planning is the further example in the Howell Report of 'the importance of proper, legal contracts and the need to protect the rights of individuals and teams' demonstrated by the All England Women's Lacrosse Association (AEWLA). The Association explained to the Committee of Inquiry how a properly drawn legal contract helped to prevent a commercial sponsor from interfering either with the technical conduct of a major event for its own marketing ends and it also ensured payment of the sponsorship fee. The event was the first World Tournament for women, held at Nottingham in 1982.

An American company manufacturing plastic lacrosse sticks wanted to accelerate the conversion from wooden to plastic sticks by creating a brand-name link with the international federation. After payment of the first sponsorship instalment fee the American manufacturing company threatened to withdraw as sponsor unless all players used their sticks even though there was no contractual obligation to do so. After negotiations the manufacturing company realised that it could not enforce this requirement. The result was an amendment to the International Women's Lacrosse Federation constitution. A clause was inserted to ensure that no company can have a monopoly on sponsorship or any influence over the use of equipment.

That example of purported interference and control of sport by commercial interests raises a cascade of moral questions concerning the operation of sponsorship. The Howell Report investigated this position thoroughly, which is discussed in its Chapter 13, under the

SPECIMEN SPONSORSHIP CONTRACT:
Checklist (from the Central Council of Physical Recreation:
The Howell Report) 1983
[p 339 supra]

Table 5.1 Contract Checklist
from David Way (sports sponsorship consultant)

1. **Title:** The precise title of the event and the degree of emphasis given to the sponsor should be agreed. Will they, for instance, receive 'equal billing' in the title?

2. **Duration:** The precise duration of the sponsorship with start-finish dates.

3. **The Event:** Details of the event/competition should be included.

4. **Fees:** Details of fees and dates when payments become due must be covered. If the fee is linked to the RPI then specify the month when new figure will be taken.

5. **Option to Renew:** The first option to renew the contract should be given to the current sponsor(s). State deadline. If existing sponsor(s) declines then the event should not be offered to another potential sponsor at terms which are more beneficial without the existing sponsor being given first option on those better terms.

6. **Governing Body's Authority:** Is the governing body authorised to sign on behalf of participating clubs/teams/players? State position clearly.

7. **Information:** Organisers to keep sponsors informed, in advance if possible, of any changes affecting the event. Copies of all sponsor press releases to go to sponsor.
   Sponsors to keep organisers informed of any press releases, information, developments affecting the event. Copies of all sponsor press releases to go to organisers.

8. **Cancellation:** Sponsor may withdraw support. How much prior notice required? Payments required? These payments will probably be linked to involvement of a new sponsor.

9. **Promotion:** Sponsor's use of competition/event/competitors for promotion and publicity purposes. Any limitations?

10. **Conflict of Interests:** Should there be any restrictions concerning competitive products?

11. **Television Cover:** Clearly the situation regarding television covers companies, channel, duration, live or highlights. Firm commitments are to be avoided but television companies will usually state their 'intention' to cover.
    The financial consequences (if any) of loss of television should be covered in the contract.

12. **Television Boards:** If television boards are to be used their size/precise location should be given. The use of imprecise terms like 'prime sites' should be avoided.

13. **Sponsor's Facilities:** Will free/reduced price tickets/passes/seasons be available?
    Will entertaining facilities be available for company personnel/company guests?

14. **Shared Sponsorships:** Shared sponsorships should be avoided, but if an event has more than one then arrangements concerning all sponsor benefits must be agreed beforehand. This applies especially to identification in the title, print and television bannering.

15. **Problem Products:** Both sides should try to anticipate possible problems related to products – drink/tobacco/gambling and young people, for instance.

ASTON VILLA FOOTBALL CLUB

SPONSORSHIP CONTRACT

Between Aston Villa Football Club plc and:

Company Name :

Address :

Telephone Number :

Invoicing Address (if different from above) ....

FOR THE:

Please reserve the ***   match

Aston Villa versus

To be played on

Number of Guests in Sponsors Party

SPONSORSHIP COST   V.A.T. will be added where applicable.

DEPOSIT PAID

Signed ....

Name ....

Position ....

Date ....

Signed on behalf of Aston Villa Football Club

Name ....

Date ....

title 'Ethical Considerations'. It concluded with a recommendation, which has yet to be implemented, that the Government should refer to the Office of Fair Trading for full examination of the relationship between important sporting events in the United Kingdom and whether any monopoly situation exists. In the years since the Report was published, commercial involvement has hardly decreased; and another angle was aired in Sir Denis Follows' Philip Noel-Baker Memorial Lecture on the theme, 'Whither Sport?'

It extracted this section when Follows said:

'Nearly every top level performer has his agent. If he is an individual performer, his agent contracts his appearance. As a result in certain sports, the governing body has ceased to govern. The agent or the entrepreneur cracks the whip assisted by the television producer. We have now reached the stage where the sport at the top level has become almost completely show business with everything that one associates with show-biz – the cult of the individual, the desire to present the game as a spectacle, more money, less sportsmanship, more emphasis on winning.'

Here, too, however, 'the need for water-tight contracts and the employment, if necessary, of sound professional advice' cannot be overemphasised. It was illustrated vividly when one of GO Smith's successors as England's centre-forward and captain decided to go to court during the period after the World Cup competition of 1982 over a commercial contract indirectly associated with sponsorship contracts.

Kevin Keegan sued his former public relations and promotion company Public Eye Enterprises Ltd in breach of contract, in Leeds Crown Court, after the World Cup had ended. He had begun the action with two claims. One was for damages that Public Eye Enterprises had not performed sufficiently a representation and oral term of a written Agreement dated 16 November 1972 that it would guarantee him £30,000 over the next two years. The other was that the company held £3,714.79 on his behalf, but that it had failed and refused to hand it over. The case lasted over six working days, including evidence and legal argument. McCowan J's judgment delivered on 27 October 1982 covers 38 pages of typescript, and the Court of Appeal transcript judgments number 12.

Yet one key issue went to the heart of the case. Keegan admitted in evidence that he had wrongly believed a written agreement for five years lasted for only three.

At the trial and during evidence nothing was heard further about the claim for damages, which Keegan's counsel told the court was not to be pursued. The other claim was amended to £4,709.81, and was admitted, subject to set-off under a counterclaim by Public Eye

Enterprises Ltd. This amounted also to two claims. One was that
Keegan had broken his agreement with the company and entered into
numerous commercial contracts of a nature deemed to be controlled
by the written agreement of 16 November 1972. The other was that a
former director of the company, Harry Swales, had induced Keegan
to break his contract with it and damages were claimed against both
of them.
The judge was not unfamiliar with the football field in court. He
had acted as counsel for the wounded plaintiff in *Lewis v Brookshaw*
(see Chapter 6, 'Participation Problems', page 177) at Lewes Assizes
and in London's High Court during 1969 and 1970 when Rees J had
awarded £4,000 for deliberate violent foul play creating a civil assault.
On this occasion he made three crucial findings on what was a
commercial agreement which were not challenged in the Court of
Appeal (which was concerned solely with technical financial issues).

(1)   The written agreement dated 16 November 1972 was a sole
       agency agreement. This gave Public Eye Enterprises Ltd exclus-
       ive control over the off-field and non-sporting contractual ac-
       tivities it covered, during the five-year operation until 16
       November 1977.

(2)   Keegan was in breach of contract because he entered into
       contracts without the prior knowledge and approval of Public
       Eye Enterprises Ltd before that five-year period had expired.

(3)   If Keegan had been correct that the written agreement lasted for
       only three years and not five it would have terminated on 16
       November 1975 and not in 1977; and in those circumstances
       Keegan would have been free to enter into contracts without
       obligation to Public Eye Enterprises Ltd as soon as the three-
       year period ended. The judge's verdict after hearing evidence
       and examining documents during the six days' hearing ruled
       against this; and he made an order against Keegan for an
       account and against Keegan and Swales for damages to be
       assessed (*Keegan v Public Eye Enterprises Ltd* (by original
       action) and (by counterclaim) *Public Eye Enterprises Ltd v
       Keegan and Swales* (1984) CAT No 84:575; (1982) Times, 28
       October; Yorkshire Post, 21 October 1982).

The uninitiated may be assisted to know that Sir Patrick Hastings, the
leading advocate with Norman Birkett during the years between the
two World Wars, and afterwards for a period, used to say: There is a
bull point in every case. One of his regular junior counsel, Theo
Matthew, immortalised the profession in his classic *Forensic Fables*,
under the pseudonym 'O', with a moral at end of each Fable. The
moral which is to be extracted from the *Keegan* case is an addition to

the CCPR – David Way contract check list. Read and remember what has been signed; and do not omit to check it when a row erupts about it.

Annexed to the page in the CCPR Howell Report on which that check list appears is a comment under the heading Integrity of Sport. The paragraph records,

'Throughout this Report, one main area of concern is the preservation of the integrity of sport. The fears voiced by Victor Head (author of *Sponsorship: The newest marketing skill*: cited in Chapter 2 'Growth of Sponsorship') that "sport could soon be run for the benefit of the promoting company and not primarily in the interests of sport itself" are understood by the Committee.'

On the other hand, promoting and sponsoring companies are in a powerful position to benefit sport when sport fails to benefit and protect itself. David Miller in *The Times* on the opening day of the new Barclays League football season wrote on 15 August 1987,

'I wish that Barclays, with their vested interest, would have conditional clauses written into the prize money benefits which penalise bad behaviour on and off the field.'

Perhaps one day they and others will, and thus steer sport into a foul-free fund dimension once more. Analogous to the well-known off-field legal concept applied often to easement, negligence and nuisance: the sponsorship categories are never closed. Alongside its phenomenal growth the Sports Council established in 1982 a Sports Sponsorship Advisory Service, with the services of a consultant, Mr Derek Etherington; and in November 1985 the CCPR implemented one of the 73 Recommendations of the Howell Report, to

'encourage the establishment of an Association of Commercial Sponsors of Sport in order to further the interest of sport itself and sponsoring companies.'

Under the presidency of HRH the Duke of Edinburgh the Institute of Sports Sponsorship was launched by the Central Council of Physical Recreation in 1982. Its guide published in 1989 under the title of *The Search for Sports Sponsorship* covered in general terms what are particularised in the 75 specimen precedents contained in the two volumes of Fosbrook and Laing (supra at page 340 above), ranging from agency, via exclusivity to the video and non-theatrical market. One developing area not covered by either is what has become known as Ambush Marketing. This is the trespassing and hijacking of existing sponsored rights without authority, ie a classic example being purported use of the Olympic Games symbol licensed to users whose exclusivity is infringed by copying of it.

Licensing

The licensing of intellectual property rights in connection with sport and sporting events is becoming an ever more popular phenomenon. Copyright, logos, patents and trade marks are licensed to persons or organisations who wish to exploit a name, reputation, event or personality and thus, the merchandising of national and international sports events, emblems and mascots and personalities is now the norm for many major sporting events. Merchandisers may take licences of these emblems or mascots and put them on their products so that the product may be associated with the particular event.

For example the Barcelona Olympics produced the mascot 'Cobi' based on a Catalan mountain dog. More than 1,200 products were licensed with this symbol. The international Olympic rings are also licensed for commercial exploitation on a grand scale. The governing body of European football has an emblem for each of its events and a mascot 'Bernie' which is available for merchandising purposes. These are just three examples of many which illustrate the extent of sports licensing.

As Iain C Baillie explains in the Introduction to *Licensing – A Practical Guide for the Businessman* under the heading

'**What is licensing**'
Licensing is a branch of the law of contracts. The contract is a specific form of agreement and strictly speaking embodies a licence; ie permission from an owner of a right to another to use part of that right. The other side of the contract is the obligation assumed by the receiver of the permission (ie the licensee) in return for the permission.
... it is the contract which defines the obligation of the parties. The "right" backs up the contract and can be used separately for enforcement if there is a breach. The "weaker" the right the weaker the contract and its back-up enforcement.
As in most areas of the law, licensing has no exact boundaries but a useful definition is a revocable right to do or secure that which you otherwise cannot do or secure.'

Together with those formal and structured developments, that growth is evidenced by the in-depth studies which have emerged during the two decades since England's success in the 1966 World Cup. Without claiming the list to be exhaustive, the following may assist readers wishing further guidance.

1 1966 Peter R Hunt MCAM, FIPR   *Public Relations Aspects of Sponsoring Sport*
2 1972 The Sports Council   *An Inquiry into Sponsorship*

3	1981 HM Treasury Memorandum (of evidence to House of Commons Committee)	Taxation in the Context of Private Sponsorship and of Gifts of Art Objects to Public and Private Institutions
4	1981 *Economist* Intelligence Unit Ltd: Jean Simkins	Sponsorship 1980/81
5	1983 The Central Council of Physical Recreation	*The Howell Report*
6	1984 Stephen Townley and Edward Grayson	*Sponsorship of Sport, Arts and Leisure: Law, Tax and Business Relationships*
7	1987 Iain C Baillie	*Licensing; A Practical Guide for the Businessman*
8	1988 Victor Head	*Successful sponsorship*
9	1989 The Central Council of Physical Recreation	The Search for Sports Sponsorship
10	1989 Deborah Fosbrook and Adrian C Laing	*Vol 1 The Media Contracts Handbook*
11	1990 Deborah Fosbrook and Adrian C Laing	*Vol 2 The Media Contracts Handbook*

5 SPONSORED TAX LAWS

Introduction

The developing nature of this area means that conflicts of attitudes will inevitably arise. Thus the valuable EIU *Special Report on Sponsorship 1980/81* claims

'Sponsorship is not the same thing as advertising. Although for some companies sponsorship expenditure comes out of the same budget as advertising, it is important to be aware of the division of the two.'

Irrespective of that division in economic or marketing circles, so far as the Inland Revenue is concerned, the equally valuable HM Treasury Memorandum of Evidence to the House of Commons Education, Science and Arts Committee identified for allowable tax deductible expense explains:

'in computing business profits for tax purposes...the business purpose – generally advertising – must be the sole purpose for which the purpose is made.'

Ordinarily these issues would fall into the next chapter, Chapter 14, 'No fine on fun'. However, since this particular aspect of fiscal policy and practice commanded the specific attention of the Treasury-Revenue evidence to the House of Commons Committee with an emphasis on private sponsorship, it is convenient to conclude this chapter with an awareness of the authoritative guidance given from such a source.

6 SPONSORED TAX LAWS

Taxation in the Context of Private Sponsorship and of Gifts of Art Objects to Public and Private Institutions is the title of a joint HM Treasury – Inland Revenue Memorandum comprising of documentary evidence submitted during 1981 to a relatively little-known but crucially important House of Commons Education, Science and Arts Committee on the Public and Private Funding of the Arts (Session 1980–81 (1982) HC 49–11 at pp 291–292). It did not identify Sport in any way at all; but the taxation principles which it summarised clearly for that Committee's guidance are equally applicable to sport.

The same may be said of the evidence given to the Committee by a former Chairman of the Arts Council, Lord Goodman, who was also Chairman of the Association of Business Sponsorship and the Arts (ABSA), and, also, of the statement made by the then Norman St John Stevas MP, a former Minister for the Arts during an interview with Victor Head, the author of *Sponsorship: The newest marketing skill*, both during 1981. The questions posed an issue which is relevant equally to both spheres, and so, too, are the answers (today as correct as they were when given in 1981).

[*Question*]	[*Answer*]
Much heat is generated over the question of changes in tax laws to encourage more sponsorship. Do you feel that perhaps not enough emphasis is placed on the fact that sponsorship expenditure can be regarded as a form of advertising promotion and so qualify for tax exemption in the appropriate way (eg 52% for companies paying corporate tax)?	Since it took office in 1979, the Government has reduced the minimum qualifying period for covenanted payments to charities from over six years to over three years and introduced tax relief on the higher rates of income tax in respect of covenanted payments by individuals up to an annual ceiling of £3,000. [NB Further increased to £5,000 from 6 April 1983 in Finance Act 1983, s 23 (2)]. These concessions were designed to ease the position for donations, and the arts benefit considerably as most arts organisations are registered charities. There are signs that they are not widely enough known and used.

That part of the answer that 'most arts organisations are registered charities' creates a prima facie differential from sport, save and except that the concluding sentence is equally applicable to sport, ie 'There are signs that they are not widely enough known and used.' For whereas sport per se is not yet recognised as a valid charitable concept, sport qua education has qualified charitably for over seventy years without full advantage ever having been taken of this position, either intellectually or practically (see Chapter 1 'Genesis', Chapter 2, 'Under starter's orders').

The former Minister, as Mr Norman St John Stevas, concluded thus:

> [*Answer*] (concluded)
> 'You mention the provisions under section 130 of the Incomes and Corporation Taxes Act 1970 (now section 74 of the Income Tax and Corporation Taxes Act 1988) whereby *revenue expenditure* [NB author's emphasis] incurred "wholly and exclusively" for the purposes of a trade can be offset against tax. The Inland Revenue has instructed its Inspectors to advise companies at the outset whether sponsorship deals should qualify in this way, so there is now every opportunity for companies to frame their proposals so as to get the maximum tax relief. I hope businesses are aware of this concession by the Inland Revenue.'

Identical advice was tendered by Lord Goodman in his own evidence testified at about the same time in 1981 to the House of Commons Education, Science and Arts Committee which was cited by the author in the chapter entitled 'Tax, VAT, Hope and Charity' in *Sponsorship of Sport, Arts and Leisure: Law, Tax and Business Relationships* [1984] by Stephen Townley and Edward Grayson at page 261. In the present context, and with words which are equally applicable to sports sponsorship, Lord Goodman told the Committee (HC 49–11, pp 291–292 at para 742) inter alia.

'There is some recognition needed of the Inland Revenue. There is a lot of discussion about whether there should be more generous terms made available for subsidies to the arts...In fact, taxation relief for companies is pretty adequate. You can get taxation relief for any activity that bears a relationship to what you are doing. You can get taxation relief from any payment under a covenant. So it is a thin excuse for people to say there is no tax relief.

There is one very important matter that the head of the Inland Revenue made. He agreed they would notify all their Inspectors of Taxes to tell companies in advance if they inquired whether a particular contribution would be tax deductible or not. I do not think that is sufficiently generally known. If a company has any doubt, therefore, Somerset House has instructed the Inspectors of Taxes that they should advise whether that doubt is real or not.'

'Company' in that context, of course, is interchangeable with any other identifiable legal persona. Clubs which are legally identifiable as unincorporated associations and known technically and realistically only through their members are nevertheless trapped within the statutory definition of 'company' for all tax purposes. Indeed, although at common law, in equity, and under property legislation they hold land only through trustees, for direct tax purposes, the club itself as an unincorporated association is the chargeable person (*Worthing Rugby Football Club Trustees v IRC* [1985] STC 186; *Carlisle & Silloth Golf Club v Smith* [1913] 21 CB 75).

With this crucial caveat, and against the background of the authoritative sources cited above, the joint HM Treasury-Inland Revenue Memorandum takes on an almost familiar ring. Under the subheading of Evidence to the House of Commons Education, Science and Arts Committee of Note by H M Treasury the Memorandum begins with an explanation of how

'It sets out the position on sponsorship and gifts under present taxation arrangements and has been prepared in conjunction with the Inland Revenue'.

Summarised here is the sequence of published headings:

Private sponsorship

(i) Covenanted payments: which bring into operation the whole range of charity law.
(ii) Business expenses: the conventional and traditional legitimate allowances of a revenue (as distinct from capital) nature

Gifts (which are more usual in the Arts than the Sports scene), ie
CTT (Capital Transfer Tax)
CGT (Capital Gains Tax)

When the Memorandum expands into details, the sub-heading *Business expenses* inevitably develops Mr Norman St John Stevas' well-known 'wholly and exclusively' text in the following way, with words which are equally applicable to sponsored sport:

'A sponsorship payment will normally be a deductible expense in computing business profits for tax purposes if it is of a revenue nature (ie not a capital payment) and is incurred wholly and exclusively for the purpose of trade. The first condition means that no deduction is allowable for any lump sum donation towards, for example, the building or modernisation of a theatre, or the purchase of a work of art. The second condition means that the business purpose – generally advertising – must be the sole purpose for which the payment is made. The expenditure will not be admissible if it is incurred for a dual purpose – eg both promoting a business and promoting a charitable or benevolent object.'

The contrast between revenue and capital payments is of particular significance and importance in the sporting world, with its special developing problems under the volatile climate of safety of sports ground proposals following from the Interim and Final Reports of Mr Justice Popplewell and Lord Justice Taylor and their respective Inquiries into Crowd Safety and Control at Sports Grounds. See Chapter 5, 'Public protection', pp 133–139.

Neither the Inquiry nor its reports was concerned directly with financial methods for implementing its Recommendations. Sport's own dramatic tragedies during 1985 which culminated in the fatalities at Bradford and Birmingham, in England, and later at Brussels, highlighted the Safety of Sports Grounds Act 1975 which followed the Ibrox Stadium, Glasgow, deaths in 1971, ten years before the Committee's Report in 1981. It also exposes the limitations built in to that 'first condition [in the Treasury – Revenue Memorandum] ... that no deduction is allowable for any lump sum donation towards, for example, the building or modernisation of a theatre.'

Successive Finance Acts have been prepared to treat for *capital* allowance purposes certain expenditure, on buildings, as being plant (unless a deduction can be made elsewhere) to which safety certificates apply under the sports ground safety legislation (see here the retrospective effects of section 40 of the Finance Act 1978, upon section 49 of the Finance (No 2) Act 1975) and ultimately section 119 of the Finance Act 1989 now all consolidated with the Capital Allowances Act 1990, 55, 69, 70, following recommendations in the *Final Hillsborough Taylor Report* paragraph 115 [cm 962, January 1990].

The national awareness of the need for some form of financial assistance to modernise antiquated sports stadia also merits assessing how far the debatable decision of the Burnley Football Club's grandstand tax disallowance should be re-argued. Mr Justice Vinelott's different interpretation of crucial *sporting evidence* overruled the factual findings of the distinguished Special Commissioners. Presided over by the late H H Monroe QC, together with his successor, Mr

R H Widdows, they held on the evidence before them that the then new building structured before the 1975 safety legislation did qualify for a repair allowance, although it was disallowed under the head of plant. (See *Brown v Burnley Football and Athlete Co Ltd* [1980] 3 All ER 244, [1980] STIC 424. and also *Tax 'Anomaly'*: para 115, page 19 *Final Hillsborough Taylor Report* (supra)).

The judge disagreed with their actual findings. This was inconsistent with the recent re-emphasis by the House of Lords in *Cole Brothers v Phillips* ([1982] STC 301) that the crucial importance of commissioners' conclusions on admissible evidence will not be overturned lightly. The detailed care with which the experienced Special Commissioners assessed the evidence relating to the Bob Lord stand's location within the famous Turf Moor ground at Burnley emerges from the law reports and raises the query why the club did not adapt the precedent from the game's ruling body at Lancaster Gate for its House of Lords charity appeal to seek financial assistance from the Sports Council and the CCPR, and challenge the divergence of judicial opinion at least in the Court of Appeal.

The Howell Report (p 39) stressed

> 'It is the responsibility of sports organisations to limit tax liabilities in respect of sponsorship income ... They must always obtain proper professional advice concerning taxation.'

So, too, should sponsors and potential sponsors. In particular the borderline between business and entertainment issues, which is easily blurred and therefore capable of entering the disallowed areas under traditional tax law and practice, needs only to be mentioned for demanding specialised and practical professional advice. A classic and well-reported trap is the sponsor which attempts to indulge in racehorse ownership under sponsorship colour. Recreation is disallowed; legitimate advertising accepted. Accordingly, the Jockey Club changed the Rules of Racing to permit company ownership, and thereby sponsorship, through the advertising of horses in training and thus complement the long-standing sponsorship of famous races. How many people outside the racing fraternity know that the celebrated European Champion, Moorstyle, before it was retired to the National Stud at Newmarket, was sponsored by a Yorkshire-based furniture company, whose fortunes were not hindered by the local and international success of its four-legged investment?

7 CHARITY

No less in need of specialist advice is the lamentable story of sport's neglect of its opportunities to take full advantage of the manner in which sport as an education concept has been open to development for over seventy years. In 1976 the valuable *Report of the Goodman Committee*, published by the National Council of Social Service on *Charity Law and Voluntary Organisations*, recommended, inter alia, that

'the encouragement of sport and recreation should be recognised as an independent charitable object provided the necessary element of altruism and benefit to a sufficient section of the community are present. In so far as the existing law does not make this clear it should be amended.'

At the time when these thoughts were formulated the FA Youth Trust Deed case was en route from Mr Justice Walton via the Court of Appeal to the House of Lords. We know now from earlier citations in this text how the concept of an educational sporting charitable trust confirmed Mr Justice Eve's landmark decision in *Re Marriette* ([1915] 2 CH 284), where he held that a gift for providing squash courts in an Aldenham School was charitable on the ground that sport was part of the curriculum of such an establishment.

When the joint Treasury – Revenue Memorandum on Arts Sponsorship explained at the outset of its explanation that

'A payment in sponsorship of the arts may qualify for tax relief in one of two ways,'

it prefaced the Business expenses category with Covenanted payments. The opening sentence under that latter heading proclaimed

'Many of the bodies which promote activities in the field of the arts are established charities.'

In the FA Youth Trust Deed decision of the House of Lords (*IRC v McMullen* [1981] AC 1 at 17), Lord Hailsham of St Marylebone explained,

'I do not think that the courts have as yet explored the extent to which elements of organisation, instruction, or the disciplined inculcation of information, instruction or skill may limit the whole concept of education. I believe that in some ways it will prove more extensive, in others more restrictive than has been thought hitherto.'

For 'courts' should be read Sport and the Law together. Amateur administrators and professional lawyers have been jointly guilty of the omission inferred by the Lord Chancellor, who, as Chapters 1 and 4 explain, when Minister for Science and Education in 1962 under Mr Macmillan's premiership, created the role of a Minister with special responsibility for Sport. Indeed, so too was the House of Lords itself which resisted the temptation to tackle the Recreational Charities Act 1958 during its own deliberations because of inadequate evidence in the FA Youth Trust case. This had to await *Guild v IRC* [1992] 2 All ER 10. On that occasion an offer to the House of Lords from the Irween House of the Court of Session duly resulted in the 'interests of social welfare' criteria contained in s 1 (1) [of the 1958 Act] being upheld after a bequest 'to be used in connection with the Sports Centre [then] in North Berwick' to include also a concept of 'some similar purpose in connection with sport'. Bearing in mind the problems for defining sport, as the author wrote in the *New Law Journal* 15 January 1993 'whenever this legal googly will bowl the courts, as some day it will, watch this space for another potential entrant to the House of Lords Sport and Law lottery'.

The establishment of charitable status would have four clear advantages for any sporting organisation, namely,

(1)   Statutory exemption from most forms of direct taxation.

(2)   Covenanted payments which, as the joint Treasury – Revenue Memorandum explained, enables a sponsored recipient to obtain repayment of the tax deducted by the Inland Revenue from a sponsoring company.

(3)   Mandatory 80 per cent rate relief under the Local Government Finance Act 1988, 547, for sporting organisations registered with the Charity Commissioners.

(4)   Discretionary 100 per cent rate relief for non-registered sporting organisations effectively executing charitable functions, such as evening and weekend sporting education facilities, to schools whose playing fields and gymnasia are closed outside normal school hours.

The practical methods of achieving these desiderata are spelt out more emphatically in Chapter 14, 'No fine on fun'; but it is noteworthy at this stage to explain that the green light for progress was shone for sport by Mr Charles Weston, the Charity Commissioner who was responsible for the Trust Deed's registration in 1972, at a CCPR seminar organised after the House of Lords FA Youth Trust decision. He advised the hiving-off process, whereby a section of a club or organisation can be separated from its main body administratively for specific educational purposes. The FA's own school at the National Sports Centre at Lilleshall in Shropshire, sponsored by General Motors, is a classic illustration. The Midland Bank sponsorship of the Metropolitan Police five-a-side youth soccer tournament is another; and the Lloyds Bank Masters Chess Tournament is on all fours with Vaisey's judgment in *Re Dupree's Will Trusts* ([1945] Ch

16) that a chess tournament for young people in Portsmouth was ideally educational. As the author has explained at the end of his contribution to the British Association for Sport and the Law's *Sport and the Law* journal for November 1993 (p 90) on the *Guild Case*, a Home Office publication entitled *Voluntary Action* has thrown doubt or at least begun a debate on the future existence of current charity structure and the law.

8 VAT AND SPONSORSHIP GENERALLY

Value Added Tax replaced Entertainment Tax and Selective Employment Tax as an administrative headache for British sport, as well as the remainder of the leisure industry, resulting from Britain's entry into the Common Market under the European Communities Act 1972. For sponsorship purposes it applies to those services supplied by businesses which meet the registrable turnover limits established at the time of writing at £35,000. The business element at the heart of sponsorship inevitably creates a potential taxable supply.

The absence of that key business factor destroys the need for registration within the VAT tax band. England's High Court confirmed this when it upheld an appeal to a VAT tribunal by a country landowner against a Customs and Excise assessment in respect of shooting rights to friends and relatives for a fee. A supply of services was admittedly provided; but was it for a business? The Customs and Excise commissioners said it was. The documentary and oral evidence tendered by the landowner and his accountants satisfied the tribunal and the High Court that no advertisement or other commercial insignia existed (*Customs and Excise Commissioners v Lord Fisher* [1981] 2 All ER 1). The position of Sporting Rights generally is now regulated by H M Customs and Excise leaflet No 742/2/92.

When the business element exists, and the statutory ceiling of £35,000 is reached, then sporting organisations carried on commercially charge VAT at the standard rate of 17.5 per cent on taxable supplies; and generally they can deduct any VAT charged on supplies to them, except on business entertainment.

9 VAT AND SPORT GENERALLY

The Aston Villa specimen sponsorship contract reproduced above includes VAT in its charges for services supplied; and the developing dimension of this new kind of tax alien to traditional Anglo-Saxon commercial and legal sources demands a mixture of specialist legal and accountancy services at every level of activity. Three further illustrations demonstrate this from the standpoint of organisation or administration, sporting competition rules, and the EEC itself.

1 *Organisation or administration*
Sport's special constitutional structure should always be recognised and considered. The Watchet Bowling Club in Somerset was assessed by the customs authorities liable for registration. They ignored the sporting and accounting realities that two separate sections existed affiliated to the two national bodies, indoors and general: the English *Indoor* Bowling Association (EIBA) and the English Bowling Association (EBA). The supplies of each unit individually was below the registrable VAT threshold, although together they qualified within it. The VAT Tribunal confirmed that neither was registrable as a taxable person (*AG Hayhoe (on behalf of Watchet Bowling Club and Watchet Indoor Bowling Club) v Customs and Excise Commissioners*, VAT Tribunal ref LON/80/341, 13 January 1981).

2 *Sporting competition rules*
The Union of European Football Associations (UEFA) regulations mandatorily required competing clubs and associations to reciprocate hospitality during competitive fixtures. Thus they were upheld by the Scottish Court of Session and a London VAT Tribunal respectively as recoverable input tax which the customs authorities had disallowed for the Celtic Club and the Football Association (*Celtic Football & Athletic Co Ltd v Customs & Excise Commissioners* [1983] STC 420; *Football Association Ltd v Customs & Excise Commissioners* London VAT Tribunal/83/484).

3 *The EEC*
A hotel sale to a North Wales fishing club was exempt from VAT. The Tribunal applied a little known paragraph (h) under Article 13 of the Sixth EEC Council directive concerning land which had not been built on, in that case a river bed and adjoining land comprising supply of a fishery and fishing rights (*Parkinson v Customs & Excise Commissioners* (1985) Times, 8 November).

In an authoritative manner comparable to the joint Treasury – Revenue Memorandum, HM Customs & Excise Commissioners published a VAT Leaflet, No 701/41/90. It contained specific guidance for Sponsorship Rights in what was formerly No 701/5/81, the leaflet entitled *An Annex*. Its concentrated layout and style of language have been deliberately rearranged and divided into subparagraphs here (with added emphasis) for easier readability as follows:

'The tax value for the *supply* of sponsorship *rights* includes not only

(1) the money received from the sponsor, but also

    (2)   (i)   (a) any payments made by the sponsor
                  (b) to third parties
                  (c) in respect of the expenses
                  (d) of staging a competition or event
    and   (ii)   (a) the value of any prizes
                  (b) given to the team competitions
                  (c) taking part
                  (d) under the terms of the sponsorship agreement.'

Thus, all and each of these elements has to be calculated, assessed and taken into account by all parties to a sporting sponsorship agreement if appropriate to the particular sponsorship transaction. Comprehensive analysis here can never cover all contingencies, just as no medical textbook can provide for every prognosis. Awareness of potentialities is the most realistic target which can be contemplated.

Indeed, that awareness at the time of writing in the late summer of 1993 becomes more acute each day with the Parliamentary Question and Answer as recorded in Hansard for 22 July 1993 relating to 'the liability to VAT of amateur sports and cultural activities in the public sector' from Mr Roger Gale MP (North Thanet).

> *Treasury*
> C – North Thanet
> 439 *Mr Roger Gale*
> 'To ask Mr Chancellor of the Exchequer, what plans he has to change the liability to VAT of amateur sports and cultural activities in the public sector'.
> *Sir John Cope*
> 'I am discussing with my Rt Hon Friend the Secretary of State for National Heritage a VAT exemption for the supply of certain services by non-profit making organisations and local authorities to persons who take part in sport or physical education. This would be a limited exemption to be introduced by Treasury Order. The precise scope of the exemption would be determined after we have discussed with the representative sports bodies the services and sports to be included.
> We shall also be holding discussions with a view to examining the case for exempting certain cultural services and associated goods supplied by public authorities.'

In due course publication of the Value Added Tax (Sport, Physical Education and Fund Raising Events) Order 1994 was laid before Parliament and came into effect from 1 April, 1994 as SI 1994/68. Its general significance is considered in Appendix 12.

10 CONCLUSIONS

It is appropriate that the last word on this technical but nevertheless crucially important area of sports sponsorship within the framework of Sport and the Law should come from the Howell Report. In the section dealing with tax implication, Chapter Seven under the heading of 7.8 *Corporation Tax* it states (p 41):

> 'Any sporting body which at the end of an accounting period has a liability for the payment of corporation tax may well question whether their affairs have been ordered to their best advantage ... We believe this approach to be more realistic to this problem than expectation of any early government policy to provide special exemption for sport or its sponsors.'

Such pessimism may now soon be overtaken by events in motion to occur after publication. In substance it is not far removed from Lord Goodman's evidence to the House of Commons Education, Science and Arts Committee (at page 361, supra). Not for the first time the two worlds merge on common ground for the community's cultural benefit.

Chapter 14

No fine on fun
(Changing laws for sport beneficially and charitably)

1 INTRODUCTION

No Fine on Fun: The Comical History of the Entertainment Duty (1957) was the title of a polemical publication from Sir Alan Herbert, barrister, author, one-time MP, librettist, humourist, satirist and lone campaigner. Lawyers and laymen still admire his many *Misleading Cases* and his *Uncommon Law*. Laymen and lawyers still enjoy his partnerships with Vivian Ellis and their melodies from *Bless the Bride* and *The Water Gypsies*.

No Fine on Fun crystallised and climaxed his sustained attacks upon the Entertainment Duty imposed by Parliament on a target area built-in to its title imposed as a temporary pretext as a patriotic First World War contribution from all amusements during 1916. Alan Herbert's campaign destroyed it.

Today sport has been replaced with equally crippling fiscal burdens.

Sir Denis Follows died in 1983. Before then, in Sir Alan Herbert's tradition, he left this message with that Philip Noel-Baker Memorial address at Loughborough College in March of that year, part of which has already been cited in Chapter 2, 'Progressive perspective' *supra* at p 31:

'For years I have been shouting from the roof tops against the iniquitous taxation system of this country so far as sport is concerned. When I tell you [1983] that of the £888,000 raised by the British Olympic Association in 1980 to send out teams to the Olympic Games, to maintain the sporting prestige of this country, we paid £176,000 in tax, you can understand my indignation and concern. Any sports organisation in this country which is a non-profit distributing body should be relieved of all forms of taxation of the revenue it raises; and for good measure no sports body should be required to pay 15 per cent VAT on the admission charges to sports gatherings.

In 1957 [the year of *No Fine on Fun*] a Conservative administration abolished entertainment tax because the tax was killing sport and entertainment. How much more vital is it in 1983 that entertainment tax in the guise of VAT should be taken off the back of sport? We in sport have long argued that if the Government did not take so much out of us

371

in taxation we should not be crying out for so much to put back through the Sports Council and local government.'

Belatedly, after a sustained CCPR and National Playing Field Association campaign, VAT for non-profit-making Sport, Physical Education and Fund-Raising Events has been alleviated as from 1 April, 1994 with retrospective effect as explained earlier in Chapter 13, 'Sponsored gentless and players' at p 369 and in Appendix 12.

Yet other fiscal burdens still remain and the position of local authorities in relation to this VAT re funding still awaits clarification at the time of going to press.

Ten years after Fallows' plea as reported by Robert Hardman in *The Daily Telegraph* for 15 September 1993

'At yesterday's annual general meeting of the British Olympic Association, the treasurer reported a respectable pre-tax 1992 profit of almost £1.3 million. However, exactly half of that must go to the Treasury in corporation tax.

The BOA, unlike their profligate big brother, the International Olympic Committee, do not throw money around. Their annual salary bill is the same as one day's worth of IOC self-indulgence. They prop up the starry-eyed ambitions of all those unknowns we only hear about once every four years and sink much of their money into grass roots improvements (£700,000 on their medical trust last year, for example).

Mr Major has shown himself willing to make much larger tax concessions for racing and football in previous Budgets – and he will grandly wave a cheque for £75 million, payable to Manchester, in front of the IOC members at Monaco. So why not give a relatively inexpensive boost to a body who represents almost every sport in the land by awarding the BOA some sort of tax exemption?

I am not suggesting the sort of spending spree which goes on abroad– £500 per month to the Olympic athlete in Germany, $15,000 to every gold medallist in America etc. But a £640,000 tax break for the BOA would be worth considering, not least because it might generate even more in donations. People are more inclined to give to an organisation which is not, in turn, going to pass on large sums to the taxman'.

In the same spirit as already cited earlier in these pages in a different context at page 255 in Chapter 9, Peter Lawson, the Secretary of Britain's Central Council of Physical Recreation, at an international Symposium on Sport and the Law at Monaco in early 1991, organised by the International Athletic Foundation, explained

'though in Britain we have mixed fortunes in our sports events and competitions, there is one league that we have consistently headed for many years. It is called the European Sports Taxation League. We are probably the hardest hit sporting nation in Europe and we have not bothered to extend our researches beyond Europe because of the bad news we receive so close at home. The fact of the matter is that sport is very, very big business world-wide. Certainly it is very, very big business in the United Kingdom. My government loves sport. They absolutely are delighted with it, but not for the reasons the average sports lover would commend. It is because sport through one form or another of taxation produces for the Chancellor of the Exchequer each year £2.5 billion. Now that is all forms of taxation including of course, and one must be fair here, a legitimate and proper rake-off from the betting and gambling that goes on in sports-related competitions, but it is a massive sum of money.'

Furthermore, notwithstanding that the world of sport has to compete with the arts for government largesse, and that plums can be extracted from the Treasury pie, complete exemption from financial liabilities cannot or would not be claimed by even the most optimistic advocate for sport in the 1990s. What sport does demand is special treatment professionally at every level in which it impinges on the wider boundaries of society, medicine, physical education and not least of all taxation.

Thus, it was announced in July 1993, that following CCPR discussions with Government Ministers and H M Customs and Excise Officials, the Treasury explained its intention to introduce a limited exemption for supplies of services to amateur sports clubs and cultural activities in the public sector and in the House of Commons on 22 July the Paymaster-General, Sir John Cope, stated in reply to a Parliamentary question,

'I am discussing with my Rt Hon Friend the Secretary of State for National Heritage a VAT exemption for the supply of certain services by non-profit-making organisations and local authorities to persons who take part in sport or physical education. This would be a limited exemption to be introduced by Treasury Order. The precise scope of the exemption would be determined after we have discussed with the representative sports bodies the services and sports to be included. We shall also be holding discussions with a view to examining the case for exempting certain cultural services and associated goods supplied by public authorities.'

Those discussions took place during mid-September 1993 and the consequences were not publicised and implemented to take effect until after 1 April, 1994 as explained at page 369 above. Among them will be repayments of overpaid VAT since 1 January, 1990 when Customs and Excise levied tax in breach of EC Directives. These require services closely linked to non-profit-making sport to be exempt from VAT when provided by non-profit-making organisations or local authorities. The UK Customs and Excise and Treasury requirements which require many such services to be taxed were thereby out of line with the EEC Directive explained in Appendix 12. The mechanics of monies to be repaid may require return to the persons against whom the demand was levied before any organisation concerned may consider retention for itself.

One of the key factors is that this exemption will extend only to relevant income generated by non-profit-making bodies which inevitably includes clubs or organisations where any surplus income is ploughed back for the benefit of the members. The detailed change in the VAT structure and back payments will be implemented by Treasury Order after these pages have appeared or are being prepared for publication and it may be anticipated that many hours and days in negotiations and consultation will be spent in arriving at conclusions which inevitably will vary between differing categories of taxpayers potentially affected by these innovations.

As these pages should have shown already, sport is a very special social animal; and although the needs of differing individual and corporate personalities require no different taxation and legal services from those outside the sporting world, the variations within this area require recognition professionally.

Thus, a year before the manuscript for the first edition was completed in October 1987 Richard Baldwin, B Comm, FCA, ARII, one of the co-authors with Richard Harvey ACA of *Tax and Financial Planning for Sportsmen and Entertainers* (1987), at a CCPR Taxation and Sport Seminar held in London on 6 November 1986 at the Queen Elizabeth II Conference Centre stated

> 'I recently reviewed the audited accounts of six governing bodies and these appeared to indicate that all six were treated slightly differently from a corporation tax viewpoint.'

Nearly seven years later, again, Richard Baldwin was associated with a Report from his specialist football industry accountant firm, Touche Ross, entitled 'The Taxman Cometh! The importance of PAYE to football clubs.' *The Guardian* for 26 July 1993 as reported by Don Atkinson explained

> 'An Inland Revenue crackdown is set to close dozens of football clubs unless they put their tax affairs in order, Touche Ross, the accountancy firm, has warned';

and he concluded by citing

> Richard Baldwin, a Touche partner said:
> 'Not only do clubs have to collect and account for PAYE and National Insurance on payments to employees, they also have to complete the paperwork required by the Revenue.
>
> This is often a minefield for staff who may not have the time or expertise.
>
> In particular, allowances and expenses should be supported by documentary proof, he said.'

Significantly this corroborates what a decade earlier the then Rt Hon Denis (now Lord) Howell MP told the CCPR Annual Conference at Bournemouth on 25 November 1983 when questioned during a public discussion about financial aspects of his own CCPR Committee of Enquiry into Sports Sponsorship. He explained spontaneously

'I remember going to see the Financial Secretary to the Treasury to tell him that one sports body was paying far too much corporation tax to the Government. Corporation tax is paid on trading and the reason you have to pay it is that if you do not pay it, it is unfair to the trader's fellow competitors. The Financial Secretary to the Treasury happened to be a first class accountant in private life and he told me that if any sports body pays corporation tax it obviously needs better professional advice.'

To be fully effective such advice must harmonise legal and accountancy disciplines, in the manner that surgery needs skilled anaesthetic assistance if patients are to be assured of safe surgical treatment.

Accordingly, the purpose of this chapter within the scope of this particular book's comprehensive range can be only to highlight those areas for which professional experiences, instructions and observations have demonstrated since the first edition was published in January 1988, a need for general attention and comment. Any specific requirements not covered by such a general approach would merit that 'better professional advice' recommended to Lord Howell.

2 TAXATION PRACTICE GENERALLY

Effective practice and operation of the tax law for the public generally and the sporting world particularly demands two levels of awareness whether acting personally or representatively through a governing body or professional trade union or association. One is the traditional barrister-solicitor-accountant expertise. The other is knowledge of attitudes adopted by an ever-increasing army of tax and VAT commissioners and inspectors and charity commissioners, all battling for or against the taxpayer in the middle. This leads on accordingly to one oft-forgotten reality which cannot be ignored, whether in sporting or wider social spheres.

As a branch of law, taxation affects everyone journeying from the cradle to the grave, and even there, too (see *Clore Estate* litigation: *Stype Investments v IRC* [1984] STC 609: [1985]STC 394). Only traffic laws, touching pedestrians as well as vehicle users, equal this. Nevertheless, even this similarity is differentiated by one crucial and fundamental operation. Symbolically for sport and the law it has been summarised graphically by the future Master of the Rolls, Sir John Donaldson, as Lord Justice Donaldson, before he succeeded Lord Denning, when he said in *IRC v Garvin* [1980] STC 296 at 313:

> 'There is a certain fascination in being one of the referees of a match between a well-advised taxpayer and the equally well-advised Commissioners of Inland Revenue, conducted under the rules which govern tax avoidance. These rules are complex, the moves are sophisticated and the stakes are high.'

Sadly, but realistically, this equation can concern only a litigation Superleague. The available services are not always 'equally advised'. Indeed, more often than not the balance between the payer and the Revenue is decidedly unequal at the level where fairness is required most urgently, ie at the lowest litigiously contentious, but, for the practitioner, most significant level: the General or Special Commissioners, where the hard factual evidence to which so much tax law is related must be adduced.

Thus, on the one hand, the United Kingdom courts have repeatedly refused to accept evidence on appeals to judges from tribunal levels not produced at the earliest possible Commissioner hearing. They also have repeatedly emphasised how findings of facts before Commissioners have to stand unaltered on appeal, unless there is no supporting evidence for them (*Cole Bros Ltd v Phillips* [1982] 55 TC 188). Yet no legal aid exists for any professional assistance of any kind at those levels to taxpayers, many of whom cannot afford representation of any description if they wish or need it. On the other hand, however, the House of Lords, since both Sir John Donaldson's sporting image in *IRC v Garvin* (supra) and the Cole Bros Ltd ruling, has berated the Revenue for not being represented professionally at that earliest possible level in *Reed v Nova Securities Ltd* (1984) STC 124. The House of Lords thus confirmed the principle applied by the Court of Appeal in J P R Williams libel action, when it rejected the *Daily Telegraph's* fresh evidence, available but not relied upon at the initial trial. For it attempted to use that evidence for seeking a retrial (which it obtained on the different ground of the judge's misdirection to the jury about the amateur rules of Rugby Union football), after Dr (now Mr) J P R Williams' libel damages award, as already explained in Chapter 6, 'Participation problems'. Evidence on appeal which could have been obtained with diligence at an earlier hearing is usually too late for use as a second bite at a cherry, even if it could tip the balance of judicial digestion for a verdict, on the principle that there must be an end to litigation.

Another illustration of a potential costs injustice is where the Football Association funded the initial stages of its Inland Revenue battle to confirm the Charity Commissioners' registration of its

Youth Trust Deed. The final round of appeals in the House of Lords was affordable only with support from the Sports Council and CCPR. Sport therefore does not differ from any other fiscal sphere whereby different circumstances demand differing levels of collective or individual advice and funding of a professional nature. The tax and VAT problems of sport and recreation are as diverse and varied as countries and individuals who all create separate and contrasting, although frequently overlapping, fiscal issues. Furthermore, the growth of international sporting competitions and prizes means that double taxation issues and separate taxations in different countries must be considered closely, with a further awareness of what Richard Baldwin's differentiates in treatment 'from a corporation tax viewpoint'. Throughout this chapter the reader is credited with the personal knowledge of the usual tax charges, ie

(1) Personal   Income Tax
                       Capital Gains Tax
                       Inheritance Tax
                       Rating Taxes
                       Value Added Tax

(2) Clubs   As above and also

(3) Companies   Corporation Tax

Accordingly, the structure of these pages will follow the pattern of chapters dealing with active action within sport, namely
Chapter 4, 'Parent, school and club partners';
Chapter 5, 'Public protection';
Chapter 6, 'Participation problems'.

3 PARENT, SCHOOL AND CLUB PARTNERS
(Chapter 4)

(1)   The bracketing of clubs with companies stems from the author's professional experiences, instructions and observations since the first edition manuscript was completed in October 1987. This is that notwithstanding the now 80-year-old and unchallenged precedent of *Carlisle and Silloth Golf Club v Smith* [1913] 3 KB 75, uncertainty still persists how, for fiscal purposes, the sources and existence of unincorporated associations are the artificial creation of statute within the definition of 'company' for the purpose of the Income and Corporation Taxes Act 1988 and Taxation of Charitable Gains Act 1992, and thereby accountable for corporation tax on any income or chargeable gains which may be obtained.

Any doubts or questions about the fact of an unincorporated association not having a separate legal entity (and being recognised in law only through its individual members or representatives) were dispelled in the network of various appeals involving the Worthing Rugby Football Club during the 1980s. The Club's unsuccessful appeal against a Development Land Tax Act ruling and the Revenue's successful appeal relating to capital gains re-affirmed the Carlisle Silloth Golf club principle that it is the *association* and *not* the *individual* members who are liable to tax, despite the fact that an unincorporated association does not have a separate identity. This position contrasts sharply with the potential personal liability in contract and tort as illustrated by the Blackburn Rovers collapsed grandstand case on *Brown v Lewis* (1896) 12 TLR 455 (*Carlisle and Silloth Golf Club v Smith* [1913] 3 KB 75 (income); *Worthing Rugby Football Club Trustees v IRC* [1985] 1 WLR 409 (capital gains); *Frampton v IRC* [1987] STC 273 (Development and Tax) Value Added Tax Act 1983, s 31 (3). An unincorporated association must still be represented by counsel and not a member before the courts (although not the commissioners) because it is not a litigant in person – *Animal Defence and Anti-Vivisection Society v IRC* (1950) 66 TLR (Pt 1) 1112.)

(2)   As already explained in Chapter 4, 'Parent, school and club partners', sections 47 (1) and (2) of the Local Government Finance Act provided for rate relief by local authorities when premises were linked to charity status, now as guided by the House of Lords in its two landmark decisions a decade apart from each other in 1981 and 1992. The FA Youth Trust case of *IRC v McMullan* [1981] AC 1 and the *North Berwick Sports Centre* decision in *Guild v IRC* [1992] 2 All ER 10 have respectively given bona fide claimants for charitable status with a sporting flavour an authentic foundation: the FA decision re-affirmed the then 65-year-old decision of *Re Mariette* [1915] 2 Ch 384 that physical education is as validly charitable as the teaching of Latin or Greek; and the *North Berwick* judgment extended the 'interests of social welfare' contained in section 1 (1) of the Recreational Charities Act when considering a bequest to 'be used in connection with the Sports Centre (then) in North Berwick' to include also a concept of 'some similar purpose in connection with sport'. How to define 'sport', as the author and others have questioned in these pages and in the *New Law Journal*, 15 January 1993, can yet await a House of Lords hat-trick on sporting charitable decisions.

(3)   For present purposes, however, a mandatory relief of 80 per cent of the rate levied on premises occupied by a charity wholly or

mainly used for charitable purposes can be obtained from the appropriate rating authority. It can also be granted a discretionary relief to 100 per cent for the first of the following three categories specified in section 47 (2) of the Local Government Finance Act 1988, namely

(i)   charities;

(ii) organisations not established or conducted for profit and whose main objects are charitable or are otherwise philanthropic or religious or concerned with education, social welfare, science, literature or the fine arts;

(iii) clubs, societies or other organisations not established or conducted for profit and whose premises are wholly or mainly used for the purposes of recreation.

At present politically, attempts to extend the mandatory relief area to all non-profit-making organisation have failed. Thus, during a House of Commons debate initiated by the then Mr Denis Howell, MP on Sports Facilities during late November 1991, the Labour Party spokesman Tom Pendry explained that Government sources had told him in respect of an earlier written answer

'about the total number of sports clubs that received rate relief in 1991, but what they refused to tell me – despite an explicit request on my written question, although I have since discovered the answer as a result of pressing other departments – is that the survey showed that 1,136 voluntary sports clubs applied for rate relief in 1991 under the present system but were denied.'

Subsequently, in the early summer of 1993 the CCPR Annual Report for 1991–92 recorded how its own

'survey reveals a bleak picture. Findings based on returns from 3,200 clubs revealed that 24.5% of clubs received no rate relief whatever. 33.5% of clubs receive less than 50% rate relief. Only 31.5% of clubs receive 50–100% rate relief'.

(4)   One mechanism for attempting to qualify for charitable rate relief stems from the wise advice given at an earlier CCPR Taxation and VAT conference at London's Waldorf Hotel in 1980. On that occasion the principal Charity Commissioner, Mr Charles Weston, whose encouragement for registration of the FA Youth Trust Deed in 1972 was endorsed ultimately by the House of Lords in *IRC v McMullan*, recommended an administrative mechanism for attempting to achieve authentic charitable educational sporting status: hive off a section of a club or other organisation, administratively and physically.

This method and result were achieved by a bowls club at Watchet in Somerset extraneously to charitable issues and intentions. It emerged during a successful appeal to a VAT Tribunal against a Commissioners of Customs and Excise assessment upon the club for VAT purposes (*AG Hayhoe (on behalf of Watchet Bowling Club and Watchet Indoor Bowling Club) v Customs and Excise Commissioners*, VAT Tribunal ref LON/80/341 13 January 1981 (unreported)).

The Club was structured in two separate sections, and affiliated to the two national governing bodies under its two separate sections, indoors, and general: the English Indoor Bowling Association (EIBA) and the English Bowling Association (EBA). Proof by oral and also detailed documentary accounting and administrative evidence of the two separate club sections satisfied the VAT Tribunal and the Customs and Excise assessment on the club as a registrable VAT unit was discharged. Neither of the two separate entities was compulsorily eligible for that tax.

Questions have been raised about the practical and legal implementation of Mr Weston's guidance. Thus, if the physical accommodation can be provided in the manner that clearly existed at Watchet, trustees who hold properties in accordance with traditional land law concepts, transcending the artificiality produced by the Court of Appeal in *Worthing Trustees v IRC*, could be appointed to more than one unit without creating any conflict of interest or legal objections to Mr Weston's concept.

4 PUBLIC PROTECTION (Chapter 5)

Two contrasting decisions impinging upon the issue of public protection illuminate the artificial and arcane world in which taxation law is administered and practised, separate and apart from legislative links today with EC law directives, outside the mainstream of ordinary legal life and experience. One concerns the famous Burnley Football Club. The other demonstrates how a little-known tennis coaching property in the Midlands with which it will be more convenient to begin was foot faulted because of an absence of professional advice. It also illustrates the problems created by the limitations to Sir John Donaldson's fascination in *IRC v Garvin* (supra) when a taxpayer in person does not qualify for his standpoint of being a

'referee of a match between a well-advised taxpayer and the equally well-advised Commissioners of Inland Revenue, conducted under the rules which govern tax avoidance'

where the

'rules are complex, the moves are sophisticated and the stakes are high'.

(1)   Thus, *Thomas v Reynolds and Broomhead* ([1987] TC No 3080: (1987) 119 Taxation 77) may be of concern to more people in sport than the actual taxpayers associated with the result.

Walton J in London's Chancery Division of the High Court described it as 'a rather unfortunate little case,' for the taxpayers. It could also be unfortunate for sport generally, although concerned immediately with tennis coaching. Through no fault at all of the learned judge, it may also be unfortunate for the image of the law. For it emphasises the imbalance caused by the House of Lords attitude in recommending revenue representation before the Commissioner while legal aid does not exist for taxpayers at that crucial level. No detailed formal report of the judgment in the official Tax Cases appeared until June 1987 (TC No 3080), although a valuable commentary in the weekly journal *Taxation* from which a citation is taken below was published on 24 April 1987.

The Inspector of Taxes had appealed against a ruling of the General Tax Commissioners at Scarsdale in Derbyshire. It had favoured the taxpayers, Messrs Reynolds and Broomhead. They traded in a partnership business as qualified tennis coaches. In order to provide winter services to their pupils they had bought during their tax year ending 31 March 1982, an inflatable cover of high-grade polythene, together with the necessary equipment to inflate it, and a hut for storage when the cover was not in use. By personal appearance without representation they claimed a first year capital expenditure allowance under section 41 (1) of the Finance Act 1971. Subsection (1)(a) provides its availability where

'a person carrying on a trade incurs capital expenditure on the provision of machinery or plant for the purpose of trade.'

The General Commissioners found in favour of the taxpayers. The Revenue appealed, represented by solicitors and Counsel experienced in taxation affairs, challenging the Commissioners' decision. The key issue was how the General Commissioners in accordance with correct judicial principles had applied the relevant law to the facts provided before them by the taxpayers. Because Parliament has never defined either machinery or plant, the Courts have been obliged to define this particular gap themselves. A cluster of reported cases, including *Brown v Burnley Football Club* (infra), culminating in the *Cole Bros v Phillips* (supra) in the House of Lords differentiates between 'plant' and the 'ambience' or 'setting' for carrying on the business concerned. Their Lordships decided that the ultimate conclusion is essentially a question 'of fact and degree for the Commissioners to decide' ([1982] TC 307 at 307 (j)).

Two practical questions which Walton J had to decide were

(i)   whether the inflatable cover

'is plant, because quite clearly, although the machinery by which the balloon is inflated is machinery it is by no means obvious that the cover itself, the air balloon, is plant'

(ii)   also

'whether upon the facts found in the Case Stated by the General Commissioners the air cover has any direct part to play in the business carried on'.

Apparently the facts found by the General Commissioners based on the information supplied by the taxpayers resulted in finding that the inflatable cover's primary function was to provide shelter. Before Walton J the taxpayers, appearing in person, added valuable

'various facts which are certainly not covered in the Case Stated ... unfortunately I can pay no attention although I have not the slightest reason to suppose that they are untrue.'

The learned judge was trapped by the House of Lords ruling in *Cole*'s case that any appellate court would be bound by the General Commissioners' findings. The principle which arises is clear: there must be an end to litigation.

The draconian imposition of the principle at the stage between Tax Commissioners and the High Court is inconsistent with other procedures with which litigants, and especially those unable to afford High Court representation and ineligible for legal aid, could be familiar. Appeals from magistrates' courts to Crown Court, and many interlocutory/interim appeals in civil proceedings at County Court, High Court, and even Court of Appeal levels, permit additional evidence not available or used at an initial stage. The exclusion of this practice from revenue appeals creates an injustice and inconsistency which so far has failed to excite reforming zealots warmly concerned with human rights yet less concerned with the public's rights of evidence in tax litigation.

The additional facts which Walton J felt constrained to reject for his judgment related to beneficial lighting conditions, dipping outside floodlights, and general coaching advantages: all directed to meeting the legal criteria for 'plant'. The *Taxation* journal under a main headline 'Winners lose' claimed in its 'Commentary' paragraph:

'The inference is that Mr Justice Walton considered that the taxpayer should have won their case, but he was bound to hold in favour of the Revenue because they had not put the correct facts to the General Commissioners.'

Even if the taxpayers had been served by professional assistance there is no guarantee that the limitations of human communications would have disclosed the material facts at the crucial initial stage: a situation which the late Mr Simon Burns, defence solicitor in Woolmington (supra), cited anecdotally in Chapter 3, at p 79, would have recognised. Nevertheless, the circumstances leading to Walton J's inevitable judgment are unsatisfactory, as indeed is this whole legal taxation sporting area. It must await another set of comparable facts, and opportunity to consider Vinelott J's judgment on the Burnely case in the Court of Appeal or even the House of Lords.

During the Chancellor of the Exchequer's autumn budget proposals for November 1993 it was announced that buildings and structures would not thereafter qualify as plant for tax reliefs although this would not affect expenditure for those purposes already qualified, and also the 'repair' circumstances considered below in the *Burnley Football Club* case.

(2) At Burnley the famous football company club directors decided in 1969 on architectural advice that the part of their playing area premises at Turf Moor known as the Brunshaw Road stand which had been built in 1912 could no longer be regarded as safe, and consequently arranged for its demolition, at a replacement cost of £209,365. In due course that sum was argued as a basis for deduction from the company club's profits for corporation tax purposes as either

(a) a 'repair of premises' allowance under section 130 of the Income and Corporation Taxes Act 1970 or

(b) capital expenditure on the provision of plant for the purposes of the Club's trade under section 41 of the Finance Act 1971.

Before the Presiding Special Tax Commissioner, Hubert Monroe QC and his successor, R H Widdows, the club failed to establish its claim for plant, but succeeded to establish, with the author's emphasis,

'*On the facts we find the Stadium to have been the profit-earning entity*, the premises occupied for the purposes of the Club's trade to which paragraph (d) section 130 refers. The actual playing field together with the surrounding stands and terraces was where, to use a colloquialism, it all happened: the spectators paid their money to occupy the stands and terraces so that they might watch the players on the field and, as spectators and supporters, participate in the matches put on by the Club. *We find the stadium, as we have defined it, to be the premises and the stand to be physically, commercially and functionally an inseparable part.* On that footing it seems to us that the replacement of the Brunshaw Road stand qualifies as "repairs of premises" and we so hold.'

In accordance with the appellate procedure in revenue cases the Crown declared its dissatisfaction with that finding as 'being erroneous in point of law'. Vinelott J adjudicated, again with the author's emphases,

'The question "What is the whole, the entirety, the entity which is said to have been repaired by replacement of part?" cannot be answered by any one yardstick or rule of thumb. It must, in the words of Lord Reid, "be answered in the light of all the circumstances which it is reasonable to take into account" (see *Regent Oil Co Ltd v Strick* [1965] 3 All ER 174 at 179, [1966], AC 295 at 313).

Application of the principle enunciated in para 9(11)(3) of the case [stated] would not, as it seems to me, have pointed to the playing field and the surrounding stands and terraces which the Special Commissioners take in [it] to constitute the "entity" or "premises" which were repaired. The profit-earning undertaking comprehended also a car park, changing rooms, baths and, more remotely, a gymnasium. All were, as I see it, equally part of the "profit-earning entity" ... It may be that, for instance, a sports stadium designed and built as a single building would constitute separate "premises", and that replacement or renewal of a part, more or less extensive, would be a repair of the premises as a whole, though it is not easy to see why, in such a case, a car park, baths and changing rooms forming an integral part of the structure should not be as much part of the stadium as the spectators' seats and the ground itself. However, in the recent case the premises occupied by the club comprised a number of distinct structures. It was not designed, far less built, in accordance with a single plan. For instance, the Cricket Field stand was added in 1969. Each separate part of the whole had its own distinct function. *No part, except the football pitch itself, was necessary to the performance of the club's central activity of arranging professional football matches as a spectacle. The club could have continued its activities without affording covered seats for those of its supporters prepared to pay for that amenity.* It could have leased a part of its ground to another prepared to afford that or other amenities, as I believe is sometimes done by racecourse owners.

In my judgment, therefore, the erection of the new Brunshaw Road stand *was not* a 'repair' *of any larger entity*, whether identified *as the whole* premises *occupied by* the club for the purposes of its business or as the field and surrounding *stands* and *terraces* alone.'

As I have reached the clear conclusion that the erection of the new stand was not a repair, the further question whether, if it had been a repair, it could nonetheless have been expenditure of a capital nature does not arise for decision. It is also a question which can only be asked on the hypothesis, in my judgment false, that the erection of the new stand was a replacement of part of some larger whole. It would I think be undesirable that I should express any opinion whether, if the hypothesis had been well founded, the expenditure would have been expenditure of a revenue or capital nature, having regard to the interval between the erection of the old stand and the erection of the new stand,

and to the enduring nature of the new stand. *(Brown (Inspector of Taxes) v Burnley Football and Athletic Co Ltd* [1980] 3 All ER 244 at pages 255–256).

That judgment was delivered after the Ibrox Stadium disaster of 1971 and Lord Wheatley's Report on it which led to the Safety of Sports Grounds Act 1975. The Bradford City and Hillsborough Sheffield disasters with their respective reports from Mr Justice Popplewell (1985) and Lord Justice Taylor (1989 and 1990) with their consequential legislation were yet to come, and the impact which the tragedies on those occasions made on the judicial and public consciousness did not exist when Mr Justice Vinelott reversed the experienced Special Commissioner's fact findings to hold

'No part, except the football pitch, was necessary for the performance of the club's central activity of arranging professional football matches as a spectacle. The club could have continued its activities without affording covered seats for those of its supporters prepared to pay for that amenity.'

Nevertheless it is difficult to ignore the opinion that if the Burnley Football Club had appealed to the higher courts either a *Wooldridge v Summer* finding in which the learned judge drew the wrong inferences of fact from the evidence would have resulted, or an echo would have been heard of Viscount Dunedin's House of Lords view of the Court of Appeal in the *Seymour v Reed* (1927) AC 554 tax-free cricketers' landmark decision at pages 560–561,

'honestly, had it not been for the fact that honourable judges, whose opinions I respect, have come to another conclusion, I would have thought the contention was quite preposterous.'

Parliament and the Government have since those crowd disasters and subsequent successive legislation (see Chapter 5, 'Public protection') attempted to alleviate the financial inhibitions caused by this reversal of the very experienced Special Commissioner's careful factual conclusions. First the Finance (No 2) Act 1975, s 49 prior to the Burnley decision and consistent with the Safety of Sports Ground Act 1975 amended the capital allowance rules to provide for tax relief when safety certificates existed; and ultimately section 119 of the Finance Act 1989, now all consolidated in the Capital Allowances Act 1990s 69, 70, following recommendations in the Hillsborough Taylor Report. For clubs and stadia owners whose premises do not qualify for football ground tax reliefs, the judicial Burnley blockage remains unless and until attempts are made to reverse it on a further appeal, if necessary to the House of Lords as experienced in *Seymour v Reed* and ultimately in the FA Youth Trust and North Berwick Sports

Centre charity (supra cases), where earlier decisions were reversed by
Britain's court of last resort. The FA Youth Trust experience of
supportive funding from the Sports Council and the Central Council
of Physical Recreation could encourage such a course, and a valuable
and practical critique of the position generally appears in the *British
Tax Review* (1990) No 11 at pages 329–334.

5 PARTICIPATION PROBLEMS (Chapter 6)

Seymour v Reed (supra: [1927] AC 554 already considered in earlier
pages is inevitably the starting point, with its reversal of the Court of
Appeal majority and restoration of the eminently experienced tax
judge, Rowlatt J who had affirmed the General Tax Commissioners'
decision. This was that the proceeds of James Seymour's benefit
match at the traditional Canterbury Cricket Week in 1920 were a gift
or donation from an appreciative public subscription and not assessable to tax as income. More recently history's wheel turned full circle
after the transfer from Nottingham Forest to Southampton of the
England international goalkeeper, Peter Shilton. On that occasion in
early 1991 the House of Lords again reversed the Court of Appeal to
establish on this occasion that a £75,000 payment to him from Forest
to encourage his transfer and thus reduce its wage bill was not as
claimed, and argued, a golden handshake. It was held to have been an
emolument from his employment under section 181 (1) of the Income
and Corporation Tax Act 1970 and thereby liable to tax (*Shilton v
Wilmshurst* [1991] 3 All ER 148, [1991] STC 88). A constructive
critique of the decision appears from John Tiley, Cambridge University's Professor of the Law of Taxation in the Taxation section of
the *All England Law Reports Annual Review* (1991) at pages 36–347
and more generally in the author's Sport and the Law pages at page
309 and in the 1990 volume at pp 245, 248.

In the years between these pages in Chapter 1, 'Genesis', I have
already explained how advisers to the Professional Footballers Players' and Trainers' Union hopelessly tried to equate the footballers'
discretionary but contractually tied benefit payment position with the
cricket circumstances (see *Davis v Harrison* (1927) 43 TLR 623: *Davle
v Duff: Corbett v Duff: Feeburg v Abbott* (1941) KB 730 and pages
supra), until the author's articles in the *Football Association Bulleting*
(April 1953) and *Rating and Income Tax* (1953) led to the Peterborough United non-Football League experiment in *Rigby v IRC*
((1959) Peterborough Citizen and Advertiser 16 June, 24 July) and
the ultimate deletion of all contractual elements from professional
football players contracts. Thus the Football Association's appreciation to its World Cup winning players in 1966 with a £1,000 bonus
payment outside the match fee was held by Brightman J to have had

'the quality of a testimonial or accolade outside rather than the quality of remuneration for services rendered'

Moore v Griffiths [1978] 3 All ER 309 at page 409 (b–c) consistent with the *Seymour v Reed* tax-free cricketers' benefit principle and thereby not assessable to tax. No appeal was lodged by the Revenue against either of these Peterborough United and 1966 World Cup decisions based upon the *Seymour v Reed* precedent. Two further appeals, however, reversed High Court rulings in the Court of Appeal.

In *Moorhouse v Dooland* [1955] 1 All ER 93 the Professional League cricketers' *contracted* benefit was equated with the old-styled footballers' contractual regulated payments and was thereby held subject to tax. A decade later, a trend for *amateur* rugby union players to move over into professional rugby league which has been doubtless encouraged by the Court of Appeal's decision in *Jarrold v Boustead* [1964] 2 All ER 76 can be seen from its decision that inducement payments to amateur rugby union players to become professional players under rugby league professional rules were treated as once and for all capital payments and not subject to income tax. Of this decision in relation to Shilton v Wilmshurst (supra), Professor Tiley's All England Law Reports Annual Review 1991 commentary says it 'was not cited but presumably remains in place' because the House of Lords decision 'leaves intact the tax-free status of the compensation for giving up a senior position' (*Pritchard v Arundale* [1971] 3 All ER 1011).

A final example of the manner in which tax laws today are entwined with high-profile and high-earning sportspersons appears from an interest-free loan from Arsenal Football Club to its Republic of Ireland International, David O'Leary, of £266,000 repayable on demand to a Channel Islands Trustee for the benefit of the employees. The loaned money was invested in a Jersey Bank, and interest accrued to the employee. A Special Commissioner's conclusion was upheld on appeal in the High Court that the income arising from the settlement arrangement stemmed from the employment source and was chargeable under Schedule E and not from the bank deposit under Schedule D, Case V, *O'Leary v McKinlay* (1991) *Tax Journal*, 7 March [1991] STC 42.

Since 1987 rules have existed for withholding of tax at source on payments to non-resident entertainers and sportsmen for which a special Foreign Entertainers Unit was set up to administer the new scheme at 5th Floor, City House, 140 Edmund Street, Birmingham B3 2JH (telephone 021 200 2616). The burden of collection lies upon the organiser or arranger of the circumstance creating the occasion. The significant of this development was highlighted and recorded in

Hansard for 21 May 1993 Vol 225, No 184, col 286 and in *Taxation* for 3 June 1993, that the amount of tax and interest (taking repayments into account) obtained from foreign entertainers and sportsmen by the Revenue's specialist unit has steadily increased. In the first year of operation, 1987–88, the unit brought in £6,921,507 plus £3,178,043 tax and interest from the previous year. For 1992–93 the unit received £19,953,506 plus £508,569 relating to the previous year.

Finally, no picture of fiscal revenue matters in relation to Sport and the Law would be complete without sadly recording how the circumstances leading to the Swindon Town Football Club's experiences before the High Court and the FA Appeals Committee resulted directly from Football League investigations into financial irregularities which ended ultimately with a criminal trial and Crown Court conviction and jailing of the former chairman. Payments had been made to players without deduction of tax and a prosecution was brought for conspiracy to defraud the Inland Revenue. In due course the sentence of 12 months was halved on appeal *R v Brian Hiller*: (1992) Times, 30 July, 11 December. Furthermore, at the time of writing nearly two years later, similar circumstances cannot be discounted.

6 VALUE ADDED TAX GENERALLY

(1)   The proposed intention of

> 'a VAT exemption for the supply of certain services by non-profit-making organisations and local authorities to persons who take part in sport or physical education',

as announced by the Paymaster-General in the House of Commons on 22 July 1993, does not detract from the application of this particular European impact on British cultural life and all other sporting areas since the tax came into operation in the United Kingdom on 1 April 1973 with the passing of the Finance Act 1972 which became law on 27 July 1972.

(2)   A decade later it was subsequently consolidated in the Value Added Tax Act 1983. Statutory instruments, EC directives, VAT leaflets and VAT tribunal and High Court ruling all the way up to the House of Lords added to the 51 sections and 11 Schedules contained in the 1983 Act.

(3)   Accordingly, within the context of attempting to create a level of awareness within these pages, a sample selection of three precedents from the cases, and a fourth example of the impact from a

sporting political lobby, must suffice to demonstrate how this particular law is operated and practised within a sporting context.

(4) For more detailed guidance in addition to specialist advice the reader is referred to the Customs and Excise leaflets which are available from all of their offices under their titles of Value Added Tax, VAT Leaflets:

Youth Clubs No 701/35/84: 1 January 1984
Sponsorship No 701/41/90: 1 February 1990
Letting of facilities for Sport and Physical Recreation No 742/1/90: 1 March 1990
Clubs and Associations No 701/5/90 1 June 1990

7 VALUE ADDED TAX CASE EXAMPLES SPECIFICALLY

(1) *Customs and Excise Commissioners v Lord Fisher* [1981] 2 All ER 147 was a High Court decision upholding a VAT Tribunal that although shooting rights of a family, established where pheasants supplied ample targets, were organised in a business-like way, and guests contributed to the cost, they did not convert pleasure and socially enjoyable activities into a business. Accordingly, they were not concerned with the making of taxable supplies for a consideration and thereby assessable for VAT.

(2) *Celtic Football and Athletic Club Ltd v C & E Commissioners* [1983] STC 470 and *Football Association v C & E Commissioners* (1985) VAT Tribunal Reports 106 established that the contractual obligations imposed by the Union of European Football Associations (UEFA) requiring reciprocal hospitality arrangements for home and away competition fixtures excluded the services provided by the host association from qualifying as a business entertainment which would ordinarily have been excluded as a deductible input tax.

(3) *Customs and Excise Commissioners v Professional Footballers' Association (Enterprises) Ltd* (1992) Times, 11 March, the House of Lords, Court of Appeal majority all upheld a VAT Tribunal finding that an awards dinner including trophy presentations was for a consideration rather than a supply of goods for no consideration and therefore not assessable for VAT. A valuable commentary on the Court of Appeal state of play from Mr John Newth in the *Taxation* journal for 10 September 1992 explained before the House of Lords confirmation that

'The trophies awarded by golf clubs (including the British Open), football clubs (including the Cup Final), tennis clubs (including Wimbledon), schools and many other sporting and other clubs and associations would all come within the ambit of a value added tax charge should the House of Lords reverse the decision in the Lower Court.'

It did not, and after the Commentary's preliminary observation,

'The result will be awaited with bated breath as the House of Lords decision has serious implications for the leisure industry',

those concerned were able to breath again without the burden of this charge.

(4)   Also breathing again in a limited manner are members of the bloodstock industry, for whose campaign to alleviate the imbalance between European VAT charges Lord Oaksey provided powerful Appendices in the 1978 (*Sunday Telegraph*) and 1988 (Butterworths) *Sport and the Law*

EC Council Directive 77/388 (Sixth Directive, art 9(2)(d)) [itself deleted by Tenth Council Directive 84/386, art 1] resulted in a European Court of Justice judgment that ocean-going sailing yachts, even if used for sporting purposes concurrently with commercial enterprises must be regarded as forms of transport (*Hamann v Finanzamt Hamburg-Eimsbuttel* (Case 51/88) [1991] 193 Simon's Tax Cases). The reference procedurally was routed under EEC art 177 (see Chapter 10, 'Single European market and UK sport' pp 270–271 supra for UK precedents) and the failure to be freed from VAT burdens *at present* has an echo of *Re Hodge* (1895) with the failure of the yacht's prize then to qualify for charitable status.

CONCLUSION

The fluidity at the time of writing which surrounds the fiscal attitudes towards British sport at Government level was emphasised by the support promised for the Manchester Olympic Games bid and the creation of the National Lottery Act which received the Royal Assent on 21 October 1993. By reason of delay due to the Maastricht debates it has been anticipated that operations for a National Lottery will commence in Autumn 1994. So far as sport is concerned, the CCPR's Annual Report for 1991–92 published in the early summer of 1993 while the Bill was passing through Parliament explained

'When first announced there were to be three beneficiaries – sport, the arts and heritage. There are now five – sport, the arts, heritage, charities and the Millenium Fund. The CCPR believes that it is of crucial importance that sport as a beneficiary should be locked into the arrangements through primary legislation.'

Four days after the Bill became law the Secretary of State for the Department of National Heritage appointed a former audit partner with the accountants Price Waterhouse, and subsequently a financial director in the retail and insurance world, Peter Davis, as financial director. He explained during an interview with *Leisure Management* in December 1993 how his first task was to produce a Draft Invitation to Apply (ITA) and a Draft Licence to Run the National Lottery. This would result in contending applications for operating the National Lottery under a two-tiered system which is provided for under sections 5 and 6 of the Act.

With an enthusiastic optimism he explained how

'The DNH's research has picked up on the best and worst points of other lotteries [ie from overseas], and with this knowledge we intend to create the best lottery in the world.... . The Secretary of State's conservative estimate is £1.5b a year, but there are other prosecutions based on foreign lotteries which suggest a figure nearer the £5b mark'.

The details will be revealed after these pages are published.

Together with the mechanism available for funding for Sport from the Foundation for Sport and the Arts, the Government's Pound for Pound Sponsorship Scheme and the Football Trust, Sir Alan Herbert and his successors would have been vindicated.

Part VI

Conclusion

Chapter 15

Whither Sport and the Law?

1. INTRODUCTION

The National Lottery etc Act 1993 received the Royal Assent on Trafalgar Day, 21 October 1993, while these pages were in preparation. Its detailed mechanism for implementation will be created after this book appears; and how the world of sport is treated by the administrators of its funds could affect the manner in which British sport develops towards and into the 21st Century.

John Goodbody, wrote in *The Times* after the Chancellor of the Exchequer, Kenneth Baker QC MP's November 1993 budget, crystallising the key problem which has remained unanswered ever since Lord Hailsham of St Marylebone identified over thirty years ago the absence of any 'coherent body of doctrine, perhaps even a philosophy of government encouragement'. Then he conceived the idea of 'a need, not for a Ministry, but for a focal point under a Minister'; and recent Government proposals subsequently announced on 8 July 1994, and summarised at page 425 below, for reassessing the future structure at Government level for British Sport, do nothing to diminish Goodbody's basic criticisms hereafter which echo Lord Hailsham's 30 years old complaint of 'lack of an overall strategy'; 'no proper co-ordinated policy'; 'the chaos will continue'.

...

Peter Brooke, the national heritage secretary, yesterday reiterated the government's view that the proceeds from the national lottery, when it starts next year, will not be used to replace public funding for the arts, sport, heritage and the millenium fund.

...

In future, the government may not increase money to the Sports Council as much as it would have done previously, because capital projects will be financed by the lottery.

The heritage department is also aware that the real problem of sport's funding is the lack of an overall strategy. There are too many agencies: the four Sports Councils, the Foundation for Sport and the Arts: the Football Trust and local authorities, let alone private sponsorship and organisations like the Sports Aid Foundation.

As a result of this, there is no proper co-ordinated policy. Available money is not always properly directed.

The government is now re-examining the proper structure for British sport. It may realise that, until it appoints a minister OF sport, not FOR sport, with a budget and executive powers, the chaos will continue.'

What John Goodbody could have added, too, within the constitutional legal framework of Cabinet Government, is that until such a minister obtains full Cabinet status with power to co-ordinate all the strands which Lord Hailsham identified in *The Door Wherein I Went* and cited at pp 42–43 above, and reiterated in his Memoirs, *A Sparrow's Flight*, with the oft-forgotten realism, 'Organised sport is undoubtedly part of our national culture', there will be no chance of any progress being made with the various fragmented unincorporated agencies identified by John Goodbody. That must exist notwithstanding the intervening thirty years since Lord Hailsham together with Lord Howell and Sir Neil MacFarlane became the only government ministers on either side of the political spectrum to recognise in book form what another great pioneer Sir Ludwig Guttman, explained in his *Textbook of Sport for the Disabled*, published in 1976.

He ended his opening chapter 'Reflections on Sport in General', as a prelude to his more detailed excurcus dedicated to his life's work at the National Spinal Injuries Centre, Stoke Mandeville Hospital, Aylesbury, Buckinghamshire, under two sub-headings: Sport and Ethics:

'Today sport plays an ever-increasing integral part in the life of the individual, as it does in the life of nations, and represents as much a positive element in the culture of our modern life as it did in the culture of ancient nations. It must be remembered that physical education in ancient times was of a religious nature, and the sports festivals of ancient nations, whether in Asia or Greece, were based on ethical principles dedicated to the gods.'

Finally, targeting the real basis of his own disciplines, Sport and Training he began,

'Training in sport, defined as "education to efficiency through exercises", has, in the course of years developed into an important branch of applied physiology';

and he finished with a complete rebuttal to all who mislead themselves and others into a self-induced deception that sport can ever be inflated in its importance to humanity and society.

'... trainers should not lose sight of the psychological state of the trainee and of the fact that the human body is not an automated machine, but that physical performance is a medium of self-expression – a creative outlet which helps to develop personality and character, thus contributing to human development.'

That is the practical ideal transcending all other ideas and theories on sport and Guttman ended his 'Reflections in Sport in General' thus:

'These are the virtues which distinguish the real sportsman from a man whose motivation is simply to practise physical exercises for health reasons. But training in sport is also a contest against an opponent, which above all compels courtesy and must be a contest without hate, for sport is not warfare. Naturally, training for sports competitions will encourage the display of the whole of the one's energy and the inflexible will to set up higher standards and new records, to win and also to do one's best for the organisation and, indeed, the country one represents, but it is also an education in accepting a final decision without conceit of despondency.'

2. SPORT IN SOCIETY TO-DAY

Paradoxically and perversely the value of sport and its ethical, educational and social benefits for the health, welfare and enjoyment of the nation never appear to command the attention at the highest government levels which the successful precedents of Lord Hailsham and Lord Howell would have suggested perpetuation. Indeed, notwithstanding the creation of the Sports Council in 1971 during Sir Edward Heath's premiership and subsequently Lord Wilson's elevation to the status of Minister of State with access to Cabinet papers, of Lord Howell as Denis Howell, the longest serving Minister with responsibility for Sport (with the concurrent impact of sport's importance on the international scene) no Prime Minister appears ready to recognise and fill the gap identified by Lord Hailsham. Indeed, the current position was crystallised graphically by Peter Corrigan in the *Independent on Sunday* for 24 October 1993, a calender month short of a day before the fortieth anniversary of the day when English soccer bit the Hungarian dust at Wembley Stadium from the Magyar magic of Puskas, Hidegkuti & Co with the memorable 3–6 defeat for the first time against a continental side on English soil. He explained significantly and simply,

'Sports-lovers about to rush out to spend £25 on Margaret Thatcher's book had better be braced for disappointment. I managed to sneak into a bookshop to buy an unsigned copy and trawled through in vain for mention of the subject closest to our hearts.

I could find nothing in the Baroness's burly tome, for instance, about the six Ministers for Sport she used up in her lust to impose her will on our sporting scene. There is not a word about football hooligans and her

single-handed but sorrowful attempt to bring them to heel with identity
cards.

On page 88 is the briefest of reference to her attempt to prevent the
British team's attendance at the Moscow Olympics of 1980 in support of
President Carter's boycott of the event. But we get no further insight
into that doubtful episode, although she concedes with an almost
audible sniff, that most of the team went in any case. Posterity might
have been better served had she mentioned that one of them was Seb
Coe who won a gold medal and who is now an up-and-coming Tory
MP.

Perhaps Lady Thatcher's reluctance to enlist sport's ability to bring
light and inspiration to the most dreary of publications can be explained
by the fact that on each of the rare surges she made into the sporting
arena she came a cropper. This might have cheered us up at the time but
in retrospect it was a shame. Just a little success might have encouraged
her to look more kindly on this area of her realm, in which case her
Downing Street years might not have been so damaging to the nation's
sporting health, especially at school level.

We have much still to hope for from John Major's more enlightened
attitude, but the failure of Manchester's Olympic bid, which he supported with genuine enthusiasm, may seriously have dampened his
crusading zeal.

. . .

Under Major, sport was moved to the new Heritage department when it
came under the sympathetic supervision of David Mellor . . . and since
his departure any priority physical recreation was beginning to enjoy
has not been pressed so heartily'.

In October 1994, however, the genuinely sports-loving Prime Minister, John Major, appeared to press a hopeful button for the future
with his announcement at the Conservative Party's Bournemouth
Conference for including Sport and Physical recreation in the
National Curriculum in every school for children between five and
sixteen, but subject always to facilities and particularly school playing
fields accessibility.

Thus, the key question for Whither Sport and the Law? which was
posed in 1983 by Sir Denis Follows at the end of his Philip Noel Baker
address still demands answering today,

'Where is sport going? I say that at the top level it has ceased to be sport
– it has become a branch of the entertainment industry . . . but for 99% of
the participants, we, the devotees of sport and recreation, have a
responsibility to ensure that the young of this country are brought up to
observe the basic principles of fair play and sportsmanship – a respect
for others and for authority'.

Sadly and overwhelmingly that respect for others and for authority
has not only been eroded at the tope level (where) it has ceased to be
sport. Prevention of that erosion has been impaired by the undoubted

failure of sporting governing bodies at both domestic and international levels to impose their authority and uphold the Rule of Law within sport. Hence Lord Howell's recognition in his Foreword

> ' "the law does not stop at the touchline" ... a reality too long ignored by many administrators of the old school – "leave us to look after our affairs, we can sort things out." '

FIFA's World Cup 1994 decision to operate overdue red card sanctions created precedents causing contention and confusion within the game. It also stirred other disciplines and particularly rugby union to re-assess how to 'sort things out'.

Thus, three years after Sir Denis Follows' apprehensions were expressed in his survey Whither Sport, W G Grace's modern biographer, Eric Midwinter, social historian, author and educationist, already cited in Chapter 13. 'Sponsored Gentlemen and Players', posed the problem in the opening pages of *Fair Game: Myth and Reality in Sport* in 1986:

> 'Modern sport is in a mess. It is too often the focus of issues which are beyond its grasp. This would not matter too much save that there are considerable human hazards at stake. There are risks of personal damage, social disorder and other ills, commercial avidity and political dangers. The existence of these real threats demonstrates how far sport has spread beyond its proper narrow boundaries.'

Seven years later at the end of 1993, David Miller was writing in the *Times* as cited in the Introduction in a similar vein. That citation led to the conclusion in this comparable chapter in the first edition that such a mess can be cleared up if its principal elements which clearly transgress the Rule of Law can be identified as surely they can, and were later and will again here be classified as sport's Four Vices, thus:

(1) Violence

(2) Drugs

(3) Commercial exploitation

(4) Political violation;

Significantly, none of them was ever within the purview of the Wolfenden Committee, its evidence or its Report in 1960. Yet its terms of reference created in October 1957 by the then CCPR directed it

> 'To examine the factors affecting the development of games, sports and outdoor activities in the United Kingdom ... and ... to make recommendations ... in promoting the general welfare of the community.'

Further significantly none of them was within the purview of that schoolboy Second World War correspondence enjoyed by the author with England's greatest centre-forward of the Victorian era and later headmaster of the present school for England's future King William III, Ludgrove in Berkshire referred to in the Introduction and as Chapter 1 'Genesis', explains, is the origin of this book in *Corinthians and Cricketers*.

That comparable chapter in the first edition explained how these four evil elements crept into sports insidiously from that decadent permissive society so recklessly and irresponsibly and thoughtlessly described by the then Home Secretary and now Chancellor of Oxford University, Lord Jenkins of Hillhead, as cited on page 14 to the Abingdon Labour Party (*The Times* 21 July 1969 p 3) to be 'the civilised society'. This doubtless influenced the equally reckless, irresponsible and thoughtless amateur and professional sports administrators to fail to recognise such influences and halt the slide, as should have happened if the domestic Rules of Law within sport and the national law outside it as a last resort had been upheld with any concept of civilised behaviour.

Professional golf, as we saw in Chapter 3, 'Under starters' orders', with its ideal Constitution, Code of Ethics and disciplinary practices, has been free from the social and legal outrages which have disgraced professional soccer and tennis and amateur rugby football in the years since the Wolfenden Committee reported in 1960. Many will recall how no really effective action was taking by the rugby union authorities after the then celebrated referee Norman Sansom dismissed Geoff Wheel (Wales) and Willie Duggan (Ireland) for fighting at Cardiff's National Stadium in the Wales versus Ireland rugby international during early 1977. Ten years later the Rugby Football Union hierarchy at Twickenham, led by the President, Alan Grimsdell, son of Arthur Grimsdell, one of England's and Tottenham Hotspur's greatest captains throughout the history of each of these traditional soccer sources, forestalled future risks of potential criminality in the name of their own great game; they banned from selection for the next international the principal offender, his captain and other players whose playing and social misconduct shocked the sporting public during the Wales versus England international at Cardiff early in 1987. Yet in early December 1993 the England captain Will Carling in the *Mail on Sunday* was condemning the New Zealand All Blacks visitors as being remembered

> 'mostly as a dirty side. That is sad for them, but I think they deserve it. Some of their play has been beyond the conventions we obey and I feel more sad about the damage they have done to rugby's image.
> This tour was a great showcase for the game, but how many mothers will now be saying "I don't want my son to play rugby"' ...

The Phil de Glanville and Kyran Bracken incidents (each creating serious injuries witnessed worldwide on television), went beyond the unwritten code among players.

Rugby's problems is that when it comes to touring teams there is no independent disciplinary board'.

In a similar context later in the season in *The Times* sports letters pages for 3 February 1994, the Head Master of St Paul's School, Mr R S Baldock, wrote after violent foul play during Wales versus Scotland rugby international,

'If acts of violence like those perpetuated most obviously by the Welsh hooker but also by other players involved in both matches are not condemned there can be no good reason for parents to support the continued existence of games in schools.'

Yet even if there had been, it would never have been able to compensate the victims in the manner provided for by the civil and criminal compensatory courts and board and tribunals.

Professional soccer is in the same condemnatory category. As long ago as 1981 the distinguished anthropologist and former professional football club director, Desmond Morris in *The Soccer Tribe* cited Professor Colin Tatz that

'A violent assault which is outside the rules of the game is also outside the rules of the law, and therefore amenable to its jurisdiction and punishment'

As Desmond Morris recorded (p 158), the Professor

'was brusquely answered by the Secretary of the English Football Association, which replied,
    'Legal intervention in sport ... has become the hobby-horse of many publicity seekers. Justice on the field is undeniably rough justice, but it is accepted in sport and is something on which it relies totally".'

A decade later this enlightened administrator's successor was condemned from all resposible refereeing and playing sources within the game for his arguably inadmissible evidence which endorsed elbow to head conflicts on the field in the *R v Blissett* prosecution at Salisbury Crown Court towards the end of 1992. It was rebutted by the Professional Footballer's Association's recommendations that such tackles should be outlawed a year later after similar incidents and injuries towards the end of 1993. Almost simultaneously with that decision came the announcement of a *reported* but exagerrated out-of-court settlement award in Scotland's Court of Session of £900,000 by Motherwell Football Club for serious damage to nerves, tendons and ligaments suffered by a former Celtic under 20 representative player, *Steve Murray*, The Herald, Glasgow, 24 November 1993. The realistic figure was nearer £250,000.

The capacity of the law to intervene in sport was recognised in tennis when anti-apartheid demonstrators interrupted play sufficiently during a Wimbledon doubles match between Davidson and Bowrey and Pilic and Drysdale to merit a public order prosecution which ended in the House of Lords as *Brutus v Cozens* [1973] AC 845. Conversely no one had the moral or public service courage to initiate comparable proceedings against the even more offensive publicised and televised public misconduct by reputedly celebrated professional players, who were clearly candidates for the legal process.

One of the reasons for this abdication of responsibility creating the four vices of Violence, Drugs, Commercial Exploitation and Political Violation was explained in the first edition in this chapter as perhaps an uncertainty or ambiguity about the role of sport in society today, and especially in the intervening thirty-six years which have passed since the CCPR appointed the Wolfenden Committee in 1957. This aspect was demonstrated in an area where the author joins issue with and parts company from Eric Midwinter's other admirable analysis, when he wrote in the passage immediately following that cited above (on p 394):

'Modern sport has been allowed to assume a seriousness which is inflated beyond belief in the life of individuals, of nations and of the world. It is totally out of keeping with its true nature.
The myth of sport is that it is meaningful. At core it is not. It is, or should be, merely diversionary for player or watcher. The reality of spirt is that people believe or presume it is meaningful, and, for varying motives, they act accordingly.'

This contention contains a basic flaw which perhaps explains the failure of those administrators and participants who have allowed the corrosive and destructive elements identified above to creep into sport and cause Midwinter himself to acknowledge it 'is in a mess', and Pickering to ask, as cited in the Introduction to this book 'Have we slipped down the slippery path that far there is no return?' For Midwinter ignores one undoubted but unrecognised or unfashionable fact. In a secular-orientated society sport, within the rules of fair play, is the only visual guide to millions for differentiating between right and wrong, for recognising authority, in the brief life span from the cradle to the grave.

Thus the Feltham Young Offenders Institute in Middlesex has encouraged rugby football coaching as a rehabilitative element in its battle for reformation; and a little known but important publication in 1990 from the Centre for Criminological Research at Oxford University developed this concept on a wider canvas in a Report by

David Robins, a Football trust Research Fellow, under the title *Sport as Prevention: The Role of Sport in Crime Prevention Programmes Aimed at Young People* (1990).

C B Fry, too, was an author and educationist. He was also a living example of social history, chosen by J B Priestley in his *Survey of The English* published in 1973, alone among our own time alongside representatives from all ages, Raleigh, Pepys, Dr Johnson, Charles Lamb, Michael Farady and R F Burton in the chapter entitled A Portrait Gallery. Fry wrote in his Foreword to *Corinthians and Cricketers* shortly before he died in 1956:

'these field games, being quite a major interest indeed perhaps the major interest, of a people who have won two world wars, cannot be of negligible inherent value humanly considered.'

Because the current conflict of attitudes towards the role of sport in society today it is essential to consider this position in order to understand its relation to law when assessing the future of each in relation to the other, and how together they operate for the benefit of sport in particular and society in general. Effectively at this stage the most illuminating way will be to proceed with an explanation that Midwinter's 'mess' and Pickering's 'slippery path' have been created by sport's own four vices already cited which continue to transgress the Rule of Law and poison society.

3. SPORT'S FOUR VICES: AND HOW TO DEAL WITH THEM

(1) Violence

(i) Within sport itself

(a) Referees and administrators. Consistency is an ideal which can only be aimed for with little hope of perfect attainment. Criticisms of the professional judiciary and the controversial debate about powers for a Court of Appeal on the initiative of the Attorney-General to reconsider allegedly too lenient sentences after mature reflection demonstrate the problems of sporting referees and umpires giving decisions with serious consequences in a blaze of publicity with considerable financial consequences flowing from errors. Every sporting discipline can point to its own examples. No benefit to sport would exist here for raking the embers of burn-out episodes. Six general principles must be identified.

1. The laws and rules of all sports, except for special modifications because of age, size and disability and specially exempted occasions, apply equally at village green and national stadium levels.

2. Referees, umpires, touch judges, linesmen as much as the players participate for their love of sport, with no comparable financial reward to those under their authority at the public level.

3. Administrators and critics should support the referees and umpires except for a flagrant mistake or misjudgment amounting to gross error or negligence. Thus, in one publicised soccer precedent the referee admitted that he wrongly penalised a player whose offence was ultimately expunged. On the other hand, the referee who sent off the field for the first time a player in the FA Cup Final of 1985 obtained an agreed amount of £1,000 damages for libel; and the referee who sent off two internationals at Cardiff in 1977 for fighting was barred from refereeing a subsequent international for England against France because the French Federation President protested that the referee was too strict!

4. The dynamic growth of sport should inspire administrators to recognise the need for amendments to *penal* playing laws and their administration. Thus professional rugby league introduced the 'sin bin' principle, borrowed from the most violent forms of body contact sports, ice-hockey and water-polo, to douse its more heated confrontations; and amateur rugby union has given authority to touch judges at international levels to act effectively. This is not yet possible at lower grades because of limitations upon numbers of available trained personnel, with a similar verdict awaiting at grass roots level the outcome of FIFA's 1994 World Cup initiatives.

5. Even if referees fail to observe an offence, administrators should act to uphold the Rule of Law when serious breaches occur.

6. Players should be aware not only of the laws of their particular game. They and their officials should also be aware of the manner in which he law of the land transcends and overrides the law of any field of play. Two well-known examples demonstrate this, in addition to *R v Bishop* (1985) supra. One concerned the renowned Liverpool Football Club and the 1978 Football League Cup Final at Old Trafford, Manchester. The other concerns the sorry saga of Leeds United.

(b) Liverpool   On 22 March 1978 Nottingham Forest beat Liverpool 1–0 by a disputed penalty goal. The causation was seen by millions on television. The controversy surrounded an allegation that the tackle which led to the penalty award took place outside the penalty area, but the referee behind the actual play was too far back to adjudicate correctly. On the following day the late Denis Lowe was not alone when in the *Daily Telegraph* (23 March 1978) he reported that the offender,

'Phil Thompson, whose foul on John O'Hare was adjudged by the referee to have been committed inside the penalty area, said: "It was never a penalty. I admit it was a professional foul, but it was outside the box."'

The extent and nature of that 'professional foul' was corroborated three years later by Thompson's colleague, Phil Neal, in a book entitled *Attack from the Back*. The blurb on the jacket described the author as 'one of the finest exponents of fullback play in modern football. He is also a keen student of the game, and in one of the most intelligent books ever written about football he analyses the role he plays so well.' It also concludes that

'This thoughtful study of modern football will appeal not only to Liverpool fans but to all followers of the game, and will be immensely helpful to aspiring footballers at all ages and at all levels'.

Unfortunately, it omitted a Government health warning for reasons which will now become apparent. At page 87 appears this blow by blow account of the events leading to the penalty, under the chapter heading of Penalties.

'John O'Hare was clear. There is no worse sight for a defender in football than the man who has left the defence behind and has only the keeper to beat. As John roared in on our goal, we saw Phil Thompson tearing across the park, hell bent on stopping him. There was only one way it could be done and Tommo did it, to a tee. A yard outside the box he committed a really wicked foul on O'Hare, who went through the air as if he had been fired from a cannon to thud down in the penalty area. The game has its divers, but there was no question of John O'Hare diving that night. Running at full stretch, he was well and truly clobbered with malice aforethought by Tommo. There is no other way to describe it.'

Not so. There was another way to describe it, as that author cheerfully obliged in the paragraph immediately following, and in the next chapter entitled Referees. The paragraph below explained

'All that Pat [the referee: Mr Partridge] could have seen that night was a deliberate, dirty foul resulting in a man landing like a ton of coal in the box.'

The next chapter, 'Referees', recorded at page 98:

'I have no idea what sort of view Partridge [the referee] had of the incident, but it certainly looked bad from any angle: a wilful tackle, a bloke hurtling through the air to land with a fearful smack inside the box, the screams of thousands of outraged Forest fans. The result was almost bound to be a penalty.'

Now it is possible that when Mr Thompson admitted in 1978 to his professional foul, and Mr Neal corroborated it in 1981, they were both unaware that they were respectively admitting and confirming the existence of the identical offences which landed David Bishop in the dock at Newport Crown Court and the Court of Appeal criminal division. Nevertheless they and all readers who were enticed by the blurb on the book jacket to consider that the 'thoughtful study of modern football ... will be immensely helpful to aspiring footballers of all ages and at all levels' may realise how helpful these citations can be, perhaps in a manner not anticipated by Phil Neal. For they spell out very clearly a direct route to a criminal prosecution, and in the event of broken limbs, a potential claim for damages in a civil court.

These matters of criminal and civil liability in law have been fully explored in Chapter 6. 'Participation problems', and need not be repeated here. They are noteworthy only for the professional precision with which Neal faithfully fulfils the blurb on the book jacket, transposed to corroborate and confirm his colleague Thomson's reported admission: he analyses the role 'so well'. Neither player appears to have been aware of the extent to which they were emulating the celebrated unawareness of Moliere's character, M Jourdain, in *Le Bourgeois Gentilhomme*: 'Good Heavens! For more than forty years I have been speaking prose without knowing it.'

Equally noteworthy, however, was the curious absence of any action by the local police authority in Manchester, where Old Trafford, the scene of the crime, was situated. For two years later, on Saturday 16 February 1980, at Twickenham, the Irish international rugby referee David Burnett, dismissed from the playing field a Welsh international player for an offence against England. Four days later, Wednesday 20 February 1987, the following letter appeared prominently in *The Times* to the Editor over the address of the Chief Constable's Office from the Chief Constable of Manchester, and the Chief Constable himself, Mr James Anderton.

'Is it any wonder there is violence in the streets and on the picket lines? It is any wonder young people resort to gratuitous, sadistic violence when they see it practised deliberately in the name of sport?

What happened on more than one occasion, in a very recent Rugby International (report February 18) was positively disgraceful. Judged by the television recording of that match some players must now be surprised they are not facing charges of criminal assault. It is high time the powers in the game clamped down and sorted out the trouble matches. Responsibility for this cannot be avoided by calling Rugby "a man's game'. That was a view once taken of war.'

Mr Anderton had been appointed Chief Constable of Manchester in 1976, and had been Deputy since 1975. Whatever was the reason for reticence over the criminal assault committed and reportedly admitted at Old Trafford on 22 March 1978, the opening lines of that letter have a direct relevance to the next example of circumstances where the Rule of Law should prevail, and failed to do so with significant consequences.

(c) Leeds United. In the case the Liverpool experiences cited above should be considered exceptional in the world of modern English professional football a more extended impression was given by a contribution to the *Daily Express* on Tuesday 25 August 1987 at pages 30–31 which has been cited already in the Introduction. The former Leeds United and Eire international, John Giles, wrote of his club's progress in the 1970s,

> 'I get a rush of pride when I think of the great years with Leeds United. I also feel shame ... now I can see clearly enough that we stretched the rules to breaking point ... We went too far, too ruthless. I went too far ... We did and we prospered. We never thought there might be a day when we would wonder if the price was too high.'

The answer to that wonderment is crystallised in the following paragraph in *Soccer Match Control* by Stanley Lover published in 1986, at page 144, the standard work on soccer refereeing.

> 'Specific acts of gamesmanship, cheating or professional fouls – whatever label one wishes to give them – can be observed in junior football and even in school games within twenty-four hours of being seen on television. Recently an eight-year-old schoolboy returned home after playing for his school team and was heard to boast that he had committed "a pro foul" on an opponent to stop a goal.'

Mr Lover does not state whether this was inspired from Phil Neal's text cited above. In fact, he continued,

> 'His justification was that he had seen his idol, a professional of a Football League First Division team, do the same thing a week earlier. Many referees have reported examples of dissent by schoolboy footballers which, a few years ago, were unheard of. One referee was reported to have to dismiss his own son for swearing during a friendly match.'

A similar example was cited in February 1986 at the Sport's Council's Recreation Management Seminar at Harrogate. The schoolmaster explained how he had remonstrated with a pupil against spitting during a school match. The response was that the big boys did it as seen on television. Thus the spitting image had become reality. In a similar vein, a 17 year-old tennis player during 1984 was banned by the Lawn Tennis Association for three months for making obscene gestures and throwing his racket. The precedent for this misbehaviour would not be difficult to find for regular sporting fans.

If these accounts needed corroboration, the author received it during the robing-room talk which the cameraderie of the Bar produces while awaiting the commencement of cases already prepared in detail overnight to be heard after delays in court timetables. When the talk turned to football in early 1987 the author discovered his barrister opponent under the adversarial litigation system, James Scobie, to be captain of the Old Etonians in the Arthur Dunn Cup Competition, still enjoying the legacy of R C Gosling's philanthropy explained in Chapter 13 'Sponsored Gentlemen and Players', albeit a far cry in time from their six FA Cup Final appearances and one success at Kennington Oval over a century ago. When the author enquired that no doubt the Corinthian sportsmanship and chivalry according to the Laws of the Game still endured from the Gosling-Fry vintage years, the response was shattering. 'Don't you belive it. We are as ferocious as any professionals.' When asked why and how, the reply was no less awesome. 'You perhaps don't realise that when we were at school during the early 1970s the yardstick for success was Leeds United', including of course John Giles. Thus does another form of professional friendship bridge the generation gap, and destroy a romantic sporting illusion.

That foul play evidenced from Liverpool and Leeds United is no different ethically, morally and legally from the foul play title which Tom Donohue and Neil Johnson used to describe their book cited in Chapter 7. 'Sports Medicine and the Law' with its sub-title: 'Drug Abuse in Sports'. At national level as distinct from sport that particular social evil is controlled by the law from Parliament: The Misues of Drugs Act, 1971.

Foul play on the field is controlled by the Offences Against the Person Act1861 and its application by the judges at common law as laid down in *R v Bradshaw* (1878), *R v Moore* (1898) and *R v Venna* (1975), as explained in Chapter 6, 'Participation problems'. It has been re-affirmed by the Law Commission's Consultation Paper No 218 *Consent and Offences Against the Person* published while these pages were in their final stage of preparation. If the prosecuting authorities and sentencing policies of the courts are hesitant to use this armory to end these social and sporting menaces the author has attempted to simplify its availability into a double-barrelled draft Act of Parliament: a Safety of Sports Persons Act, to complement and supplement the Safety of Sports Ground legislation, initially of 1975 and now updated in 1987 by the Fire Safety and Safety of Places of Sport Act 1987. Its piecemeal implementation did not begin until 1 January 1988 (see SI 1987/1762), and sunsequently has been reinforced by the Football Spectators Act 1989 and the Football

(Offences) Act 1991 and 1992, and further associated Statutory Instruments.

(ii) Outside sport

If sport cannot control itself adequately to protect itself, and more significantly its victims, from unlawful conduct committed in the name of sport, then the national Law must be wheeled on to the field of play, if only to prevent the corrosive and corrupting effect upon future generations in the manner evidenced here. Road traffic legislation has progressed from the red flat in the Corinthians hey day during the 1980s to compulsory disqualifications for drugged and drunken drivers to penalise such universally acknowledged anti-social behaviour. Why should sporting offenders be excluded from this principle?

When the author was preparing initially with Lord Havers and also ultimately Peter Shankland, *The Royal Baccarat Scandal* and its Tranby Croft house party and High Court trial dramas (concerning an alleged cheating at cards on the eve of the Doncaster St Leger horse race classic on 9 September 1890), preparations were also in hand for the first series of *Sunday Telegraph* articles linking Sport and the Law under that title. Both publications appeared in 1977. When the more general survey on Sport and the Law was published in booklet from a year later in 1978, the contrast between the punishments for sporting-social misconduct in Victorian England and the permissive society of the 1960s and 1970s was startling. The Plaintiff in the Baccarat Case, Sir William Gordon-Cumming, Bart., a noble Scottish sporting landowner of ancient lineage, lost his High Court slander action in June 1891 to clear his name against the allegation of cheating, wrongly in the opinion of the joint authors and his own counsel at the time, Sir Edward Clarke, the Solicitor-General of the day. Within hours of the jury's verdict he was kicked out of the Scots Guards with whom he had served with bravery and distinction in the Victorian African Wars and ostracised for the remaining forty years of his life by the society in which he had been one of the privileged members of the Marlborough House set centred around the Prince of Wales, later King Edward VII. In our own time, as John Giles explains,

'we stretched the rules to breaking point ... and we prospered.'

Against those contrasting backgrounds the draft Safety of Sports Persons Act was prepared and placed in an Appendix to the 1978 *Sunday Telegraph* production in booklet form. Its purpose was to focus attention upon the existing law and to aim for automatic mandatory suspension from play in the manner equivalent to the mandatory disqualification imposed by Parliament reflecting society's will upon drugged and drunken drivers (with certain special exceptions) and Victorian Society's ostracism for foul play at the card table. Its implementation would displace the discretionary power which at present is available to allow courts a free rein to perpetuate a permissive society's penal policy. An immediate sanction would align this social evil with its motoring equivalent under the penal policy contained progressively in Road Traffic and Transport enactments.

Furthermore, the draft Act was designedly and deliberately aimed also at a similar withdrawal of discretion from the courts for sporting violence off the field. The Public Order Act 1986 absorbs the exclusion order discretion which Parliament gave to the courts for offences under its licensing legislation and to Scotland during 1980. It falls short of the mandatory jurisdiction created by Parliament for all courts when disposing of driving offences.

The double-barrelled purpose to hit field and crowd violent offenders is to target all who are convicted of sporting violence and (save for comparable road traffic exceptions) withdraw any discretion from the courts for loss of liberty by attendance or detention centre orders. The Court of Appeal has exhorted against leniency by lay justices. Offenders have ridiculed them and publicly stated they expected severer sentences than probation orders or fines. The draft Act fulfils their expectations with proposed *compulsory* attendance or detention sentence orders to be implemented at times of sporting fixtures. In this way the soul searching for the reasons which cause sporting violence can be short-circuited. Mr Justice Popplewell stated in his Final Report that he had read about thirty or forty sources on the causation of crowd hooliganism and doubted if he was any the wiser. He might not have been aware that the ground records crowds for all the leading professional football clubs were established during the depressed inter-war years between 1919 and 1939; and that so far as the author has been able to trace no attempt has been made anywhere to evaluate their development and existence without any reported record of unlawful or anti-social actions associated with them. The statistics are contained in the three schedules in Appendix 5 whilst Appendix 14 contain the draft Act. Countless survivors from those record crowds are still alive and available for the social-historians who are genuinely concerned about and interested in seeking the truth behind the contrasting phenomena of violent-free sporting supporting crowds between 1919 and 1939 and the social disease which has afflicted them by a minority infection since the 1960s.

(2) Drugs

While this chapter was being completed the sad story outline in Chapter 7 'Sports medicine and the law', has been sustained with a continuing controversy about the extent of the problem; the absence of hard evidence, and the reported death of the first proven fatality in Britain from anabolic steroids. The existing law laid down by Parliament in 1971 under the Misuse of Drugs Act would appear to have been overtaken by chemical and sporting ingenuity. The genetic consequences which the European horse-racing authorities have recognised in contrast to the American states, which permit racing by horses injected with Bute and Lasix to conceal pain, have been ignored for humans. The state of play in this area and the way ahead would appear to point in only one direction. A full in-depth enquiry receiving medical, chemical and legal evidence, to be commissioned by either the Sports Council, the CCPR, severally or jointly, or by Parliament or the Government with power to call witnesses.

Lord Diplock was a member of the Wolfenden Committee on Homosexual Offences and prostitution which reported in 1957 [Cmnd 247]. Inter alia it recommended legislative changes to free this practice between consenting adults from legal and social obloquy. He would tell his Middle Temple Bar students at their Cumberland Lodge week-end seminars in Windsor Great Park, who enquired how the Committee arrived at its conclusions, that on the medical evidence they had no alternative but to recommend the amending legislation. Only by a comparable in-depth investigation can the extent and remedies for the never-decreasing drug menace to sport and the society it serves be adequately assessed and attempted to be controlled and curtailed.

Within sport, the various International Federations battle against fragmented differences of drug testing arrangements, litigation challenges, debatable administrative practices, and so long as national law enforcement agencies through prosecutions of civil claims for damages are discouraged from intervening, the war between offenders and authority will continue.

(3) Commercial exploitation

Four separate and independent areas here demand attention and action.

(1) Property development
(2) Sponsorship
(3) Television
(4) Government

1. Property development

Planning permission, and opposition to applications for it as contemplated by Lord Denning in *Miller v Jackson* (supra) and as operated by Ian Wooldridge and the *Daily Mail* for the War Memorial Recreation ground at New Milton in Hampshire, are the key to protecting sport here. While this chapter was being prepared for the first edition in 1988 the then forty-year-old Harringay Arena Greyhound racing stadium in North London was closing down with a loss of communal identity and, employment to staff and ancillary activities associated with dog racing. Its replacement with appropriate planning permission is to be a supermarket. Furthermore the Register of Playing Fields published during 1993 awaits legislative endorsement, while their administrative destiny remains ultimately in the hand sof the Department of the Environment, the Department of Education and Science and local auhtorities, but never with the Secretary of State or his Under-Secretary at the Department of National heritage which houses today the Government sport portfolio.

2. Sponsorship

David Miller's proposal in *The Times* for conditions imposed by commercial sponsors built in to the sponsorship contract cited in Chapter 13 'Sponsored Gentlemen and Players' is essential if sponsorship is to play a positive role for the sporting moral and ethical advantages it can bring to sport, instead of treating it like any other commodity in the market place. This would be consistent with the opening Conclusion in the Howell Report to its Chapter Thirteen entitled Ethical Considerations (page 87).

> 'The interests of sport, sports people, sponsorship practitioners and the public demand the highest degree of professional practices and ethical standards. In this regard, it is the overriding duty of those controlling sport, nationally and internationally, to initiate machinery whereby such standards may be established and maintained.'

That essential Conclusion was prefaced with a paragraph which explained the obvious for those requiring the need for it to be spelt out.

> 'Without doubt, enormous sums of money have been and are being poured into the promotion of sport. Yet if the affairs of sport at top level are not to descend into a commercial circus it is vital to public interest, the protection of individual sportsmen and sports women and the credibility and integrity of the controlling organisations of sport that adequate initiatives are taken to ensure an acceptance and maintenance of ethical standards by all those involved and acting on behalf of sport.

To underline the importance we attach to this view, we wish to state our principal conclusion at the outset of our discussion of these matters.'

One practical administrative machine which had existed even before the establishment of Denis Howell's Committee of Enquiry into Sports Sponsorship in 1981 was initiated by the sponsors of the oldest originally amateur competitive league in Southern England, the Isthmian League, now the Diadora League, the Berger Paint Company. For the Berger Isthmian League sponsors created an imaginative concept which so far as the author is aware has rarely been repeated, although its true sporting advantages are self-evident.

A Fair-Play Award Scheme was structured. It was geared to a financial pool. Every field offence which resulted in a booking by the referees had the additional consequence of a deduction from the pool. The club with the least number of deductions at the end of the season obtained the greatest share in the pool. The author recalls clearly this period of its existence when the then little-known Leatherhead Football Club was making a national name for itself in various FA Cup competitions. Its chairman, Tom Dixon, would become upset and agitated when players received a censure of booking by the referee. 'There goes another fifty pounds lost from the Fair Play Award Scheme', with phraseology less structured. The principle, however, meets the Howell Report and David Miller's criteria. The Central Council of Physical Recreation's Charter for Fair Play created the same ideal and has been adopted internationally. Furthermore the Council of Europe produced a detailed *Code of Sports Ethics* which it sub-titled *Fair Play – the Winning Way*. What each lacks in a manner consistent with so much of sports approach to the Rule of Law within Sport is a criterion of effectual sanctions for enforcement as created for FIFA in the 1994 World Cup. An example of how effective sanctions range of off-the-field penalties has been created by one of the last bastions of *amateur* sport is the British Amateur Rugby League Association (BARLA).

Adjoining Mr Howell's Birmingham constituency, however, is the Aston Villa Football Club. It provided the Football League's founder President, William MacGregor. It has also provided the first, so far as the author is aware, four-handed funding of recreational services attached to such a club: the Aston Villa Leisure Centre paid for the Club: the local authority, the regional Sports Council and a private source: Associated Dairies Group Limited – an ideal partnership.

Finally, as the pressures in competitions intensify to satisfy the demands of sponsors, investors, the conflicts between health, endurance and capacity to compete as identified in Chapter 7, 'Sports medicine and the law' and Chapter 8, 'Women in Sport and the Law' will explode one day with contractual disputes.

3. Television

The ambivalent approach by sport to those phenomena is evidenced by the contrasts between the blessing given to it by the Wolfenden Report in 1960 (paragraph 222 at pages 84 and 85) and the warning by Sir Denis Follows in 1983,

> 'The very nature of sport is being changed by the advent of television. The Olympic Movement itself depends now for its very existence on television money, 80% of which comes from the United States.'

Two years later this was confirmed by Francis Wheen's *Television: A History* (1985). He explained how the American ABC's input of $225 million was the largest single contribution towards the 1984 Los Angeles Olympic Games (the rest of the world's television companies contributed just $125 million); and then he wrote (page 241):

> 'When ABC is paying the piper so handsomely, it expects to call the tune. At the Winter Olympics in February 1984 (which ABC had acquired for $92 million) there were frequent complaints from performers and journalists about the network's heavy handed behaviour. At one point Princess Anne's private detective asked an ABC man to stop poking his camera in her Royal Highness' face [The Princess Royal attended in her dual capacities as the active President of the British Olympic Association and as a former competitor]. 'Listen buddy', came the reply,
> "We're ABC television. We bought the Olympics. And we do what the hell we like."'

Wheen's *History* continued with its record of the next notch in the hostage of sport to commercial convenience:

> 'ABC has already demonstrated the truth of that by having the 1988 Winter Olympics in Calgary lengthened so that they extend over the three week-ends of prime viewing time. The organisers of the Winter Olympics objected to this interference at first, until they saw the size of ABC's bid of $309 million.'

Wheehan concluded this section of his *History*:

> 'It all seemed a far cry from John Logie Baird's first flickering picture of the Epsom Derby half-a-century earlier [in 1931]; but as one ABC executive put it
> "To bring the best athletic competition in the world back to the United States and at the same time receive high ratings – nothing could be greater".'

Equally, nothing could be greater than the depth of degradation with which these figures emphasise the refusals of the Los Angeles organisers to fund the Wheelchair Olympics, the Paralympics, as explained at pages 195–196 in Chapter 7, 'Sports medicine and the law'. It is not clear on what basis the funds necessary to hold those Games in the United States were sought and rejected. Nevertheless, the philosophy behind the profitability suggests that any request would have been refused even if accompanied by Bing Crosby's rendering of 'Buddy can you spare a dime'.

Against this background, Ron Pickering's citation of Peter Corrigan's insight becomes clear: 'Sport took its soul to the pawnbrokers so long ago that finding the redemption ticket is not going to be easy'. The commodity should be redeemable every four years when the contracts expire – unless the commercial moguls controlling the Olympic Games have mortgaged their inheritance from Baron de Coubertin's legacy to television companies for eternity. In the absence of such feckless irresponsibility even for profit seeking sporting administrators the key question commercially for sport is simple: does sport at any level need television more than television needs sport or vice versa? The equation should be resoluable by a negotiated contract in favour of sport if sport has the will to achieve it.

There is, however, one vital aspect concerning television and sport which is always ignored and now must come into the open. What is the role of the commentator who witnesses and reports upon criminal foul play? Should he or she ignore it and thereby condone it? Should he or she discourage it and expose it for its criminality. These permutations should not be dismissed as irrelevant or fanciful. The law of aiding and abetting in the United Kingdom has not been withered by television or commercial considerations, and the robust judicial attitude of Lord Goddard in *Wilcox v Jeffery* cited in Chapter 6, 'Participation problems' is still the law. It upheld the conviction of the *Jazz Illustrated* proprietor who knew that Coleman Hawkins' appearance on stage was in breach of the Aliens Order restriction on employment. He could have booed, as Lord Goddard adjudged, and did not. He was guilty of aiding and abetting. Television commentators please note, when witnessing criminal foul play, and commenting on it.

4. Government

Government exploitation of sport for over seventy years since its earlier imposition via Entertainment tax in 1916 to its retention through other taxes has been sustained throughout these pages since the earliest citation at page 2 in the opening chapter, 'Genesis' identifies from David Miller in *The Times*

'that sport's VAT/income tax contribution to Government of £2.4bn is greater than the auto industry, that its consumer expenditure £3.2bn (excluding gambling) is more than books/magazines, DIY or records/tapes'.

The point need hardly be made that notwithstanding the Heysel Stadium tragedy, that the death rate from sports generally bears favourably to that from the motor industry. As Sir Denis Follows said in *Whither Sport,*

'the amount of money spent by Government on sport and sports facilities is miniscule in proportion to the importance of sport to the community. Governments, no matter what their political colour, really in truth take sport for granted or as a milch cow to provide them with revenue ... In days of high unemployment recreation facilities provide a means whereby, particularly, the youth of the country may let off steam and hopefully through wise leadership learn the true lessons of sports discipline and tolerance.

And what do we in sport get in return for all the efforts we put into its management, direction and control – our voluntary service? Taxation as if we were running a business; Any revenues raised by sport are taxed as if they were business profits ... Any sports organisation in this country which is a non-profit distribution body should be relieved of all forms of taxation on the revenue it raises'.

The proposed VAT concessions for harmonisation with EC directives are a step in the right direction, alongside the Foundation for Sport and the Arts and the Government Pound for Pound Scheme.

Realities of Government expenditure constraints and the Treasury's sticky paws must be geared to one further factual foundation to discourage optimism in this particular field. The Government portfolio for sport, as we have seen, was charged in 1986 to a Parliamentary Under-Secretary with only 20% of his time allocated to sport, the remaining 80% scattered in the directions clarified in the citation from the evidence to the House of Commons Environment Committee at page 20 above. By 1994 the Parliamentary Under-Secretary shares sport within an Arts National Lottery Sport Group specifically within the framework of an even wider portfolio within the Department of National Heritage which is responsible, as explained in *Whitaker's Almanack 1994.*

Aspects of government policy previously covered by six other government departments. It is responsible for government policy relating to the arts, broadcasting, the press, museums and galleries, libraries, sport and recreation,heritage and tourism. It funds the Arts Council of Great Britain and other arts bodies, including the National Heritage Memorial Fund. It also funds the Museums and Galleries Commission, the national museums and galleries in England, the British Library, the Sports Council, the British Tourist Authority and the English Tourist Board, and the British Film Institute. It is responsible for the issue of export licences on works of art, antiques and collector's items.; the Government Art Collection; the built heritage, including the Royal Parks and the Historic Royal Palaces Executive Agencies; and statistical services including the International Passenger Survey and broadcasting statistics. The Department is also responsible for policy and implementation of the National Lottery and the Millenium Fund.'

This analysis emphasises how significantly neither the Under-Secretary nor his Minister, the Secretary of State, has any direct or even indirect constitutional connection with the Departments for Education and Science concerning school sport and playing fields, or the Department of the Environment concerned with local authority playing fields and other Departments explained in Appendix 7.

(4) Political violation

Wheeler and others v Leicester City Council (supra) should be a sufficient encouragement to all who are victims of manipulation of sport for political purposes, however well- or ill-intentioned. There is another, however, which exists in all the principal sources, but is rarely, indeed, never so far as the author is aware cited for its sporting significance. It concerns one of cricket's greatest heroes to all true sports lovers: Lord Constantine of Maravel and Nelson, MBE, better known as Learie.

During the Second World War he had booked accommodation at London's Imperial Hotel, Russell Square, for himself and his family during 1943 for playing in a charity cricket match. At that time the Allies' Second Front against Nazi Germany was in focus and many American allied servicemen were stationed in the United Kingdom. Sadly, some of them who had doubtless danced to Cab Calloway's black musicians, and felt vicarious patriotic pride in the triumphs of Joe Louis and Jesse Owens, objected to the presence in the hotel of the Empire's greatest all-round cricketer at that time. Assisted by sympathetic lawyers he sued the hotel at common law for wrongfully refusing to receive and lodge him and his family. After two days of legal argument and evidence Birkett J found the case proved and awarded damages, albeit of a nominal amount. Neither side appealed (*Constantine v Imperial Hotels Ltd* [1944] 1 KB 693). For Constantine and sport the result was even more significant than his many Test match triumphs for his native West Indies and his ultimate call to the Bar by Middle Temple and election to its governing body as an Honorary Bencher in addition to his Life Peerage. He had proved that sport and the law know no racial boundaries when the law is operated effectively and correctly in the interests of the wider social scene as well as sport. Within sport itself, the power politics at international level which have witnessed the dominance of International Federations were graphically documented during 1992 by Viv Swinson and Andrew Jennings in *The Lords of the Rings*.

4. CONCLUSION

Wither sport and the law: what direction should sport take today? Whatever route is taken, the Rule of Law, on and off the field, alone can and must guide it within a rapidly revolving social setting whose pace can hardly match the kaleidescopic changes daily imposed on the public mind and eye. Ron Pickering's warning in 1985 that sport need a massive re-think is evidenced by four separate situations which emerged nearly 40 years ago in 1957 with no apparent inter-connection. Yet on reflection they prove and illuminate how sport and society and the law have all changed at the public and private level and point the clear way ahead.

(1)   The Wolfenden Report on Homosexual Offences and Prostitution (Cmnd 247) was published.

(2)   The Wolfenden Report on Sport and the Community was commissioned by the CCPR.

(3)   The Sportsman's Book Club edition edition of *Corinthians and Cricketers* was published.

(4)   Radar was used in Britain as a speed check on motorists.

The last of these three *published* items ended with a citation from the reminiscences, *Almost Yesterday*, of the then doyen of modern sporting writers, Trevor Wignall. His columns in the *Daily Express* were woven into Fleet Street's fascinating tapestry alongside his renowned editor, Arthur Christiansen and its legendary proprietor, Lord Beaverbrook.

> Those who assert that the playing of games is not very different from what it was one hundred years ago are not far wrong ... the kicking of a goal by Tom Lawton, or the heading of it, is much the same as it was when G O Smith was banging them in, and the scoring of a century by Walter Hammond calls forth the same strokes that were employed by W G Grace. Sport has undoubtedly been developed out of all recognition, but not so much in its expositions as in the finer workmanship that has been acquired, and in the enormous crowds it bails and holds'.

Those crowds are even greater today – because of television. The kicking of a goal and scoring of a century and the strokes they require are still the same as in the days of G O Smith and W G Grace. Yet the extent to which sport has developed out of all recognition thirty-seven years later since the citation in 1957 is seen through its administrative structure concurrent with the changes in society generally.

G O Smith and W G Grace were at the peak of their powers in 1896. Dr W G Grace captained England against Australia led by G H S Trott in all three Test Matches played that summer. G O Smith as an undergraduate from Oxford University was England's centre-forward alongside a mixture of his fellow Corinthians and the leading professionals of the day in all three home internationals which alone were played at that time. Against the auld enemy Scotland, at Parkhead, Celtic Park, Glasgow, he was one of six Corinthians chosen with five professionals three months before he hit a memorable 132 in Oxford's fourth innings to help win the Varsity match against Cambridge.

1896 was also a landmark year for the area of law which touches the hem of the majority of citizens universally and with uniformity: driving. Two distinguished Professors, D W Elliott and the late Harry Street explained in their survey *Road Accidents*, published in 1968:

'The history of the criminal law about driving shows a gradual development from the range of offences provided by the law as it existed in a pre-motoring age, a range which, as one would expect, was ill adapted to deal with the new phenomenon of highways crowded with powerful and fast motor vehicles ... Until 1896 it was an offence to drive a horseless carriage at more than 4 mph outside town and 2 mph inside them.'

The need for motoring law and techniques to protect the public to keep pace with each engineering development is stated here only to emphasise the contrasts in time. The radar trap in 1957 and the debates after it suffice to recall the degrees of change since the days of W G Grace and G O Smith in 1896.

If society's conscience towards criminally fouling footballers of all codes had kept pace with its readiness to pressurise Parliament into action against foul driving and drunk and drugged motorists, then many more international footballers (and perhaps a few coaches and managers and directors as aiders and abettors) would have preceded David Bishop into the dock of different criminal courts throughout the land. By their example Bishop might have been warned to avoid the act which so many have committed before to so many, but for which so few have been punished by the courts, as they could and should have been for violation of sport as well as the law. When a distinguished rugby administrator complained that the decision to prosecute Bishop did more harm to rugby football than the punch which set the law in motion it was necessary to point out through the correspondence columns of the *Daily Telegraph* that if the complaint was not in contempt of court, and it might have been, it certainly was in contempt of sport.

In 1896, too, Oscar Wilde was languishing in Reading Gaol, resulting from convictions a year earlier after a second trial at Central Criminal Court, a previous jury having failed to agree upon a verdict. The second trial took place during the last fortnight in May 1895 when W G Grace was racing towards his 1,000 runs which opened up the avenues for his near £10,000 bounty later that summer, and the double standards which allowed retention of his amateur status. Wilde's prosecution took place in a climate of social hostility which would be less severe today; but an Irish biographer of Wilde, Richard Pirie, writing of his fellow countryman in 1983 noted

'the double standard of the day whereby Wilde was kept as a fashionable plaything while he amused, as in Wilde the saboteur of public morals'.

Time has demolished the basis for any ambivalence towards Grace's status, and also possibly to a lesser degree, helped by Wolfenden, the attitudes which destroyed Wilde. Yet in the same period which has shrunk the intervening years, sport, with so many fragments framing it, has failed to build its fences with sufficient will and authority to prevent control on the field as well as off it from being challenged by criminality copied at the most crucial level of all: in the playgrounds and classrooms. Blackmail or threats towards it appeared to shadow preparations for nearly every cricket tour outside the white Commonwealth during the period of South Africa's exclusion from the community of sporting nations. Innuendoes and disputed degrees of evidence about drugs are aired without any attempt by authoritative sources to get a grip by establishing a committee of any kind, whether in the style of Wolfenden's or Howell's qua sport, or under Parliamentary surveillance. While all the time asset strippers and property developers are operating the planning laws to their commercial advantage without any feel for sport or its public, who are uncoordinated and unaware of how to fight this insidious enemy, except at times when the CCPR, NPFA or the *Daily Mail* can raise a battle cry loud enough to stir the local planning authority before the Department of Environment is allowed to have the last word, except when its legal errors (not known) throw a lifeline to the courts.

When the law is invoked in a genuine attempt to protect sport, its use is criticised gratuitously and erroneously as acting intrusively in the manner experienced in *Cowley v Heatley* (1986) during the Commonwealth Games, or on similar false premises after *R v Bishop* (1986). Yet no greater illustration exists today for a need to allow the law into sport readily rather than grudgingly – for it is certainly here to stay – than through the personnel of the Corinthians and the professions they pursued off the field of play when playing for England, too.

Their goalkeeper, W R Moon, founded the well-known Bloomsbury firm of solicitors, Moon Gilkes & Moon. The famous A M and P M Walters brothers at full-back (Morning and Afternoon as they were known) entered the two different branches of the profession. A M founded the firm which became Walters and Hart. P M practised at the Chancery Bar, became a Bencher of his Inn of Court, Loincoln's and a hero to the great golf correspondent and fellow barrister, Bernard Darwin, who reminisced frequently about visits to his chambers in his many writings. Tinsley Lindley, G O Smith's immediate predecessor at centre-forward for England the Corinthians also played for Nottingham Forest, as an amateur. He became a successful barrister on the Midland Circuit, and also son-in-law of the proprietor of Punch, Sir Francis Burnand, who decreed pronunciation of his name after the port proved fitness to join the ladies. His photograph in wig and gown alongside that of Montague Shearman, the earliest chronicler of *Athletics and Football, The Badminton Library* (887) can be seen to-day in a montage of the Midland Circuit from 1913 in the Robing Room at Derby Crown Court. Their centre-half over many years, Charles Wreford-Brown, moved from successive captaincies of Charterhouse, Oxford, Corinthians and England, to chairmanship of the FA Council before and during the Second World War while establishing the City firm of Devonshire & Co. Yet he alone was required to lend his expertise to sport: as Honorary Legal Adviser to the National Playing Fields Association.

Today, because 'Sport has undoubtedly developed out of recognition' since those Corinthian days of G O Smith and W G Grace, their professional services and those of their contemporaries are crucial for the administrative survival of sport at all levels. Each of the traditional professions which these amateur Corinthian internationals adorned while playing alongside their professional team colleagues for England is equally essential for sport's future existence as sport, and not merely as a tradeable commodity in a sordid marketplace. The schoolmasters such as G O Smith himself and Fry are vital to steer pupils, players and administrators along the paths of propriety, according to the rule of fair play. The banker of Gosling's lineage is essential for funding facilities which successive governments of all political colouring and their bureaucracies have failed at local as well as national levels to provide for the grass-roots demands of the rapidly changing standards of sporting participants; sport's self-evident need to-day for medical wisdom of the kind developed by their Oxford and Corinthian contemporary at wing-half, Farquhar Buzzard. By the time he died at the end of 1945 as an eminent neurologist and Sir Farquhar, he had been Regious Professor of Medicine at Oxford University and Physician to two Kings of England, H M George V and H M George VI. His life-long devotion to football, however, was evidenced by the prelude to his outstanding contributions to medical literature and thought in his *Who's Who* entry. It listed proudly in addition to his Oxford Soccer Blues his appearance in two of the earliest FA Cup Amateur winning XI's and three London Senior Cup Finals.

Sport needs all of these, and all the other associated professions, for whom this book identifies it is intended, as explained in the Introduction if it is to preserve its true integrity and identity in a rapidly dominating commercial market forces world. Lawyers to free it from the feudal grip of administrators in the Banks, Eastham, Nagle, Packer and Welsh FA line of litigation. Schoolmaster leaders to point the way in the modern traditions created ideally by Rous, Follows, Altham and their successors, to teach those who have to be reminded from time to time or throughout their lives of the basic difference between right and wrong. Doctors to heal the wounded from foul play or natural causes in the tradition of Tucker's insight into Compton's knee-cap problem from his rugby days with England; and financiers to benefit sport as well as themselves in the style of Barclays investment in the eccentric finances of professional football to catch up with the legacy left by the member of the family associated with their Gosling's Branch in Fleet Street, perpetuating the memory of another creative schoolmaster amateur international footballer alongside the outstanding professionals of his day, Arthur Dunn. Above all else sport needs a revival of Lord Hailsham's awareness, cited on the opening page, of the absence of a 'coherent body of doctrine, perhaps even a philosophy of government encouragement'.

So, in the end, we return to the beginning. Whither Sport. Whither Sport and the Law. In this Chapter 15 'Whither Sport and the Law' in the first edition I wrote;

'Has the time come now to move on from the need spelt out by Lord Hailsham of "a focal point under a Minister" to beyond a Parliamentary Under Secretary with 80 per cent of his time allocated to matters other than sport as evidenced by the former Junior Minister, Mr Richard Tracey, MP to the House of Commons Committee cited above. Furthermore, has the time come to transfer the 20 per cent of time available for sport away from the Department of the Environment?'

The answer appeared to have been provided by transferance of the Sport and Recreation Division (SARD) services within the Whitehall machine with the Department of National Heritage and its Minister with Cabinet Status in 1992 after a brief period at the Department of Education and Science. The Secretaries of State for Wales, Scotland and Northern Ireland are responsible for government policy in Sport and their countries [see Appendix 8 on Scotland from Kerrigan QC] and in Northern Ireland the Department of Education makes direct grants towards the capital cost of facilities for local authorities and voluntary sports bodies.

Notwithstanding the elevated status of the DHH Minister at Cabinet level, his portfolio shares sport with arts as in Appendix 7, with only a junior minister allocated exclusively in England and Wales for sport. Furthermore, in this Chapter 15, 'Whither Sport and the Law', in the first edition it was necessary to write;

'the most supreme irony of all these situations is contained in the Letter of Responses to the Chairman of the House of Commons Environment Committee after the 1985 Report from the then Senior Minister concerned, the Secretary of State for the Environment, Mr Nicholas Ridley dated 24 June 1986, and published 2 July 1986 [HC 504]. Inter alia it states,

'Sport plays a vital role in everyday life. We recognise its importance to people in the national and international scene. At home sporting activity provides a healthy and enjoyable leisure pursuit; sport promotes civic and national pride; it can assist social and community aims; it has a significant impact upon the economy. Internationally, sport can extend British influence and prestige and promote trade and stability – not least in the Commonwealth.

To play these various important roles, sport requires, as your Committee recognised, public support and sometimes guidance. The Sports Council is the public agency, which is the primary source of this support and advice. Mine is the sponsoring Department; the Minister for Sport and I are concerned to give the sports movement and associated industry the necessary help and support and to promote their efficiency and contribution. We do so in cooperation with the Sports Council and with other government Departments, with responsibilities affecting sport, in particular with FCO, Home Office, DES, DE and DTI.'

It will be noted that the list of "other Government Departments" with which Mr Ridley and the Minister for Sport claimed to cooperate did not include the DHSS, concerned with drugs; HM customs and Excise concerned with VAT; or the Inland Revenue and the Treasury and the Chancellor of the Exchequer concerned with all of sport's unco-ordinated complaints about oppressive taxation. Hence the comment ... above to the effect: "Who speaks for Sport in Cabinet or elsewhere for VAT and tax concessions?"

Furthermore, the role of Home Office Ministers on violence; of DES for school sport (and the Committees criticisms of the two Departments, Mr Ridley's and the DES, before the joint seminar at the DoE in December 1986, explained above); and of the Foreign and Commonwealth Office's direct association with the South African and other overseas sporting scenes, all suggest an element of hyperbole in Mr Ridley's description of "cooperation".'

Thus, Lord Hailsham's claim in 1962 cited at page 43 above:

'that recreation generally presented a complex of problems out of which

modern government was not wholly free to opt, and which government
funds were, in fact, and were likely to continue to be committed in one
way or another ...'

has been more than confirmed by the intervening years crystallised in
the above statement of policy in 1986.

Nearly eight years after that Ministerial survey of the sporting
scene viewed from the grandstand at Westminster and Whitehall
Lord Hailsham's additional recognition cited on page 1, of the absence of any

'coherent body of doctrine, perhaps even a philosophy of government
encouragement',

still remains justified. Indeed, a joint Department of the Environment, Welsh Office and Scottish Education Department Consultation Paper in 1987 entitled 'Competition in the Management of
Local Authority Sport and Leisure Facilities' for their privitisation
resulted in a Parliamentary Order in 1989 under the Local Government Act 1988, which directed all non-educational sport and leisure
facilites into the commercial market place to competitive tender
(CCT) by 1993. This re-alignment and shifting of the balance at the
Governments insistence from local authority sources to private commercial operators invited by the Department of the Environment to
tender for sport and leisure alongside 'refuse collection, street cleaning, cleaning of buildings' and their associated activities, to cite its
own Consultation Paper, was compounded by the further evidence of
the absence of any 'coherent body of doctrine perhaps even a philosophy of government encouragement,' which is neatly cummarised in
Paragraph 1.7 of a Report dated 23 December 1993. It was prepared
by the Comptroller and Auditor-General at the National Audit
Office, Sir John Bourn, under section 6 of the National Audit Act for
presentation to the House of Commons in accordance with Section 9
of the Act with the title, 'The Sports Council: Initiatives to Improve
Financial Management and Control and Value for Money'.

'Restructuring of The Sports Council

1.7 In November 1991 the Government issued a document, Sport and
Active Recreation, which set out their policies and priorities for sport.
These included the restructuring of the Council into a Sports Council
for England and a United Kingdom Sports Commission. During the
course of the National Audit Office's examination the Government
announced that it no longer intended to proceed with the planned
restructuring. Instead, fresh arrangements were to be considered to
ensure a United Kingdom dimension for sport. Following on from this,
the activities and general structure of the Council will also be reviewed.'

A separate section and series of Paragraphs in the Report appear under the heading 'Funding Arrangments with the Central Council of Physical Recreation.' So far as these pages are concerned they reflect what the *Guardian's* distinguished Sports Politics Correspondent John Rodda described as 'the peculiar complexities of sporting policies', with which this book, as distinct from Parliamentary legislative political sources, is not concerned. For the Parliamentary announcement in July 1994 already referred to above explaining the creation of a new United Kingdom Sports Council and English Sports Council, was accompanied by a publicly disclosed letter from the new Secretary of State for National Heritage. It recognised specifically how 'the current arrangements generate confusion and cut across proper lines of accountability and responsibility'. How far the proposed 'new arrangements' also specified will create a healthier sporting climate must now await events.

Away from Government sporting administration, however, and directly in the legal penalty area significantly while these pages were in their stages of preparation one of the Secretary of State's ministerial colleagues, Attorney-General Sir Nicholas Lyell, QC, MP, was reported in the *Guardian* (2 February 1994) as having referred to the Court of Appeal Criminal Division under section 36(1) of the Criminal Justice Act 1988 as 'unduly lenient' a two years probation order imposed on a 22-years old, Jason Piff at Gloucester Crown Court in September 1993. Playing for the Fox and Hounds team in Cheltenham, Gloucestershire, he had admitted causing serious harm to Anthony Dalessandro, aged 29, who played for another amateur side, Charlton Kings. The victim had suffered from a clash between the two players a fractured left cheek bone, a shattered eye socket and other injuries which resulted in months of treatment.

The Lord Chief Justice, Lord Taylor of Gosforth, said the idea must be scotched that anyone who intended serious harm could expect to avoid a custodial sentence and be put on probation in the hope that he would respond satisfactorily; and a compensation order of £500 was cancelled (*R v Piff* (1994)).

Almost symbolically, a century earlier in October 1887, one of his predecessors as Attorney-General, Sir Richard Webster QC, MP, who had won by 40 yards the two miles race in a time of 10 mins 48.25 seconds for Cambridge University against Oxford in the 1865 Varsity Athletics Match, and later became Lord Chief Justice as Lord Alverstone, wrote in an Introduction from the Temple to the young barrister Montague Shearman's *Badminton Library: Athletics and Football*, with words of equal importance today,

'We are brought face to face in England, and other populous countries, with the difficult problem which is called into existence by over-population, and the utter absence of space and opportunity for the youth of the present day to find sufficient scope for his energies. The tendency to crowd into the curriculum of both school and college a large and ever-increasing number of subjects has rendered the strain of education far heavier than in times gone by, and this tension will certainly increase. In old days, when a fair grounding in Greek and Latin, or a moderate knowledge in mathematics, was a sufficient preparation for almost any profession (the brilliant few being left to excel in those subjects by the sheer force of their natural abilities), the culture of the body and the simultaneous development of physical and mental strength were of less importance, or at any rate their value was less recognised.'

With a further comparable relevance to today's circumstances, as a classic illustration of what may be categorised as 'back to basics', he concluded with;

'one word upon that which may be called the moral aspect of athletics. That their practice tends to encourage self-control, self-reliance, without undue confidence, and a proper appreciation of other men's merits, there can be no doubt; moreover, they promote that spirit of good-fellowship which enables the beaten man to go up and honestly congratulate the victor who has conquered him; but, beyond this, as I have already said, the contests and gatherings offer the opportunity of making lasting friendships and connections which are often of the greatest value in after life. A reputation once earned by the boy or man in such pursuits follows him to other professions, and has more than once contributed in no small degree to early success in the work of life.'

Such thoughts from the pioneering creative days of British and international sport during the 50 years of Queen Victoria's reign and the fifth year of the immortal Corinthian Football Club's foundation, have an echo of the Corinthian values cited by Ron Pickering in his 1985 address to the CCPR, Peter Bills' sub-title to his biography of France's Rugby hero, Jean-Pierre Rives, and the London *Evening Standard*'s plea in 1991;

'is there a way back to a golden age, to the Corinthian era?'

From a different angle they also reflect what *The Times* explained in a leading article after Jayne Torvill and Christopher Dean had won the British ice dance championship in the early days of 1994, stating how the former world professional celebrities

'by the increasingly absurd rules distinguishing amateurs from professionals, they have now been officially revirginalised . . . .
  But what they do is sport as well as show-business. While they are on the ice, they balance on the razor edge of grace under pressure. The earliest athletics festivals invented by sporting man held contests for poetry and dancing as well as running and throwing things. So, like

modern ice dance, they too had judges employed to give their export opinions on artistic impression.

Much modern sport has become grimly competitive, with its football hooligans, petty chauvinists, steroids, and glum professionals obsessively working towards the big money. In it there are no points for graceful losers, only for determined winners. Torvill and Dean brought grace and a genteel intimation of sex into their sport. Their skating is breathtakingly dangerous and skilful, and they introduced a new glamour and more dramatic poses, even though they sometimes still look more like wrestlers than Fonteyn and Nureyev. They are two bodies in dancing unison, and their comeback in sporting middle age gratifies the middle-aged crowd's Peter Pan instinct.

If what Torvill and Dean do on ice is deemed merely middlebrow showbusiness, sport could do with more of it. When taken to its logical conclusion, all sport is absurd. But sport is more about emotion than logic. If other sports gave marks for artistic impression, David Gower would still be batting, Henri Leconte would always win Wimbledon, Severiano Ballesteros would win championships more often than he does, and Jeremy Guscott would be shimmying through the midfield for all eternity. And the sporting firmament would be brighter.'

That brightness will return when the Rule of Law within Sport at all levels, playing, refereeing and umpiring and administratively, is recognised as essential for its survival. Indeed as the former Chairman of the Sports Council and England Rugby Football Union President and captain of England, Dick Jeeps, CBE wrote as long ago as 1978 in his foreword to the 76-page *Sunday Telegraph* edition of *Sport and the Law*

Sport belongs to the real world and its rapid development in recent years has made ignorance of the law among decision-makers unacceptable.'

Thus it is possible to end this edition with the same optimism with which I concluded six years ago in January 1988.

'Happily for sport, while Whitehall and Westminster were confirming Lord Hailsham's prevailing "confusion and doubt" cited at [page 16, above, this edition] above, United Kingdom and European and USA golfers were reviving hope for all who at times despair for preserving the true spirit of sport at the public level, in the public eye. It came with professional golf's Ryder Cup and the universal acclaim for both the European winners and the USA losers. It also emphasised the Rule of Law as the answer to Ron Pickering's need for "a massive re-think" based on Peter Corrigan's quest for a redemption ticket since "Sport took its soul to the pawnbrokers so long ago".

Of that joyous sports event David Miller wrote, also in *The Times*, while these pages were being organised (Tuesday 29 September 1987, page 44), 'It is my privilege as well as my job to be at many international events, yet I have witnessed no Wimbledon, no Olympic Games, no

World Cup of football where for three days I lived, minute by minute
from breakfast till teatime, in such suspense along with a crowd of
20,000.

More than that, there is another aspect which the Americans do not
fully appreciate [the non-reference on any one of their breakfast television sports-broadcasts to be the occasion] not only because of their
baseball-football-basketball obsession; though in this they are in company with many others. It is that professional golf is almost the only
major sport in which the players unwaveringly stick to rules.'

They have to, of course. Their Code of Ethics and Constitution
proclaim:

'... the words Professional Golfers' Association must be and remain a
hallmark of service, honesty, fair dealing and courtesy'.

Thus Counsel for the Prosecution the Nottingham County Court
libel action (Chapter 12, at p 329, above) explained:

'Golf is a game based on honour and trust. Cheating is not only
outlawed by the laws of the game, it is repugnant to the whole spirit and
ethos of the game.'

It was expressed even more widely by the Rt Rev and Rt Hon Dr
Graham Leonard, former Bishop of London, and an Honorary
Bencher of the Middle Temple (18 September 1987) at Westminster
College, Fulton, Missouri prior to his conditional ordination as a
Roman Catholic priest, now happy to be known as Father Graham
Leonard (BBC Sunday: Radio 4: 1 May 1994). He cited Cicero's
famous definition in his *de Republica*:

'True law is right reason in agreement with nature; it is of universal
application, unchanging and everlasting; it summons to duty by its
commands and averts from wrong-doing by its prohibitions ... And
there will not be different laws at Rome or at Athens, or different laws
now and in the future, but one eternal and unchangeable law will be
valid for all nations and all times, and there will be one ruler, that is,
God, over us all, for He is the author of the law, its promulgator and its
enforcing judge.'

Those within sport, and anyone beyond it, who may seek an alternative route to the Great Umpire in the sky, will find it appropriately
within the context of this book in the first known public Letters
written to the Corinthians:

'Know ye not that they which run in a race run all,
But one receiveth the prize?
So run, that ye may obtain.

And every man that striveth for the mastery is temperate in all things.
Now they do it to obtain a corruptible crown: but we an
  incorruptible'

[*Corinthians*: First Letter from St Paul Chap 9 Verse 24:25]

Appendices

Contents

SPORT

LAW

Appendix 1

The Corinthian ideal

Hubert Doggart, OBE
'Corinthian and Cricketer', past President of MCC and
ex-Headmaster of King's School, Bruton

For a sportsman to be called a Corinthian is perhaps the highest accolade he can receive. We recall from the last quarter of the Victorian age, for instance, the sporting prowess of C B Fry, a Corinthian to his fingertips, and G O Smith, the finest amateur centre-forward of his day, to whom Edward Grayson once paid a seminal visit on leave-out from school. Both could be said to have upheld the Corinthian ideal.

Today the word 'Corinthian' has ringingly favourable overtones, but it was not ever thus. In the Greek language, 'to be a Corinthian' was to suggest a lowly man or woman, or both together, whose idea of sporting activities was decidedly below the belt. In his letters to the Christians in Corinth St Paul stresses that they must be on their guard – against their own divisions as well as against the seedy diversions available at the drop of a hat.

Words, as Philip Howard tells us in his books and articles, often undergo a rich sea-change. At the inaugural meeting of the Corinthian Football Club, called by N L Jackson, the honorary assistant secretary of the Football Association, in Paternoster Row, London, in 1882, the name 'The Wednesday' was discarded and, by a happy chance, 'The Corinthian Football Club' decided. To the proposer, Mr H A Swepstone, the name may well have seemed a halfway house between Spartan and Athenian, with a healthy dose not only of sporting prowess but also of the 'Muscular Christianity' of the day.

The word 'Corinthian' can cross frontiers. When Mr Peter Bills wishes to pay Jean-Pierre Rives, the great French Rugby player and sportsman, a special compliment, he sub-titles his book, 'A Modern Corinthian', implying those standards of 'sport for sport's sake' achieved by the Corinthian teams, of the 1880s and the 1920s especially.

Bills expresses it word-perfectly at the end of the book:

'All his career Rives has fought to enshrine a special spirit, a joyous approach. He will be remembered as a man who cherished such spirit, in himself and in others. His lasting testimony to the game is not of tries scored or matches played or jerseys swapped: such are peripheral matters. It was always 'spirit' which motivated Rives, that is love for the game, played in the finest traditions with love for those involved, even one's fiercest opponents.'

The same kind of tribute could surely also be paid to the 'legendary' Bobby Jones, that outstanding Amateur golfer for the United States, whose sense of fair play, exceptional character and four Grand Slams (as they are now called) in tournament victories in 1930 are writ large in the annals of sport. Thus, we have an American Corinthian and a French Corinthian as well as those English Corinthians who have given their name to the ideal which is the subject of this appendix.

I was fortunate to be reared in a Corinthian environment, having Graham Doggart as my father, Gilbert Ashton as my prep-school headmaster, Colin Hunter as my housemaster at Winchester, and Hubert Ashton as my godfather – all four of them fine 'Corinthians and Cricketers', as Edward Grayson called his excellent book in 1955. It is true that they lived in a more innocent age in terms of sport and life, when the Corinthian ideal came to them more naturally, but that, for us, is the nub of the matter.

In his chapter in the first edition of *Sport and Law* entitled 'Genesis' (and in the Introduction to this edition), Edward Grayson has a delightful list of those 'concerned with, affected by or interested in whatever is believed or understood to be sport'. Alliteratively and engagingly it includes 'the tea ladies and the team agents', and he concludes: 'in fact, participant at every level from aspiring and fading stars with feet of clay to all who know that, in the beginning and at the end, sport exists for fun and the never changing ideal embodied in "mens sana in corpore sano"'.

Those in the list (the tea-ladies almost certainly excluded, since they know it already!) need to be constantly reminded of the Corinthian ideal. For without it – in this more complex, more commercial, more cynical, and more street-wise age – sport can so easily cease to be true to the practical hopes and personal dreams of its founders. Cricket – though, of course, sponsors are a blessing rather than a blight – can all too easily become market-led rather than cricket-led. And, mutatis mutandis, all other sports can also. We need a crusade to stop this happening.

From that list, those involved in the administration of sport have a self-evident duty to see the wood from the trees and to stop sporting 'Dutch Elm Disease' – with no aspersion being cast on the Dutch – from spreading. But I choose to select three specific groups whose efforts could be harnessed to stop the rot and ensure the survival, relatively intact, of the Corinthian ideal.

First, the doctors, whose Hippocratic oath can be construed as an upholding of the Corinthian ideal in medicine. Second, the lawyers, who once played without a thought that their services qua lawyers would be needed, but cannot now be sure. And, third, schoolteachers, whose *raison d'être* could be called 'the upholding of the Corinthian ideal in body, mind and soul'. To the barricades, then, in the cause of the Corinthian ideal!

Appendix 2

Sportsmanship and respect for authority

Doug Insole
Former Essex and England cricketer and amateur footballer

During the period of about 50 years which covers my involvement in the playing and administration of football and cricket at senior level there have been fundamental and wide-ranging changes in the attitudes of players in both games, even though the laws encompassing fair and unfair play have in each case remained unaltered throughout.

Many powerful influences, all of them reflected in society generally, can be cited as contributing towards what undoubtedly amounts to a significant deterioration in what might be described loosely as 'sportsmanship' coupled with, and probably consequent upon, a steadily decreasing respect for the laws of the game and for those appointed to ensure that those laws are applied.

The law and its custodians, on and off the field, are being tried to the limit and not infrequently to the point at which umpires and referees, but especially the latter, are being abused to such an extent that they decide to sever their connections with a 'sport' which has such unpleasant associations.

I have little doubt that the so-called glory of winning and the alleged ignominy attached to losing are the most important factors in the current approach to sporting contests. Big money is, of course, a crucial factor where it exists, but lack of respect for authority in almost all sports is as pronounced at the bottom of the scale as it is at the top. It can justifiably be said that performers in the lower echelons are simply imitating those who play at the highest level, but money and national prestige are a relevance only where star professionals are involved.

My own clear recollection of early experiences in top level sport – amateur and professional – is that dissent and the disputing of decisions was almost non-existent and that a substantial majority of players were prepared to assist the officials in charge of a match in taking decisions. An obvious example of this tendency is that batsmen frequently – in fact, usually – 'walked' when they snicked the ball to the wicket-keeper. It was customary if a catch was made close to the ground, or if it was unseen by the batsman, for the fielder to be asked if the catch had been cleanly taken and for the batsman to depart, if the answer was in the affirmative, without reference to the umpire. Fielders, similarly, would make it known immediately if what appeared to have been a catch was in fact a 'bump' ball. The claiming of a catch when the ball had not carried was almost unheard of, but not quite. There were one or two performers in the English first-class game who were regarded with some suspicion, and Frank Chester, widely regarded as the best umpire ever, told me that in a Test Match in 1948 he was asked by his colleague at the bowler's end whether a possible catch at the wicket had actually 'carried' to the keeper. Chester had seen clearly that the ball had bounced a couple of feet in front of the wicket-keeper and as a result his pronouncement of 'not out' was loud and disapproving. At the end of the over he was informed very firmly by the Australians that the umpire's job was simply to announce a decision, and not to make moral judgments.

Cricket, of course, is the only major sport in which the appeal is part of the formal structure of the game, and this in itself is a cause of controversy and of potential animosity. The very act of appealing means that the fielding side – often, in these days, in concert and unanimously – claims that the batsman is out and, much more often than not, the umpire is obliged to disagree with them. Concerted appealing, combined with premature celebration and much congratulatory embracing, is a fairly recent and entirely unacceptable means of putting pressure on the umpire and so influencing him to make wrong decisions. It is intimidation aimed at bringing about a miscarriage of justice and it is the aspect of 'gamesmanship' that umpires regard as the most objectionable of all.

In soccer, too, there was in the early days of my participation a ready acceptance of the referee's decision and even a general inclination to take the most obvious decisions for him. There was nothing quite as obvious as the occasion on which the Corinthian goalkeeper moved out of his goal to allow his opponents to score from the penalty spot and do something to expunge the disgrace of having committed a foul in the penalty area – that goes back a bit further still. But players would acknowledge a corner, or a goal-kick, or a throw-in by presenting the ball to the opposition to enable them to get on with the game. With very few exceptions a player who had injured an opponent would, at the very least, inquire after his health. That this kind of friendly gesture so rarely happens in these days is perhaps not surprising in that the assailant has probably committed an intentional, 'professional' foul and that the victim may be feigning fatal injury in order to influence the referee to dismiss the offender from the field of play. No wonder that the game is littered with disciplinary hearings and appeals procedures at which legal representation on both sides is now commonplace.

The shadow of the law influences the judgment of sporting administrators the world over. Recourse to the legal process in the settlement of what might previously have been regarded as 'internal' matters is almost the norm. Most governing bodies have recently tried to enshrine within their Rules the principle that clubs will not sue if decisions within the game go against them, but feelings sometimes run so high that the law of the land is called into play to settle 'sporting' disputes.

The modern administrator is constantly seeking the advice of lawyers about the 'reasonableness' of rules and regulations applying to his particular sport in order to avoid possible legal implications arising as a result of sporting legislation.

It would be comforting to think that what may broadly be described as 'the Corinthian spirit' may one day be revived, but for a number of reasons such a development seems a very remote possibility.

'Player power', which has played such an important part in the deterioration of behaviour in sport, could in theory be kept in check by administrators and governing bodies, but firm action is unlikely when spectators at sporting events often approve, support and give every indication of admiring those performers who challenge authority in the most ostentatious manner. To take effective punitive action against the stars of a sport which is anxious to attract and to retain public interest in a highly competitive world is a step that most administrators would take only with the greatest reluctance, and under extreme pressure. Their situation is made no easier by the fact that the media is inclined to recruit these 'characters' and to invite them to project their image of the sporting ethic to the world at large.

The situation may well be irretrievable unless respect for the law returns to society as a whole but happily there are still clubs, organisations and individuals prepared to perform within the spirit and according to the laws of their chosen sports. While they and the concept of sportsmanship still exist, they must be given all possible help and encouragement.

What is crystal clear is that modern attitudes, the worst aspect of which include such legally unacceptable practices as the professional foul and the use of drugs to enhance performance, must be altered if the word 'sport' is to retain anything of its original and time-honoured meaning.

Appendix 3

Violence, drugs and trial by television

Dr John Davies
Hon Medical Officer WRU, IRB and Chairman Medical
Commission on Accident Prevention Sport's Committee

As we approach the end of the century, we enter a new millennium hopefully having learnt a great deal from the achievements and mistakes that have been made in the past. Sport is no exception to the labyrinth of cultural and sociological changes that have taken place, and in many ways reflects these changes in so many different ways. The advent of the telecommunication industry, as one example, into sports is having far-reaching effects if only for the following reasons.

Many amateur sports are achieving exposure on a global scale, and one has only to look at rugby union, where the present Five Nations Championship commands a viewing audience of 200 million each match. Instant replays and highlights of the best moments to be savoured are alas tarnished by occasional needless acts of violence or professional foul and trial by television has now arrived, with video recordings used as evidence in disciplinary hearings. To the role of the administrators in sport has been added a new dimension of judgmental ability and possibly involving legal procedures of civil and criminal liability.

A further area of grave concern to many sports is the introduction of drug testing to participants, many of whom partake in sports and in certain parts of the world where the drug testing procedures are unfamiliar and no government agencies exist. The injection of substances, potions or elixirs to try and enhance performance has existed for centuries. However, the advent of modern powerful drugs such as anabolic steroids and stimulants with potentially life-threatening side-effects has created the era of the chemical athlete and a molecular war with the laboratories and drug detection authorities. During the last few years there have been instances of wide discrepancies by tribunals of governing bodies of sport with regard to penalties and sanctions imposed in the event of positive dope tests and the legality of resolutions imposed by governing bodies has also been challenged. In professional sports such as athletics, this has led to multi-million dollar law suits, and even in rugby union, an amateur game, players have been represented by leading not inexpensive legal counsel.

The two areas outlined above, in trial by television involving possible civil and criminal liability, and the issue of drugs in sport, both raise more questions than answers. It is into these areas that both the medical and legal professions have combined in an advisory capacity to sport in general.

The recognition of sports medicine as an integral part of preventive medicine worldwide, and its acceptance as a speciality with the creation of postgraduate degrees and diplomas, follows the traditional pathway of medicine. This is with regard to responding to healthcare demands in society, and in this instance, the sporting population.

The famous quote 'the Law follows medicine, albeit slowly, but limping a bit, and in the rear' is very apt, with interest now shown by the legal profession in the sporting scene. The recent formation of the British Association for Sport and Law augurs well for the future and follows the pathway pioneered by the medical profession in eventually having sports medicine recognised as a speciality.

It has been my great pleasure to have collaborated with Edward Grayson over the years as co-authors of *Medicine, Sport and the Law* and *Medico-Legal Hazards of Rugby Football Union*, and this second edition of *Sport and the Law* reflects not only his unbounded enthusiasm, but his chosen profession's demand for knowledge on this subject.

Many sports are entering dangerous waters and with the threat of increased exposure as outlined above, medico-legal expertise and support, together with administrators of great character and strength are all necessary for healthy survival.

Appendix 4

Women in sport: Introduction to the Brighton Declaration

Julia Bracewell
Non-practising Barrister, Gouldens Solicitors, Member of the British Sports Council, Olympic fencer and practitioner in sport and the law, Committee member of the British Association of Sport and the Law

I was honoured to head the Drafting Group at The Sports Council's International Conference 'Women, Sport and the Challenge of Change' and be responsible for presenting this Declaration to the delegates. This conference was held at the Grand Hotel, Brighton, 5–8 May 1994 and attended by over 280 delegates from 82 countries from all regions of the world who were key decision and policy makers representing governments, international and national sporting federations and non-governmental groups involved in sport. The delegates examined ways in which women's involvement in sport could be enhanced and the sporting culture changed to reflect women's values and needs.

The delegates agreed to a declaration which set out the aims for work in this area internationally with guiding principles to achieve these aims. This become the Brighton Declaration.

It focuses on sport in the widest sense, covering competitive sport, physical recreation, non-competitive activities conducted on an informal basis and activities engaged in primarily for health and fitness benefits. Research suggests that women prefer social to competitive sport. My drafting colleague, Sue Baker-Finch from the Australian Sports Commission, told how a cross country competition in Australia attracted 8 women competitors! A fun run on the same course with creche facilities attracts 400 women every Sunday. To encourage women to be involved, sport should consider marketing itself appropriately and provide the opportunities required by women.

The Conference was concerned with bringing about change to ensure appropriate sporting services and facilities are provided to women and that women have the opportunity to take part in sport at all levels and in all functions and roles. Change will be accelerated if resources are devoted to it.

Bringing about change also involves a change in attitudes. But both the Namibian Minister for Sport and Youth and the Norwegian Minister for Culture stressed the importance of legislation in facilitating change in their keynote speeches.

The Declaration could prove to be the catalyst for such legal change since it is the culmination of separate national and regional developments in women and sport which were brought together for the first time in an international forum. The Declaration requires organisations and governments to implement necessary policies or programmes to bring about the requisite change.

At this stage, as a lawyer, I am aware that the Declaration has no legal effect. To be legally binding, countries and sporting organisations will need to adopt or ratify it in accordance with their own constitutions, rules or regulations. Already, this has been done by the Sports Council, the Scottish Sports Council, the government of British Columbia and are International Triathlon Union.

Like other international sporting documents, eg the European Sports Charter, the Declaration does not address the issue of legal sanction, nor does it impose duties. It requires parties ratifying it to adopt their own procedures. But the question needs to be asked, if it is not enforced what remedies are available and who has jurisdiction to try the issue or hear any claims? The main strength of the Declaration is that it reflects the views of a very influential international gathering and is evidence of the international sporting community's views on good practice in this area.

The Conference agreed to set up an international working group, one of whose objectives is to present the Declaration to the UN's conference on women in Beijing in 1995. This is important for some of the Countries who attended. Adoption of it by that conference will not by itself make it binding internationally. A further UN instrument or treaty to which states subscribe will probably be necessary. If these principles are applied internationally the Declaration may become part of law by customary use and practice.

Interestingly whilst some women regard themselves as marginalised in sport, sport itself is rarely at the centre of developing general national and international policies although sport's contribution to society and health seems not to be disputed. The key required now is to open the way to link the role of women and sport into the more general women in society debate. UN treaties already exist eg the Convention on the Elimination of all Forms of Discrimination Against Women and many states have legislation such as our own Sex Discrimination Act.

A seminar on whether Equal Opportunities' legislation was a help or hindrance in this area was also held. The European Sports Conference, which the Sports Council chaired for two years, recommended that research should be undertaken to look at the effect of legislation on sport. No funding has yet been secured.

If women are to be encouraged to pursue a career in sport, sport will need to tackle the issues of recruitment, development and retention, which are issues employers in the business world are dealing with.

Attitudes and prevailing conditions in my own sport, fencing, have enabled me to compete at the highest levels including the World Championships and the Olympic Games. But sport is so much more than competition and in other countries, women do not have the same opportunies I have had. Women need sport for the self fulfilment, enjoyment and general wellbeing physical activity brings. But sport also needs women, their values and experiences. This Declaration is an attempt to set down guidelines on how to encourage, develop and retain women in all aspects of sport internationally and to ensure the sporting culture reflects women's needs.

THE BRIGHTON DECLARATION
ON WOMEN AND SPORT

INTRODUCTION

The first international conference on women and sport, which brought together policy and decision makers in sport at both national and international level, took place in Brighton, UK from 5–8 May 1994. It was organised by the British Sports Council and supported by the International Olympic Committee. The conference specifically addressed the issue of how to accelerate the process of change that would redress the imbalances women face in their participation and involvement in sport.

The 280 delegates from 82 countries representing governmental and non-governmental organisations, national Olympic committees, international and national sport federations and educational and research institutions, endorsed the following Declaration. The Declaration provides the principles that should guide action intended to increase the involvement of women in sport at all levels and in all functions and roles.

In addition, the conference agreed to establish and develop an International Women in Sport Strategy which encompasses all continents. This should be endorsed and supported by governmental and non-governmental organisations involved in sport development. Such an international strategic approach will enable model programmes and successful developments to be shared among nations and sporting federations, so accelerating the change towards a more equitable sporting culture worldwide.

BACKGROUND

Sport is a cultural activity which, practised fairly and equitably, enriches society and friendship between nations. Sport is an activity which offers the individual the opportunity of self-knowledge, self-expression and fulfilment; personal achievement, skill acquisition and demonstration of ability; social interaction, enjoyment, good health and well-being. Sport promotes involvement, integration and responsibility in society and contributes to the development of the community.

Sport and sporting activities are an integral aspect of the culture of every nation. However, while women and girls account for more than half of the world's population and although the percentage of their participation in sport varies between countries, in every case it is less than that of men and boys.

Despite growing participation of women in sport in recent years and increased opportunities for women to participate in domestic and international arenas, increased representation of women in decision making and leadership roles within sport has not followed.

Women are significantly under-represented in management, coaching and officiating, particularly at the higher levels. Without women leaders, decision makers and role models within sport, equal opportunities for women and girls will not be achieved.

Women's experiences, values and attitudes can enrich, enhance and develop sport. Similarly, participation in sport can enrich, enhance and develop women's lives.

THE DECLARATION

A. SCOPE AND AIMS OF THE DECLARATION

1. Scope

This Declaration is addressed to all those governments, public authorities, organisations, businesses, educational and research establishments, women's organisations and individuals who are responsible for, or who directly or indirectly influence, the conduct, development or promotion of sport or who are in any way involved in the employment, education, management, training, development or care of women in sport. This Declaration is meant to complement all sporting, local, national and international charters, laws, codes, rules and regulations relating to women or sport.

2. Aims

The overriding aim is to develop a sporting culture that enables and values the full involvement of women in every aspect of sport.

It is in the interests of equality, development and peace that a commitment be made by governmental, non-governmental organisations and all those institutions involved in sport to apply the Principles set out in this Declaration by developing appropriate policies, structures and mechanisms which:

- ensure that all women and girls have the opportunity to participate in sport in a safe and supportive environment which preserves the rights, dignity and respect of the individual;
- increase the involvement of women in sport at all levels and in all functions and roles;
- ensure that the knowledge, experiences and values of women contribute to the development of sport;
- promote the recognition of women's involvement in sport as a contribution to public life, community development and in building a healthy nation;
- promote the recognition by women of the intrinsic value of sport and its contribution to personal development and healthy lifestyle.

B. THE PRINCIPLES

1. Equity and Equality in Society and Sport

a)   Every effort should be made by state and government machineries to ensure that institutions and organisations responsible for sport comply with the equality provisions of the Charter of the United Nations, the Universal Declaration of Human Rights and the UN Convention on the Elimination of All Forms of Discrimination against Women.

b)   Equal opportunity to participate and be involved in sport, whether for the purpose of leisure and recreation, health promotion or high performance, is the right of every woman, regardless of race, colour, language, religion, creed, sexual orientation, age, marital status, disability, political belief or affiliation, national or social origin.

c)   Resources, power and responsibility should be allocated fairly and without discrimination on the basis of sex, but such allocation should redress any inequitable balance in the benefits available to women and men.

2. Facilities

Women's participation in sport is influenced by the extent, variety and accessibility of facilities. The planning, design and management of these should appropriately and equitably meet the particular needs of women in the community, with special attention given to the need for childcare provision and safety.

3. School and Junior Sport

Research demonstrates that girls and boys approach sport from markedly different perspectives. Those responsible for sport, education, recreation and physical education of young people should ensure that an equitable range of opportunities and learning experiences, which accommodate the values, attitudes and aspirations of girls, is incorporated in programmes to develop physical fitness and basic sport skills of young people.

4. Developing Participation

Women's participation in sport is influenced by the range of activities available. Those responsible for delivering sporting opportunities and programmes should provide and promote activities which meet women's needs and aspirations.

5. High Performance Sport

a)   Governments and sports organisations should provide equal opportunities to women to reach their sports performance potential by ensuring that all activities and programmes relating to performance improvements take account of the specific needs of female athletes.
b)   Those supporting elite and/or professional athletes should ensure that competition opportunities, rewards, incentives, recognition, sponsorship, promotion and other forms of support are provided fairly and equitably to both women and men.

6. Leadership in Sport

Women are under-represented in the leadership and decision making of all sport and sport-related organisations. Those responsible for these areas should develop policies and programmes and design structures which increase the number of women coaches, advisers, decision makers, officials, administrators and sports personnel at all levels with special attention given to recruitment, development and retention.

7. Education, Training and Development

Those responsible for the education, training and development of coaches and other sports personnel should ensure that education processes and experiences address issues relating to gender equity and the needs of female athletes, equitably reflect women's role in sport and take account of women's leadership experiences, values and attitudes.

8. Sports Information and Research

Those responsible for research and providing information on sport should develop policies and programmes to increase knowledge and understanding about women and sport and ensure that research norms and standards are based on research on women and men.

9. Resources

Those responsible for the allocation of resources should ensure that support is available for sportswomen, women's programmes and special measures to advance this Declaration of Principles.

10. Domestic and International Cooperation

Government and non-government organisations should incorporate the promotion of issues of gender equity and the sharing of examples of good practice in women and sport policies and programmes in their associations with other organisations, within both domestic and international arenas.

Appendix 5

Hooligan-free football ground records in England and Wales (1919–1939)

Prepared by **Harry Grayson**
Solicitor, William Relton & Co, London

Note: This Appendix was prepared for the First Butterworth edition at the author's specific request for the period 1919–1939 during national unemployment of an estimated 3 million; but no recorded violence or crime appears at any of the crowd attendance records in the schedule listed below. It is retained here to illustrate the point made in Chapter 15, 'Whither Sport and the Law?', which refers to Mr Justice Popplewell's experience (shared by the author) of having read 30 or 40 sources on the causation of crowd hooliganism, and doubted if he was any the wiser.

The hard facts contained in this Appendix had been included with the (at present unfulfilled) hope that they may perhaps stimulate research among the many survivors from these record attendances (including the author!) for comparison with the current crowd consequences of the self-styled permissive society. It is an area for research so far untapped by seekers of the truth behind one of sport's many ailments.

LIST IN ORDER OF CROWD SIZE

Club	Crowd		Date	Occasion
1	Manchester City	84,569	3 Mar 1934	FA Cup 6
	(British record for any game outside London or Glasgow)			
2	Chelsea	82,905	12 Oct 1935	FA Cup 5
3	Manchester United	76,926	25 March 1939	FA Cup
	(Wolves v. Grimsby Town)			Semi-Final
4	Sunderland	75,118	8 Mar 1933	FA Cup 6
5	Tottenham Hotspur	75,038	5 Mar 1938	FA Cup 6
6	Charlton Athletic	75,031	12 Feb 1938	FA Cup 5
7	Arsenal	73,295	9 Mar 1935	Div. 1
8	Sheffield Wednesday	72,841	17 Feb 1934	FA Cup 5
9	Bolton Wanderers	69,912	18 Feb 1933	FA Cup
10	Birmingham City	68,844	11 Feb 1939	FA Cup 5
11	Newcastle United	68,386	3 Sep 1930	Div. 1
12	Sheffield United	68,287	15 Feb 1936	FA Cup 5

13	Huddersfield Town	67,037	27 Feb 1932	FA Cup 6
14	West Bromwich Albion	64,815	6 Mar 1937	FA Cup 6
15	Blackburn Rovers	61,783	2 Mar 1929	FA Cup 6
16	Wolverhampton Wanderers	61,315	11 Feb 1939	FA Cup 5
17	Burnley	54,775	25 Feb 1924	FA Cup 3
18	Stoke City	51,380	29 Mar 1937	Div. 1
19	Fulham	49,335	8 Oct 1938	Div. 2
20	Milwall	48,672	20 Feb 1937	FA Cup 5
21	Oldham Athletic	47,671	25 Jan 1930	FA Cup 4
22	Leicester City	47,298	18 Feb 1928	FA Cup 5
23	Plymouth Argyle	43,596	10 Oct 1936	Div. 2
24	Bristol City	43,335	16 Feb 1935	FA Cup 5
25	Preston N.E.	42,684	23 Apr 1938	Div. 1
26	Barnsley	40,255	15 Feb 1936	FA Cup 5
27	Brentford	39,626	5 Mar 1938	FA Cup 5
28	Reading	33,042	19 Feb 1927	FA Cup 5
29	Grimsby Town	31,657	20 Feb 1937	FA Cup
30	Chesterfield	30,968	7 Apr 1939	Div. 2
31	York City	28,123	5 Mar 1938	FA Cup 5
32	Newport County	24,268	16 Oct 1937	Div. 3. (S)
33	Exeter City	20,984	4 Mar 1931	FA Cup 6
34	Wimbledon	18,000	1932/33	FA Amateur Cup

AUTHOR'S COMMENT

During the course of my [the author's] professional experience at Leicester Crown Court concerning football-related crowd offences at the end of the 1991–92 season, when Leicester City played Newcastle United in a potential Football League Second Division promotion context, the generous assistance of Prosecuting Counsel Mr Stuart Rafferty from the Specialist Criminal Chambers at No 1 High Pavement, Nottingham NG1 1HF, the Crown Prosecution Service and Detective Sergeant Prior of the Leicestershire Constabulary, produced the following important analysis after evidence from a special video, 'Operation Hawk', increased the average numbers of arrests on that special occasion:

'I have examined the number of football related arrests over the last five years.

The numbers are as follows:

1988/89 season	1989/90 season	1990/91 season	1991/92 season
91	117	94	107 (excluding the 128 prisoners from the 2.5.92)

This compares with only 19 arrests during the 1992/1993 season. I believe that the "high profile" press coverage of "Operation Hawk" must have contributed to this large reduction in the number of football related arrests.'

DS 447 Prior

See also *Leicester Mercury* 28 August 1993.

Appendix 6

Soccer behaviour

Jack Rollin
Editor of Rothmans Football Yearbook

During the inter-war years, two-fifths of the 88 Football League clubs attracted their highest attendance figures. None of these events were accompanied by serious crowd disturbances. However, during the same period there were minor incidents at other venues, involving a handful of spectators which resulted in the closure of grounds for short periods.

In an era of strict discipline and general respect for authority, the Football Association's response was in keeping with the nature of the offences. Usually a two-match ban on home games was sufficient punishment. In some instances, clubs were even able to rearrange fixtures, while others had to play on a neutral ground.

Millwall, who had experienced one closure in 1920, found themselves fined £50 in 1934 in addition to another ban and erected a tunnel for match officials to enter the pitch. The referee had been the target of misbehaviour.

The other clubs affected were: Wolverhampton Wanderers 1919, Crystal Palace 1920, Stockport County 1921, Queen's Park Rangers 1930 and Hull City 1934. Rowdiness and pitch incursions were the primary cause.

The dismissal of players was rare, punishment severe. Jack Barrick, who towards the end of his refereeing career controlled the 1948 FA Cup Final, had sent off only six players in over 23 years. It was not unusual for suspensions to last for several months.

Frank Barson was probably the most suspended player during the period with twelve dismissals. Unfortunately, he used a strong shoulder charge which was sometimes interpreted as foul play. Playing for Watford against Crystal Palace in the opening game of the 1928–29 season, he was cautioned early on by the referee. Shortly afterwards Joe Davison, who bore some resemblance to Barson, tackled a Palace player apparently legitimately, only to find himself sent off. According to the official history of Watford Football Club, the referee was alleged to have said: 'Off you go, Barson!' Such was his reputation.

Davison received a 14-day suspension and a few weeks later on 29 September 1928, Watford were beaten 6–2 at home by Fulham. Barson was sent off after a collision in which his legs became entangled with those of a Fulham player. Both sets of players pleaded on Barson's behalf and the referee needed police protection at the end of the match. Subsequently a petition with 5,000 signatures was sent to the Football Association claiming that Barson had been the victim of his own reputation. But the FA upheld the referee's decision. The player received seven months' suspension.

Watford had had only one other dismissal since 1912 and that had been in 1923. The same month as the Barson incident, Cecil Poynton was sent off playing for Tottenham Hotspur against Stoke City. It was to be nearly 35 years before another Spurs player was dismissed, the longest such period enjoyed by a Football League club.

In the inter-war years, clubs were often ruthless in dealing with indisciplined players. Tommy Black's tackle on Walsall winger Gilbert Alsop which resulted in a penalty kick during Walsall's famous 2–0 FA Cup win over Arsenal on 14 January 1933, resulted in manager Herbert Chapman banning him from Highbury. Black was transferred to Plymouth Argyle within a week.

The quickest sending-off remains at 20 seconds from the kick-off. Ambrose Brown of Wrexham was dismissed by referee Bert Mee of Mansfield at Hull on Christmas Day 1936 in a Division Three (North) match.

Much of the good conduct of spectators emanated from an orderly society, the majority of whose members obeyed the Rule of Law and fully expected harsh treatment if they erred. The father–son predominance among football crowds helped sustain this atmosphere, though barracking and good-natured banter were traditional features.

In contrast, the last 30 years have seen a radical change in the composition of crowds, the largest percentage of those watching have been teenagers and young people without their parents. The lowering of standards of behaviour at home, school and in workplaces has created a climate where indiscipline has flourished.

The media, particularly television, have been responsible for promoting tribal-like allegiances to clubs, often at the expense of the uncommitted football follower who has become an endangered species.

In the 1992–93 season, the number of arrests at first-class League and Cup matches totalled 6,329, compared with 6,378 the previous season. But there were a series of incidents in city centres involving football followers, sometimes prior to and often hours after matches had finished, which were not reported as being related to the game.

Moreover, the increasing use of stewards by clubs to offset the escalating cost of policing matches, has obscured the problem, because they were only able to eject unruly spectators, not charge them.

Hooliganism is at best being contained and the National Criminal Intelligence Service has its own football unit, which is kept busy during the season. During the 1993–94 season undercover police officers seized pocket rocket launchers, CS gas sprays, hammers, knives and martial arts equipment among other weapons. Hypodermic needles were even used at a pre-season friendly.

The vast majority of matches are still trouble-free, but Superintendent Brian Appleby, head of the football unit was quoted in the *London Evening Standard* of 27 August 1993 as follows: 'There are small groups, totalling about 500 people who are capable of orchestrating violence, whether against each other, decent fans or other members of the public miles away from the grounds.'

The post-war years have seen an increase in the number of players sent off in Football League matches. Pressures caused by the fear of defeat and with a much faster game being developed have been contributory causes. The maximum wage was lifted in 1961.

The number of players dismissed in Football League matches are as follows:

1946–47	12	1954–55	13	1962–63	35	1970–71	28
1947–48	5	1955–56	20	1963–64	45	1971–72	36
1948–49	10	1956–57	15	1964–65	46	1972–73	83
1949–50	14	1957–58	27	1965–66	46	1973–74	76
1950–51	7	1958–59	20	1966–67	50	1974–75	97
1951–52	14	1959–60	19	1967–68	48	1975–76	89
1952–53	15	1960–61	18	1968–69	51	1976–77	100
1953–54	14	1961–62	25	1969–70	37		

Figures doubled in the 1980s

1981–82	132	1984–85	163	1987–88	195	1990–91	202
1982–83	211	1985–86	185	1988–89	172	1991–92	244
1983–84	150	1986–87	193	1989–90	161	1992–93	226*
						1993–94	233*

* includes FA Premier League

Appendix 7

Structure of Government departments relevant to Sport and the Law

Compiled by **Edward Grayson**

'Sadly the government system for running the civil service in general is now very outdated. It seems that as soon as someone in any governmental department gets to know and understand the system, they promptly get moved to a different job and department. Any business that was run in this way would be bankrupt very quickly. But this is the way the system works at the moment and so it has to be accepted.'

From Jemima Parry-Jones, *Falconry – Care, Captive Breeding*, 1991.

The structure of Government departments relevant to Sport and the Law is set out on the following pages 458 and 459.

ORGANISATION OF THE DEPARTMENT OF NATIONAL HERITAGE

[from Civil Service Yearbook 1994, as amended by Government announcements, July 1994]

INCLUDING INTER ALIA SPORT AND RECREATION CIVIL SERVICE DIVISIONS MAY 1994 [as amended July 1994]

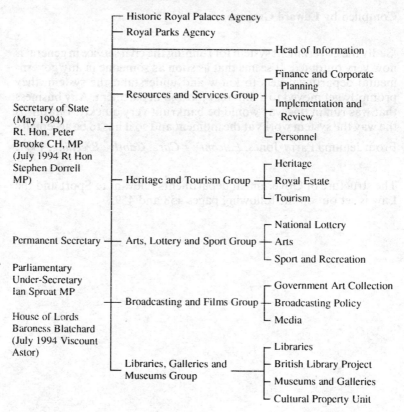

CIVIL SERVICE SPORT AND RECREATION DIVISION [without Department of National Heritage]
Sport and recreation policy, sponsorship of Sports Council and Football Licensing Authority. Safety of sports grounds. Local authority and private funding of sport, including business sponsorship of sport. International matters.

Head of Division (Grade 5)	*Telephone:* 071–211 6078	*Fax:* 071–211 6149
Miss A. J Stewart	GTN 211 6078	

SARD A
Sponsorship of the Sports Council. Sports Council PES/vote and PES coordination. Sports Council restructuring. British Sports Forum/CCPR issues. Honours. Regional Sports Councils. Sport for Women.

Grade 7	*Telephone:* 071–211 6093	*Enquiries:* 071–211 6096
T Dyer	GTN 211 6093	GTN 211 6096
	Fax: 071–211 6149	

GOVERNMENT DEPARTMENTS RELEVANT TO SPORT AND THE LAW EXCLUDING DEPARTMENT OF NATIONAL HERITAGE

1	Attorney-General's Office	Crown Prosecution Service and appellate right against lenient sentences for criminally violent foul play
2	Ministry of Agriculture and Fisheries	Sport and recreation on agricultural and recreation land
3	Department of Education and Science	School sport and physical education at local and higher education authorities
4	Department of Environment	Planning permission for school and physical recreation playing facilities
5	Department of Health and Social Security	Health and fitness through sport and physical education
6	Employment Department Group (EDG)	Comprises the Employment Service, the Health and Safety Commission (and its executive arm the Health and Safety Executive) and the Advisory, Conciliation and Arbitration Service ACAS
7	Foreign and Commonwealth Office	Overseas issues including diplomatic associations
8	Home Office	Law and order, police powers and charities
9	Lord Chancellor's Department	Law Commission and Consultation Papers on public order and consent to criminal violence in sport
10	Department of Trade and Industry	Health and Safety Executive, health and safety legislation
11	Department of Transport	Transport and traffic in relation to sporting events
12	Treasury	Inland Revenue and VAT in relation to sport and recreation
13	Welsh office	Local issues affecting Principality
14	Scottish Office	All matters affecting Scotland
15	Northern Ireland Office	All matters affecting Northern Ireland

SARD B
Sport for people with disabilities. Sport in the inner cities. Children's play and playground safety. Ethics and fair play in sport. Doping. Water sports safety. Coaching, sports science, sports medicine. Swimming pool and leisure byelaws.

SARD C
Funding of sport including local authority expenditure, sports sponsorship, the Sportsmatch Scheme. Foundation for Sport and the Arts, Sports Aid Foundation, National Lottery (sports aspects). Facility provision and playing fields. Countryside and water recreation. Participation (including promotion of physical fitness). Research. Taxation.

Grade 7	*Telephone:* 071–211 6086	*Enquiries:* 071–211 6085
T Baden	GTN 211 6086	GTN 211 6085
	Fax: 071–211 6149	

SARD D
International matters, Council of Europe/EC BOA. Football policy, Governing body issues. Safety at sports grounds, Football Licensing Authority, Football Stadia Development Committee, Football Trust.

Grade 7	*Telephone:* 071–211 6099	*Enquiries:* 071–211 6099
N Mackay	*Fax:* 071–211 6149	GTN 211 6099

Appendix 8

The position in Scotland

Herbert A. Kerrigan QC, MA, LL B (Hons)
Middle Temple, Barrister

In a brief appendix all one can hope to do is outline something of
the Scottish system of law and practice and highlight one or two
points which may be of interest to supplement the text which has gone
before. The reader will appreciate that Scotland has a fiercely
independent system of law and practice which delights in export
and has learned to tolerate import. The jurisprudential boast is
that we resort to principle, in criminal law of the Institutional Writers
such as Hume and Alison and in civil law to Roman Law and
particularly to its Reception into our practice, and that we sparingly
illustrate that principle by the best of the decided cases. In reality
there is superimposed an ever increasing burden of Statute much,
though not all, of which is common to the United Kingdom but some
of which will occasionally be interpreted differently north of the
border.

1 CRIMINAL LAW AND PRACTICE

This area affords the greatest opportunity for differences. There are
two main reasons for this. The first has been alluded to which is that
the criminal law is based on the works of Institutional Writers who in
restating the law and practice as then existing developed concepts
almost totally independently of criminal jurisprudence in our nearest
neighbour. Whilst criminal procedure is in the mostly statutory (the
Criminal Procedure (Scotland) Act 1975 as amended being the main-
stay) the criminal law survives relatively intact and indeed some of the
concepts developed judicially in Scotland were subsequently
imported into the law of England by Statute (eg the concept of
diminished responsibility). The second reason for this is the fact that
there is effectively no appeal beyond the Criminal Appeal Court in
Edinburgh. Whilst this is now subject to the currently limited influence of Europe it is free, unlike civil law, of the influence of the House
of Lords to which there has never been any right of appeal in criminal
matters.

The system of prosecution in Scotland

A radical feature of the Scottish system is that for all effective purposes prosecution is public at the instance of the Lord Advocate in solemn procedure or of his appointee in each Sheriffdom of Scotland, the procurator fiscal, in summary procedure. There has only been one wholly exceptional recent case where the High Court of Justiciary sanctioned a private prosecution. A case comes to the attention of the police, who report the matter to the procurator fiscal. The procurator fiscal will deal with the matter by way of a complaint before the District or Sheriff Court if it is a clear case for summary prosecution. He may refer certain cases to Crown Office in Edinburgh either for guidance or, more rarely, because there is a directive to that effect. If a case clearly is going to proceed under solemn procedure (ie for eventual trial by judge and jury) the procurator fiscal will present a Petition to the Sheriff Court. The fiscal will report such a case to Crown Office in due course where, unless it is a case which must proceed in the High Court (eg murder, rape, incest), Crown Counsel will decide whether it proceeds to Sheriff and Jury or to the High Court of Justiciary. It is thus apparent that there is no point at which the accused has any right of election of the method of trial.

Time limits

In solemn procedure following the presentation of the Petition where the offence or the offender's antecedents require that he be kept in custody there will be a remand for further examination of a week. The accused will then be committed until liberated in due process of law. This committal bears no resemblance whatsoever to committal proceedings in England which are quite unknown in Scotland. The significance of it is that where an accused remains in custody his trial must commence within 110 days of committal or he is forever free of process in respect of that offence. If he enjoys bail then his trial must commence within one year from the date of his first court appearance on Petition. These time limits are only sparingly extended in circumstances where delay is due to no fault which can be attributed to the Crown or simply to pressure on the system.

There is no prescription of crime at common law in Scotland; thus any common law crime can be prosecuted under solemn or summary procedure at any time even long after its commission.

In summary proceedings the general rule is that a complaint must be served within six months of the commission of a statutory offence. If the accused is in custody on a summary matter, his trial must commence within forty days of the complaint being brought into court. In a non-custody case there is no time limit for the trial to commence and there is currently concern that due to pressure of business on the summary courts long delays (by Scottish standards) are occurring and some cases are actually now being heard beyond the time limits which would be permitted in indictable offences.

Notice to the accused

In solemn procedure the Petition will narrate the charge the accused faces. At least thirty days before the trial date (and sadly all too often as a matter of practice little more than that) the indictment, the list of witnesses and the list of productions will be served on the accused. The prudent solicitor enjoying the co-operation of the local procurator fiscal will have obtained a preliminary list of witnesses. Unless the Crown chooses to lodge a statement of a particular witness as a production for their purposes witness statements are and remain confidential to the Crown. The defence has the indictment and access to the productions (generally copies of the documentary productions will be provided in due course). The solicitor has then to locate all witnesses and take statements from them. These may vary from statements given to the Crown. There may be, by grace not by right, instances where the Crown will give the defence sight of particular precognitions (statements) for example of a victim of sexual abuse or of a reluctant witness. There is a right to precognosce on oath before a Sheriff a reluctant witness. Generally speaking disclosure is very limited in Scotland compared to current practice in England and it is not a feature, in the author's considered view, that reflects well on the Scottish Legal System. The time available for preparation is increasingly causing concern. On the one hand both the public interest and the interests of an accused in custody dictate that the speediest disposal of a case is vital, but on the other it is very difficult to get all essential preparation completed (particularly scientific work) within the time limits.

In summary procedure the complaint narrates the charge. The Lord Advocate has recently instructed that statements of witnesses the Crown intend calling are to be made available to the defence upon application to the fiscal.

The criminal courts in Scotland

(i) The District Court serviced by lay justices (though Glasgow boasts some stipendiary magistrates) has a sentencing power of sixty days imprisonment or a fine at level 4 on the standard scale.

(ii) *The Sheriff Court* is serviced by sheriffs and temporary sheriffs and has a dual function.
      The Sheriff sits summarily and has a sentencing jurisdiction at common law of three months (six in certain limited circumstances) imprisonment. Certain statutes give slightly greater powers. A fine currently of £2000 can be imposed.
      The Sheriff sits with a jury on indictable cases. There are 15 jurors in a criminal case in Scotland. There are three verdicts open to a jury. Traditionally these were proven and not proven; verdict of not guilty rather drifted in from England on a Judicature Act, introduced more by accident than design. For conviction at least eight must be in favour of a verdict of guilty. Upon conviction the Sheriff can sentence an accused person to up to three years imprisonment or an unlimited fine or both. If it is considered that the sentencing power qua imprisonment is inadequate the accused can be remitted to the High Court of Justiciary for sentence.

(iii) *The High Court of Justiciary* sits as a trial and appeal court.
      One of the Lords Commissioner of Justiciary will sit with a jury. His sentencing power is limited only by statute.
      The justiciary appeal court comprises of three Lords and will be chaired generally either by the Lord Justice General or by the Lord Justice Clerk. Increasing numbers can be constituted to review previous decisions. This court is, for all practical purposes, the court of last resort and hears appeals from the District Court, The Sheriff Court and the High Court of Justiciary.

The criminal law

One can do no more here than highlight certain areas which are more likely than others to be of interest to the sportsperson.

Breach of the peace

In Scots Law breach of the peace is wide ranging – though not quite as wide as the Aberdeen Magistrate's comment, which did not find favour in the Appeal Court, that 'a things a breach'. It covers conduct which would objectively be considered to be a breach of the public peace or which might lead to conduct which itself would be a breach of the peace and can even encompass behaviour carried out in private if it is of such a nature as would lead to a breach of the peace. I shall endeavour to illustrate this in the context of sports activities and as soccer has provided most of the decided cases that is probably the simplest example.

Conduct on the way to the ground

'Breach of the peace means breach of public order and decorum, accomplished always by the qualification that it is to the alarm and annoyance of the public. Articulate noises and cries not calculated to be offensive to anyone have been held not to amount to breach of the peace. On the other hand where the brawling is of such a kind to be offensive and alarming, it is not necessary that those who hear it should be alarmed for themselves. It is enough that offensive language should be uttered in a noisy and clamorous manner so as to cause reasonable apprehension in the minds of those who hear it that some mischief may result to the public peace.'[1]

In this area it is always stressed that each case is a matter of its own facts and circumstances and this case was one of loud language and oaths emanating from a house in the quiet town of Stranraer at 3am. It would be a very different matter in judging the conduct of part of a crowd making its way to a soccer stadium but there is the potential for breach of the peace. A relevant factor (though not essential) would be if police considered that warning should be given to a particular group for good reason and that warning was ignored. In the case of *McGivern v Jessop*[2] a group of twenty football 'casuals' [described by Lord Brand[3] as youths 'whose object was to make trouble for fun'] shouted obscenities at Celtic supporters. The Sheriff took the view that this conduct upset the supporters and that it was likely to cause them to respond causing further disorder. The Appeal Court did not demur from that view nor from the sentence of three months' detention imposed on the 19-year-old offender. Conduct on a bus by setting off a firework in *McLean v McNaughton*[4] is an obvious example of a breach of the peace (in that case it caused great consternation as exhibited by the elderly passenger shouting 'Bombs') and the accused's lack of remorse when interviewed for social work, and detention centre reports confirmed his sentence of three months' detention. Where there has been trouble and the police are apprehensive it will break out again thus requiring people to move on can result in a charge of breach of the peace as in *Montgomery v McLeod*[5] where following disturbance in a car park and there was concern of recurrence.

[1] *Ferguson v Carnochan* 16 Rettie (Justiciary) 93.94 per Lord McLaren.
[2] 1988 Scottish Criminal Case Reports 511.
[3] At 513.
[4] 1984 SCCR 319.
[5] 1977 SCCR 164 (S).

Conduct near the football ground

In *Duffield v Skeen*[1] two accused placed themselves outside Celtic
Park. They shouted slogans about the ending of British rule in
Northern Ireland and other slogans which were supportive of the
IRA. Whilst one could detect instantly the element of breach of the
peace (indeed how it might have provoked riot) at Ibrox Park, the
Sheriff found in fact that the huge majority of Celtic supporters
would have been disgusted at such conduct and thus it was considered
to be a breach of the peace. It was also considered to be evidentially
relevant that the police had warned the accused about their behaviour
but that they had persisted in it none the less. In *Alexander v Smith*[2]
the accused supported the National Front and sought to sell its
literature outside a football ground. There was evidence that many
supporters exhibited annoyance at the presence of such vendors and
at that which they were selling. Thus conviction for breach of the
peace was upheld.

Conduct on the football field itself

Procurators fiscal have prosecuted players in respect of breach of the
peace (also of assault) in respect of their conduct on the field. One of
the most notable prosecutions was *Butcher v Jessop*[3] where in the
course of a Rangers–Celtic 'Old Firm' game played before 45,000
there was what was described as a seven second flare-up of tempers.
The goalkeeper struck with his elbow the chin of an opposing player,
seized him by the throat and threw him to the ground. Another player
then struck the unfortunate on the chest. The Sheriff convicted of
breach of the peace and the Appeal Court upheld that conviction.
Assault had not been charged and the Appeal Court was quick to
dissociate itself from the Sheriff's apparent inclusion of assault within
the framework of the breach of the peace. The view was that the
conduct on the park was such that it breached the peace and could
have led to further breach of the peace.

Locker room conduct

A peeping Thomas or Thomasina paying prurient attention to the
players changing would suffer conviction as in *Rafaelli v Heatley*[4]
where a peeping Tom suffered punishment for his 2/3 minutes attention at the partially opened curtains of an Edinburgh lady engaged in
undressing at 11.30pm. In that case Lord Justice Clerk Thomson said:

[1] 1981 SCCR 66.
[2] 1984 Scots Law Times (Notes) 176.
[3] 1989 SCCR 119.
[4] 1949 SLT 284.

'Where something is done in breach of public order or decorum which might reasonably be expected to lead to the lieges being alarmed or upset or tempted to make reprisals at their own hand the circumstances are such as amount to a breach of the peace.'[1]

The case of *Young v Heatley*[2] resulted in thirty days' imprisonment for a deputy headmaster who discussed his and their masturbatory and or homosexual experiences with a number of adolescent pupils. Lord Justice General Clyde[3] considered breach of the peace made out albeit the conduct was in private with only one boy present at the time in that 'the disgusting nature of the suggestions made, the fact that they were made within hours of each other with a number of adolescent boys, the fact that they were to pupils by a deputy headmaster to whom they would normally have looked for help and guidance'. Presumably the major risk was the fact that it was likely to cause a violent response either by the boys (though there was no such finding in fact) or their parents. Thus such conduct by a person in whom young people had trust in a sports context might well receive the same response.

Assault

There have been prosecutions for assault in sports circumstances. An assault is any wilful attack on the person of another with evil intent. An assault cannot be consented to. In *Smart v HMA*[4] Lord Justice Clerk Wheatley said 'if an attack on the other person is done with evil intent, that is intent to injure and to do bodily harm then, in our view, the fact that the person attacked was willing to undergo the risk of that attack does not prevent it from being the crime of assault', distinguishing the sporting situation by observing that there 'the intention is to engage in the sporting activity and not evilly to do harm to the opponent'. Clearly public interest is the determining feature in considerations of this sort. Likewise public policy arguments were persuasive of the Court in England in the later case of *The Attorney General's Reference (No 6 of 1980)*[5] dealing as it did with questions of murder and manslaughter.

Various forms of aggravated assault can also be prosecuted as a result of assaults perpetrated within the sporting context where the act and evil intention as defined above exist. If death results following an assault the charge would normally be culpable homicide although it could be murder if the Crown could prove either intention to kill or

[1] At 285.
[2] 1959 JC 66.
[3] At 70.
[4] 1975 JC 30; 1975 SLT 65.
[5] [1984] QB 715.

such gross and wicked recklessness as to show a disposition so depraved as to be regardless of whether the victim lives or dies. Where an accused person pleads guilty to an assault it was held in the case of *HMA v Christopher Tees* that an accused can be charged with the culpable homicide of the victim notwithstanding the earlier sentence.[1] In that case the Crown's acceptance of a deletion of attempted murder precluded him being charged with murder but that is possible on the general authority of *Tees*.

2 CIVIL LAW AND PRACTICE

The existence of the House of Lords as the ultimate appellate tribunal for both Scotland and England means that there is little disparity in application of civil law in areas of common law. There are areas and concepts which are peculiarly Scottish but there are few which impinge on sports law.

The civil courts in Scotland

The Sheriff Court

The greatest volume of civil work is undertaken by the Sheriff. There is a Small Claims Court where litigants are encouraged on a do-it-yourself basis with an upper limit of £750. There is Summary Cause Procedure with its simplified rules for resolution of cases from £750 to £1500. The bulk of the work is undertaken in terms of the ordinary rules. In that respect there is an option as to whether an action should be raised in the Sheriff Court or the Court of Session and a watchful eye has to be kept on the question of expenses.

The Sheriff Principal

The Sheriff Principal as well as having an important administrative function within each sheriffdom also hears appeals from the Sheriff's

---

[1] In that particular case Lord Cullen (High Court of Justiciary, Glasgow 16 December 1993) responded to the author's plea that he impose precisely the same sentence as had earlier been imposed as the accused had pled guilty to an assault to severe injury, permanent disfigurement and danger to life and had received a sentence (of seven years' imprisonment) which recognised the victim's lack of quality of life. At the time of writing Mr Tees has the unique distinction of having two convictions for separate crimes arising out of the same factual circumstances.

decisions though an appellant can choose to proceed directly to the
Court of Session.

The Court of Session

THE OUTER HOUSE
The Lords of Council and Session (the same personnel as function in
the High Court) sit at first instance to hear civil cases in the Outer
House of the Court of Session. Whilst they generally sit alone there is
procedure for jury trial (with a jury of 12).

THE INNER HOUSE
Whilst there is limited business which originates in the Inner House its
principal function is to deal with appellate business from the Sheriff
Court and the Outer House of the Court of Session. It sits in two
divisions. The First Division is presided over by the Lord President.
The Second Division is presided over by the Lord Justice Clerk.

THE HOUSE OF LORDS
The House sits as a court of appeal from the Court of Session and
functions in similar fashion as it does when sitting in English cases.

The law of delict or reparation

The law of delict applies many of the principles of tort with which the
practitioner in England is familiar and which have been recounted in
careful detail and accurately by Edward Grayson in the text of this
book. Earlier tendencies by Scottish Judges to be more sparing with
awards of damages are gradually being corrected and the apparent
excesses of juries in libel actions south of the Border do not occur as
civil jury trial in personal injury cases is a comparatively rare event
though settlements in such cases are generally higher than where a
Judge alone hears the case. Damages for sports loss occur but rarely
as an incidental to a personal injuries claim.

In one recent case, *Gorman v Inverness Farmers Dairy*,[1] a jury (of 12
in a civil case) awarded £193,000 to a farmer who was also a European
Champion and Commonwealth bronze medallist clay target shooter.
He was injured in a road traffic accident which ended his competitive
life, depriving him of cash and other prizes. General damages of
£10,000 were awarded for pain, suffering, loss of amenity and loss of
opportunity of competing at international level. The pursuer suffered
multiple fractures of right arm and elbow, requiring pinning for two

[1] 8 December 1993, unreported other than by Senior Counsel's Note in the New Law
Journal, 19 February 1994.

years and thereafter leaving him with permanent disability, limited flexion and continuing pain.[1] The jury took the view that £2,700 was appropriate for past and £16,000 for future farming losses. His wife's assistance in helping him with driving and running the farm merited £5,150 past and £2,000 for future services. Prize money and prize loss was valued at £10,000 for past and £18,000 for future loss whilst the services he is unable to render merited £2,500 for past and £15,000 for future loss. The defenders are seeking a fresh total which is the method of appeal and which if successful results in a fresh assessment by a new jury with consequences with regard to expenses. The curious feature of the procedure is that by convention neither counsel nor judge may indicate other than in very, very general terms figures appropriate to the case. In theory a process of high awards being granted and subsequently challenged could be endless. In practice the question of expenses determines sensible resolution between the parties.

Scottish Judges in the House of Lords have done much to export Scottish Legal concepts perhaps most notably by figures such as Lord Reid, and of course the present Lord Chancellor practiced exclusively at the Scottish Bar.

Administrative law

There are particular aspects of administrative law which affect sports law. One or two examples must suffice here.

Local government law

The Local Government (Scotland) Act 1973 places statutory duties on local authorities to make provision for sports and leisure facilities within the community. It is to be hoped that the Government will in their proposed reform of local government in Scotland be sensitive to the continuance of those statutory obligations and that those with interest in sports will be vigilant to ensure that they are.

Rating and valuation law

Sports grounds and facilities in Scotland enjoy much more favourable treatment in rate relief than their counterparts in England. The regulating principle, as explained in *Armour on Valuation*,[2] is the comparative principle whereby assessment is made by taking

---

[1] He also had serious head and knee lacerations and still wakes at night requiring to take painkillers.

[2] Eg at page 331 of the 4th edition which has a peculiar authority in that it was edited by the present Lord Chancellor, Lord Mackay of Clashfern, by Lord Clyde and by Lord President Hope. The destiny of the editors of the 5th edition remains to be seen.

comparison with another suitable subject making allowance for differences in size. Seating, accommodation for spectators as well as unit floorage areas are all taken into account.

Sports regulation

The Scottish Sports Council

The Scottish Sports Council has vital administrative differences from that in England. It also has direct access to the Scottish Office and the Secretary of State for Scotland which is thought to be a facility of advantage to sport in Scotland.

Self-regulation

Many sporting bodies have Scottish Associations. Those which have disciplinary tribunals which are regarded as private and domestic not exercising functions of a public nature are not subject to judicial review. Review is however open by ordinary action of reduction on similar grounds to judicial review – viz. *St Johnstone Football Club v Scottish Football Association* 1965 SLT (Notes) 35.

This appendix simply seeks to serve as an introduction to the reader of the general framework in Scotland and a few of the terms we use.

Appendix 9

House of Lords Summary – decisions overturned

Seymour v Reed [1927] AC 554 Professional cricketer's tax free benefit.
Reversal of lower court
Rowlatt J Upheld by House of Lords.

Tolley v Fry [1931] AC 330 Defamation decision of trial judge reinstated; retrial ordered.
Reversal of lower court
Acton J Defamation direction upheld by House of Lords.

Bolton v Stone [1951] AC 850 Cricket ball hit out of ground not establishing negligence or nuisance.
Reversal of lower court
Oliver J Negligence and nuisance rejected and upheld by House of Lords.

Inland Revenue Commissioners v City of Glasgow Police Athletic Federation [1953] AC 380 Police force athletic, sports and general pastimes association rejected as charitable. Reversal of first decision of the Court of Session affirmation of Special Commissioners.

Brutus v Cozens [1973] AC 854 Anti-apartheid demonstrators disrupted Wimbledon men's doubles tennis match
Reversal of divisional court
Magistrate's dismissal of insulting behaviour charge affirmed.

Inland Revenue Commissioners v McMullen [1980] AC 1 Sporting educational trust funded by football for general sporting sources
Reversal of Court of Appeal confirmation of lower court
Walton J Rejection of Charity Commissioners registration of charity and overruled by House of Lords.

Wheeler v Leicester City Council [1985] AC 1054 Reversal of local authority's decision penalising amateur rugby club's players' decision to play for England in South Africa funded from private sources.
Reversal of Court of Appeal confirmation of lower court
Forbes J Affirmation of City Council overruled by House of Lords.

Shilton v Wilmhurst [1991] All ER 148 1991/STC 88 Professional International goalkeeper's golden 'hello' taxable as emolument from employment.
Reversal of Court of Appeal confirmation of lower court Millet J Reversal of Tax Commissioners in turn reversed by House of Lords.

Guild v Inland Revenue Commissioners [1992] 2 All ER p10 Social Welfare extended beyond Sports Centre under Recreational Charities Act 1958.
Reversal of Court of Session of Inner House
Tax Commissioners confirmed by Court of Appeal but reversed by House of Lords.

NB *Customs & Excise Commissioners v Professional Footballers' Association (Enterprise) Ltd* [1993] STC 86 For the first time House of Lords upholds lower court, Nolan J and also Court of Appeal majority, all confirming VAT Tribunal decision that an awards dinner ticket price payment including trophy presentations was for a consideration rather than a supply of goods for no consideration (for the provision or supply of the trophies on the cost of which no VAT was payable separately).

Judicial review of the decision of sporting bodies

Catherine Bond
Solicitor, Jaques & Lewis

The question of whether sporting bodies' decisions are susceptible to judicial review is one which the courts have dealt with on many occasions in recent years. However, time and time again the courts have refused to allow judicial review to extend its parameters this far. This appendix is designed to give an overview of this topic by providing a summary of the legal arguments which have taken place in court in the last ten years. One of the main attractions and advantages which judicial review offers above the writ is that of a swift remedy. This is probably the reason why so many have challenged the precedent that sports governing bodies' decisions cannot be challenged by way of judicial review.

GENERAL BACKGROUND TO JUDICIAL REVIEW

Judicial review is the process by which the High Court exercises a supervisory jurisdiction over:

(i) proceedings and jurisdiction of inferior courts;
(ii) tribunals;
(iii) bodies or persons carrying out quasi judicial functions; and
(iv) bodies or persons who perform public acts and duties.

The last three groups can all be applicable to sporting bodies, so why not allow judicial review of their decisions?

Many forward the argument that sporting bodies should be able to sort their problems out within their own ranks and if the courts were to interfere in any way, it should be through the route of private law in contract. Judicial review certainly should not be perceived as a great evil which would take away the power of the individual sporting bodies to the mercy of the courts. In *R v Secretary of State for Education and Science ex parte Avon County Council*, Glidewell LJ commented on the role of judicial review:

'It is not intended to take away from those authorities the powers and discretions properly vested in them by law and to substitute the courts as the bodies making the decisions. It is intended to see that the relevant authorities use their power in a proper manner.'

Is there any reason why in addition to the route of private law in contract and negligence, 'public' sporting bodies should not be subject to the same supervision? The questions which the courts have to consider in the judicial review function are questions of legality and not of fact. The courts are concerned with the decision-making process and not concerned with the decision itself. These fundamental concepts of judicial review do not offend good sporting practice.

The traditional test for establishing whether a body is subject to judicial review is the source of its power. The power must derive from either statute or prerogative. In *R v Panel on Take-Overs and Mergers, ex parte Datafin plc* ([1981] 1 All ER 564) Lloyd LJ discussed the scope of judicial review. He stated that on one hand, there were bodies whose source of power was statute or subordinate legislation, who would of course be subject to judicial review, and on the other hand there were other bodies whose source of power is purely contractual and therefore would not be subject to judicial review. Lloyd LJ went on to say that within these two extremes there may be bodies who exercise public law functions or their functions will have public law consequences and that may be sufficient to bring the body into the scope of judicial review. This case dramatically changed the jurisdictional question for judicial review and brought the question of whether a sporting body could ever be subject to judicial review to the fore.

One of the most forceful arguments for allowing sporting bodies to be subject to judicial review is that it is in the public interest to do so because the enormous power which is now vested in some sporting bodies should be subject to scrutiny by the courts. However, in *R v East Berkshire Health Authority ex parte Walsh* ([1985] QB 152 at 164; [1984] 3 All ER 425 at 430), Sir John Donaldson said that there was no warrant for equating public law with the interest of the public: 'If the public through Parliament gives effect to that interest by means of statutory provisions, that is quite different, but the interests of the public per se is not sufficient. The crucial consideration will be whether the decision made by the body is made under a statutory power.' Thus, the source of power is still considered to be an important criteria when considering the applicability of judicial review even after the *Datafin* case.

The arguments for and against the use of judicial review in a sporting context can be illustrated by following the most recent cases on the subject and following the progression of argument. The cases start with *Law v National Greyhound Racing Club Ltd* in 1983 and finish with the most recently reported case on this subject, *R v Disciplinary Committee of the Jockey Club; ex parte Aga Khan* decided in December 1992.

1 *Law v National Greyhound Racing Club Ltd* [1983] 3 All ER 300

The defendants, the National Greyhound Racing Club Ltd, were a limited company acting as the judicial body for greyhound racing in Great Britain. The plaintiff was a trainer whose licence had been suspended by the defendant as prohibited substances had been found in a greyhound which had been in the charge of the plaintiff. The plaintiff issued an originating summons seeking, inter alia, declarations that the stewards' decision was void and ultra vires.

The National Greyhound Racing Club applied to strike out the claim for want of jurisdiction on the ground that judicial review under s 31 of the SCA 1981 should have been sought. This contention was rejected at first instance and then by the Court of Appeal. Lawton LJ held that the stewards' powers were derived from contract which is a private law and a stewards' enquiry concerned only those who voluntarily submit themselves to the stewards' jurisdiction. Lawton LJ stated that there was no public element in this jurisdiction, even though the consequences of the powers did have benefits which affected the public.

Slade LJ re-emphasised Lawton LJ's argument by saying that the NGRC's authority to perform judicial or quasi-judicial functions in respect of persons holding licences from it is not derived from statute, statutory instrument or the Crown and as such, the case is a claim against a body of persons whose status is essentially that of a domestic as opposed to a public tribunal.

2 *R v Jockey Club ex parte Massingberg-Mundy* [1990] COB 260

The applicant sought judicial review of a decision that his name be removed from the list of those qualified to act as chairman of a panel of local stewards on the grounds of lack of natural justice. Notably, the divisional court held that if the matter were free from binding authority, the court might (per Neill LJ) or would (per Roch J) have concluded that at least some of the decisions of the Jockey Club were susceptible to judicial review. This was because the Jockey Club held a position of major national importance and it held near monopolistic powers in an area in which the public had a general interest and in which many persons carried their livelihoods. The court stated that whilst some decisions of the Jockey Club were capable of being susceptible to judicial review, the question being considered in this instance did not have any public element in it at all and as such did not have any bearing on judicial review.

3   *R v Jockey Club, ex parte RAM Racecourses Ltd* [1991] COD 346

The applicants were a racecourse management company who sought judicial review of the decisions of the Jockey Club not to allocate at least 15 racing fixtures to it at Telford Race course. On the jurisdictional question, Stuart-Smith LJ felt bound to follow the *Massingberg-Mundy* decision and added that but for that authority he would have held that the Jockey Club was amenable to judicial review. Simon Brown J felt similarly so inclined criticising the grounds of the decision in *Massingberg-Mundy* and stating that the court could have distinguished *Law* in the light of *Datafin*. He said that he was much attracted to the idea that

'Jockey Club in discharging its functions of regulating racecourses and allocating fixtures is strikingly akin to the exercise of a statutory licensing power. I have no difficulty in regarding this function as one of a public law body, giving rise to public law consequences. On any view it seems to have strikingly close affinities with those sorts of decision-making that commonly are accepted as reviewable by the courts.'
    Plainly the Jockey Club for the most part takes decisions which affect only – or at least essentially – those who voluntarily and willingly subscribe to their rules and procedures. The wider public have no interest in all this, certainly not sufficient to make such decisions reviewable. But just occasionally, as when exercising the quasi-licensing power here under challenge, I for my part would regard the Jockey Club as subject to review.'

However, the Divisional Court still felt bound to follow its previous decision.

4   *R v Football Association of Wales ex parte Flint Town United Football Club* [1991] COD 44

The applicant was a football club which was a member of the Football Association of Wales playing in the Welsh Amateur League. The applicant sought to change football leagues. The respondent league argued that the applicant required their permission which incidentally had also been given to other clubs. Permission was not granted by a committee as a result of a proposed reorganisation of the football league in Wales. The applicant appealed to a commission of the respondent association who upheld the decision. The applicant sought judicial review of the decision of the committee and the commission. Again the court reiterated the *Law v National Greyhound Racing Club* decision and stated that even though the law had developed since this case, the courts were still bound by precedent. Indeed, a contractual relationship had been established between the applicant and the respondent and so it was not possible to distinguish *Law* in the way Simon Brown J had suggested in *R v Jockey Club, ex parte RAM Racecourses Ltd.*

5   *R v Football Association Limited ex parte Football League Limited* [1992] COD 52

The FA wished to create a new Premier League for the 1992–93 football season. The Football League Ltd is the most important football league sanctioned by the FA and it sought judicial review of the FA's decision. Rose J held dismissing the application:

'Despite its virtually monopolistic powers and the importance of its decisions to many members of the public who are not contractually bound to it, it is, in my judgment, a domestic body, whose powers arise from and duties exist in private law only.'

Rose J referred to other major popular sports:

'But they are all essentially forms of popular recreation and entertainment and they are all susceptible to control by the courts in a variety of ways. This does not, of itself, exempt their governing bodies from control by judicial review. Each case will turn on the particular circumstances.'

6   *R v Disciplinary Committee of the Jockey Club, ex parte His Highness the Aga Khan* [1993]

The Aga Khan's filly, Aliysa, won the Oaks at Epsom in 1989. In tests after the race, a metabolite of camphor was found in the filly's urine and the Aga Khan sought leave to move for judicial review of the respondent's decision to disqualify the filly and fine the trainer. The Court of Appeal in December 1992 upheld the Divisional Court in dismissing the application. The Master of the Rolls held that notwithstanding the fact that the Jockey Club was created by Royal Prerogative and it exercised broad and monopolistic powers over a significant national activity, it is still not in its origin, history, constitution and not least of all its membership, a public body.

Yet again, the court refused to state categorically whether sporting bodies would ever be susceptible to judicial review. The Master of the Rolls stated:

'It is unnecessary for purposes of this appeal to decide whether decisions of the Jockey Club may ever in any circumstances be challenged by judicial review and I do not do so.'

However, Farquarson LJ did give more reasoning on this point by suggesting that the question of whether the Jockey Club was susceptible to judicial review did not have to be answered on an all-or-nothing basis:

'While I do not say that particular circumstances would give a right to judicial review, I do not discount the possibility that in some special circumstances the remedy might be. If for example the Jockey Club failed to fulfil its obligations under the charter by making discriminatory rules, it may be that those affected would have a remedy in public law.'

7 Finnigan v New Zealand Rugby Football Union [1985] NZLR 159

As a final case in this list and in contrast to the conclusions which the English courts have reached so far in *Finnigan*, the New Zealand courts found that the New Zealand Rugby Football Union was subject to judicial review. This was on the grounds that the Union was in a position of major national importance, even though it was a private and voluntary sporting association. The plaintiffs who were members of local rugby football clubs and linked to the Union by contract were held to have standing to challenge the decision of the Rugby Union to send a team to tour South Africa. Since there was also a contractual relationship present, it would seem that the English courts would currently never follow this New Zealand line of reasoning.

SHOULD JUDICIAL REVIEW BE APPLICABLE TO SPORT?

The arguments which pervade either side apparently seem to be evenly balanced. On the one hand it is argued that sporting bodies' decisions are subject to attack using the private law route and on the other hand it is argued that the courts should be able to intervene on powers which are often monopolistic and have an undeniable effect on the public.

Rose J in *R v Football Association Limited ex parte The Football League Ltd* stated a compelling practical argument:

'But, for my part, to apply to the governing body of football on the basis that it is a public body, principles honed for the control of the abuse of power by government and its creatures would involve what, in today's justifiable parlance, would be called a quantum leap. It would also, in my view, for what it is worth, be a misapplication of increasingly scarce judicial resource. It will become impossible to provide a swift remedy, which is one of the conspicuous hallmarks of judicial review, if the courts become even more swamped with such applications than they are already. This is not, of course, a jurisprudential reason for refusing judicial review, but it will be cold comfort to the seven or eight other substantive applicants and the many more ex parte applicants who have had to be displaced from the court's lists in order to accommodate the present litigation to learn that, though they have a remedy for their complaints about the arbitrary abuse of executive power, it cannot be granted to them yet.'

This is indeed a powerful argument, yet it does not tackle the real jurisdictional question. The law should not be prevented from developing and allowing people to use judicial review purely for the reason that it might inhibit the progress of applicants who are currently allowed to resort to its use.

Many sporting bodies such as the Football Association and the Jockey Club have extraordinarily wide powers which affect hundreds of thousands of people within this country on a regular basis. A powerful and cogent argument was put forward in this case that those who contract with the Jockey Club have no alternative but to accept the obligations imposed since the Jockey Club's powers are monopolistic. This would therefore undermine the reality of consent in a contractual situation. Farquarson LJ argued that nearly all sports are subject to a body of rules to which an entrant must subscribe and dismissed this argument. This is true, however, and the reality of the situation with the Jockey Club is that an individual simply does not have an alternative set of rules to abide by if he wants to be involved in the horse-racing industry in this country. As such, monopolistic powers exist which may be open to abuse by the sporting body and the use of judicial review would appear to be appropriate in such circumstances.

If a contractual relationship does exist then there is a form of redress. However, this leaves open the situation where a private law remedy does not exist. It seems just that the judicial review remedy should be available when a private law remedy is not. This view that judicial review should be used where a contractual situation does not exist has not been specifically dismissed by the higher courts and is one which may well be tested in the future.

In such a non-contractual situation, the Divisional Court in *RAM Racecourses* reluctantly felt bound by its own decision in *Massingberg-Mundy* even though the *Massingberg-Mundy* decision was criticised.

If a contractual relationship does exist, it would be necessary for an applicant to argue his case to the House of Lords in order to overturn the Law and *Aga Khan* decision if the facts could not be distinguished. So far applicants have not appeared willing to face up to the reality that they have to reach the higher courts in order to have a chance of overturning the binding precedent which steadfastly exists in this area.

The jurisdictional boundaries of judicial review should not be extended to include sporting bodies just because it is convenient for people to have further redresses to the courts when wrongs are done unto them. However, there may be circumstances where a person is affected by a decision of a sporting body which does have a significant public role and therefore its actions and business has a significant affect on the public at large and there is no remedy in private law available with which to gain redress. For example, a situation could arise in which a football supporter would wish to question a decision of the Football Association. As no contract would arise between the parties and since the FA is not a body susceptible to judicial review, the supporter would have no remedy. In such circumstances, it would be impossible to predict which way the courts would turn – judicial review or no recourse in law at all? Even after *Datafin* which widened the judicial review boundaries the courts still feel bound by *Law* which was decided before *Datafin*. The courts have subsequently balanced these two authorities providing dicta that judicial review may be relevant to sporting bodies in limited circumstances.

Appendix 11

'Physical Education is Education like Latin and Greek' (Re Mariette [1915] 2 Ch 284 at 288–289)

(1) MR JUSTICE EVE

Eve J. The admonition with which Mr. Clayton[1] commenced his argument is by no means to be disregarded. One must be careful not to allow one's natural inclination to give effect to a gift of this sort to lead one to disregard well-established principles. The gift[2] in question is a gift by a gentleman who had served this school for twenty-four years as an assistant master[3] and who had obviously come to entertain for it in a marked degree that affection which most men feel for the old school, and which would certainly tend to increase in the case of a man who had given the best part of his life to its services. The amount is to be laid out in the erection of additional fives courts at the school, and the question is whether it is a gift which in law can be supported or whether it is void as not being charitable and tending to a perpetuity. It is a gift to an institution which admittedly is a charity within the Statute of Elizabeth, but I accede to the argument of the residuary legatees that it is quite possible that a gift to a charity may be of such a character as not to be in itself a charitable gift. On the other hand I think in considering whether a gift is charitable or not one must not confine oneself to the character of the gift itself, but must pay regard also to the character and objects of the charity who are the intended recipients of the gift.

The object of this charity is the education, in the widest sense, of boys and young men between the ages of ten and nineteen. No one of sense could be found to suggest that between those ages any boy can be properly educated unless at least as much attention is given to the development of his body as is given to the development of his mind. It is necessary, therefore, in any satisfactory system of education to provide for both mental and bodily occupation, mental occupation by means of the classics and those other less inviting studies to which a portion of the day is devoted, and bodily occupation by means of

---

[1] Counsel for objectors to the bequest as a charity.
[2] '£1,000 to the Governing body of Aldenham School for the purpose of building Eton fives courts or squash rackets courts, or for some similar purpose that shall be decided by a majority of the housemasters at the time of my death.'
[3] Edgar Henry Mariette.

regular and organized games. To leave 200 boys at large and to their own devices during their leisure hours would be to court catastrophe; it would not be educating them, but would probably result in their quickly relapsing into something approaching barbarism. For these reasons I think it is essential that in a school of learning of this description, a school receiving and retaining as boarders boys of these ages, there should be organized games as part of the daily routine, and I do not see how the other part of the education can be successfully carried on without them. It is not disputed that if this sum – I am dealing now with the 1000*l*. – had been left to the charity, for the general purposes of the charity, it might have been applied to any of the purposes to which moneys coming to the hands of the governing body are in fact applied; it might have been expended in the repair or in additions to the class-rooms, laboratory, and other buildings of that sort; or it might equally, as it seems to me, have been applied to the repair or enlargement of the swimming bath, the gymnasium, the fives courts, or other buildings employed in those branches of education which have exclusively to do with the bodily welfare of the students. I cannot, in these circumstances, bring myself to think, because the testator has indicated his intention that in the hands of the charity this money shall be used for the particular purposes stated in his will, that the gift is thereby vitiated. On the contrary I think the gift is a good charitable gift. It is a gift to a charity for purposes which seem to me to be included in the objects of the charity.

The same reasoning applies to the 100*l*[1]. It is given not to the charity but to the headmaster, but it is given for a purpose which, though not quite so specific as the purpose for which the 1000*l*. is given, is in my opinion within the objects of the charity, that is to say, the advancement of bodily and physical development of the students. I think both legacies are valid charitable legacies, and I so hold.

I have said nothing about the 100*l*. for the classical prize; that is clearly good, and the contrary has not really been argued.

---

[1] '£100 to the headmaster for the time being of Aldenham School upon trust to use the interest to provide a prize for some event in the school athletic sports every year agreed upon by the committee of the athletics sports.'

THE ERRATIC CHART

Date	Charitable	Non Charitable	Source
(1895)		Yacht-racing Prize (Cup)	*Re Nottage: Jones v Palmer* [1895] 2 Ch 640
(1915)	School Fives Court (Aldenham School)		*Re Marriette: Mariette v Aldenham School Body* [1915] 2 Ch 284
(1925)	Army Regimental Fund for promotion of sport		*Re Gray: Todd v Taylor* [1925] Ch 362
(1929)		County Cricket Nursery Fund	*Re Patten: Westminster Bank v Carlyon* [1929] Ch 276
(1945)	Chess tournament for under 21-year-olds		*Re Dupree's Deed Trusts* [1945] Ch 16
(1953)		Police Recreation	*IRC v City of Glasgow Police Association* [1953] AC 380
(1957)	University Rugby		*Kearins v Kearins* (1957) SR (NSW Australia) 286
(1978 1979)		FA Soccer Youth Trust	*IRC v McMullen* [1979] 1 WLR 130, CA
(1980)	FA Soccer Youth Trust		*IRC v McMullen* [1981] AC 1, HL
(1992)	Sports Centre Recreational Charities Act 1958		*Guild v IRC* [1992] 2 WLR 10, HL

Appendix 12

VAT rebate for sport and physical recreation
Edward Grayson

1. The VAT Statutory Instrument from the Treasury 1994/687 Value Added Tax (Sport, Physical Education and Fund-Raising Events) Order 1994, explained briefly in the main text above, contains the well publicised VAT exemptions in certain regulated circumstances for non-profit making sports clubs and other physical education services supplied by non-profit making organisations, which exclude local authorities, government bodies and the national Sports Councils.

2. The details are contained in HM Customs and Excise VAT Notice 701/45/94, containing 19 pages and nearly 60 paragraphs of complex detail. They will give rise doubtless to as much thought and perhaps legal argument as the Central Council of Physical Recreation and National Playing Fields Association and their representatives required to persuade HM Customs and Excise and the Treasury why the exemptions had to be backdated to 1 January 1990 or any date between then and 31 March 1994 at the option of the particular organisation registered for VAT. For Paragraph 3 at Page 1 explains

'Although European Council (EC) agreements in 1978, allowing the United Kingdom to tax all sporting services, were amended with effect from 1 January 1990, it was generally understood that this did not necessitate any change in the existing arrangements. Following a legal challenge, it is now accepted that the EC agreements require Member States to exempt supplies of sporting services by NPMOs (non-profit making organisations) in most circumstances.'

3. Within the space and context of this Appendix it would be unwise and impractical to attempt a general and what inevitably must be a selective analysis of the overall position, because every organisation to which this exemption order can apply will have different and differing internal arrangements and structures to consider. On one particular issue, 'a legal challenge' outside the terms of the Order with which this Appendix is alone concerned has surfaced already within sporting administrative circles. It is crystallised in the form of one of the 21 questions and answers listed in Annex A at Page 11, as follows:

Does the organisation have to pass the repayable VAT on to the users of its services?
15. This is a matter for the organisation and its users to decide and *not* for Customs, which is accountable only to the organisation which accounted for the VAT.

4. Further Annex D at Page 17 contains as follows:

LIST OF SPORTS ACTIVITIES WHICH QUALIFY
FOR EXEMPTION

Aikido	Gymnastics	Real Tennis
American Football	Handball	Roller Hockey
Angling	Hang/Para Gliding	Roller Skating
Archery	Highland Games	Rounders
Arm Wrestling	Hockey	Rowing
Association Football	Horse Racing	Rugby League
Athletics	Hovering	Rugby Union
Badminton	Hurling	Sailing/yachting
Ballooning	Ice Hockey	Sand & Land
Baseball	Ice Skating	Yachting
Basketball	Jet Skiing	Shinty
Baton Twirling	Ju Jitsu	Shooting
Biathlon	Judo	Skateboarding
Bicycle Polo	Kabaddi	Skiing
Billiards	Karate	Skipping
Bobsleigh	Kendo	Snooker
Boccia	Korfball	Snowboarding
Bowls	Lacrosse	Softball
Boxing	Lawn Tennis	Sombo Wrestling
Camogie	Life Saving	Squash
Canoeing	Luge	Street Hockey
Caving	Modern Pentathlon	Sub-Aqua
Chinese Martial Arts	Motor Cycling	Surf Life Saving
Cricket	Motor Sports	Surfing
Croquet	Mountaineering	Swimming
Crossbow	Movement & Dance	Table Tennis
Curling	Netball	Taekwondo
Cycling	Orienteering	Tang Soo Do
Dragon Boat Racing	Parachuting	Tenpin Bowling
Equestrian	Petanque	Trampolining
Exercise & Fitness	Polo	Triathlon
Fencing	Pony Trekking	Tug of War
Field Sports	Pool	Unihoc
Fives	Quoits	Volleyball
Flying	Racketball	Water Skiing
Gaelic Football	Rackets	Weightlifting
Gliding	Racquetball	Wrestling
Golf	Rambling	Yoga

Thus, the variations in the structure, framework and constitution of any 'organisation which accounted for the VAT' and to 'which (Customs) is accountable only' will be as divergent as the 113 different sports activities listed above.

5. Yet even within the short period of time which has elapsed since the Order was published with effect from 1 April 1994, sharp differences of legal opinion have surfaced publicly in attempts to answer the question left in Customs response number 15 cited above. In substance it boils down to: who is the ultimate owner of the money claimable from and repayable by Customs to the multitudinous organisations servicing the sports activities, which qualify for exemption cited above in relation to membership subscriptions? Indeed, one commentary has suggested

'Legal opinion on the ultimate ownership of the rebates is divided as no precedent exists'

with the final observation that only a VAT tribunal could create a guideline.

6. Such generalities have ignored the hard-core legal realities, whether the organisation is structured as a company, club or in any other lawful framework. For just as sporting culture and mythology believed that the violent misconduct on the field of play was beyond criminal and civil courts, correspondingly the well-established principles blending common law and equity in one established authority for the last sixty years have been overlooked, or sidelined, in attempts to answer the question posed and sidetracked in response by Customs. In *Harmer v Armstrong* [1934] Maughan J explained in relation to this dual dimension how the defendant in the case before him

'must in my view be treated as having entered into the contract as agent for and in a fiduciary position towards the plaintiff,'

and in the Court of Appeal Lord Hanworth, one of Lord Denning's predecessors as Master of the Rolls, re-affirmed,

'The Plaintiffs in the action sought a declaration that the defendant entered into and took the benefit of the agreements in issue as agent and trustee for the Plaintiff himself.'

7. The declaration was granted, and thus *any organisation* which seeks to retain money repaid to it by Customs on behalf of its members must obtain the approval in appropriate form, such as special resolutions or in whatever acceptable formula can be devised,

of the true owners on whose behalf the money was originally collected for Customs and under the terms of the Order to be reclaimed.

8. No doubt many organisation's members will be prepared to waive their rights for repayment for the benefit of the appropriate organisation. Yet the position can create unexpected problems for the unwary; and one example has emerged when lady members of clubs, with no voting rights, would be faced with a decision deciding the destination of money due to them for which they would be disenfranchised.

9. Procedurally such matters of ownership would not be arguable before a VAT Tribunal. A court, small claims, county court or High Court, and preferably in the Chancery Division, would be the appropriate venue.

10. The non-existence of precedent as one commentator has suggested creates no problem. For first principles, as explained in *Harmer v Armstrong*, suffice. The only problem will be for organisations to seek the agreement or approval of their respective members to avoid creating a breach of trust in equity, a breach of contract or conversion at common law. If criminality were to rear its ugly head, that would be within the unhappily conventional context of dishonestly appropriating someone else's property. Within a true sporting spirit off the field, none of these thoughts should surface, so long as the true hard-core legal position is recognised and understood from the outset, as explained here.

Appendix 13

Sanctions for fair play in sport
Edward Grayson

1. The concept of fair play in sport is the ideal result of operating the Rule of Law within any sport on and off the field of play. To that end the Central Council of Physical Recreation created a Charter of Conduct and the Council of Europe created a Code of Sport's Ethics.

2. The Charter referred in paragraph 1 to

'rules ... properly enforced'

and the Code referred to

'sanctions applied'.

3. Neither completed the logical corollary to each ideal, namely, what are the consequences of proper enforcement and applying sanctions?

4. The gap was filled with admirable timing for the 1994 World Soccer Cup Competition in the USA by the little known International Football Association Board, which monitors the Laws of the Game, as distinct from FIFA which hitherto has been remiss in enforcing them. This the whole world witnessed in 1966 when the jewel in Brazil's crown, Pele, was hacked and assaulted off the England field by brutality which today would end in either a criminal prosecution or civil claim for damages.

5. At its annual meeting in FIFA House, Zürich, Switzerland, on 5th March 1994, the International Football Association Board made a number of amendments to the Laws of the Game and International Board decisions. The Board also issued two important instructions. All amendments, decisions and instructions **must be enforced from 1st July 1994**.

Instructions for referees

1. Reckless Challenges
The Board showed much concern about the increasing tendency among players to move their arms and elbows, without due care,

too near to opponents whilst competing for the ball. Referees should, therefore, take stringent measures against the offenders by applying the sanctions available to them under Law XII.

2. Kicking an opponent
The Board discussed the increasing number of incidents where violent challenges were made **from behind** with little or no attempt to play the ball. It emphasised the fact that the current Laws of the Game forbid such actions and condemn it as Serious Foul Play.

Such violent and unacceptable challenges can result in serious injury. Referees must apply the sanctions laid down in Law XII and **send off** any player guilty of this offence.

The International FA Board gave FIFA permission to implement the aforementioned amendments as from the first match of the 1994 World Cup Finals on 17th June 1994.

6. As these pages have argued from the commencement in the Introduction, the Rule of Law on the field of play is essential for the Rule of Law in society generally. It is also arguable that if the 1994 IFAB sanctions had been in force during 1966, Brazil with Pelé could even have won the World Cup on that occasion as they have in 1994. Certainly these sanctions prove how fair play can flourish if, and only if, effective sanctions exist to punish offenders who break the law during play.

THE CENTRAL COUNCIL OF PHYSICAL RECREATION

A CHARTER OF CONDUCT FOR ALL THOSE INVOLVED IN SPORT AND PHYSICAL RECREATION

TERMS OF THE CHARTER

General

Members of governing bodies, officials, competitors and spectators are perceived by the general public as representatives of their sports and must always attempt to set a good example, particularly to the younger generation, by the way in which they carry out their duties and responsibilities both on and off the field. The media plays a particularly vital role in this respect. It is urged, in keeping with the spirit of the Code of Practice agreed by Editors of national newspapers, to maintain the highest standards of responsible journalism in its reporting of sport and in its comments on sporting personalities.

Governing Bodies

1. Must ensure that their rules are fair, thoroughly understood by competitors and officials, and properly enforced.
2. Must make every effort to ensure that the rules are applied consistently and with absolute impartiality.
3. Must make every effort to impress upon participants and officials the absolute need to maintain the highest standards of sportsmanship in the organisation and practice of their sport.

Coaches

1. Must insist that competitors understand and abide by the principles of good sportsmanship.
2. Must not countenance the use of drugs by competitors.
3. Must never employ methods or practices that might involve risks to the long-term health or physical development of their charges.
4. Must not attempt to manipulate the rules to the advantage of their charges.

Competitors

1. Must abide by both the laws and the spirit of their sport.
2. Must accept the decisions of umpires and referees without question or protestation.

3. Must not cheat and in particular must not attempt to improve their performance by the use of drugs.
4. Must exercise self-control at all times.
5. Must accept success and failure, victory and defeat with good grace and without excessive display of emotion.
6. Must treat their opponents and fellow participants with due respect at all times.

Sponsors and Promoters

1. Must not seek improperly to influence the outcome of non-professional competitions by financial inducements.
2. Must understand and agree that the administration, operation and arrangements for the conduct of competitions and events are the exclusive responsibility of the governing bodies.

Conclusion

In order to bring about the raising of standards of behaviour across the wide spectrum of sport in Britain, the CCPR expects all governing bodies of sport and recreation, clubs, teachers, coaching organisations and spectators to give study to the Charter and take the necessary action to incorporate its relevant principles into their own rules and codes of practice and appeals to the Press Council to do the same.

COUNCIL OF EUROPE
CODE OF SPORTS ETHICS

In setting a proper context for fair play
Sports and sports-related organisations have the following responsibilities:

- to publish clear guidelines on what is considered to be ethical or unethical behaviour and ensure that, at all levels of participation and involvement, consistent and appropriate incentives and/or sanctions are applied.
- to ensure that all decisions are made in accordance with a code of ethics for their sport which reflects the European Code.
- to raise the awareness of fair play within their sphere of influence through the use of campaigns, awards, educational material and training opportunities. They must also monitor and evaluate the impact of such initiatives.
- to establish systems which reward fair play and personal levels of achievement in addition to competitive success.
- to provide help and support to the media to promote good behaviour.

Sport is governed by a set of rules and, often unwritten, principles of behaviour which usually come under the banner of Fair Play. Sadly, it is often these principles which are not strictly adhered to in a range of sports. The Council of Europe's Code of Sports Ethics is a valuable reminder of the need to demonstrate and practice ethical behaviour in Europe.

The Sports Council has been delighted to play a significant part in drawing up the Code and fully endorses its content.

Appendix 14

Draft Safety of Sports Persons Act: prepared by Edward Grayson

Author's Note: For the 1st edition, published in 1988, I wrote: 'It is at least arguable in 1987 that no responsible citizen would object to compulsory disqualification for drunk and drugged drivers as an automatic penalty upon proof of a road traffic offence (except in special circumstances such as malicious or irresponsible "lacing" of drinks). In 1987 it is also arguable that fewer citizens would protest against breathalyser tests than those who complained against their purported interference with personal freedoms and liberties upon their introduction twenty years earlier by the Transport Minister, Mrs Barbara Castle, under the Road Safety Act, 1967.

Accordingly, the question arises in 1987 whether any responsible citizen would object to the author's proposal initiated in 1977 and converted into concrete form as an Appendix to the slender *Sunday Telegraph* version of *Sport and the Law* in 1978 in the circumstances explained in Chapter 15 'Whither Sport and the Law'. As appears there, the idea was inspired by the contrast between the wide ranging discretionary penalties imposed by sporting sentencing tribunals for what may be described as "field" offences, and the equally discretionary penalties imposed by magistrates and crown courts for "crowd" offences, on the one hand; and the fate of the unsuccessful plaintiff who failed to clear his name of the allegedly unjust charge of cheating at cards in the Tranby Croft Baccarat Case [*Gordon-Cumming v Green and others* (1891) 7 TLR 408], and the *Royal Baccarat Scandal* (at pages 329 and 409 above).

The initial publication of the book in 1977 coincided with the initial series of *Sunday Telegraph* articles under the *Sport and the Law* title; and the contrast between the Plaintiff's peremptory military and social dismissal within hours of the jury's adverse verdict after a six-day trial in 1891 and the mid-1970s soft options which operated at all levels of sentencing against violent "field" and "crowd" offenders was too much for the author to stomach without an attempt to propose a practical alternative. Its advocacy regularly in the same [*Sunday Telegraph*] source where it began, and elsewhere, during the intervening ten years has not been answered by the Exclusion Order principle in recent licensing and public order legislation. An overriding discretion whether or not to operate that sentencing disposal still remains. If the public's attitude and will towards these offenders is, as is argued, consistent with its attitude to drunken and drugged motorists, then Parliament should reflect it by legislative withdrawal of that discretion and its replacement with mandatory sanctions.'

That *mandatory* (as distinct from discretionary) power still remains for implementation, notwithstanding recent legislation. More significant, however, is the absence generally throughout the administrative sports world of an effective *penal* policy with a coherent code of sanctions.

One notable exception is that provided appropriately by one of the last bastions of the true *amateur* sport, the British Amateur Rugby League Association. Their Mandatory Suspensions as at November 1993 are listed after my draft Statute, and as their Chief Executive, Maurice F. Oldroyd wrote to the author on 16 November 1993:

> 'It is also worth noting that our rules state that "automatic sine die suspension *shall* be given to a player found guilty of assaulting an appointed match official . . . In the case of sine die suspensions, these will not be lifted until at least a period of 5 years has elapsed" (rule 26(v), page B15 in the 1993 BARLA handbook).'

AN ACT TO PROTECT ALL PERSONS ENGAGED IN AND CONCERNED WITH SPORTING AND RECREATIONAL ACTIVITIES FROM INJURY CAUSED TO THEM BY OTHER PERSONS CONCERNED WITH SPORTING OCCASIONS

1. Any person deliberately or recklessly causing any harm or injury in any manner whatsoever to any person concerned with, before, during or after any sporting or other recreational activity shall be guilty of an offence.
2. The said offence shall be committed by any participant during the course of any authorised sporting or recreational activity when it occurs in breach of the rules or laws of such sporting or other recreational activity.
3. The penalty for such offence committed by any participant during the course of such authorised lawful sporting or recreational activity shall be automatic suspension from further participation in the activity irrespective of any punishment pursuant to the rules or laws of such sporting or recreational activity and of any other statutory or civil cause of action or complaint.
4. The penalty for conviction of any offence committed by any non-participant before, during or after the course of any such

authorised lawful sporting or other recreational activity shall include disqualification from or further attendance at any such sporting activity from the date of such conviction and also compulsory attendance at an appropriate attendance or detention centre to be designated by the Secretary of State on every Saturday afternoon between the hours of 2.00 p.m. (14.00 hours) and 5.00 p.m. (17.00 hrs.), and every evening between the hours of 7.00 p.m. (19.00 hrs.) and 10.00 p.m. (22.00 hrs.) for a period of 12 months from the date of such conviction; and in default of the availability of such attendance or detention centres, a community service order for the same time within the same period shall be directed.

BRITISH AMATEUR RUGBY LEAGUE ASSOCIATION
MANDATORY MINIMUM SUSPENSIONS AND FINES

Offence	Suspension Matches	Minimum Fines
Biting	8	£24.00
Butting	8	£24.00
Fighting	2	£6.00
Abuse – Foul Language (General)	3	£9.00
Abuse – Foul Language to Referee	6	£18.00
Abuse – Referee (not foul language)	4	£12.00
Gouging	Sine-Die	–
High Tackle	6	£18.00
Kicking – Vicious	8	£24.00
Late Tackle	4	£12.00
Off the ball incidents	8	£24.00
Persistent technical offence	1	£3.00
Persistently disputing decisions	2	£6.00
Punching	2	£6.00
Retaliating	2	£6.00
Running In	2	£6.00
Spearing or Dumping	4	£12.00
Spitting	2	£6.00
Stamping	6	£18.00
Stepping on player	6	£18.00
Stiff Arm	6	£18.00
Tripping	3	£9.00
Use of Elbows	5	£15.00
Use of Knees	8	£24.00
Other Conduct Warranting Dismissal	Discretionary	–

Team Offences

Brawling £75.00
*Defined as 3 or more players fighting. On
second or subsequent reports of brawling the
Coach will be required to attend the
Discipline Committee Meeting.*
Abandoned Game £100.00

How It All Began (1953)

During Edward Grayson's early days of practice at the Chancery Bar from Chambers in Lincoln's Inn, before departing to the Temple, he prepared for publication as *Corinthians and Cricketers* what had been his Second World War schoolboy correspondence with England's leading centre-forward at the century's turn, G. O. Smith, the Gary Lineker of his day. 'G. O.' like W. G. Grace, known by his initials and also as 'Jo' Smith, retired after 21 England appearances, many as captain, with only three home international matches played each season from 1894–1901, to become headmaster of the future King William III's preparatory school, Ludgrove in Berkshire, on the death of its founder, Arthur Dunn. C. B. Fry contributed the Foreword, and research for the two games in the book produced the legal puzzle and paradox that while professional cricketers' benefit matches were tax-free, professional footballers' (and parsons' Easter offerings) were subject to tax.

Encouraged by the then FA Secretary, Sir Stanley Rous, two articles were written for analysing and attempting to solve the puzzle. The first appeared in the *FA Bulletin* for April 1953, while the joint Oxbridge team, Pegasus, were winning the F.A. Amateur Cup for the second time in three years before 100,000 at Wembley Stadium. The second, in *Rating and Income Tax* for 8 October 1953 Volume 46, p 652. Within two months a House of Commons question to the then Financial Secretary to the Treasury, on 26 November, crystallised the issues with the following succinct exchanges [Hansard: Vol. 521 26 November 1953: Cols. 504–505/House of Commons Oral Answers]

Cricketers' Benefits (Tax) [col 503]

Mr Hamilton asked the Chancellor of the Exchequer if he is aware that the benefits payable to professional footballers are liable to Income Tax, whilst benefits paid to professional cricketers are not so liable; and what steps he contemplates to remedy this anomaly.

Mr Boyd-Carpenter: The discrimination is not, as the hon. Member suggests, between cricketers and footballers. It is between on the one hand, payments to either cricketers or footballers which accrue by reason of the terms of the employment and are taxable, and, on the other hand, payments which accrue by way of gift of personal testimonial and are not taxable.

Mr Hamilton: Is the Minister aware that if a footballer gets a benefit after five years' service he gets £750 which, after taxation, comes to rather less than £500, and that a professional cricketer, who may get £12,000 or £13,000, receives it free of tax? Does the Minister say that that is not an anomalous situation, however he might defend it? Would he ask his right hon. Friend to have this matter looked into further before next April?

Mr Boyd-Carpenter: [Col 505] It depends in every case, regardless of which sport is concerned, on whether the man gets his benefit as part of the terms of his employment, in which case it is as properly taxable as any other part of his income, or whether he gets it as a gift, in which case it is quite properly, under the present law, not taxable.

Mr K Thompson: Is the Minister prepared to distinguish, for the benefit of the House, between the uncontracted benefits of the cricketer and the receipts of a vicar at the time of the Easter offerings?

Mr Boyd-Carpenter: There is nothing about vicars in this Question.

Six years later, as explained earlier in the main text, a tax test case experiment to align the two disciplines operated by Peterborough United, then outside the Football League, resulted in the Inland Revenue's acceptance of the thrust of the two articles by adapting for professional footballers the cricketing circumstances. This was exclusion *from the terms of employment*, as explained above of any benefit provisions, and more readily capable of facilitation in the then Midland League regulations, where Peterborough then played. They also resulted in life-long friendships until death with the late James Guthrie, then Chairman of the then Professional Footballers' and Trainers' Union (now the PFA), and the first shots fired to establish restraint of trade under professional footballers' standard form of contract in *Aldershot v Banks* (1955) [pages 295 supra] a Group Accident Insurance scheme for professional footballers affirmed in *Alder v Moore* (1961) and also with the Pegasus founder and future FA Council chairman, Sir Harold Thompson. Attempts to establish his romantic Oxbridge creation of the 1950s as a sporting education charity were rejected by the Revenue and unchallenged solely through lack of funds. It was not fought as it could have been with encouragement from the New South Wales Equity court confirmation as charitable of a bequest to the Sydney University Rugby Club (1957), until after registration of the FA Youth Trust Deed two decades later in 1971. After an eight year battle against the Revenue through all court levels the House of Lords in *IRC v McMullan* [pages 379 supra] overruled the Revenue, the High Court, a Court of Appeal majority and confirmed the Charity Commissioners Registration of what had been claimed in vain nearly thirty years earlier.

The *Rating and Income Tax* article for 8 October 1953, reproduced here verbatim, extended in more formal style what had appeared in the *FA Bulletin* for April 1953. It is the acorn from which this second edition oak tree of 506 pages has grown. It also explains how Sport and the Law can develop if the appropriate facts are recognised, identified and threaded constructively and progressively to the relevant and applicable law, notwithstanding earlier errors and omissions when earlier assessments have ignored or failed to spot the ball.

TAXATION OF FOOTBALLERS' BENEFITS

By EDWARD GRAYSON, MA (Oxon), Barrister-at-Law

ON the 24th July of this year [1953] awards were published by the Industrial Disputes Tribunal, to which the Ministry of Labour and National Service under the Industrial Disputes Order, 1951, had referred a claim by the professional Association Football Players' and Trainers' Union 'for certain specified terms and conditions of employment.' The tribunal, rejecting a claim that the benefit moneys and accrued shares of benefit moneys payable to a player on his transfer from one club to another should be made obligatory, observed: 'it was the union's view that all players should as of right be entitled to benefit payments for meritorious service.' Presumably the submissions of the Football Association and the Football League were accepted, viz., 'that payments of benefits are the reward for meritorious service and that to make them compulsory would be a negation of that principle.'

Sixteen months earlier in March, 1952, the report was published (H.M.S.O., 9d.) of a committee of investigation appointed by the Ministry of Labour under the Conciliation Act, 1896, to inquire into a difference in the football industry. Paragraph 46 contained figures showing that no more than 14 per cent. out of 3,200 to 3,500 registered professional footballers for the years 1948–51 received payments of benefit moneys. Nevertheless, for over a quarter of a century the courts have held that the obviously non-compulsory and gratuitous payments to professional footballers 'for meritorious service' are taxable, while the corresponding payments made to professional cricketers are not. How this arises typifies the refinements distinguishing similar circumstances under income tax law.

WRITTEN AGREEMENTS

The liability to tax in both cases arises under Schedule E of the Income Tax Acts. Section 156 of the Income Tax Act, 1952, which deals with Schedule E, provides : 'Tax under this schedule shall be charged in respect of every public office or employment of profit.' This was formerly the heading to Schedule E of the Income Tax Act, 1918. Rule 1 of sch. 9 to the Income Tax Act, 1952 (formerly r.1 of the rules applicable to Schedule E under the Income Tax Act, 1918) provides : 'Tax under Schedule E shall be annually charged on every person having or exercising an office or employment of profit mentioned in Schedule E ... in respect of all salaries, fees, wages, perquisites or profits whatsoever therefrom for the year of assessment ...' So when George Harrison received £650 from and in pursuance of a written agreement with the Everton Club by way of an accrued share of benefit on his transfer, Rowlatt, J., restored an assessment under Schedule E which the General Commissioner had discharged, observing : 'He has earned this just as much as he has earned anything else in the service of the club' (*Davis* v. *Harrison* (1927) 11 T.C. 707, 723).

Subsequently most contracts dropped that written agreement. Under reg. 45 of the Football League, formerly reg. 61 and previously reg. 9: 'Clubs may enter into agreements with players after three playing seasons' continuous service providing for a benefit after five playing seasons' continuous service'; and provision is also made for a 'benefit match arranged to augment a benefit for a player and collections.' Further, by reg. 47, previously reg. 63, when a player is transferred by a club, the club *may* pay him a percentage proportionate to the amount which the club had guaranteed him, or would have been likely to guarantee him, for a benefit.

ABSENCE OF WRITTEN AGREEMENTS

Accordingly, the Football League consented in 1936 to Manchester City paying £200 to F. W. Corbett as an accrued share of benefit on his transfer to Lincoln City, and £650 to William Dale as a benefit after five years' continuous service; and to Notts County's arranging a benefit friendly match for Alfred Feebury, the net proceeds of which were made up to £350 by the club under a voluntary guarantee. In each case the payment was assessed under Schedule E, not in one sum, but as arising evenly over the five-yearly period following reg. 63. In the cases of Corbett and Dale the General Commissioners held the amounts received to be taxable as 'wages earned as professional footballers in the service of the club'; and in Feebury's case as moneys forming 'part of the appellant's emoluments or profits of employment.'

In *Corbett* v. *Duff*; *Dale* v. *Duff*; *Feebury* v. *Abbott* (1941), 34 R. & I.T. 189, Lawrence, J., upheld these findings. He first applied the principles stated by the House of Lords in *Cooper* v. *Blakiston* (1909),

5 T.C. 347, 355, and *Reed* v. *Seymour* (1927), 11 T.C. 630, 646: 'namely, that if the payment though voluntary is remuneration for the office or employment, it is taxable; but if it is personal in the sense that it is given to the person not as a holder of office or employment, but as a personal testimonial, it is not.' Then he held: 'in face of the terms of regs. 61 and 63, and the facts stated in the cases as to the understanding amongst professional football players, it is impossible to hold that any of the three payments to the appellants in question was not paid in respect of, and as remuneration for, the appellant's employment as a football player.... The only difference between the present case and *Davis* v. *Harrison* is that in that case a formal agreement under reg. 61 had been entered into. But that agreement was not acted upon and the case is really on all fours with *Corbett's* case.'

DISTINCTION FROM SEYMOUR'S CASE

Yet that agreement in *Harrison's* case, if not directly acted on, certainly caused the payment of £650, as Rowlatt, J., pointed out in his judgment at p. 721. Further, whatever may be 'the facts stated in the cases as to the understanding amongst professional football players' before 1939, they do not reflect the position of 86 per cent. of the players employed between 1948 and 1951; and how a distinction can be made between the facts and circumstances in the Feebury and Seymour benefits is unexplained in the judgment of Lawrence, J., or elsewhere.

In *Reed* v. *Seymour* the House of Lords, at p. 645 *et seq.*, a week before the decision in *Davis* v. *Harrison*, reversed the Court of Appeal and restored Rowlatt, J.'s order. This upheld the General Commissioners' findings that the Kent batsman, James Seymour, should not pay tax on the sum representing the gate money from his benefit of nearly £1,000 after Kent played Hampshire in 1920. Viscount Cave, L.C., said (p. 646): 'The question to be answered is, as Rowlatt, J., put it: "Is it in the end a personal gift or is it remuneration!" If the latter, it is subject to the tax; if the former, it is not. Applying this test, I do not doubt that in the present case the net proceeds of the benefit match should be regarded as a personal gift and not as income from the appellant's employment. The terms of his employment did not entitle him to a benefit, though they provided that if a benefit were granted the committee of the club should have a voice in the application of the proceeds.'

CONCLUSIONS

Undoubtedly, *Harrison's* terms of employment did entitle him to a benefit, but it is open to doubt whether those terms before Lawrence,

J., likewise entitled the players concerned to a benefit. Certainly to-day the position is completely reversed, with the players attempting to complete their terms of employment by expressly requesting, in vain, that their benefits should be made obligatory. In the quarter of a century since *Reed* v. *Seymour* and *Davis* v. *Harrison* the facts surrounding footballers' benefits have completely changed. Even allowing for Lawrence, J.'s conclusions, it would appear from the facts declared by the Ministry of Labour's recent reports that their proper presentation before the Commissioners and, if necessary, the courts, would have a greater opportunity than ever before of destroying the distinction between the two kinds of players' benefits, a distinction which merits Viscount Dunedin's opinion, in *Reed* v. *Seymour* (p. 647), of the purported taxation of cricketers' benefits: 'Preposterous.'

Table of Statutes

Table of Statutory Instruments

Table of Commissions, Inquiries and Reports

Table of Treaties

Table of Cases

Index